Bf 8.00

Progressivism in Ohio
1897-1917

PROGRESSIVISM
IN OHIO

1897-1917

□ □ □

by HOYT LANDON WARNER

OHIO STATE UNIVERSITY PRESS
FOR
THE OHIO HISTORICAL SOCIETY

FOR MY WIFE

PREFACE

THE PROGRESSIVE ERA is one episode in the long history of liberal reform in the United States. It began about the turn of the century and ended with the entry of the United States into the First World War. Although the term "progressive" did not come into general use until the years 1910–11, it has been applied retroactively in this work to cover the entire reform movement from its beginnings just prior to 1900. The application of the label to the whole period seems justified as a means of differentiating the progressive movement from the immediately preceding Populist movement, for the two are distinct, even though much of the Populist program became the mainspring of action by the progressives. Furthermore, to differentiate also the general movement from the party of the same name formed in 1912 to support the presidential candidacy of Theodore Roosevelt, the term "progressive" in lower case has been used when referring to the former and the term capitalized when designating the latter.

General histories of this movement have appeared as well as special studies of individuals and states, but this is the first devoted exclusively to the progressive movement in Ohio. The movement began as a civic revival in Toledo, Columbus, and Cleveland, led respectively by Samuel Milton Jones, Washington Gladden, and Tom L. Johnson. These leaders were pioneers in the movement, not only in Ohio but also in the country as a whole, and came to have a national reputation. They were invited to speak on their reform experiments throughout the land; thus, they helped to spread the spirit of reform. They became good newspaper copy. Some of them, notably Jones, Gladden, Frederic C. Howe, and Brand Whitlock, wrote prolifically on the programs and personalities of the movement in Ohio.

Jones and Johnson carried reform into the state, when they found that the cities were held in leading strings by the governor and the General Assembly. The reform spirit that they introduced gained momentum in the administrations of Governor Judson Harmon (1909–13) and reached its flowering in the Ohio Constitutional Convention of 1912, which wrote many of the progressives' demands into the fundamental law of the state, and in the first administration of Governor James M. Cox (1913–15), when the constitutional changes received the needed implementation by the executive and the legislature. These reforms were widely reported in national magazines, and Ohio continued to enjoy a nation-wide reputation as a leader in the progressive movement. The well-deserved publicity that Cox received for his share in advancing the reform program helped him to win the Democratic nomination for President in 1920.

There are several special problems which challenge the historian of this era—problems which Professor Richard Hofstadter has perceptively outlined and given some tentative answers to in his study entitled *The Age of Reform*. Earlier political revolts had been triggered by hard times, but progressivism began in a period of general prosperity. Why, then, was there discontent and the demand for reform? Professor Hofstadter has pointed to what he calls the "status revolution" for at least a partial answer. Briefly, his argument is that the groups who had long supplied political leadership in America—lawyers, clergy, teachers, the gentry, and small businessmen in family concerns—felt that they had been superseded in the post–Civil War decades by the captains of industry and the gaudy, newly rich, and the old leaders were determined to regain their birthright. They had not joined in the Populist protest because they had been alarmed by the violence of the labor unrest following the Panic of 1893, but the prosperity that had begun just before 1900 made the times seem safe for them to air their grievances. Moreover, the movement coincided with the coming of age of the first generation of upper-class dissenters who had been born and raised during the period of the status revolution.

Their aim was to restore the economic individualism and political democracy that were generally believed to have existed before in America and to have been threatened, if not partially destroyed, by the rule of the great monopolistic corporations and corrupt political machines. The restoration of the old economic and political system would bring back a kind of morality and civic purity that had been lost. If monopoly and every form of special privilege were abolished, once more economic success would be related to personal character and would constitute a reward to the industrious and the deserving. If the political boss and machine were driven from power, the citizen would regain the ideal of personal responsibility for and active participation in government. One aim of this study will be to examine the relevance of Professor Hofstadter's analysis to progressivism in Ohio.

In addition he and other historians have raised questions that relate to the nature and adequacy of the economic and political programs of the progressives. These historians have remarked upon the ambivalence of the progressives' attitude toward trusts, immigrants, and labor unions, upon their alleged failure to reach immigrant workers, and upon their excessive faith in mechanical governmental reforms. Were the Ohio progressives subject to the same ambivalence and limitations?

But this is not alone a "problems" study. Its aim is also to re-create a period that is remarkable for the political personalities it produced, remarkable for its program of political education of the citizens, and remarkable for its constructive reforms.

The core of this book is the author's doctoral dissertation, "Ohio's Crusade for Reform, 1897–1917," submitted to the Department of History of Harvard University in 1950. The original study, however, has been completely revised and rewritten to incorporate materials that have become available since the dissertation was completed. They include the letters and papers of several participants, notably Samuel Milton Jones, Tom L. Johnson, Newton D. Baker, Theodore E. Burton, and Walter F. Brown; and numerous monographs which cast fresh light on the men and events of this era in both Ohio and the nation.

A significant contribution of this study is the interpretive material acquired by the author in interviews, ten to twelve years ago, with the then surviving progressives and other participants, many of whom have since died. I wish to acknowledge my indebtedness to the following persons who answered my questions and shared with me their recollections: Edward F. Alexander, Alfred A. Benesch, Herbert S. Bigelow, Henry Percy Boynton, Robert J. Bulkley, James M. Cox, Hal DeRan, John D. Fackler, Arthur C. Fricke, Carl D. Friebolin, Robert N. Gorman, Joseph C. Hostetler, Graham P. Hunt, S. Gale Lowrie, William F. Maag, Jr., Carl Matson, Charles A. Otis, Jesse Dowd Stafford, Leo Weidenthal, and Peter Witt.

Many of those I interviewed also wrote me letters amplifying what they had said orally. There are still a few others with whom I was only able to correspond, namely, Elizabeth J. Hauser, Robert Crosser, and Florence E. Allen. To them I also express my thanks for their contributions.

I am grateful to a number of persons who have given me permission to use the letters and papers of some of the principals of the period: to Joseph C. Hostetler for the Newton D. Baker Papers (now in the Library of Congress); to Mrs. Helen Witt Cummins for the papers of her father, Peter Witt; to Mrs. Mary B. Pomerene and Phillip R. Shriver for the Atlee Pomerene Papers (now in the library of Kent State University); to Mrs. Jane Stockwell Covert for the scrapbooks of her father, John S. Stockwell; to Frederick Hilles for the papers of his father, Charles Dewey Hilles; and to Mason Jones and James H. Rodabaugh for the Samuel Milton Jones Papers.

Many librarians have assisted me with patience and generosity: Robert Wheeler, custodian of newspapers, and Elizabeth C. Biggert, custodian of manuscripts, Ohio Historical Society Library, Columbus; Virginius C. Hall, director of the Historical and Philosophical Society of Ohio, Cincinnati; Mrs. A. L. White and John J. Horton of the Western Reserve Historical Society Library; Lee Wachtel, librarian of the Municipal Reference Library, Cleveland; C. S. Metcalf, librarian of the Cleveland Public Library; the staff of the Bowdoin College Library; and the staff of the Kenyon College Library.

A number of my contemporaries have shared with me their knowledge of the period and have given me useful biographical suggestions: O. Garfield Jones, Randolph C. Downes, Richard Hofstadter, John M. Blum, Everett Walters, Phillip R. Shriver, and Henry J. Caren. I owe a special debt of gratitude to those who have saved me from error and have helped to clarify points that were obscure by reading the manuscript: Arthur M. Schlesinger, Sr., who directed my doctoral dissertation; Carl Wittke, C. H. Cramer, and Robert H. Bremner, each of whom read the manuscript in its entirety; Eugene C. Murdock, who read the chapters on the political career of Tom L. Johnson in Cleveland and in the state; and Jack F. Isakoff, who examined the chapter "Municipal Home Rule."

My last acknowledgment is made to the two persons who have contributed the most to this study. James H. Rodabaugh has given me constant encouragement in preparing my dissertation for publication and has gone over the final draft with many suggestions for its stylistic improvement. My wife, Charlotte Collins Warner, has not only done much of the drudgery of typing and correcting, but she has also helped me through the bad moments when my spirit and interest flagged.

My friends share in whatever merit this study may have but I alone am responsible for any errors of fact or judgment.

HOYT LANDON WARNER

Kenyon College
June 6, 1962

CONTENTS

Progressivism in Ohio

1897-1917

CHAPTER ONE

OHIO UNREFORMED

To REFORMERS, Ohio in 1900 was a self-satisfied state, content to be governed by big business, which seemed as firmly in the saddle as it had ever been since its rule began in the 1880's. The economy of the state had recovered from the depression of the mid-nineties and was about to enter a period of remarkable expansion and prosperity. The right of the captains of industry to rule had not gone undisputed but they had successfully survived each challenge. Farmers and the urban middle class continued to look to them for political leadership; labor, lacking organization and class consciousness, was generally a pawn in their hands.[1]

Although these powerful industrial leaders worked through both major parties, the Republican was the one they had created in their own image in Ohio. They were attracted to that party because it had certain assets that the Democrats lacked. The Republican party had a fund of good will inherited from the Civil War; it was the Grand Old Party that had saved the Union. The aura of victory had made it *the* political institution. "One became, in Urbana and in Ohio for many years, a Republican just as an Eskimo dons fur clothes," Brand Whitlock wrote in his reminiscences.[2] Its high tariff stand was popular; much sympathy for protection existed among the small businessmen and farmers; even laborers in the iron and steel mills were persuaded by the argument that the tariff assured them a full dinner pail. The party's position on currency questions was

3

sufficiently ambivalent not to give offense in most elections, yet when a sound currency was threatened as it was by Bryan's free-silver campaign in 1896, the leaders swung the party behind gold. Since the Civil War the Republicans had carried Ohio in every presidential election and all but three state elections. In 1900 a Republican native son, William McKinley, had been re-elected President; both of Ohio's United States senators, a majority of the representatives in the House, the governor, and the state legislative leaders were Republican as well. Adding to the party's popularity was the mounting prosperity, a successful war against Spain, and the prospects of trade expansion in the Philippines and China.

The most powerful Republican leaders in the state at the turn of the century were Senators Joseph Benson Foraker and Marcus Alonzo Hanna. Foraker was a corporation lawyer from Cincinnati and a professional politician who had been twice governor and had been elected senator in 1896. An able administrator, he had made a good record as governor, but he was best known for his oratorical powers and skill in appealing to the old-soldier vote by waving the bloody shirt of rebellion. So thunderous and direful were his speeches that he won the sobriquet of "Fire Alarm Joe." He had exploited his political prominence to make a personal fortune as an attorney for corporations seeking political favors, never seeming to question the propriety of mixing business and politics. During his years in the United States Senate he continued to receive a retainer from the Standard Oil Company and various public utilities. Yet what attracted him to politics more than money was prestige and power.[3]

Mark Hanna was a retired Cleveland businessman who had first gained renown when he saved the nation from the menacing challenge of Bryanism and Populism in 1896 by managing the election campaign of his friend, William McKinley. To continue to defend the established order against further assaults by free-silver heretics and other faddists became Hanna's mission. In his own light he was a patriot. A businessman in politics, he gave to the task all the energy and acumen which had brought him wealth in coal, iron, and steel. A frank materialist, he made his appeal directly to people's pocketbooks. He articulated a philosophy that had been implicit before and developed an organization to perpetuate it. Just as he once persuaded the workers in his coal mines and iron furnaces, so he persuaded the people of Ohio to shun false prophets and to keep in power the leaders of industry and finance by identifying the prosperity of the country with business prosperity. His election to the United States Senate in the bitterly contested fight of 1897–98 had brought him to the peak of his influence in the state. His power in Ohio now matched his power in the nation, and he enjoyed wearing his double crown.[4]

Foraker and Hanna had been political rivals since 1888, when Hanna first boomed McKinley for President and ignored the claims of Foraker, but they feuded over political power, not principle. Whenever the interests of the business community were threatened or the party was in jeopardy from meddling reformers, the two dropped their enmity and both sought to ward off the challenge. Hanna blessed and courted George B. Cox, the political boss of Cincinnati, who was also Foraker's closest ally. There were no more loyal Republicans nor ardent defenders of the established order than these two senators. They built a party organization that extended its sway into almost every courthouse and city hall in Ohio.[5]

Opposing this Republican juggernaut were the Democrats, weaken by factionalism, bereft of any inspiring program, and weighted with liabilities out of the past. They carried the taint of disloyalty from the Copperhead movement of the Civil War period, they had taken the unpopular side on the tariff issue in opposing protection, they had been branded with radicalism since Bryan campaigned for free silver in 1896.[6] The party in Ohio reflected all of the divisions that split the Democrats nationally. There were the Gold Bugs, who were bitter against Bryan; the sincere advocates of free silver, particularly numerous among the farmers in the northwestern counties of the state, who praised the Nebraskan; the city radicals, who cared little about the monetary plank but supported Bryan because he was a symbol of protest against the power of the trusts and the bankers; and the professionals who climbed aboard the Bryan band wagon for reasons of political expediency.

Among the political opportunists temporarily allied with Bryan was John R. McLean. By 1900 he had come to wield great power in the Democratic party of the state through his own

5

newspaper, the *Cincinnati Enquirer,* his support of certain county weekly journals, and his lavish distribution of funds at election time. Although he continued to maintain a voting residence in Cincinnati, he had been residing since 1885 in Washington, D. C., where he had become enormously wealthy by developing the district's public utilities. Politics to him meant place and power. He had aspired to a seat in the United States Senate in 1885 and to the governor's chair in 1899, unsuccessfully trying to buy his way each time.[7] His hopes, though unfulfilled, were not unjustified. Twice his own party had responded to the Midas touch, electing to the United States Senate Henry B. Payne, "the Standard Oil senator," in 1884 and Calvin S. Brice, an absentee utility magnate, in 1890.[8] Despite the lip service McLean paid to Bryan in 1896, his (McLean's) opinions on economic issues were those of the other captains of industry. All that separated him from the Foraker-Hanna Republicans were party labels and a deep-seated partisanship bred in the Civil War.

During the 1890's, challenges to the rule of the businessmen-in-politics came from party mavericks who responded to the fears of some farmers, small merchants, and the white-collar class that the giant trusts were becoming too big and powerful; they were a threat to the American way of free competition and must be checked. The dissenters attacked big business along three lines: they commenced antitrust action, struck at tax favoritism, and exposed the misalliance of business and bosses in the cities.

The Ohio campaign against monopolies is instructive of the difficulties Republican reformers faced within their own party. In 1890 the Republican attorney-general, David K. Watson, had brought suit against the Standard Oil Company of Ohio—a unit of that first great monopoly, the Standard Oil Trust. The action had been initiated without consultation with the party leaders, who were surprised and irate. Hanna remonstrated with Watson and warned him that it would affect his public career. But the conscientious attorney-general was not to be intimidated and took his case before the Ohio Supreme Court, which ordered Standard of Ohio to withdraw from the trust because it was a monopoly in violation of the common law.[9] Several years later another Republican attorney-general, Frank S. Monnett, brought

6

further legal proceedings, charging that Standard had not carried out the earlier order and was in contempt of court. The case ended in a deadlock, the judges dividing three to three. But by this time the Standard Oil Trust had changed its structure by incorporating all of its components into a giant holding company under the laws of New Jersey, which permitted the new company to hold stock in an Ohio company and do business in the state.[10]

The action against Standard had been brought under the common-law doctrine of monopoly, but this was soon re-enforced by a state antitrust statute of 1898, the terms of which were as broad as the federal Sherman Act in prohibiting all combinations in restraint of trade. Under the new law Monnett instituted suits against three other units in the Standard combination which were accused of secret price-fixing. Senator Foraker, then retained as counsel for the Standard Oil Company, intervened to curb the overzealous attorney-general and to request a delay in the proceedings. When Monnett refused, Foraker, according to Monnett, threatened political reprisal and did take a hand in the arrangements to defeat the attorney-general's renomination by the Republicans in 1899. Before the suits could be heard, Monnett's term expired and his Republican successor allowed them to lapse.[11] The antitrust campaign in Ohio was bound to end in frustration, for no single state could curb the monopoly power of great industrial aggregations like Standard Oil; the national government alone had the means, if it wished, to exercise them.

Another evil that distressed the dissenters was the extent to which the public utility companies, especially the railroads, and substantial property owners escaped their fair share of taxation in Ohio. The problem was made more pressing as the state faced an empty treasury and frequent deficits because of the failure of the legislature to find new revenues to meet the legitimate growing needs of the state as well as to pay for some of their own extravagances. Twice in the 1890's Republican-controlled legislatures appointed tax commissions that exposed the facts of tax favoritism and recommended reforms in the cumbersome methods and machinery of taxation.[12]

The existing system had grown in topsy-turvy fashion and was expressive of its origins in an earlier age when Ohio was

7

rural and held to the Jacksonian conviction that any man could judge the value of his neighbor's property. The county auditor, assisted by a panel of citizen assessors, appraised the real property in each county every ten years—often enough for the relatively stable agrarian society of the past but not for the booming industrial economy in which commercial property values were skyrocketing overnight. In between the decennial appraisals, the county auditor sat annually with similar boards of citizens to make additions or decreases in the value of real and personal property.[13] Excluded from their calculations was the property of railroads which was separately assessed by the auditors of the counties through which each line ran. Other utilities, like telephone, telegraph, and express companies, were valued by an ex officio state board composed of the state auditor, attorney-general, and treasurer. These officers, busy with their other duties and too indifferent to make a scientific study of taxation, tended to accept the tax return as filed by each utility.[14]

As slipshod as the machinery were the various methods of assessing property and business enterprises. Ohio's constitution then called for taxation "by a uniform rule [of] all moneys, credits, investments in bonds, stocks, joint stock companies or otherwise; and also all real and personal property according to their true value in money."[15] The constitution makers, in endeavoring to be explicit and inclusive enough to catch all familiar forms of property within the tax net, had failed to anticipate certain developments. They had not foreseen the growth of the public-utility corporation, much of whose "true value" was attributable to the worth of its franchise or good will—items not enumerated in the tax article. Because of the constitutional silence, the mode of taxing such businesses had been left to the discretion of the legislature and the courts, with the judges having the final word.

The Ohio Tax Commission of 1893 complained that the judges had raised a "fog of doubt" in construing the tax clause.[16] Still, much of the blame for the existing confusion rested on the legislators themselves. In 1894, for example, the General Assembly passed the Nichols Law taxing the telephone, telegraph, and express companies doing business in the state, and the statute was so phrased as to include the franchise value of these enterprises. The Ohio Supreme Court sustained the act and thereby made it legal for the legislature to tax the franchise value of all other utilities.[17] But these corporations balked at paying the tax increases such a change would produce and bargained to retain the old method of assessment by accepting an additional light excise tax. It was reported that they had agreed in 1896 to an excise tax of one-half of 1 per cent on their gross earnings in return for a pledge from the Republican leadership that the Nichols Law would never be extended to them.[18]

For many years thereafter they continued to be appraised under the general property laws at what their physical equipment would bring in a bankruptcy sale. Their valuable franchises went untaxed except for the modest levy on their gross earnings. A number of studies revealed the extent to which the railroads and other utilities escaped their proper share of the tax burden.[19]

Railroads, for example, according to the report of the state tax commission of 1893, were appraised for very little more than that of the livestock of the state in 1892, and the assigned value of three of the major lines had declined between 1878 and 1892 despite an increase of more than 50 per cent in their gross receipts. "There seems to be constantly at work," the commission added, "influences which pull down and keep down the appraised values of these properties."[20] The commissioners might have carried their candor one step further and disclosed what the "influences" were, for it was no secret that the railroads gave free passes, free vacations, and campaign funds to county officers and state officials in return for tax favors.[21]

Nor was this the end of the tax inequities; vacant lots and commercial properties were undervalued in every city. The legislature had failed to spell out a "uniform rule" for assessing such property. By default local tax boards and assessors were allowed wide discretion in determining their own system, with the result that great variations existed in the assessed value of the same kind of land between city and city.[22]

There was evasion in reporting every kind of intangible personal property. The tax commission of 1893 estimated that only 20 per cent of the money deposited in the banks of the state was reported and that the gravest evasions occurred in the five most populous urban counties—Cuyahoga, Hamilton, Lucas, Franklin, and Montgomery.[23] The owners of stocks and bonds, regarding the general property tax as confiscatory, had concluded, according to the Cleveland Chamber of Commerce, that it was "entirely justifiable to conceal, to evade, to resort to every subterfuge, to lie outright, and even to commit perjury, in order to escape this burden of taxation. . . ."[24] A tax-inquisitor law, designed to supplement the effort of tax officers to force such intangibles out of hiding, proved a feeble stopgap. The effect of these inequalities and evasions was to place the heaviest share of the tax load on the small homeowner and the farmer, who had the least to conceal.[25] By 1900 little more progress had been made in tax reform than in abolishing monopolies.

A third source of concern to the political dissenters was the tie between big business and the city boss and the corrupting influence they exercised upon municipal government. The cities of the state were the focal points of the industrial expansion and the accompanying population explosion and were the first to feel the stress and strains of the industrialism which had revolutionized the country since the Civil War. Conditions in Ohio's municipalities were but a reflection of those in the nation at large. Some were as boss-ridden as any in the United States, notably Cincinnati and Dayton; others like Toledo, Cleveland, Columbus, Youngstown, and Canton oscillated between bursts of reform and vassalage to a boss or a machine; still other small cities such as Marietta, Zanesville, and Springfield kept relatively free from bossism.[26]

The decade of the nineties brought sharply into focus for the first time many of the problems that had been accumulating in the post-Civil War era. So diverse were the difficulties that the citizens were easily confused and diverted from a sustained attack on any one evil. Unscrupulous politicians and businessmen were able to take advantage of this situation and draw attention away from their malpractices by raising the hue and cry on some other emotional issue.

Two such issues that created a turmoil in Ohio were the revival of a nativist, anti-Catholic movement and the intensification of the liquor question. The new immigration from the predominantly Catholic areas of Central and Southern Europe had aroused the alarm and hostility of certain American Protestants in the Midwest, and a secret organization, the American Protective Association, had been formed in the early 1890's to keep Catholics out of political office and political employment of any kind. It attracted a sizable following throughout rural Ohio and in three cities, Columbus, Youngstown, and Toledo, supported as it was by many Protestant ministers, a number of newspapers, and politicians of both parties who yielded to this epidemic of bigotry for personal gain.[27] The need to suppress this virulent form of bigotry absorbed the energy of urban reformers and left them with little strength to attack other abuses.

Equally emotional and equally divisive was the perennial liquor issue. The good people of the cities, many of whom had come from a farm or a small town, were appalled by the saloons which had become both numerous and unsavory. The patrons were principally laboring men who looked upon the saloon as a local club. Brewers, distillers, and saloon-owners had a large investment which they wished to protect against the assaults of the temperance and prohibition people. Inevitably the battle became a political one; both sides adopted tactics that gave offense. The Ohio Anti-Saloon League, which had been founded in Oberlin in 1893, exercised a powerful influence in the state. It demanded that every candidate for state or local office declare himself on the liquor question. Opportunistic politicians who did not wish to offend such a potent pressure group became officially "dry" and received the political support of the League, even though they might have the reputation of being "dripping wet" in private. On the other hand, those who were conscientiously opposed to legal prohibition—the goal of the League— were branded as "wets," no matter how abstemious they might be in their personal drinking habits.[28]

The methods adopted by the liquor interests, however, seemed even more offensive and certainly crasser. Some of the most respectable saloons violated the evening and Sunday-closing laws; the worst were linked with gambling and prostitution. All sought political protection and resorted to bribery to obtain it. Certain cities in Ohio had the reputation of being wide-open towns, notably, Cincinnati with its large concentration of Germans, and Toledo and Canton with their high percentage of mixed foreign residents. The corruption destroyed the integrity of the police force which, too often, became a body of bribe seekers instead of a law-enforcement agency. Many a municipal election witnessed an attempt of the "outs" to defeat the "ins" by promising to "throw the rascals out" and "to clamp down the lid" on the saloons. But too frequently the "outs," once they were in office, were no better than the administration they had replaced, and the misalliance between saloonkeepers, gamblers, and brothel-owners, on the one hand, and politicians, on the other, remained.[29]

The record of broken promises and failures caused some of the middle class to question the argument of the prohibitionists and do-gooders that the drinking habits of a community could be radically altered by legislation. These doubters wished to remove the issue from the political limelight and handle the saloon problem in a way that the great majority would support. At a minimum they wished to disassociate saloons from gambling and prostitution and to free their regulation from bribery. Furthermore, to these same skeptics the liquor question seemed to be a distraction that was making people lose sight of more serious forms of graft and corruption.[30]

As the needs of the cities multiplied and municipal business became more valuable, businessmen were willing to pay bribes for contracts to supply sewer pipe and street paving, to insure the city property, or to provide textbooks for its schools. But even more of a scramble took place in the fight for the most valuable prizes that urban governments had to dispense—the franchises to furnish the citizens with electricity, gas, transportation, and, in some cases, water. In their eagerness for these utilities the people had initially been generous with the companies in setting rates and other service requirements. By the 1890's, moreover, such technological advances as the electrification of street railways and the improved technique of laying pipe lines for natural-gas concerns had greatly increased the profits and the values of such utility properties. The consolidation of companies which took place, notably among street-railway lines, also produced economies in operation. Finally, the ever increasing concentration of people meant more users for each unit of physical plant. The result was inflated profits and inflated values far in excess of the actual plant investment—values which the companies labeled in their books "franchise value" or "good will." In turn the franchise value and good will were capitalized in the form of stock—"watered stock"—so called because it did not represent any physical property or actual money investment. Because these franchises promised such riches, public-service corporations were becoming more rapacious and notorious in the methods they employed. Sometimes they resorted to direct bribery of municipal councilmen, sometimes they worked through a local boss or machine. The effect was to corrupt city government on a grand scale. Bosses, machines, and rings, supported by funds from the private utilities, became the characteristic rulers in the cities of Ohio and the nation.[31]

This dominance was further promoted by the cumbersome, obsolete governmental machinery that existed in most of the municipalities of the state. Many of the existing structures dated from the pre-Civil War era when they had been adequate for the small homogeneous communities of that day, but they had proven unequal to the needs of the greatly expanded polyglot urban centers of 1900. City charters frequently divided legislative powers between the common council and a board of aldermen, distributed executive authority among the mayor and separate boards, some elective, some appointive, and spread the appointing power among the council, tax commissioners, probate judge, and governor. Such a dispersion of responsibility and authority made it difficult for poorly organized groups of good citizens to locate those responsible for misdeeds and to institute reform. On the other hand, the political boss could impose his organization upon the scattered parts and weld them into a unified machine that would serve his ends.[32]

In Ohio the corollary between unreformed charters and unreformed politics was strikingly revealed in Toledo, Dayton, and Cincinnati. In all three the bosses and machines identified themselves with the dominant Republican party, although their partisanship did not prevent them from collaborating with like-minded Democrats when political needs dictated. The boss of Toledo in the mid-nineties was Guy Major, a successful linseed oil manufacturer and a Foraker partisan, who was twice elected mayor by riding on the coattails of the American Protective Association. As the power of that organization declined after 1895, so did Major's political strength. He was succeeded by Hanna partisans: George P. Waldorf, collector of internal revenue, and his protégé and successor, Walter F. Brown. The machine dispensed city jobs in return for votes, distributed contracts by favor, and squeezed the gamblers and prostitutes. Its graft, however, was relatively puny, and its corruption was tempered by inefficiency and the genuine opposition of the Democrats.[33]

Dayton was ruled by Joseph E. Lowes, whose political power had a unique base: the four to five thousand veterans in the nearby National Soldiers' and Sailors' Home who had long been persuaded to vote Republican by the party's liberal pension policy and were kept in line by more favors. Doc Lowes, as he was popularly known, was in politics not for personal office—that he refused—but to advance his business interests. He developed a well-knit Republican organization, neutralized the opposition of the Democrats by sharing patronage with them and backing their candidates for office in a "nonpartisan" way, and was thereby able to win bigger prizes than his counterparts in Toledo. Through his control of the city council he obtained franchises worth thousands of dollars for two street railways, an electric-light company, and a natural-gas company, in all of which he was personally interested.[34]

But the most boss-ridden city of the three was Cincinnati, ruled by George Barnsdale Cox, who boasted of being its boss. The machine that he organized achieved national notoriety; it was so widely publicized that it became the model which politicians in other cities sought to copy.[35] Cox secured his hold on the "Queen City" in the late 1880's by stepping into a political vacuum left when the McLean-Campbell Democratic gang, who had been ruling the city, was ruined by a scandalous miscarriage of justice which had caused a riot in 1884.[36] But more than the turn of circumstance was involved in the new boss's rise to power. He had attracted the attention of a fellow Republican and townsman, the then Governor Joseph B. Foraker, whose ambition was to be United States senator. Having failed twice to carry his native city during the era of Democratic dominance, Foraker was determined to reverse that trend, and Cox, he concluded, was the one man capable of organizing the vote for him. His method of aiding Cox is instructive. In 1886 he used the power of his office to persuade the legislature to abolish the Cincinnati Board of Public Works, an elective body, and create a board of public affairs appointed by him as governor. He threw the patronage of the new board, some twelve hundred to two thousand jobs, to "Old Boy" Cox, who was thereby able to expand greatly his control over the city government and be assured of a predominance over other contestants.[37]

The machine Cox constructed was pyramidal in structure with himself at the apex, the undisputed leader, who operated from his office over the Mecca saloon, where he passed on candidates and gave his orders for the day to his lieutenants. Tall, large-framed, with heavy features and florid complexion, cold and gruff in manner, he looked and acted the part of a powerful political boss. Skillful in electing others, he was unable to elect himself to public office once he had become prominent; therefore he was obliged to operate behind the scenes. His personal success as party boss derived from his ability as an organizer, the iron discipline he imposed upon his followers, his loyalty to his friends, and strict fulfillment of his promises.

Immediately beneath him were his three lieutenants: Garry Hermann, to whom was delegated the patronage and all other matters pertaining to city hall as well as the collection of campaign funds; Rudolph Hynicka, in charge of county patronage and problems, keeper of the card catalogue that contained information on most of the adult males of Hamilton County; and Mike Mullen, once a henchman of the Democratic machine, now Cox's legislative whip in the city council. In successive layers below were the ward captains, frequently holders of important municipal or county offices; precinct leaders and committeemen; and, forming the base, the five thousand petty job-holders, each of whom owed his position to Cox and in return was required to deliver four to five votes for the machine candidates at election time.[38]

This tight, disciplined organization was only one source of Cox's political strength. The large German element, once Democratic, had begun to drift into the Republican fold following the excesses of the McLean-Campbell gang in the mid-eighties. These prosperous small tradesmen and homeowners were given further encouragement to shift their party allegiance by Cox's low-tax policy and his lax enforcement of the Sunday-closing laws for saloons that enabled them to observe a Continental Sabbath to which they were accustomed. Moreover, he favored their leaders in selecting nominees for mayor and liberally awarded city and county advertising to the German-language press. Cox also benefited from the Republican tariff policy, which could not be too strongly protectionist to please the manufacturing interests of the city. By introducing the tariff issue in municipal elections, he was able to persuade many a prejudiced voter to cling to the Grand Old Party instead of chasing after the Democratic free traders. This tie with the business community, so vital to his continued power, he encouraged in other ways. He catered to the utilities and other interests seeking favors from the city, granted them franchises written according to their specifications, winked at legal infringements, prevented nuisance and reform legislation, and protected their low tax assessments.[39]

Technically the Cox machine operated within the law. Its take or so-called graft was derived from five sources: contributions from job-holders and favored businesses, especially utilities and breweries; betting on local elections; buying and selling of public-utility stocks in advance of franchise changes; letting of contracts to friendly bidders; and interest from banks on deposits of public money, a perquisite of office by long standing custom.[40]

There had been uprisings against his rule in the 1890's; one of them temporarily dethroned him in 1897, but the fusion administration elected under the leadership of the affable but weak Gustav Tafel was soon destroyed by defections stimulated by Cox. By 1900 his power was once again secure at home and had extended into the state itself through his ties with Senator Hanna as well as with his first mentor, Senator Foraker.[41]

If the tales of these three cities seemed to prove a correspondence between unreformed charters and unreformed politics, the contrary proposition that political reform was an axiom of charter reform was not necessarily true; the histories of Cleveland and Columbus were cases in point. In 1891 the legislature had approved a new fundamental law for Cleveland that was a model of governmental organization. It swept away numerous boards, concentrated executive authority in the mayor and department heads appointed by him, and vested legislative power in a medium-sized council elected by wards.[42] Still, an ambitious young Republican mayor, Robert S. McKisson, had been able to use—or *abuse*—the new structure to consolidate his personal power over the party organization and to challenge that of Senator Hanna in his home city. Government under McKisson and his Democratic successor, Mayor John Farley, seemed as inefficient and corrupt as those of earlier administrations under the unreformed charter. In 1899 Cleveland had its "gas ring," the "notorious thirteen," in the council chamber who threatened not only to yield to the extravagant demands of the private gas companies but also to hustle through a favorable franchise renewal to Mark Hanna's street railway company.[43]

Columbus had followed the Cleveland trend by modifying its charter to tighten lines of authority and responsibility. Yet again clean, efficient government had not followed. At the turn of the century it was alleged that a councilmanic ring was seeking a corrupt bargain with those utilities which held franchises that were about to expire and wanted to assure renewals on terms favorable to them.[44] Neither Columbus nor Cleveland was in the same grip of boss rule as were the other three cities; nevertheless they also were in need of someone to clean house and protect the public interest.

A further obstacle to good urban government was the complete subordination of the cities to the General Assembly. Ohio municipalities were too often the prey of self-seeking politicians in Columbus who harassed them with so-called ripper bills— bills which changed for partisan advantage the machinery of government or shifted from mayor to governor the power to appoint certain officers, such as happened with Cincinnati's Board of Public Service. Cities were beholden to the legislature for every grant of power, whether to build a bathhouse, erect an electric-light plant, shift funds from one account to another, or alter the duties and powers of a municipal officer.[45] This subordinate role was characteristic of the great majority of cities in the United States. By 1900 only four states had adopted what the urban reformers wanted: "constitutional home rule," which they defined as the outright grant in the fundamental law of the state of municipal powers independent of legislative sanction.[46]

In the opinion of reformers, Ohioans were shutting their eyes to these pressing problems of monopoly, taxation inequalities, and corrupt, inefficient city government, which had been allowed to continue by the leaders of the Republican party in alliance with big business. If the people could be made to see the magnitude of these evils, little would be left of the popular mood of self-satisfaction that then prevailed. It became the mission of a handful of men to open their eyes, to change the public temper from one of contentment to one of discontent with things as they were, and to win support for the remedies that they proposed to cure the existing evils.

1. The political dominance of big business is stressed in Eugene H. Roseboom and Francis P. Weisenburger, *A History of Ohio* (Rev. ed.; Columbus, 1958), 243–44, and in Philip D. Jordan, *Ohio Comes of Age: 1873–1900* (*A History of the State of Ohio,* ed. Carl Wittke, Vol. V [6 vols.; Columbus, 1941–44]), 189–219, 293–94.

2. Brand Whitlock, *Forty Years of It* (New York, 1914), 27.

3. This sketch is drawn from the perceptive and impartial biography of Foraker: Everett Walters, *Joseph Benson Foraker, an Uncompromising Republican* (Columbus, 1948), 2–4, 111–26, 251–55.

4. The commentary on Hanna is based on the appraisals by Herbert Croly, *Marcus Alonzo Hanna, His Life and Work* (New York, 1912), 465–79, and William Allen White, *Masks in a Pageant* (New York, 1939), 193–94, 201–21.

5. Walters, *Foraker,* 80–82, 98–110, 127–40; Croly, *Hanna,* 120–39; Roseboom and Weisenburger, *History of Ohio,* 252–54.

6. Roseboom and Weisenburger, *History of Ohio,* 243–44, 246–52.

7. Biographical accounts of McLean range from those of undue admiration to those of hypercriticism. Friendly to McLean are: the obituaries in the *Cincinnati Enquirer,* June 10, 1916, and *Cincinnati Times-Star,* June 10, 1916; and Thomas E. Powell, ed., *The Democratic Party of the State of Ohio* (2 vols., n. p., 1913) I, 372–73. Hostile to McLean is Allen C. Myers, *Bosses and Boodle in Ohio Politics* (Cincinnati, 1895), 213–14.

8. Myers, *Bosses and Boodle in Ohio Politics,* 260–61, 267–73, 280–90. Payne's election in 1884 is also reviewed in Henry Demarest Lloyd, *Wealth against Commonwealth* (New York, 1894), 374–85.

9. Roseboom and Weisenburger, *History of Ohio,* 256; Wade H. Ellis, "The History of the Standard Oil Company in Ohio," *Ohio Magazine,* IV (January, 1908), 2–10; *State v. Standard Oil Co.,* 49 Ohio State Supreme Court Reports 137 (1892).

10. Roseboom and Weisenburger, *History of Ohio,* 256.

11. *Ibid.,* 256–58; Walters, *Foraker,* 276. The Valentine Anti-Trust Act is in 93 Ohio Laws 143 (1898).

12. The tax commissions were appointed in 1893 and 1898. The best critical analyses of Ohio's finances and tax structure are in: *Report of the Tax Commission of Ohio* (1893); Frederic C. Howe, "Taxation of Quasi-Public Corporations in the State of Ohio and the Franchise Tax," *Annals of the American Academy of Political and Social Science,* XIV (September, 1899), 157–80; Harley Leist Lutz, *The State Tax Commission* ("Harvard University Economic Studies," Vol. XVII [Cambridge, 1918]), 479–81.

13. 94 O.L. 336 (1900); *Bates' Annotated Revised Statutes of Ohio* (3rd ed., 1902), secs. 2805 and 2805a.

14. The system had been adopted in piecemeal fashion over a span of years beginning with railroads and later extended to other utilities. The major statutes are: 59 O.L. 88 (1862) and 62 O.L. 110 (1865) for railroads; 90 O.L. 330 (1893) for express, telegraph, and telephone companies; 91 O.L. 408 (1894) for sleeping-car companies; 92 O.L. 89 (1896) for freight-line and equipment companies.

15. Ohio Constitution of 1851, Art. XII, sec. 2.

16. *Report of the Tax Commission of Ohio* (1893), 6.

17. 90 O.L. 330 (1893). The act was sustained by the Ohio Supreme Court in *State* v. *Jones,* 50 Ohio 492 (1894), and by the United States Supreme Court in *Adams Express Co.* v. *Ohio State Auditor,* 166 U.S. Supreme Court Reports 185 (1897).

18. Such an allegation was made in 1902 during the contest to amend the tax laws (*Cincinnati Enquirer,* January 21, February 14, 1902).

19. Thomas McDougall, *Address on the Taxation of the Property of Street Railways, Gas, Electric Light and other Quasi-Public Corporations before the Senate and House Committee on Taxation at Columbus, February 25, 1896* (Cincinnati, 1896), 15. McDougall spoke of himself as a "citizen and tax payer and a Republican." Corroborating evidence is presented in: Henry C. Wright, *Bossism in Cincinnati* (Cincinnati, 1905), 103; Howe, "Taxation of Quasi-Public Corporations in the State of Ohio and the Franchise Tax," 170–71; Charles C. Williamson, *The Finances of Cleveland* ("Columbia University Studies in History, Economics and Public Law," Vol. XXV, No. 3 [New York, 1907]), 70; P[eter] W[itt], *Cleveland before St. Peter* (Cleveland, 1899), 44.

20. *Report of the Tax Commission of Ohio* (1893), 59.

21. Tom L. Johnson, *My Story* (New York, 1911), 139, 142.

22. Williamson, *The Finances of Cleveland,* 66; *Report of the Tax Commission of Ohio* (1893), 24–25.

23. *Report of the Tax Commission of Ohio* (1893), 30, 41.

24. "Taxation: Report of the Special Committee," *Cleveland Chamber of Commerce Reports and Addresses* (1895), 10.

25. *Ibid.,* 17–20.

26. Political conditions in Cincinnati are described in Wright, *Bossism in Cincinnati, passim,* and Harold Zink, *City Bosses in the United States, a Study of Twenty Municipal Bosses* (Durham, N. C., 1930), 260–65; those in Dayton in Harold A. Stone, Don K. Price, and Kathryn H. Stone, *City Manager Government in the United States, a Review after Twenty-five Years* (Chicago, 1940), 180–82, and in reports by W. S. Couch in *Cleveland Plain Dealer,* September 6–8, 1905; those in Toledo in Wendell F. Johnson, *Toledo's Non-Partisan Movement* (Toledo, 1922), 51–53, in James H. Rodabaugh, "Samuel M. Jones — Evangel of Equality," *Northwestern Ohio Quarterly,* XV (January, 1943), 25–27; and in reports by W. S. Couch in *Cleveland Plain Dealer,* August 30–31, 1905; those in Cleveland in Johnson, *My Story,* 114–16, Frederic C. Howe, *The Confessions of a Reformer* (New York, 1925), 82–94, and Carl Lorenz, *Tom L. Johnson, Mayor of Cleveland* (New York, 1911), 21–26; those in Columbus in Washington Gladden, *Recollections* (Boston, 1909), 328–39; those in the other Ohio cities in reports by W. S. Couch in *Cleveland Plain Dealer,* September 5, 10–12, 14, 1905.

27. An account of APA activity in Columbus is in Gladden, *Recollections,* 361–65; in Youngstown in Hoyt Landon Warner, *The Life of Mr. Justice*

Clarke (Cleveland, 1959), 17–19; in Toledo in an article by Negley D. Cochran in *Toledo Bee,* March 23, 1899, and in Harvey S. Ford, "The Life and Times of Golden Rule Jones" (Ph.D. dissertation, University of Michigan, 1953), chap. v, pp. 4–5.

28. Roseboom and Weisenburger, *History of Ohio,* 244, 343–45; James M. Cox, *Journey through My Years* (New York, 1946), 179–80.

29. Cox, *Journey through My Years,* 160; Roseboom and Weisenburger, *History of Ohio,* 239–40, 244.

30. Johnson, *My Story,* 122; Brand Whitlock, *On the Enforcement of Law in Cities* (Indianapolis, 1910), 26, 43, 49–50, 72-79; Whitlock, *Forty Years of It,* 283.

31. Since the privately owned utilities were a major target of attack by Ohio's municipal reformers, the literature on this theme is voluminous. Extensive treatments of the problem are in: Johnson, *My Story,* 28–47, 89–107, 145–66, 206–63; Whitlock, *Forty Years of It,* 322–48; John M. Killits, ed., *Toledo and Lucas County, Ohio, 1623–1923* (3 vols.; Chicago, 1923), I, 581–86; Gladden, *Recollections,* 338–50; Washington Gladden, "The Influence of Public Service Corporations on City Government," *Proceedings of the National Conference for Good City Government* (1900), 164–75; Frederic C. Howe, "The City of Cleveland in Relation to the Street Railway Question," *Bulletin of the Municipal Association of Cleveland* (1897); Elliott Hunt Pendleton, "Cincinnati's Traction Problems," *National Municipal Review,* II (October, 1913), 617–68.

32. The decentralization of administration in Ohio cities is fully discussed in Samuel P. Orth, *The Centralization of Administration in Ohio* (New York, 1903), 15–17, and in an article by the same author, "The Municipal Situation in Ohio," *Forum,* XXXIII (June, 1902), 430–37.

33. Guy Major's rise and decline are described in Ford, "Golden Rule Jones," chap. v, pp. 4–5. Waldorf, Brown, and their political organization are critically analyzed in: Johnson, *Toledo's Non-Partisan Movement,* 17, 51–53; report by W. S. Couch in *Cleveland Plain Dealer,* August 30–31, 1905; *Toledo Bee,* March 8, 1899; Ford, *op. cit.,* chap. xiv, p. 1; *Toledo News-Bee,* January 10, 1904. A laudatory sketch of Waldorf, typical of county histories, is in Harvey Scribner, ed., *Memoirs of Lucas County and the City of Toledo* (2 vols.; Madison, 1910), II, 415–18.

34. Report by W. S. Couch in *Cleveland Plain Dealer,* September 6–8, 1905; *Dayton Daily News,* October 26–27, 30, November 1–3, 1905; the author's interview with James M. Cox, June 29, 1949.

35. Frank Parker Stockbridge, "The Biggest Boss of Them All," *Hampton's Magazine,* XXVI (May, 1911), 616–17; Zink, *City Bosses in the United States,* 273; Lincoln Steffens, "Ohio: A Tale of Two Cities," *McClure's Magazine,* XXV (July, 1905), 293–311.

36. Wright, *Bossism in Cincinnati,* 17–18.

37. *Ibid.,* 30–31; Zink, *City Bosses in the United States,* 260–62; Walters, *Foraker,* 116–17. Walters, while acknowledging that Cox was Foraker's most consistent and strongest supporter, points out that the Senator had other political friends around the state upon whom he also relied for support.

38. This sketch of Cox and his organization is drawn from Wright, *Bossism in Cincinnati,* 63–66, from Zink, *City Bosses in the United States,* 259–61, 268, 273–74, and from George Kibbe Turner, "The Thing above the Law, The Rise and Rule of George B. Cox and His Overthrow by Young Hunt

and the Fighting Idealists of Cincinnati," *McClure's Magazine*, XXXVIII (March, 1912), 580–82.

39. Cox's courting of the German element is described in Wright, *Bossism in Cincinnati*, 124. Four nominees for mayor backed by Cox were of German descent. In addition to liberal awards of advertising, the editors and principal stockholders of the German-language press received good city positions. Cox's emphasis on low taxes, lax enforcement of the Sunday-closing laws for saloons, and tariff protection is stressed in: Max B. May, "Taxation in American Cities: Cincinnati," *Annals of the American Academy of Political and Social Science*, XXVIII (1906), 158–59; Stockbridge, "The Biggest Boss of Them All," 620; report by W. S. Couch in *Cleveland Plain Dealer*, August 9, 1905. His catering to the utilities and other business interests is discussed in Zink, *City Bosses in the United States*, 271.

40. Herbert F. Koch, "An Ohio Warwick: Something of the Life and Times of George Barnsdale Cox" (MS in the Historical and Philosophical Society of Ohio, Cincinnati), 20–21.

41. Wright, *Bossism in Cincinnati*, 42–45, 47–48; Charles P. Taft, *City Management, the Cincinnati Experiment* (New York, 1933), 10–11.

42. "An act to provide a more efficient government for the cities of the second grade of the first class [Cleveland]," 88 O.L. 105 (1891).

43. Croly, *Hanna*, 242–66; Johnson, *My Story*, 112–19; Lorenz, *Johnson*, 21-26; *Cleveland Press*, December 6, 1900. The rise and fall of the McKisson machine are discerningly appraised in Thomas F. Campbell, "Background for Progressivism: Machine Politics in the Administration of Robert E. McKisson, Mayor of Cleveland 1895–1899" (Master's thesis, Western Reserve University, 1960).

44. Gladden, *Recollections*, 328–39; Alma Jagsch, "Washington Gladden, a Prophet of Social Justice" (Master's thesis, Ohio State University, 1935), 31–32.

45. The abuse of ripper bills was frequently discussed and deplored in the press: for example, *Ohio State Journal* (Columbus), January 1, February 9, 1900, May 1, 1902; *Cleveland Press*, February 14, 28, 1900; *Toledo Blade*, April 29, 1902. Much of the time of the Ohio General Assembly was absorbed in legislating for cities.

46. Augustus Raymond Hatton, "Constitutional Municipal Home Rule," in Woodruff, ed., *A New Municipal Program* (New York, 1919), 78–82 and nn. 1, 82. The four states were Missouri (1875), California (1879), Washington (1889), and Minnesota (1896).

CHAPTER TWO

THE REFORM AWAKENING IN TOLEDO AND COLUMBUS
1897 ■ 1904

In Ohio as elsewhere in the North the reform awakening which gave rise to the progressive* movement began in the cities as a revolt of the middle class against the rule of big business and big bosses. Leadership, it has been shown by Richard Hofstadter[1] and others, came from the elite of this class: men of inherited wealth and established businesses as well as men of prominence in the professions—lawyers, editors, preachers, and educators. Few, if any, came from the ranks of labor. Most were native Americans in their mid-thirties, who had had a college education and were Protestants in religion, Republicans in politics. They were the natural leaders, accustomed to political prestige and power. But they had come to feel that they were being displaced by the new rich, the captains of industry, who were corrupting politics and destroying traditional values.

The leadership of the progressive cause in Ohio conforms somewhat to this pattern. Lawyers predominated, accounting for twenty-eight or about one-third of those active in the movement; the eleven businessmen constituted the next largest category, though few had inherited an established business;

---

* Since the term "progressive" is used to refer both to a general movement and a particular political party, the following practice will be observed in this book to distinguish between the two usages: (1) When *uncapitalized*, it refers to the broad movement of reform which cut across party lines. (2) When *capitalized*, it refers to the party of that name founded in 1912 to back Theodore Roosevelt for the Presidency of the United States.

newspapermen numbered five; educators and ministers numbered three each. Ohio departed from the norm in having eight
union-labor men who contributed significantly to reform. These
leaders were for the most part native-born Protestants in their
thirties, but less than half were college educated, and the combined total of progressive Republicans and Theodore Roosevelt
Progressives did not exceed one-third; the rest were Democrats.[2]

The most important exceptions to the pattern, however, were
the three men who initiated the reform impulse in their respective communities. Two of them, Samuel Milton Jones of
Toledo and Tom Loftin Johnson of Cleveland, were businessmen who had not inherited but had made their wealth and,
what is more, made it under the protective system of "special
privilege"—patent and franchise monopolies—the very system
that they and other reformers were to decry as the source of
political corruption. They differed in other ways as well: both
lacked a college education and were older than the usual leaders,
Jones was Welsh-born, and Johnson was a Democrat. The third,
Washington Gladden, pastor of the First Congregational Church
in Columbus, did conform more closely but even he deviated in
one respect: he was sixty-four when he entered politics—much
older than the usual progressive.[3]

These leaders in Ohio, like others in the North, made common
cause with the small businessmen and white-collar class—the
most rapidly increasing element in the population of the country
—who began to fear not only big business but also big labor.
These middle-class groups believed that the monopolistic price
structure of the trusts and the rising wage scales imposed by
the unions were responsible for the inflation which was squeezing
their pocketbooks.[4] Yet it was again somewhat distinctive of
the Ohio reformers, particularly in Toledo and Cleveland, that
they succeeded in reaching below this level to the laboring men
themselves and detaching many of the recent immigrant workers
from the control of the local bosses.[5]

The ideology of the movement in Ohio was partly secular,
partly religious. In differing proportions these progressives drew
their inspiration from American radical thought—Henry George's
theories in particular—and the precepts of Jesus as found in the
Sermon on the Mount. Instinctively the reformers, whether
businessmen or preachers, gave a religious tone to the movement.

23

Participants spoke of conversion to reform principles as "seeing the light," and "getting religion," borrowing the language of evangelists to heighten the fervor of the temporal crusade. The leaders believed that moral and spiritual regeneration would accompany and be abetted by social and political reform. They were dedicated to a vision that man could be regenerated, poverty eliminated, and democracy revitalized.

These men might be "revolutionists" in their dream of founding a perfect society in this imperfect world, but unlike the Marxian Socialists, they were not revolutionists in method. Instead they believed in the efficacy of education and in gradual change, through the enactment of a limited, practical program of reform.

The most moderate parts of their platform were the ideas inherited from Grover Cleveland Democracy and Mugwump Republicanism: civil service reform, the elimination of special favors to business, like the tariff, and the restoration of competition by antitrust legislation. More radical were the planks taken directly from the Populists: government ownership of natural monopolies, the eight-hour day, the direct election of United States senators, the direct primary, and the initiative and referendum. The most radical of all were the reforms that Jones, Johnson, and, to a lesser extent, Gladden, introduced in their own cities. No longer content to have municipal government play the traditional role of policeman, they proposed to make it an active agent of reform. They believed that the municipality should own and manage all the needed services of transportation, water, light, and gas; that it should provide abundant recreational facilities such as parks and playgrounds, concerts and lectures; and that it should adopt a radically improved method of treating the destitute and delinquent members of society. To these reformers the city, instead of being a cause of despair, should become the hope of democracy. Later these same men extended their campaign to the state when they realized that the cities would not be free until the state itself was free from bondage to big business.

Although the first of the Ohio leaders appeared on the political scene prior to 1900, the movement did not gain momentum and breadth until the first decade of the new century. Not until then did the members of the middle class consider the times safe enough to introduce reforms. The return of prosperity had by that time eliminated the labor violence and the specter of revolution that had haunted the middle class in the depression years of the mid-nineties. Memories of the Homestead riots, the Pullman strike, and the march of Coxey's army on Washington had receded into the past. The din of the Populist agitation had quieted. Bryan, the latter-day Populist and champion of cheap silver, had been defeated; the currency issue was settled in favor of sound currency. The economy was prosperous enough to withstand the mild shocks from the social and political changes the middle-class reformers might introduce.[6]

The first stirring of reform occurred in Toledo in 1897 more by accident than by design. Leadership came unexpectedly from a relative newcomer to that city, Samuel Milton Jones. A resident of less than five years, he had won some renown in business circles as a manufacturer who had introduced advanced labor theories and made them pay, and in church circles as a man who was deeply concerned with the problems of applied Christianity. Politically he was unknown. Nevertheless, the extraordinary happened: the first political convention he had ever attended chose him as its nominee for mayor. The stage had been set for his selection as a dark-horse candidate by the division among Toledo Republicans.

The Hanna faction, led by George Waldorf and Walter F. Brown, was looking for a candidate to replace Guy Major, the incumbent mayor, who had become a political liability because of his loose administration and his long identification with the discredited American Protective Association; it turned to James Melvin. Challenging the power of the bosses and the Hanna machine were two other factions: the Forakerites, who were backing Lem P. Harris, city clerk, in the expectation of regaining power and prestige, and a group of independent businessmen hopeful of cleaning up the party, who were supporting one of their own, John Craig.

For five ballots the convention was deadlocked. However, Melvin had been slowly gaining, and the two opposition factions realized that they must unite if they were to defeat the machine. Thereupon Craig's manager, James M. Ashley, Jr., withdrew his candidate's name and presented Jones's instead. Simultaneously the Forakerites shifted from Harris to Jones, and a loud demonstration was generated for "S. M. Jones, the businessman and a true friend of labor." On the sixth ballot he won. He had received the nomination because it was believed he could command the labor vote and, once in office, would give the city a clean, "business" administration, and at the same time restore party patronage and prestige to the Foraker faction.[7]

Few persons knew what to make of this unsophisticated candidate who had been dubbed "Golden Rule" Jones for pleading for fair play for labor and a better social order. But the politically inexperienced nominee possessed instinctively the talent of a seasoned campaigner. In this first contest he set the keynote for all the others that were to follow. He spoke plain truths to his audiences about the right to work and the unemployment problem, about the inequalities in taxation. These were the real issues, he insisted, and were not to be drowned out by the clamor over the tariff and the currency. His unorthodoxy aroused the opposition of the utility interests, and his identification with "good" government inspired the enmity of the saloonkeepers, who supposed that he was another moral reformer. But supported by labor and by a large section of the middle class whose natural propensity was to vote Republican, he carried the election against his Democratic opponent by the narrow margin of 518 votes out of the 20,614 cast. With all of the exuberant pride of a schoolboy winning his first victory, he wired Washington Gladden, "I am elected in spite of six hundred saloons, the street car company and the devil."[8]

The mayor-elect was then fifty-one, a big man with brawny hands, large blue eyes set in a genial face, and a manner that was frank and direct. He had great energy and a practical shrewdness that had enabled him to rise from humble beginnings to become a man of means. His parents had brought him by steerage from his native Wales to America in 1849 when he was three. They settled on a farm in Lewis County, New York, where he received his only formal education, thirty months at the local school. Finding farming chores uncongenial, he left home at fourteen to work as a sawmill hand and three years later as a greaser and wiper on a steamboat—jobs that satisfied his mechanical bent. At nineteen he went to Titusville, Pennsylvania, where the oil fever was at its height, and within a few years had established himself as an oil driller with wells of his own. His first marriage took place there in 1875, a marriage whose sorrows left their scars upon him. First his only daughter died, then four years later his wife died, leaving him with two sons to raise alone.

In an effort to free himself from the poignant associations of his Pennsylvania home the widower, with his two boys, moved in 1885 to Lima, Ohio, the center of a new oil strike. There Jones drilled the famous Tunget Well, which produced over six hundred barrels a day. With a small group of other oil producers he formed the Ohio Oil Company, which sold its interests in 1889 to the Standard Oil Company for $650,000. During the next three years Jones continued to live in Lima, active in church and civic affairs. In 1892 he married Helen Beech, a schoolteacher who shared his love of music, and moved to Toledo, his new wife's home. There, two years later, he began a new and very profitable business, the Acme Sucker Rod Company, to manufacture oil-drilling machinery that he had patented.[9]

When this newcomer first appeared in Toledo, he seemed scarcely distinguishable from other prosperous, civic-minded businessmen of the city. He had given no hint of the distinctive opinions that were to set him apart from these men and to affect the politics of his adopted city. But he was soon to witness conditions that profoundly influenced his thought and actions. He opened his factory in 1894, a year of depression and unemployment. Men came in streams begging for work. "The actual contact with ragged starving men," he wrote, "willing and anxious to do any kind of work," made him acutely conscious for the first time in his life that the existing social arrangements "did not square with any just conception of democracy or brotherhood."[10] He determined to make what restitution he could within his own plant.

At once Jones investigated the wage structure, and learning that some men were working for as little as a dollar a day, he announced that in his factory the "going wage" would be replaced by a "living wage." He set the minimum wage first at a dollar and a half, then raised it to two dollars a day, for all who had been employed a year. Gradually other benefits were added, some unique at that time: the eight-hour day and forty-eight-hour week, a week's vacation with pay for all who had been with the company six months, a 5 per cent cash dividend at Christmas, lunches at cost, and a cooperative insurance plan to pay for sickness and injuries. These benefits, Jones insisted, were not inspired by generosity nor donated as charity; they were an effort to make a fairer distribution to the men of the wealth their labor created.

Jones's burgeoning social philosophy was reflected in other ways in the conducting of his factory. Appalled by the practice in neighboring establishments of printing a long list of rules, most of which ended with the threat of dismissal, he determined to have only one rule in his factory, the golden rule: "All things whatsoever men do to you, do ye even so to them." This was painted on a piece of tin and nailed to the factory wall. No applicant for a job was questioned on his religion, morals, or habits. Discipline was maintained on the co-operative principle; there were no bosses, timekeepers, or time clocks. Neither child labor, piecework, nor any system of contract labor was countenanced.

His men, Jones discovered, needed more than material benefits; they needed education in the spirit of liberty, equality, and brotherhood. Men applying for work in his factory had a groveling sense of inferiority toward him as an employer. To overcome this attitude among his own workers he planned outings with them and invited them to his house. In their weekly pay envelopes he inserted short essays on democracy, co-operation, and love. He and other speakers addressed the men and their families on the same themes on Sunday afternoons in Golden Rule Park, which had been laid out in a corner of the factory lot. There also the Golden Rule Band played and a chorus sang Jones's own songs about love and brotherhood. A room above the shop, which he christened the Golden Rule Hall and Dining Room, was set aside as a place where the factory hands might mingle and talk with distinguished guests present at Jones's invitation. These accessories to his factory were his particular delight; they provided a practical demonstration of his theories on brotherhood.[11]

Jones's experience as an employer was the first step in his social awakening. It was closely accompanied by a second when he turned to other social thinkers for ideas to confirm and widen his own. He founded the Society of Applied Christianity and brought before that body at his own expense speakers who were known for their concern about the Christian's social responsibility: Josiah Strong, Washington Gladden, Jane Addams, Graham Taylor, and many more. He began delving into the works of sociologists, social psychologists, political scientists, and economists, including Frank Parsons, John A. Hobson, James Bryce, Sidney and Beatrice Webb, and John R. Commons.[12] He made himself familiar with the writings of Henry George, whom Jones praised as "one of the noblest spirits the social reform spirit has known," though he found inadequate the remedy of the single tax and differed fundamentally with George on the method of achieving equality by restoring competition.[13] On the other hand, he found the ideas of Henry Demarest Lloyd altogether compatible. Not only did Jones believe Lloyd's exposure of the "crimes" of the Standard Oil Trust in *Wealth against Commonwealth* to be "unanswerable," but he agreed with Lloyd that the ideal social order was a "Co-operative Commonwealth" that would bring out man's full capacity to love his neighbor.[14]

He received inspiration and guidance from the prose writings of Emerson, Ruskin, Bellamy, and Howells and from the verses of the English and American poets of the mid-nineteenth century, for he had an inborn Celtic love of lyrics and song. Walt Whitman became his favorite poet; Jones kept an autographed, well-marked copy of the *Leaves of Grass* close at hand. It was Whitman's praise of the common man and cry for comradeship that appealed to the Mayor. Side by side with Whitman's poems was a well-thumbed New Testament which he read with his "reason and common sense, dismissing all nonsensical theological notions," but seeking out its message of brotherly love. He found more influential than any other novelist Count Leo Tolstoy, especially his last book, *The Resurrection*. But the writer to whom he owed the most was George D. Herron, the Christian socialist minister. It was he who had brought Jones from "the darkness of individualism into the real light of social relationship." Herron's appeal for unity among men, his denunciation of self-interest and materialism, his emphasis on the stewardship of wealth struck responsive chords in Jones's own thinking. These were his guides to politics, to economics, to life.[15]

In an autobiographical volume called *The New Right*[16] Jones attempted to draw together his social philosophy. This and a collection of essays written for the enlightenment of his factory employees and published under the title *Letters of Love and Labor*[17] comprise the bulk of his formal writing. Even in these works Jones failed to systematize adequately his thought, for he lacked formal training and relied upon intuition more than logic in attacking problems.

He was very much a child of the Anglo-American intellectual environment of the nineteenth century in accepting its optimistic view of mankind and its faith in the moral and social progress of man here and now. The perfect society was to be achieved, according to him, both by the regeneration of the individual and by changes in the social environment. Everyone, he believed, was capable of being redeemed by love. To his friend Washington Gladden, he declared his faith in its redemptive power: "I think Emerson was right when he said 'love is the only basis upon which we may hope to build an enduring state' and back of him Jesus was emphatically right in saying, 'Ye must be born again.'"[18] But Jones did not expect the rebirth to be instantaneous; it would only come by the slow process of education and evolution. Government had a responsibility to teach people the brotherhood of love and to guide them by molding love into law. Eventually, he hoped, individuals would come to know that they cannot separate religion from politics or business from religion.[19]

He saw the ideal state as a co-operative commonwealth in which public co-operative capital would replace private competitive capital, and all men would enjoy the greatest of human rights, the right to work. This did not imply drudgery for eight to ten hours a day, he explained, "but the right to participate in creating the world about us"—the kind of work William Morris defined "when he said that 'art is the expression of man's joy in labor.'"[20] Moreover, since work, as he believed, was the source of all wealth, the workers would be able to retain all the fruits of their toil. There would be no need for charity; paupers, tramps, and criminals would disappear. All would live together as a loving family of equals, each having access to everything needed for the fullest development of his soul and body.[21]

Jones's blueprint of the ideal community is a familiar one, not unlike Bellamy's and Lloyd's. It also bears a marked similarity to Marx's communist utopia. But Jones was otherwise far apart from the orthodox Socialists and rejected their doctrines of class warfare and revolutionary change. Instead, he insisted upon a step by step approach toward his goal.[22]

He would correct at once the most distressing problem of unemployment by adopting the eight-hour day universally; but if unemployment persisted, he would reduce hours even more. He would encourage all laborers to join trade unions because of the great good they had accomplished and the feeling of solidarity they fostered—a step in the direction of universal brotherhood.[23] Another step forward, he believed, would be to "abolish every form of special privilege—all patent laws, all tariff laws, all grants of franchises." These were the source of the trusts. Nevertheless, he did not believe in destroying these giant monopolies. Much as he decried their evils, he defended their growth as a logical, even desirable, economic development in man's progress toward the destruction of the fierce warfare of competitive capitalism. His solution for the problem of the trusts was to have the people own them as they owned the post-office "trust." Government ownership of the flour and steel industries would bring the same benefits as the municipal ownership of gas or street-railway lines. Economically it would enable the people to recover the values they had created and to gain efficiency by substituting co-operation for competition. Morally and politically its virtue would be to awaken a sense of pride among citizens through common ownership and to give a practical demonstration of brotherhood by having the government seek the good of all against the individual.[24]

It is evident from his advocacy of public ownership that Jones believed in the efficacy and potential goodness of the political state. Indeed it was for him the only organization of which all the people were a part, the only one through which all might be served, and the only agency through which the people could express their love for one another. But more and more he had come to believe that the only proper function of the state was to administer "all the necessities that are common to all the people" and not to be a "government by force."[25] Furthermore, much as he might respect the *ideal* state as a potent instrument for good, he pleaded for the right of the individual in the *existing* state to judge its law according to his own conscience and determine what he shall obey and what he shall defy. Not until there was a changeover from private to public ownership of utilities and trusts, not until the government ceased to be "an instrument of the cunning few for the purpose of plundering the poor" would good laws and a good state be assured.[26]

So far the common people in their ignorance and delusion had failed to act. But Jones was confident that they would respond to the appeals of leaders like himself who were dedicated to the people's cause and were without consciousness of class. The working people would rise to the challenge, he explained, not because they were intrinsically more moral or intelligent than the rich but because they had the advantage of their environment which developed the sturdy social virtues of neighborliness and faith in one another. He would not organize them into a political party, however, for to him the party idea seemed "an effort to divide a social body, to separate men that are brothers and ought to live brotherly, an effort to line them up into organizations as fighters and haters when we should be doing all in our power to go together as lovers and friends."[27] Partisan politics, he prognosticated, would yield in time to nonpartisanship; and political campaigns, instead of being contests for place and power between Democrats and Republicans, would become great forums for the enlightenment of the people in the cause of liberty, equality, and love. Another argument he advanced in favor of the nonpartisan principle was that it would make elections more democratic. For the same reason he supported the initiative and referendum, which would enable the people to legislate for themselves. He had a boundless faith in the capacity of the common man to rule and therefore found appealing any reform that would increase democracy.[28]

Jones made no claim to consistency; he was the first to admit that his conduct fell short of his ideals. His business prospered behind patent walls that he would abolish together with all forms of special privilege. Party politics offended him, yet he did not hesitate to take sides in campaigns, first with the Republicans, later with the Democrats in order to back Bryan for President in 1900 and Tom Johnson for governor in 1903. The system of charity angered him; nevertheless, the mayor's office during his incumbency became a charity bureau through which he dispersed every cent of the salary he received from the city. He turned against the churches, yet insisted at the same time that he was becoming more and more of a true Christian. His anarchical view of the law seemed to free the individual from the responsibility of obeying laws against his conscience, but as mayor he enforced statutes in which he personally did not believe.[29]

Such, in brief, were the ideas of Mayor Jones. However, he had not had the occasion to state or even consider all of them before taking office in 1897. The man's social conscience and philosophy continued to develop during his political career, which was to extend through the remaining seven years of his life.

Throughout his four terms as mayor he endeavored to make Toledo a model co-operative commonwealth. The eight-hour day was introduced in the departments of police and water and was prescribed on all work privately contracted by the city. Municipal services were expanded to provide playgrounds, golf links, free concerts, and kindergartens in the schools.[30] Jones made a strong effort to promote municipal ownership of an artificial-gas plant and an electric-light plant. Unfortunately, a disastrous experience with a city-owned natural-gas pipeline in the early 1890's had prejudiced a majority of Toledoans against municipal enterprises, and both were defeated.[31] It was impossible for him to press for city ownership of the street-railway system, which the laws of Ohio did not permit. But he did pursue the next best alternative—a reduction in fares that would return to the people the "unearned increment" or profit from the franchise monopoly. In this contest he had the backing of a majority of the citizens, who had suspected for some time that the traction company had been reaping exorbitant profits from the prevailing fares. In 1903 the city council passed an ordinance which cut the rate schedule, although not enough to suit the Mayor, who vetoed it.[32] The issue of the street-railway fares was unsettled at the time of his death; it remained a problem that his successors were to find equally unyielding and were unable to resolve for many years. Jones carried the fight for the municipal-ownership principle outside of Toledo through the League of American Municipalities and the similar organization in Ohio, in both of which he took an active interest.[33]

The reform which has become inseparable from his name, and which he left as his major legacy to Toledo—the nonpartisan principle—grew directly out of his political experience as well as his philosophical convictions. During his first two years in politics when he still wore the Republican label, he clashed with Senator Mark Hanna, who seemed to the Toledo mayor to be the symbol of the self-seeking rich man in politics. Because of his antipathy to Hanna, Jones became allied, albeit somewhat ambiguously, with the opposing Foraker faction and engaged in an intraparty contest that was uncongenial to him, and in which he was an inept participant. Hanna regarded him as a renegade and marked him for political destruction. The Senator's lieutenants helped defeat the Mayor's renomination by the Republicans in the spring of 1899 and routed Jones's hopes for being the party's nominee for governor that same summer. To this point he had weighed the possibility that he might follow in the footsteps of his friend and fellow-Republican, Governor Hazen S. Pingree of Michigan, who had succeeded in leading his party down the path of reform, first as mayor of Detroit and then as the head of his state. But now Jones left the Republican party, never to return. He might have crossed over to the Democratic side where there were some kindred spirits, but he hesitated because of John R. McLean, who seemed to be a man of the same stamp as Hanna.[34]

In the Toledo mayoralty election of 1899, Jones ran for the first time as an independent and won overwhelmingly, polling nearly 70 per cent of the votes. Interpreting his victory as a triumph of nonpartisanship, he was encouraged to run for governor as "The Man Without a Party" in the fall of 1899. It was in this campaign that he became a confirmed advocate of the principle. Although he did not win in the state as he had in Toledo, and although he later supported the Democrats on particular issues, he remained unswerving in his allegiance to his new commitment.[35]

Jones's vivid sense of brotherhood with all mankind led him to look upon the fallen members of the community—prostitutes, drunkards, gamblers, and petty criminals—as the victims of society who had long been subject to ill-treatment. One source of abuse was the brutality and irresponsibility of the police, which the Mayor sought to remedy by improving the quality of the force through the merit system and a shorter working day and by limiting their power to do physical violence by exchanging canes for clubs. He appointed men of like sympathies, Benjamin Raitz and Perry Knapp, as superintendents of police. Another source of ill-treatment of the social pariahs, in Jones's eyes, were the moral reformers who wanted to force men to be good by punitive blue laws. He refused to listen to these busybodies and tailored his enforcement policy to his own theories, halfheartedly cleaning out gambling places, wine rooms, and brothels, and defending the saloon as the poor man's club and refuge. Good government to him did not mean "clamping down the lid"; the objective should be rather greater freedom from restraint and more of the spirit of brotherhood. But it seemed to the ministers and good people of Toledo that he was tolerating a wide-open town. They were doubly distressed because they had voted for him in 1897 in the belief that he was a like-minded moral up- lifter. In the next mayoralty campaign they took their revenge by importing a professional revivalist, Samuel Porter Jones, to berate the Mayor for being a tool of the saloon interests.[36]

Still their concern on this count was soon overshadowed by their alarm at Jones's open contempt for the system of "police- court justice," which he began voicing in his third term. Prior to that time he had confined his attention to its worst abuses by eliminating the wholesale beatings and arrests of drunk and disorderly persons, by assuring humane treatment of the in- mates of the workhouse, and by providing legal aid out of his own pocket for those who could not afford it.[37] Now he turned on the system as a whole. He condemned it for discriminating between rich and poor—sending the poor man to prison and allowing the rich man to walk away free upon paying a paltry fine. He castigated imprisonment for crime as a fraud that had failed as a method of reform. Under the charter he as mayor could preside over the police court in the absence of the regular judge. As often as the opportunity came, he used the occasion to emphasize his views by dismissing all the defendants who appeared before him. In one session he shocked the community by freeing two men who had pleaded guilty to burglary charges because, as he said, though they deserved imprisonment it would be of no help to them.

Jones insisted that the way to rid the community of criminals was to provide opportunities for men to earn an honest liveli- hood. Change the economic system and the need for police courts and jails would disappear, for all men were sound of heart, he believed, and would lead upright lives in the proper social environment. Meanwhile he could show his faith in the goodness of humanity by protecting tramps and petty thieves from the injustices of the existing system.[38]

The Mayor's conduct angered the respectable element. They condemned his theory as being palpably false. Times were prosperous, work was plentiful, and still men begged and stole. But they condemned him even more for bringing the city into disrepute as a kind of asylum for petty criminals.[39] Desperate to curb the Mayor, they backed a ripper bill, which passed the state legislature in 1902, stripping him of his power over the police board and the police court. But in lending their support to such legislation they overplayed their hand. They gave Jones the opportunity to divert attention from himself and law enforcement to the issue of democratic rule versus boss rule, for he accused the local politicians of both parties of being responsible for destroying the old board in order to regain patronage over the police department, which he had placed on the merit system.[40]

The Mayor, who had been in ill health for a year and had contemplated retiring, determined to run a fourth time in the spring election of 1903 to vindicate himself and his principles. As before, he ran alone without a slate of candidates for other offices and without a formal organization. He was aided only by a few Toledo friends and a handful of speakers from outside. Among his supporters were: William Cowell, a former editor of a labor paper, who had been responsible for launching the Mayor into politics in 1897; Brand Whitlock, a young Democratic lawyer, who had been drawn to Jones because of a common sympathy for the outcasts of society and because of a mutual enthusiasm for Whitman, Tolstoy, and other writers with a social vision; and a few Republicans like A. D. Fassett, Elisha B. Southard, and John B. Merrell, a former police commissioner—men who placed loyalty to Jones above loyalty to the party.[41]

The strategy of the Republicans and Democrats was to select as their nominees businessmen of impeccable respectability and to deny newspaper backing to Jones. As a result the Mayor's only press support came from a foreign-language journal. The Republican *Blade* even refused to mention his name, but its

policy of silence boomeranged, for it made a martyr of Jones
and greatly strengthened his cause with the common people.
Negley D. Cochran, the editor of the Democratic *Bee,* who had
endorsed Jones in 1901, now turned against him. Although the
editor respected the Mayor as a humanitarian, a foe of bigotry,
and a champion of the people's rights against the utility interests, Cochran felt that Jones was damaging the city's name by
harboring violators of the law. The *Bee,* however, gave the
Mayor's campaign ample coverage.[42]

Jones countered the hostility of the press by increasing the
tempo of his campaign. He spoke daily from street corners, at
manufacturing plants during the noon hour, and at halls in
the workingmen's districts at night. His meetings were more
educational and religious than political in character. The sincerity and earnestness of his delivery, the simplicity of his
phrases made him a compelling speaker. He was the idol of
the foreign-born, who eagerly responded to his homilies on
liberty and brotherhood that were liberally sprinkled with quotations from Emerson, Whitman, and the Bible. Band music
and songs performed by men from his factory added to the
popularity of his meetings. But to win he needed more than
the votes of the immigrants. He carried the election by a substantial plurality because he also appealed to many white-collar
workers and small businessmen. They preferred a mayor who,
no matter how eccentric his views might be on law enforcement, was sincerely trying to apply the golden rule and make
"the outer world fit the inner vision." [43]

However, in running alone, Jones had let the other city
offices go by default to candidates of the Republican machine
who won all but one of them. Such divided control of the municipal government substantially nullified the Mayor's jubilant
claim that the people in electing him had "served notice on the
political machines of the city that their services are no longer
needed." Moreover, the people were soon to lose the leadership
of their beloved mayor; within fifteen months of re-election he
was dead.[44]

One other contribution by Jones to the reform awakening
remains to be told. Not only was he the first of the municipal
reformers in Ohio, but he was also the first to recognize the
need to carry the battle to the state if the cities were to be free

from the dominance of big business and its political allies. His chance to make a state-wide campaign came in the gubernatorial contest of 1899.

The large vote by which he had been re-elected mayor in the spring of that year had placed him in the political limelight. He was encouraged to run for governor on the Republican ticket by some of the Forakerites and on the Democratic ticket by Negley Cochran, the head of the local anti-McLean faction.[45] But Jones did not have a chance of acceptance by the leaders of either party. Senator Hanna denounced him as a "moral crank" and supplied the money that was decisive in helping to elect a hostile delegation from Lucas County (Toledo) to the Republican state convention. Long before that body met even Senator Foraker had publicly read the Toledo mayor out of the party for "his municipal ownership nonsense and other Populistic fads." It was, therefore, no surprise that Jones was ignored. The party's nomination for governor went instead to George K. Nash, the choice of Mark Hanna and of George B. Cox, who controlled the convention.[46] But this was not the only decision by the Republicans that offended the Mayor. He thought the "cheekiest" thing they had done was to condemn the trusts and indulge in self-glorification over the antitrust laws in their platform and then turn around and defeat Frank S. Monnett, the incumbent attorney-general, "who had done more to enforce the laws against the trusts than any attorney general the state ever had." Jones was convinced that the Hanna-Cox ticket should be defeated because it did not represent "a single moral principle." [47]

After witnessing the eclipse of his hopes for making the Republican party an instrument for progress, he was still undecided on what course to follow to unite the reform forces. Should he cast his lot with the Democratic party, as Cochran urged? He knew that he had no chance for the Democratic nomination, for though he had become an apostate from Hanna Republicanism, he had been too recently identified with that party. The two leading Democrats for the governorship were John R. McLean, the ambitious non-resident with plenty of money and few scruples, and Colonel James Kilbourne, a Columbus manufacturer with an enlightened labor record and a reputation for honesty and incorruptibility. It was widely rumored that Jones would support Kilbourne, if the latter were nominated, but at no point did the Mayor make such a pledge.[48]

On the contrary, by mid-summer he was all but committed to run for governor as an independent candidate. Two considerations weighed most heavily in his decision. One was the stream of letters urging him to make the race—an expression of "the voice of the people" which was irresistible to him. The other was unmistakable evidence that McLean would be the Democratic nominee—a prognostication that was confirmed when that party met on August 28. Without waiting for the Democrats to act, Jones had made a formal announcement the week before that he would run for governor as a nonpartisan.[49]

Already he had enough signatures on nominating petitions to secure a place on the election ballot. Unbeknownst to him he had received undercover aid in circulating the petitions from the McLean men, who were hopeful that Jones's candidacy would divide the Republican vote. But his principal and genuine support came from labor. There had been talk in the spring of a complete labor ticket in the forthcoming election, and he had already addressed a convention called to consider such an independent movement, but nothing came of it. Nevertheless, without formal endorsement, the "Golden Rule" Mayor was regarded as the candidate of labor.[50]

His platform was designed to appeal not only to workingmen but to middle-class reformers as well. It included pledges to promote public ownership of all utilities, direct primaries, direct legislation, and acceptance of the nonpartisan principle, in addition to planks that applied to labor alone: the eight-hour day, union standards for skilled employees, elimination of the contract system on public works, abolition of prison labor, and state aid for the unemployed. In the campaign he concentrated on the abolition of parties, the political change most important to him, although he did not neglect public ownership of utilities and labor reforms.[51]

At the outset Jones was handicapped by lack of money, organization, and newspaper support. His campaign director, William Cowell, complained that there were not enough funds to supply the demands for literature or to pay the traveling expenses of speakers. Abandoned by the Forakerites, Jones received no open support from professional politicians. His speakers were all

volunteers from outside of the state and were generally known radicals: William J. Ghent, George D. Herron, Herbert N. Casson, and Clarence Darrow, who had defended Debs in the Pullman strike. For this very reason Henry Demarest Lloyd had declined to assist, fearful that his own radicalism might prove injurious to the Mayor's cause. Jones himself campaigned hard, particularly in the rural areas, where he was little known, covering half of the eighty-eight counties. People were impressed, he noted, "with the religious enthusiasm that seemed to characterize the meetings." [52]

He threw a scare into both the Republican and Democratic camps. Hanna increased the party funds in Cincinnati, Toledo, and Cleveland in an endeavor to hold the labor vote, and pressure was brought on the express and railroad companies to keep their employees in line. President McKinley, Theodore Roosevelt, and other prominent Republicans were brought into Ohio to divert attention from Jones and his reform issues to national questions of the Philippines and of trade. The Democrats followed similar tactics. McLean sought to lure the labor vote from Jones by promising most of the same reforms and purchasing the support of some union leaders. He ordered the editors of the Democratic papers that he subsidized to ignore Jones. William Jennings Bryan entered the campaign on McLean's behalf and helped to shift the emphasis to the Philippine issue and anti-imperialism. Speakers for both parties tried to belittle Jones by dismissing him as a kindly but impractical dreamer who was running alone without a slate of other candidates for the state offices or the legislature and who had no hope of election himself. A vote for such a man was a vote wasted, they insisted. [53]

On election day the unusually heavy balloting indicated that the Republican and Democratic managers alike were making the final effort to defeat the Jones threat by getting their partisans to the polls. They succeeded: Nash won with 417,199 votes, McLean ran second with 368,176, and Jones third with 106,721. The farmers had once again remained "true blue" to the Republican party, persuaded, according to one of its observers, that "the high prices of wool and wheat were better arguments than any cry of anti-Hannaism or anti-imperialism." But Jones had the satisfaction of making a dent in the Republican urban vote by carrying his own city as well as Cleveland, the home of Mark Hanna.[54]

As in the case with other third-party movements in American history, the election figures did not truly measure Jones's significance. He led an educational campaign for the acceptance of principles and reforms which, though considered radical then, were in large part written in the statute books within a decade and a half. He befriended the workingmen when they had few champions and detached some of them from their allegiance to the ward bosses.[55] He stirred dissent against the Hanna brand of Republicanism. By campaigning against parties he helped to weaken the intense partisanship of the time and to stimulate independence in voting, even if he won little support for the nonpartisan idea. His example encouraged reformers in other urban communities, not only in Ohio but in the nation. Thereafter Jones enjoyed a national reputation. He was invited to speak all over the country and to write for the leading magazines concerned with reform, and he played a prominent part in the proceedings of the League of American Municipalities.[56]

One of those inspired by Jones's example was Washington Gladden, a minister of the social gospel, who consented to run as an independent reform candidate for the municipal council in his adopted city of Columbus in 1900. The city's relations with the public-service corporations had reached a critical point. Important franchises were expiring, and the fate of the municipal light plant was in jeopardy. A ring of councilmen, it was alleged, were seeking re-election through a corrupt bargain with those utilities which would be applying to the council for franchise renewals, and one of those councilmen was from Gladden's district. As a man of standing in the community, Gladden felt an obligation to serve the city in its hour of need. An encouraging letter from Jones helped to strengthen his decision. Although nominally a Republican, he was supported by a nonpartisan association of neighbors who made a door-to-door canvass on his behalf. He was elected as an Independent, defeating the regular Republican nominee by a majority of seventy-three votes.[57]

The new Councilman, with his bald head, patriarchal white beard, and stocky frame, was a familiar figure to most citizens of the capital city. Not only was he prominent at home, but he enjoyed a reputation throughout the country for his fearless protests against cant and injustice and for his intense interest in labor and humanitarian reforms. His social conscience had been first awakened by the temperance and anti-slavery crusades which in the early 1850's swept the region of Central New York State, where he had been reared. Brought up in a household of bookish New England Calvinists, he had developed a religious and moral sensitivity which made him quick to respond to these humanitarian causes. He joined a newly formed Congregational church composed of reformers as militant as himself. It was this association that inspired Gladden to choose the ministry as a career; at the age of twenty he began preparing for it at Williams College. Like Jones, he was moved by a faith in man's capacity to be regenerated by the power of Christian love and "to realize the Kingdom of God in this world." [58]

The conviction that religion should lay "hold upon life with both hands" possessed him the rest of his days.[59] In the spirit of the ministers of the early New England Congregational church and of the preachers of the latter-day social gospel, he was the temporal as well as the spiritual guide to his congregation. The pages of his autobiographical *Recollections* bear witness to his lively interest in political and social issues. During his ministry in North Adams, Massachusetts, immediately after the Civil War, the labor problem was thrust at him in aggravated form when a local shoe factory introduced Chinese coolies as strikebreakers to displace the native workers. In New York, where he served as the religious editor of the *Independent* for a brief period, he was shocked by the exposure of the notorious Tweed Ring. He used the editorial page to arouse a stunned and helpless public to act against the members of the Ring and to send the guilty men to jail. The year after the Panic of 1873 he had returned once again to the active ministry, accepting a call to a church in Springfield, Massachusetts. The city was feeling the effects of the hard times, and the unemployed were restless. Gladden was asked to address them. Although he promised them little, he agreed to make their cause the subject of his next Sunday sermon—a daring concession in a day when any expression of sympathy for labor from the pulpit was frowned upon. He pleaded with his congregation to find work for the jobless, and several responded. Two years later he published a series of talks on the subject, entitled *Workingmen and Their Employers*, which afterwards seemed to him timid and not as sympathetic to labor unions as they might have been. Yet they were tokens of his conviction that "the application of the Christian law to social questions is not a recondite matter." [60]

His ministry in Columbus, which began in 1882 when he was forty-six, was the fulfillment of all that had been tendentious in his life before. Not only was his church at the center of the city geographically, but he made it also a center of interest in the political and social problems of the community. In 1893 he showed that he had the courage of his convictions when his was one of the few voices raised against the bigotry of the American Protective Association, then particularly active in Columbus, where the supreme vice-president of the association, the Reverend Adam Fawcett, had his church. For his pains in exposing Fawcett and the association, Gladden was accused of being a jackal of the Catholic church, in black conspiracy with Romanism, and the mere thought of considering him as a candidate for the presidency of Ohio State University was denounced by the pro-APA majority in the state legislature. But in two years time the movement was dead, and the condemnation turned to praise as people recalled his courageous opposition to that wave of intolerance.[61]

The suffering of the workers in the Panic of 1893 and the depression that followed affected Gladden much as it did Jones; the minister came to adopt labor views that were as advanced as those of the Toledo manufacturer. Gladden became an insistent advocate of the trade union and of collective bargaining. "It is ridiculous," he wrote, "to talk of freedom of contract between employer and employee, when the employer is a great corporation, and the employee is a single individual. The freedom of the man outside the gates is simply the freedom of taking what is offered or starving." The law must confirm and employers must recognize the right of working men to bargain collectively, if the wage system were to be maintained. He supported the eight-hour day and a Saturday half-holiday to give factory workers a chance for recreation and sports. Strikes, he believed, should be called sparingly and conducted without violence; arbitration was his preferred method of settling disputes.

Although he rejected the socialist state, he urged government interference to protect the working class "from the brutalizing effects of unhindered competition": sweatshops, dangerous machinery, child labor, and long hours for women. Also he insisted that the government had a responsibility to provide work relief for the unemployed in times of depression.[62]

Not only did Gladden challenge contemporary views on labor, but he also endeavored to upset complacent thinking on other political and economic questions. In 1893 he published an article recommending a co-operative league between churches and other agencies to promote good government. He aroused an interest among the members of the Columbus Board of Trade in drafting a new charter for the city which would effectively concentrate authority and responsibility. At the Milwaukee convention of the National Municipal League in 1900 he gave an address entitled "The Influences of Public Services on City Government," in which he concluded that they were debauching municipal democracy by illegitimate and subterranean methods of bribery and corruption. As the bribe givers, the public-service corporations were more to blame than the bribe takers. The remedy for the situation was municipal ownership, for the people must recover the rich franchise monopolies before the pressure of private greed destroyed city government. In other writings he logically extended the public-ownership concept to railroads, the telegraph and telephone systems, and natural resources. The essence of economic democracy, as he saw it, was popular control of the monopolies of goods and services necessary to the well-being of the people. In addition he urged government regulation of trusts in other fields of industry.[63]

When Gladden entered upon his duties as councilman in 1900, he welcomed the opportunity to put his theories into practice. He was made chairman of the committee on gas and electricity and was a member of another on street railways. A fight was then being waged over renewing the franchise for the traction company. He exposed the fallacies in its pleas for high fares, yet at the same time he rejected as impractical a proposal by Tom L. Johnson of Cleveland to buy the traction system and operate it on a three-cent-fare basis. Instead he proposed a compromise plan of reducing fares in relation to the company's earnings, which the council adopted. This settlement removed from Columbus politics an issue which kept the voters of Toledo and Cleveland agitated for more than another decade.[64]

The preacher-in-politics took an even more vigorous part in the settlement of the city lighting question in which the principle of municipal ownership was at stake. Bonds for a municipal light plant had been voted in 1896, and a small plant had been constructed which was capable of lighting only a third of the city's street lamps; power for the remainder was furnished by a public-service corporation, the franchise of which expired in 1901. In the summer of 1900 the municipal plant closed down because the council refused to vote funds on the grounds that it was a failure. Gladden prepared to meet this challenge to his theory by visiting municipal electric plants in Detroit, Springfield, Dayton, and Chicago and gathering valuable material on their operating costs. Armed with these figures and with the specific recommendation of a Chicago expert on the amount needed to make the Columbus plant a success, Gladden introduced an ordinance to issue bonds worth $132,000 to erect a light plant large enough to furnish power to all of the street lamps of the city. The council passed the measure unanimously, and later the people voted their endorsement.[65]

Gladden refused to stand for re-election in 1902, for he found the demands of office too heavy on top of his ministerial work. Moreover, he was disillusioned by the partisanship, the ignorance, and the selfishness he found on the council. Unless he was joined by other good men, it was futile, he felt, for him to continue. Although he never held political office again and thus failed to lead a party of reform, he continued to be an effective crusader for his principles by other means. He lobbied for reform before the council and state legislature, served on committees to endorse good candidates, presided at civic-reform meetings, and acted as a mediator in strikes. In his Sunday evening lectures, which were printed in Monday morning's press, he constantly pleaded for labor's rights, municipal ownership, direct democracy, and a better tone in politics. By such deeds and words he kept the reform spirit nourished in Columbus.[66]

When Gladden retired, he knew there were others elsewhere who would carry forward the civic revival in Ohio. Not only was Jones still at the helm in Toledo, but Tom L. Johnson, who was to become the most aggressive Ohio leader of reform, had been elected mayor of Cleveland the year before.

1. Richard Hofstadter, *The Age of Reform: From Bryan to F. D. R.* (New York, 1955), 148–63. Confirmation of Hofstadter is to be found in an analysis of the leaders of the Progressive party made by Alfred D. Chandler, Jr., "The Origins of Progressive Leadership," in Elting E. Morison and John M. Blum, eds., *The Letters of Theodore Roosevelt* (8 vols; Cambridge, 1951–54), VIII, Appendix III, 1462–65, and in an examination of the leaders of the progressive movement in California by George E. Mowry, *The California Progressives* (Berkeley, Calif., 1951), 86–88.

2. This analysis is based on an examination of the careers of over ninety individuals who actively contributed to the progressive movement in their community, the state administration, the legislature, the Constitutional Convention of 1912, or the party organization. The selection has been necessarily somewhat arbitrary, and it has not been possible to find the desired data on every individual.

TABLE OF OCCUPATION AND PARTY AFFILIATION OF LEADERS
OF THE PROGRESSIVE MOVEMENT IN OHIO

Occupation	Democrats	Republicans	Progressives
Lawyers	20	3	5
Businessmen	7	4	3
Editors	3	0	2
Ministers	2	1	0
Educators	1	1	1
Laborers	6	1	1
Unknown	24	6	0
Total	63	16	12

Only four are known to have been foreign-born: two in Wales, one in Scotland, and one in Germany. The number of non-Protestants is not readily ascertainable but so far as is known only two were Catholics and two Jews. Ten were in their forties and five were fifty or older.

3. Johnson, *My Story*, 1–47; Samuel M. Jones, *The New Right* (New York, 1899), 39–63; Gladden, *Recollections*, 282–84, 378–80.

4. Hofstadter, *The Age of Reform*, 168–72.

5. See pp. 37, 39, 41, below.

6. The contemporaneousness between the return of prosperity and the timing of the progressive movement was first pointed out in Hofstadter, *The Age of Reform*, 165.

7. The Republican factional strife is discussed in *Toledo Commercial*, February 26, 1897, and in Rodabaugh, "Jones—Evangel of Equality," 25–27. The proceedings of the Republican convention are described in *Toledo Blade*, February 25, 1897.

8. Jones has left his personal comments on the campaign in *The New Right*, 80–82, and in his correspondence. For example, S. M. Jones to J. B. Hodsdon, June 22, 1898, in the Samuel Milton Jones Papers (MSS in the Toledo Public Library, Toledo, Ohio [hereafter referred to as Jones Papers]). The election results are reported in *Toledo Bee*, April 8, 1897. The telegram to Gladden is quoted in John B. Merrell, "Samuel M. Jones: The Mayor," *Commons*, IX (August, 1904), 352.

9. This biographical sketch is drawn from Jones, *The New Right*, 39–60. The facts on the sale of the Ohio Oil Co. to the Standard Oil Co. are taken from the *Toledo Blade*, July 13, 1904. The two sons were Percy (b. 1879) and Paul (b. 1884). He had a third son by his second wife, Mason (b. 1897).

10. Jones, *The New Right*, 120, 129.

11. *Ibid.*, 61–63; Washington Gladden, "Mayor Jones of Toledo," *Outlook*, LXII (May 6, 1899), 17–18; Frank T. Carlton, "The Golden Rule Factory: The Late Mayor Jones' Contribution toward the Solution of Industrial Problems," *Arena*, XXXII (1904), 408–10; Robert H. Bremner, "The Civic Revival in Ohio: Samuel M. Jones: The Man without a Party," *American Journal of Economics and Sociology*, VIII (January, 1949), 153–57.

12. Nevin O. Winter, *A History of Northwest Ohio* (3 vols.; New York, 1917), II, 1323; Rodabaugh, "Jones – Evangel of Equality," 28–29.

13. Jones, *The New Right*, 234–39; S. M. Jones to W. L. Torrance, March 11, 1898; S. M. Jones to Bolton Hall, June 21, 1898, Jones Papers.

14. Jones, *The New Right*, 249, 256.

15. Jones's correspondence contains many references to books that had influenced his life. For example: S. M. Jones to W. H. Waddell, October 12, 1898; to H. A. Tobey, November 16, 1898; to Rev. Marion Hyde, November 7, 1901, Jones Papers. To William Dean Howells Jones wrote that he had read Howells' articles in magazines for many years and had recently "enjoyed to the fullest" *A Traveller from Altruria* (S. M. Jones to W. D. Howells, December 21, 1898, Jones Papers). An account of Jones's first meeting with Walt Whitman and of the Mayor's slow acceptance of the *Leaves of Grass*, which had seemed to him on first reading unpoetic, is told in Ernest Crosby, "Golden Rule Jones, the Late Mayor of Toledo," *Craftsman*, VII (1904–5), 682. Jones's commentary on the approach to the New Testament is in S. M. Jones to W. H. Waddell, October 21, 1898, Jones Papers. Jones corresponded with Tolstoy: S. M. Jones to Count Leo Tolstoy, September 8, 1898, Jones Papers.

Jones spoke of Herron's transcendent influence to several correspondents, including the minister himself (S. M. Jones to W. A. Kling, February 15, 1898; to W. T. Stead, May 11, 1897; to George D. Herron, October 25, 1897, Jones Papers).

16. New York, 1899. In preparing this work Jones had editorial assistance from Herbert N. Casson and William J. Ghent. The volume contains an Introduction and a chapter on "Co-operation and Profit Sharing" by N. O. Nelson, a St. Louis businessman, who shared many of Jones's enlightened views on the labor problem.

17. 2 vols.; Toledo, Ohio, 1900–1901.

18. S. M. Jones to Washington Gladden, February 19, 1900, Washington Gladden Papers (MSS in the Ohio Historical Society, Columbus [hereafter referred to as Gladden Papers]).

19. Samuel M. Jones, "The Way to Purify Politics," *Independent*, LIV

(February 27, 1902), 512–13; Samuel M. Jones, "The Non-Partisan in Politics," *ibid.*, LV (August 20, 1903), 1965; S. M. Jones to L. A. Russell, July 24, 1900, printed in *Cleveland Press*, August 25, 1900.

20. Jones, *The New Right*, 150, 247–49.

21. *Ibid.*, 66; Samuel M. Jones, "The Right to Work," *Sunday Journal* (Toledo), January 8, 1899.

22. Jones rejected the Socialists on two counts: their emphasis on the class structure of society and their doctrinaire sectarianism (Samuel M. Jones, "The American Workingmen and Religion," *Outlook*, LXV [July 14, 1900], 640; S. M. Jones to M. J. Rountree, December 9, 1899, Jones Papers). His friend Eltweed Pomeroy accurately characterized him as "a philosophical anarchist," "not a socialist." He pointed out to Jones: "You do not believe the way Debs does at all but more the way that W. J. Bryan thinks. You are attracted to Debs by his strong humanitarian spirit and if you vote for him, that will be the reason and not because you believe the remedies he believes in."—Eltweed Pomeroy to S. M. Jones, April 3, 1900, Jones Papers.

23. Jones, *The New Right*, 187, 202, 207–8, 215; Jones, *Letters of Love and Labor*, I, 69, II, 2–5.

24. Jones, *Letters of Love and Labor*, I, 104; Jones, *The New Right*, 66, 223–26, 261–63, 277–78; editorial in *Columbus Citizen*, October 20, 1899; S. M. Jones to H. D. Davis, March 23, 1898, and S. M. Jones to Josiah Strong, November 15, 1898, Jones Papers.

25. S. M. Jones to Elizabeth J. Hauser, December 1, 1899, Jones Papers; Jones, *The New Right*, 78, 375–77.

26. Jones made an open declaration of his anarchical view of the law while he was mayor in a letter published in *Toledo Bee*, June 29, 1902. His criticism of government in his own time was made in a speech on "Political Liberty," delivered before the League of American Municipalities and reported in *Cleveland Plain Dealer*, August 24, 1901, and in Jones, *The New Right*, 233, 377.

27. S. M. Jones to Washington Gladden, February 19, 1900, Gladden Papers; Jones, *The New Right*, 451–53; S. M. Jones to Mr. Cadwallader, October 30, 1899, Jones Papers.

28. Jones, *The New Right*, 379–81.

29. Jones's inconsistencies were noted in Crosby, "Golden Rule Jones," 687–88. The business benefits to the Mayor from the patent law were aired in the press in an exchange of letters between Jones and Charles Dick, chairman of the Ohio Republican Executive Committee, published in *Toledo Bee*, October 24, 27, 1899.

Characteristically, the Mayor wrote that he was "ready to turn over my interest in the Acme Sucker Rod patent and business to the city of Toledo just as soon as the city of Toledo is ready to take and carry on the business for the benefit of all the people." His remarks on the churches and his own Christian spirit are in S. M. Jones to W. H. Kinnier, November 11, 1897, Jones Papers.

30. Jones, *The New Right*, 83, 99–105, 362–63, 367, 508–9; Brand Whitlock, " 'Golden Rule' Jones," *World's Work*, VII (September, 1904), 5309; Samuel M. Jones, "Government by the Golden Rule," *Munsey's Magazine*, XXVIII (1902–3), 508–9. In addition to promoting the eight-hour day in his own factory and in the departments of the city, he launched a campaign to promote it among the oil producers. There are many letters on the subject

in his correspondence files, including one to Samuel Gompers, October 29, 1897. The campaign came to nought (S. M. Jones to W. W. Norton, March 28, 1898, Jones Papers).

31. Jones, *The New Right*, 95–99; *Toledo Bee*, July 21, August 3, December 12, 19, 29, 1899; *Toledo Commercial*, October 28, 1899; April 13, 1900. Jones was himself critical of the city's decision to enter the natural-gas business because it had lacked an assurance of an adequate supply of gas when the operations began in 1891. Moreover, it meant competing with a private utility, the Northwestern Natural Gas Co., to which the city had granted a franchise, and which was supplying gas at a reasonable rate and offered to continue at such a figure. But his objection applied to the natural-gas plant alone and not to municipal ownership of other services. (S. M. Jones to M. Compton, October 22, 1897, Jones Papers.) He continued to hold this same view on the natural-gas plant as late as 1903. The grant of a franchise was a partnership and the city should not compete with its "partner," was his conclusion. (S. M. Jones to E. W. Bemis, September 9, 1903, Jones Papers.) The controversy over the natural-gas plant in Jones's administrations, as well as its previous history, is reviewed in Robert H. Bremner, "The Civic Revival in Ohio: Gas and Ice Monopolies in Toledo," *American Journal of Economics and Sociology*, X (July, 1951), 417–24.

32. *Fourth Annual Message of Mayor Samuel M. Jones* [1900] and *Fifth Annual Message of Mayor Samuel M. Jones*, February 24, 1902, Jones Papers. Jones reviewed the battle in the council and his veto of the franchise in his private correspondence (S. M. Jones to N. O. Nelson, September 9, 1903, and to C. R. Woodruff, September 24, 1903, Jones Papers). Detailed reviews of the street-railway franchise fight are to be found in Rodabaugh, "Jones — Evangel of Equality," 39–41, and in Ford, "Golden Rule Jones," chap. xvi, pp. 16–19.

33. S. M. Jones to Robert E. McKisson, October 12, 1898; S. M. Jones to C. R. Woodruff, September 24, 1903, Jones Papers.

34. Jones called himself a "Lincoln Republican." He discussed his brand of Republicanism and his hostility to Hannaism in letters to several friends: S. M. Jones to J. C. McKinney, January 12, 1898; to J. L. Cowles, January 13, 1898; to Ernest Hammond, January 4, 1898; to Thomas Slade, March 22, 1898, Jones Papers. Jones's relations with the Foraker faction are discussed critically by Ford, "Golden Rule Jones," chap. vii. Jones presents his view of the Republican city convention of March 3, 1899 in *The New Right*, 86–91, and in S. M. Jones to Hazen S. Pingree, March 6, 1899, Jones Papers. The Republican leaders were critical of Jones for accepting his defeat with such poor grace and bolting the ticket (Walter F. Brown to S. M. Jones, March 8, 1899; J. M. Ashley to S. M. Jones, March 10, 1899; George P. Waldorf to S. M. Jones, March 11, 1899, Jones Papers). In letters to friends Jones expressed his antipathy to McLean and some of the activities of the Democrats (S. M. Jones to J. F. McNamee, June 26, 1899; S. M. Jones to N. O. Nelson, July 12, 1899, Jones Papers).

35. Jones's growing commitment to the nonpartisan principle can be traced in his correspondence in 1899, particularly in his letters to N. O. Nelson, August 11, 1899, to Eltweed Pomeroy, August 26, 1899, and to Rufus W. Weeks, October 16, 1899, Jones Papers. The election returns for the mayoralty race in 1899 are reported in *Toledo Blade*, April 14, 1899, and in Jones, *The New Right*, 111. The vote was Jones (Independent) 17,782, Russell (Republican) 4,472, Dowling (Democrat) 3,293.

36. Jones described his reforms in *The New Right*, 99–105. He expressed his distaste for blue laws and defended the saloons many times. For example: *ibid.*, 159; *Toledo Blade*, February 3, 4, 1898; S. M. Jones to G. A. Burgess, March 17, 1898; S. M. Jones to N. O. Nelson, July 13, 1898, Jones Papers. The Mayor lampooned the revivalist, Samuel P. Jones, in *The New Right*, 106–7. The latter's meetings were always newsworthy. For example, the *Toledo Blade*, March, *passim*, April 1, 1899, and the *Toledo Bee*, February 19, March, *passim*, 1899.

37. Jones, *The New Right*, 362–63, 367; Whitlock, " 'Golden Rule' Jones," 5309–10.

38. Jones, *The New Right*, 99–105; Whitlock, *Forty Years of It*, 119–21; Crosby, "Golden Rule Jones," 541–43.

39. *Toledo Blade*, April 30, 1900.

40. Jones made this charge in an open letter printed in the *Toledo Bee*, June 29, 1902. He expressed his strong resentment of "this act of usurpation" to his friends (S. M. Jones to Ernest H. Crosby, April 25, 1902; to Tom L. Johnson, May 2, 1902, Jones Papers). The statute is in 95 O.L. 203 (1902). It received bipartisan support; a Republican introduced it and a prominent Democrat enthusiastically praised it (*Ohio State Journal* [Columbus], March 21, 1902; *Toledo Blade*, April 12, 1902).

41. Jones discussed his decision to give up retirement and to run again with his friends (S. M. Jones to N. O. Nelson, March 18, 1903; to Tom L. Johnson, March 21, 1903, Jones Papers; S. M. Jones to Washington Gladden, April 23, 1903, Gladden Papers). His support is described in *Toledo Bee*, March 19, 1903; *Cleveland Plain Dealer*, April 12, 1903.

42. Jones was, of course, sensitive to the press silence and criticism and felt a sense of martyrdom (S. M. Jones to Tom L. Johnson, March 21, 1903, Jones Papers). Cochran gave this criticism of the Mayor in an editorial, *Toledo Bee*, March 19, 1903. Jones exaggerated when he said that every paper was "closed tight" against him, for the *Toledo Bee* gave his campaign ample coverage and did print his letter accepting the nomination, although it charged the regular advertising rate (Jones, "The Non-Partisan in Politics," 1964–65; *Toledo Bee*, March 14 – April 4, 1903). The Republican candidate was John W. Dowd, whom Jones much admired (S. M. Jones to J. W. Dowd, April 9, 1903). The Democrat was Charles M. Edson, cashier of the Dollar Savings Bank.

43. There are many accounts of Jones's techniques in this campaign as well as previous ones. Among the most colorful are: Whitlock, *Forty Years of It*, 126–35; Whitlock, " 'Golden Rule' Jones," 5310–11; Herbert N. Casson, "Draining a Political Swamp," *Arena*, XXI (1899), 769–70; *Cleveland Plain Dealer*, April 12, 1903. The *Blade* commented on the strength of Jones's support among small businessmen, *Toledo Blade*, April 7, 8, 1903. See also the congratulatory letters to Jones, April 8–30, 1903, Jones Papers. The election results were: Jones (Non-Partisan) 10,350, Dowd (Republican) 7,501, Edson (Democrat) 4,266, Bragg (Socialist) 539.

44. Republicans won all the other city offices and had a majority of ten on the council and dominated the board of public service. The Jones quotation is from his statement published in *Toledo Bee*, April 7, 1903. Jones died July 12, 1904.

45. *Toledo Blade*, April 5, 1899.

46. Jones commented on his defeat in the Lucas County Republican pri-

maries in letters to Arthur Brisbane, May 13, 1899, and to J. K. Hamilton, May 16, 1899, Jones Papers. Hanna's part in his defeat is reported in William C. Beer to John McCall, November 11, 1899, printed in Thomas Beer, *Hanna* (New York, 1929), Appendix, 308. Foraker's remark was published in the *Toledo Blade*, May 22, 1899. Jones had been critical of Foraker because of his work for the fifty-year-franchise bill for the Cincinnati street railway in 1896 (S. M. Jones to L. D. Thurstin, October 30, 1897, Jones Papers). The Republican state convention is reported in the *Toledo Bee*, June 3, 1899, and the *Toledo Blade*, June 3, 1899.

47. S. M. Jones to L. C. Meeker, June 3, 1899; S. M. Jones to Charles E. Jewell, June 6, 1899, Jones Papers.

48. Jones concurred in these opinions of McLean and Kilbourne (S. M. Jones to John F. McNamee, June 26, 1899; S. M. Jones to N. O. Nelson, July 12, 1899, Jones Papers). The rumor that Jones would support Kilbourne was reported in the *Columbus Citizen*, November 10, 1899, and in Powell, *The Democratic Party of the State of Ohio*, I, 374. Meanwhile Negley Cochran was trying desperately to stop the McLean boom (*Toledo Bee*, July 6–19, August 20–24, 1899). But he did support McLean in the campaign (*ibid.*, October, 1899, *passim*).

49. Jones spoke many times in his letters of the popular tide running in his favor and of his sense of duty to respond (S. M. Jones to N. O. Nelson, June 20, 1899; to Eugene V. Debs, June 22, 1899; to A. F. Otte, July 12, 1899; to Eltweed Pomeroy, August 26, 1899, Jones Papers). The Democratic state convention is reported in the *Toledo Blade*, August 29, 1899. McLean was nominated on the first ballot with a large plurality over Kilbourne. Jones's formal announcement was printed in *Toledo Bee* and *Toledo Blade*, August 23, 1899.

50. McLean's part in circulating Jones's petitions was revealed by Lewis Bernard, the Democrat's manager (*Cincinnati Times Star*, June 10, 1916). Jones's effort to head a labor party and his support by labor is discussed in Ford, "Golden Rule Jones," chap. xi, pp. 18–40.

51. The platform was contained in the official announcement of his candidacy (*Toledo Bee*, August 23, 1899).

52. Cowell's remarks were reported in the *Toledo Blade*, November 8, 1899. Jones stated that his total expenses were less than $10,000 (S. M. Jones to George Herron, November 16, 1899, Jones Papers). He described the progress of the campaign to his friends (S. M. Jones to John H. Thomas, October 12, 1899; to N. O. Nelson, November 17, 1899, Jones Papers). Lloyd's comment was made to Gladden (H. D. Lloyd to Washington Gladden, October 5, 1899, Gladden Papers).

53. The Republican and Democratic campaigns are covered respectively in the *Toledo Blade* and *Toledo Bee*, September–October, 1899, *passim*. Hanna's role is reported in William C. Beer to John McCall, November 11, 1899, printed in Beer, *Hanna*, Appendix, 304–325. Cochran of the *Toledo Blade* violated McLean's instructions and gave Jones excellent coverage because the Mayor's acts were newsworthy in Toledo (*Toledo Bee*, October 4, 1899). A sample of the efforts to belittle Jones is in the *Toledo Blade*, October 28, 1899.

54. The election results were printed in the *Toledo Bee*, November 20, 1899. The quotation of the Republican observer is from William C. Beer to John McCall, printed in Beer, *Hanna*, Appendix, 322. Jones expressed his

elation at defeating Hanna in Cleveland to W. R. Raymond, November 8, 1899, Jones Papers.

55. The significance of Jones's campaign in appealing to the immigrant voters in Cuyahoga County (Cleveland) is discussed in Wellington G. Fordyce, "Nationality Groups in Cleveland Politics," *Ohio State Archaeological and Historical Quarterly,* XLVI (1937), 124–25.

56. Jones's letter files contain numerous invitations to speak, many more than he could accept. The Bibliography lists the articles Jones wrote for *Arena, Independent,* and *Outlook.* His activity on behalf of the League of American Municipalities was reported in S. M. Jones to Clinton R. Woodruff, September 24, 1903, Jones Papers.

57. Gladden acknowledged Jones's inspiration in a sermon he gave on the Toledo mayor shortly after the latter's death, reprinted in *Toledo News-Bee,* July 19, 1904. The political situation in Columbus and Gladden's campaign are described in: *Cleveland Press,* February 16, 1900; "Dr. Gladden's Election," *Outlook,* LXIV (April 14, 1900), 855–56; Gladden, *Recollections,* 336–39, 378–80. See S. M. Jones to Washington Gladden, February 19, 1900, Gladden Papers.

58. The data on Gladden's early life is drawn from Gladden, *Recollections,* 1–84.

59. *Ibid.,* 63.

60. The labor situation in North Adams is recounted in *ibid.,* 171–73, his editorials on the Tweed Ring in *ibid.,* 204–8, his talks to labor during his pastorate in Springfield and his appraisal of them in *ibid.,* 248–55.

61. *Ibid.,* 282–84, 358–65; Jagsch, "Washington Gladden," 13–26. His denunciation by the legislature and subsequent elimination by the trustees, who were sympathetic to his brave stand but listened to political expediency, is told in Alexis Cope, *History of the Ohio State University, 1870–1910 (History of the Ohio State University,* ed. Thomas C. Mendenhall, Vol. I [5 vols.; Columbus, Ohio]), 153–55.

62. The quotations are from Washington Gladden, *Organized Labor and Capital* (Philadelphia, 1904), 54, 57. Gladden wrote extensively on the labor problem in *Social Facts and Forces* (New York, 1897), and *The Labor Question* (Boston, 1911), a collection of five articles which had first appeared under various titles in *Outlook,* XCVII (February 25, March 4, 18, April 15, 1911), 465–71, 497–502, 589–95, 827–32; XCVIII (May 6, 1911), 35–40. He discusses his aversion to socialism in his *Recollections,* 306–8.

63. Washington Gladden, "The Cosmopolis City Club," *Century Magazine,* N.S., XXIII (January, 1893), 395–406; Gladden, *Recollections,* 328–30; Washington Gladden, "Public Service Companies and City Governments," *Outlook,* LXVI (October 27, 1900), 502–8; *Ohio State Journal* (Columbus), September 21, 1900; Gladden, *Social Facts and Forces,* 104–5, 113–14.

64. Gladden's part in the street-railway settlement is told in his *Recollections,* 340–41, and in the *Ohio State Journal,* January 1–4, 11, 15, 27, February 5, 1901. Johnson discusses his proposal in *My Story,* 156–57. Jones confessed his surprise to Johnson at Gladden's rejection of Johnson's offer (S. M. Jones to Tom L. Johnson, February 5, 1901, Jones Papers). The franchise as passed provided for five-cent cash fares with transfers, seven tickets for twenty-five cents with transfers, until the annual gross earnings of the company reached $1,750,000; thereafter eight tickets for twenty-five

cents with transfers. It was not until 1912 that the lower rate became effective. (*Ohio State Journal*, February 5, 1910)

65. Gladden's contributions are reported in the *Ohio State Journal*, February 11 and April 22, 1901, and in Gladden, *Recollections*, 345–46. The actions by the council and the people are recounted in the *Ohio State Journal*, February 12, March 19, 1901; March 18, April 8, 1902.

Also during Gladden's term the council renewed a natural-gas franchise on terms favorable to the people, but Gladden confessed that his part in the negotiations was not very creditable. On the advice of his constituents he voted to accept the gas company's offer, while the majority of the council held out for lower rates, which were eventually won. (Gladden, *Recollections*, 343–44)

66. He stated his reasons for declining to run in Gladden, *Recollections*, 351, and in the *Ohio State Journal*, January 13, July 13, 1902. Gladden's Sunday-night sermons were carried regularly each Monday in *ibid.*, 1900–1912, *passim*.

CHAPTER THREE

CLEVELAND:
"THE CITY ON A HILL"
1901 ∎ 1909

IN THE FALL OF 1900, after an absence of six years, Tom Loftin Johnson had returned to Cleveland to devote himself to the cause of reform by taking part in municipal politics. He was already well-known as a former congressman and as an eccentric millionaire who had become a disciple of Henry George. Johnson had recently sold the last of the street-railway lines and steel mills which had been the source of his wealth, in order to free himself from business cares.[1] His opportunity to enter upon his new political career was, however, as fortuitously timed as had been that of Samuel Jones in Toledo.

Within weeks of his return he was unexpectedly importuned to run for mayor. There had been a popular outcry during the summer of 1900 against attempts to force through the city council a franchise renewal favorable to Mark Hanna's street railway. A faction among the Democrats, sensing the political advantage of capitalizing on this protest, was looking for a candidate who would have the energy, knowledge, and money to lead the fight. The availability of Johnson seemed heaven-sent; they seized upon the retired millionaire who knew the street-railway business from top to bottom and who seemed eager to champion the people's cause in this contest.[2]

Johnson, who had known Hanna for twenty years and did not underestimate him as an opponent, realized from the outset that it would be "a very hard fight." "But," he wrote to his friend Samuel Jones, "I have learned the lesson from you that fear of defeat must never retard one from going into a contest and I am going into this in earnest. I have no doubt that much of what is done here will bear fruit with you and help you in the good fight that you are undertaking in Toledo." [3]

On February 6, 1901, Johnson allowed himself to be "surprised" at his home by the Committee of Fifty, bearing a petition of several thousand signatures drafting him as the Democratic nominee for mayor. Producing from his pocket a prepared statement, he read his acceptance speech, which announced the platform on which he would campaign: a business administration, home rule, a three-cent fare for street railways, municipal ownership of public utilities, the equalization of taxes, and the single tax. Radical as this platform was, every plank except the single tax was familiar campaign talk in Cleveland. William Akers, who was to be Johnson's Republican opponent, came out for three-cent fares and a municipal light plant.[4]

Johnson's prospects were promising. He enjoyed a well-established reputation in both political and business circles. Twice he had been elected to Congress from one of the Cleveland districts and had endeared himself to the party professionals by his lavish expenditures. Charles P. Salen, who had managed those campaigns, had launched the Johnson boom for mayor in the hope that the candidate's wealth would again fill the party coffers. His candidacy was further aided by strife among the Republicans, which weakened his opponent. On the other hand, Johnson helped to heal the factionalism which had plagued his own party. A Bryan supporter since 1896, Johnson commanded the support of the silver wing, which had threatened to bolt if the incumbent mayor, John Farley, a Gold Democrat, had been renominated. Even though Farley became a dissenter himself and tried to develop a Democratic movement for the Republican Akers, the old mayor was so discredited by his inefficient administration and favoritism to the railroad interests that his endorsement was a bane rather than a blessing. The influential Democratic paper, the *Cleveland Plain Dealer*, gave Johnson its backing.[5]

Because of his former prominence in the transport industry of the city, the nominee could also count on the support of some of his old business friends who regarded him as a bargain mayor. Others, notably Mark Hanna, took seriously his commitment to Georgian doctrines and advised their friends to vote against this dangerous man. Another group at the opposite end of the political spectrum also accepted his beliefs as sincere. Peter Witt and Tom Fitzsimmons, old Populists and managers of Jones's successful Cuyahoga County campaign in 1899, threw themselves behind Johnson's election. They made a nonpartisan fight for him in the immigrant-labor wards as they had for Jones.[6]

In the campaign Johnson was accused of being a tax dodger and of being a hypocrite in now advocating a three-cent fare, whereas, as an owner of street railways, he had charged a higher rate. Instead of responding in kind, with smear charges against his Republican opponent, Johnson answered the criticisms directly and briefly, then addressed himself to educational talks on the swollen values of public-utility franchises that went untaxed, the inequalities of taxation in general, and the need for public improvements. He disappointed the professionals by keeping his campaign expenditures within the limits prescribed by the Corrupt Practices Act and by refusing to promise any jobs. At the election on April 1 he won by a plurality of six thousand votes. He carried the immigrant wards of the West Side by three thousand and made heavy inroads in the East End wards, bulwarks of Republicanism. With characteristic impetuosity, Johnson, instead of waiting the customary two weeks, took office two days later to prevent a threatened action he considered hostile to the city's interest.[7]

What was the true character of this new mayor? Was he a dangerous radical, as Mark Hanna insisted, or a politician ambitious for personal honor and success as most of the newspapers believed?[8] His past career had been so paradoxical that mixed interpretations of his character and motives were inevitable.

Tom Johnson had been born on July 18, 1854, the son of an Arkansas cotton planter and slaveowner. His earliest memories were of the Civil War, which began when he was seven. While the father served in the Confederate army, the family led a nomadic existence. When peace came, the Johnsons were in Staunton, Virginia, where they remained for the next four years, too poor to move from their temporary home. Tom experienced there the gnawing uncertainty of poverty and also received his first lesson in monopoly, as a newsboy. A railroad conductor, taking a fancy to him, agreed to give the boy exclusive rights to sell the newspapers which the train brought from other cities. Since these were the only papers available in Staunton, and the demand was brisk, Tom was able to collect a handsome premium. Although five weeks later a change in conductors abruptly ended the scheme, Tom, meanwhile, had earned eighty-eight dollars, enough to enable the family to move to Louisville, Kentucky, where the father hoped to make a fresh start among relatives and friends. In his autobiography Johnson says that he never forgot the lesson of this first business venture: to place his money and energy behind a business where there was little or no competition.[9]

In Louisville Tom soon took a job with a street-railway company owned by two friends of his father, Biderman DuPont and Alfred V. DuPont, advancing from office boy to secretary, then to superintendent of the road. While in the service of the DuPonts he invented a fare box which netted him twenty to thirty thousand dollars. With this saving and a loan of thirty thousand dollars from Biderman DuPont, Johnson in 1876 purchased the majority of the stock of an Indianapolis street-railway company, thus embarking upon his own at the age of twenty-two. Three years later he entered the street-railway field in Cleveland.[10]

The most aggressive of the several companies then existing in Cleveland was one in which Mark Hanna was interested. Hanna's company initiated the fight against this interloper and won the first round, but Johnson came back, winning rounds two and three. After his defeat in their third clash, Hanna proposed that the two form a partnership, for, as he pointed out, to join his own talent in finance and politics to Johnson's skill as a street-railway manager would make a profitable combination. Johnson, however, declined, giving as his reason that they were too much alike, that they "would make good opponents, but not good partners."[11] Opponents they remained, in business and politics. The battleground for their fight was the Cleveland City Council chamber, where they vied for franchises. Mark Hanna taught Johnson to play politics as the only means of remaining in the Cleveland transit field. Johnson never resorted to bribery, yet whenever he wanted favors from the council, he contributed to the campaign funds of both parties, a form of indirect corruption against which he later inveighed.[12]

In the late 1880's Johnson invented a girder groove rail, "a steam railroad 'T' rail with a street-railroad wearing surface," and an associate, Arthur J. Moxham, invented a process to roll it. After contracting with a steel company to manufacture these rails for a year, the profits were so attractive that in 1889 the two men built their own mill outside Johnstown, Pennsylvania. Six years later Johnson expanded his steel operations, erecting a new mill at Lorain, Ohio, a village west of Cleveland on Lake Erie. In locating his plant here he revealed his business acumen and foresight, for only a few others in 1895 recognized the natural advantage of this site in insuring low transportation costs of raw materials.[13]

While pursuing his steel enterprises he was no less vigorous in the management and promotion of his street-railway interests. Selling his Indianapolis system at a good profit, he bought a part interest in the Sixth Street Line in St. Louis. His Cleveland lines were electrified and merged into a corporation, popularly known as "The Big Consolidated," at a substantial advantage to Johnson. In 1894 he also accepted the management of the Detroit street-railway system, purchased by the R. T. Wilson Company of New York, in which Johnson had a large interest. A dilapidated, run-down road, operating with horses and mules, Johnson rebuilt it into a modern, efficient system, electrically equipped throughout. His last venture as a private street-railway manager was in Brooklyn from 1896 to 1898. In the latter year he began disposing of all his business interests and investing his fortune of two to three million dollars in government bonds.[14]

Johnson abandoned active business because, as he later declared, "the requirements of my work didn't square with my principles . . . so I gave it all up to find peace and freedom of mind." [15] His inward conflict had been increasing for some time, although only a few business associates and intimate friends knew of the intense conviction with which he maintained his principles, even in the face of harm to his business interests.[16] To the general public he was a familiar businessman hero in the Horatio Alger tradition, who could be expected to devote his declining days to good works of charity, endowing hospitals and colleges, collecting art treasures, dabbling in politics. It was scarcely suspected that he would war against those monopolies which had brought him fortune and become the champion of social democratic reform. His enemies always suspected his sincerity. Yet his political career is a testament to the genuineness of his new faith. The man responsible for his conversion was Henry George.

Johnson, in his autobiography, has told the story of his chance introduction to George's writings. In 1883 on one of his frequent business trips between Cleveland and Indianapolis, a news vender offered him a book called *Social Problems* by a new author, Henry George.[17] Thinking that it was another jeremiad against the social evils of vice and crime, Johnson was about to turn it down when the conductor of the train persuaded him that the book would interest him since it dealt with street railways, taxation, and land. Johnson read it almost without stopping and bought all the other books, including *Progress and Poverty,* that George had written. To Johnson, George's analysis and solution "sounded true—all of it." Nevertheless he was reluctant to believe it. Distrustful of his own judgment of a theoretical dissertation, he persuaded his lawyer and his business partner to read *Progress and Poverty.* Both assured him that George was logically consistent. Since Johnson had been certain from the outset that the basic facts were right, this now convinced him that the argument was sound.[18]

Johnson offered little explanation why George's ideas attracted him so immediately and powerfully, yet there are certain clues. He had an alert, inquiring mind that had been devoted almost exclusively to engineering and business problems, but it was capable of responding to the challenge of broad social questions. Furthermore, because he lacked formal education and an interest in reading, he had not previously explored the realm of political and social theory. Purely by chance he happened upon George as his guide. George appealed to him because he struck a responsive chord of humanitarianism that the younger man scarcely knew he possessed and because his message, though buttressed with erudition, was simple and direct. It was easy for Johnson to grasp George's "proof" that monopoly was a social wrong, to contrast that with the opposite belief he had long held, and to discover that his old view was egocentric, antisocial, and destructive. It was no more difficult for him to

59

grasp George's specific and practical remedy: the elimination of the land monopoly by the single tax and thus the restoration of equal opportunity to all.

The effect of these ideas on Johnson was soon reinforced by the power of George's personality. The two men met in 1885 and began a friendship which strengthened with the years until George's death in 1897. Their relationship was one of pupil and teacher; Johnson was thirty-one, George forty-six in the year they met. The older man drew Johnson into politics first as a financial backer, later as a speaker in his campaigns in New York. Under George's inspiration Johnson ran four times for Congress from the Twenty-First Congressional District of Ohio. Defeated in 1888, he ran successfully in the next two elections, then failed of a third term in the Republican landslide of 1894. During his four years in the House of Representatives he consistently voted for tariff reductions, including that on the steel rails he manufactured. He and five collaborators read into the *Congressional Record* George's treatise, *Protection or Free Trade;* and the six parts were assembled in a pamphlet of which Johnson distributed over a million copies, each selling for one cent. In 1897 Johnson was manager of Henry George's last campaign for mayor of New York, the strain of which cost George his life.[19] Johnson had remained in business throughout this formative period of his political development on the theory that making money to promote the cause would be his most effective contribution. By 1898, however, he was confident that his political apprenticeship was complete, that he should follow the advice of his teacher and lead a political crusade of his own for the Georgian reforms, and that the place to begin was the city.[20]

When Johnson assumed the duties of mayor of Cleveland, he was forty-seven and in the prime of life. He was of medium height, comfortably stout, his expanded girth a witness to his love of good food. His curly black hair, finely cut nose, mouth, and chin gave his features a Grecian cast in profile. His eyes were bright, always darting about. Genial and jovial, he generally wore a smile, an irresistible smile that disarmed enemies and heartened supporters. His manner was unaffected and easy unless aroused; then he could be gruff though never abusive. He treated opponents fairly.[21]

Johnson's formal schooling lasted only a little more than a

year, but with characteristic drive and energy he sought to remedy this by self-improvement after he entered politics. He considered his four years in Congress the equivalent of a college education, with Henry George, his frequent visitor in Washington, as tutor. While mayor, he hired a teacher and learned French at the breakfast table, and at night, before retiring, he did a stint in a volume on political science.[22]

In this and other ways he resembled his Toledo counterpart, Samuel M. Jones, with whom he had formed a friendship in the Bryan campaign of 1900.[23] The two men were attracted to each other by their common interests and background. Both had a natural curiosity, a habit of close observation, and an aptitude for mechanics. In addition, Johnson was an able mathematician and an expert in electricity. Both were self-made, successful businessmen who had turned reformers. But Johnson was pre-eminently the practical man, while Jones mixed with his innate practical sense a large measure of Celtic mysticism and lyricism. Johnson did not share Jones's love of music and poetry. Both were humanitarians, but Jones's love of humanity came from the heart, Johnson's more from the mind. Jones was pacific by nature and disliked opposition; Johnson was a fighter who thrived on competition. Although Jones's attributes for leadership were considerable, Johnson possessed them in fuller measure: buoyancy of spirit, personal magnetism, showmanship, a sense of humor, a sense of justice, a rugged constitution, tremendous capacity for work, a talent for organization, and executive ability.[24] One day Johnson defined executive ability: "It's the simplest thing in the world; decide every question right half the time. And get somebody who can do the work. That's all there is to executive ability."[25]

Johnson knew how to delegate power and select good men. He surrounded himself with a brilliant coterie, attracted, or "hypnotized," as his enemies claimed, by his magnetic personality. Many were young, recent graduates from college, whose social conscience had been aroused by the new spirit of protest that was challenging complacency on the campuses. The original group included: Newton D. Baker, Frederic C. Howe, and Edward W. Bemis from Johns Hopkins; Charles William Stage and John N. Stockwell from Western Reserve in Cleveland. Later, still younger men were added to the fold: Carl Friebolin, also from Western Reserve; Robert J. Bulkley and Alfred A. Benesch from Harvard; and Robert Crosser from Kenyon in Gambier, Ohio. Johnson was teacher as well as comrade to these young men; he taught them practical civics.[26]

Others gathered to the circle of advisers and friends were students of social problems known for their high-mindedness and civic sense: Peter Witt, a voice for reform since the 1890's; the Reverend Harris R. Cooley, minister of Johnson's church; William J. Springborn, a Republican convert and efficient manager of municipal enterprises; Daniel E. Leslie, guardian of the city park system; Fred Kohler, the chief of police with a national reputation for his reforms; Carl Nau, watchdog of the city's finances; Antoine Biderman DuPont, the son of Johnson's first benefactor and his traction expert in the street-railway fight; and the Mayor's private secretary, Walter Burr Gongwer, a young reporter of promise whom the *Plain Dealer* reluctantly released.[27] These men from many walks of life were inspired by a common ideal: the success of the city experiment. They liked their work; they talked shop at their parties. "Theirs," wrote Lincoln Steffens, "is a sense of pride and preoccupation such as I have never felt." [28]

Of this wide circle four stand out, pre-eminent in their devotion to Johnson and in their contribution to the cause: Baker, Cooley, Witt, and Howe. Johnson's chief lieutenant and heir was Newton D. Baker. He was born in 1871 in Martinsburg, West Virginia, a border community where feelings aroused by the Civil War and Reconstruction ran high. Baker's own family had been split by the war. His grandfather Elias Baker had remained loyal to the Union but his own father, after whom he was named, served in the First Virginia Cavalry. Although the father accepted the Northern victory, he continued to be a staunch Southern Democrat and inculcated in his son a strong sense of loyalty to that party.

In other ways Newton Baker, Sr., who was a doctor and a man of culture, influenced the son. He helped to mold the boy's taste for history and government, and he picked out the new Johns Hopkins University as the college the young man was to attend. There the son took courses with Professor Woodrow Wilson in political science and listened to the professor at the dinner table in the boarding house where they lived together.

Young Baker graduated in 1892, took a year of postgraduate study in jurisprudence and Roman law, and, finally, another year at William and Mary in an accelerated course in American law.

Upon admission to the bar in 1894, the young lawyer opened an office in Martinsburg, where he practiced law for the next five years with one interruption in 1896–97 when he went to Washington, D.C., to become private secretary to Postmaster-General William L. Wilson in President Cleveland's cabinet. In 1899, at the age of twenty-seven, he decided to seek another community — one with brighter prospects than the declining Martinsburg could offer. At the urging of his fraternity brother, Fred Howe, and a prominent Democratic lawyer, Martin A. Foran, the young attorney chose Cleveland.

Baker's short, slender frame and agile movements gave him a boyish appearance, although there was nothing juvenile about his face. His dark hair, sensitive brown eyes, strong chin revealed spirituality and strength. A story that is told of his entrance into Cleveland politics was built upon his Puck-like figure. One day Judge Foran, unable to make a scheduled political address, asked Baker to pinch-hit for him. The chairman of the meeting, an old time Democrat, introduced Baker in this patronizing, curt way: "Mr. Foran is sick and cannot appear. He's sent his boy to speak for him. Come on, boy, and tell'em what you know." The crowd laughed as the wispy Baker came forward, but that speech made the reputation of Judge Foran's "boy." It was different, it was compelling. Baker's oratory was not of the old school; his delivery was clear-toned, graceful, simple, and convincing.

When Johnson returned to Cleveland and was elected mayor, Foran told him about Baker. The young lawyer had already begun to interest himself in the social and civic work of Cleveland. Fred Howe invited him to join a social service club at the YMCA, which conducted a vigorous program for the welfare of children and workingmen. Johnson, immediately attracted to Baker, brought him into the administration first as the legal adviser to one of the tax boards and then, when an opening occurred, as assistant law director.[29]

In later years, when Baker had become a conservative on economic issues, there was speculation among his old friends on why he had ever joined the Johnson reform movement. His interests were bookish, and his temperament was cautious and judicious. His one previous experience had warned him, he confessed to a friend, that he was not a politician. In 1896 he had followed the conservative course, bolting the Bryan ticket and voting with the Gold Democrats. Yet his choice in 1901 was deliberate; he rejected an offer to join a law firm with one of the most lucrative practices in Cleveland to accept a poorly paid legal post in the city government. No doubt his decision was prompted as much by his heart as by his mind. He was moved by the suffering and wretchedness of the poor of Cleveland, which he experienced for the first time. But the most impelling influence was unquestionably Tom Johnson, whom Baker came to love with a devotion that few men inspire. Responding to Johnson's tutelage, the young lawyer became a convert to the principles of Henry George and to the Mayor's "Democratic selective socialism," as Baker once called it. Baker's political creed was simple: "I am a follower of Tom Johnson." He won the confidence of the Mayor as no other man did, and his loyalty never wavered.[30]

In 1903 he was elected to head the city's law department, where he served for four consecutive terms, surviving Johnson's defeat in 1909. A tireless, efficient worker, Baker bore the burden of the law suits and injunctions with which the public utilities pelted the city during Johnson's administration, and he was in the thick of every campaign, preaching the Johnson causes. His diction was so beautiful that radical ideas from his lips lost their terror. He was a fighter whom opponents respected because he was fair and without personal malice. His was a great contribution to the Cleveland experiment as Johnson's principal aide and later his successor in the mayor's office.[31]

The second man in the Johnson "cabinet" was Harris R. Cooley, a graduate of Hiram College and Oberlin Theological Seminary and a former pastor of the Cedar Avenue Disciple Church of Cleveland. The friendship between the two began in the early 1880's when Johnson became one of Cooley's parishioners. Since his student days Cooley had developed a strong interest in social work. His father, the superintendent of Cleveland's Bethel Union, had introduced him to the problems of a charity organization, and several trips to England brought him firsthand knowledge of the social settlement movement and the Salvation Army. He shared Samuel Jones's belief that the teachings of Jesus could be made to work in industrial and social relations. He shared Tom Johnson's commitment to the teachings of Henry George.[32]

In 1901 the Mayor appointed Cooley director of the department of charities and correction because "he is just the man to carry out my ideas of reform in the treatment of the unfortunate. . . ." Many were scornful at first of this "preacher-in-politics," but his character and ability won the confidence of the people. He served until the end of 1909. With a minister's gift for imagery and parable, he could rend the hearts of his listeners with tales of misery and misfortune and then inspire them with a vision of what the city could do for the fallen members of society. The council never refused an appeal from him for appropriations. His service to the humanitarian cause in Cleveland was exceptional, and his work won national notice.[33]

The most fiery radical as well as the most colorful personality of the Johnson circle was Peter Witt, whose inheritance and background prepared him for the role he was to play. He was born a rebel; his parents were exiled German Forty-eighters. One of eleven children, he was forced by his father's inability to feed so many mouths to leave school and go to work at thirteen; thus he knew early the sting of poverty. After trying various trades he learned that of an iron molder, only to have this means of livelihood cut off in his early twenties when he was blacklisted for organizing a strike. Embittered by such treatment, he became a determined foe of the industrial order that had outlawed him. He joined the Populist crusade against the hated monopolists and discovered that he had a talent for speaking and organizing that was serviceable in politics.[34]

He and Johnson first met in 1894 at a tent rally that the then congressman was leading in his campaign for re-election. Witt and some friends appeared during a long harangue by a Democratic henchman and began to heckle the speaker. Instead of ordering them out of the tent, Johnson invited Witt to come to the platform and speak his mind. Such fair play inspired mutual respect and understanding which ripened into friendship. The two soon discovered another tie: their common allegiance to the theories of Henry George.[35]

Johnson praised Witt as a man of "sturdy honesty" and "unswerving fidelity to principle." In any job he tackled, Witt showed marked ability and ingenuity, first as head of the "Tax School" in Johnson's first administration and then as city clerk from 1903 to 1909. His specialty was publicizing the taxation issue. In campaign talks he introduced stereopticon slides to illustrate his tax lecture and lashed out at tax dodgers, excoriating them with his epithets.[36]

Conservatives anathematized him as an anarchist. Within the Johnson circle he spoke his mind with the same vehemence, lecturing anyone, from the Mayor down, who he felt was at fault. Publicly he ripped apart Charles Salen, Johnson's chief lieutenant in the state Democratic hierarchy, for a breach of faith. Privately he voiced his suspicions of Newton Baker's sincerity. The Johnson group passed off his remarks as the barbed thrusts of the court jester, but his later political career suffered from the indiscretions into which his quick, sharp tongue betrayed him. To the Johnson movement he was important as a gadfly, as an orator who dramatized the reform issues, and as a dynamic lieutenant who commanded the loyalty of the immigrant workers.[37]

The student of the Johnson experiment was Frederic C. Howe. He was born in 1867 in Meadville, Pennsylvania, the only son of a respected middle-class merchant. In his autobiography he described the environment of his youth as "a comfortable little world, Republican in politics, careful in conduct, Methodist in religion." There he lived until he graduated from the local Allegheny College. Then at the age of twenty-two he left Meadville to begin the slow, painful process of unlearning the canons he had been taught. He enrolled at Johns Hopkins to work for a Ph.D. in history and politics, spent a summer at the University of Halle in Germany, and supported himself as a newspaper reporter. Although he had trained himself for a career in journalism, he could not find a job in that field in the hard times of 1892–93. Disillusioned by this failure, he turned to the study of law at the University of Maryland and New York law schools. In 1894 he settled in Cleveland, joining the firm of Harry and James Garfield, sons of the former President. His association with the Garfields was a happy and profitable one. But Howe was driven by his Methodist-Quaker inheritance to do more than make a success of the law; he threw himself into social settlement work and assumed the secretaryship of the Municipal Association of Cleveland, which had just been founded to promote good government.[38]

In 1901, the year Johnson campaigned for mayor, Howe ran for council as a reform candidate on the Republican ticket. After hearing one of Johnson's talks he was so impressed by the directness and simplicity of the message that he called upon him at his office. In the course of that conversation Howe, who had admired the logic of *Progress and Poverty* but had remained unconvinced by its message, was converted to the Georgian faith. The young lawyer whose mind had been stripped of old shibboleths was poised and eager for conversion to a new set of values, but he needed Johnson as a catalyst. Howe became one of the Mayor's most grateful pupils; his affection for the older man was only exceeded by that of Baker. In the city council, to which he was elected, Howe became a spokesman for the Mayor and shifted his allegiance from the Republicans to the Democrats. Later he served the Johnson cause in the Ohio Senate, 1906–8. He also served as one of four assessors in a scientific reappraisal of Cleveland real estate in 1910, an account of which he entitled, "Single-taxing a City"—at best a half-truth. Taxation was one of his major interests, and to that subject he contributed several significant studies.[39]

In his sincere, candid autobiography Howe has attempted to analyze his own complex nature and his reactions during the period when he was a member of the Johnson circle. Both a lawyer and a politician, he tells us that he liked neither the law nor politics. Perhaps his distaste for both arose from the duality of his career, which, in retrospect, seemed to him almost schizophrenic. As a lawyer he served railroads and public utilities; as an investor he bought their securities and built a comfortable estate upon their earnings; but as a Johnsonian Democrat he fought on the side of the people against the special privileges of those same corporations. Intellectually he was able to rationalize this duality by the same defense that Johnson has made familiar: the money he took from privilege would give him the greater freedom to fight privilege. Emotionally, however, this split existence took its toll. He could barely tolerate the snubs from old friends and the social ostracism which his political principles and activities brought upon him. For that reason he was glad in 1910 to abandon the law, politics, and the Cleveland scene itself for New York and to make a fresh start in journalism, which had remained his first love.[40]

Long before he departed, however, he had already made his mark as one of the most persuasive publicists for municipal reform. In 1905 he published *The City the Hope of Democracy,* which marshaled in scholarly form all the arguments to support the thesis of the Cleveland group that the city was the dominant force in our twentieth-century civilization and there democracy would be reborn—"a democracy that will possess the instincts of the past along with a belief in co-operative effort to relieve the costs which city life entails." Howe instilled into this book his passionate love for the city and painted glowingly his vision of what the cities across the land could become. The essay had a profound effect beyond the Johnson circle; it influenced the thinking of a generation of Americans. Moreover, it was the first of a series of studies that Howe made of cities in Britain and Europe.[41]

Johnson's talent for inspiring followers was extraordinary. A leader of the Ohio single-tax movement, he aroused many men to champion George's ideas. Besides his four closest advisers he was instrumental in converting: Carl Nau, Antoine Biderman DuPont, Robert Crosser, mentioned above; Elizabeth J. Hauser, a leading woman suffragist and an editorial assistant to Johnson in the preparation of his autobiography; and Lincoln Steffens, who had come to Cleveland to expose Johnson and remained to admire him. The Mayor drew into city and state politics other single taxers: William Radcliffe, an effective street-corner orator for the Johnson movement; James B. Vining, active in the low-fare fight for street railways and later an officer in Baker's administration; Herbert Bigelow and Daniel Kiefer of Cincinnati. Brand Whitlock, the Toledo mayor and single taxer, leaned heavily upon Johnson and his circle for inspiration, advice, and campaign assistance. Johnson gave encouragement to Mark Fagan, a George disciple in New Jersey, in his campaign for reform. Following his defeat for re-election in 1909, Johnson was treasurer of the Joseph Fels Fund of America, established by the wealthy manufacturer of naphtha soap to promote the single tax. In two journalistic ventures Johnson financially sup-

68

ported Louis F. Post, friend and disciple of Henry George.[42]

Johnson's loyalty to Georgian doctrine was unflagging; his last public address was delivered at a single-tax rally in Cleveland. Although he never made it a central issue in his campaigns, he sought to educate the people to this philosophy and lay the groundwork for its ultimate adoption by means of such preparatory legislation as direct primaries, the initiative and referendum, home rule for cities, and tax reform. In the words of an admirer, he did more through his political campaigns and his services as congressman and mayor to promote the political growth of George's ideas in the United States than any other person. This is too sweeping a dictum in the light of the services of other single taxers, but certainly George's influence on Ohio reform would never have been as pervasive without Johnson.[43]

Doctrinaire single taxers criticized the Cleveland mayor's methods and activities as leading to fruitless compromise. They wanted none of his halfway measures; they disapproved of his association with the Democratic party. Johnson, however, would have nothing to do with organizing a single-tax party.[44] With his intuitive political sense he adopted the most direct way to win victories for his ideas: to infiltrate and capture the organization of the Democratic party and make it a vehicle for his purpose. He selected that party not only because of his personal identification with it but also because in Ohio it had attracted a group of like-minded men eager for change.

During his first term in the mayor's office Johnson gained control of the Democratic city and county committees and built an organization loyal to him, which he and his successor, Newton Baker, dominated for fifteen years. Johnson succeeded in spreading his authority to the state Democratic organization for two years, 1902–3, long enough to bridle the power of John R. McLean in party councils. Many of Johnson's methods were scarcely distinguishable from those of his opponents. He bossed party conventions, wrote the platforms, prepared the slate of candidates, and expected the convention to rubber-stamp his work. The professional Democratic politicians, interested in office and patronage and indifferent to his program, accepted this dictation so long as Johnson mustered the votes for victory at the polls. They measured men and ideas by their popularity.[45]

Nevertheless, in other respects Johnson's methods differed

radically from those of the conventional boss. Primary elections were conducted honestly. Compulsory political assessments from public employees were forbidden; the heaviest burden of campaign expenses Johnson carried himself until his financial reverses in 1908 made that no longer possible. The breath of bribery or scandal never touched any convention Johnson dominated. To Johnson, loyalty to the party meant loyalty to the principles of the party platform. Those who were unfaithful he exposed and drove from political life. Faithful party henchmen were rewarded by being given priority in patronage and job appointments, but the men chosen had to be capable. Johnson never hesitated to select an able Republican for an important post, nor would he permit a conscientious city employee to be removed because of his party label. As his movement progressed in Cleveland, he gave less and less consideration to place hunters in the party and became increasingly nonpartisan in all except name. Johnson transformed the local Democracy of Cleveland and Cuyahoga County into a party in his own image, dedicated to social reform.[46]

Johnson was successful in public life not only because of his remarkable talent as an organizer and leader of men but also because of the simplicity and directness of his goal. He did not suffer from any multiplicity or confusion of ideas; he was steadfastly faithful to the beliefs of his mentor, Henry George. There was one social wrong, the inequality of opportunity; one social remedy, to restore equality of opportunity and secure for each worker the product of his labor by eliminating monopoly and special *privilege*. The term "Privilege"* meant the same to him as it did to Jones and Gladden; it applied to all businesses which profited from the labor of others because of legal protection from competition. The benefits the law conferred, Johnson grouped into five categories in order of their importance: the under-taxation of land—particularly, idle land—which was the foundation of "land monopolies"; other forms of tax favoritism, such as tariff protection, which created "tax monopolies"; special grants to railroads, which were the bases for "transportation monopolies"; franchise grants to urban utilities, which led to "municipal

---

* To give emphasis to the importance Johnson assigned to the term "Privilege," his practice of capitalizing it has been followed.

monopolies"; and patent restrictions, which undergirded "patent monopolies."[47]

To Johnson the greatest movement of the times was the struggle of the people against Privilege. So far, Privilege had had the best of the contest because it was alert and quick to act and had been backed by the press, legislature, and courts. He conceived it to be his mission to assume leadership of the people's cause, to awaken them to this threat to their liberty, and to channel their latent power in support of a change that would bring them relief. How was the battle to be won? Not by political changes—replacing the present owners of monopolies by more virtuous men or exchanging a Democratic for a Republican political boss—but only by an *economic* change would the people be able to rout their adversary. The economic reform that would benefit the people of Cleveland most directly was public ownership of the street railway, electric, gas, and telephone utilities, then in private hands. Such a change would eliminate franchise grants, which were at the root of the trouble. The people would benefit economically in reduced rates and improved service, and they would also profit politically by removing the most corrupting influence in municipal government.[48]

Johnson, like the other two leaders in Ohio, was a "gas and water socialist," but in no sense a Marxist. He wanted to destroy Privilege in order to restore the fullest opportunity for competition among what he called "honest" forms of capital. He did not object to capital accumulation by individual effort, even to the combination of small units for greater efficiency and service. In making such an allowance he was at variance with the extreme antitrust advocates, who would abolish by law every combination that restrained competition in any way. To Johnson such legislation was too sweeping and non-discriminatory. He preferred to concentrate his attack against those trusts that existed because of law-made favors or restrictions.[49]

Because of his single-minded dedication to one remedy, he had much less to say on labor questions than did Jones and Gladden. Moreover, while he was not unsympathetic, he lacked their deep concern for the workingman. As an employer Johnson had always paid good wages and encouraged his men to join unions. Although he did not think that trade unionism would ever solve the basic problem of labor, he did believe in unions as a means of achieving the solidarity and uplift of the workers. The true solution for labor, as for all groups, was the elimination of monopolies.[50]

To open the war against Privilege, Johnson chose the street railways of Cleveland as his first target because of his intimate knowledge of their operation and structure. He might have been deterred from this choice by the impossibility of imposing his favored solution of municipal ownership on the traction lines, which the Ohio statutes did not then permit. But he had already conceived a scheme by which he might accomplish many of the same benefits through another approach that he had developed in Detroit with the assistance of that city's reform mayor, Hazen S. Pingree. It will be recalled that Johnson in the mid-nineties completely modernized the Detroit street railways for a private concern. Mayor Pingree became convinced that the new, efficient system could operate profitably at reduced fares, and to his surprise the traction manager agreed, for Johnson had by then come to look upon street railways with their exclusive franchise grants as "municipal monopolies." Both men believed that the fare might be cut from the prevailing rate of four or five cents to three, thereby restoring to the public the socially created franchise value without impairing a fair return to the owners on actual investment. It was Pingree who persuaded another private company to introduce the first three-cent fare on a cross-town line in that city. The success of this operation convinced Johnson of the feasibility of such a rate. It was also in collaboration with the Detroit mayor that Johnson devised another innovation that would be a step closer to municipal ownership: the formation of a holding company to operate the entire street-railway system for the public at cost. In 1899 the two co-operated in trying to sell the Detroit transit network to such a holding company, but the sale was defeated after the opposition claimed that the purchase price was too high. Nevertheless, Johnson's faith in this solution remained undimmed.[51]

For nine years the fight raged in Cleveland between the Mayor and the private owners of the traction lines. Its details, which have been recorded many times by both participants and observers, lie outside the concern of this book.[52] It is sufficient to say that it aroused the citizens of Cleveland in a way that few other issues have before or since. It was a central question in all five of Johnson's campaigns for mayor; it was fought in the newspapers, the council chamber, and the courts. The city streets became the scenes of near-pitched battles. It required all of the Mayor's daring, energy, and knowledge to win a temporary victory in 1907 for his solution: the operation of the consolidated street railways of the city by a holding company on a three-cent-fare, or cost, basis. But mismanagement, misjudgment, a costly strike, and inattention to public relations produced a popular revulsion against the Mayor's remedy. The people, in a referendum election, voted down the franchise grant to the holding company. Nevertheless, Johnson had only lost a battle, not the war. The final settlement which came in 1910, after he was out of office, incorporated his principles. The new franchise set a fair return of 6 per cent on actual investment and substituted a sliding scale for a fixed rate to assure such a return. For a three-year period from 1911 to 1914 the actual fare was three cents, with free transfers, thus proving the reasonableness of Johnson's prediction.

The street-railway contest has been criticized for the intensely hostile feelings it aroused and for the legacy of enmities it left. The Mayor has been accused of insincerity, duplicity, demagoguery, even nepotism and peculation—charges which the record does not sustain. The most he was guilty of was poor judgment, lack of tact, obstinacy, and a certain business impropriety. He himself shrugged off the false accusations, confident that his purpose was worthy and high-minded. To him and his group the fight was a great educational campaign, exposing, on the one hand, the nature and power of Privilege, and, on the other, awakening a popular interest in the importance of municipal ownership.[53]

He was able to give an even more direct stimulus to the acceptance of this principle by demonstrating the practical benefits of municipal ownership in the operation of those services that the Ohio statutes then permitted cities to own and manage. A start was made in providing light and power by the annexation to Cleveland of two villages that already possessed municipal light plants. However, the further expansion of the city's system of electric power, which the Mayor fervently desired and the private electric utility as fervently opposed, had to be subordinated to the prolonged street-railway fight. But there were other activities where the resistance was less and the public demand greater. The city, for example, bought out a private garbage company and made refuse collection a municipal service; it took over street-cleaning and the lighting of street gas lamps, instead of jobbing the work to private contractors.[54]

Indirectly Johnson endeavored to inspire confidence in municipal ownership by making Cleveland one of the best-governed cities in the country. He determined to eliminate politics from the municipal water works, which had become a nest of party hacks. Edward W. Bemis, an economist trained in public-utility statistics and devoted to municipal ownership, was placed in charge. People scoffed at this "professor-in-politics." There was near rebellion in the ranks of the Democratic organization when Bemis proceeded to substitute the merit for the spoils system, turning loose a Kansas cyclone in the water-works office. Johnson backed him to the hilt, overruling the persistent demands for place and patronage from his own partisans, to whom Bemis was anathema. The water-works department was placed on a scientific, business basis; a water-intake tunnel running out in the lake, the construction of which had been stalled by graft and incompetence, was completed, and water rates were reduced.[55]

What Bemis accomplished for the water department, William J. Springborn achieved for the department of public works. He, too, shared Johnson's belief in the wisdom of municipal ownership and wished to demonstrate how efficiently municipal enterprises could be run. This former Republican administered with great practical skill the municipal garbage plant and light works; he pushed the program of clean, well-paved and lighted streets, protected by adequate drains. The same honesty and efficiency was introduced into the department of health by the appointment of the German-born Dr. Martin Friedrich. Building inspection was completely reorganized under a new code which strengthened the city's hand in eradicating tenement rookeries. A purchasing department was established to introduce business methods and gain the economies from large-scale buying.[56]

As these reforms suggest, the Mayor looked upon Cleveland as a great corporation with himself as chairman of the board, the other city officers as directors, and the people as stockholders. In the spirit of a business executive with the best interest of his stockholders at heart, he supported actions that seemed to run counter to his principles. It was the cause of some wonderment that this advocate of municipal ownership should endorse a franchise grant to the East Ohio Gas Company to supply natural gas to the city's residents and the city itself. Not only did this mean admitting a new private utility, but also it meant admitting one that was affiliated with the unpopular Standard Oil Trust. But Johnson explained that his purpose was to promote the public welfare by introducing a cleaner, cheaper form of fuel and light, and that there was no other source available. To achieve this immediate goal he was willing to subordinate his long-range objective. Again for similar reasons he favored an extension of the Belt Line Railroad in Cleveland because an extension of rail facilities would stimulate the industrial expansion of the city and invigorate its economic life.[57]

Honesty and efficiency in the management of municipal government and the promotion of the community's economic well-being were important, but the realization of Johnson's vision of "a City on a Hill" demanded something more. The city should bring beauty and pleasure into the lives of its citizens and a spirit of humanity toward the underprivileged. Johnson made a reality of the Cleveland Group Plan, to which many contributed. The plan embraced the symmetrical grouping of the principal public buildings about a mall lined with formal shade trees, extending from the lake to the public square. It was unique in this country when originated, though other cities soon adopted similar improvements.[58] Johnson made the parks recreation centers for the people, removing the "Keep off the Grass" signs and greatly expanding their facilities. Under the direction of Superintendent of Parks Daniel E. Leslie, playgrounds, sport fields, tennis courts, bathhouses, and gymnasiums were built, and municipal band concerts inaugurated. The city contributed as never before to the joy and health of the community.[59]

In the development of its parks and playgrounds Cleveland followed other cities in the land,[60] but in its handling of underprivileged groups it stood in the forefront. What Jones did for Toledo, Johnson and Cooley did for Cleveland in introducing a number of daring humanitarian reforms. In their fulfillment Johnson supplied the political backing, Cooley the planning and administration. The two approached the problem from the same premise as did Jones: the source of poverty and crime was the unjust social conditions that denied men the opportunity to earn a comfortable living; since society was to blame, delinquents were not to be treated as objects of charity but were to be given hope and fresh opportunities which the world had previously denied them. The spirit of Christian brotherhood with all men should replace the notion of self-righteous almsgiving to the poor and retribution to the evildoers. Johnson and Cooley sought to realize their ideals by a varied program.[61]

Pardons and paroles were liberally granted to free men imprisoned for lack of money to pay court fines—a system that seemed to the two reformers tantamount to imprisonment for debt. When Johnson sat as magistrate of the police court, he was as generous as Jones in granting reprieves and in paying fines from his own pocket. After 1903 a "sunrise court" was introduced, which enabled persons arrested for intoxication the first time to plead guilty, sign waivers of their right to appear when tried, and be released by the police. This system of waivers was further extended in 1908 under the "Golden Rule" policy of Chief of Police Fred Kohler. The substance of his policy was this: patrolmen were to be given large discretion in making arrests; only as a last resort were they to take offenders into custody; juveniles apprehended were to be sent home to their parents; intoxicated persons were escorted home, or retained, if necessary for their safety, and given a waiver of trial; those charged with a misdemeanor were to be released after signing the "Golden Rule" book unless evidence indicated the crime was committed with malice aforethought or with the intent to injure property or persons. Although this practice coincided with Cooley's humanitarian program, Kohler found other reasons to support his system. Quite simply he defended it as one of common sense that brought results. The "Golden Rule" policy was watched all over the United States and adopted in modified form in some cities. In Cleveland it raised a tempestuous controversy which stormed about the character of Kohler as much as about the policy itself.[62]

Johnson had made him chief of police in 1903, partly in restitution for an injustice, partly in recognition of his ability, vigor, and self-reliance. A martinet, he was hated by the police force for his insistence on strict military discipline and for his capriciousness. Also something of a sycophant, he knew how to impress people in authority. He won Johnson's respect and confidence because he carried out to the letter the Mayor's policy toward saloons, gambling, and vice. Johnson knew that he could no more eliminate drinking and private gambling than he could abolish prostitution, but he determined to eliminate their most offensive and vicious side. He ordered gambling places and assignation-houses to separate from saloons; if the owners were recalcitrant, he stationed a uniformed policeman before the doors to take down the names of all who entered. This technique was so effective that gambling places closed and houses of prostitution no longer operated in conjunction with saloons. Slot-machine operators were forced out of business. The practice of blackmailing bawdyhouses by periodic police raids to collect large fines was stamped out. So long as Kohler was chief, he would not countenance the slightest suspicion of graft among the men of the department. He won from Theodore Roosevelt the encomium of "the best chief of police in America." In Newton Baker's administration Kohler's career as chief of police came to a sad end; he was removed from his post because of a scandal involving his personal life.[63]

Another and equally important part of the Johnson-Cooley program was the establishment of a farm colony outside of Cleveland to care for the aged, the sick, and the delinquent. Cooley, who had recommended the plan and for whom the farm colony was named, had two motives for this back-to-the-land movement: to furnish land that would afford the inmates the greatest opportunity to use whatever talents they possessed, and to cure the mentally and physically ill. On a two-thousand-acre plot at Warrensville three clusters of buildings were located, separated by fields and forest. Designed in the Spanish-mission style, with plastered walls and roofs of red tile, they were simple and dignified. One group provided a home for the aged poor, the second was a tuberculosis sanatorium, and the third the workhouse and reformatory.

Cooley rhapsodized on the wonders of these model communities. Hardened criminals were to be reformed by placing them in "sun-dungeons," glass-enclosed rooms in the towers of the reformatory, where the therapy of light and air would effect a cure. If this was sentimental, wishful thinking, not all of Cooley's ideas of penal reform were so naive. His aim was the reformation and rehabilitation of character—to make men. He freed the Correction Farm of the trappings of a prison: no striped clothing, no chains, no weapons for the guards. The work in the fields built up the bodies of the inmates; a night school, organized in the House of Correction, taught the illiterate to read and write; a Brotherhood Home in the city furnished lodging for released prisoners and served as an employment agency. On the same principle Cooley operated a Boys Farm at Hudson for minors sent from the juvenile court. He substituted humaneness and dignity for callousness and petty cruelty in the treatment of all the wards of the city. The Cooley plan, which followed, but in certain respects excelled, European farm colonies, attained a fame which crossed the ocean; visitors came to inspect it from many lands. It placed Cleveland in the vanguard of penal and welfare reform.[64]

This sums up Johnson's achievements in his adopted city. Like all visionaries, he failed to realize the dream that inspired him. Privilege he failed to abolish; inequality and poverty remained. His work was that of "seed-plowing, planning, and pioneering."[65] His battle for municipal control of street railways and municipal ownership of light and other services illustrated how the fight against Privilege might ultimately be won. The management of Cleveland during his nine years set a new standard for municipal service in cities. The Cooley-Johnson reforms brightened the prospects for a more humane treatment of society's wards everywhere. Johnson and his "City on a Hill" were a beacon light to reformers in other cities: Joseph W. Folk in St. Louis, Samuel M. Jones and Brand Whitlock in Toledo, George W. Guthrie in Pittsburgh, Edward F. Dunne in Chicago, and William B. Thompson in Detroit.[66] "Cleveland shared Tom Johnson with all its sister municipalities," the *Kansas City Star* declared. "Not another city entered a franchise fight, or planned an extension of activity for the general well being, or sought a square deal in any form, that it did not receive help and inspiration from Cleveland's public servant."[67] Yet the force of his personality and ideas was not confined to the urban sphere.

His contributions to the regeneration of Ohio, though less brilliant, were of a magnitude to place him in the front rank of the state's reformers.

1. Johnson, *My Story,* 107–9.
2. *Ibid.,* 109–16.
3. Tom L. Johnson to S. M. Jones, January 8, 1901, Jones Papers.
4. *Cleveland Press,* February 7, 11, 1901.
5. Lorenz, *Johnson,* 27; Eugene C. Murdock, "Cleveland's Johnson: Elected Mayor," *Ohio Historical Quarterly,* LXV (January, 1956), 28–43; *Cleveland Plain Dealer,* March 12, 1901. Johnson had solicited its support and the paper supported him for election but did not endorse all his views. This marked the beginning of a relationship that was beneficial to both. He profited politically from its aid in his five campaigns for mayor and one for governor; the paper prospered by espousing the cause of the popular mayor, forging ahead to become the leading Cleveland morning daily (Archer H. Shaw, *The Plain Dealer, One Hundred Years in Cleveland* [New York, 1942], 282–83). Johnson also received fair reporting and lukewarm editorial support from the *Cleveland Press* of the Scripps-McRae chain (*Cleveland Press,* March 11, 1901).

6. A prominent Republican banker, Myron T. Herrick, stated that in electing Johnson, Cleveland would be getting a $100,000 executive for $6,000 (Charles E. Kennedy, *Fifty Years of Cleveland, 1875–1925* [Cleveland, 1925], 139. Johnson comments on Hanna's view of him in *My Story,* 115–16. Another Republican who feared that the "resourceful" Johnson would be a threat to his party's supremacy in the county was Congressman Theodore E. Burton, who had campaigned four times against his opponent for his seat in the House of Representatives, splitting the victory in these contests. Burton defended Akers against the charge that he was affiliated with the discredited McKisson faction and urged his business friends to band together for the good of the party, not only in Cleveland but in the state and the nation. T. E. Burton to Henry S. Blossom, March 25, 1901; to Charles A. Brayton, March 25, 1901; to James Quayle, March 27, 1901; in the Theodore E. Burton Papers (MSS in the Western Reserve Historical Society, Cleveland, Ohio [hereafter referred to as Burton Papers]).

Information on the support of Witt and Fitzsimmons was obtained in the author's interview with Peter Witt, March 8, 1946, and from the *Toledo News-Bee,* April 11, 1911. The two men borrowed their organization plan from the Toledo Non-Partisans and were aided in applying it by William Cowell, Jones's campaign manager.

7. The campaign and election results were reported in the *Cleveland Plain Dealer,* February 25, March 13–18, April 2, 3, 1901; and in Johnson, *My Story,* 110–12. The threatened action was the execution of an ordinance passed by the council conveying title to certain steam railroads to a strip of filled land along the lake front worth several million dollars. As a private citizen Johnson brought an injunction restraining Mayor Farley from signing the ordinance. Since the injunction expired at noon on April 3, 1901, Johnson took office that morning. The law set no definite date but allowed the mayor-elect to enter upon his duties as soon as he was qualified by the election board. (Johnson, *My Story,* 117–18.)

8. Typical examples of newspaper commentary are in *Cleveland Plain Dealer*, April 3, 15, 1901, the *Cleveland Leader*, February 8, 1901, the *Toledo Blade*, April 3, 1901, and the *Ohio State Journal* (Columbus), November 10, 1901.

9. The data on Johnson's early life is drawn from his autobiography, *My Story*, 1–8.

10. *Ibid.*, 9–17.

11. *Ibid.*, 25.

12. *Ibid.*, 21, 48.

13. *Ibid.*, 29–33, 90, Appendix, 315–16.

14. *Ibid.*, 31–33, 86–107; Howe, *The Confessions of a Reformer*, 145.

15. Interview with Johnson, *Cleveland Plain Dealer*, November 20, 1908.

16. Johnson, *My Story*, 89. His partner, Arthur J. Moxham, wrote, "During Tom Johnson's business life in steel his emphatic, radical beliefs and policies brought him frequently into trouble, and at times even into financial danger. I could speak of more than one close crisis where the choice practically lay between all the financial help he needed for his business enterprises, to be won by stultifying himself in his political faith, or, as an alternative, financial opposition which at the time looked as though it would be fatal."— Interview with Arthur J. Moxham, April 11, 1911, printed in *ibid.*, Appendix, 315.

17. New York, 1883.

18. Johnson, *My Story*, 49–50. Other accounts of the exchange between Johnson and Moxham and his lawyer, L. A. Russell, on George's philosophy are told in Howe, *The Confessions of a Reformer*, 96–97, and in Louis F. Post, *The Prophet of San Francisco* (New York, 1930), 132–33. *Progress and Poverty* was published in New York, 1879.

19. Johnson has told of his meeting and campaigning with Henry George in *My Story*, 51–58, and of his experience in Congress in *ibid.*, 59–81. Champ Clark remembered Johnson's fight against a tariff on steel rails at a time when he was the second largest producer of these items in the country. To Clark it was the mysterious workings of God. (Champ Clark, *My Quarter Century of American Politics* [2 vols.; New York, 1920], I, 318–19).

20. Johnson, *My Story*, 107.

21. Whitlock, *Forty Years of It*, 152; Lorenz, *Johnson*, 125–26.

22. Lorenz, *Johnson*, 134; Johnson, *My Story*, 63, and Elizabeth J. Hauser, Introduction to *ibid.*, xxvii.

23. Neither man accepted Bryan's free-silver panacea, but they supported the Commoner because of his stand against monopoly and imperialism. Johnson stated his view of Bryan in *My Story*, 108–9. Jones expressed his attitude on free silver to S. M. Biddison, April 16, 1898, Jones Papers, and his admiration for Bryan to Hazen S. Pingree, October 20, 1900, and to Tom L. Johnson, November 13, 1900, Jones Papers.

24. This appraisal of Johnson is drawn from Lorenz, *Johnson*, 47–48, from Paul Leland Haworth, "Mayor Johnson of Cleveland," *Outlook*, XCIII (October 23, 1909), 469, and from Brand Whitlock, "Tom Johnson of Cleveland," *Human Life*, V (August, 1907), 3. Edward W. Bemis, a professional statistician, college professor, and co-worker with Johnson from 1901 to 1909, declared that the Cleveland mayor was "the greatest administrator, the most efficient executive, greater than Jefferson, Jackson, Altgeld, Pingree, or

Jones."–Edward W. Bemis, "Tom L. Johnson's Achievements as Mayor of Cleveland," *Review of Reviews,* XLIII (May, 1911), 558. Two perceptive appraisals of Johnson have recently appeared: Robert H. Bremner, "The Civic Revival in Ohio: Reformed Businessman: Tom L. Johnson," *American Journal of Economics and Sociology,* VIII (April, 1949), 299–309; Eugene C. Murdock, "Cleveland's Johnson," *Ohio Archaelogical and Historical Quarterly,* LXII (October, 1953) 323–33.

25. Whitlock, *Forty Years of It,* 207.

26. *Cleveland Plain Dealer,* January 1, 1916; Howe, *The Confessions of a Reformer,* 127–28; the author's interviews with Alfred A. Benesch, March 8, 1946, and Robert J. Bulkley, July 31, 1949; Robert Crosser, "Cleveland's Great Mayor Tom L. Johnson," a speech delivered in the House of Representatives, March 19, 1946, *Congressional Record,* 79th Cong., 2d Sess., 2437–38.

27. Johnson, *My Story,* 173–181; Lorenz, *Johnson,* 51–81.

28. Lincoln Steffens, *The Struggle for Self-Government* (New York, 1906), 188–89. Whitlock corroborated this view of the Johnson circle (Whitlock, *Forty Years of It,* 173). See also Steffens, "Ohio: A Tale of Two Cities," 293–311.

29. Accounts of Baker's early life and descriptions of his appearance and oratory are in: Brand Whitlock, "Newton D. Baker," *American Magazine,* LXXII (1911), 559–60, and *Forty Years of It,* 171; Burton J. Hendrick, "Mayor Tom's Successor," *World's Work,* XXVII (April, 1914), 670, 675–76; C. H. Cramer, *Newton D. Baker: A Biography* (Cleveland and New York, 1961), 13-33, 70-75; N. D. Baker, Jr. to N. D. Baker, Sr., November 14, 1896; to Frederic C. Howe, November 22, 1898; to Martin A. Foran, December 19, 1898; in the Newton D. Baker Papers (MSS in the Cleveland City Hall, Cleveland, Ohio [hereafter referred to as Baker Papers, CCH]). The account of his first political address in Cleveland is taken from *Cleveland Plain Dealer,* November 8, 1911.

30. The speculation was begun by Lorenz in his biography of Johnson, Lorenz, *Johnson,* 70–74. The remarks on his temperament and political deficiency are drawn from N. D. Baker to W. Calvin Chesnut, December 29, 1895, Newton D. Baker Papers (MSS in the Library of Congress [hereafter referred to as Baker Papers, LC]); and from Hendrick, "Mayor Tom's Successor," 671–74. Baker explained to his father why he had bolted the Bryan ticket and also reaffirmed his faith in the tenets of Grover Cleveland Democracy: free trade, civil service reform, and "a scientific and safe currency" (N. D. Baker, Jr. to N. D. Baker, Sr., November 14, 1896, Bakers Papers, CCH). His devotion to Johnson is confirmed in Lorenz, *Johnson,* 70–74, and in Baker's biographical article, "Tom Loftin Johnson," *Dictionary of American Biography* (21 vols.; New York, 1928——), X, 122–24. Baker later confessed that his conversion to the single tax had been somewhat superficial because he never understood the intricacies of the doctrine (N. D. Baker to F. C. Howe, April 29, 1912, Baker Papers, CCH). Baker's credo is in Hendrick, "Mayor Tom's Successor," 671, and in N. D. Baker to F. C. Howe, May 6, 1904, Baker Papers, CCH.

31. Johnson, *My Story,* 173; Howe, *Confessions of a Reformer,* 190; Lorenz, *Johnson,* 74; N. D. Baker to Gilbert H. Stewart, February 5, 1906, Baker Papers, CCH.

32. Cooley's background is related in the *Cleveland Plain Dealer,* April

13, 1901, in Harris R. Cooley, "After Twenty Years," *ibid.*, December 2, 1934, and in Jean A. Herring, "Harris R. Cooley" (Master's thesis, Ohio State University, 1949), 1–23. He expressed his belief in the efficacy of the teachings of Christ in a letter to S. M. Jones, January 10, 1901, Jones Papers.

33. Johnson's remark is quoted in Kennedy, *Fifty Years of Cleveland,* 140. Appraisals of Cooley's work are found in Johnson, *My Story,* 109–10, and in Lorenz, *Johnson,* 57.

34. The account of Witt's early life is drawn from Lorenz, *Johnson,* 75–76, and from Carl Wittke, "Peter Witt, Tribune of the People," *Ohio Archaeological and Historical Quarterly,* LVIII (October, 1949) 362–64.

35. Johnson, *My Story,* 84–85. Witt was first introduced to Henry George's philosophy by Dr. L. B. Tuckerman (Wittke, "Peter Witt," 364).

36. Johnson's praise is in Johnson, *My Story,* 85–86. His work in behalf of tax reform is described in Lorenz, *Johnson,* 76–79. Witt wrote a book in which he mockingly and scathingly exposed the city's tax dodgers, *Cleveland before St. Peter* (Cleveland, 1899). It was written before Johnson returned to Cleveland to lead the reform movement. Ironically, he was among those accused by Witt of tax dodging (*ibid.,* 46–48).

37. Lorenz, *Johnson,* 80–81, 136; N. D. Baker to Daniel Kiefer, June 17, 1908, Baker Papers, CCH; *Cleveland Plain Dealer,* October 19, 1907; the author's interview with Charles A. Otis, October 4, 1949.

38. Howe's early life is told in his autobiography, *The Confessions of a Reformer,* 1–84.

39. *Ibid.,* 95–99, 127, 136. "Single-taxing a City" is the title of chap. xxii in *ibid.* Howe explained that the assessors took "the first step toward the single tax by increasing the valuation of land and reducing the valuation placed on improvements," but neither buildings nor personal property were left untaxed as George advocated.

40. *Ibid.,* 115–16, 199–207, 224–25.

41. Frederic C. Howe, *The City the Hope of Democracy* (New York, 1905), 7. He described the growth of democracy in the cities of Europe in *The British City: The Beginnings of Democracy* (New York, 1907), *European Cities at Work* (New York, 1913), and *The Modern City and Its Problems* (New York, 1915). Howe's concern for the city and his general philosophy are ably discussed in Robert H. Bremner, "Honest Man's Story: Frederic C. Howe," *American Journal of Economics and Sociology,* VIII (July, 1949), 413–14, 419–22.

42. Johnson's influence and leadership were recounted in Howe, *The Confessions of a Reformer,* 184, in J. B. Vining to S. M. Jones, November 9, 1899, Jones Papers; and in the author's interview with Herbert Bigelow, September 26, 1949. Whitlock's reliance on the Johnson circle is revealed in his letters: Brand Whitlock to Harris R. Cooley, March 12, 1906; to Tom L. Johnson, April 10, 1906; to Tom L. Johnson, November 19, 1907; to Peter Witt, September 30, 1909; in the Brand Whitlock Papers (MSS in the Library of Congress [hereafter referred to as Whitlock Papers]). The first three of these letters are reprinted in Allan Nevins, ed., *The Letters and Journal of Brand Whitlock* (2 vols.; New York, 1936), I, 52, 56–57, 83. Johnson's impact on Fagan is reported in Ransom E. Noble, Jr., *New Jersey Progressivism before Wilson* (Princeton, 1946), 93. His association with the Fels Fund and support of Post is told in Johnson, *My Story,* 54–55, 306–8.

43. The admirer was Louis F. Post, who made the statement in a signed

article in *The Public*, XIII (June 10, 1910), 537. A comprehensive review of the contributions of other single taxers is in Ransom E. Noble, Jr., "Henry George and the Progressive Movement," *American Journal of Economics and Sociology*, VIII (April, 1949), 260–67.

44. Johnson, *My Story*, 107. Johnson made clear at once his opposition to a single tax party (*Cleveland Plain Dealer*, March 29, 1901).

45. Even the editor of the paper most friendly to Johnson in Cleveland called him a "political boss," a "political dictator" (*Cleveland Plain Dealer*, March 23, 1902). It was a cause of some confusion to precinct workers everywhere that the reformers like Johnson, La Follette, Folk, and Theodore Roosevelt were just as dictatorial as the old-time bosses, Hanna, George Cox, and Matthew Quay (*ibid.*, April 11, 1909).

46. In 1902, for example, Johnson issued an order prohibiting the collection of compulsory political assessments and fired the superintendent of the street department, a prominent Democrat and Catholic, for violating the order (*Cleveland Plain Dealer*, July 21, August 9, 1902). The next year in the Democratic primaries he campaigned to defeat this same superintendent and another Democrat who had once been a member of a notorious group in council suspected of bribery in connection with the gas franchise (*ibid.*, March 9, 10, 14, 17, 18, 1903). Johnson appointed four Republicans to important posts: William J. Springborn, director of public works department; Daniel E. Leslie, director of parks department; Myron B. Vorce, building inspector; and Fred Kohler, chief of police. In 1907 the Mayor endorsed for re-election four Republican councilmen who had supported the low-fare movement. (Johnson, *My Story*, 179–84; *Cleveland Plain Dealer*, August 20–21, 1907).

47. Elizabeth J. Hauser, Introduction to Johnson, *My Story*, xxv–xxvi; Tom L. Johnson, Foreword to *ibid.*, xxxv–xxxvii.

48. Johnson, Foreword to *ibid.*, xxxvii–xli.

49. Johnson expressed his opposition to socialism in replies to Socialist hecklers at his political rallies in the 1902 and 1903 campaigns (*Cleveland Plain Dealer*, November 1, 1902; *Cincinnati Enquirer*, October 4, 1903). His opposition to sweeping antitrust legislation was stated in an address he made before the National Anti-Trust Conference, Chicago, February 13, 1900, reprinted in *The Public*, XIV (April 21, 1911), 373–74.

50. Elizabeth J. Hauser, Introduction to Johnson, *My Story*, xxi–xxii. His remarks on unionism were made at a political meeting in the 1901 campaign, reported in the *Cleveland Plain Dealer*, March 19, 1901. In Congress Johnson had voted for a bill to establish the eight-hour day for government employees and he had protested against the brutality of the police in the handling of Coxey's Army on May 1, 1893 (Gordon R. Rawlinson, "Tom Johnson and His Congressional Years" [Master's thesis, Ohio State University, 1958], 64, 105).

51. Johnson, *My Story*, 91–97; Lorenz, *Johnson*, 17–18.

52. The Cleveland street-railway fight has been voluminously reported. The newspapers of the city, especially the *Plain Dealer* and the *Leader*, gave excellent day-by-day coverage of the conflict bcause it made dramatic copy. There are several survey accounts. Sympathetic to Johnson, in addition to his own account in *My Story*, 156–66, 221–94, are two articles by Edward W. Bemis: "The Street Railway Settlement in Cleveland," *Quarterly Journal of Economics*, XXII (August, 1908), 543–75; "The Cleveland Street Railway

Settlement," *ibid.*, XXIV (May, 1910), 550–60. Lorenz is on the whole favorable to the Mayor in *Johnson*, 139–84. Hostile to Johnson are Haworth, "Mayor Johnson of Cleveland," 469–74, and Warren S. Hayden, "The Street Railway Situation in Cleveland," *Proceedings of the Cincinnati Conference for Good City Government and the Fifteenth Annual Meeting of the National Municipal League* (1909), 403–16.

53. These criticisms of the battle and of Johnson personally were made in Hayden, "The Street Railway Situation in Cleveland," 415–16; in the author's interview with Charles A. Otis, who was one of Johnson's leading opponents, October 4, 1949; and in the *Cleveland Plain Dealer*, November 10, 11, 1908. Statements in his defense are to be found in: Johnson, Foreword to *My Story*, xl–xli, 282; Bemis, "Johnson's Achievements as Mayor of Cleveland," 560; Lorenz, *Johnson*, 65–66, 180–82, 195; Peter Witt, "The Man Who Died," *Cleveland Press*, April 10, 1914.

54. Johnson recounts the fight for a municipal electric plant in *My Story*, 216–19. The details were reported in: *Cleveland Plain Dealer*, March 18, July 28, 29, August 3, October 28, November 1, 2, 5, 1903; November 10, 1904; January 31, February 6, 7, 14, 21, March 12, 21, 1905; November 6, 7, 1907; *Report of the Special Committee on the Proposed Municipal Electric Plant*, Cleveland Chamber of Commerce, July 25, 1903, 4–5; H. T. Newcomb, *Municipal Socialism, the Conservative Victory in Cleveland* (Washington, D.C., 1905), 46–48. The account of the other services managed by the city is in Lorenz, *Johnson*, 64.

55. Lorenz, *Johnson*, 51; *Cleveland Plain Dealer*, November 1, 1907; Williamson, *The Finances of Cleveland*, 185, 196. The attacks of the Democratic Buckeye Club on the Bemis administration of the water works department reached their peak in the spring and summer of 1902. In the council the Democrats defeated an ordinance to reorganize the department. As a result of this open revolt, Johnson demanded and received the resignation of two Buckeye Club leaders from their administrative posts: J. Martin Thumm, chief clerk of the water works department; and George Faerron, city sealer. (*Cleveland Plain Dealer*, March 18, 21, July 22, 23, 1902.)

56. The work of Springborn and Friedrich is told in Lorenz, *Johnson*, 52–53, 57–58, and in Johnson, *My Story*, 179–180. The new building code is in the *Cleveland Plain Dealer*, November 1, 1907; March 29, 30, 1908. The reorganization of the purchasing department is reported in *Annual Report, City of Cleveland* (1908), Div. XVI, pp. 3, 9–10; *ibid.* (1909), Div. XVI, pp. 3, 6.

57. The grant of a franchise to the East Ohio Gas Co. was fought by the artificial-gas companies and the coal dealers. One councilman confessed that he had been offered a bribe of $5,000 to vote against the franchise. It was alleged, on the other hand, that the Standard Oil Co., which owned the East Ohio Gas Co., had given Johnson $1,000,000 for his support. (Johnson, *My Story*, 212–16; Lorenz, *Johnson*, 61–62.) Johnson's support of the Belt Line is stressed in Lorenz, *Johnson*, 62.

58. The Cleveland Group Plan idea was initiated by Fred Howe and Morris Black, who were familiar with group planning of public buildings in European cities. They prepared illustrated stories on the grouping of public buildings in Vienna, Paris, Budapest, Dresden, and Munich for the Sunday papers, persuaded the Cleveland Architectural Club to hold a competition for plans, and enlisted the support of the Cleveland Chamber of Commerce.

Elbert H. Baker, the lessee and editor of the *Cleveland Plain Dealer*, was influential in gaining Johnson's enthusiastic support for the Group Plan. The law authorizing the plan provided for the appointment of a three-man commission by the governor. In order to insure the selection of a strong commission, Johnson worked in harmony with the Cleveland Chamber of Commerce, knowing that their endorsement would be decisive with Republican Governor Nash. The three men endorsed and appointed were Arnold W. Brunner, architect of the Cleveland Federal Post Office and Court House; Daniel H. Burnham, one of the architects for the Chicago Columbian Exposition of 1893; and John M. Carrere, architect of the Buffalo Pan-American Exposition of 1901. (Howe, *The City the Hope of Democracy*, 243–45; Shaw, *The Plain Dealer*, 278; *Cleveland Plain Dealer*, June 1, 3, 21, 1902.) The Group Plan is described in Daniel H. Burnham, John M. Carrere, and Arnold W. Brunner, *Report on the Group Plan of the Public Buildings of the City of Cleveland* (2d ed.; 2 vols.; [Cleveland], 1907), I, 1–3.

59. Lorenz, *Johnson*, 53–54.

60. Boston was the leader in the park movement (Howe, *The City the Hope of Democracy*, 245–46).

61. Johnson, *My Story*, 173–74; *Annual Report of the City of Cleveland* (1903), 1009–10; Howe, *The City the Hope of Democracy*, 214–38.

62. Johnson's and Cooley's policy of liberal pardons and paroles is described in: *Cleveland Plain Dealer*, November 15, 16, 28, 1901; June 15, August 16, 1902; interview with James B. Morrow, printed in *ibid.*, August 16, 1908; Kennedy, *Fifty Years of Cleveland*, 141; *Annual Report of the City of Cleveland* (1903), 941–42; *ibid.* (1905), Div. XIV, p. 13. Kohler's "Golden Rule" policy and his defense of it are presented in Johnson, *My Story*, 182–83, in William J. Norton, "Chief Kohler of Cleveland and His Golden Rule Policy," *Outlook*, XCIII (November 6, 1909), 537, and in the *Cleveland Plain Dealer*, January 6, 1909. According to Alfred A. Benesch, however, the two men who were the real authors and instigators of the waiver system were Emmanual Levine and William A. McGannan, judges of the municipal court (author's interview with Alfred A. Benesch, March 8, 1946).

63. Johnson's favorable appraisal of Kohler is in *My Story*, 181–82; Roosevelt's praise of the Cleveland chief was printed in the *Ohio State Journal*, March 18, 1913. The criticism of Kohler was made by Alfred A. Benesch. Johnson's plan for enforcing the separation of saloons and houses of prostitution and gambling was borrowed from his father who had first applied it and found it to be effective when he was chief of police of Louisville (Johnson, *My Story*, 122; *Cleveland Plain Dealer*, April 11, June 21, August 7, 1901). The Cleveland Civil Service Commission found Kohler guilty of "gross immorality and conduct unbecoming an officer and gentleman," and discharged him from office (*ibid.*, March 18, 1913).

64. Descriptions of the Cooley Farm Colony and its operation are in "Report of the Division of Charities and Correction," *Annual Report of the City of Cleveland* (1909), Div. VIII, pp. 4–9, and in Johnson, *My Story*, 175. Cooley's ideas on the rehabilitation of criminals are in: Lorenz, *Johnson*, 55–56; Johnson, *My Story*, 175–76; Harris R. Cooley, "New Deal in Crime as Practiced in Tom L. Johnson's Day," *Cleveland Plain Dealer*, April 7, 1935; Robert H. Bremner, "Harris R. Cooley and Cooley Farms," *American Journal of Economics and Sociology*, XIV (October, 1954), 71–75. The fame of the Cooley plan is reported in Bemis, "Johnson's Achievements as Mayor

of Cleveland," 559, in Lorenz, *Johnson*, 57, and in the *Cleveland Plain Dealer*, September 23, 1906.

65. Lincoln Steffens to Tom L. Johnson, September 1, 1909, in Ella Winter and Granville Hicks, eds., *The Letters of Lincoln Steffens* (2 vols.; New York, 1938), I, 224.

66. Testimony of Folk in a Cleveland address, *Cleveland Plain Dealer*, November 4, 1905; Brand Whitlock to Lincoln Steffens, September 23, 1909, Whitlock Papers, printed in Nevins, ed., *The Letters and Journal of Brand Whitlock*, I, 220; speech of Guthrie at memorial meeting for Johnson in Pittsburgh, *The Public*, XIV (May 12, 1911), 439. The Johnson group's assistance of Dunne in the Chicago street-railway fight and of Thompson in his campaign for re-election in 1908 is reported in *Cleveland Plain Dealer*, June 8, 12, 1905, and October 19, 1908, respectively.

67. Editorial in *Kansas City Star*, April 11, 1911, reprinted in *The Public*, XIV (July 21, 1911), 725.

CHAPTER FOUR

THE FIRST CAMPAIGN
FOR TAX REFORM
1901■1902

THE ISSUE which first compelled Johnson to enter state politics was taxation reform, a fundamental problem to a disciple of Henry George. The Mayor would have preferred to concentrate his attention on Cleveland alone, where he knew many grave tax inequities existed, but he soon learned that it was impossible to change conditions in Cleveland without reforming the tax structure of the whole state. The cities had to be made free from state control, free to adopt their own methods of taxing themselves, if the ultimate goal of the single tax were to be achieved.[1]

The cities were chosen as the experiment stations by Johnson and the other followers of Henry George because they believed that the application of the single tax would be easiest and the benefits would be greatest within urban communities. In the large municipalities the rise in land values was most dramatically revealed. These were values which, according to the single taxers, were created by the pressure of population and municipally financed improvements, such as police and fire protection and water and sewer lines—in short, were socially created. Yet the beneficiaries were the landowners, who had done nothing to create such values. The George disciples proposed to tax this "unearned increment" and return to society the values society had created. This proposal seemed both morally right and the most promising in practical results.[2]

Frederic C. Howe, an idealistic spokesman for the Ohio

followers of George, has written glowingly of the train of consequences that would follow after the cities had adopted the
single tax. It was expected to solve automatically all the urban
problems. It would eliminate political corruption by making
rational and clear the methods of taxation; it would go a long
way towards abolishing poverty, vice, and slums by forcing idle
land into productive uses—the building of factories and model
tenements—thus giving the poor more work and more living
space; it would provide a continuously growing source of revenue
to meet the city's needs, for the constant rise in urban land values
through population expansion would mean greater tax collections. The city's land would become the city's treasure.[3]

Closely related to the "unearned increment" of land values
was the value of the franchises granted to utility companies to
use the public highways. These rights of way in the city streets
were site values in another form. The one kind owed its value
to society as much as did the other. Furthermore, the grant to
supply transportation, gas, water, and electric lighting was a
more thoroughgoing monopoly than the land.[4] Ideally, these
service monopolies should be under municipal ownership. But
if that were not possible, their franchise values at least should
be taxed. So rapid and continuous had been the rise in land
and franchise values in American municipalities that Howe did
not believe it would be necessary to recover the increases which
had occurred in the past. Cities would have enough revenue,
he thought, if they continued their present property taxes and
then added all future gains annually.[5]

It was the wish to start taxing this untapped treasure that
determined Johnson's line of attack in Cleveland. He began
at once to expose the gross undervaluation of commercial property and idle land within the city. A week after taking office in
April, 1901, the Mayor established a bureau in the city hall,
known as the Tax School, to lay the groundwork for his campaign. Peter Witt, who had already made a name for himself
by publicizing tax dodgers, was placed in charge, while Newton
Baker was assigned to aid in the legal work. Johnson's purpose
was to expose and publicize the existing tax inequalities on land
and improvements and at the same time to educate the public

on the taxation question. Ward by ward, on maps sixteen feet square, clerks copied the *assessed value* of each lot and building in the city, and experts gathered statistics on the *market price* of the properties. Taxpayers were invited to see these displays, criticize the existing tax appraisals, and suggest changes in valuation. By means of these discussions a unit value for each foot frontage of land by one hundred feet in depth was established for every block in the city. This method, called the "Somers unit system" of taxation after its author, W. A. Somers, appealed to Johnson because it achieved an accurate appraisal of land and separated the assessment of land from its improvements, the first steps toward the single tax. The new values thus computed were plotted on the maps for each individual holding, enabling a rapid, visual comparison between the assessed and the market values. Wide variations were revealed; at one extreme, property was assessed at 2 per cent of its sales price; at the other, at 68 per cent higher than the market.[6]

Newspaper publicity, Peter Witt's stereopticon lectures, and individual letters to taxpayers helped to spread the results among the citizens. In the aggregate the new valuations did not much exceed the old, but a greater uniformity and a shift in the incidence of the tax burden had been achieved. On the West Side, for example, where the homes of workingmen predominated, tax values were generally reduced; on the other hand, in Ward Two, the city's commercial and financial heart, assessed values were as uniformly boosted to conform to the market price. A howl arose from the owners whose property assessments were radically increased. One of the large holders who was also high in Republican counsels petitioned for an injunction to end the operations of the Tax School. Vulnerable to attack because it had been financed with funds voted by the council without statutory authorization, the Tax School was forced to disband by the court in December, 1902, but by then its task of determining the value of every foot of Cleveland property according to the Somers unit system had been completed.[7]

Meanwhile it was Johnson's task to persuade the existing tax bodies to adopt its scientific appraisals. He first approached the Cuyahoga County Decennial Board of Equalization, which had just completed its reappraisal in 1900—a reappraisal that had increased the total valuation of city property but had not altered the old disparities. When this Republican-dominated board refused to listen to his pleas, he went over its head to the Ohio Decennial Board of Equalization, which eventually did make a blanket increase of 12.5 per cent.[8]

Since, however, this did not touch the existing inequalities, the Mayor turned to the one channel still open to him, the annual city board of equalization. Opportune vacancies, two of which he had had a hand in creating, enabled him to appoint four members and thus control this seven-man board. As soon as the legal authority of the decennial appraisers expired on December 31, 1901, he was confident that the city board would adopt the work of the Tax School, which they had already endorsed. Such expectations were frustrated when the Republican legislature in May, 1902, abolished the body he had appointed, replacing it with a board of review chosen by state officers.[9] Nevertheless, Johnson's efforts had not been in vain. The Tax School revealed to Clevelanders and other Ohioans the slipshod methods being used and the consequent inequalities in property assessment. Ultimately its proposals were incorporated into a revision of Ohio's tax laws.[10]

Simultaneously with this contest against the wealthy landowners, Johnson jousted with the public utilities. The five gas, light, and street-railway companies were notorious tax dodgers, escaping with assessments of 10 to 20 per cent of their true value. Although the undervaluation of these utilities had been public knowledge for some time, the Mayor was the first to make a concerted effort to correct it. He proposed a solution that had been suggested a half-dozen years before: the taxation of these public-service corporations according to the unit rule of the Nichols Law, which would include the worth of their valuable franchises.

Since the taxable property in dispute was personal, jurisdiction belonged to the annual city board, to which Johnson had just appointed a majority of his own men. During June, 1901, he briefed its members on the proper method of taxing utilities and forearmed them to resist the companies when the latter presented their usual low returns. At the hearings in July, Johnson appeared with Professor Edward W. Bemis, who had been hired as a tax expert, "the only such expert on the people's side," to appeal for a much higher valuation of these properties. By a partisan vote of four to three the Johnson appointees on the board raised the tax values to the figures recommended by the city's experts. The increases, amounting to more than $16,400,000 or 450 per cent, were immediately challenged by the corporations, and the Cleveland Street Railway Company asked for a temporary injunction against the payment of the new assessment.[11]

It was not necessary, however, for the utilities to continue the expensive litigation in the courts, for upon appeal they obtained relief from the Republican-dominated state board of tax remissions. At the hearing lawyers for the defendant corporations insisted that the city had exceeded statutory authority in computing the new returns, that it was, in effect, adopting the unit rule of the Nichols Law, which did not apply. Newton Baker, representing the city, quoted from the opinion of the United States Supreme Court in a test case of the Nichols Act that "it is a cardinal rule which should never be forgotten that whatever property is worth for the purposes of income and sale it is worth for purposes of taxation." That rule, the city's attorney insisted, applied, irrespective of the Nichols Law, to these utilities. On February 1, 1902, the state board announced its decision, remitting the increase because the Board of Equalization had "exceeded its powers and acted without authority of law." [12]

Johnson flatly charged the Republican state governmental officials with playing politics and paying off the generous campaign contributions of the Cleveland utilities with this political favor—an accusation not unfounded. Although there was a legal question whether the assessment of franchise values demanded by the city should have been sustained, the remission of the whole amount was an act of deliberate prejudice, for the very next year the two Cleveland street-railway companies voluntarily doubled their returns. Over a four-year period, between 1900 and 1904, the five companies increased their assessed values from $4,500,000 to $7,800,000, adding $60,000 a year to the city's tax collections.[13] Johnson's example inspired similar action in Columbus and Toledo, and he assisted Mayor Jones by sending Professor Bemis to present the city's case before the Toledo Board of Equalization. Finally, in 1910 the Ohio legislature adopted Johnson's proposed method of taxing utilities as the law of the state.[14]

The Cleveland mayor's third round was with the railroads. Again the tax favors they enjoyed had been thoroughly aired by Republican-dominated tax commissions in the nineties, but no adequate remedy had yet been imposed. The powerful railroads, allied with the county auditors and the Republican state administration and favored by friendly judges, had thus far been able to resist tax increases. Undaunted by this combination, Johnson sought to challenge all the lines that were assessed in Cuyahoga County, of which Cleveland is the county seat. He was armed with statistics that Bemis had prepared when he appeared before the several boards of county auditors in May, 1901, to testify against the low tax returns each line presented. According to his evidence the Valley Railroad, for example, was assessed at $5,500 per mile instead of its true value of $65,000 per mile. Another line, the Cleveland Belt and Terminal Railroad, returned a total valuation of $19,655, although the property had recently been sold for $400,000. The auditors listened stolidly to Johnson's statistics and arguments, refused to call for the companies' books as he demanded, then voted increases of approximately 1 per cent.[15]

The results were not surprising, for, although they were public officials, the county auditors were in reality minions of the railroads, nominated and elected with campaign funds supplied by the companies, furnished with passes, and not uncommonly sent to the seashore for a summer vacation at railroad expense. At the hearings on the tax return of the Cleveland, Lorain, and Wheeling Railroad, Johnson was able to publicize one of these evils by drawing from each auditor the admission he had a pass from the line.[16]

An opportunity to bring more cities into his battle against the railroads came when Johnson was invited to address the League of Ohio Municipalities, which was then meeting in Cleveland. This organization of mayors, of which Samuel Jones was a co-founder, had been formed to discuss and promote municipal reforms of every kind. Johnson described his experiences with the county auditors and urged that a committee of mayors carry the issue to the state board of equalization for railroads. If that body refused to act, they would seek redress in the courts, and if all else failed, at least they would have given the existing low valuations of railroads forceful publicity. His motion was carried unanimously, and the committee of five selected included himself and Mayors Jones of Toledo and John N. Hinkle of Columbus.[17]

On September 5, 1901, Johnson, as a representative of the league, together with his two aides, Bemis and Baker, appeared before the state board; Mayor Jones, Colonel James Kilbourne, from Columbus, and various railroad men witnessed the heated session. Bemis presented the evidence of undervaluation, citing statistics to show that the railroads of the state were assessed at only 21 per cent of their true value. But this issue was pushed to one side when the board insisted that it lacked power under the law to increase the total appraisal of the county auditors. Baker argued that it had the power. Ohio Attorney-General John M. Sheets, however, insisted on a literal interpretation, maintaining that the board's only authority was to equalize differences in values made by the several auditors of the counties through which the lines ran. Even if a return for a railroad was omitted altogether, he claimed the board could not require correction of the omission. At the end of this exposition Baker charged the attorney-general and the board with having made up their minds on the question before the hearing took place. Johnson added heat to the argument by accusing two members of accepting an invitation from a certain railroad official to make a trip to California in his private car. When Bemis pointed out that the board had in the past advanced the appraisals of county auditors by small amounts, the attorney-general admitted the fact but declared that the increases were so slight that the practice was never questioned.[18]

After the hearing Johnson filed a brief with the board elaborating the verbal arguments. On October 1, 1901, Attorney-General Sheets rendered a formal opinion reiterating his previous position that the board lacked legal authority to raise the appraisals, an opinion Johnson castigated as "nothing but the flimsiest sort of subterfuge." And he added, "The board didn't want to raise the valuation because they had received favors for which they were grateful; the Republicans didn't want to oppose these roads, and so the opinion was written." At the same time, he announced that this decision did not end the matter.

93

As a taxpayer he brought a mandamus suit to compel the state board to boost the aggregate appraised values of the railroads. The Ohio Supreme Court, on February 4, 1902, refused to grant the writ on the ground that the board could not act as a body of appraisers under statutes which prescribed their duties as equalizers; relief could come only from the legislature.[19]

This last conclusion of the Supreme Court of Ohio confirmed what had become apparent to Johnson after the first few months of his fight in Cleveland. The evils of local tax injustice could not be abolished until the state laws and administration were reformed. Such changes, in turn, could not be achieved without educating the citizens of the whole state, not Cleveland alone. "What is most needed," he told the League of Ohio Municipalities, "is to bring these matters before the people, and we can trust them when they once understand the subject to see that right is done." [20]

Johnson soon had his opportunity. On July 9, 1901, the Democratic state convention met in Columbus to nominate a governor and other officers and draft a platform. The Mayor, who was indifferent to the selection of candidates, concentrated on placing his ideas on tax reform in the platform. Because of the sudden death of his brother, he could not be present himself, but he was represented by Charles P. Salen, chairman of the convention, and by two other Clevelanders, Echo M. Heisley and Newton Baker, who were members of the resolutions committee.[21]

A contest developed in that body between the Johnson wing and the conservatives, whose spokesman was Judson Harmon. The latter were determined to prevent an endorsement of Bryan's Kansas City platform and the national Democratic standard-bearer himself. Although the Johnson men were friendly to Bryan, they had no interest in his free-silver crusade. A compromise was reached in the committee: the conservatives were given their way in drafting statements on national issues, the Johnson radicals were allowed to incorporate their favorite state planks. One struck at railroad abuses, demanding the removal from office of any public official accepting a free pass or other favors from a railroad. Two were aimed at tax reform, requiring publicity of the books of public utilities and access to their records by state or local officials, and the assessing of steam and electric railroads, including their franchises, in the same proportion as the market value of farms and homes. A fourth urged a referendum election, upon petition of 5 per cent of the voters of a city, on all renewals or extensions of street-railway franchises. A fifth called for the nomination of United States senators by state party conventions.

There were other planks in the platform which Johnson had not specifically requested but which he wholeheartedly endorsed: home rule for cities, a declaration against the protection of any product manufactured by trusts, and a pledge to labor to oppose all class legislation.[22]

On the floor of the convention, William L. Finley, leader of the Bryanites, unsuccessfully challenged the omitted endorsement of the Commoner and his platform, but there was no vocal opposition to the Johnson planks. The nomination for governor went by acclamation to Colonel James Kilbourne, whom John R. McLean had defeated in the Democratic convention two years before, a selection satisfactory to all factions. Even McLean's *Cincinnati Enquirer* had nothing but praise for Kilbourne who was, in its words, "eminently qualified to stand on a platform designed to reunite all the forces of democracy. . . ."[23]

When the campaign opened unofficially late in the summer, the Democratic orators relied on the time-honored practice of attacking the national administration for its sins and subordinating state issues. An assassin's bullet on September 6, killing President McKinley, however, changed the character of their strategy. Because of Kilbourne's refusal to continue attacks on the administration of the martyred President, the Democrats had to shift to state problems. At the formal campaign opening in Bucyrus, October 22, Kilbourne made taxation his central theme, though he did not neglect trusts and the tariff, and Johnson, speaking from the same platform, devoted his entire speech to the tax question, a concentration on that reform which was displeasing to the Republicans.[24]

In their convention in June the Republicans had renominated George K. Nash for governor, John M. Sheets for attorney-general, Walter D. Guilbert for auditor, and Isaac B. Cameron for state treasurer, the very men who, composing the state tax board, had thwarted Johnson's attempts to make the railroads bear their fair burden. Aware that the Democrats would pounce upon the taxation question, the Republicans had declared for tax reform in their state platform. They had recommended levies on business instead of assessments on real and personal property as sources of state revenue and a constitutional amendment to remove all legal doubts about the power of the legislature to tax franchises and every other form of property; they denounced schemes which would place the whole burden on real estate, a direct slap at Johnson's single-tax theories. But as far as possible in the campaign the Republicans preferred to keep clear of this touchy subject. Their stump speakers focused on the tariff, prosperity, and the re-election of Foraker to the United States Senate; they exploited the noble character of McKinley and the tragedy that closed his career. Mark Hanna, dominant in party circles, stressed the slogan he had coined, "Let well enough alone." "This is no time," he added, "to bring into this contest any side issues of state affairs, such as taxation, three-cent fares, Henry George theories, or anything else of that kind," and he warned the people not "to chase after the Johnson steer." [25]

Except for the speech at Bucyrus, Johnson confined his campaigning to Cleveland, concentrating on two objectives: education of the people on the tax question and the election of the Democratic slate of delegates to represent Cuyahoga County in the General Assembly, all of whom he had personally approved. Nightly, during the final two weeks, he pitched his big tent, first used in his congressional campaigns, in different parts of the city, conducting meetings which were more in the nature of forums on taxation than poltical rallies. Baker, Cooley, and Witt were regular speakers on the rostrum with Johnson. Baker lucidly and urbanely presented the legal aspects and the general view of the tax problem; the tender, religious Cooley stressed the moral side; and Witt gave blackboard talks, punctuated with sarcasm, on the tax inequalities in the particular district where the tent was pitched. Without so labeling them, Johnson emphasized the Georgian principles behind the tax-reform measures. Unequal to sustained, flowing oratory, he made his points briefly in easy, conversational tones, then filled out his time answering questions, a technique he had developed when campaigning for Henry George. Questions stimulated Johnson's thought. Although friends spotted in the audience would frame some to enlarge upon a particular point, not all the questions came from sympathizers, for he invited hecklers to parry with him. In this manner he capitalized on a weakness and enlivened his meetings.[26]

When the returns were counted on election night, November 5, the Democrats had carried Cuyahoga County, electing four state senators, ten state representatives, one judge of the Cuyahoga County Court of Common Pleas, and all the county officers including the auditor, a key official in taxation. In addition, the party won in Franklin County, but elsewhere the election poll was gloomy for the Democrats. The remaining big-city counties went Republican, as did the state as a whole; a total of sixty-one of the eighty-eight counties were in the Republican column, four more than in 1899.[27]

Newspapers credited the Republican victory variously to the assassination of McKinley, prosperity, and Hanna's technique of smearing the Democrats as dangerous incendiaries. The Democratic *Cleveland Plain Dealer* belabored the state managers of its party for rejecting Johnson's advice to make taxation the single issue and, instead, encouraging the spellbinders to mouth "the old platitudes, making pretense of fighting . . . on the old issues and invoking the shades of the dead and gone to keep their party followers in line." "If Mayor Johnson's policy had been adopted and carried into effect throughout the state as it was in this county," the editor concluded, "there would be a Democratic governor and a tax reform legislature at Columbus in the coming year."[28]

Instead, the General Assembly which met on January 6, 1902, was safely Republican: the House, sixty-eight Republicans to forty-two Democrats, organized by the Hanna faction; the Senate, twenty-one Republicans to twelve Democrats, controlled by friends of Foraker, who was easily re-elected United States senator over his Democratic opponent, Charles W. Baker of Cincinnati. Johnson established headquarters in a house on East Broad Street near the State House to assist the Cuyahoga delegation in preparing and promoting bills which embodied the platform pledges.[29]

On the eve of the first day for introducing legislation, the Republican *Ohio State Journal* lamented, "Gloomy announcement is made that tomorrow will be 'Johnson day' in the house and a choice assortment of Cuyahoga anti-property bills will be unloaded on the several committees of that body."[30] True to this prediction, the Cleveland members dropped in the hopper bills to permit municipal ownership of street railways, to require a referendum vote on all street-railway franchises, to eliminate property-owner consents in making street-railway grants, to enforce complete publicity of all public service–corporation books, to prohibit public officials from accepting railroad passes, and to establish a passenger rate of two cents per mile on rail lines.[31]

The editors of the *Ohio State Journal* were not the only Republicans to take alarm at the Cleveland bogeyman. In the House the party leaders announced that no more bills would be passed under suspension of the rules for fear that a Johnson bill might sneak through before they were aware of it. "We look with suspicion on anything that emanates from Tom Johnson," said Representative Andrew G. Comings, a merchant of Oberlin, "and we insist that all measures shall go to the regular committees, where they can be carefully scrutinized." All local bills for Cleveland were to be approved by two prominent Republican businessmen of the city, Myron T. Herrick and Homer H. Johnson, for, as Comings again explained, "You cannot expect this Republican majority to accept the word of the Cleveland members that the bills which they introduce are acceptable to the people of Cleveland until confirmation is given us by representative Republicans of the city." Comings and George H. Chamberlain, an Elyria lawer who performed a similar service in the Senate, were dubbed the "guardian angels" of Cleveland by the wrathful Democrats, and denounced for destroying the rights of the people to true representation.[32]

Despite the unwanted solicitude and interference the Cuyahoga delegation fared well on local measures authorizing the city government to construct bathhouses, appoint the Group Plan Commission, and increase levies for libraries and schools. But their other bills were given short shrift, most of them dying in committee. Johnson pleaded with the municipal affairs committee for his bill to permit municipal ownership of street railways to no avail, only one Democrat voting to report out the measure. The explanation of the fate of the railroad bills was epitomized in a mock resolution offered by a Democrat from Seneca County: "Resolved, That the heartfelt thanks of this body are hereby extended to all the transportation companies of Ohio for courtesies received [free passes], and in return we present an unbroken record of legislative favors as proof of our gratitude." This was greeted with a cry of disgust from the Republicans, who promptly voted to table the motion.[33]

Johnson's primary interest was not in these measures but in taxation, an interest shared by other members of his party and by the Republicans as well. This was the principal theme of Governor Nash's message to the legislature and of Speaker William S. McKinnon's acceptance speech. By the end of January the administration had initiated the first part of its program: a bill introduced by Ralph D. Cole boosting the excise tax from .5 to 1 per cent on all public service–corporations, and another presented by Frank B. Willis levying a tax of one-tenth of 1 per cent on all other incorporated businesses. A month later, bills for the remainder of the program had been framed: an excise tax of 2.5 per cent on the gross receipts of foreign insurance companies, and a reduction in the state levy on real and personal property from 2.89 to 1.35 mills, the latter retained wholly for educational purposes.[34]

The Johnson Democrats were not appeased by these measures, which only halfheartedly attempted to correct the existing inequalities. To the Republicans' surprise neither were the rest of the Democrats. Fully expecting an opposition tax bill to originate among the Johnson delegates, the Republicans were ready to brush it aside with a few smear epithets. However, when the Johnsonites yielded the honor of introducing a comprehensive, alternate bill to their party colleagues, Representative Roscoe L. Carle of Seneca County and Senator William E. Decker of Paulding County, the majority party had to give the proposal proper consideration. The Carle-Decker measure, applying the unit rule of the Nichols Law in the assessment of all public service–corporations, railroads included, received the strong backing of the Johnson wing, the approval of the party leaders of the state, and the support by caucus action of every Democratic member of the Assembly.[35]

At a joint hearing of the House and Senate tax committees prominent Democrats spoke in its support—Judge Robert M. Ditty of Columbus and Charles W. Baker, as well as Bemis and Johnson. In his address Johnson supported the Democratic measure as a means of making the railroads and the public-service corporations in the cities bear their proper burden; he attacked the Cole bill for not taxing the utilities enough, and the Willis bill for taxing on the basis of the par value of the stock rather than earnings, a procedure which could have the effect of driving competitive business from the state.[36]

Opposition to the administration tax program was not confined to Democrats; a faction within the Republican party balked, and the utilities were hostile. They considered the Cole bill to be a breach of the promise that the Republicans had made in 1896 not to tamper with the excise tax. However, a special message from Governor Nash, party caucuses, and vigilance by the party leaders kept the Republican members in line. On April 10 the Nash program was adopted by a straight party vote, and the Carle-Decker bill was defeated at the same time.[37]

This was not the only blow Johnson suffered in his battle to remove tax inequalities. On March 27 the Republicans introduced in the Senate a ripper bill which would substitute for the decennial and annual city boards of equalization, appointed by mayor or council, a board of review to be chosen by the state board of appraisers at any time a county auditor requested. The new body was to consist of three men, no more than two of whom could be from the same party. Johnson criticized the bill for running counter to home rule in taxation. In the Senate the Republicans offered little resistance, but those in the House balked at this ripper legislation. On the final ballot in the lower chamber the roll had to be called many times before the bill passed by one vote.[38]

The first auditor to make application under the act was Republican William Craig of Cuyahoga County; another early request came from the Republican auditor of Lucas County. If the bill was aimed at curbing the power of Mayors Johnson and Jones, as was widely contended, it was a marked success. In the case of Cleveland the act seemed all the more iniquitous, for it allowed an auditor defeated at the polls to throw out the existing board and commit the city to a new one appointed by the same state officers who had already declared their bias in remitting the tax increases on the five Cleveland utility corporations.[39] Defeated but not disheartened, Johnson prepared to renew the battle for just taxation when his attention was temporarily diverted from that issue by an Ohio Supreme Court decision tearing down the governmental structure of Cleveland and every other city in the state.

1. Johnson, *My Story*, 125; Frederic C. Howe, "The Best Governed Community in the World," *World's Work*, III (February, 1902), 1726.

2. Howe, *The City the Hope of Democracy*, 251–52, 261. There is an excellent analysis of the single tax philosophy and of the aims of the Cleveland tax reformers, which has provided many helpful suggestions to this author, in Robert H. Bremner, "The Civic Revival in Ohio: The Single Tax Philosophy in Cleveland and Toledo," and "Tax Equalization in Cleveland," *American Journal of Economics and Sociology*, IX (April, 1950), 369–76; X (April, 1951), 301–4.

3. Howe, *The City the Hope of Democracy*, 191–92, 205–7, 225, 237, 249–50, 263, 277.

4. *Ibid.*, 264–66.

5. *Ibid.*, 266–68.

6. Johnson, *My Story*, 125–28, 292; *Cleveland Plain Dealer*, April 11, 30, 1901; Bemis, "Johnson's Achievements as Mayor of Cleveland," 559–60. Somers had first applied his system in St. Paul, Minnesota, and was invited by Johnson to assist in its application in Cleveland.

7. Johnson, *My Story*, 129–30; *Cleveland Plain Dealer*, April 30, October 5, 10, 1901; September 29, December 21, 23, 1902. The injunction suit was brought by Willard J. Crawford. Not only did he seek to close the Tax School, but he also tried to compel the return of the money illegally spent. However, the judge of the court of common pleas refused to compel the repayment, and the higher courts sustained his ruling. (*Proceedings of the City Council of Cleveland*, XXXV [1902–3], 249-50; *Annual Report of the City of Cleveland* [1904], 1120.)

8. Johnson criticized the work of the county board in his annual message to the council, reprinted in the *Annual Report of the City of Cleveland* (1901), ix. A *Plain Dealer* editorial condemned the results as "the most chaotic and illogical appraisement of real property that a poor system had ever produced in Cleveland" (*Cleveland Plain Dealer*, September 7, 1901). The state board first made a blanket increase of 25 per cent, but a lobby of businessmen sent to Columbus by the chamber of commerce succeeded in having the amount cut in half (*ibid.*, April 19, 20, May 7, 1901).

9. See p. 100, below.

10. Appraisals of the work of the Tax School are in Johnson, *My Story*, 129, and in Williamson, *The Finances of Cleveland*, 82. The Tax School attracted the attention of reformers in Detroit and New York, who sent experts to Cleveland to examine the application of the Somers unit-value system (*Cleveland Plain Dealer*, August 9, November 19, 1902).

11. Johnson's arguments and the action taken by the board are reported in the *Cleveland Plain Dealer*, July 17, 19, 20, 23–24, 26, 31, 1901. The returns of the five companies were increased as follows: the Cleveland City Railway Company from $600,000 to $5,605,191; the Cleveland Street Railway from $1,625,510 to $8,676,759; the Cleveland Electric Illuminating

Company from $474,882 to $1,347,000; the Peoples Gas Company from $360,245 to $1,074,000: and the Cleveland Gaslight and Coke Company from $1,500,000 to $4,286,400. The Cuyahoga County Court of Common Pleas refused to grant the injunction (*ibid.*, July 31, 1901). Johnson's praise of Bemis is in Johnson, *My Story*, 132.

12. Baker quoted from *Adams Express Co.* v. *Ohio State Auditor*, 166 U.S. 185 (1897). The hearings and the board's decision were reported in the *Cleveland Plain Dealer*, January 18, February 2, 1902, and the *Ohio State Jounral* (Columbus), February 2, 1902.

13. In his revision of the returns for these five utilities, as well as in his estimate of the values of railroad property, Johnson attempted to make synonymous franchise value and physical assets, thus circumventing the refusal of the legislature to apply the unit rule of the Nichols Law in assessing these companies. Such an identification, however, is not supported by most economists, who make a clear distinction between the two. The point is discussed in Lattimer Johns, "Taxation of Railroads in the State of Ohio" (Master's thesis, Ohio State University, 1912). The increase by the companies in their returns was noted in the *Cleveland Plain Dealer*, August 1, 1902, and December 1, 1904, and in Johnson, *My Story*, 130.

14. *Ohio State Journal*, August 5, 1902; *Toledo Bee*, August 2–4, 1901. The tax legislation of 1910 is in 101 O.L. 399 (1910).

15. *Cleveland Plain Dealer*, May 4–5, 10–11, 16, 18, 22, 1901; Johnson, *My Story*, 132–44.

16. Johnson, *My Story*, 139; *Cleveland Plain Dealer*, May 22, 1901.

17. *Cleveland Plain Dealer*, May 16, 1901. Jones's part in the founding of the League of Ohio Municipalities is told in the *Toledo Bee*, February 9, 1898, and the *Toledo Blade*, February 9, 25, 1898.

18. *Cleveland Plain Dealer*, September 6, 1901; Johnson, *My Story* 139–42. Bogart considered Sheets's position untenable. See Ernest L. Bogart, *Financial History of Ohio* ("University of Illinois Studies in the Social Sciences," Vol. I, Nos. 1 and 2 [Urbana, Ill., 1912]), 325.

19. Johnson's comments were quoted in the *Cleveland Plain Dealer*, October 2, 1901. His reasons for bringing the mandamus action are stated in *My Story*, 142; the case is reported in *State of Ohio* ex rel. *Johnson* v. *Annual State Board of Equalization of Railroads*, 65 Ohio 544 (1902).

20. Quoted in the *Cleveland Plain Dealer*, May 16, 1901.

21. *Ibid.*, July 9, 10, 1901; Powell, ed., *The Democratic Party of the State of Ohio*, I, 379.

22. *Cleveland Plain Dealer*, July 10, 11, 1901; *Ohio State Journal*, July 10, 1901; *Toledo Bee*, July 10, 1901.

23. *Cincinnati Enquirer*, July 11, 1901; Powell, ed., *The Democratic Party of the State of Ohio*, I, 379–80.

24. *Toledo Bee*, October 23, 1901.

25. The Republican state convention is reported in the *Cleveland Plain Dealer*, June 24–26, 1901. The Republican campaign and Hanna's speeches are in *ibid.*, October 20–21, 26, 1901, and the *Toledo Bee*, October 23, 27, 1901.

26. Johnson's campaign is described in Johnson, *My Story*, 83, in Lorenz, *Johnson*, 88, and in Whitlock, *Forty Years of It*, 170. It was extensively reported in the *Cleveland Plain Dealer*, October 15, 18–19, 22, 24–25, 1901.

27. *Cleveland Plain Dealer*, November 6, 7, 1901; *Toledo Bee*, November 6, 1901; *Ohio State Journal*, November 6, 7, 1901; *Cincinnati Enquirer*, November 6, 7, 1901. The vote was: George K. Nash (Republican) 436,092; James Kilbourne (Democrat) 368,525; E. Jay Pinney (Prohibition) 9,878; John Richardson (Union Reform) 2,718; J. H. T. Juergens (Socialist Labor) 2,994; Harry C. Thompson (Socialist) 7,359 (*Report of the Secretary of the State of Ohio* [1906], 119). Brand Whitlock, candidate for state senator on the Democratic ticket, was defeated in the Republican landslide in Lucas County.

28. *Cleveland Plain Dealer*, November 7, 1901; *Toledo Bee*, November 6, 1901.

29. *Cleveland Plain Dealer*, November 7, 1901; January 2, 5, 15, 1902; *Ohio State Journal*, January 5, 15, 1902. The vote for senator was Foraker 87, Baker 53.

30. *Ohio State Journal*, January 14, 1902.

31. *Cleveland Plain Dealer*, January 8, 15, 22, February 21, 1902. Representative Edward J. Bracken of Franklin County also introduced a bill to permit municipal ownership of street railways.

32. Comings' remarks were quoted in *ibid.*, January 25, 26, 1902. The work of the "guardian angels" was reported in *ibid.*, January 29, February 13, May 13, 1902.

33. The legislative measures were reported in *ibid.*, May 10, 12, 1902, Johnson's pleading in *ibid.*, February 28, 1902, the resolution by the Seneca County Democrat in the *Cincinnati Enquirer*, May 13, 1902. Moreover, the Cuyahoga County delegation with their other Democratic colleagues were unable to prevent the adoption of three measures considered reactionary: the repeal of the Garfield Corrupt Practices Act; a bill to make potentially more costly a test in the courts of the validity of legislation; and a curative act validating bonds, franchises, grants, and privileges issued under acts later declared illegal by the courts (*Cleveland Plain Dealer*, March 26, April 25, May 7, 1902). The statutes are in 95 O.L. 77, 316, and 444 (1902), respectively.

34. Governor Nash's message and Speaker McKinnon's speech were reported in *Ohio State Journal*, January 7, 1902, the tax legislation in *ibid.*, January 26, March 1, 1902.

35. The text of the Carle-Decker bill was fully discussed in *ibid.*, February 15, 1902. Attorney-General Sheets and several Republican members of the legislature favored the extension of the Nichols Law principle at some future time, but were content for the present with the administration tax proposals. Governor George K. Nash said he knew nothing about the Carle-Decker measure, but disapproved of it as a Democratic bill. (*Ibid.*, February 15, 16, 1902; *Cincinnati Enquirer*, February 15, 1902)

36. *Ohio State Journal*, March 12, 1902.

37. *Ibid.*, February 20, 26, April 2, 11, 1902. The bill to reduce the state levy from 2.89 to 1.35 mills was the only administration tax measure for which the Democrats were willing to vote (*Cleveland Plain Dealer*, April 17, 1902). The tax statutes are in 95 O.L. 124, 136, 290, 324, 327, 439 (1902).

38. *Cleveland Plain Dealer*, March 28, May 2, 1902; special article by W. S. Couch, who in 1902 was the *Plain Dealer* correspondent in Columbus

and an accurate observer, in *ibid.*, October 20, 1909. The act is in 95 O.L. 481 (1902).

39. *Cleveland Plain Dealer*, May 3, 16, 1902; *Toledo Bee*, June 2, 1902. By June 1 boards of review had been appointed also for Elyria, Lorain, Zanesville, Portsmouth, and Gallipolis (*ibid.*, June 2, 1902). A year later the Ohio Supreme Court held invalid all special legislation creating city boards of equalization. The effect of this decision was to make mandatory the appointment of boards of review in all cities of the state by the state board of appraisers. (*State of Ohio* ex rel. *Kemp* v. *Clarke*, 68 Ohio 463 (1903); *Toledo Bee*, May 22, 1903)

CHAPTER FIVE

THE FIGHT TO FREE
THE CITIES
1901⬛1902

ONE MONTH after Johnson had registered his second victory at home in the election of November, 1901, a news dispatch from Columbus announced that a quo warranto suit had been filed with the Ohio Supreme Court to test the constitutionality of the Cleveland charter. The suit had been initiated by an obscure attorney, C. D. Gibbon, and another man whom the press referred to as "a Republican and a taxpayer," but it was soon evident that powerful forces were behind them when Attorney-General John Sheets was persuaded to take charge. Johnson was certain the street-railway companies were the real instigators. Lawyer Gibbons admitted that before filing he had consulted a few prominent anti-Johnson Democrats and Republicans, including Mark Hanna, to solicit legal and financial aid and had confided to them that his purpose was to knock out the form of government which had fostered the growth of the Johnson machine. Whoever the ring leaders were, their intent was obviously to "get" Johnson. The moment was propitious to strike, for the Ohio Supreme Court had been showing increasing evidence that it was ready to destroy the system of special legislation for cities, of which the Cleveland charter was a product. Although Johnson deplored the system in general as the source of many municipal evils—in particular the vicious ripper bills— he was unwilling to let go Cleveland's excellent plan of government without a protest. His decision to defend the city had broad popular support, for the citizens were justly proud of their form of government and were suspicious of the motives of those behind the assault.[1]

Before that suit could be heard by the state supreme court, a companion case had originated in Toledo. It will be recalled that a ripper bill passed the legislature in 1902, replacing Toledo's elective police board, over which the mayor presided, with a commission appointed by the governor. Although the change had been urged by many of the respectable citizens because of the Mayor's open contempt of the police-court system, Jones was certain that the persons truly responsible for the attack upon him were the patronage-hungry politicians who wanted to regain control of the police department and restore the spoils system that he had abolished. Certain that right was on his side, he decided to fight back. He persuaded the old board to refuse to recognize the authority of the new commission or the governor's power to appoint it. In an open letter he defended his own conduct as consistent with the will of the people of Toledo and condemned that of the opposition as the violation of home rule. For his defiance of the law he was upbraided by both the Republican *Blade* and the Democratic *Bee* and branded as an egotist, a publicity seeker, and an anarchist— editorial criticism that stung the Mayor. Soon the newly appointed commissioners brought a mandamus suit in the Ohio Supreme Court to compel him and the old board to turn over command of the police department to them. Jones retained Brand Whitlock to represent him in the litigation.[2]

This had not been the only ripper bill passed in the 1902 legislative session. The tax boards of the cities were shifted from local to state control, and Cleveland also had its park board metamorphosed. So numerous were these bills that even some Republican newspapers took alarm. The *Toledo Blade* deplored especially a bill to substitute boards for single directors to head the Cleveland departments of public works and public safety, introduced by Senator Patterson of Pike County without consultation with the members from Cuyahoga. An editorial in the *Ohio State Journal* urged the Assembly to kill all "the rippers," adding, "There is no popular demand for any of these bills and the interest of good government cannot in any way be subserved by their passage." No doubt the legislators were deterred from passing any further rippers by the pending cases before the supreme court challenging the constitutionality of special acts.[3]

The plain intent of the Ohio Constitution had been to protect cities from legislative tampering by prohibiting the General Assembly from passing any *"special* act conferring corporate powers,"[4] but the constitutional injunction had long been circumvented by legislative action and judicial acquiescence. The legislature had proceeded to classify cities by population and to write special laws for municipalities of each class as though they were intended for general application. By 1900 the number of categories for cities had grown to fourteen and the *Ohio Code* was strewn with special laws for each municipality.[5]

The Ohio Supreme Court had originally upheld the classification system on the assumption that cities, as they grew in population, would adopt the form of government prescribed for the next class in size. When the General Assembly began subdividing classes into grades, grades into sub-grades, writing "general laws" for cities with a population of not less than 10,956 nor more than 10,960, it became apparent that the court's prophecy would not be fulfilled. Nevertheless, as late as 1895 the supreme court in a Cincinnati case continued to close its eyes to the obvious violation of the constitutional intent on the theory that such legislation had been so long recognized and the city governments were so linked to it that "the evil consequences to be apprehended from overturning the established rule would greatly exceed any likely to result from adhering to it."[6]

However, within the next seven years the court did upset what seemed to be its settled policy. The reversal did not occur as suddenly as it appeared to the uninformed, for it had been foreshadowed in dissenting opinions. Justice John A. Schauk had twice dissented from the majority view, and in the second case had been joined by two other justices.[7] By the time the Toledo and Cleveland cases were heard in June, 1902, the court majority had switched to the dissenting view.[8] It was appropriate, therefore, that Justice Schauk was assigned to speak for the majority, declaring both the Toledo Police Board Act and the Cleveland charter invalid because they were clearly special legislation conferring corporate powers in the violation of the Ohio Constitution.[9] Since the effect of the decision in the Cleveland case was to threaten the validity of the charter of every city in the state, the court suspended the execution of its decision until October 2, 1902, to give the legislature time to act.[10]

Mayor Jones, rejoicing in his victory, commented, "Even supreme court judges are men. . . . The supreme court is bound to be right once in a while. It is good to overthrow precedent." Johnson, although defeated and still distrustful of the motives of those back of the Cleveland suit, also praised the court for knocking out special legislation and expressed his hope that the Assembly would draft a flexible municipal code or at least adopt the federal-plan charter for all the cities of the state.[11]

The main hope of the two mayors and other reformers was pinned on the adoption of a municipal code prepared by Judge David F. Pugh of Columbus and Edward Kibler of Newark, a bipartisan commission of two, which the legislature of 1898 had authorized Governor Asa Bushnell to appoint. After two years of effort they had prepared a code embodying very advanced principles: abolition of classification; municipal control by the local council, not the state legislature; a federal-plan organization with concentration of executive power in the mayor and of legislative power in a small council; a nonpartisan ballot; adoption of the merit system; submission of franchises and bond issues to popular vote; and extension of municipal ownership to street railways and telephones. Nevertheless, the Pugh-Kibler bill had several strikes against it. In the first place it was over-detailed and cumbersome, running to 1,185 sections and 260 pages. Secondly, many of its features were so radical as to arouse the organized resistance of two groups: the politicians who balked at the nonpartisan ballot and the merit system, and the public-service corporations, who resented any extension of municipal ownership. Introduced in the state Senate in 1900 by Senator Warren G. Harding as an administration measure, it was passed, then recommitted to the municipal corporations committee on the same day. Such action, prompted by the street-railway lobby, meant the death of the bill for that session In their 1901 platform the Democrats endorsed the bill and condemned the Republicans for its defeat.[12]

During the interim between the 1900 and the 1902 legislative sessions, a committee of five, commissioned by the Ohio Bar Association, had trimmed its bulk and had also eliminated two of its most controversial features—nonpartisan elections and the municipal-ownership clause. Reduced in size and strength, it was presented to the Assembly in 1902, where it lacked friends among the big-city delegations. The Cincinnati members opposed it because of George B. Cox's continued hostility; the Johnson men from Cleveland declared it worthless without the municipal-ownership provisions; Columbus delegates disliked the merit system; only the Toledo representatives favored it. By the time it was reported on the floor of the House, some two hundred amendments had been added in committee. Frightened by its complexity and possible ambiguity, the representatives refused to bring it to a vote. Nevertheless, despite the fate of the bill, there was considerable sentiment in the House for municipal government reform.[13]

The decisions of the supreme court in June, occurring after the adjournment of the regular session, reopened the issue of a new municipal code. No longer could the legislature dodge the question; action was imperative. On July 22 Governor Nash summoned a special session for August 25 to draft a charter of government for the cities. Throughout the summer various groups and individuals were busy framing proposals. Governor Nash assigned the task of preparing an administration measure to Wade H. Ellis, assistant corporation counsel of the city of Cincinnati, and State Senator Nicholas Longworth, assisted by a committee of the Ohio Bar Association, Attorney-General Sheets, and Special Counsel Smith W. Bennett. The State Board of Commerce, a private organization representing various business interests, drafted a bill of its own.[14] When the appointed day came, four proposals were ready.

The bill sponsored by the State Board of Commerce and presented by Representative William W. Chapman, embodied a maximum of home rule. Under its terms each city was directed to call a charter convention to draft its own governmental organization, the only stipulation being that there must be a mayor and a council. It granted broad powers to cities to make and enforce local, sanitary, police, and other regulations not in conflict with general laws, and to create debts and levy taxes subject to such limits as the legislature might prescribe. Johnson, who had concluded from his experiences in the regular session that it would be futile to present his own proposal, endorsed it with minor reservations, for it was a long step toward his ultimate goal of complete freedom for cities to manage their own internal affairs.[15] In essence it foreshadowed the home-rule amendment ratified by the Ohio voters in 1912.

An alternate proposal, drafted by Judge George B. Okey of Columbus, was patterned after the State Board of Commerce bill, with the addition of a municipal-ownership clause and specific limitations on the rates charged by utilities, i.e., a maximum four-cent fare for street railways. Called the York bill after its legislative sponsor, Charles I. York, of Ottawa County, this likewise received the blessing of reform groups.[16]

The Nash bill, bearing the patronymic of the governor and the sanction of Foraker, Hanna, and George Cox, provided for a uniform organization for all cities, with powers specifically enumerated. Modeled after the government of Cincinnati, the proposal called for a mayor, council, elective city solicitor, auditor, and treasurer, elective boards of public works and public safety, and civil service for the police and fire departments. In presenting the proposal Wade Ellis remarked, "We have not attempted to devise any novel plan for the government of Ohio municipalities." Certainly it was not novel, for it added no new powers and saddled the cities with a "board plan," discredited by every student of municipal affairs and by thoughtful conservatives interested in the responsibility and efficiency of city government.[17]

The fourth measure, drafted and introduced by Representative W. E. Guerin, Jr., of Erie County, borrowed from the Nash bill the enumeration of municipal powers but proposed a modified federal plan of single heads in place of boards, the directors of the departments of law and accounts to be elective, those of public safety and public improvements appointive.[18]

While confessing himself no friend of the federal plan, Governor Nash had originally favored an outline code which individual cities could fill in, but he had been dissuaded by constitutional doubts — doubts confirmed by a public statement of Justice Shauck and a brief prepared for the attorney-general by Smith W. Bennett. It is possibly true that the Ohio Constitution did not permit as much elasticity in framing municipal governments as the home-rule bills advocated; nevertheless, there was legal precedent for permitting more flexibility than existed in the ironclad administration proposal. In his message to the special session Governor Nash attempted to discredit the home-rule plans by urging the Assembly to "stand rigidly by the principles of the constitution" and not waste their time on schemes which flew in the face of the commands of the highest court.[19]

When the legislature convened on August 25, the numerically large House referred the four bills to a committee of twenty-three appointed by the speaker, fifteen Republicans and eight Democrats; the small Senate considered them sitting in committee of the whole. All of the major-city counties had one representative on the special house committee except for Hamilton County, which was given two. Among the Democrats were such ardent partisans of municipal reform as Charles W. Stage from Cuyahoga County, Edward J. Bracken from Franklin County, and William F. Maag from Mahoning County, the publisher of the *Youngstown Vindicator*. From August 27 to September 10 the committee in public meetings listened to the testimony of a host of special pleaders. There was abundant support for home rule: from W. L. Hughes, a representative of the League of Ohio Municipalities, Washington Gladden, H. H. McMahon, a Columbus lawyer, Professor John A. Fairlie of the University of Illinois, Johnson and Baker, Harry A. Garfield, a Republican attorney from Cleveland, and Harry Thomas of the United Trades and Labor Council of Cuyahoga County.[20]

Gladden did more than support home rule before the committee; he pleaded for it from his pulpit and in open letters to the press. Taking the text for one of his sermons from the words of the Prophet Micah, "The voice of Jehovah crieth unto the city, and the man of wisdom will fear thy name," he told his congregation that "the divine voice must admonish those who are charged with this responsibility that they give the people of the cities the rights and privileges that belong to them as citizens; that they make it legally possible for the cities to govern themselves . . . [for] the foundation principle of our democratic republic is local self-government."[21]

Many shades of Cleveland opinion were present to advocate a federal-plan charter and a city-wide merit system: representatives of the Municipal Association, a delegation from the Cleveland Chamber of Commerce, and Johnson, Baker, and Witt. Witt expressed the strangeness he felt at being on the same side as the Chamber of Commerce, but he presumed that every person in Cleveland held the same opinion on the merits of the federal plan. Moreover, the contrasting system of government by boards was condemned: Baker called it a "two-headed calf," Gladden and Mayor John N. Hinkle of Columbus decried it as the least desirable form of government. But the board plan had its defenders; speeches were made on its behalf by Mayor Julius Fleischman of Cincinnati and E. M. Thresher of Dayton.[22]

A strenuous struggle developed over the franchise question, a reflection of the street-railway fight in Cleveland and of a special situation in Cincinnati. Lobbyists for the traction interests began infesting Columbus on the day the session opened. At the behest of his friends, Guerin had included in his bill a curative provision to reinstate a fifty-year franchise of the Cincinnati street-railway company, which had been declared void by the circuit court. The franchise had been granted originally under the Rogers Law, of infamous memory to reformers, an act manipulated through the legislature of 1896 by the traction companies, with the aid of Foraker, and repealed at the next session. This attempt to restore such an "iniquitous franchise" aroused the ire of Baker and Johnson, who delivered tirades against the curative proposal.[23]

Furthermore, both sides in the Cleveland street-railway battle recognized that this was an opportunity to improve their positions. Hanna appeared before the committee to ask for perpetual franchises subject to a revision of rates every ten years. He defended his request as a means of preserving his "savings bank" (The Cleveland City Railway Company) from the ravages of "politicians" (Johnson and his boys) and of insuring the people better service. A caustic editorial in the *Cleveland Plain Dealer* commented on the spectacle of the junior senator from Ohio combining the arts of a cheap lobbyist with the additional power of his political office to obtain a perpetual franchise. Aroused by Hanna's maneuver, Johnson descended upon the committee to demand that the laws be eased in favor of new street-railway lines and that all franchises, original grants, renewals, and extensions be submitted to vote of the people. He made a plea for the municipal ownership of street railways, a recommendation also supported by Gladden, Harry Thomas, and Bracken. Fearful of the effect on public opinion, the Republican leaders persuaded Hanna to drop his perpetual-franchise idea, at the same time agreeing to dismiss all changes in the existing legislation on street railways except for passage of the curative act.[24]

Talk as they might, the municipal reformers in 1902 could not impress their views on the majority, safely controlled by the Republican machine. On September 8 and 9 the Republicans in the Senate and on the House special committee voted overwhelmingly to proceed on the basis of the Nash bill, and in later meetings they defeated proposals to substitute a home-rule amendment. The administration measure, with the curative bill tacked on, passed the Senate September 30 by a vote split along party lines, twenty-one Republicans for, twelve Democrats against. On the same day the House added the curative proposal as an amendment to the bill, forty-seven Republicans and eight Democrats in the affirmative, twenty-five Democrats and nine Republicans in the negative. Johnson, who had earlier issued a warning of vengeance against party corruptionists who voted for the curative bill, declared that the eight Democratic traitors were marked men, and that he would fight them with all his strength should they seek office again. A week later the House passed the bill, but, while accepting the curative amendment, it had rejected the board plan and had substituted instead single directors to head the departments of public works and public safety.[25]

To reconcile the conflicting Senate and House versions, a conference committee composed of nine Republicans and one Democrat who had voted for the curative bill was appointed. After verbal pressure from Governor Nash and Hanna, and telegrams from bankers, lawyers, and ministers, the House members yielded and agreed to the administration's board plan or "Cox's curative code," as Charles Stage dubbed it. The final vote came on October 21. Four Republicans caused a near sensation in the Senate by switching their votes to the opposition, but two of them soon returned to the fold, enabling the conference report to pass. In the House the atmosphere was tense as the Democrats taunted their opponents with the charge that they were "slaves of the bosses." But when the roll call was taken, the conference report passed sixty-four to thirty-five. This time only three Democrats joined the solid phalanx of Republicans.[26] As the House adjourned, the Democrats regaled the opposite benches with a derisive parody of the doxology:

Praise Cox to whom all blessings flow;
Praise him, ye people of O-h-i-o;
Praise Hanna, Nash and all the host,
But praise George B. Cox the most.[27]

This feeling that the Republican bosses and George B. Cox in particular had dictated the final results ran high among the opponents of the new code. The Johnson group, moreover, was convinced that the board plan had been deliberately selected to minimize the Mayor's power. Their bitterness was given expression in an editorial in the pro-Johnson *Cleveland Plain Dealer*:

> To this degradation has the Republican party of Ohio been brought by the petty spites and bungling management of its leaders, of whom better things might have been expected. Its managers wear the collar and obey the commands of a Cincinnati boss who holds no official position in the state. The Republican legislators take their orders from the same boss instead of from their constituents. All the cities in the state, from the biggest to the smallest, are to be saddled with a system of municipal government unwieldy, costly, open to the raids of political spoilsmen, unscrupulous contractors, and corrupt officials, that this boss may still hold Cincinnati at his mercy. Cleveland has been robbed of the best system of government it ever had and is to be given the worst, at the dictation of the Cincinnati boss. . . . [28]

Such hostile reactions were not confined to the local press or to reformers. The new code was condemned by two Republican papers in Chicago and by the *Springfield* (Mass.) *Republican,* which echoed the sentiments of the *Plain Dealer,* lamenting "this perversion of a great opportunity in municipal reform for low partisan ends," namely, "of keeping the spoils of the cities in Republican hands and the grip of the bosses upon municipal rule." [29]

Clinton R. Woodruff, of the National Municipal League, who had spent several days in Ohio during the summer to advocate adoption of the League's model municipal code, deplored the work of the Assembly, accepting the popular verdict that it was a "Cox code." He singled out for condemnation four main aspects: the enumeration of specific grants of power to cities instead of the preferred general grant, the profusion of elective officers, the retention of the antiquated board system, and the inadequate civil service provisions. In particular he denounced as "a vicious denial of the principle of home rule" the provision that the members of the board of public safety should be appointed by the governor if the mayor, the original appointing agent, should fail to obtain the endorsement of two-thirds of the council for his nominees. Another student of municipal affairs, Delos F. Wilcox, termed the code's machinery of elective officers and boards "the most striking example of deliberate dissipation of responsibility to be found." [30]

That the Republicans were nettled by these criticisms was apparent in the apologetic tone they adopted toward their handiwork. In the introduction to his annotations of the *Ohio Municipal Code* published the following year, Wade Ellis marked out the general line of defense: the Assembly was faced with an emergency demanding prompt action and did the best job possible in the brief time allotted; the board plan was traditional, the federal plan experimental and unfamiliar; much of the criticism could be discounted as coming from scholarly citizens of states far to the rear of Ohio in municipal progress; finally, the code with its imperfections was a long step forward and did end the evils of legislative tampering by ripper bills.[31]

There is no question that the Republicans had some merit on their side. The new code did improve the governmental organization of Dayton and Toledo, for example; it reduced the council to a unicameral body, partially elected at large, and increased its powers; it made mandatory the merit system for the police and fire departments in all cities; and by establishing a uniform law, it put a stop to ripper bills.[32]

But in the eyes of the municipal reformers, the Republicans had betrayed the people of the cities by imposing a code which had been tailored to suit George B. Cox and which failed to make any significant advance toward home rule. Johnson accepted the results as a challenge. He and his lieutenants determined to publicize the indifference of the Republicans to the cause of municipal freedom and to develop an irresistible demand throughout the state for home rule.

1. *Cleveland Plain Dealer,* December 12, 1901; C. D. Gibbons to the editor of the *Plain Dealer,* issue for July 18, 1902. Hanna angrily denied meeting Gibbons but refused to make further comment (*ibid.,* July 19, 1902).

2. Jones's actions and his defense were reported in the *Toledo Bee,* April 12, May 1, 15, June 29, 1902. Editorial criticism of the Mayor appeared in the *Toledo Blade,* May 6, 1902, and the *Toledo Bee,* June 29, 1902. The suit was brought by the commissioners of the new board and styled *State of Ohio* ex rel. *Knisely* v. *Jones,* 66 Ohio 453 (1902). Whitlock discusses his part in *Forty Years of It,* 136–37. Preparation of this brief had a profound effect on Whitlock. It aroused his interest in the problems of city government and made him see the necessity of acquiring home rule for municipalities. This point is discussed in Robert H. Bremner, "The Civic Revival in Ohio: The Artist in Politics: Brand Whitlock," *American Journal of Economics and Sociology,* IX (January, 1950), 248. The controversy is referred to in Chap. II, p. 36.

3. The revision of the tax boards is discussed above in Chap. IV, p. 100. The statute on the Cleveland Park Board is in 95 O.L. 823 (1902). The change was to make the offices of park commissioners appointive by the judge of the probate court instead of elective, as they had been before. The denunciations by the *Blade* and *Ohio State Journal* of the abuses of ripper legislation are in the *Toledo Blade,* April 29, 1902, and the *Ohio State Journal* (Columbus), May 1, 1902, respectively. Moreover, it is evident that the legislators saw the handwriting on the wall, for they approved two significant statutes establishing uniform legislation for cities. One was the Longworth Bond Act, codifying the piecemeal statutes specifying the purposes for which municipal bonds might be issued; the other was the Price Accounting Act, which prescribed a uniform system of accounts for all cities and counties and created a state audit bureau to inspect and supervise such activity (95 O.L. 318 and 511 [1902], respectively). The importance of the Price Act as a fiscal reform is discussed in John A. Fairlie, "Financial Provisions of the New Municipal Program," in C. R. Woodruff, ed., *A New Municipal Program* (New York, 1919), 205–6.

4. Ohio Constitution of 1851, Art. XIII, sec. 1.

5. *Bates' Annotated Revised Statutes of Ohio* (3d ed.; 1902), sec. 1546–48. The abuse of classification is discussed in Orth, "The Municipal Situation in Ohio," 431.

6. *State of Ohio* v. *Cincinnati,* 52 Ohio 419 (1895).

7. *State of Ohio* ex rel. *Sheets* v. *Cowles,* 64 Ohio 162 (1901).

8. The court shift had already been disclosed in two unpublicized decisions. In the first, handed down in March, 1902, a law authorizing Toledo to issue bonds for a bridge had been held unconstitutional (*Platt* v. *Craig; Jones* v. *State of Ohio* ex rel. *Walbridge,* 66 Ohio 75 [1902]). In the second, a special law relating to the Cincinnati hospital was invalidated on June 24, two days before the Toledo and Cleveland decisions (*City of Cincinnati* v. *Trustees of the Cincinnati Hospital,* 66 Ohio 440 [1902]).

9. The court presented an opinion only in the Toledo case (*State of Ohio* ex rel. *Knisely* v. *Jones,* 66 Ohio 453 [1902]).

10. *State of Ohio* ex rel. *Sheets* v. *Beacom,* 66 Ohio 491 (1902).

11. Jones's remarks were reported in the *Toledo Bee,* June 26, 1902, Johnson's in the *Cleveland Plain Dealer,* June 29, 1902.

12. Able discussions of the Pugh-Kibler bill for Ohio cities are in Orth,

"The Municipal Situation in Ohio," 435–36, in Clinton R. Woodruff, "Municipal Government in Ohio," *Yale Review*, XII (1903–4), 127–28, and in the *Sunday Journal* (Toledo), November 26, 1899. The legislative history of the bill in the 1900 session is reported in the *Ohio State Journal*, January 26, April 12, 1900. The Democratic platform endorsement is in the *Cleveland Plain Dealer*, July 11, 1901. Jones's interest in this bill is revealed in his correspondence: S. M. Jones to Albert Shaw, April 11, 1899; to John R. McLean, November 10, 1899, Jones Papers.

13. The revision of the committee of the Ohio Bar Association and the endorsement of the revised code by that association as well as by the Ohio Board of Commerce is reported in the *Ohio State Journal*, January 10, February 2, 1902. Its reception and ultimate rejection by the House is told in *ibid.*, March 11–12, 14, 28, April 17, 1902, and in the *Cleveland Plain Dealer*, April 17, 1902.

14. Wade H. Ellis, ed., *The Municipal Code of Ohio* (Cincinnati, 1903), xxi–xxii. Both Ellis, a former Democrat, and the Republican Longworth were close associates of George B. Cox, beholden to him for political advancement (Wright, *Bossism in Cincinnati*, 111, 115–16; Turner, "The Thing above the Law," 588–89).

Equally conservative on economic issues were the three corporation lawyers who served on the Ohio Bar Association committee: John W. Warrington of Cincinnati, a close associate of Foraker; Thomas H. Hogsett of Cleveland; and E. B. King of Sandusky. The drafting committee of the State Board of Commerce was composed of Judge Gilbert H. Stewart, chairman, H. H McMahon, E. M. Thresher, and Allen Ripley Foote of Chicago. (*Ohio State Journal*, August 10, 1902)

15. The content of the bill was reported in *Ohio State Journal*, August 10, 28, 1902, and in *Proceedings of the Special Committee on the Municipal Code* (75th General Assembly, Extraordinary Session, 1902), 73–79 (hereafter referred to as *Proceedings on Municipal Code*). Johnson's endorsement and a discussion of his tactics is in the *Cleveland Plain Dealer*, August 11, 1902.

16. *Ohio State Journal*, August 28, 1902; *Toledo Bee*, August 28, 1902.

17. *Ohio State Journal*, July 27, August 16, 1902. Ellis' remarks are quoted in *Proceedings on Municipal Code*, 40–41.

18. *Proceedings on Municipal Code*, 479–95; *Ohio State Journal*, September 5, 1902.

19. Governor Nash's views and message were reported in the *Cleveland Plain Dealer*, July 8, 11, August 29, 1902, and the *Ohio State Journal*, August 13, 1902; Justice Schauk's in the *Cleveland Plain Dealer*, July 10, 1902; Bennett's in the *Ohio State Journal*, August 10, 1902. Precedent for allowing cities more discretion was unearthed by Representative Aaron E. Price of Athens, who found ten court decisions in support of granting city councils power to expand municipal government if necessary. In one of the cases Nash had been one of the attorneys seeking to establish such a conclusion. (*Cleveland Plain Dealer*, September 7, 1902)

20. The organization of the House and Senate is described in *Cleveland Plain Dealer*, August 27, 1902, and the *Ohio State Journal*, September 10, 1902. The support for home rule is reported in *Proceedings on Municipal Code*, 516 (Hughes), 528 (Gladden), 79 (McMahon), 255–56 (Fairlie), 402–12 (Johnson and Baker), 347 (Garfield), 568 (Thomas).

21. Sermon reprinted in the *Ohio State Journal*, September 8, 1902; letter of July 5, 1902, printed in *ibid.*, July 13, 1902.

22. The remarks of the defenders of the federal plan are reported in *Proceedings on Municipal Code,* 334, 363–73, 376, 385, 402–12, 534–37, 571–72, those of the supporters of the board plan in *ibid.,* 161–63, 445.

23. Present to represent the street-railway interests of their respective cities were: Andrew Squire, of Cleveland; Henry J. Booth, of Columbus; Benson Foraker, of Cincinnati, Senator Foraker's son; and Walter Brown, of Toledo (*Cleveland Plain Dealer,* August 27, 1902, and special article by W. S. Couch, *ibid.,* August 30, 1905). The Guerin curative provisions are reported in *Proceedings on Municipal Code,* 379–80. The Rogers Law and Senator Foraker's part in its adoption are described in Walters, *Foraker,* 124–26, and in Steffens, *Struggle for Self-Government,* 169–70. Baker's and Johnson's criticisms are in *Proceedings on Municipal Code,* 404–7, 414–21.

24. Hanna's request and the *Plain Dealer* editorial reaction are in the *Cleveland Plain Dealer,* August 28, 29, 1902, respectively. Johnson's rebuttal is reported in *Proceedings on Municipal Code,* 414–21, the support for a municipal-ownership provision in *ibid.* 423, 521, 567, 838. Such a resolution was defeated thirteen to four (*ibid.,* 838). The decision to drop the perpetual-franchise idea was reported in the *Cleveland Plain Dealer,* September 6, 1902, and the *Ohio State Journal,* September 25, 27, 1902. One Republican congressman, Theodore E. Burton, wrote a number of confidential letters to members of the Assembly urging them to oppose the bill. (T. E. Burton to W. S. Harris, September 4, 1902, Burton Papers) The letter to Harris contained the notation: "Same letter written to Wm. H. Crafts, H of R, Chas. A. Judson, Senate, Geo. H. Chamberlain, Senate."

25. The proceedings in both houses were reported in the *Ohio State Journal,* September 9–10, 16–17, 1902, the votes in *ibid.,* October 1, 8, 1902, and the *Toledo Bee,* October 1, 1902. Johnson's declaration of vengeance on the eight Democrats was made in campaign speeches at Fostoria and Marion (*Cleveland Plain Dealer,* September 27, October 2, 1902).

26. The pressure on the conference committee members was reported in *Cleveland Plain Dealer,* October 13, 22, 1902, and the *Ohio State Journal,* October 14, 18, 1902. The vote on the committee's report is in *ibid.,* October 22, 1902, the *Toledo Bee,* October 22, 1902, and the *Cleveland Plain Dealer,* October 22, 1902.

27. *Cleveland Plain Dealer,* October 23, 1902.

28. *Ibid.,* October 19, 1902. Similar criticisms were made in the *Toledo Bee,* October 18, 22, 1902.

29. Undated editorial quoted in the *Cleveland Plain Dealer,* October 21, 1902. The next day the *Plain Dealer* quoted editorials of the same tenor from the *Chicago Evening Post* and the *Chicago Post.*

30. Woodruff's commentary is in Woodruff, "Municipal Government in Ohio," 136–38; Wilcox's remark is quoted in John R. Schindel, "The Paine Law in Ohio," *Proceedings of the Cincinnati Conference for Good City Government and the Fifteenth Annual Meeting of the National Municipal League* (1909), 252. Woodruff visited Ohio in the summer of 1902 and knew the problems of the municipal code first hand (*Cleveland Plain Dealer,* July 23–24, September 15, 1902).

31. Ellis, ed., *The Municipal Code,* xxix–xxxii. Hanna's praise of the code was quoted in the *Cleveland Plain Dealer,* October 26, 1902.

32. 96 O.L. 20 (1902), secs. 116–18 (council), secs. 156–86 (merit system for fire and police).

CHAPTER SIX

JOHNSON'S STATE CAMPAIGNS
1902∎1903

In July, 1902, three months before the special legislative session had sealed the fate of the cities, Johnson had made up his mind to invade the state again in support of his principles. This time he was determined to make a major assault. His plan of campaign was to repeat what he had done in Cleveland: to remodel the Democratic party of Ohio into a crusading organization for reform and to break the hold of the Republicans upon the voters by exposing the true character and aims of the leaders of that party.

It was an off-year election, with only a few offices to be filled, the principal one being that of secretary of state. Johnson was pleased since it would allow him to test his strength in a preliminary skirmish before engaging in a major fight.[1] As early as January he had participated in a conference of Democratic leaders to establish permanent headquarters and an organization to give continuity to the party's work between campaigns. Although he failed to dominate the selection of the state executive committee, he was able to name one member, Charles Salen, and to prevent the appointment of Lewis Bernard, watchdog of the interests of John R. McLean.[2]

The dominance of the Cincinnati publisher in party affairs had long been opposed, for he was suspected of every political heresy from working to defeat a Democratic state ticket to dealing with Boss Cox for the control of Cincinnati. Furthermore, his counsel was always negative, a long series of "don'ts." But the professionals were afraid of him, since every candidate who offended or even failed to consult him had been knifed on election day by his forces. It was with relief and approval, therefore, that the party leaders watched Johnson open war on McLean.

In June the Cleveland mayor, carrying the attack into the newspapers, said of his Cincinnati adversary: "A man who is in politics as the representative of no issue or principle, and stands merely for himself and his selfish ambitions, is not a source of strength to his party, no matter how lavishly he may scatter his money to promote his personal ends. Mr. McLean has never since his connection with Ohio politics . . . stood for any issue except John R. McLean."[3] Clearly such a man had no place in the same party with himself.

An opportunity to renew the attack occurred July 2 on the occasion of a Democratic clambake, the summer substitute for the anniversary banquets of the winter. Most of the party big-wigs attended, with the notable exception of McLean. Excusing his absence because of a prior engagement, he sent a letter, a mixture of platitudes and warnings, urging the party to unite on "sound doctrine," to rely on "enduring principles," and to shun "irregular inventions" and "doubtful alliances." The principal speakers made harmony their theme, but not Johnson. Taking as his subject "The Mission of Democracy," he denied that harmony in itself was an essential part; the free traders of Ohio could not harmonize with the protectionists of Louisiana; nor could he harmonize, he implied, with McLean. No, the true mission was to stand squarely on live issues, two of which were now at hand, namely, taxation and home rule for cities. Those who called them fads did not know the temper of the people; those who derided them as newfangled notions were ignorant of history, for home rule had long been a principle of the Democratic party, and equal taxation was an ideal for which men of every political faith had striven for years. And what side should the Democracy take on these issues? The side of the people.[4]

This cry to action was hailed by Negley Cochran, the staunchly Democratic editor of the *Toledo Bee* and an old foe of McLean. He praised Johnson's talk as "healthy and vigorous and full of life," and admonished those Democrats who could not take the speech "to buy a new backbone." Cochran concurred with the Cleveland mayor that "the Democratic party must protect the people against the persistent assaults of selfish interests who want laws made giving them an advantage over their fellows, [for] if the Democratic party won't protect the people, then no party will."[5]

When the Democratic state convention met at Cedar Point, on the shores of Lake Erie, September 2, the press had already forecast that it would be a Johnson convention throughout. Reports from Washington, D. C., the home of McLean, stated that he was willing to give Johnson all the rope needed, confident that the Clevelander would hang himself; then the party regulars would return on bended knee to the McLean camp. The other leaders had indicated a willingness to follow Johnson's lead. Not only did Johnson serve as temporary chairman and deliver the keynote speech, but he also succeeded in nominating most of his candidates on the ticket and in getting his platform adopted.[6] Several planks dealt with taxation. Two demanded that the corporations bear their just burden and that all railroads and other utilities be assessed at their "saleable value" and be required to open their books to public officials. A third plank endorsed a constitutional amendment to permit classification of property and separation of state and local taxes. Other planks advocated municipal home rule as provided in the Ohio State Board of Commerce and the Okey-York bills, then pending before the special session of the legislature; supported the popular ratification of franchises and condemned perpetual ones; denounced free railroad passes, trusts, imperialism, and the unholy alliance between Boss Cox and the two Ohio senators for the purpose of furthering their own interests at the expense of the people.

All these were approved without protest; the only murmur of dissent arose over the endorsement of Bryan and the Kansas City platform, which this time the conservatives reluctantly agreed to in the interest of party harmony.[7] With the exception of McLean's *Enquirer,* which echoed Republican criticism, the major Democratic papers approved the resolutions as being "pertinent to conditions" and meeting "the living issues of the day with candor and force." Home rule, just taxation, and franchise reform were the battles cries of the campaign.[8]

To aid him in carrying these issues to the people, Johnson selected as the party nominee for secretary of state a man who made his debut in state politics at the convention, Herbert Seeley Bigelow, of Cincinnati. The two had met in 1900 at a conference of the Anti-trust League in Chicago and again at the Democratic national convention in Kansas City, and had formed an acquaintance that blossomed into a friendship when they discovered a mutual enthusiasm for the single tax. In the spring of 1902 Johnson asked Bigelow to find a local attorney who would be eager to run for secretary of state as a champion of reform. The Mayor wanted a Cincinnati candidate in order to extend the geographical support for his program and to give effective leadership to the forces challenging McLean and Cox in their own stronghold. When Bigelow could find no one else, he decided to make the race himself.[9]

The slender, fair-haired Bigelow was then thirty-three; he possessed a restless, independent spirit and he was bursting with youthful idealism. He had run away from his own parents at the age of nine and had been adopted by a childless couple who not only gave him their name and a home but also sent him to the preparatory school and college of Oberlin, and then to Adelbert College of Western Reserve University in Cleveland, from which he graduated in 1894. That fall, after marrying an Oberlin classmate, he entered Lane Theological Seminary in Cincinnati. A year later the trustees of the Vine Street Congregational Church invited him to serve as a supply minister during the illness of their regular pastor, and made the appointment permanent in 1896. Having caught some of the old abolitionist spirit in his Oberlin days, Bigelow gloried in the past tradition of the Vine Street Church, once a southern terminal of the Underground Railroad, and determined to renew its ante bellum spirit. He resented what he considered to be the existing complacency of many of the congregation who seemed to feel that all human slavery had been abolished with the freeing of the Negroes. It was not long before the radical minister was clashing with his conservative parishioners.

He preached a sermon in praise of Bryan during the 1896 campaign and was pointedly reminded that this was "a Republican church." He began holding prayer meetings on Sunday evenings in front of the church on Vine Street, then as now a commercial thoroughfare, attracting a street crowd of a desultory character, which he would then invite inside. Again he was admonished for his zeal because the regular parishioners complained that the pew cushions were becoming infested with vermin. The rumble against him developed into a roar when he invited an educated Negro into the church membership. The man's entry was opposed; Bigelow threatened to resign, denouncing the opposition for failing to keep faith with the tradition of the church; the Negro was admitted, then tactfully withdrew. But some of the congregation never forgave their pastor and soon trumped up heresy charges against him. He agreed to stand trial before a board of ministers if his accusers would declare the real reason for their action. However, when they refused, he would not appear. In time the case collapsed for lack of evidence.[10]

These actions shocked Bigelow, for to him they were contrary to the spirit of Christ's teachings. Was there something wrong with Christianity or with the way it was applied? It was some time before he found answers to this question. His fame as an orator attracted new members to the church, and those who had opposed him gradually withdrew. The church began to take on new life, absorbing the zeal of the earnest minister. Still he was not satisfied, since evangelical religion seemed to be a palliative rather than a force to create the conditions for human brotherhood. At this critical time in his thinking (the year was 1897), he was persuaded to reread George's *Progress and Poverty* by one of the new members, George VonAuer, and became converted to the single-tax faith with a suddenness only matched by Johnson's experience. Later Bigelow said of his conversion to George's theories:

> I came to the conclusion about which I now have not the slightest doubt, that the world is suffering more from the lack of a social conscience and a sound political economy than from the lack of agencies to give aid and comfort to the victims of social wrongs; that freedom of opportunity is the brand of charity that is needed. I saw, at last, that religion has vastly more to do with the question of wages than with the question of the Trinity. I saw more religion in the Declaration of Independence than in all the creeds. I began to realize that unless the church substituted for lifeless doctrines the doctrine of the sovereignty of the people and made it her business to guard

popular liberties against the encroachments of subsidized politics, her name would become the synonym for treason and her
doors the gates of hell.[11]

Increasingly the interest of the young social-gospel minister
and the congregation itself turned from the problems of the
world hereafter to those of the world about them. No longer
was the binding faith among them a theological creed; instead
it was the acceptance of a common view towards political, economic, and social issues. The weekly prayer meeting became
the Thursday Evening Economic Club; the pulpit was opened
to laymen, particularly those of an unorthodox point of view—
Clarence Darrow, Lincoln Steffens, Brand Whitlock, and many
others. During 1899-1900, when Bigelow became a leader in
the anti-imperialist battle to grant independence to the Philippines, protest meetings held in the church took on the fervor
of the old antislavery days. The congregation freely allowed
their minister to leave the pulpit for the hustings. Bigelow took
the stump for Bryan in 1900. In his campaign for secretary of
state in 1902 the members permitted him to make the basement
of the church his headquarters, several actively engaging in the
fight. One of them, Daniel Kiefer, a clothing merchant and
convert to the single-tax doctrine, became Bigelow's closest political associate and remained so for many years.[12]

In naming Bigelow for the top place on the ticket Johnson
had made a daring choice. Bigelow had several counts against
him: a youthful appearance, the profession of the ministry, and
a background of Republicanism. Reared in the tradition of Lincoln and freedom, he had clung to the Republican party despite
his unwillingness to subscribe to the new tenets of Hanna and
Foraker. In 1900 he was one of the rump group of Silver Republicans who held a convention simultaneously with that of
the Democrats in Kansas City, nominating Bryan for President
and Charles A. Towne for Vice-President. But by 1902 he had
broken his last ties with the Republicans.

On the other hand, there were points in Bigelow's favor. He
had shown that he was no political tyro when he successfully
challenged the powerful Bernard-McLean machine and brought
to the state convention a large delegation from Hamilton County
committed to his candidacy. His chief asset, however, was his

ability as a speaker. His oratory had the rounded phrases, the fervid eloquence of Bryan, with whom he has been favorably compared. One of the remarks in his acceptance speech at the Democratic convention was long a favorite quotation among the Johnsonites. After commenting on Hanna's demand for a perpetual franchise, he said that he was reminded of the rhyme:

> Hark, hark, the dogs do bark,
> The beggars are coming to town,
> Some in rags, some in tags,
> Some in velvet gowns. . . .

Then he continued, "So long as we have beggars in velvet gowns eating unearned bread at the front doors of the legislature we must expect to have beggars in rags and tags eating crusts of charity at the back doors of the nation."[13]

Negley Cochran's *Toledo Bee*, after surveying the work of the convention, declared that a new era in Ohio politics had been born; the bosses had been driven to the rear, and new leaders had stepped forward to show the people their true interests and how to govern themselves.[14] Johnson, though not running for office, was the recognized head of the ticket and the dominant figure in the campaign. Defiant of the conventional, he proposed to tour the state in a highspeed, red, Winton car, known as the "Red Devil," frightening to men and horses on the country roads. The rest of the Johnson caravan consisted of eight stout wagon teams to haul his famous tent. The Republicans scoffed, but soon Senator Hanna was also appearing in a "canvas auditorium."[15]

Johnson and his "preacher-in-politics," the label with which the press promptly tagged Bigelow, opened their campaign in Lorain. A crowd of six thousand overflowed the tent, and the air was hot and oppressive until a thunderstorm came, causing the gasoline lamps to flicker and almost drowning the speakers' voices. From there the caravan rolled on to Norwalk, then to Bellevue, where the rain-washed air was cool and invigorating, and "a more ideal evening could not be imagined." The itinerary included the important towns of the north- and central-western sections of the state where lay the strength of Bryan Democracy.

Until October 10 Johnson and Bigelow remained together. Then, after splitting to extend their coverage, they rejoined once more for an intensive three days in Cincinnati, where extra aid was critically needed, since the local Democratic committee was in the hands of the McLean gang.[16]

The major theme of the early campaign was taxation. Johnson attacked the auditors in county after county for accepting railroad passes and failing to assess railroads in the same manner as other property. No more tenderness was shown Democrats than Republicans. He made the Democratic nominees for auditor in Henry and Defiance counties, both party strongholds, fidget in their seats until they screwed up their courage to pledge themselves to value railroad property justly and refuse passes, while in Van Wert County he went after the scalp of the incumbent Democrat for failing to perform his duty in this respect. Although the radical *Toledo Bee* applauded the nerve and courage of "the bounding Tom L.," other Democratic papers maintained a disapproving silence.[17] When the eight party renegades in the legislature voted for the Cincinnati curative bill at the end of September, Johnson added them to his baiting list, singling out for special attention William C. Gear of Wyandot County, who had broken his promise to his constituents not to vote for the measure unless a referendum clause was added to the bill.[18]

In addition to the rural communities, Johnson covered all the major cities of the state except Dayton. At Toledo Jones and Bryan spoke in Johnson's tent, the Toledo mayor giving a characteristic talk on independence in voting, the Nebraskan praising the state platform and candidates and exhorting the people to vote for reform.[19]

The Cincinnati meetings were stormy; Johnson launched into a diatribe against McLean and the *Enquirer,* spurning their friendship, even inviting their hostility. He urged them to move to the Republican party where they belonged and thereby make room for all "who labor for the rights of the people and not for personal and selfish ends to come together under the standard of the New Democracy." Nor did he spare Boss Cox, Senators Hanna and Foraker, and the Republican legislators from Cincinnati who had helped pass the curative act. The *Enquirer* retaliated by printing reports of the Johnson-Bigelow meetings on the back pages, while giving much more prominence to the Republican rallies.[20]

During the final days Johnson campaigned in Cleveland, aiming his jabs particularly at Mark Hanna, whom he compared to Nicholas Biddle, the man President Andrew Jackson had defeated in the bank-recharter fight in the 1830's. Both mixed business and politics for personal profit, the one to promote the United States Bank, the other his Cleveland street railway; both vowed the destruction of those inimical to them. Mr. Hanna, the Mayor concluded, might profit by Biddle's experience.[21]

In this attack Johnson had found a major target, for the Senator was not only the greatest power in the Ohio Republican party but also its chief attraction. It had been rumored that Hanna's power was based entirely on his national patronage and would decline with the death of President McKinley, but his role at the Republican state convention in May, 1902, belied the report. His control rested on a firm base: the confidence of the delegates in his acknowledged ability as an organizer and speaker and his proven loyalty to the men he endorsed. At the convention Foraker had made no contest and Cox's strength was limited to the eighty-five delegates from Hamilton County.[22]

At the formal campaign opening at Akron in September Senator Hanna set the Republican keynote with an exhortation to "stand pat!" He and other speakers played variations on this theme, alternately embellishing the character of McKinley, stressing prosperity, and painting the dire calamity of a Democratic victory. As the campaign wore on, the Republicans grew more personal in their attacks, roundly denouncing Johnson as a "demagogue," "hypocrite," "liar," and "a bigger humbug than P. T. Barnum." State issues could not be ignored altogether; Hanna frequently defended himself on the franchise issue; and other party members answered directly the questions of taxation, home rule, and the curative law which Johnson raised.[23]

The election results were similar to those of the year before, with Bigelow carrying Cleveland and Cuyahoga and his rival, Lewis C. Laylin, capturing all the other large-city counties and the state as a whole. In the congressional contests the Republicans made a similar sweep, winning seventeen of the twenty-one districts. The Democrats lost ground in Franklin County but gained in those rural counties where Johnson held his tent meetings. In Hamilton County Bigelow was the lowest on the Democratic ticket, losing by a margin of 27,500 votes, a result the *Enquirer* gloatingly reported. Recriminations flew back and forth. The Bernard forces ascribed the defeat to Johnson's personality and his attack on Democratic auditors; Harvey Garber, a Bryan Democrat, called John R. McLean, in turn, "the Benedict Arnold of the party." But Johnson, outwardly unruffled, was already looking forward to next year's campaign, dismissing the defeat with the declaration that "truth loses some battles but no wars."[24]

During the winter of 1903 the independent conservatives within the party, those who wanted neither McLean nor Johnson, grew restive. A rash of editorials broke out in the press against Bryan and the Cleveland mayor. The latter's sweeping victory in the spring mayoralty election, however, restored him to leadership and placed him in direct line for the gubernatorial nomination in the fall.[25]

Although formal announcement of his candidacy was not made until August, 1903, in a sense he opened his campaign in May, invading Richland County in his "Red Devil" to defeat the nomination to the lower house of William H. Earhart, one of the eight Democratic blacksheep in the last session. In this venture he raised more dust than billowed about his car on the country roads. Many in the party were incensed at this interference; even the friendly Negley Cochran reprimanded him for violating the principle of home rule. Johnson defended his action on the grounds that it was just as important to select a proper legislative candidate in Richland as in Cuyahoga, if desirable laws were to be passed.[26]

To calm ruffled tempers Charles Salen, a suave professional politician, the only one with whom Johnson collaborated, albeit intermittently, went forth on a pacification mission. So adroit was his handling of the situation that he persuaded a number of Democratic politicians from all over the state to meet in Johnson's home on July 23, 1903, to urge upon the Mayor the gubernatorial nomination and to outline campaign policy. During the next month Johnson further advanced his candidacy as well as his principles by addressing county conventions in Stark, Champaign, and Medina counties. He invited Bryan to speak

with him at the Champaign meeting, to the distress of the conservatives. On August 8 the Cleveland mayor formally announced his candidacy.[27]

When the Democratic conclave assembled in Columbus on
August 25, he was in complete control, McLean again refusing
to challenge his leadership. The only opposition came from the
supporters of John L. Zimmerman, a conservative identified with
manufacturing and utility interests in Springfield, Ohio, who
urged the party to return to the principles of Thurman, Pendleton, and Tilden. As the proceedings progressed, the hostility
between the Johnson men and the minority faction grew to
large proportions. At the outset the seats of one hundred and
forty-five Zimmerman delegates were contested, the bulk of them
from Hamilton County; none were admitted because of Johnson's control of the credentials committee, an action deeply resented by his opponents. An *Enquirer* headline screamed,
"Henry George's Apostle Is Master of a Machine."[28]

The adoption of the platform, bearing witness to his author-
ship in almost every line, raised another storm. A brief opening
paragraph dealt with national issues: endorsement of the Kansas
City platform and criticism of the Republican administration for
the high tariff, imperialism, ship subsidies, lack of antitrust
action, and government by injunction. Then followed a declaration that state questions were paramount, especially home rule
and equal taxation. The corrupt alliance between the managers
of the Republican party and the great corporations was condemned, and, by contrast, the enforced political demise of the
eight Democratic renegades was upheld as exemplary. Specific
planks included those on taxation, home rule, franchises, and
the abuse of railroad passes, repeated from the 1902 resolutions,
plus others favoring a passenger rate of two cents per mile on
railways, a salary instead of a fee system for county officers, the
initiative and referendum for all municipal legislation, and endorsement of United States senators by party convention.[29]

On the whole the reaction to the platform in the Democratic
press was favorable. The *Dayton Daily News,* for example,
pointed out that the so-called Johnson fads were being adopted
in many places in the land: the initiative and refendum in
Oregon; a complete system of direct democracy, including recall
of officials, in Los Angeles; an act to decide by referendum the

question of municipal ownership of utilities in Chicago; and a municipal home-rule amendment in Colorado. But the conservatives at the convention were beside themselves. Michael A. Daugherty of Fairfield County declared the platform was "a rabid, unreasoning attack and indiscriminate assault upon the corporations of the state," that its "sentiment of disloyalty" and "false note of communism" were comparable to Vallandigham's platform of 1863 which cast suspicion on the party's attachment to the Union. Zimmerman declared that he would not accept nomination upon such a set of resolutions.[30]

His withdrawal ended any hope of defeating Johnson, who was therewith nominated by acclamation, and the rest of his ticket was chosen by substantial majorities. Although the method of selection differed little from the ward-caucus technique of any petty politician, the slate was a strong one: Frank B. Niles of Toledo, a friend and supporter of Samuel Jones, for lieutenant-governor; Frank S. Monnett, an ex-Republican, for attorney-general; Edward J. Dempsey, a Cincinnati judge with a fine record on the bench, for justice of the Ohio Supreme Court; and John H. Clarke, whose nomination aroused a major furor, for United States senator.[31]

The conservatives were opposed to the endorsement of any candidate for the senatorship, preferring to leave the party representatives in the legislature free to act, but the most heated struggle occurred within the Johnson ranks. The Bryan wing was indignant at the selection of Clarke, who had bolted the party in 1896 on the free-silver issue. Johnson, however, was adamant, and on the second ballot his "Gold Bug" candidate received the necessary votes.[32]

At the time of his selection John Hessin Clarke was within a month of his forty-sixth birthday, well known in political circles and enjoying a wide reputation as a lawyer. The erectness of his bearing, his large head, his face with its intense penetrating eyes, square jaw, and compressed lips suggested a man of forceful character and definite opinion who could command respect more readily than warm friendship.[33]

He and the Cleveland mayor had been political friends since the 1890's, joined together by similarities of political beliefs and parallels in their backgrounds and careers. Clarke was born and reared in the village of New Lisbon (now Lisbon), Ohio, county seat of Columbiana County, where his father, a native of the North of Ireland, had become a successful lawyer and had won election as prosecuting attorney and then judge of the county court of common pleas. Despite the father's humble beginnings the family enjoyed a highly respected position in the community during John Clarke's boyhood. He gained further prestige by attending Western Reserve College, then at Hudson, Ohio, from which he graduated with honors in 1877. His education there was excellent preparation for the legal career that he had long ago decided to enter in emulation of his father. He practiced briefly in Lisbon, for close to two decades in Youngstown, and after 1897 in Cleveland; by each change he achieved a more important and remunerative practice as a trial lawyer in the field of corporation law. In 1903 he was general counsel for the Nickel Plate Railroad and an attorney for other railways and the Pullman Company. However, he was no more a typical successful corporation lawyer than Johnson was a typical successful businessman.

Clarke had definite political principles and he did not let "pocketbook interests" divert him from the promotion of what he believed to be just causes. Born into the Democratic fold, he had remained there because the Democrats in Ohio supported principles to which he subscribed—the Grover Cleveland program of low tariff, antimonopoly, and anti-imperialism.

Off and on since 1880 Clarke had been active in the party, writing editorials in support of its platform and candidates in the *Youngstown Vindicator,* in which he became a stockholder and an intimate of the owner-manager, William F. Maag. The young attorney worked on the resolutions committee at nominating conventions and spoke during compaigns. At the Democratic state convention of 1894, he had joined with Johnson to reprimand the Democratic United States Senator from Ohio, Calvin S. Brice, for his dereliction in the senatorial battle to lower the tariff. Standing in front of Brice, the convention chairman, Clarke delivered a famous philippic against the Senate as a "richman's club," "the nesting place of trusts . . . to defeat the will of the people." "When a Senator is to be elected," he declared, "the question is no longer what is his worth, what are his talents, what service has he done the state, but what is he worth (in dollars)?" The speech made Clarke's reputation as a dramatic orator and as a champion of integrity in politics.[34]

Two other events were to contribute to his political prominence, one favorably, the other adversely. In the mayoralty election in Youngstown in the spring of 1896, he played a major part in a successful campaign against bigotry, defeating a bid for control of the city government by the American Protective Association. He not only risked his own political reputation, but he staked as well the future welfare of the *Vindicator,* the mouthpiece of the anti-APA forces. But that same summer he deserted the national party after the nomination of Bryan on a free-silver platform and became a leading figure in Ohio of the Gold Democratic faction. Again principle—and fear of the Populist "rabble" —determined his course. In 1900 he had won partial reinstatement as a regular Democrat by supporting Bryan and anti-imperialism, overlooking this time the free-silver issue which the Nebraskan had insisted on resurrecting.[35]

Clarke, by this time, had begun to enlarge the scope of his interest in reform—a change that was characteristic of upperclass liberals in general. He was aided in the process by Johnson's expositions of political problems in his campaigns during the preceding two years. The railroad attorney was prepared to accept the Mayor's fundamental premise that government must intervene to fight special privilege and to create a better world for the common man. Furthermore, the two were in agreement on the principal planks in the program of reform. Both had long opposed a protective tariff, trusts, and imperialism; now they shared in common support for tax reform, for more direct democracy, and for humanitarian labor measures. To be sure, Clarke differed with Johnson over the single tax, municipal ownership, and the facts of railroad taxation. But only on the last point had their differences been publicly aired and then in a manner that did not affect their respect for one another. Moreover, the railroad lawyer supported the Mayor's demand for reform in the method of assessing railroads as well as other corporate property, for abolition of the abused free pass, and for adoption of a passenger fare of two cents per mile.[36]

Clarke was elated by his senatorial nomination, for he had long hoped for this prize. He did not underestimate the difficulty of defeating the Republican incumbent, Mark Hanna. But, as he remarked in his speech of acceptance, he would make his fight against Hanna the senator, not Hanna the man. He would endeavor to persuade the voters that the Democrats were more trustworthy public servants and that their platform promised more for the public welfare.[37]

Many other Democrats, however, left the Columbus convention prepared to defeat everything that had been done there, openly predicting the annihilation of the new movement. Johnson would concede nothing; he defended the "Red Devil campaign" in Richland County against the renegade Earhart, and he insisted on the complete acceptance of the platform principles as a test of party loyalty, inviting those who differed to secede. His dictatorial tone aroused the ire of Negley Cochran, an admirer the year before, who now accused Johnson of making "personal enemies with a lavish disregard of the consequences" and of "running down men who have crossed his path to such an extent that self-preservation will band his victims together to politically assassinate him at any risk." In conclusion, the Toledo editor declared, "Here is Johnson's weakness. He can crush but not conciliate."

A different response came from the *Dayton Daily News*, published by James M. Cox, a young man with political ambitions. In an editorial introducing Johnson to the Dayton public, the paper praised his high standing in Cleveland, endorsed the issues for which he fought, and ended with a prophecy: "Tom Johnson may be defeated, but he will stir this state to its very depths and the principles of home rule, equal taxation, and safeguards against robbery, extortion and blackmail in courthouses will prevail, and Tom Johnson's championship will have praise and encomium not bound by party limit. It may not come now, but come it will."[38]

Once again the Mayor publicized his campaign by traveling from town to town in the "Red Devil" automobile until a general breakdown late in September forced the car's retirement. The tent caravan, however, was abandoned in favor of the more certain, if less picturesque, railroad transport of the big canvas. Johnson stepped up his tempo and extended his itinerary of the year before. Speaking four to seven times a day, with a tent meeting almost every night, he wove his way through fifty-six counties, expanding his coverage to include the eastern and central portions of the state as well as every major city. Many of his meetings were enlivened by Peter Witt's stereopticon pictures of the properties of local tax dodgers.

Clarke's itinerary and daily stint of speeches were only a little less strenuous. The senatorial nominee was helped by Bryan, who spoke twice on Clarke's behalf in the hostile, pro-silver part of the state in an effort to clear the former Gold Bug of the stigma of apostasy.[39]

The two principal candidates elaborated upon the platform planks, stressing especially taxation, home rule, the two-cent railway fare, and the Cox-Hanna-statehouse alliance. Their purpose, they kept reiterating, was to educate the people, to make them think and vote intelligently, and to elect legislators of principle. Although they had proposed to refrain from personal attacks, they did not carry out their promise altogether. Johnson condemned by name the Republicans and Democrats alike who had voted for the curative act. Clarke was goaded by his rival into violating his expressed intention to shun personal attacks. When Hanna had the "effrontery" to accuse him of being a sycophant of the railroads he served and of not being trustworthy as senator, the Democratic candidate replied by reasserting what he had been saying for years—that the private interests of his clients had never influenced his political views, but that, contrariwise, Mr. Hanna was a "corporation senator" in the worst sense of the term. So persuasively did Clarke develop the latter point that his rival never repeated the charge again.[40]

Although men in the thick of a campaign can scarcely avoid the self-deception that theirs is certain to be the winning side, the two nominees must have had more than a suspicion that the chances for a Democratic victory were dim. Certainly the opening at Akron, where the local committee made no preparations to receive the visiting speakers, was not calculated to encourage optimism. The meetings in Toledo were reported as frosty. Jones again supported Johnson, as well as Clarke, Niles, and Monnett, offering to campaign for them in the counties where his popularity had been greatest in 1899. At the cost of an intraparty feud, the Johnsonian Democrats in Lucas County effected a fusion with the Jones nonpartisans. Everywhere the courthouse politicians were disappointed by the tight rein Johnson kept on the purse strings. Local committees even had to raise seventy-five dollars to help defray expenses in each county

where the big tent was pitched. Not a penny was given to the
Democrats in Cincinnati, thus adding fuel to the discontent of
the old McLean faction.[41] But the most formidable obstacle
was the unshaken faith of most Ohioans in the Republicans as
the party of prosperity and respectability.

In June the Republicans had nominated the following: for
governor, Myron T. Herrick, a highly respected Cleveland
banker, who was acceptable to Hanna; for lieutenant-governor,
Warren G. Harding, the politically ambitious editor and publisher of the *Marion Star* and a member of the Foraker faction;
for state auditor, Walter Guilbert, the incumbent and a special
foe of the tax reformers; for state treasurer, William S. Mc-
Kinnon, former speaker of the House and an intimate of incumbent Isaac B. Cameron, whose term was expiring; and for
attorney-general, Wade Ellis, who was being rewarded for
writing the "Cox code," his enemies alleged.[42]

Although Mark Hanna was endorsed for re-election to the
United States Senate, his political power had actually declined,
for he had lost ground to his political rival, Senator Foraker.
Late in May he had been outmaneuvered by the senator from
Cincinnati, who, intent on nipping the presidential ambitions
of Hanna, had announced that he would seek a declaration by
the state convention endorsing Theodore Roosevelt for President
in 1904. In a public statement disavowing any aspirations of
his own for that high office, Hanna tried as adroitly as he could
to fend off such a pledge, wiring the President of his course.
Roosevelt drafted a curt reply, handing a copy to the press, in
which he insisted that since the issue had been raised, "those
who favor my administration and my nomination will favor
endorsing both, and those who do not will oppose." Crowded
into a corner, Hanna had to yield with the best grace possible.
Again to preserve harmony at the convention he had to concede to Foraker the Harding nomination.[43]

In the eyes of the Hanna men the primary goal of the
campaign was his return to the United States Senate. They
insisted on stressing the national issues at the expense of the
state issues in the platform. They persuaded cabinet officers
and congressmen to speak in Ohio on the importance of the
senatorial election; Foraker took up the theme; and Hanna himself, though tired and ailing, was on the stump for six weeks.

In his keynote address he added a new variant—"Hands off"—to the phrases, "Let well enough alone" and "Stand pat," and in his speeches he rang the changes on the nobleness of McKinley and on Republican prosperity.[44]

He answered Democratic attacks by lampooning and vilifying Johnson, whom he venomously but picturesquely characterized as "a carpet bagger followed by a train of all the howling vagrants of Ohio, with a crazy quilt ticket and pretending to stand upon a pessimistic, socialistic and anarchistic platform." In other speeches he exploited the ignorance and prejudice of his audience by declaring that "the Socialist party in the United States has for the first time a national leader . . . Tom L. Johnson," and he begged them "to rise and kill the attempt to float the flag of socialism over Ohio . . . . Socialism is only a short step from anarchy and you should rise up to suppress it if for no other reason than our late president, the honored McKinley, was a victim of that damnable heresy." Herrick also took up the hue and cry, distorting his opponent's single-tax theories beyond recognition to frighten rural audiences. Late in the campaign the Republicans accused Clarke of favoring the black-listing of union labor—an accusation that was no more than a campaign canard, but it hurt. Yet the Republican hopes of victory did not rest on such violent appeals to passion and bias alone; funds were lavishly spent to intensify organization work among the voters, especially in the counties where the opposition appeared to be making the strongest impression.[45]

These tactics bore fruit. The Republicans made a clean sweep of the state offices and won an overwhelming majority in the legislature. Herrick led the ticket with a plurality of 113,812, the largest ever given an Ohio governor; the rest followed close behind. The heaviest Democratic losses were not in the rural counties, twenty-six of which the party carried, but in the urban ones of Cuyahoga, Franklin, Lucas, and Hamilton. A substantial body of electors in Cleveland, who had helped re-elect Johnson mayor in the spring, rebuked him for seeking to desert his post by voting the straight Republican ticket, thus enabling that party to carry the county offices and legislative delegation. The anti-Johnson Democrats in Franklin County switched to the Hanna-Herrick camp. The Toledo fusion movement failed miserably, ending in "con-fusion," as one wag had prognosticated. Every ward in Cincinnati went Republican as McLean achieved his revenge.[46]

No sooner had the votes been counted than post-mortems began to fill the press. Republicans attributed their landslide to party harmony, the intelligence of the voters, "their loyalty to sound business principles and good government"—arguments the Democrats promptly disputed. The losers detected more sordid motives for the triumph of their opponents in their unprecedented expenditure of funds and, as Clarke commented, in "the adroit appeal of Senator Hanna to the cupidity and fears of the people." Johnson, however, was the chief scapegoat. The victors claimed that his socialistic fads had frightened the voters away, while members of his own party condemned him for splitting their ranks by dragging in Bryanism, attacking party renegades, and discussing the single tax, although denying it was a campaign issue.[47]

The truth was that Ohio was not yet prepared for the Mayor's progressivism. No breath of the new liberalism which was affecting the La Follette Republicans in Wisconsin had stirred among the Republicans of Ohio. Johnson had miscalculated the degree of acceptance of his new philosophy within his own party. Much more spade work needed to be done.

However, the political Cassandras who prophesied the Mayor's doom were only half right. Although he never regained his power in the state organization of the party, nevertheless the issues for which he continued to battle became accepted, and even his opponents enacted many of them into law. The trend of the times was with him, as he so confidently believed; the Republican triumph was destined to be short-lived.

1. Johnson, *My Story*, 195–96. Under the Ohio election laws of the time the secretary of state was elected in alternate years to those in which the governor and other principal officers were chosen. In 1902 other officers to be elected were: a justice of the Ohio Supreme Court, the dairy and food commissioner, and one member of the state board of public works.

2. Powell, ed., *The Democratic Party of the State of Ohio*, I, 406–7; *Toledo Blade*, January 16, 1902. The Democratic executive committee consisted of William J. Frey, chairman, Charles W. Baker, Harvey C. Garber, Charles Salen, and William R. Burnett.

3. Johnson's remarks on McLean were quoted in the *Cleveland Plain Dealer*, June 19, 1902; the appraisal of McLean appeared in *ibid.*, June 18, 1902.

4. McLean's letter, Johnson's speech, and the other activities of the clambake were reported in the *Cleveland Plain Dealer*, July 2, 1902.

5. *Toledo Bee*, July 3, 1902.

6. Accounts of the convention and of the dominant role played by Johnson are in: Powell, ed. *The Democratic Party of the State of Ohio*, I, 392–93; *Ohio State Journal* (Columbus), July 11, September 1, 1902; *Toledo Bee*, September 2, 3, 1902; *Cincinnati Enquirer*, September 3, 4, 1902. Johnson succeeded in nominating candidates of his own choice for most of the offices: Herbert S. Bigelow, secretary of state; Michael Donnelly, justice of the supreme court; Joseph Pater, member of the board of public works. He failed in nominating his choice for dairy and food commissioner, but acquiesced in the nomination of Philip H. Bruck.

7. The platform was reported in *Cincinnati Enquirer*, September 3, 4, 1902, and the *Toledo Bee*, September 2, 1902. Some politicians believed that Johnson's endorsement of the Kansas City platform was not only a bid for support from the Bryan wing of the Democracy in Ohio but indicated a desire to inherit the mantle of the Nebraskan in the country at large. On the other hand, Bryan had been greatly disappointed by the omission of any reference to the Kansas City platform in the state resolutions the year before and had asked for an endorsement, a request difficult to deny to the titular head of the party. (*Cincinnati Enquirer*, February 25, September 1, 1902).

8. Democratic reaction was reflected in *Cincinnati Enquirer*, September 3, 1902, the *Dayton Daily News*, September 3, 1902, the *Youngstown Vindicator*, September 4, 1902, the *Cleveland Plain Dealer*, September 4, 1902, and the *Toledo Bee*, September 4, 1902. The typical Republican reaction was reported in the *Ohio State Journal*, September 4, 1902.

9. The account of the beginnings of Johnson's relations with Bigelow is taken from the *Ohio State Journal*, February 13, 1900, and the author's interview with Herbert S. Bigelow, September 26, 1949.

10. Information on Bigelow's early life and relations with his Vine Street Church congregation was obtained from Frank Parker Stockbridge, "Ohio Wide Awake," *Everybody's Magazine*, XXVII (November, 1912), 700–702, and from the author's interview with Herbert S. Bigelow, September 26, 1949. His own father's name was Seeley; he was adopted by Mr. and Mrs. Alpheus A. Bigelow.

11. Quoted in Stockbridge, "Ohio Wide Awake," 703–4. Bigelow's conversion to the single tax is told in *ibid.*, 702–4.

12. *Ibid.*, 704–5.

13. Quoted in the *Cleveland Plain Dealer*, September 3, 1902. The appraisal of Bigelow's liabilities and assets is drawn from Stockbridge, "Ohio Wide Awake," 704–5, from Johnson, *My Story*, 196, and from the author's interview with Edward F. Alexander, September 28, 1949. Bigelow's challenge to the Bernard-McLean machine is told in the *Cincinnati Enquirer*, August 29, 1902, and the *Cleveland Plain Dealer*, August 29, September 3, 4, 1902. The Bigelow forces did not win quite half of the delegation, but even this was a triumph over the powerfully organized McLean organization.

14. *Toledo Bee*, September 4, 1902.

15. The campaign and Johnson's caravan are described in the *Cleveland Plain Dealer*, September 2, 4, 6, 1902, and in Johnson, *My Story*, 196, pictures facing 194, 204.

16. Campaign news was good copy and was copiously reported in all the leading newspapers. Some of the best reporting was in the *Cleveland Plain Dealer,* September 10–October 28, 1902, *passim,* and the *Toledo Bee,* September 1–October 28, 1902, *passim.*

17. *Toledo Bee,* September 18, 1902; *Cleveland Plain Dealer,* September 17–21, 1902.

18. *Cleveland Plain Dealer,* September 27, 1902; *Ohio State Journal,* October 2, 1902. The next week in Wooster Johnson attacked another one of the Democratic renegades, Urias F. Wells, of Wayne County (*Toledo Bee,* October 7, 1902).

19. *Toledo Bee,* September 14, 1902. Because of a prolonged illness Jones was unable to campaign for the Johnson ticket outside of Toledo.

20. Johnson's remarks were quoted in the *Cleveland Plain Dealer,* October 24, 25, 1902. The *Cincinnati Enquirer's* treatment of the Johnson meetings is to be seen in the issues for October 24–26, 1902.

21. *Cleveland Plain Dealer,* October 28, 1902.

22. *Ibid.,* May 29, 1902.

23. Hanna's remarks were quoted in *ibid.,* September 28, 1902. Other campaign attacks on Johnson were reported in *ibid.,* September 28–October 28, 1902, *passim,* and the *Ohio State Journal,* September 28–October 28, 1902, *passim.* Hanna defended himself in the *Cleveland Plain Dealer,* October 25, 1902. William R. Hopkins, a bright, young Republican lawyer, debated with Johnson on taxation, home rule, and the curative law in Gray's Armory, Cleveland, the night of October 28 (*ibid.,* October 29, 1902).

24. The election results were reported in the *Cleveland Plain Dealer,* November 5, 6, 1902, the *Ohio State Journal,* November 6, 1902, the *Dayton Daily News,* November 5, 1902, and the *Toledo Bee,* November 5, 1902. The official count for secretary of state was: Laylin (Republican) 436,171, Bigelow (Democrat) 345,706, Andrew L. White (Prohibition) 12,336, Max S. Hayes (Socialist) 14,359, Theodore Adams (Socialist Labor), 2,983 (*Report of the Secretary of State of Ohio* [1906], 119). The election commentary is drawn, respectively, from the *Cincinnati Enquirer,* November 5, 6, 1902, and the *Toledo Bee,* November 5, 1902. Johnson's statement was quoted in the *Ohio State Journal,* November 6, 1902.

25. Criticism came from William J. Frey and Charles E. Peoples at a meeting in Columbus of the Ohio Democratic Editorial Association on March 20. Their remarks loosened the pens of other editors who joined in the condemnation of Bryan and Johnson. (*Cleveland Plain Dealer,* March 21, 1903; *Cincinnati Enquirer,* March 21, 1903). Johnson's victory in Cleveland was reported in the *Cleveland Plain Dealer,* April 8, 1903. The *Springfield* (Mass.) *Republican* foresaw even a national role for Johnson, commenting that he was "the most promising successor to Bryan in the Democratic leadership which the radical wing of the party has in sight."—Editorial reprinted in the *Cleveland Plain Dealer,* April 12, 1903.

26. *Cleveland Plain Dealer,* May 21–22, 24, 1902. Cochran's reprimand appeared in the *Toledo Bee,* May 22, 1903, Johnson's defense, in Johnson, *My Story,* 197.

27. *Cleveland Plain Dealer,* July 24, 31, August 6, 8, 13, 23, 1903. The editors of the *Plain Dealer* tried to dissuade Johnson from running on the grounds that this action would divert his attention from city affairs and would be interpreted as a move to further his personal ambitions for high

office and fame. See Kennedy, *Fifty Years of Cleveland,* 148–49. Kennedy was co-editor of the *Cleveland Plain Dealer* from 1898 to 1907.

28. McLean's indifference was reported in the *Cleveland Plain Dealer,* September 26, 1903, Zimmerman's opposition in *ibid.,* August 26, 1906. Johnson's control of the convention is described in *ibid.,* August 26, 1903, and in Powell, ed., *The Democratic Party of the State of Ohio,* II, 455–58. The *Cincinnati Enquirer's* protest is in the issue for August 26, 1903. The men to whom Zimmerman referred were former United States senators from Ohio, George H. Pendleton and Allen Thurman, incorruptible Jeffersonian Democrats, who had unsuccessfully fought against the "boodlers" in the party, such as Henry B. Payne, Calvin S. Brice, and Samuel J. Tilden, Democratic nominee for President in 1876, defeated by Rutherford B. Hayes.

29. *Cleveland Plain Dealer,* August 27, 1903.

30. Favorable press reaction appeared in the *Dayton Daily News,* August 31, 1903, the *Cleveland Plain Dealer,* August 28, 1903, and the *Youngstown Vindicator,* August 27, 1903. The criticisms by Daugherty and Zimmerman are in the *Cleveland Plain Dealer,* August 27, 1903, the *Ohio State Journal,* August 27, 1903, and Powell, ed., *The Democratic Party of the State of Ohio,* I, 394.

31. The rest of the ticket was composed of Charles A. Kloeb, auditor of state; T. H. B. Jones, member of the board of public works; Volney J. Dahl, treasure of state; and J. H. Secrist, school commissioner (*Cleveland Plain Dealer,* August 26, 27, 1903).

32. Clarke's nomination was opposed by the following members of the Johnson camp: William L. Finley, leader of the Bryan wing; William W. Durbin; Harvey C. Garber, chairman of the state central committee; and John J. Lentz. They supported two other candidates, Lentz and George M. Saltzgaber, temporary chairman of the convention. Aware of the resistance to Clarke, Johnson had first offered the senatorship to John W. Bookwalter, who refused it. The Cleveland mayor had also urged Samuel M. Jones to run against Hanna, but when the Toledo mayor insisted that he must stand as a nonpartisan Johnson realized that this would be an insurmountable handicap and that he must find another candidate. (*Toledo News-Bee,* June 27, July 6, 11, 1903; *Youngstown Vindicator,* August 25–27, 1903; *Ohio State Journal,* August 25, 27, 1903).

33. The biographical sketch of Clarke which follows is drawn from Warner, *The Life of Justice Clarke,* 1–52.

34. *Youngstown Vindicator,* September 19, 20, 1894.

35. The battle against the APA is told in *ibid.,* March 16—April 6, 1896, and summarized in *ibid.,* March 27, 1938. Clarke's bolting of the party over the issue of free silver is reported in *ibid.,* July 29, 1896.

36. The relations between Clarke and Johnson are discussed in Warner, *The Life of Justice Clarke,* 32–34, 48–49.

37. *Youngstown Vindicator,* August 27, 1903.

38. Democratic dissatisfaction and Johnson's defiance of all criticism were reported in *ibid.,* August 27, 1903, and the *Cleveland Plain Dealer,* August 27, 1903. Cochran's accusations are in the *Toledo News-Bee,* August 27, 1903, Cox's praise in the *Dayton Daily News,* August 27, 1903. On June 1, 1903, the Scripps-McRae League purchased the *Toledo Morning Times,* the *News,* and the *Bee,* consolidating the latter two under the editorship of Negley D. Cochran, the former publisher and editor of the *Bee.* See John

H. Doyle, *A Story of Early Toledo* (Bowling Green, Ohio, [1919]), 131–32.

39. The Johnson–Clarke campaign was covered with thoroughness by the *Cleveland Plain Dealer*, September 6–October 31, 1903, *passim;* other reports are in *Toledo News-Bee*, September 1, October 11, 1903, the *Cincinnati Post*, October 27, 1903, and the *Dayton Daily News*, September 30, 1903. Johnson describes the campaign in *My Story*, 199–203.

40. Johnson's indulgence in personalities was reported in the *Cleveland Plain Dealer*, October 18, 21, 1903, Clarke's personal reference to Hanna in the *Youngstown Vindicator*, September 10, 1903.

41. The opening meeting at Akron was reported in the *Cleveland Plain Dealer*, September 10, 1903. Jones supported Johnson enthusiastically, but ill health once again prevented him from speaking for the Cleveland mayor outside of Toledo (S. M. Jones to N. O. Nelson, October 17, 1903; to Tom L. Johnson, October 29, 1903; to Messrs. Kiefer and Bigelow, October 30, 1903, Jones Papers). An account of the intraparty feud in Toledo is given in the *Toledo News-Bee*, November 1, 1903. Johnson's tight control of the purse strings is described in Johnson, *My Story*, 199, 201, and in the *Columbus Daily Press*, November 9, 1903.

42. The remarks on Herrick are drawn from Croly, *Hanna*, 428; the charge against Ellis is implied in Wright, *Bossism in Cincinnati*, 115–16. The rest of the ticket was composed of Augustus M. Summers, justice of the supreme court; George N. Watkins, member of the board of public works; Edwin D. Jones, school commissioner (*Cleveland Plain Dealer*, June 4, 5, 1903). A recent investigator disputes the widely held view that Herrick was a protégé of Hanna. According to this contention Hanna's choice for governor was Charles Dick, but the Senator reluctantly accepted Herrick when he found the latter had organized widespread support for his candidacy through the good offices of Theodore Burton, who was not in sympathy with the senator from Cleveland (Wilbur D. Jones, "Marcus A. Hanna and Theodore E. Burton," *Ohio State Archaeological and Historical Quarterly*, LX [January, 1951], 16–17). The reasons for the political enmity between Hanna and Burton are sketched in Forrest Crissey, *Theodore E. Burton, American Statesman* (Cleveland, 1956), 132–37.

43. Foraker's maneuver and Hanna's response are given in Walters, *Foraker*, 201–3, Croly, *Hanna*, 420–27, and John M. Blum, *The Republican Roosevelt* (Cambridge, 1954), 50–53. The text of Roosevelt's reply is quoted in Croly, *Hanna*, 425, and in Theodore Roosevelt to Henry Cabot Lodge, May 27, 1903, in Elting E. Morison and John M. Blum, eds., *The Letters of Theodore Roosevelt* (8 vols.; Cambridge, 1951–54), III, 481. Hanna's comment on Harding's nomination is reported in the *Cleveland Plain Dealer*, June 5, 1903. Congressman Burton later explained to Roosevelt that his endorsement for president was not the real issue between Foraker and Hanna; rather it was control of the party machinery (T. E. Burton to Samuel Mather, January 20, 1904, Burton Papers).

44. *Cleveland Plain Dealer*, June 4, 5, August 28, September 20, October 7, 13, 1903. Hanna received offers of help and testimonials both from his conservative friends and the Republican insurgents-to-be: Senators Jonathan Dolliver, Albert J. Beveridge, Moses E. Clapp, and George F. Hoar (Croly, *Hanna*, 431–32).

45. Hanna's vilification of Johnson was quoted in the *Cleveland Plain Dealer*, September 20, 30, 1903, and Johnson, *My Story*, 201, Herrick's in

the *Cleveland Plain Dealer*, September 20, October 1, 1903, the accusations against Clarke in the *Youngstown Vindicator*, September 28, 1903. The expenditure of funds was treated in the *Cleveland Plain Dealer*, October 25, 1903. Johnson's campaign manager, Charles Salen, in an open letter charged the Republicans with expenditures of $100,000 in Cuyahoga County, $25,000 in Hamilton County, $15,000 in Lucas County, $12,000 in Franklin County, and $6,000 in Montgomery County.

46. The election results were reported in the *Cleveland Plain Dealer*, November 5, 1903, the *Ohio State Journal*, November 4, 1903, the *Toledo News-Bee*, November 4, 1903, and the *Cincinnati Post*, November 4, 1903. In Toledo it was clear to the Democrats that they had lost by fusion, that Jones could not deliver the nonpartisan vote he received to any other candidates. Jones himself thought it was the fault of the Toledo Democrats and that the party might as well give up the ghost in that city. (*Cleveland Plain Dealer*, November 5, 1903). The official tabulation for governor was: Herrick (Republican) 475,560; Johnson (Democrat) 361,748; Nelson D. Creamer (Prohibition) 13,502; Isaac Cowan (Socialist) 13,495; John D. Goerke (Socialist Labor) 2,071 (*Report of the Secretary of State of Ohio* [1906], 119).

47. Republican claims and Democratic rebuttals were printed in the *Cleveland Plain Dealer*, November 4, 5, 1903, the *Toledo News-Bee*, November 4, 1903, and the *Cincinnati Enquirer*, November 4, 1903, and in Powell, ed., *The Democratic Party of the State of Ohio*, I, 394–95. Clarke's remark was quoted in the *Youngstown Vindicator*, November 4, 1903.

CHAPTER SEVEN

ROUTING THE BOSSES
1904■1905

In 1904 the Mark Hanna brand of Republicanism was supreme
in Ohio. Built on the hard rock of practical politics, it appeared
to be an edifice that could weather any storm, yet in the succeeding year its foundation began to crumble as the currents
of reform washed against it with gathering momentum. No fore-
boding of such an outcome, however, disturbed the Republicans
when the Ohio General Assembly met in the House of Representatives on January 12, 1904, to elect a United States senator.
In contrast to the one-vote margin at his first election in 1898,
Mark Hanna was re-elected this time by a resounding vote of
115 to 25, the largest majority any senator ever received in Ohio.[1]

The overwhelming endorsement no doubt would have helped
Hanna recover whatever political prestige he had lost in the
previous May when Foraker, it will be recalled, forced the Cleveland senator to suppress his own presidential ambitions and commit himself instead to the candidacy of Theodore Roosevelt. But
little time remained in which to test the extent of Hanna's
political recovery, for his physical strength was fast ebbing. As
the committee ushered him to the platform for his acceptance
speech before the assembled legislators, all could see that he
was an old man, his age accentuated by the drag of his right
foot, and the furrowed, sagging skin of his face. Only the sharp,
clear, brown eyes intimated his indomitable will and mental
vigor. In five weeks he lay dead of typhoid fever, his passing
mourned in his native state and in the nation, by foe as well

143

as friend. Friends lamented the loss of a confident leader; foes, such as Johnson, expressed their respect for the memory of an opponent worthy of their mettle.[2]

Although rumors circulated that his demise would lead to wrangling among his partisans and to disintegration of the system he had built, nothing of the sort occurred at the time. The Foraker faction tried to strengthen its position without success. No break appeared in the ranks of the Republican legislators when General Charles F. W. Dick, of Akron, was elected to succeed Hanna in the United States Senate, reportedly in fulfillment of the latter's dying wish. Dick, a political wheelhorse of the McKinley campaigns and four times a congressman, was several cuts below his predecessor in stature. He filled the office Hanna left vacant but not his political role. As a prophecy of events to come it was noteworthy that no man was big enough to inherit the dead leader's mantle. Instead, it was shared by a triumvirate of Dick, Herrick, and George Cox, with the Cincinnati boss holding the balance of power. Moreover, Senator Foraker with his share of federal patronage was still a figure to be reckoned with in the councils of the party.[3]

In the legislative session of 1904 the citizens had their first view of the new leadership in action; what they saw did not encourage them to clamor for more. With a majority of four to one in the House and seven to one in the Senate, the Republicans were able to have things their own way without interference from meddlesome reformers.[4] Johnson had no voice in the proceedings whatsoever.

Although the legislators had performed their most important function in the election of Hanna and then Dick to the United States Senate, and were committed to a program of economy and cautious change, there were a few matters on which action was imperative. One of these was a recodification of the existing school laws, a mass of special legislation which fell under the ban of the Ohio Supreme Court's decision in the Toledo and Cleveland cases of 1902. The question was whether the Assembly should adopt the Cleveland plan of a small board elected at large and a superintendent in whom was vested responsibility and power, or the Cincinnati scheme of a large board and a superintendent with limited authority. A school code embodying the Cleveland setup was introduced by a Cuyahoga representative, bearing the endorsement of civic organizations, the State Board of Commerce, and known to be favored by Governor Herrick. Under pressure from the Cincinnati boss an administration "compromise" bill was introduced in the Senate providing for the adoption of the Cincinnati plan for cities with a population of over fifty thousand, and the small-board plan for all other political entities, an arrangement that underscored the intent of satisfying George Cox.[5]

To many educators it seemed a travesty to model the state school system after that of a city where the educational facilities were notoriously shabby and backward. Once the pride of the state, the Cincinnati schools had deteriorated under political manipulation, mismanagement, and financial starvation. Boss Cox had only two interests in them: to provide jobs as rewards for the party faithfuls, and to squeeze what financial favors he could from book publishers. In his battle to retain the existing structure, one of Cox's most aggressive allies was the firm supplying texts for the Cincinnati schools, the American Book Company, which maintained two lobbyists in Columbus during the legislative session.[6]

The "Cox Code," as the administration school bill was derisively called, passed the Senate but was defeated in the House. A conference committee finally developed a plan, which was adopted, providing for a school board of flexible size for large cities, partially elected at large, partially by wards, while retaining the small board for communities under fifty thousand, as had been proposed in the original administration bill. The school board was given full authority over the educational system, although it could delegate power to a superintendent appointed by it. A feature retained from the old code was the privilege of voting for school board members granted to women over twenty-one. Again, as with the Municipal Code, Cox had his way, although this time the options did not saddle the other cities of the state with the Cincinnati system.[7]

Important as this measure was to him, his primary interest in this session, it was alleged, was in a bill to lease the state canal between Dayton and Cincinnati to a company in which he was a substantial stockholder for the purpose of using the berm as a roadbed for a steam railroad. He wrote letters to members of the Assembly urging support of the proposal and encouraged company officials to use their wiles as lobbyists. In Dayton the bill aroused a furor, and delegations from that city descended on Columbus to fight it. So strong was the popular outcry that it was tabled and never heard of again.[8]

Another measure which aroused public enmity toward the Republican politicians was the Chapman bill to change the time of municipal elections from spring to fall to coincide with the state ones. In commenting upon the bill the *Cleveland Plain Dealer* conceded that it had the virtue of diminishing the expense and disturbance of frequent elections, but such worthy considerations were not the reasons for its introduction. "Among Republican politicians," the *Plain Dealer* continued, "there is no concealment of its purpose being wholly political and that it is intended to curb the 'pernicious' habit of independent voting in municipal elections, a habit which shows an alarming tendency to increase and which, unless effectively checked, may extend to other elections." In other words, its intent was to check the power of Jones in Toledo and Johnson in Cleveland.

This supposition gained credence, when at the hearings before the House committee on elections the only speakers for the bill were Republicans from those two cities. Strong pleas against the proposal were made by Washington Gladden, who had previously attacked it in the press, by the secretary of the Cleveland Municipal Association, and by a representative of the Columbus Board of Trade. Although individual Republican legislators made verbal protests against the administration pressure to support the bill, few had the courage to vote against it, and the measure passed with a comfortable margin in both houses. But whatever expectations its framers may have had, their hopes were quickly dimmed by the adoption of the Ricketts Resolution initiating a constitutional amendment to shift the state elections from the odd- to the even-numbered years, the effect of which would be to separate again voting on municipal and state affairs.[9]

If the Chapman measure was an oblique attack on the principle of home rule, the Hypes bill was a frontal one. It provided for a complete revision of the election code, sweeping away the city boards of elections appointed by the respective mayors, replacing them with bipartisan county boards of four members selected by the secretary of state upon the recommendation of the state executive committees of the two leading parties, and requiring the registration of voters in cities with a minimum population of fourteen thousand. In the final rush of business the measure was carried.[10]

One more threat against the cities was a bill, drafted by Judge William B. Sanders, one of the attorneys for the Cleveland Street Railway Company, to create a state franchise commission to determine the conditions and regulate the rates under which quasi-public corporations were to operate in the state. Infuriated by what he considered "a vicious and infamous attack on home rule," Johnson called it "the worst measure of its kind ever offered for the consideration of any state legislature," an opinion echoed in a *Toledo News-Bee* editorial. Fortunately for its opponents the proposal died in committee, never coming to a vote on the floor.[11]

Amidst the welter of gloom which this session cast upon the reformers, a few pieces of legislation were passed which lifted their spirits. One of these laws, which was drafted by Brand Whitlock, permitted all the large cities to establish juvenile courts like the one in Cleveland which had been first introduced by special act in 1902; another sanctioned municipal group-planning commissions for every city; a third provided for optional primary elections and extended to them the coverage of the state corrupt-practice laws; and a fourth required state officials to place all state moneys in banks which had bid for the privilege of being state depositories.[12] Nothing was done, however, to appease the reformers in taxation. They disapproved of the law passed imposing a 2 per cent levy on all inheritances over three thousand dollars and they regarded as a mere sop an amendment to the Cole Act extending the 1 per cent excise tax to water transportation, heating, and cooling companies.[13]

The chief criticism of the session was not leveled at the legislators. With the exception of the Hamilton County delegates, of whom it was said that they "could vote for no bill without communicating with Cincinnati," the press praised the other members of the General Assembly for their independence from the bosses. Instead, it was directed at the leaders themselves for their intervention on behalf of measures to promote their personal gain or to foster narrow partisan advantage, regardless of what the effect on the public good might be.[14]

A party that continued to bow to this brand of leadership might expect voter resistance ahead; nevertheless the Republicans refused to read the signs. At their state convention at Columbus on May 17, 1904, where harmony and peace reigned among all factions, Foraker, Dick, Herrick, and Cox were honored by election as delegates-at-large to the Republican national convention, and the control of these four over the state organization remained unbroken. The entire proceedings were described by a Republican paper as "very tame, very humdrum, very much prearranged": the slate of state officers was approved without a contest and the platform was a routine announcement, pledging support for President Roosevelt's candidacy, endorsing Governor Herrick and Senators Dick and Foraker, and commending the legislature for fulfilling its platform pledges.[15]

On the Democratic side, 1904 was scarcely more propitious than the previous year for the radical wing of the party. Since it was a presidential year, interest in state issues tended to recede into the background without being replaced by a compensating absorption in national affairs. There was no agreement among the Ohio reformers on a presidential candidate to boom. Bryan, about whom they had rallied before, was considered by many of them to be "unavailable" after his two defeats. The state convention which met on May 23 was described as "leaderless" and was applauded for returning to "historic and conservative Democracy." Although many delegations, including those from Cuyahoga, Hamilton, Montgomery, and Franklin counties, had their seats contested, the issue was quickly settled by a deal between Charles Salen and Lewis Bernard to seat the regular organization from each county. Since this meant sacrificing the Bigelow faction from Cincinnati, Johnson protested but finally acquiesced because altogether the arrangement favored a majority of his supporters. The platform was mainly confined to generalities, attacking the Republicans for their extravagance, taxation methods, and disregard of home rule, and promising reforms in each case under a Democratic administration. Johnson won a minor victory by persuading the convention to add a resolution in favor of a two-cent railroad fare, but he failed in his efforts to prevent a pledge that bound the Ohio delegation to the unit rule at the national convention. In the selection of delegates-at-large Johnson received a further rebuff when the convention chose as one of the four, Charles Salen, who had offended the Mayor by working with Bernard. The other three were John A. McMahon of Dayton, Will S. Thomas of Springfield, classed as conservatives, and Edmond H. Moore of Youngstown, who was not identified with either wing.[16]

Johnson cut no figure at the Democratic national convention in St. Louis, which he attended as a delegate from Cleveland. He was voted down for membership on the resolutions committee; his archenemy, John R. McLean, was elected a national committeeman; his presidential choice, Joseph Folk of Missouri, received no support from other members of the Ohio delegation. The state's forty-six votes went, under the unit rule, to the conservative Alton Parker, the ultimate convention choice. Johnson hailed the platform which Bryan had had a hand in formulating as a great document because of its two declarations that tariff protection is robbery and that all should enjoy equal opportunity.[17] Johnson and the radical wing of the Ohio Democracy were sufficiently mollified by the platform to support the party nominee, but their campaigning on his behalf lacked conviction.

In the election Theodore Roosevelt swept Ohio, carrying into office the Republican state candidates as well as most of their county nominees. The victorious party won in seventy-one of the eighty-eight counties, receiving the unprecedented plurality of 255,421 votes of the 1,000,000 cast. Many Bryan Democrats rebuked their party for selecting the conservative Parker by either remaining away from the polls or voting for Roosevelt, who carried nine counties which had been faithful to the Democrats before.[18]

In interpreting the Republican triumph the staunchly partisan *Ohio State Journal* declared that it was not an endorsement of "stand pat protectionism" nor any other doctrine in the platform, but it was a tribute to "the sterling Americanism of Theodore Roosevelt and his personal platform of a 'square deal' to every class of citizen and to every worthy and legitimate interest in the nation." Although the party politicians must have looked askance at these remarks, many Ohioans shared this view, applauding the President in his crusade for the rights of all.[19] In this sense his victory was a harbinger of the moral resurgence which in another year had gathered enough momentum to overturn the bosses of the state. Paradoxically, it was Theodore Roosevelt's own party that was to suffer the most.

Roosevelt was only one of the many forces awakening and quickening the conscience of the Ohio electorate to the social and political injustices of the day. The Johnson campaigns had brought home to the people a few truths. The muckraking magazines were then reaching the peak of their militancy in exposing the corruption and greed in politics and industry across the land. In 1905 *McClure's Magazine* published Lincoln Steffens' article, "Ohio: A Tale of Two Cities," praising the Johnson administration in Cleveland but presenting a withering condemnation of Cincinnati under Boss Cox's rule.[20] The Ohio press was catching the crusading spirit. The *Cleveland Plain Dealer* underscored the scope of the reform movement in the selection of its news articles, highlighting Joseph W. Folk's election as governor of Missouri in 1904, the triumph of Mayors Edward F. Dunne in Chicago and George W. Guthrie in Pittsburgh in 1905, as well as the fight being waged against boss rule in New York, Philadelphia, Indianapolis, Baltimore, and San Francisco. During the late summer of 1905 the *Plain Dealer* turned to muckraking with daily articles written by one of their veteran reporters, William S. Couch, exposing the boss-ridden conditions in each Ohio city where they existed. Though not so vivid in style, they rivaled Steffens' work in their frank and meticulous reporting of the facts.[21]

An even more potent journalistic force in stimulating the moral revival in Ohio politics was the Scripps-McRae League, which had proven itself worthy of the motto: "With a mission and without a muzzle." The chain, which consisted of the *Cleveland Press* and *Cincinnati Post* in 1900, had expanded to include the *Toledo News-Bee* and *Times,* purchased in 1903, and the *Columbus Citizen,* acquired a year later partly upon the insistence of Washington Gladden. At the beginning of 1905 a special telegraphic line was opened connecting these papers, thus enabling a swifter co-ordination of policy. Catering to the lower middle class and the workingman, they reached an audience which the *Cleveland Plain Dealer* and the muckraking magazines seldom touched. Emotional in content, colloquial and terse in style, their articles and editorials carried a punch that could hardly fail to arouse the reader. So long as the able, eccentric Edward W. Scripps remained responsible for their policy, they followed his enlightened thinking on social and political affairs. Although all the Scripps-McRae papers contributed to the moral uprising, the two most important were the *Toledo News-Bee* and the *Cincinnati Post,* by virtue of their position in cities where the crusade against bossism was most intense.[22]

The Toledo situation was an anomalous one, for simultaneously with Jones's personal triumphs the Republican machine had succeeded in dominating most of the other municipal offices and the city council. It was the Mayor's rejection of a party organization that had produced this grave state of affairs.[23]

Control of the Republican organization had passed from George P. Waldorf to Walter Folger Brown, who was a Harvard-educated lawyer, polished in manner and speech—a new type of boss in contrast to the crude, unlettered George Cox. The difference was only superficial, however, for Brown copied Cox's methods in order to enhance his own power in the party in Toledo. In revamping the local machine he was aided by three lieutenants: Charles Nauts, clerk of the city council, Frank Baird, state oil inspector, and Sam Cohn, a Hungarian-born Jew, who was the popular superintendent of the state free employment agency in Toledo. The machine was closely allied with the utility interests, the breweries, and other corporations seeking favors, many of which were the clients of Boss Brown, who used his political power to promote their interests. It was this union which appeared to be such a source of strength that led to his downfall.[24]

After the municipal election of 1903 the Republican organization seemed impregnable; it had a majority of ten on the council, a number sufficient to override the veto of the mayor, the only obstacle to their complete domination. Thus solidly established, Walter Brown sought to obtain a franchise renewal for his client, the Toledo Rail and Light Company. This attempted "grab" was defeated first by the veto of Jones, then after his death in the summer of 1904 by the veto of the acting mayor, Robert Finch, a Republican who had the backbone to defy the machine. The council was stayed from passing the ordinance over these negatives by a "petition in boots," a mass protest of citizens who were organized and drilled by a prominent attorney, Johnson Thurston, and shouted their disapproval outside the council chamber.[25]

But more decisive action than this was required if similar crises were to be avoided in the future and the spadework of Jones in promoting municipal reforms and nonpartisanship were to survive. Elisha B. Southard took the lead, calling together old associates of Jones to discuss a plan of action. Among them were: Johnson Thurston, important as a legal adviser; William Cowell, Jones's manager; Oren Dunham, an ex-newspaper man; Ambrose A. Moody; Frank Geer; and Albert E. Overmyer—almost all of them nominal Republicans. Sharing Jones's aversion to the usual party organization, in which the tail wags the dog, they developed a scheme which would allow the initiative to come from the people themselves. A call went forward for neighboring meetings in each precinct to select two delegates to attend city-wide conventions at which issues were to be discussed and candidates selected. On August 29, 1904, the Independent Voters, the label chosen by the new party, held their first general meeting and adopted a brief platform of three planks advocating home rule, nonpartisan nominations, and popular referendum on all franchises. Determined to concentrate on local issues, the party emphasized the platform first, the candidates second. In seeking nominees they adhered to the principle that the office should seek the man, depending on neighborhood groups to suggest suitable persons, who were then screened by an investigating committee. It was the most democratic plan of any political organization in the state.[26]

In the election of November, 1904, the Independents placed a full slate of councilmanic candidates in the field and marshaled their partisans to the polls with the skill of political veterans. In spite of the Republican attempt to confuse the elecorate by introducing a bogus Independent ticket, the Independent Voters elected a councilman-at-large and two councilmen from the wards. In addition, their educational campaign aided in the defeat of every councilman who had supported the Republican machine in its traction fight. A measure of their strength was the difference between Theodore Roosevelt's plurality in Toledo of nearly 13,000 votes and that of their candidate for councilman-at-large, Adam Schauss, who defeated his Republican opponent by 2,384. The results sounded the death knell of the

Walter Brown Republican organization as an influential force in local politics.[27]

This triumph gave the Independents a great start, but it is doubtful whether they could have sustained their movement without the two men who then joined their cause, Negley D. Cochran and Brand Whitlock. In contrast to the originators of the party, both were Democrats. Negley Cochran, the older of the two, was born in 1863, and spent his childhood in Wheeling, West Virginia, where his father was a judge and superintendent of a Methodist Sunday school. Graduating from the University of Michigan at the age of twenty, he began his newspaper career in Toledo, a career which was to endure for more than half a century. At first a reporter on the *Toledo Commercial* and the *Toledo Blade*, then managing editor of the former, he later shifted to the *Toledo Bee*. In 1897, with the aid of some associates, he purchased the *Bee* and transformed it. Under his direction it became a crusading, independent Democratic paper and retained this character after it merged with the Scripps-McRae chain in 1903 and took the new title *Toledo News-Bee*.[28]

Cochran was of a passionate nature, and he relished a fight. He struck at the bigotry of the anti-Catholic movements which raged in Toledo periodically. He maintained a running war against the ministers of the city for their self-righteous smugness and carping criticism of Whitlock for failing to stamp out the saloons and vice. The enemy of social injustice and wrong, he began as early as 1897 flaying the traction interests for their attempts to saddle the people of Toledo with high fares in order to pay dividends and interest on stocks and bonds which represented two-thirds "water" and one-third actual investment. In the crisis over the street-railway issue in 1904, it was his flaming news stories and editorials which aroused the people to the danger of the franchise "grab" and kept them on their guard until the threat had passed. Because of Cochran's ability to give fire and zest to his work, Edward Scripps considered him one of his greatest editors.[29]

His relations with Jones had been somewhat mixed. The editor admired the Mayor's humanitarianism, opposition to cant, and championship of the people's interest against the utilities. But Cochran's partisanship stood in the way of a close friendship. In Jones's first two mayoralty campaigns, for example, the publisher had thrown the support of his paper behind the Democratic candidates. But after the Mayor had broken completely with all factions of the Republicans and declared his nonpartisanship, the editor tried to draw him into the Democratic fold without success, although in 1900 Jones did support William Jennings Bryan and Cochran himself, who ran unsuccessfully for Congress. In return the publisher persuaded the Democrats to endorse Jones for mayor in 1901 after he had once again been nominated by petition as a nonpartisan candidate. But two years later Cochran had deserted Jones for the Democratic nominee, complaining that the Mayor's sympathy for the tramps and petty criminals was threatening the whole system of law enforcement — the very government itself — in Toledo. Furthermore, Cochran differed from Jones in insisting upon the practical necessity of a party organization. Perhaps, fundamentally, it was impossible for two such strong personalities to work in harness together; Cochran liked to dominate, but no man could rule the free, stubborn spirit of Jones. A party, however, dedicated to promoting the ideals they shared was certain to enlist Cochran's support.[30]

In Brand Whitlock, who was titular head of the Independent movement from his election as mayor in 1905 until his retirement in 1913, he found the very man with whom he could team in relative harmony. It was a case of opposites complementing one another. Cochran was bold and defiant, Whitlock cautious and conciliatory; Cochran loved the hurly-burly of politics, Whitlock found it uncongenial; Cochran supplied the emotional drive and color, Whitlock the intellectual arguments and air of respectability. The common denominator between them was their interest in the poor and the outcast, and their hatred of hypocrisy, social injustice, and economic inequality. It has been said that Cochran made Whitlock politically. In a sense he did, but Whitlock was no puppet; he pursued his own counsel, developed his own program, and held the confidence of the people for eight years because he was independent, honest, able, and served them well.[31]

The wonder is that this sensitive man, slender and austere in bearing, fastidious in dress, and aristocratic in taste, ever entered politics. He was born in Urbana, Ohio, on March 4, 1869, the son of Elias D. Whitlock, a Methodist minister. From

his father he received a respect for learning and some unshak-
able religious convictions. However, not all was harmony between the two. As Brand grew up, he reacted strongly against
his father's fundamentalism and strait-laced morality. More
congenial to the young boy was his maternal grandfather, Joseph
Carter Brand, in whose home he frequently summered. The
older man imparted to his grandson the fervor and excitement
he had felt as an abolitionist, an agent of the Underground Railroad, and an officer in the Civil War. Also he first introduced
the youth to the cosmopolitan culture of Europe that he had
experienced while traveling abroad and serving as the United
States consul in Nuremburg.[32]

Brand Whitlock's education in politics began in 1887 when
he left home for Toledo to become a reporter on the *Toledo
Blade.* There he met Frank Hurd, a former Democratic congressman, who was a brilliant and persuasive opponent of the
tariff. He converted the malleable young Whitlock to free trade
and weaned him away from his inherited Republican faith.
Through Hurd, Whitlock obtained a job four years later on
the *Chicago Herald,* an outstanding Democratic paper. His
experiences as a reporter as well as his association with a challenging group of newsmen in Chicago's Whitechapel Club
widened his intellectual and political horizon.

In 1892 he met another of the men who were to influence
his life, John Peter Altgeld, then running for governor of Illinois.
A wealthy lawyer and a judge, Altgeld was also a strong humanitarian, known for his radical labor views. Although the owner
of the *Chicago Herald* was hostile to Altgeld, toward the end
of the campaign Whitlock was allowed to print some articles
on the candidate. So pleased was Altgeld with these columns
that after his election he offered to make the young reporter
his private secretary, but he refused the offer. Later, however,
he accepted a position as head clerk in the office of the secretary
of state.

Whitlock's experiences during his four years in Springfield,
Illinois, had a profound effect on his future career. The highly
impressionable temperament of this young man made him ex-
ceptionally sensitive to the pull of any given environment. He
shared Altgeld's travail in pardoning the three remaining men
convicted of bomb-throwing in the Haymarket Riot; he imbibed

some of the passionate convictions with which the governor defended labor and struck at economic inequality; he became wise to the political tricks of privileged groups to defeat reforms; he began his long friendship with Clarence Darrow, who helped shape his literary tastes as well as his social thinking; he prepared himself for the law; and he married Ella Brainerd, of whom a friend later wrote, "She was half of his heart, half of his head, and more than half of his courage." [33]

In 1897 when he returned to Ohio, he was disillusioned with politics in general and the Democratic party in particular. He was embittered by the party's betrayal of tariff reform, by the graft that existed in the Illinois legislature, and by the vicious reprisals taken upon Altgeld for pardoning the three Haymarket anarchists. He might have gone back to journalism, but he shied from it because of its long hours and low pay. Instead he entered the profession for which he had most recently prepared himself, the law, opening an office in Toledo. Within a few years he had won a reputation for his courtroom eloquence in defending criminals and in pressing the damage claims of workingmen injured on the job. It was his interest in the derelicts and the poor that brought him to the notice of Samuel Jones. The new Mayor invited the young attorney to speak at Golden Rule Park and by 1900 had drawn Whitlock back into politics as an active supporter of himself and his independent movement.

The ties between the two were further strengthened by their enthusiasm for Tolstoy, Whitman, Emerson, and other writers with a social message. Whitlock contributed to Jones's literary education, just as Jones deepened Whitlock's humanitarian sympathies. Their friendship grew. The young lawyer continued to campaign for the Mayor, substituted as police magistrate in the latter's absence, and became the Mayor's legal counselor. When Jones died on July 12, 1904, Whitlock was the principal speaker at the funeral ceremonies and was considered by many to be the political heir of the dead leader.[34] But would he accept the role?

His years in Toledo had been richly productive in a literary way; his short stories had gained acceptance; his fine political novel *The Thirteenth District* had won acclaim; and he was in the midst of a second, *The Turn of the Balance,* an indictment of society's handling of criminals. To assume leadership of the

Jones movement would mean the curtailment, if not the end, of his leisure for writing.[35] The insistence of Cochran, supplemented by the pleading of Tom Johnson and Lincoln Steffens, and the assurance that the people wanted him, however, made him yield to what his conscience dictated to be his duty. In the autumn of 1905 he was nominated for mayor by petition on the Independent Voters ticket, heading a complete slate of candidates for all the offices to be filled.[36]

Grave as the Toledo situation was in 1904–5, the plight of Cincinnati seemed even more critical to reformers. The Toledo Independents had the record of Jones's victories and the inspiration of his ideals to carry them forward; the Cincinnati reformers had only a legacy of defeats and lacked a Jones to lead them. Machine domination in Toledo was sporadic; boss rule in Cincinnati had been entrenched for many years.

George B. Cox, undisputed boss since the late 1880's, had achieved the pinnacle of his power. He had gained prestige at home by becoming president of the Cincinnati Trust Company in 1903. His political control had passed beyond Cincinnati and Hamilton County, and now extended through southern Ohio to the state capital itself. One of the Hanna lieutenants, delegate-at-large to the party national convention, respected and feared by the governor, the legislators, and the United States senators from Ohio, he was formidable. Perhaps it was this very excess of power that frightened people to revolt and led to his undoing.[37]

Three conditions, however, made the task of the reformers a prodigious one: the "craven" apathy of Cincinnati businessmen, big and small; the collusion between Cox and the McLean-Bernard regular Democratic organization; and the superficial respectability of Cox's rule. There were no scandals such as had precipitated the courthouse riot in 1884, nor was the "sporting" element permitted to operate in a flagrant way. The police force was kept reasonably efficient, and was forbidden to make nuisance raids on gambling dens and houses of prostitution to collect petty graft. Whatever these establishments paid for protection went directly to the top in the form of campaign contributions.[38] The reformers had to break through public indifference, demonstrate the malign character of the Cox machine, and, most important, develop their own organization.

The opposition to Cox was badly split. The efforts of the Tom Johnson wing, led by Herbert Bigelow and Daniel Kiefer, to rout the Bernard-McLean forces and remodel the local Democracy into a militant reform organization had been only partially successful. They had weakened Bernard's hold but not destroyed it. Bigelow and Kiefer lacked the stuff that makes great leaders. The preacher, a brilliant agitator for reform, was egotistical and impractical, with little talent for compromise; the retired clothing merchant, a devout, orthodox single taxer, was a genius as a money-raiser but could inspire no large following. Furthermore, these "Vine Street radicals," tarred with the single-tax brush and advocating such radical measures as municipal ownership of utilities and the initiative and referendum, could enlist no co-operation from the conservative wing. They were considered a weird lunatic fringe by such aristocratic Democrats as Judson Harmon, one-time attorney-general in Grover Cleveland's cabinet; Melville E. Ingalls, then president of the Big Four Railroad; Judge Hiram Peck, a corporation lawyer; and his son John Weld Peck, the leading street-railway attorney. The only point the conservatives and radicals shared was opposition to McLean and Cox. Holding the balance between these extremes were the professional politicians, Tom Noctor, a personable Irishman, and Henry Heilker, a German-Catholic lawyer. Interested in patronage, not principle, they gave their support to whatever group appeared to have the strength to win.[39]

In 1903, however, the several factions were so evenly balanced that none could control the executive committee or the party machinery. As a way out of the dilemma, a new committee of twenty-six men who were outside of the warring factions was appointed to organize the mayoralty campaign. They agreed upon a nonpartisan ticket labeled the Citizens Municipal party and headed by Melville E. Ingalls. Although the various Democratic factions promised to support this slate, they reneged on their pledges. Cox's candidate, Julius Fleischman, a wealthy, respected manufacturer, defeated Ingalls by a plurality of 15,500. The latter gained some votes in Republican strongholds but not enough to offset his losses in the Democratic wards.[40]

After the election the disheartened Democratic politicians left the burden of continuing the crusade against Coxism to a group of college intellectuals. They reorganized and reduced the committee of twenty-six to nine members, each dedicated to reclaiming the city from the Cox machine. Their guiding spirit was a Democrat, Elliott Pendleton, a nephew of former Senator George B. Pendleton. Tall, aristocratic in mien, a graduate of Harvard, and a talented amateur actor, he lent an aura of respectability to the movement. But, more than this, he contributed a contagious enthusiasm for reform and displayed a fearlessness that strengthened the timid in opposing the bosses. He financed and edited the *Citizens Bulletin,* a weekly devoted to good citizenship and an exposé of the Cox regime. The gang sneered at this erudite sheet, which had a quotation from Seneca's *Pilot* at the top of its editorial page and other excerpts from Virgil, Plato, and John Fiske liberally sprinkled through its columns. Nevertheless, it appealed to members in the upper bracket of the business community and brought home to them the serious faults of the existing administration. Pendleton, either by inclination or design, ignored radical, controversial issues; instead he stressed the need for better schools, improved street paving, greater economy and efficiency in city departments—reforms to which all good citizens could subscribe. Even though the Vine Street radicals found his program inadequate, they respected his sincerity and his fearlessness in leading the attack on Cox.[41]

In 1904 the *Citizens Bulletin* was the only voice against bossism in Cincinnati. Charles P. Taft's *Cincinnati Times-Star,* which had roundly abused Cox early in his career, had been won over when the boss restored its political advertising and backed its proprietor for Congress. For reasons of party expediency a second Republican paper, the *Cincinnati Commercial-Tribune,* edited by Murat Halstead, had also capitulated to Cox. John R. McLean's *Cincinnati Enquirer* kept a sphinxlike silence on municipal matters. Fearing for its survival, Milton McRae had even muzzled the *Cincinnati Post,* heretofore a consistent foe of Cox. When Edward Scripps discovered this in 1905 he countermanded his partner's instructions, ordering the editor, John Vandercook, to take up the cudgels against Cox and rain harder blows than before. Writing about the incident six years later, Scripps explained, "I felt I would rather lose the *Post* as a business than possess it as a fat, greasy, prosperous prostitute." During the campaign of 1905 the paper blazed at Coxism with every journalistic device, including caricatures of the Boss in cartoons drawn by the famous Homer Davenport. Scripps, in addition, contributed money to the reform campaign, and J. Chandler Harper, general counsel of the Scripps-McRae League, organized the Honest Election Committee of Cincinnati to fight for a free ballot and a fair count.[42]

A magazine article and a book issued in 1905 further publicized the Cincinnati situation. The article was Steffens' aforementioned "Ohio: A Tale of Two Cities," published in *McClure's Magazine*. It had been almost ready for publication in January, 1904, then set aside after Hanna's death, and finally released in the summer of 1905, when sentiment against bossism was riding high both in Ohio and the country. The book was *Bossism in Cincinnati* by Henry C. Wright, a social worker and secretary of the Citizens Municipal party. He exposed the methods and evil character of the Cox machine more thoroughly, if less dramatically, then did Steffens.[43]

Cox promptly bought a copy of Steffens' article and tried to shrug off the indictment as "full of falsehoods." Mayor Fleischman also attempted to discredit the report by stating that the author had only talked with him for fifteen minutes and that his investigations had been superficial, intended merely to prove his preconceptions.[44]

But most Cincinnatians thought differently; they were shocked by the evidence that George Cox and his gang had dragged the fair name of the "Queen City" through the mire. One of his Democratic allies, Lewis Bernard, was the first to feel the change in the public temper. At the Democratic city convention which met on September 29, 1905, Bernard's men were beaten and the opposing factions took control, nominating a slate of honest, moderate reformers. Edward J. Dempsey was the unanimous choice to head the ticket. A respected judge of the Cincinnati Superior Court who had protected the interest of the city against the utilities and a friend of Clarence Darrow, he was acceptable to both conservatives and radicals.[45] The harmony achieved at the convention set the stage for a united attack against the Cox regime by all the opposition elements of the city.

This wave of sentiment against bossism was not confined to Toledo and Cincinnati, where the problem was most acute. Infectiously it spread from city to city, from urban to rural districts, until it became a central theme in the politics of the state. Nevertheless, the four top Republicans, ignoring the changed temper of the times, ran their state convention in Columbus on May 24 in a smoothly regimented manner. Herrick and other incumbents were renominated; the only major change was the substitution of Andrew L. Harris for Warren G. Harding for the office of lieutenant-governor. Charles Dick wrote the platform, which contained more platitudes and weasel planks than concrete promises. The only excitment was produced by William Howard Taft, the chairman of the convention. This native son of Ohio was then secretary of war and an intimate of President Roosevelt; therefore, any policy pronouncement he might make carried great weight. In his keynote address he defended the need to grant the Interstate Commerce Commission the power to fix railroad rates, a proposal then pending before Congress and one that Senator Foraker was known to oppose.[46]

A month later, on June 27, the Democrats held their state convention in the capital city. As was the case the year before, no individual or faction had the strength to dominate; it was a "bossless" conclave. There was a spirited race for the gubernatorial nomination, but it left no bitterness. The contestant with the largest number of instructed delegates was John M. Pattison, a Civil War veteran, lawyer, and president of a Cincinnati insurance company. He had been prominent in Democratic politics between 1873 and 1893 and served twice in the state legislature and once in congress. Known as a dry, he drew support from the rural counties but none from the large city districts. His leading opponent was John C. Welty of Canton, a favorite with many of the Democratic bosses and the liquor interests. Johnson, who had refused to endorse Pattison for fear temperance would become the paramount issue, threw the vote of the Cuyahoga delegation to Brand Whitlock, whose only other support came from Lucas and Ottawa counties. On the second ballot Pattison was nominated. His acceptance speech helped to mollify his opponents, since he devoted a third of it to an attack on the corrupt organization of the state under the rule of Coxism, soft-pedaled temperance, praised Bryan and even Roosevelt, and endorsed the platform point by point.[47]

The platform was principally the handiwork of Johnson, who

served on the resolutions committee. As clear and precise as the Republican one was vague and platitudinous, it repeated former pledges to grant maximum home rule to cities, to tax all utilities at their saleable value, including franchises, to separate state and local taxes, to prohibit the abuse of railroad passes, to substitute a salary for the fee system in compensating county officers, and to allow the use of the initiative and the referendum on questions of public expenditures and franchises. Again the Republican bosses were condemned for the graft and corruption prevailing under their rule and for their attempt to steal the canals. The only important plank not repeated was the pledge of a two-cent railroad fare, which Johnson, in the interest of party harmony, did not press. Two significant new resolutions advocated the direct election of United States senators and permissive municipal ownership of utilities after a referendum vote.[48]

In contrast to 1903 the platform was adopted unanimously, blessed by conservatives as well as radicals. The moderate Pattison was an enthusiastic advocate of home rule and the initiative and referendum. The inclusion of a municipal-ownership plank revealed how far the party had swung in the direction of Johnson's principles. This spirit of harmony prevailed throughout the proceedings; the bitterness toward Johnson was laid aside. The convention chairman, Michael A. Daugherty, his harshest detractor in 1903, introduced him, in Steffens' words, as "the best mayor of the best governed city of the United States," a greeting which produced a great ovation from the delegates. By the end of the convention he had regained much of the prestige he had lost after his defeat two years before. One other event augured well for a harmonious, united party. A letter from John R. McLean announced his resignation from the national committee, thus severing his last tie with the Ohio Democracy.[49]

When the convention disbanded, the *Toledo News-Bee* prophesied: "The time is ripe for a reform revival. The air is humid with the spirit of protest against political and financial corruption." Pattison echoed the same sentiment to Whitlock in a letter that revealed how close the nominee's sympathies were to those of the other reformers:

The old time politician, however able and valuable in ordinary campaigns, will not secure many votes in this one. The

real battle must be fought by men who stand for something and
in whom the people have absolute confidence . . . and a fight
[must] be made in favor of clean politics and honest Government in all public offices, both City and State. We should
stand squarely against Coxism and Bossism and all that they
imply, whether in Cincinnati or Toledo. . . . [50]

Throughout the summer, long before the official campaign
opening, events began to corroborate these surmises. From his
pulpit a Republican preacher flayed Cox as Ohio's political
czar; Republican laymen, prominent in their communities, explained that they intended to bolt the ticket because they were
weary of machine rule. In the northwest counties of the state
the political weather for Herrick was distinctly squally. The
feeling against the Governor was increasing in the Western
Reserve. Early in September Arthur L. Garford, chairman of
the Republican executive committee of Lorain County, sent him
a disheartening survey of the local feeling, which was typical in
the northern part of the state. Oberlin, he reported, was in a
turmoil over the temperance question, and a number of prominent workers were opposing the Governor's re-election because
of his alleged tie with the liquor interests; in industrial Lorain
the foreign voters appeared to be safe, but there was determined
opposition in the businessmen's wards; much the same feeling
existed in Elyria where Herrick was opposed by churchmen for
his attitude on the Brannock local-option bill, by horsemen for
his veto of the bill to legalize betting pools at race tracks, and by
a miscellaneous lot who were tired of "Boss Cox and his dominating influence in the state." Only in the small towns were
the conditions normal. In addition the Republicans were plagued
with financial troubles because a number of former contributors
had refused to respond.[51]

At their campaign opening in Newark on September 23, the
Democrats added heat to the sentiment that was crystallizing.
Pattison condemned Herrick's record, and Johnson spoke on the
text, "Boss or Leader." On the stump Pattison made bossism
and temperance the two issues, his own views being the party
plank on the latter question. At a number of meetings Republican supporters monopolized him; the phrase, "I am a Republican but for you, Mr. Pattison," grew monotonous. Although
no orator, he had a warm smile and a hearty handshake, and

his appeal for nonpartisan support attracted many voters.[52]

For their part the Republicans tried to laugh aside Coxism as an issue, adopting the familar Hanna technique of underscoring the tariff and the threat to prosperity should the Democrats win. Typical was the campaign opening at Bellefontaine on September 23, where Vice-President Charles W. Fairbanks and Senator Foraker, after endorsing Herrick, concentrated on national issues. But as the clamor against bossism grew more insistent the Republican orators could no longer dodge the issue; Dick was forced to defend Cox boldly.[53] On October 21 at Akron, Taft, who had been persuaded to return to Ohio again to campaign for the ticket, once more startled the party leaders by launching into the state situation with a vengeance. In his speech, the main purport of which was to impress his audience with Herrick's integrity and independence of Cox, he made the candid admission: "If I were able . . . to cast my vote in Cincinnati at the coming election, I should vote against the municipal ticket nominated by the Republican organization." He continued with a picture of the strangling effect of Cox's control on party nominations and elections, which drove young independent candidates out of politics. Such a denunciation was wholly unexpected and caught the Republican leadership by surprise. Herrick and Dick were frozen into silence, for Taft's insurgency was anathema to them. Although the Republican press in the northern part of the state praised the Secretary of War's courage in making the attack, his own half brother's newspaper, the *Cincinnati Times-Star,* refused to print or comment on the speech.[54] It was widely believed that Taft was speaking not only for himself but for Roosevelt, and that it was Taft's opening bid for the presidential nomination in 1908.[55]

From that point on the Republicans seemed to grow evasive and to falter, while the Democrats gained strength and confidence. In the final week Pattison made a successful tour through the Republican Western Reserve, and Joseph Folk of Missouri invaded the state for a two-day campaign with major speeches in Cleveland and Cincinnati. At the latter meeting his condemnation of Coxism and his plea for nonpartisanship were supplemented by a letter from Governor Robert M. La Follette of Wisconsin stressing the same issues.[56]

When the voters went to the polls on election day, November

7, the impact of the anti-bossism campaign had taken effect. Pattison won with a plurality of 42,647 out of a total vote of approximately 960,000, carrying fifty-seven of the eighty-eight counties. Cuyahoga and Lucas, Republican in 1903, switched to the Democratic column, Hamilton remained Republican by a narrow margin, Franklin and Montgomery by somewhat larger majorities. Nevertheless, the most surprising shift had occurred in the areas outside the major cities: twenty-five "safe" Republican and five doubtful counties lined up for Pattison. Not in years had Ohio witnessed such a wave of independent voting. It was clear, however, that the disgruntled Republicans in switching their votes only intended to give Herrick and the top leadership a rebuke, for they proceeded to elect the rest of the party's state ticket by majorities of 29,000 to 46,000.[57]

Spokesmen for the losers, wasting few words in apology, confessed that they had been hit by a tidal wave of moral reform. Temperance and bossism, they agreed, had been the decisive issues which wrought the havoc. In the future it would be wise, they concluded, to lend an ear to popular clamor and deal openly with the people. One of the prominent Republican papers, the *Cleveland Leader*, recommended that the present leaders retire in the best interests of the party and let Taft take the helm and introduce the Rooseveltian brand of Republicanism into Ohio.[58]

The upheaval in the state was more than matched in the municipal elections in the big cities. In Cleveland Johnson was returned to office with the largest majority of his career over his opponent, William H. Boyd, once associated with the McKisson machine; also the entire Democratic municipal, county, and legislative tickets were victorious. The Democrats elected mayors in Columbus and Dayton, where anti-bossism and graft had been major questions. The Toledo Independents, who had conducted their campaign on the sole issue of freedom from boss rule, made a clean sweep of the municipal offices and elected eight councilmen, four county officers, a state senator, and two representatives. Whitlock's plurality over his Republican opponent, Robert Finch, was four thousand votes. From Cincinnati, however, came the most astonishing returns: Edward Dempsey and the entire Democratic municipal, county and legislative tickets were elected. This "furious revolt" was attributed to Taft's attack on Cox, Governor Folk's speech denouncing bossism and appealing for a nonpartisan vote, and the work of the Honest Election Committee in fighting fraudulent registrations and policing the voting booths. On election night, when the trend at the polls was obvious, although the tabulations were far from complete, George Cox hoisted the white flag, announcing his retirement from active political life.[59]

To the reformers the redemption of the people from the state and city bosses marked a long step toward the millenium. Johnson jubilantly declared, "The reign of the grafters and boodlers in Ohio is over forever," a statement more remarkable for its optimism than its prescience.[60] Never one to bask in the sunlight of victory, he promptly began to marshal his forces for the coming legislative session, hopeful that his program would be translated from the blueprint stage into a reform edifice.

1. *Cleveland Plain Dealer,* January 13, 1904; *Ohio State Journal* (Columbus), January 13, 1904. Although the Democratic legislators declared they were ignoring the endorsement of John H. Clarke by the state convention, they nevertheless agreed to support him in caucus and cast their twenty-five votes for him (*Ibid.,* January 3, 1904).

2. Hanna's health had been declining since 1899 and was particularly poor during the latter part of 1903; he died on February 15, 1904 (Croly, *Hanna,* 449–51; *Cleveland Plain Dealer,* February 16, 1904). The eulogies of Hanna are summarized in Croly, *Hanna,* 456–58; Johnson's sentiment was stated in Lorenz, *Johnson,* 114.

3. Dick was elected United States senator to fill Hanna's unexpired short term as well as the long term by a full party vote on March 1 (*Cleveland Plain Dealer,* March 2, 1904). A biographical sketch of Dick and a discussion of his relations with Hanna and the other Republican leaders are in *ibid.,* February 21, 23, March 2, 1904, the *Ohio State Journal,* February 17, 21, 25, 1904, and Walters, *Foraker,* 207.

4. The composition of the General Assembly was: Senate, twenty-nine Republicans and four Democrats; House, eighty-eight Republicans and twenty-two Democrats. The senators and representatives from the five largest urban counties were all Republicans. (*Ohio Election Statistics* [1904], 25–27)

5. Governor Herrick in his inaugural address had outlined a legislative program which included revision and recodification of the school laws, a state depository law, the compulsory examination of state banks, improvements in the control of corporations, a revision of the election laws, and better regulation of street railways to protect capital and to secure more efficient service at a reasonable cost (*Cleveland Plain Dealer,* January 5, 12, 1904). The two school plans were reported in *ibid.,* January 9 and February 5, 1904, respectively.

6. The school situation in Cincinnati and Cox's control was reviewed in

articles by Ben F. Allen and W. S. Couch, who conducted special investigations of Cincinnati for the *Cleveland Plain Dealer* in 1904 and 1905 (*ibid.*, February 8, 1904; August 14, 1905). The low tax rate and its effect on the schools is discussed in Max B. May, "Taxation in American Cities: Cincinnati," 158–59. The lobbying activity of the American Book Co. was reported in the *Cleveland Plain Dealer*, February 29, 1904.

7. The course of the bill through the legislature is told in the *Cleveland Plain Dealer*, March 31, April 15, 25, 26, 1904. The text is in 97 O.L. 334 (1904). The plan for school boards for large cities provided for two to seven members elected at large and two to thirty elected by wards.

8. The history of the company, Cox's stock interest in it, and his pressure on the legislators to pass the bill are recounted in an open letter from Harry R. Probasco, an anti-Cox Republican of Cincinnati, to Charles Dick, printed in the *Youngstown Vindicator*, November 2, 1905. Cox's lobbying activity among the legislators was reported in the *Cleveland Plain Dealer*, March 24, 25, 1904, the *Ohio State Journal*, March 25, 1904, and the *Dayton Daily News*, March 24, 1904. It was alleged that Herrick also had stock in the company.

9. The *Cleveland Plain Dealer's* criticism is in the issue for January 16, 1904. The intent of the framers was noted in *ibid.*, March 4, 1904, and the *Toledo News-Bee*, March 6–7, 13, 1904. The pleas against the proposal by Gladden and others were reported in the *Cleveland Plain Dealer*, February 28, March 4, 1904, and the *Ohio State Journal*, March 4, 1904. The vote on the measure was seventy to thirty-seven in the House, fifteen Republicans joining twenty-two Democrats in opposition. These Republicans were from closely contested or normally Democratic counties (*ibid.*, March 11, 1904). The Ricketts Resolution was reported in *ibid.*, March 11, 1904.

10. *Cleveland Plain Dealer*, March 19, April 24, 1904. The text is in 97 O.L. 185 (1904).

11. Johnson's criticism was reported in the *Cleveland Plain Dealer*, April 11, 1904, and in the editorial of the *Toledo News-Bee*, April 9, 1904. See also the *Cleveland Plain Dealer*, April 9, 11, 1904. David Eley, a Democrat from Ashland County, introduced a bill to permit municipal ownership of street railways after a referendum vote, which was buried in committee (*ibid.*, April 17, 1904).

12. The juvenile-court legislation was reported in the *Cleveland Plain Dealer*, April 21, 1904, and in Brand Whitlock to Ben Lindsey, June 3, 1907, and Brand Whitlock to William Allen White, April 8, 1908, in Nevins, ed., *The Letters and Journal of Brand Whitlock*, I, 79, 91. The text is in 97 O.L. 561 (1904). The other legislation was reported in the *Cleveland Plain Dealer*, April 23–24, 1904, and the *Ohio State Journal*, April 26, 1904. The texts are in 97 O.L. 516, 107, 535 (1904), respectively.

13. *Cleveland Plain Dealer*, April 26, 1904. The texts are in 97 O.L. 398 and 324 (1904), respectively.

14. The Republican was Representative Elijah W. Hill, who was quoted in the *Cleveland Plain Dealer*, February 1, 1906. The praise for the independence of the legislators from the bosses came from the *Toledo News-Bee*, April 26, 1904. *The Dayton Daily News*, however, thought that it was "the most reckless and incapable legislative body that ever assembled in Columbus." *Ibid.*, April 26, 1904. Newton D. Baker, who as Cleveland's city solicitor had to struggle to interpret the bills passed, also complained that the

Assembly had left a "heritage of bad legislation and confusion."—N. D. Baker to Frederic C. Howe, May 6, 1904, Baker Papers, CCH.

15. The quotation is from the *Ohio State Journal*, May 19, 1904. That paper gave the most detailed report of the convention (issues for May 17–19, 1904). The nominees for state offices were: Lewis G. Laylin, secretary of state; Horace Ankeny, dairy and food commissioner; Richard B. Crawford, member of the board of public works; and William T. Spear, justice of the supreme court.

16. The quotation is from the *Cleveland Plain Dealer*, May 17, 1904. The deal between Salen and Bernard on seating contested delegations, the adoption of the platform, and the selection of the delegates-at-large were reported in *ibid.*, May 24–26, 1904, and the *Ohio State Journal*, May 25–26, 1904. The nominees for state offices were: Alfred P. Sandles, secretary of state; Quinton M. Gravatte, dairy and food commissioner; W. H. Ferguson, member of the board of public works; and Philip J. Renner, justice of the supreme court.

17. Johnson's role and enthusiastic endorsement of the platform and Bryan's hand in writing it were reported in: *Cleveland Plain Dealer*, July 11–12, 1904; *Toledo News-Bee*, July 6, 1904; Paul W. Glad, *The Trumpet Soundeth: William Jennings Bryan and His Democracy* (Lincoln, Neb., 1960), 156–57; N. D. Baker to William J. Bryan, July 12, 1904, Baker Papers, CCH.

18. *Cleveland Plain Dealer*, November 9–11, 1904; *Ohio State Journal*, November 9–11, 1904. The presidential vote in Ohio was as follows: Theodore Roosevelt (Republican) 600,095; Alton B. Parker (Democrat) 344,674; Silas C. Swallow (Prohibition) 19,339; Eugene V. Debbs (Socialist) 36,260; Charles H. Corregean (Socialist Labor) 2,633; Thomas E. Watson (People's party) 1,392. The vote for secretary of state was: Laylin (Republican) 587,568; Sandles (Democrat) 357,179; Harold K. Rockhill (Prohibition) 19,253; Alfred J. Swing (Socialist) 33,763; John H. T. Juergens (Socialist Labor) 2,534; John E. Allen (People's party) 1,093. (*Report of the Secretary of State of Ohio* [1906], 120.)

19. *Ohio State Journal*, November 9, 1904. Indicative of the attitude of Democratic reformers toward the President was Newton Baker's appraisal: "Roosevelt seems to me to be a very strong courageous man of more genius than any President we have had since Lincoln, and I have profound regret that [he is] . . . so bloodthirsty and truculent that it is unsafe for the country to have him as Chief Executive."—N. D. Baker to J. M. Dabney, September 16, 1904, Baker Papers, CCH.

20. Steffens, "Ohio: A Tale of Two Cities," 293–311. The work of the muckraking magazines is described in C. C. Regier, *The Era of the Muckrakers* (Chapel Hill, N.C., 1932), 49–58, 192.

21. Samples of the reform news printed in the *Cleveland Plain Dealer* are in the issues for April 6–7, July 20, 22, 1904, and November 6, 1905. W. S. Couch's articles appeared in *ibid.*, August 8–September 14, 1905. The largest number of articles was devoted to Toledo, Cincinnati, and Dayton, the most boss-ridden communities. He found petty graft and lax law enforcement but no bossism in Columbus, Canton, and Youngstown. Political conditions, he reported, were healthy in Zanesville, Springfield, and Marietta. Because of Couch's exposés the *Plain Dealer* took credit for starting the campaign against bossism. But this claim is pretentious, for no one event

was responsible for initiating the attack; rather it was the impact of many. (*Ibid.*, November 9, 1905.)

22. The *Toledo News-Bee* and *Times* were purchased on June 1, 1903, the *Columbus Citizen* on July 6, 1904. The League also owned the *Akron Press.* Gladden's influence in the purchase of the *Columbus Citizen* is mentioned in Milton A. McRae, *Forty Years in Newspaperdom* (New York, 1924), 209. The importance of these papers was stressed by Tom L. Johnson to Brand Whitlock, January 2, 1905, Whitlock Papers.

23. Report by W. S. Couch in the *Cleveland Plain Dealer*, August 29, 1905. After his election in 1903 Jones realized the need to do some organizing if his own work was to be carried on, but he thought in terms of founding a five-cent weekly, not in building a precinct organization (S. M. Jones to Charles Ferguson, April 7, 1903, Jones Papers).

24. This analysis of Brown, his three lieutenants, and their methods is drawn from *Cleveland Plain Dealer*, August 30, 1905, from Johnson, *Toledo's Non-Partisan Movement*, 17, 51–53, and from C. S. Van Tassel, "Sam Cohn," in *Toledo Blade*, October 14, 1936. The corrupt methods of the Republican clique were exposed by a grand jury composed of businessmen and called together by Judge Reynolds R. Kinkade to investigate city affairs in 1902. The grand jury indicted the city solicitor, Moses R. Brailey, on bribery charges; Ed Eckert, a claim agent of the traction company, for the attempted bribery of a councilman; two members of the board of revision for soliciting bribes; and an assistant street commissioner for soliciting a bribe. (Johnson, *Toledo's Non-Partisan Movement*, 52–53; *Cleveland Plain Dealer*, May 20, 1902; *Toledo Blade*, May 19, 1902).

25. In 1903 the Republican ring elected their candidates for city solicitor, auditor, vice-mayor, and board of public service. They had thirteen members on the city council to the Democrats' three. (*Toledo Bee*, April 7, 1903). There are many accounts of the Toledo street-railway fight in 1904. The best running account is to be found in the *Toledo News-Bee*, 1904, *passim*. An excellent summary is in Killits, ed., *Toledo and Lucas County*, I, 579–82. The dramatic "petition in boots" is described in Whitlock, *Forty Years of It*, 178–80, and in a report of W. S. Couch in *Cleveland Plain Dealer*, September 3, 1905.

26. The organization of the Independent Voters and the enunciation of their principles and platform are described in: *Cleveland Plain Dealer*, September 3, 1905; Johnson, *Toledo's Non-Partisan Movement*, 19–23, 33–35; Killits, ed., *Toledo and Lucas County*, I, 579–80; *Toledo News-Bee*, August 30, 1904.

27. The campaign and election were reported in the *Toledo News-Bee*, October 16, November 5–6, 1904, and in Johnson, *Toledo's Non-Partisan Movement*, 22–23.

28. This biographical sketch is drawn from the *Toledo News-Bee*, October 14–15, 1913, and from obituaries in the *Toledo Blade* and *Toledo Times*, April 14, 1941.

29. He attacked the anti-Catholic APA, for example, in the *Toledo Bee*, March 23, 1899, and the *Toledo News-Bee*, October 14–15, 1913. His defense of Whitlock against the charges of the ministers is in various news articles and editorials in mayoralty campaigns of 1907, 1909, and 1911 in the *Toledo News-Bee*. His role in the street-railway battle is told in the *Toledo Bee* and the *News-Bee*, 1897–1904, and in Whitlock, *Forty Years of*

It, 132, 176–78. Scripp's opinion of him was reported in the author's interview with Hal DeRan, of Fremont, January 28, 1950.

30. Cochran's political relations with Jones are discussed above in Chap. II, p. 37; Jones's support of Bryan, in Chap. III, p. 61. The editor's support of Jones in 1901 is reported in the *Toledo Bee,* March 16–April 3, 1901, his criticisms of the Mayor in 1903 in an editorial in *ibid.,* March 29, 1903.

31. This analysis of Whitlock's personality and character is drawn from Howe., *The Confessions of a Reformer,* 187–88, and from Newton D. Baker, Introduction to Nevins, ed., *The Letters and Journal of Brand Whitlock,* I, viii–ix, xv–xvi. An appraisal of Whitlock that parallels in most respects the one found here is in Bremner, "The Civic Revival in Ohio: The Artist in Politics: Brand Whitlock," 239–54. A well-written and perceptive biography of Whitlock by the grandson of Samuel M. Jones has recently appeared in various issues of the *Northwest Ohio Quarterly*: Samuel Milton Jones III, "Brand Whitlock," XXXI (1959), 7–37, 94–112, 126–37, 156–69; XXXII (1960), 7–14, 61–78, 117–31, 173–86; XXXIII (1961), 91–104. The claim that Whitlock owed his political success entirely to Cochran was circulated at the end of Whitlock's career as mayor. Cochran himself, after he had fallen out with his former friend, fostered the claim. (N. D. Cochran to Carl Matson, October 16, 1939, in the possession of the author.) However, in 1913, on the eve of Whitlock's retirement, when the *Toledo Blade* made such a charge by implication, Cochran urged the Mayor to make an open statement about their relationship. "The people should know," he concluded, "that you were mayor, as I know you have been mayor all these years. . . ."–N. D. Cochran to Brand Whitlock, October 6, 1913, Whitlock Papers.

32. This sketch of Whitlock's early life is drawn from his autobiography, *Forty Years of It,* 1–69; Nevins, ed., Biographical Introduction to *The Letters and Journal of Brand Whitlock,* I, xxii–xxxvi.

33. Whitlock describes at length his Springfield experiences in *Forty Years of It,* 69–101. Nevins stresses Whitlock's highly impressionable and sympathetic temperament in his Biographical Introduction to *The Letters and Journal of Brand Whitlock,* I, xxix. The remark about Ella Brainerd was made by Newton D. Baker in his Introduction to *ibid.,* I, xx.

34. The Jones-Whitlock friendship and their influence on each other is revealed in Whitlock, *Forty Years of It,* 102–40; Brand Whitlock to S. M. Jones, December 22, 1900, Jones Papers; Nevins, ed., Biographical Introduction to *The Letters and Journal of Brand Whitlock,* I, xxxii–xxxvi.

35. In his autobiography Whitlock confessed that "it has seemed to be my fate, or my weakness, which we too often confuse with fate, to vacillate between an interest in letters and an interest in politics . . . ."–Whitlock, *Forty Years of It,* 86.

36. *Ibid.,* 182–84; *Toledo News-Bee,* October 6, 1905. Cochran at first was prepared to back Robert Finch because of his firm loyalty to the people's side in the traction fight. When Finch refused to desert the Republican party, Cochran swung his support behind Whitlock. (McRae, *Forty Years in Newspaperdom,* 210–211)

37. Stockbridge, "The Biggest Boss of Them All," 616–17.

38. The "craven" apathy of Cincinnati businessmen was remarked upon by Steffens and Wright, as well as W. S. Couch in his report on the Cincinnati situation in the *Cleveland Plain Dealer,* August 24, 1905. The

collusion between Cox and the McLean-Bernard Democrats was reported in *ibid.*, August 8, 24, 1905, the *Toledo News-Bee*, October 16, 1905, and Wright, *Bossism in Cincinnati*, 109–10. The moderation and methods of Cox's rule are described in the report of W. S. Couch in *Cleveland Plain Dealer*, August 15, 16, 1905, and in Zink, *City Bosses in the United States*, 271.

39. This analysis of the factions within the Democratic party is drawn from the report of W. S. Couch in *Cleveland Plain Dealer*, August 22, 1905, and from the author's interview with Herbert S. Bigelow, Setpember 26, 1949. The characterization of Bigelow is based on the author's interviews with four men who knew him: Hal DeRan, January 28, 1950; James M. Cox, June 29, 1949; Edward F. Alexander, September 28, 1949; and Henry P. Boynton, October 3, 1949. The biographical data on Kiefer is taken from Brand Whitlock, "Daniel Kiefer," *American Magazine*, LXXIV (September, 1912), 549–53.

40. The work of the committee of twenty-six in forming the Citizens Municipal party and the defection of the Democratic factions is told in Elliott Pendleton and Others, "Militant Political Work for Better Governed Cities," *Proceedings of the Pittsburgh Conference for Good City Government and the Fourteenth Annual Meeting of the National Municipal League* (1908), 98–99. The election was reported in the *Cincinnati Enquirer*, April 2–4, 7, 1903.

41. The formation of the committee of nine is described in Turner, "The Thing above the Law," 587. The sketch of Pendleton, his methods, and contribution is drawn from *ibid.*, 586–87, from Koch, "An Ohio Warwick," 28–30, and from Wright, *Bossism in Cincinnati*, 139–40. His standing with the Vine Street radicals was stated by Bigelow in an interview with the author, September 26, 1949.

42. The indifference of the Cincinnati press to bossism was stressed by W. S. Couch in his special report on Cincinnati in the *Cleveland Plain Dealer*, August 22, 1905. The statements about the attitude of the *Cincinnati Times-Star* are based on Turner, "The Thing above the Law," 586, and Wright, *Bossism in Cincinnati*, 99; those on the *Cincinnati Enquirer* are the result of a check of its files from 1901 to 1905. The disagreement between McRae and Scripps and the quotation of the latter is taken from Negley D. Cochran, *E. W. Scripps* (New York, 1933), 56–57. The contribution of the *Cincinnati Post* to the 1905 campaign is to be seen in the issues for September–October, 1905. The work of Harper and the Honest Election Committee is reported in Cochran, *Scripps*, 63, and in McRae, *Forty Years of Newspaperdom*, 275–76. Among the other members of the Honest Election Committee were Elliott Pendleton, Henry T. Hunt, John Weld Peck, Graham P. Hunt, and Lewis C. Black, a Republican attorney (author's interview with Graham P. Hunt, September 28, 1949).

43. The Steffens article was published in *McClure's Magazine*, XXV (July, 1905), 293–311. Wright's book was published in Cincinnati.

44. Cox's remarks were reported in the *Cleveland Plain Dealer*, June 24, 1905, Fleischman's in the *Cincinnati Enquirer*, June 24, 1905.

45. *Cincinnati Enquirer*, September 30, 1905; *Cleveland Plain Dealer*, September 30, 1905. Dempsey's background was reported in the *Cincinnati Post*, October 23, 1903.

46. *Ohio State Journal*, May 24–26, 1905; Walters, *Foraker*, 210. The

other officers nominated were: W. S. McKinnon, state treasurer; Wade Ellis, attorney-general; William Kirtley, member of the board of public works; Edwin D. Jones, school commissioner; William Z. Davis, justice of the supreme court.

47. The characterization of Pattison is drawn from Powell, ed., *The Democratic Party of the State of Ohio*, I, 404–5, 410–12, and from the *Cleveland Plain Dealer*, August 20, 1905, and *Toledo News-Bee*, June 27, 1905. The characterization of Welty is from *ibid.*, June 27, 1905. Johnson's support of Whitlock is discussed in the *Ohio State Journal*, June 28, 1905; the convention proceedings, including the platform, are covered in *ibid.*, June 28–29, 1905. The nominees for other offices were: Lewis B. Houck, lieutenant-governor; Hugh T. Mathers, justice of the supreme court: James A. Rice, attorney-general; Charles E. Mason, state treasurer; Patrick McGovern, member of the board of public works.

48. *Cleveland Plain Dealer*, June 28–29, 1905. Other planks promised repeal of the school code, demanded better treatment of agricultural interests, careful inspection of state and private banks, and legislation by Congress to prohibit railroad rebates and secret contracts, and endorsed the state canal system and the constitutional amendments to exempt state and local bonds from taxation and to separate municipal and state elections.

49. The spirit of harmony and friendly treatment of Johnson is stressed in *ibid.*, June 28–29, 1905; McLean's letter was printed in the *Ohio State Journal*, June 29, 1905.

50. The *Toledo News-Bee* editorial appeared in the issue for June 27, 1905, the Pattison quotation in John M. Pattison to Brand Whitlock, July 6, 1905, Whitlock Papers.

51. The Democratic papers in northwest Ohio relished publishing the indications of Republican bickering; for example, *Cleveland Plain Dealer*, August 3, 9, 17, 19, 21–22, 26, September 4–5, 9, 18, 1905; *Toledo News-Bee*, September 18, 23, 28, 30, 1905. Garford's résumé of conditions in Lorain County is contained in A. L. Garford to Myron T. Herrick, September 7, 1905, in the Arthur L. Garford Papers (MSS in the Ohio Historical Society, Columbus [hereafter referred to as Garford Papers]). In the year of Herrick's election the voters approved a constitutional amendment granting the governor a veto power for the first time in Ohio history. For constitutional reasons he vetoed the Brannock liquor bill which would have established local option in residential areas in cities, and he refused to allow the pool-betting bill because he did not wish to antagonize the church people further.

52. *Cleveland Plain Dealer*, September 24, 28, November 5, 1905; Powell, ed., *The Democratic Party of the State of Ohio*, I, 407–8.

53. *Cleveland Plain Dealer*, September 18, 24, 1905.

54. Taft's speech was reported in the Republican *Ohio State Journal* and *Cleveland Leader*, October 23, 1905, and widely heralded in the Democratic press: *Cleveland Plain Dealer*, October 22, 1905; *Youngstown Vindicator* and *Toledo News-Bee*, October 22–23, 1905. The *Cincinnati Post* played upon the generally accepted rumor that Boss Cox had imposed silence upon the publisher of the *Cincinnati Times-Star* by printing one of Homer Davenport's most famous cartoons. It depicted the Boss, a whip in one hand, Taft's speech in the other, forcing the text down the throat of a reluctant

billy goat, labed "C. P. Taft." The caption read, "Now Eat Them Words."
—*Ibid.*, October 23, 1905.

55. Roosevelt had been informed by Lincoln Steffens that there was an alliance between Herrick and Cox and that the Governor, therefore, did not deserve any administration support (Lincoln Steffens to Theodore Roosevelt, August 7, 1905, in Winter and Hicks, ed., *The Letters of Lincoln Steffens,* I, 169–70). Nevertheless, the President believed otherwise and urged Taft to clear Herrick's name and prove his independenc of Cox. This Taft willingly did, but his support of Herrick was almost obliterated by his sensational denunciation of the Cincinnati boss. It is worth noting that Taft's insurgency against bossism was short-lived; soon he himself was accepting Cox's support. (Henry F. Pringle, *The Life and Times of William Howard Taft* [2 vols.; New York, 1939], I, 268–69)

56. Folk's campaign was reported in the *Cleveland Plain Dealer,* November 5, 1905, La Follette's letter in *ibid.*, November 3, 1905.

57. The vote for governor was as follows: Pattison (Democrat) 473,264, Herrick (Republican) 430,617, Isaac Cowen (Socialist) 17,795, Aaron S. Watkins (Prohibition) 13,061, John E. Steiger (Socialist Labor) 1,808 (*Report of the Secretary of State of Ohio* [1906], 129–35). The approximate pluralities of the Republican officers elected were: Andrew L. Harris, lieutenant-governor, 29,200; W. S. McKinnon, treasurer of state, 44,000; Wade Ellis, attorney-general, 42,500; William Z. Davis, justice of the supreme court, 44,700; William Kirtley, member of the board of public works, 46,600 (*Ohio Election Statistics* [1905], 13–22).

58. *Cleveland Leader,* November 9, 11, 1905. Herrick and Harding both emphasized the reform wave (*Cleveland Plain Dealer,* November 8, 10, 1905; *Ohio State Journal,* November 9, 1905).

59. Johnson's victory in Cleveland was reported in the *Cleveland Plain Dealer,* November 8–11, 1905. The successful candidate in Columbus was DeWitt C. Badger, in Dayton, Charles A. Snyder (*Ohio State Journal,* November 8–12, 1905; *Dayton Daily News,* October 24, November 1–6, 8, 1905; *Cleveland Plain Dealer,* August 26, 28, 1905). The campaign and triumph of the Independents in Toledo were described in the *Toledo News-Bee,* October 23, 26, November 4, 8, 1905. The defeat of Cox and his political retirement were reported in the *Cincinnati Enquirer,* October 24, 29, November 8–9, 1905, and the *Cincinnati Post,* November 8–9, 1905. The *Enquirer* reminded its readers that this was Cox's second announced retirement from politics, (*Cincinnati Enquirer,* November 8, 1905).

60. Quoted in the *Cleveland Plain Dealer,* November 8, 1905.

CHAPTER EIGHT

REFORM IN THE BALANCE
1906■1908

IN THE WEEKS following the election of 1905 the hopes of the reformers ran high that victory for their principles was close at hand. They interpreted the election results not merely as a repudiation of bossism but as a mandate for their program. Their optimism was further strengthened by the backing of the powerful Scripps-McRae papers and by the leadership which the dynamic Tom Johnson spontaneously supplied. Accompanied by five of the Cuyahoga County legislators-elect, the Cleveland mayor was in Cincinnati on November 11, 1905, conferring with John Pattison, Edward Dempsey, and the Democratic delegation from Hamilton County to map out a legislative program for the approaching session. They agreed to amend the Municipal Code, to further home rule, and to improve the election laws. Soon the irrepressible Johnson was soliciting the co-operation of two more sympathetic colleagues, Mayors-elect Brand Whitlock of Toledo and DeWitt Badger of Columbus, in promoting legislation to free the cities.[1]

The outcome of their discussions was a call to all the mayors-elect in Ohio to meet in Cleveland on December 4. Presided over by Johnson, the conference was addressed by Dempsey, who asked for a legislative investigation of Cincinnati, and by Whitlock, who emphasized the importance of city problems and the need for mayors to represent the common people of their cities before the legislature because no one else would. Before adjournment the Association of Mayors of Ohio Municipalities was formed, and a committee of the new association appointed, including Johnson, Whitlock, and Dempsey, to draft changes to the Municipal Code. Lincoln Steffens, arriving in Cleveland the next day, spoke of the historical significance of the mayors' organization as "an object lesson for the great cities and states all over the union." [2] In addition to mobilizing the mayors, Johnson rented quarters in Columbus to be able to give continuous direction to the reform battle throughout the legislative session.

Whatever Governor Pattison may have felt about Johnson's activities, he showed no sign of being offended. His own precarious health prevented any like display of energy. Sick with a mortal illness when he reached Columbus, he found it a heavy effort even to deliver his inaugural address. Whitlock, who saw him a day or so after the ceremonies, wrote Johnson, "There was really something pathetic in his weakness, something more pathetic too in the pleasure he evinced when I told him that you and I had discussed his message and decided that there were more things in it that we could approve than there had been in any other governor's message that we had ever read. Of course, I should have exempted Altgeld's messages from this statement, but I did not." [3] What, no doubt, failed to appeal to them was Pattison's insistence on greater law enforcement, a stricter observance of Sunday laws and of a Christian Sabbath, and a declaration of war on the liquor interests. But what they did applaud was his enthusiastic endorsement of the principal planks Johnson had written in the platform: home rule, tax reform, a county-salary law, legislation eliminating the abuses of railroad passes, and changes in the election laws. The moderate Pattison, they concluded, was closer to their camp than to any other. [4]

Although the reformers had a friend in the chief executive's office for the first time, they still had to face an uncertain legislature. The Senate was split, eighteen Democrats to eighteen Republicans, the thirty-seventh member, a Toledo Independent, holding the balance of power. In the House the Republicans held sixty-two seats, the Democrats fifty-seven, and the Toledo Independents two. Furthermore, many of the Democrats were apathetic toward the platform, interested solely in dispensing favors and patronage. The only members who could be counted upon to push reforms were the Cuyahoga and Hamilton County delegates and the Toledo Independents.[5]

With the vote of the Toledo Independent Sylvester Lamb the radicals fared well in the organization of the Senate. James M. Williams of Cleveland was elected president pro tempore; Fred Howe was appointed chairman of the committee on committees and succeeded in packing the important standing committees with friends of reform. In the Republican-dominated House, however, the outcome was the reverse. The majority party elected all the officers and committee chairmen and practically ignored the Hamilton and Cuyahoga delegates in assignments to important committees; none of them were placed on the committee on fees and salaries and only one, John N. Stockwell of Cleveland, on the municipal affairs committee. Although smarting from defeat, the Democrats were somewhat solaced by the revolt of certain independent Republicans against being bound by a party caucus, the system which had prevailed in the previous two sessions. It gave promise that the bosses would not be pulling the legislative strings.[6]

The primary interest of Johnson and his group lay in an attempt to amend the Municipal Code to simplify urban government and increase home rule. At the outset the prospect seemed hopeful. Not only had Pattison asked for such legislation in his inaugural, but the committee appointed by the Association of Mayors had prepared a bill incorporating the desired changes. Moreover, Attorney-General Wade Ellis, the author of the code of 1902, had approved of the revisions with the exception of the municipal-ownership clause. On January 24, Louis H. Paine, a Toledo Republican, introduced the bill in the House. It incorporated major changes; for example, the replacement of the boards of public works and public safety by single directors, and the appointment of the new directors as well as the city solicitor by the mayor; the extension of the merit system to all departments; the restoration of the former city tax commissions selected by the mayor; the grant of power to municipalities to own and operate all utilities; and provisions to strip away the legal red tape in granting street-railway franchises to new companies. The last recommendation was also incorporated in two separate bills, introduced by Pierce D. Metzger and John Stockwell, both of Cleveland, as a kind of double insurance.[7]

The first to emerge from committee was the Metzger bill to permit a popular referendum on street-railway franchises. Johnson was encouraged that the committee had recommended its passage. But the hearings and debate in the House dampened his initial enthusiasm. The measure galvanized the street-railway lobby into action. The more it worked on the members, the less hope there was for adoption of any Johnson proposals. The bill was defeated, and a month later Stockwell's companion measure to liberalize the law on street-railway franchises was voted down.[8] The Paine bill to amend the Municipal Code was stripped in committee of all the features Johnson particularly wanted. He and the other reformers withdrew their support from this truncated version, and it was allowed to die on the calendar.[9]

The voting on these measures tended to follow a rural-urban pattern. The members from the small rural counties, whether Republican or Democratic, voted against, while the delegations from Lucas, Cuyahoga, and Hamilton counties were almost solidly in favor. However, on the Stockwell bill, although the rural Democrats remained in opposition, three independent Republicans from non-urban counties in the Western Reserve had crossed over to vote in the affirmative.[10] This division is illuminating, for it reveals that support for, as well as opposition to, reform had crossed party lines. Some Republicans defied their leaders by endorsing reform, while some of the Democrats defied Johnson by opposing change.

Second in importance to municipal legislation in the eyes of reformers were changes in the tax structure. In this they achieved somewhat more, successfully passing one of their platform commitments, repeal of the inheritance tax. They objected to this levy because the income received from this source removed the pressure to increase the tax on other items such as utility franchises and railroad properties, which to them were the glaring evils to be corrected. Even this action was almost upset in the Senate by Howe and John Harper of Cincinnati, who, defiant of the party platform and caucus, opposed repeal as a matter of conscience. Threatened with retaliation against every measure he favored, Howe agreed to reconsider his position and voted for the bill on final passage.[11] He could not afford to prejudice his colleagues in advance against a proposal of primary interest to him, which he was then preparing.

Howe's measure, introduced February 14, proposed a levy of six mills on the franchise value of all quasi-public utilities, including railroads, to be determined by deducting the assessed amount of their tangible property from the market price of their stocks and bonds. Howe estimated that it would yield $3,500,000 annually and relieve the counties of raising any taxes for state purposes, thus fulfilling a second part of the Democratic program, the separation of state and local taxes. It was no secret that Johnson was the real author of the measure. Jokingly, he declared that it should be entitled, "bill to raise political h——l in Ohio." That much it did accomplish. The corporation lobby, however, was too powerful and successfully fended off any action in the Senate. Since the bill treated franchises as a form of property and sought to tax them at a rate below the state levy on other property, it probably would have been declared unconstitutional by the courts. A more realistic measure was presented by Senator Francis M. Vanover, a Wayne County Democrat, who proposed to extend the unit rule of the Nichols Law to all public utilities. This, too, shared the fate of Howe's bill.[12]

Although the Johnson men failed to tax the franchise privileges enjoyed by railroads, they did score one major triumph over the carriers. Early in the session the perennial bills for a two-cent-per-mile passenger fare were submitted. Always before they had been treated as a joke, but this year there seemed to be a spontaneous demand for such a measure. This was a curious reversal of opinion in view of the opposition to such a plank in the Democratic convention and the silence of both party platforms on the issue. On February 6, John R. Freiner, a Republican from Vinton County, presented his bill for a second reading in the House. He began, "We have all heard enough about this . . .," and before he could proceed, there was a roar of "Agreed, agreed." Making a megaphone of his hands, he shouted, "Well then vote, vote." Cries answered, "Call the roll, call the roll." Attempts to add amendments were shouted down. When the vote was announced of 107 yeas and 1 nay, cheers rang from the gallery. Two days later the Senate, which had already passed one such bill, adopted the House version unanimously. It was rushed to the governor, who signed it in forty minutes after its passage. This was the first two-cent-fare law adopted by any state, and it remained on the books until 1917.[13]

There are several reasons why this legislation went through with such a flourish. It was adopted early in the session before bickerings over other bills and patronage had created bitter feelings. Secondly, the lobbyists of the four largest railroads had ceased fighting because their companies had voluntarily refused free passes to the legislators, and there was nothing to trade. Moreover, the companies preferred to save their fire for the more dangerous threat of increased taxes. Finally, this fare was only an extension of the rate they had already adopted in selling mileage books.[14]

A second measure affecting railroads was introduced by a Wayne County Democrat, Edwin S. Wertz, to establish a state commission to regulate freight rates. In this reform Ohio was no leader; it was merely catching up with a trend initiated by more advanced states and by the federal government. The debate then raging over the Hepburn bill in the halls of Congress touched off widespread public interest in the need for firmer regulation of railroads to prevent such abuses as rebates and other secret agreements. Ohio had been particularly backward, never having gone beyond the creation in 1867 of a commissioner of railroads and telegraph with limited supervisory powers. The new bill, drafted at a conference of representatives of the major railroads and shippers, provided for a three-man commission with powers similar to those of the Interstate Commerce Commission as amended by the Hepburn Act. Since it satisfied all the interests that would be affected, the legislature passed the measure with little opposition.[15]

The reformers were only mildly interested in this legislation. Johnson had little faith that a governmental body could control the vast railroad monopolies in the public interest. He adhered to the remedies advanced by Henry George: taxation of their franchise values to recover the unearned increment for the public to whom it rightfully belonged, and the restoration of competition among the carriers by state ownership of the roadbed and free use of the tracks to all owners of rolling stock. Such changes, he believed, would destroy the evils of rebates and other forms of rate discrimination.[16]

What concerned the Johnson wing more than the Wertz bill itself was an amendment to abolish free passes that Howe attached to it in the Senate. This reform had long been one of their platform planks, and they hoped it would carry as a rider. The Senate accepted the amendment, but in the House, Democrats joined Republicans in killing it; only twenty-seven members of the lower chamber voted to punish an official for accepting what the railroads were no longer allowed to offer by a self-denying agreement.[17] Yet incongruous as this seems the Johnson followers were hardly more consistent. They demanded government action to prescribe a ceiling on passenger fares and to punish state officials who accepted passes. At the same time they were indifferent, though not hostile, to the regulating of freight rates by a public commission and the outlawing of rebates by statute. Their point of view indicates a naïveté in economic thinking of which they were not generally guilty.

The one other important victory of the reformers, in addition to the two-cent-fare law, was the passage of a county-salary act which had long been agitated for. Under the existing fee system the auditors in the large counties were clearing a net of forty to fifty thousand dollars after expenses, and the treasurers as much as thirty thousand—compensation far out of proportion to their duties or to the pay of other public officials. Johnson had been largely instrumental in placing the demand for this reform in the Democratic platform; Governor Pattison had also made a strong plea for it in his inaugural address. Three salary bills were introduced, all by Republicans. In opposition was a powerful lobby of county officers, past and present, including Lewis Bernard and Charles Salen. Despite their wiles salary legislation was enacted, providing for a sliding scale of payments with a maximum of six thousand dollars for officers in the most populous counties. Three conditions aided its passage: the popular appeal of salary reductions as an economy measure; the persistent clamor of the metropolitan press for the reform, regardless of political affiliations; and the division among the county officials. The new law actually raised the pay of most of the rural officials; it was only those from Cuyahoga, Hamilton, and a few other counties, who were adversely affected.[18] In addition, the legislature abolished one of the two state oil inspectorships, very lucrative posts under the fee system, and set a salary of $3,500 for the other.[19]

On the remainder of their legislative program the reformers did not score very well. Howe's bill to introduce the merit system in the state and Stockwell's proposal to adopt the Oregon Plan for the direct election of United States senators were buried in committee.[20] A constitutional amendment to institute the initiative and referendum passed the Senate but was ignored in the House.[21] A few minor electoral reforms were approved: a law to prohibit certain abuses imperiling the purity of elections; repeal of the Dana Law, which had prohibited the name of a candidate from appearing in more than one place on the ballot; Howe's bill to keep the Cincinnati and Cleveland polls open until 5:30 P.M.; and an act to make the ballot for school board candidates nonpartisan.[22] On the other hand, a bill to grant the mayor instead of the secretary of state the power to appoint municipal election boards, which Johnson wanted, failed to reach the floor, and mandatory direct-primary legislation was defeated.[23]

In the appraisals of this session there was no unanimity. The conservative *Cincinnati Enquirer* called it a failure, the independent Republican *Ohio State Journal* declared it a success. Both the *Cleveland Plain Dealer* and the *Toledo News-Bee* commended the legislators for their independence and backbone, for being more truly representative of the people than any of their recent predecessors. But Johnson and the other reformers were disappointed at the number of issues left unresolved.[24]

The most distressing feature of the session was the openness with which the lobbyists operated. In previous ones they did not have to work openly in Columbus because the deals had been made at election time and the stern Republican caucus rules kept party legislators in line. But in this legislature the lobby was everywhere in evidence. It was to the credit of the legislators that they had passed the two-cent-fare law and the county-salary law in the face of the lobbyists' opposition. However, the combined efforts of legislative agents representing the railroads and other utilities had prevented any tax increase or legislation to aid the cities. The one advantage of the open lobby was to throw the spotlight on weak members and expose political maneuvers which hitherto had been conducted in Washington, Cleveland, or Cincinnati.[25]

One of the most significant contributions of this legislative session to the political enlightenment of the state remains to be considered: the investigation of Cincinnati and Hamilton

County. Such an inquiry had been demanded by Mayor Dempsey immediately following his election. An appropriate resolution, drafted by the Hamilton County delegation, was introduced in the House on January 11; the Republicans, though recognizing it as a hot potato, voted unanimously in conference to support it; and on the last day of the month it passed with only five members dissenting. An amendment to extend the scope of the investigation to Cuyahoga County was defeated on the floor. The most eloquent speaker in behalf of the original resolution was Elijah W. Hill, Republican from Columbiana County. He argued that the amendment to include Cuyahoga was insincere. "Republican that I am," he continued, "I freely admit that Cleveland is a magnificent city, well governed and with its people satisfied. At its head is a mayor, who is not a gangster, but a man working for the interests of the people he serves. How different the picture of Cincinnati. We must and will have an investigation that strikes deep into the roots of the Cox system." [26]

The resolution called for a bipartisan committee of six, half to be appointed by the speaker from the House, half by the lieutenant-governor from the Senate. Since both the appointing officers were Republicans, the Democrats in the upper chamber balked at this arrangement, fearful lest a feebly constituted committee be selected, more interested in clearing Cox than in conducting a thorough investigation. This body, therefore, killed the House resolution and named a five-man committee from its own membership, three Democrats and two Republicans, to conduct the probe. [27]

At the first day's hearings on February 23 the Senate committee, called the Drake committee after its chairman, uncovered evidence that placed it in the political limelight. The testimony revealed that Rudolph Hynicka, when treasurer of Hamilton County, had pocketed thirty thousand dollars in interest on public funds from banks favored as depositories. Confronted with the facts, both Hynicka and the bankers admitted them, claiming in extenuation that they had been merely following custom. Two of the banks involved were the Cincinnati Trust Company, of which Cox was president, and the Market National Bank, in which former Mayor Fleischman had a large interest. As the committee pursued its hearings, it continued to make

182

startling disclosures. Graft and bribery were discovered in the sale of private turnpikes to the county and in the construction of bridges. The committee found that the bonding of public officials and the insuring of property were monopolized by the county officers. It unearthed evidence that Cox had tampered with justice by trying to persuade certain judges to reverse the judgment of a lower court against the engineering firm of Lane and Bodley in a suit in which the city was the plaintiff.[28]

Late in March, County Prosecutor Hiram Rulison, a Cox appointee, yielding to popular clamor, called together a grand jury to investigate the misappropriation of funds by the county treasurers revealed by the Drake committee. Leading bankers and Boss Cox himself were arraigned before the jurors, but no bills of indictment were drawn. The jury argued that the wrongdoing was "technical," a custom followed in every county in the state by Democrats as well as Republicans, and considered it sufficient that three former county treasurers had returned over two hundred thousand dollars of their illegal funds. Although some applauded this action, others spoke contemptuously of it as the "whitewash in Cincinnati."[29]

Meanwhile, foes of the investigation had not been idle. A suit was instituted to test the constitutionality of the Drake committee and tried before the Hamilton County Circuit Court, which held that the body was illegal because its functions involved a usurpation of judicial power. Although the committee tried to continue its hearings for a few days in defiance of the court, it was forced to adjourn on April 26.[30] This initial investigation was important on three counts: it led to the recovery by the county of huge sums illegally pocketed by the county treasurers; it forced the legislature to pass a compulsory county depository law;[31] and it unveiled the connection between Cox and respectable businessmen. Yet it failed in its major objective of arousing the Cincinnatians to drive from office the remaining Cox henchmen who had survived the Democratic landslide of the preceding November. When the Ohio Supreme Court confirmed the opinion of the circuit judges, Senator Thomas P. Schmidt, a member of the Drake committee, accurately prophesied that "the decision really means the rejuvenation of the Cox gang." The people, he felt, were in a comatose state, still unaware of the seriousness of conditions.[32]

If the local leaders failed to keep these disclosures alive in Cincinnati, other Democrats did their best to make political capital of them elsewhere. The battle cry at the party's state convention, which met August 21, 1906, was "Down with bossism and machine politics." Platform resolutions praised the Senate for the investigation and flayed the bosses. Johnson sought to apply the lesson to his party and free the Democratic state organization from the control of professional politicians.[33]

The leader of the latter group was Harvey C. Garber, who was an able organizer and political manipulator but devoid of principle. An admirer and student of Napoleon, he was accused by his enemies of trying to emulate the Corsican in promoting his own personal power through opportunistic tactics. He had identified himself with the left-wing reformers in the party by backing Bryan in 1896 and Johnson in 1902–3. But he had joined them, not because he was committed to their principles, but because he believed they were vote pullers. Garber had straddled on the liquor question, voting for or against the wets as the political situation demanded.[34] In 1904 he had been re-elected to Congress, the only Democrat elected from Ohio, and had managed Pattison's campaign in 1905. Throughout these years he had also served as the legislative agent for the Central Union Telephone Company, a Bell subsidiary. He had used his political influence to serve the business interests of his client after the fashion of George Cox and Walter Brown. Such lobbying activities had discredited him in the eyes of the Johnson reformers. At the time of the state convention in 1906, however, Garber's prestige was high, and he and his allies had won control of the state central and executive committees, defeating the Johnson faction.[35]

Nevertheless, there was no attempt to shackle the Cleveland mayor completely. The credentials committee seated the Dempsey-Johnson partisans from Cincinnati, who were opposed by Bernard delegates. Herbert Bigelow, Newton Baker, and Johnson were elected to the resolutions committee and given great latitude in drafting the platform. Those proposals recommended in 1905 and not adopted in the past legislative session were again demanded. Bryan was endorsed for President in 1908. The only fight occurred over the temperance question, which was becoming increasingly prominent in Ohio politics. Johnson, who looked upon it as a distraction from more fundamental issues, opposed any specific recommendation. On the other hand, the rural members, led by William L. Finley, a leading ally of Garber, demanded a strong temperance plank endorsing county local option and a high saloon-license tax. Such a resolution was voted down in the committee and on the convention floor; the Johnson view prevailed. When the conclave adjourned, the Cleveland mayor was well satisfied with the proceedings. Garber, he declared, had not controlled the nomination of state officers, and the platform was "aggressive and progressive," containing all that he wanted and nothing to which he could object.[36]

Within the Republican ranks, a few office-holders had taken heed of the moral upheaval of the preceding November and of the disclosures of Coxism at work in Cincinnati. Their leader was Theodore E. Burton, seven times congressman from Cleveland. They were demanding an end to machine rule in the state—specifically the end of the control of the state organization by Senators Foraker and Dick, who were working in an uneasy alliance after the defeat of Herrick and Cox. The crux of Burton's plan was to discredit the senators by emphasizing the hostility between them and Theodore Roosevelt, and to insist that their leadership be repudiated at home in order to gain favor with the popular President. Unfortunately Burton who was scholarly and without human warmth lacked the fire to rally others to revolt. At the Republican state convention he was beaten; Foraker and Dick with the assistance of Walter Brown and George Cox, who could still control their county delegations, won a majority of the state central committee, which promptly elected the senator from Akron chairman again. To Burton's further dismay the convention cordially endorsed both Roosevelt and the two Ohio senators in the platform, a document that gave other evidence of equivocation.[37]

The *Ohio State Journal*, critical of the Foraker-Dick leadership, declared that the petty politicians, more eager for office than for the good of the party, had rushed to the defense of the machine at the convention, but that the people would repudiate them.[38] This burst of moral indignation, however, proved a poor prophecy. The Republican independent voters, forgetful of their apostasy in 1905, returned to the fold and helped to elect Carmi A. Thompson secretary of state by a plurality of 56,390 over his Democratic rival, Samuel A. Hoskins. The victorious party carried all the other state offices and seventeen of the twenty-one congressional seats. In the rural districts the Democrats ran behind the vote for Governor Pattison, though they did almost as well as the other officers on the party's ticket in 1905. They held Cuyahoga County but only by a substantially reduced margin. Republican strength was restored in Lucas County, where both the Democratic state ticket and the Independent Voters' slate suffered defeat. In Franklin and Montgomery counties the Republicans triumphed again. The heaviest blow to reform hopes, however, was in Hamilton County, where the Grand Old Party elected its entire ticket: state and county officers, congressmen, and judges.[39] If the state results were an endorsement of Dick and Foraker, as the press contended, the victory in Hamilton County was by the same token a reacceptance of Cox.

This remarkable reversal within a year's time was in large measure the result of dissension among those who had supported Dempsey in 1905. There were many jarring elements to crack his administration apart. Reform Republicans whose votes had brought the Mayor victory wanted all partisanship eliminated from government, while Democrats besieged him to turn the Republicans out and install loyal party men. He was hounded, on the one hand, by people who had fought Cox on the saloon issue alone and wanted the lid clamped down tight, and on the other, by people who believed Cincinnati was entitled to a Continental Sunday. To get along he had to compromise, incurring the disfavor of extremists on both sides. He made partisan appointments but did his best to select good men. He enforced the midnight-closing law, destroyed public gambling places and slot machines, and refused to renew the licenses of notorious dancing halls.[40]

His administration did succeed in instilling a fresh vigor in the management of municipal affairs and in reminding the people that the city government could be an effective instrument in promoting the public welfare. The water works, begun under Gustav Tafel, were completed and a filtration plant installed, practically eliminating typhoid fever. Other health measures included a crusade against impure milk, the construction of a new hospital, the exposure of foul and disease-ridden tenements and the beginning of their elimination by new ordinances requiring proper air space and sanitation. The city was made a more attractive place in which to live by other changes, including the inauguration of a comprehensive park program, the paving and cleaning of streets, and the introduction of natural gas. The schools were improved, a concession of free transfers was wrung from the street-railway company, and a bureau of municipal research was established.[41]

Impressive as these improvements were, the Dempsey administration still failed to clean its own house. One of the newly elected officials excited derision by appealing to the notorious councilman, Mike Mullen, to sponsor legislation to increase the emoluments of his office. The taint of corruption besmirched the water-works project. The police force, often the citizen's only contact with his government, remained hostile to the new administration.[42]

Dempsey himself lacked the aggressiveness, the ideological commitment, and the vision to be the type of crusader the situation demanded. One of his close political advisers, the single taxer Daniel Kiefer, wrote to Whitlock that "he [Dempsey] is utterly dense to economic understanding. Barring that, there is no better man in public life, —better in that he has an appreciation of the rottenness of things and the need for political betterment; but the possibility of betterment through a changed order that would follow the making of our healthy minority into a majority, is as yet beyond his understanding."[43]

By the fall of 1907 Dempsey was under a heavy barrage from former partisans. Conservatives were vexed that his political confidants were Kiefer, Bigelow, and a third single taxer, Fenton Lawson, whom they derisively described as a "clique of half socialists, half reformers." Another group was distressed by the mayor's appointments and even accused him of nepotism.[44] On October first the Democrats held their city convention, renominating Dempsey for mayor, Frank L. Pfaff for vice-mayor, as well as a number of other incumbents. But nine of the nominees, among them Pfaff, sent in their resignations. An effort was made by independent Republicans and Democrats to induce Dempsey to withdraw. When this failed, a committee of fifty of them, including Elliott Pendleton and other former Dempsey supporters, met to name a City Party ticket, which Pfaff was persuaded to head. Dominated by businessmen, the new party adopted the slogan, "A dollar's worth of government for every dollar's worth of taxes," and condemned the bosses of both parties. The *Cincinnati Post* swung its editorial batteries behind the new party.[45]

The Republican machine nominated the respectable Leopold Markbreit, editor of the *Volksblatt* and city water commissioner. They had the advantage of any party out of power, namely, to attack the mistakes of those in office. Still the split among the opposition was their strongest asset.[46] When the votes were counted, the Republican candidates had won by majorities of nine to twelve thousand over the combined vote of the Democratic and City Party opponents. Cox greeted the returns as the "greatest victory for Republicanism ever known in Cincinnati." The yoke of the boss was once again around the city's neck.[47]

Fortunately for the hopes of reformers, Cincinnati's election results were not symptomatic of conditions everywhere else. In Toledo, Brand Whitlock, who had entered upon his mayoralty duties with little knowledge of municipal government and no great zest for his job, had quickly responded to the demands of his office and had won the confidence of the people. He came to share Fred Howe's belief that the city was the hope of democracy and that the failure of municipal institutions was not caused by too much democracy but by too little. An ardent admirer of Johnson, even becoming a single taxer, Whitlock leaned heavily on the Cleveland group. During his first year in office he called upon Peter Witt, Harris Cooley, and Fred Howe to speak in Toledo on various aspects of the work being done in Cleveland. Whitlock explained to Cooley how anxious he was to have him talk because he (Whitlock) was endeavoring to introduce in the charitable and correctional institutions of Toledo the same innovations that had already been started in Cleveland. In handling civic morals the Toledo mayor also pursued the policy of administrative repression that had been introduced in Cleveland, eliminating wine rooms in houses of prostitution, closing saloons at midnight, and extirpating professional gambling places. On the traction question Whitlock was happy to follow the lead of Johnson, who explained that "we are really making your Toledo fight and if you can hold things for a few months, you will find we have established here a pattern or model that it will be very easy for you to follow." [48]

Nevertheless the principal source of the Toledo mayor's inspiration and reform ideas was Samuel Jones. The same spirit of humanity and tolerance that had dominated the administration of his predecessor marked the tone of Whitlock's. Petty offenders were treated with a similar leniency. The police force was entirely disarmed, even the canes that Jones had substituted for clubs were removed. At the city workhouse the stripes were obliterated from the prisoners' garb, and a parole officer was appointed whose principal duty was to find jobs for the released prisoners. The program of expanding the public parks, playgrounds, and other facilities was continued. Whitlock chose able men to administer these reforms. Perry Knapp was retained as superintendent of police and to work in harmony with him John Joseph Mooney was chosen as director of public safety. The Mayor found the capable John Robert Cowell to manage the department of public works, and Franklin Smith Macomber to serve as director of public service in charge of the parks and similar civic enterprises. These men shared Whitlock's zeal to make Toledo a second "City on a Hill."[49]

By campaign time in 1907 there was no doubt in the minds of the Independent Voters as to who should lead their ticket. Whitlock was renominated by acclamation at the party convention together with the rest of the city officials elected in 1905. Their platform, the most radical one ever adopted by a party in Toledo, demanded a three-cent fare, a referendum on franchises, municipal ownership of street railways, and the initiative, referendum, and recall.[50] The Republicans, desperately trying to stage a comeback, abandoned the convention system which had become discredited by the manipulations of the machine and nominated their candidates at a party election conducted under the optional direct-primary law. Rudolph A. Bartley, a prominent churchman and the largest wholesale grocer in the city, won the nomination for mayor. The News-Bee accused him of being Walter Brown's candidate, but he seemed rather to be ruled by the Anti-Saloon League. He made a "lid" cam-

189

paign, promising to enforce Sunday and midnight closing of saloons, to drive the gamblers from town, and to shut up the wine rooms.[51]

Although the two candidates stumped the city and held major rallies, the chief excitement was aroused by the newspaper war between the *Toledo Blade,* champion of Bartley, and the *Toledo News-Bee,* defender of Whitlock. The *Blade* editor prodded Bartley to make law enforcement the issue. Negley Cochran shouted that this was a mere smoke screen to conceal the central question of a new street-railway franchise. Alternately he defended Whitlock against the charge of being an impractical dreamer and a condoner of vice and crime, and praised the Mayor as the guardian of the people's interest in the traction battle.[52] The election was a thundering triumph for the Independent Voters. Whitlock received a plurality of 6,735, their other candidates for city offices were elected, and together with anti-machine Republicans they won ten of the sixteen seats in the council. The Mayor credited the victory to the spirit of Jones, to the people themselves, to the host of volunteers, and to the *Toledo News-Bee* which kept the truth before the people. This encomium seemed well deserved to Cochran, who stated without modest restraint, "Brand Whitlock may well be proud of the vote of confidence which he received. To the *News-Bee,* however, justly belongs much of the credit for the Independent victory. The combination of white paper, printer's ink and brains will almost invariably defeat mere white paper and printer's ink." On the other hand, Walter Brown attributed Whitlock's victory and Bartley's defeat to the latter's endorsement of Sunday closing of saloons, which the *Toledo Blade* had forced on the Republican nominee as the price of its support.[53]

The temperance issue, which had been of slight consequence a few years before, became prominent in a number of urban elections. In Columbus the Republicans nominated Charles A. Bond, candidate of the "liberal" element and the local machine; the Democrats nominated Thomas J. Duncan, a dry. Despite the latter's endorsement by Washington Gladden and two nominally Republican papers, the *Ohio State Journal* and the *Columbus Dispatch,* Duncan lost.[54] In several small cities "lid" candidates fared as badly, suffering defeat in Canton, Springfield, Portsmouth, and Kent. However, law-enforcement mayors won in Zanesville, Coshocton, Warren, and Youngstown, and in Dayton a moderate regulator was elected.[55]

This revival of temperance agitation was inspired by the Anti-Saloon League, which had been very active in mobilizing the sentiment of religious groups against the liquor traffic, and by the moral upheaval of 1905. Large numbers of Protestant middle-class churchgoers were persuaded by the League propaganda to associate lax law enforcement and a wide-open town with boss rule and to demand that the saloons and wine rooms be closed, thereby eliminating an important prop of a political machine. To the municipal reformers, however, the rise of this issue had always been distressing. Although agreeing with the temperance people that the excesses of the liquor trade should be stamped out, they saw no reason to deprive the poor man of his glass of beer at the neighborhood saloon, even on Sunday. Their cure was economic, not personal, reform.[56] In attempting to ignore the temperance question the municipal reformers were taking the same side as the bosses, but the popular confusion which might have resulted was dispelled by their wide divergence on every other issue.

Whitlock's victory was one case in point; Johnson's in Cleveland was another. In the largest city of the state the law enforcement question was not even raised, though it had been brought forward by the opposition in earlier campaigns. Johnson, seeking election for the fourth time, stood on a platform differing little from his previous ones: settlement of the low-fare fight, now nearly won; home rule in all local affairs, including the regulation and granting of franchises; and honesty and good management in city affairs.[57]

His Republican opponent was Congressman Theodore E. Burton. Although he was unfamiliar with the city's problems, he had a reputation as a vote getter in the Cleveland congressional district that he had long represented, and was esteemed for his political independence. He only consented to "make the fight" after he had received the public endorsement of President Theodore Roosevelt and Secretary of War William Howard Taft, both of whom insisted that the defeat of Johnsonian Democracy in Cleveland was important to the Republican party nationally. No doubt Burton was also persuaded to run by the promise of a victory which would raise his political stature to the point where he might supplant as party leader in the state Foraker, Dick, and Cox, whose power he had unsuccessfully challenged the year before.[58]

In the previous spring the traction battle between Johnson and the "Concon," as the consolidated Cleveland Railway Company was popularly called, had reached a crisis, and it was well understood that the street-railway company, together with the other utility interests, was eager for Johnson's scalp. Burton, though popularly considered to be the "Concon candidate," did his utmost to disassociate himself from the company and proposed a fare that almost matched the three-cent rate that Johnson had promised. The Republicans' tactics were to play down the street-railway issue and concentrate their attack on the Johnson administration, charging waste and extravagance, ring rule, and bossism. To pictorialize the accusations, the Republican *Cleveland Leader* imported Homer Davenport, the cartoonist who had once caricatured "Boss" Hanna and "Boss" Cox, to turn about and lampoon "Boss" Johnson.

But the Mayor withstood these assaults by campaigning on his record, and won with the second largest plurality of his four elections. It was another great victory for the people, he declared, and for the free city.[59] Moreover it was a second endorsement, in a sense, of the principles that the Cuyahoga County delegates had advocated in the General Assembly in 1906, and encouraged them to renew the attack in the approaching session.

Because of a constitutional amendment ratified in 1905 shifting state elections from the odd to even years, the terms of state officers and legislators, which would normally have expired in 1907, were extended to the end of 1908.[60] Thus, the session about to meet was the second one of the Seventy-seventh General Assembly. This meant that the Cleveland delegation would be given another chance to push through the reforms which had failed in the first session.

Two days prior to the opening, the Democratic members met in Columbus to discuss policy and organization. Fred Howe, seizing the opportunity to strengthen support for the Johnson program, proposed that the party be bound by a caucus vote on all bills which would implement the platform. Although his colleagues turned him down, they did agree to appoint a five-man steering committee in each chamber to brief members and urge support for such bills, but individual members retained the right to reject the advice. In the House the party organization was recast by the selection of Edwin S. Wertz as minority floor leader in place of Daniel E. Yost, a conservative lawyer from Monroe County.[61]

The session, however, did not begin auspiciously for the reformers. They were outmaneuvered by their opponents when they endeavored to retain on the calendars old business left over from 1906; instead the calendars were wiped clean. Andrew L. Harris, the Republican lieutenant-governor, who had succeeded the deceased Pattison, openly denounced such previously proposed legislation as Howe's franchise tax and the initiative and referendum. Any measure Johnson was known to support was immediately suspect to conservatives of both parties. There was evidence that some members were more influenced by lobbyists than before. The fact that it was an election year meant that bills would be appraised for their political effect, whatever their inherent merits or faults might be.[62]

Despite these ill omens, the reformers met with remarkable success in enacting the desired legislation for cities. Profiting from their failures in 1906, they corrected their strategy and approached the problem by a process of enumeration rather than by an omnibus amendment to the Municipal Code, by parceling out the sponsorship of bills to others besides delegates from Cleveland, and by appealing for nonpartisan support from friends of reform among the opposition party.[63]

On January 20 Louis H. Paine, Republican from Toledo and chairman of the committee on cities, introduced in the lower chamber a bill to replace the municipal boards of public works and public safety with single directors appointed by the mayor, and to extend the merit system to all municipal departments. By prearrangement the Cuyahoga delegation did not enter the debate except for one dissident member, Jesse Roberts, who had fallen out with Johnson and attacked the bill for increasing the power of the mayor. Efforts to weaken the measure by amendments were, however, successfully fended off by Paine and Wertz, the floor managers. In this limited package form, these proposals, which had been defeated two years before, were accepted by a vote of sixty-eight to twenty-nine, and all but seven of the Democrats were on the affirmative side, joined by half of the Republicans and the one Independent. The vote indicated the strength of the coalition of reform-minded Republicans and the Democrats. In the Senate the bill was defeated one day, and reconsidered and passed the next by a vote of twenty-two to fifteen, the majority representing a similar alliance to the one in the House.[64]

The Hamilton County Democrats, who strongly favored the Paine bill because it was offensive to George Cox, managed to strike at the Cincinnati boss in another way by successfully amending the School Code to make a small board mandatory instead of optional as the act of 1904 provided.[65]

Although the Cuyahoga delegates tried to spread the sponsorship of municipal reform proposals among a wide group, they took under their wing bills dealing with street-railway problems. Their intent was frankly to win advantages for Johnson in his low-fare fight, which then had reached a critical stage. Metzger and Stockwell both reintroduced in the House their proposals originally presented in 1906; two more were sponsored in the Senate by another Clevelander, Thomas P. Schmidt. The House remained hostile to these "Johnson bills," but the Senate on February 6 passed unanimously one of the Schmidt measures, which proposed to modify the law on property-owner consents by abolishing the necessity of obtaining them for new grants or extensions of old ones along a street where an electric railway had previously existed. For several weeks the prospect of favorable action by the House appeared dim. Then on April 7 the bill was called from the calendar. In the bitter debate that ensued the Cleveland Mayor was the stalking-horse, but such Republicans as Robert B. Lersch of Lorain County and Carl F. Shuler of Montgomery County waived aside the Johnson bogy. Through the aid of the coalition the bill passed, sixty-two yeas to twenty-three nays. Most remarkable of all, the House version contained an amendment introduced by Paine to provide for a referendum on all street-railway franchises within thirty days of a grant upon petition of 15 per cent of the voters. This feature for which the reformers had long been contending was accepted by the Senate without discussion, and the revised bill received the governor's signature a week later.[66]

Although this was the only application of the initiative to be approved at this session, two other measures providing for direct forms of legislation received considerable support. That so much sentiment existed in favor of these proposals which conservatives condemned as tantamount to "socialism, communism and worse," was the result of Herbert Bigelow's labors.[67]

As long ago as 1899 he had begun advocating direct legislation under the banner of the Union Reform party. Later he had become secretary of various organizations which had been formed to conduct educational campaigns on behalf of the initiative and referendum. In 1906 he had taken a leave of absence from his congregation to stump the state for this reform. Associated with him in the work were other disciples of Henry George—Tom Johnson and Fred Howe of Cleveland, Fenton Lawson and George W. Harris of Cincinnati—whose primary interest was in using the device of the initiative to speed the introduction of the single tax. For fear of frightening farmers and others, however, they kept this motive in the background, emphasizing a secondary one, the desire to place political power in the hands of the people. Bigelow himself was such a persuasive speaker that he succeeded in mollifying many of the farmers as well as winning an enthusiastic response from labor groups. He also received the backing of the Scripps-McRae papers.[68]

It is significant that one of the measures Bigelow favored, a resolution to amend the state constitution to permit the initiative and referendum, was introduced in the Senate by a Republican from a small town in Licking County, W. L. Atwell. In spite of the announced opposition of Governor Harris and other conservatives, enough Republicans joined Atwell to pass the resolution on February 4 by the necessary three-fifths vote. When the resolution came to the House, opponents, instead of trying to kill it outright, adopted a favorite tactic of preserving its form but rendering it harmless. The hostile judiciary committee, which had smothered a similar resolution in 1906, revised the Senate version to require a majority of the votes cast at an election in lieu of a majority vote on the proposition as necessary to carry. Again it was a Republican, Elisha A. Tinker, a Chillicothe lawyer, who proposed to delete the crippling change made in committee, though one of its most insistent champions was a Cincinnati Democrat, Thomas B. Paxton.

On March 17 the House held a public forum, hearing addresses in favor of the original Atwell resolution by Bigelow,

Washington Gladden, and representatives of the Ohio Mine Workers and the Ohio State Grange. Gladden summarized the principal benefits to be had from direct legislation: it would cure the ills of democracy by providing more democracy, it would prevent both corrupt and special legislation, and it would educate the public. Despite these pleas the House voted for the revised version of the Senate resolution as recommended by its judiciary committee. When the Senate refused to acquiesce, a conference committee was appointed, which failed to find a compromise. There the bill died as the Cassandras had predicted. Bigelow, who had been satisfied with the House version, was incensed by what he believed to be a piece of political chicanery and declared that he would take the issue before the people at the next election. He was reinforced in this decision after the identical fate befell an initiative and referendum bill that applied only to municipalities. It became apparent that he was not indulging in idle talk when later he increased the tempo of his work for direct legislation.[69]

A companion reform that was desired by the Johnson Democrats and like-minded Republicans was the direct-primary system of nominating candidates. Direct legislation gave hope of driving Privilege from the legislative halls, the direct primary of eliminating the influence of Privilege in the nominating conventions. Having lost by a close margin in the first session, advocates of a mandatory direct-primary law were sure that this time they had the votes to win. Altogether four bills were presented, which were discussed by the House and Senate election committees in joint session. On February 27 the House passed the proposal of Hiram S. Bronson, a Columbus Republican, by a vote of ninety to twelve; on April 6 the Senate with only two dissenting votes approved the bill with minor amendments in which the House later concurred.[70]

The new law made mandatory direct-primary elections for the nomination of county, township, municipal, and school board officers, of members of the General Assembly and judges, except in the two largest counties where it was optional. State officers and congressmen were still to be nominated by delegate conventions, but the delegates were to be chosen at primary elections. The system of electing party committees and determining representation at party conventions was regularized. The "closed" primary plan was adopted, that is the voter had to declare his party allegiance and vote only for the candidates of his own party, and the plan was protected from abuse by the threat of fines. Another provision permitted the names of candidates for the United States Senate to appear on the primary ballot of each party upon petition, and stipulated that the results would be certified to the legislature. This was, however, a far cry from the Oregon Plan, which the reformers wanted. Finally, all of the legislation to protect the purity of general elections was made to apply to the primaries.[71]

One other step was taken to curb the power of Privilege in elections. An act was passed declaring contributions by corporations to political parties or candidates a corrupt practice, and officers as well as the company were made punishable in the event of violation.[72]

Efforts were revived to enact the Democratic taxation planks and correct some of the most glaring deficiencies in the taxing system. The attention given to the subject, however, seemed inadequate in view of the fresh ammunition provided friends of tax reform by the findings of the Ohio Tax Commission of 1908. This body had been appointed by Governor Harris in the fall of 1906 in response to a widespread demand for a reinvestigation of the tax structure of the state. The five members, Wade Ellis, chairman, Atlee Pomerene, secretary, George E. Marsh, Thomas H. Hogsett, and Alfred C. Cassatt, held monthly meetings for over a year; listened to proposals from representatives of farmers, laborers, businessmen, bankers, lawyers, teachers, and homeowners; and investigated the tax systems in a number of states. In November, 1907, the governor had persuaded the National Tax Association to hold a conference in Columbus for the benefit of the commission and to stimulate interest in its survey. The governor of Massachusetts presided, three other state chief executives were present, and leading tax experts and practical administrators from all over the United States participated.[73]

The tax commissioners echoed in amplified tones the complaints made by their predecessors in 1893. They noted that the same tax inequalities existed everywhere—between owners of real estate and personal property, between the individual and the corporation, and among the owners of each class of property. Their report was particularly severe on the constitutional provision that all property must be taxed under a uniform rule, a system which had "long ago served its day" and which other states had either abandoned or were struggling to abolish. Equally sharp criticism was directed by the commission at the system of appraising real estate in decennial periods. Another aspect that received censure was the method of taxing corporations, which the report described as a jumble of makeshift legislation, full of injustice and favoritism, and enforced by a random collection of ex officio boards which lacked the means of investigating returns or discovering tax dodgers.[74]

Since the tax commission reported on January 10, 1908, the legislators had had time to frame some of their recommendations into bills for submission during the session. The proposal to abolish the general property tax and to permit classification was prepared as a constitutional amendment. It met stiff resistance in the House from the rural members, who reflected the farmers' fear that personal property would escape taxation under classification and thus increase the burden on agricultural land. Nevertheless, the amendment received the required three-fifths vote of the House and later passed the Senate.[75] A second recommendation of the tax commission, to abolish the ex officio state boards and replace them with a full-time tax commission of three members, was incorporated in a bill by John Freiner, which failed even to reach the floor. A third proposal, to shorten the period between the reappraisals of real estate from ten to four years, was presented by Fred Howe, defeated, then reintroduced by Senator Samuel H. West of Logan, the Republican floor leader, and passed with only two dissenting votes. Before final passage lobbyists invaded the Senate chamber to try to stop the proposed action. One of them fumed that it was a Johnson bill and that West had made a deal with the Cleveland mayor; the senator sputtered invectives at his accuser, driving him from the room. In the House, however, the hostile lobby prevented the bill from coming to a vote.[76]

Although the tax commission had made no specific recommendation on taxing utility franchises, it had urged the classification amendment to permit the legislature to assess taxes against this form of property, should it so desire. Without waiting for such constitutional authorization, Howe reintroduced his bill on the subject, ably defending it before the Senate tax committee against attack by leading attorneys for the public-service corporations. Despite the unanimous recommendation of the committee for passage, its defeat was made a party issue by Republican senators and Governor Harris, and it lost by a vote of fifteen to twenty. Attempts to revive it later in the session were of no avail.[77]

Nevertheless corporate business did not entirely escape reform legislation. The General Assembly approved a blue-sky bill; overhauled the state banking laws and created a superintendent of banks to invigorate the system of examining financial institutions; prohibited the employment of children under fourteen (already prohibited in mines) in industrial and commercial establishments, and limited their employment generally between the ages of fourteen and sixteen; and strengthened the pure-food-and-drug code.[78] Other humanitarian measures included: acts permitting cities to regulate tenements, and counties to provide separate homes for tuberculosis patients; laws to create a bureau of vital statistics and a state board of health; a law allowing counties to prohibit the sale of liquor by referendum vote; and legislation to establish separate commissions to investigate relief for the blind, conditions in the penitentiary, and problems in the coal mining industry.[79] In the adoption of these reforms the Johnson group played a major role. Howe worked hard for the passage of the penitentiary and mining commissions; James F. Reynolds, a Cleveland machinist, fathered the amendment to the child labor law; and Senator Peter W. Ward, of Cuyahoga County, was the author of the tenement law.[80]

In addition to these commissions for exploring social and economic problems, committees were appointed to probe into political affairs. After much maneuvering a satisfactory body was named to resume the investigation of Cincinnati and Hamilton County. As a countermove the Republican whip in the House, George Little of Greene County, offered a resolution to probe Cleveland. Although the charges made sounded suspiciously similar to those advanced by the Republicans in the last mayoralty campaign, the Democrats, including those from Cuyahoga, voted solidly for the Cleveland investigation, and the Senate concurred. It was not until the final hours of the session, however, that an appropriation of $35,000 for each committee was approved.[81]

Although the Cox emissaries, who had fought the Cincinnati probe step by step, appeared to have been beaten, they had one more refuge. State Auditor Walter Guilbert, a henchman of the Republican machine, questioned the legality of the committee, refusing to pay any vouchers until the doubt was cleared. "To use a mining phrase," explained the *Ohio State Journal,* "the contention is the legislature cannot grub-stake a muckraking expedition." The courts sustained the auditor's objections, declaring the committee unconstitutional on the ground that it had no power to act after the end of the legislative session because the legislature had adjourned in May sine die; therefore it could not receive a report from the committee nor approve its findings. As a result no investigation of either Cincinnati or Cleveland was made.[82]

Concurrently with these efforts to revive the Cincinnati probe, the Democrats prepared to investigate the offices of the state treasurer and auditor. Though greatly hampered, they were at least successful in making a preliminary investigation. For some time the suspicion had been growing that the treasurer's office was a nesting place for graft and corruption and that the incumbents had been pocketing interest on public funds. In 1902 a resolution had been introduced in the House to conduct such an investigation. The finance committee, to which the measure was referred, made an inspection, reported that the treasurer's accounts were in order, and the House Republicans on a strict party alignment voted to accept this finding, which was denounced as a "whitewash" by the Democrats.[83]

The Cleveland delegation was responsible for the revival of interest in such a probe in 1908. John Stockwell initiated the activity on his own. Since he could elicit little enthusiasm from the Republican House, he passed on the job to Howe in the Senate. Accompanied by a group of newspaper men, the latter called upon the treasurer to ask to see the money reported to be in the state vaults. When this was refused, the Senator demanded, as chairman of the finance committee and as a citizen, the right to examine the ledgers. At this the treasurer grew choleric. "It's none of your damn business," he said, "either as a senator or as a citizen where I keep the money or how I run my office." In the brief time it took this remark to circulate, the

Senate as a body became committed to such a probe, voting unanimously to name a committee of three: Democrats Howe and John C. Drake, with Howe as chairman, and Republican Frank N. Patterson of Ashland County. The investigation revealed that the treasurer, William S. McKinnon, had turned over the business of the department to his deputy, Charles C. Green; that McKinnon, as treasurer, had used his position to favor McKinnon, as banker, placing state funds at low interest rates on deposit in banking institutions in which he held stock; that no proper records of interest payments were kept in the department; and that Green was either incompetent or utterly indifferent.[84]

Three weeks later the Senate increased the scope of its investigations to include the auditor's office, the bureau of inspection, and the state boards in charge of tax assessments and remissions. The House also joined in the fray, asking Auditor Guilbert to describe his methods of handling tax returns from gas, electric light, and power companies. He reported that the returns were accepted as made without further questioning until last October, when two investigators were named at the instigation of Attorney-General Ellis. His statement revealed a lax state of affairs, which to the Democrats was sufficient explanation of how Guilbert had built up a powerful personal machine. Further inquiry disclosed that he was accustomed to depositing state funds in banks in which he owned stock, holding the money at no interest for several months and finally paying the sums to the state treasurer. When asked why the amounts had not been turned over more promptly, he lamely replied, "Probably I didn't want to."[85]

The Republicans sought to discredit the proceedings of the Senate committee by crying "Politics." Governor Harris tried to cut short their highly disturbing investigations by proposing to replace them with a two-man commission appointed by himself with the Senate's consent. Patterson, the Republican member of the committee, presented a separate statement to soften the majority report filed by Howe and Drake, stressing the findings of the expert accountant hired by the committee that the treasurer and auditor were not guilty of any peculation and that no state funds had been misappropriated. Although these worst suspicions had not been proven, the Democrats were well content with the findings, for they had shown loose, irregular management and incompetence by Republican office holders.[86]

When the legislative session closed in May, 1908, the prospects of the reformers seemed bright indeed. They had succeeded in embarrassing the entrenched Republican state machine by their probes. Progress toward their goals had been accelerated by the passage of the two-cent-fare law, county-salary legislation, the Paine Amendment to the Municipal Code, the franchise-referendum act, and provision for mandatory direct primaries. Sentiment for their principles was expanding, criss-crossing party lines. Still much remained to be accomplished. Majority opinion had not yet been educated to accept all their measures, they were still a minority group within the Democratic party, and they had not yet achieved control of the state executive departments nor even complete domination of the legislature. Nevertheless, all these seemed within easy grasp as they faced the approaching state campaign.

1. *Ohio State Journal* (Columbus), November 12, 1905; *Cincinnati Enquirer*, November 12, 1905; *Cleveland Plain Dealer*, November 12–13, 1905.

2. The Cleveland conference of mayors was reported in *Cleveland Plain Dealer*, December 5, 1905; Steffens' remark was quoted in *ibid.*, December 6, 1905.

3. Brand Whitlock to Tom L. Johnson, January 13, 1906, in Nevins, ed., *The Letters and Journal of Brand Whitlock*, I, 48.

4. *Cleveland Plain Dealer*, January 9, 1906.

5. *Report of the Secretary of State of Ohio* (1906), 30–33. The membership in the House, which had numbered about 110 before, increased in this session to 121. Most of this gain was the result of a constitutional amendment adopted in 1903 which provided that each county should have at least one representative. Fred Howe commented on the apathy toward reform of his Democratic colleagues in *The Confessions of a Reformer*, 161.

6. The organization of the Senate is described in Howe, *The Confessions of a Reformer*, and the *Cleveland Plain Dealer*, January 11, 1906, that of the House in *ibid.*, January 11, 1906. The revolt of the Republicans against the caucus system is reported in *ibid.*, January 15, 17, 1906. The committee assignments in both houses were listed in the *Report of the Secretary of State of Ohio* (1906), 33.

7. Attorney-General Ellis conferred with Johnson and the other mayors on the amendment to the code. At the end of the meeting Johnson had a word of praise for Ellis. (*Cleveland Plain Dealer*, January 5, 9–10, 25, 1906) The text of the Paine bill was reported in *ibid.*, January 25, 1906, the Metzger and Stockwell bills in *ibid.*, January 23, 26, 1905.

8. *Cleveland Plain Dealer,* February 14, 20–1, March 1, 30, 1906. The changed spirit of the reformers is recorded in *ibid.,* February 24, March 26, 1906, and *Toledo News-Bee,* March 22, 1906.

9. *Cleveland Plain Dealer,* March 12, 1906. As reported out of committee, the provisions for municipal ownership and the restoration of the city tax board had been deleted.

10. The three Republicans who supported the bill were Robert B. Lersch of Lorain, Frank W. Woods of Medina, and Elijah W. Hill of Columbiana. One of the consistent foes of franchise legislation, on the other hand, was Thomas B. Paxton, Jr., a Democrat from Hamilton County (Cincinnati). (*Ohio State Journal,* March 30, 1906) The one piece of franchise legislation to pass in this session was the Hillenkamp bill, which dispensed with the requirement of a referendum in granting a franchise to a competing electric light company, (*ibid.,* March 31, 1906).

11. *Ibid.,* January 19–20, February 28, 1906. Harper held firm and voted against the repeal on the final passage.

12. *Cleveland Plain Dealer,* February 15, 1906; *Ohio State Journal,* March 30, 1906. Johnson was quoted in the *Cincinnati Enquirer,* February 15, 1906. The unconstitutionality of the bill as well as its undesirability was discussed in Wade H. Ellis, "Taxation in Ohio," *Ohio Magazine,* I (September, 1906), 285–86. The Vanover bill was reported in the *Ohio State Journal,* January 25, 1906.

13. It was reported that similar legislation had been introduced in every session for the past twenty-six years (*Cleveland Plain Dealer,* February 8, 1906). The passage of the bill in the House and Senate was described in *ibid.,* February 7, 9, 1906. The text is in 98 O.L. 4 (1906). Howe's colorful account, which telescopes the time of the adoption of the bill and claims that passage took place on the first day of the session in each house, is not corroborated by the newspaper reports. When he wrote this description nineteen years later, he must have had a lapse of memory. (Howe, *The Confessions of a Reformer,* 162)

Identical legislation which followed in other states is discussed in Grover G. Huebner, "Five Years of Railroad Regulation by the States," *Annals of the American Academy of Political and Social Science,* XXXII (1908), 146–47, 155. By 1908 eleven states had adopted such legislation and eleven others had laws specifying a maximum passenger rate between two and three cents. The Pennsylvania and North Carolina laws were declared unconstitutional by the courts on the grounds that they were confiscatory. However, in Ohio no test case was brought.

14. *Cleveland Plain Dealer,* January 26, February 8, 1906. The first annual report of the Ohio Railway Commission revealed that the passenger revenue on the railroads in the state increased approximately $1,300,000 in the first year of operation under the two cent–fare law, thus proving the contention of the legislators that the reduced rate would actually benefit the railroads (*Cincinnati Enquirer,* October 6, 1907).

15. The introduction and adoption of the bill were reported in the *Cleveland Plain Dealer,* February 8, March 31, 1906. The history of railroad regulation by the states is told in Frederick C. Clark, *State Railroad Commissions and How They May Be Made Effective* ("American Economic Association Publications," Vol. VI, No. 6, [1891]), 32–39, 52–53, and in Huebner, "Five Years of Railroad Regulation by the States," 138–39. By

1900, thirty states had established railroad commissions, thirteen of which, including Ohio's, acted only in a supervisory capacity. The other seventeen were of the type first established in Illinois in 1871 with some degree of regulatory power. After 1900 the tendency was to introduce the strong commissions of the second type and extend their control to other utilities besides railroads. Ohio was the only state in 1906 to introduce such a regulatory agency; a year later eleven others followed. The text of the Ohio statute is in 98 O.L. 342 (1906). The new railway commission was given supervision over express and freight car companies as well as railroads. It was granted authority to hear complaints and on the basis of its findings to issue orders fixing rates and services; also it could initiate rate-fixing on its own motion. Its rate orders were effective at once, although the courts could issue restraining injunctions. Railroads had to publish their rates and adhere to them.

16. Johnson, *My Story*, 149–53. However, the Johnson partisans did vote for the railway commission act, although they had taken no leadership in its adoption.

17. The fate of the railroad anti-pass amendment was reported in the *Cleveland Plain Dealer*, January 9, March 7, 31, 1906, and the *Ohio State Journal*, March 31, April 2, 1906. The granting of free passes had become so abused that all of the railroads east of Chicago had finally agreed to abolish the free pass, effective January 1, 1902. Although not properly observed at first, the agreement was reasonably well enforced by 1906. (*Cleveland Plain Dealer*, November 25, 1901; *Toledo News-Bee*, January 5, 1906.)

18. By 1902, forty-two counties had shifted from the fee to the salary system of paying their officers, but because the changes had all been made by special legislation, the Ohio Supreme Court had held them unconstitutional, along with the charters for cities. All counties had then reverted to the fee basis. (*State of Ohio* ex rel. *Guilbert* v. *Yates*, 66 Ohio 546 [1902]) Efforts to write a general salary law had preceded the supreme court decision and were renewed in the 1904 legislative session. Such a bill passed the Senate in that year but was defeated in the House by the powerful county officers' lobby. (*Cleveland Plain Dealer*, January 22, 23, March 14, April 20, 26, 1904) In the 1906 session the three bills were introduced by Benjamin Wilson of Belmont County, George A. Bassett of Lucas County, and George Little of Greene County. The power of the lobby was commented on in *ibid.*, January 28, March 15, 1906, and *Ohio State Journal*, January 27, 1906. Both houses passed separate salary bills on February 21; on March 15 the Senate accepted the House version (*Cleveland Plain Dealer*, February 22, March 16, 1906). Johnson was certain the act would raise the pay of officers in about eighty of the counties (interview in *ibid.*, March 16, 1906). The text of the law is in 98 O.L. 89 (1906).

19. *Cleveland Plain Dealer*, April 3, 1906. The text is in 98 O.L. 359 (1906).

20. *Cleveland Plain Dealer*, January 26, March 14, 1906.

21. In the Senate Howe led the fight for the resolution, which was supported by five Republicans and all of the Democrats save one. Similar proposals had been introduced in the sessions of 1900 and 1902 and then buried in committee. (*Ibid.*, March 21, 1906)

22. *Ibid.*, March 29, 31, 1906. The texts are in 98 O.L. 223, 176, 30, and 116 (1906), respectively.

23. Both the House and Senate passed mandatory direct-primary bills in different forms. A conference committee was appointed to reconcile the two versions, but the Senate refused to accept the committee's revision. Johnson was opposed to certain features of both bills. However, the Cuyahoga County delegation did not actively oppose the proposed legislation. (*Ohio State Journal*, March 15, April 1, 3–4, 1906; *Cleveland Plain Dealer*, February 28, 1906)

24. *Cincinnati Enquirer*, April 3, 1906; *Ohio State Journal*, April 3, 1906; *Cleveland Plain Dealer*, March 25, 1906; *Toledo News-Bee*, January 18, 1908.

25. Article by W. S. Couch in the *Cleveland Plain Dealer*, March 25, 1906; *Ohio State Journal*, March 13, 1906.

26. *Cleveland Plain Dealer*, January 6, 12, 17–18, 1906. Hill's speech was reported in *ibid.*, February 1, 1906.

27. *Ibid.*, February 7, 9, 1906. The committee was composed of John C. Drake, chairman, Arthur Espy, and Thomas P. Schmidt, Democrats. The two Republicans refused to join.

28. The work of the Drake commission was reported in *ibid.*, February 24, March 1, 10–11, 21, 25, 1906, and *Cincinnati Enquirer*, March 10–11, 1906. A digest of its report was published in *ibid.* and in the *Ohio State Journal*, January 15, 1908.

29. The investigation and report of the grand jury were reported in the *Cincinnati Enquirer*, March 22, April 1, 1906. Support for the jury's decision came from the *Dayton Daily News*, April 2, 1906, on the ground that the practice had been generally understood but ignored. The *Cleveland Plain Dealer* spoke of the derisive contempt for the leniency shown by the grand jury in the issue for April 1, 1906.

30. *Cleveland Plain Dealer*, April 18, 27, 1906.

31. The text is in 98 O.L. 274 (1906).

32. Schmidt was quoted in the *Cleveland Plain Dealer*, October 18, 1906.

33. *Ibid.*, August 22, 1906; *Ohio State Jounral*, August 22, 1906.

34. This analysis of Garber is drawn from the author's interview with James M. Cox, June 29, 1949, from Cox's *Journey through My Years*, 182–83, and from the *Toledo News-Bee*, February 29, 1908. An uncritical view of Garber is presented in Powell, ed., *The Democratic Party of the State of Ohio*, II, 29.

35. *Cincinnati Enquirer*, August 23, 1906.

36. *Ibid.*, August 22–23, 1906; *Ohio State Journal*, August 22, 1906; *Cleveland Plain Dealer*, August 22–23, 1906.

37. The analysis of Burton and his strategy is drawn from: *Cleveland Plain Dealer*, August 17, 1906; *Ohio State Journal*, August 18, September 12, 1906; Cox, *Journey through My Years*, 33–34; the author's interview with Alfred A. Benesch, March 8, 1946. Burton was allied with Herrick, Harry M. Daugherty, and Robert F. Wolfe, the influential publisher of the *Ohio State Journal* and *Columbus Evening Dispatch* (Walters, *Foraker*, 256–57). The proceedings at the convention were reported in the *Cleveland Plain Dealer*, September 12–13, 1906.

38. *Ohio State Journal*, September 12, 1906.

39. *Cleveland Plain Dealer*, November 7–8, 1906; *Ohio State Journal*,

November 7, 1906; *Toledo News-Bee*, November 7, 1906; *Dayton Daily News*, November 7, 1906; *Cincinnati Enquirer*, November 7, 1906. The vote for secretary of state was as follows: Thompson (Republican) 408,066; Hoskins (Democrat) 351,676; O. J. Henslee (Socialist) 18,432; A. F. Hughes (Prohibition) 11,970; Max Eisenberg (Socialist Labor) 2,211 (*Report of the Secretary of State of Ohio* [1906], 120).

40. This appraisal of Dempsey's difficulties was made by W. S. Couch in the *Cleveland Plain Dealer*, April 1, 1906.

41. The accomplishments of the Dempsey administration were recorded in: address of Elliott H. Pendleton in *Proceedings of the Cincinnati Conference for Good City Government and the Fifteenth Annual Meeting of the National Municipal League* (1909), 4–5; Taft, *City Management*, 12–13; speech of Alfred M. Cohen before the Democratic city convention, printed in the *Cincinnati Post*, October 1, 1907.

42. Report by W. S. Couch in the *Cleveland Plain Dealer*, April 1, 1906; Taft, *City Management*, 12–13. Dempsey was unable to gain complete control of the board of public safety and hence of the chief of police. The police force tried to discredit the administration by being over-zealous in enforcing the law.

43. Daniel Kiefer to Brand Whitlock, April 16, 1906, Whitlock Papers, the author's interview with Graham Hunt, September 28, 1949.

44. The conservative criticism came from Melvin E. Ingalls, quoted in the *Cincinnati Enquirer*, November 7, 1906. The charge of nepotism was reported in the *Cincinnati Post*, October 24, 1907. It was said that there were fourteen Dempseys on the public payroll. Fenton Lawson was a single taxer, Swedenborgian, and manufacturer of tinware. Wealthy and an intimate of the "hilltop aristocracy" of Cincinnati, he helped to give respectability to the Vine Street radicals. Moreover, he had a gentleness that was often wanting among reformers, which increased his usefulness to the Bigelow group. (The author's interview with Herbert Bigelow, September 26, 1949)

45. *Cincinnati Post*, October 1–3, 7–8, 10–11, 1907; *Cincinnati Enquirer*, October 9–10, 1907.

46. Cox's favors to Markbreit and other editors of the German-language press are discussed in Wright, *Bossism in Cincinnati*, 124. See also Chap. I, pp. 15, 20–21, n. 39. The points of the Republican attack were listed in the *Cincinnati Post*, October 24, 1907.

47. *Cincinnati Enquirer*, November 6, 1907.

48. Whitlock's attitude toward his job and his administration of city affairs is told in Whitlock, *Forty Years of It*, 162–63, 255–58, Whitlock, *On the Enforcement of Law in Cities*, 88–89, and "Brand Whitlock: Mayor, Novelist, Democrat," *Arena*, XXXVII (June, 1907), 193–208. His dependence on the Cleveland groups is related in correspondence: Brand Whitlock to Harris R. Cooley, March 12, 1906, and Brand Whitlock to Tom L. Johnson, April 10, 1906, in Nevins, ed., *The Letters and Journal of Brand Whitlock*, I, 52, 56–57. The Johnson quotation is in Tom L. Johnson to Brand Whitlock, October 15, 1906, Whitlock Papers. Whitlock was never an ardent believer in the single tax. He does not mention his own conversion in his autobiography, although he does speak of his preference for the single taxers over the Socialists (Whitlock, *Forty Years of It*, 313–14). A recent biographer maintains that he was a single taxer in name only, for he was

fundamentally a relativist who was not satisfied with any one doctrine (Samuel Milton Jones, III, "Brand Whitlock and the Independent Party," *Northwest Ohio Quraterly*, XXXI [Summer, 1959], 104).

49. Whitlock, *Forty Years of It*, 260; Brand Whitlock to Laurence Chambers, March 15, 1907; Brand Whitlock to Shailer Mathews, June 28, 1910, in Nevins, ed., *The Letters and Journal of Brand Whitlock*, I, 70–71, 138; *Toledo News-Bee*, September 27, 1907.

50. *Toledo News-Bee*, September 26, 1907; Johnson, *Toledo's Non-Partisan Movement*, Appendix, 71; Brand Whitlock to Daniel Kiefer, November 25, 1907, Whitlock Papers.

51. *Toledo News-Bee*, September 27, 1907; *Toledo Blade*, October 19, 23–24, 1907. The Anti-Saloon League actively supported Bartley.

52. *Toledo Blade*, October 23, 26, 28–29, 1907; *Toledo News-Bee*, October 2–3, 7, 11, 16, 26, 1907. Shortly after Whitlock took office, the *Toledo Blade* praised him for closing the saloons at midnight, eradicating the wine rooms, and driving out the professional gamblers. The Mayor confessed to Johnson that it made him very uneasy to have the approval of the *Blade*, for he believed its concern with rigid law enforcement did not proceed from any moral sense but from a desire to wreck the reform movement (Brand Whitlock to Tom L. Johnson, January 13, 1906, in Nevins, ed., *The Letters and Journal of Brand Whitlock*, I, 48–49).

53. *Toledo News-Bee*, November 6, 1907. Cochran's quotation is from *ibid.*, November 6, 1907. The *Toledo Blade* printed Brown's statement with the comment that it had been anticipated. His influence, the editor continued, had spelled defeat for every candidate suspected of being close to him. People had been led to believe that he was using the party to promote the traction company and the brewery merger. Many even thought that he preferred Whitlock to Bartley because the former favored licensing saloons. (*Toledo Blade*, November 7, 1907)

54. *Ohio State Journal*, September 13–14, 28–29, October 11, 15–16, 19, 28–29, November 6, 1907.

55. *Ibid.*, November 7, 1907; *Youngstown Vindicator*, November 1, 6–7, 1907; *Dayton Daily News*, October 22, 30–31, November 6, 1907.

56. Wayne Wheeler, superintendent of the Anti-Saloon League in Ohio, expressed his satisfaction over the number of cities in which temperance was an issue (interview in the *Ohio State Journal*, November 7, 1907). Typical of the views of reformers on the liquor question are those expressed in Johnson, *My Story*, 170, 173–74, 220, and in Whitlock, *On the Enforcement of Law in Cities*, 3–4, 19–20, 22–24, 49–50.

57. *Cleveland Plain Dealer*, October 6, 1907.

58. Burton made public President Roosevelt's letter to him (*ibid.*, September 18, 1907). It is also printed in Morison and Blum, eds., *The Letters of Theodore Roosevelt*, V, 177. There are further comments on Burton's candidacy in Johnson, *My Story*, 267-69, and in Crissey, *Burton*, 147–60.

59. *Cleveland Plain Dealer*, October 10–11, 21, November 6–7, 1907; *Cleveland Leader*, October 10–November 7, 1907; Johnson, *My Story*, 269–75.

60. The text of the amendment is in 97 O.L. 640 (1905). It was approved at the 1905 election by a vote of 702,669 for, 90,762 opposed (*Report of the Secretary of State of Ohio* [1905], 132). The text of the statute

extending the terms of state officers and members of the General Assembly is in 98 O.L. 27 (1906).

61. *Ohio State Journal,* January 5, 7, 1908.

62. *Ibid.,* January 7–8, 1908; *Cleveland Plain Dealer,* January 8, 10, 25, February 15, 1908; *Cincinnati Enquirer,* January 8, 1908.

63. F. C. Howe to Brand Whitlock, December 26, 1907, Whitlock Papers.

64. *Cleveland Plain Dealer,* January 21, March 11, April 23, 1908. The text of the bill is in 99 O.L. 562 (1908).

65. Joseph P. Kealy, a Cincinnati Democrat in the House, said of the Paine proposal, "I like this bill for the enemies it has made."—*Ohio State Journal,* March 11, 1908. The amendment to the School Code was passed in the closing hours of the session (*Cleveland Plain Dealer,* May 2, 1908). The text is in 99 O.L. 585 (1908).

66. The so-called Johnson bills are discussed in the *Ohio State Journal,* January 14, 1908, and the *Cleveland Plain Dealer,* January 14–15, 1908. The adoption of the Schmidt bill was reported in *ibid.,* February 7, April 8–9, 16, 1908. The text is in 99 O.L. 102 (1908). Johnson and others from Cleveland called upon Governor Harris to stress the importance of the bill and the need for immediate, favorable action. The Mayor spoke especially of the referendum provision, which he declared was the greatest feature of the bill. (*Ibid.,* April 15, 1908) Ironically, the first franchise to be submitted to referendum vote was the security grant made to the Cleveland Railway Company, April 27, 1908, and which formed the foundation for the lease of the Municipal Traction Company which guaranteed to operate the street-railway system at a three-cent fare. On October 22, 1908, the Cleveland electorate voted down the security franchise and brought the three-cent fare experiment to a temporary halt. Indeed, Johnson had opposed this particular application of the referendum, even though he was enthusiastic for the principle. The Cleveland street railway contest is discussed above in Chap. III, pp. 72–73.

67. These words of condemnation were uttered by Thomas B. Paxton, Jr., a conservative Cincinnati Democrat (quoted in the *Ohio State Journal,* March 19, 1908).

68. Stockbridge, "Ohio Wide Awake," 704–5; Herbert Bigelow, "From Pulpit to Stump," *Independent,* LXI (November 1, 1906), 1036; Herbert Bigelow to Brand Whitlock, December 1, 1906; January 15, 1907, Whitlock Papers; Brand Whitlock to W. A. White, April 8, 1908, in Nevins, ed., *The Letters and Journal of Brand Whitlock,* I, 90–91.

69. *Ohio State Journal,* January 14, 16, March 18–20, 26, April 3, May 2, 1908; *Cleveland Plain Dealer,* January 16, 25, February 5, 1908. The testimony of Gladden and others was reported in the *Ohio State Journal,* March 18, 1908.

70. *Ohio State Journal,* January 9, 1908; *Cleveland Plain Dealer,* February 13, 28, April 17, 23, 1908.

71. The text is in 99 O.L. 214 (1908). Stockwell did try to get the Oregon Plan adopted by a separate bill which was buried in committee (*Ohio State Journal,* January 8, 1908). Furthermore, the legislature passed a joint resolution petitioning Congress to call a convention to draft a con-

stitutional amendment providing for the popular election of senators. The text of the joint resolution is in 99 O.L. 641 (1908).

72. The text is in 99 O.L. 23 (1908).

73. *Ohio State Journal,* November 12, 1906; November 13–16, 1907; *Report of the Honorary Commission Appointed by the Governor to Investigate the Tax System of Ohio and Recommend Improvements Therein* (Columbus, 1908), 5–7 (hereafter referred to as *Report of the Tax Commission of 1908*).

74. These criticisms are to be found in *Report of the Tax Commission of 1908,* 18–21, 28–33, 34–35, and 40. One of the Republican commissioners, Wade H. Ellis, had already gone on record as condemning the inadequacies of the Ohio taxing system (Ellis, "Taxation in Ohio," 277).

75. *Cleveland Plain Dealer,* February 13, 28–29, 1908. The text is in 99 O.L. 629 (1908). The amendment was defeated in the 1908 election. Although the vote was 339,747 for to 95,867 against, it was 221,853 short of the majority of the votes cast, which the law required. A similar amendment had been defeated by approximately the same vote in 1903. (*Report of the Secretary of State of Ohio* [1908], 179–80; *Ohio Election Statistics* [1903], 29–31) The farmers' fears were expressed in Frank A. Derthick, *Revision of the Tax System in Ohio* (n. p, [1906]). Derthick was master of the Ohio State Grange.

76. *Report of the Tax Commission of 1908,* 39–41; *Ohio State Journal,* January 16, 1908; *Cleveland Plain Dealer,* February 16, April 17–18, 1908.

77. *Cleveland Plain Dealer,* January 21–22, 25, 31, February 1, 13, 1908. The Tax Commission of 1908 made two other recommendations on which no action was taken: repeal "at the earliest possible date" of the state levy on real and personal property, and publicity of tax assessments and returns (*Report of the Tax Commission of 1908,* 41–44).

78. The texts of these laws are in 99 O.L. 336, 269, 30, 257 (1908), respectively. The first Pure Food and Drug Act had been passed in 1904 (97 O.L. 116 [1904]).

79. The text of these laws are in 99 O.L. 124, 62, 296, 492, 35, 362, and 321 (1908), respectively. Howe's penitentiary bill was vetoed by the Governor (Howe, *The Confessions of a Reformer,* 165).

80. Howe's contributions are related in *ibid.,* 165, *Cleveland Plain Dealer,* January 15, 1908, and *Ohio State Journal,* May 1, 1908; Reynolds' are in *ibid.,* January 22, 1908, and *Cleveland Plain Dealer,* January 22, 1908; Ward's are in *ibid.,* March 28, 1908. Thomas Schmidt also introduced a bill to abolish capital punishment, which passed the Senate but was buried in the House (*Ohio State Journal,* March 12, 1908).

81. *Ohio State Journal,* January 29, February 4, 1908; *Cleveland Plain Dealer,* January 28, February 26, April 21, 30, May 3, 1908. The texts of the resolutions are in 99 O.L. 621 and 642 (1908), respectively.

82. *Ohio State Journal,* May 10, November 25, 1908.

83. *Ibid.,* February 18–19, 25–26, 1902; Powell, ed., *The Democratic Party of the State of Ohio,* I, 425.

84. Howe's role and the treasurer's remarks to him are drawn from Howe, *The Confessions of a Reformer,* 163–64. The probe itself is covered in the *Ohio State Journal,* February 21, 1908, and the *Cleveland Plain Dealer,* March 15, 1908.

85. The investigation of the auditor's office was reported in the *Ohio State Journal,* March 12, 1908, the *Cleveland Plain Dealer,* April 4, 1908, and the *Toledo News-Bee,* April 16–17, 1908.

86. Harris' proposal was presented in a special message to the legislature. However, no action was taken. (*Cleveland Plain Dealer,* April 1, 1908). The majority report and Patterson's separate statement was published in the *Ohio State Journal,* May 10, 1908.

CHAPTER NINE

GOVERNOR HARMON'S
FIRST ADMINISTRATION
1909■1910

LONG BEFORE the close of the legislative session in May, 1908, Tom Johnson had begun to lay plans for the nomination of a reformer of his own kind to head the Democratic state ticket. He leaned strongly toward Brand Whitlock, but drew back because of the practical obstacles to backing a Toledo Independent. Instead he turned to a little-known Canton lawyer, Atlee Pomerene, whose Democratic allegiance was unquestioned. On February 20, 1908, Johnson announced his choice; a week later a letter was in the hands of the Canton man drafting him for governor. It was signed not only by Johnson and other municipal reformers from Cleveland, Toledo, and Cincinnati but also by conservative Democratic politicians, editors, and judges. The following day Pomerene formally announced his candidacy.[1]

Although he had played no part in the state councils of the party, he had gained some recent prominence as secretary of the tax commission. In local political circles he was well known; he had been twice city solicitor, and once prosecutor of Stark County, surviving the McKinley landslide in 1896 to win that office. A graduate of Princeton and the Cincinnati Law School, where he won a prize as the best all-round debater, he had had excellent preparation for these posts, and he had earned a solid reputation for honesty and ability.[2]

Although Johnson and Pomerene may have known each other earlier, their political friendship dated from at least 1903. As chairman of a Democratic rally in Canton that year, the young attorney must have made a strong impression on the candidate for governor by his earnest and eloquent endorsement of the platform planks of tax reform, home rule, and the two-cent railroad fare. Two years later the Canton lawyer supported the same principles in campaigning for Pattison. He himself was a candidate for state senator, yet he made so little effort in his own behalf that his opponent walked away with the honor.[3] What no doubt clinched Johnson's decision to back Pomerene for governor in 1908 was his work on the tax commission and the endorsement by that body of the program which the Cleveland reformer had long been advocating.

Having publicized his choice for governor, Johnson set to work with his customary directness and energy to secure Pomerene's nomination on a radical platform by the Democratic state convention. The determined Mayor began by opening fire on the conservative Harvey Garber, then the most powerful figure in the party's state hierarchy. Johnson accused him in the press of being "a traitor to his party and its principle," of "manipulating his organization . . . to defeat legislation pledged in the Democratic platform and demanded by the people," and of attempting "to engineer weak nominations and a weak platform as a means of paying his obligations to Walter Brown . . . and other Republican organization leaders." Backing words with deeds, Johnson dispatched emissaries to three congressional-district conventions to commence the anti-Garber fight. The month of March was stormy; both sides exchanged charges and countercharges. On the 25th a harmony meeting was called in Columbus by men who had been out of party leadership for years. Johnson attended this "ghost dance," which proceeded to pass a pious resolution asking for harmony and co-operation in throwing out the boss-controlled Republican office-holders and then adjourned. Still the warfare continued with little abatement.[4]

Two other gubernatorial candidates were major threats to Johnson's choice, John C. Welty and Judson Harmon. Welty was a fellow townsman of Pomerene, and somewhat older, their wives were first cousins, their law offices were fifty feet apart, and their political pattern locally had been much the same. Outside of Canton, however, Welty was much better known than Pomerene, for the older lawyer had been a candidate in 1903 and 1905 for governor and in 1906 for Congress. Nevertheless Welty was eliminated in the Stark County primaries, when the voters elected a solid Pomerene delegation to the Democratic state convention by a majority of six to one.[5] A much more serious rival was Judson Harmon, around whom the former Pattison supporters were beginning to rally.[6]

Harmon, who had just turned sixty-two, was a commanding figure. His tall stature, powerful frame, and erect bearing gave him the appearance of a military man rather than of a politician. The first impression was confirmed by a closer observation of his features: his ruddy complexion, close-cropped mustache, mouth of a determined cast, and eyes that gazed firmly from under thick, shaggy eyebrows. Yet the austere military look would dissolve when his eyes lit with flashes of kindness and his mouth broke into a smile or hearty laugh.

He had been born in Hamilton County, the son of a Baptist minister, and graduated from Denison University and the Cincinnati Law School after working his way through both. Settling in Cincinnati to practice his profession, he became a prominent attorney and won further distinction as a judge on the benches of both the common pleas and superior courts of Hamilton County. Although he had inclined toward the Republican party in the Civil War period, he revolted against the harsh Reconstruction program of the Radical Republicans and eventually became firmly affiliated with the Democratic party. President Grover Cleveland added luster to Harmon's name by appointing him attorney-general in 1895. In that office the Cincinnati lawyer displayed his remarkable talents, initiating two famous antitrust suits which were decided on the basis of the principles he had advanced, although after his term had expired.[7]

It was on the basis of this work that President Theodore Roosevelt in 1905 appointed him and Frederick N. Judson, of St. Louis, special counselors to investigate an alleged violation of a federal injunction by the Santa Fe Railroad. The restraining order had been issued at the request of the Interstate Commerce Commission to stop that railroad from granting rebates to the Colorado Fuel and Iron Company. The facts unearthed by these two special investigators implicated Secretary of the Navy Paul Morton, who had been vice-president of the Santa Fe Railroad at the time of the alleged violation. They insisted that not only the railroad company but also the individual officers, including

Morton, should be indicted for contempt. Roosevelt refused to concede their wish, exonerating his secretary and ruling that only the corporation should be held responsible for the criminal offense, not the men themselves. Overruled by the President, the two counselors submitted their resignations in a letter in which they defended their recommendations:

> They [the great corporations] cannot be imprisoned, and punishment by fine is not only inadequate, but reaches the real culprits lightly, if at all. The evils with which we are now confronted are corporate in name, but individual in fact. Guilt is always personal. So long as officials can hide behind their corporations no remedy can be effective. When the government searches out the guilty man and makes corporate wrong doing mean personal punishment and dishonor the laws will be obeyed.[8]

The maxim that "guilt is always personal" was the standard by which Harmon judged the conduct of all officers, whether those of a corporation or of a government. He also subscribed to the corollary enunciated by President Cleveland that "public office is a public trust." In this and other beliefs as well, Harmon remained a faithful disciple of his former chief. Both stressed economy and business efficiency in the management of public affairs, fairness toward all interests, favoritism toward none, and the limited exercise of governmental power. The new political movement, espoused by the municipal reformers within his own party, towards more direct democracy and a more positive role for government both in regulating industry and providing welfare services was foreign to his thinking and seemed to trouble and confuse him.[9]

Since his return to Cincinnati in 1897, his private law practice had demanded most of his time. He had been appointed receiver of three different railroads and had made a remarkable record in restoring them to financial health and saving the interest of the stockholders.[10]

Although he had remained aloof from politics for the most part, what political activity he had engaged in had antagonized the reform wing of the party. He had opposed Johnson's program from the time it was first presented in 1901, and he continued to be hostile to many aspects of it, notably the proposals for direct legislation. Because of his opposition he stood condemned as a symbol of reaction in the eyes of Johnson, Bigelow, and the other Democratic reformers, and they were determined to defeat his nomination. Harmon's support for the governorship came from conservative Democrats in general and one prominent state leader in particular, William L. Finley, a former Bryanite, who had backed Pattison in 1905. As the sentiment for the Cincinnati candidate increased, others, including Harvey Garber, gravitated to his standard.[11]

When the Democrats assembled in Columbus for their state convention on May 5, 1908, Harmon was the favorite. He had vigorous support among the rural members, and the unanimous backing of the delegations from Franklin, Lucas, and Montgomery counties, although the delegation from his own county was split, a substantial minority opposing him. On the opening day the Harmon camp and the Johnson forces divided honors. The delegation of the Toledo Democratic organization, which favored Harmon, was seated in place of the progressive group led by Isaac R. Sherwood. On the other hand, Charles W. Stage, one of Johnson's young men, was chosen chairman of the committee on rules and order of business. Also Johnson and Baker were elected members of the resolutions committee, and even though their supporters did not dominate it in numbers, they wrote the platform.[12]

The document again called for the initiative and referendum in state and local government, home rule for cities, municipal ownership of all utilities, and a franchise tax. Its labor demands were more voluminous than before: more stringent child labor legislation, an eight-hour day on public works, an employers' liability act, and a law limiting injunctions in labor disputes. The most was made of the exposé of the state treasurer's and auditor's offices and of the selection by the Republicans of candidates who would be likely to perpetuate the existing conditions. Bryan was endorsed for President, and the state delegates were committed to his nomination.[13]

Before a vote was taken to nominate any candidate, the platform was approved by the convention. It contained several provisions known to be distasteful to Harmon, which Johnson had underscored in a bitter speech on the first day. The Clevelander accused the Cincinnati lawyer of being unalterably opposed to the franchise tax and the initiative and referendum, of representing the breweries and Wall Street railroads, and, therefore, of being an impossible choice of the Ohio Democracy. The intemperate tone and vigor of the denunciation created a near state of pandemonium. It seemed to the Harmon forces that the Cleveland mayor had broken his pre-convention promise to make a clean and open fight. On the second day he renewed the attack by innuendo when he placed Pomerene in nomination for governor. "I want to present the name of a man," he said, "who stands on every plank of the Democratic platform. He is for direct legislation, spends his time in season and out for that, is for the taxation of franchises, always was for Bryan and never rejoiced at the defeat of Bryan."[14] A member from Cincinnati made the nominating speech for Harmon. Johnson might better have held his tongue, for Harmon led Pomerene on the first ballot and won the nomination on the second.[15]

After the selection of the candidate for governor the convention sought to placate the Cleveland mayor by suggesting Senator Thomas Schmidt for lieutenant-governor and Pomerene for attorney-general. But the Mayor sulked, announcing that he wanted no further part in the proceedings. The Clevelanders tried to discredit the ticket by proposing Lewis Bernard and John Bolan for lieutenant-governor. However, David L. Rockwell, a neutral choice, was nominated on the first vote. Further balloting for officers was halted when Pomerene and A. P. Sandles, another defeated candidate for governor, asked for the floor to pledge support to Harmon. The Canton lawyer did not stop there but went on to sing the praises of Johnson and Bryan and to stress the important party principles of tax reform and direct legislation. Although the mention of Johnson's name brought cheers from friendly delegations, he sat through the speeches stolidly smoking his briarwood pipe.[16]

Nevertheless he began to pick up as the convention leaders continued to press him with concessions. The motion to endorse James E. Campbell for United States senator, favored by the reformers, carried. Garber contributed a peace offering by voting his Darke County delegation for Johnson's candidates, David S. Creamer for state treasurer and Timothy S. Hogan for attorney-general, both of whom won. As a final token of good will the Harmon men made unanimous Johnson's election as delegate-at-large to the national Democratic convention. Following this moving testimonial, Johnson mounted the rostrum and made a conciliatory speech. He praised the platform, refrained from any allusions to Harmon, and added, "I make my fights before conventions, not afterwards."[17]

Though the delegates were left in doubt as to what his future course might be, an editorial in the *Youngstown Vindicator* predicted, "Mayor Tom will be on the stump for the ticket long before election day." Undoubtedly written by Johnson's friend, John H. Clarke, it also expressed regret that the Mayor had attacked the propriety of Harmon's law practice, for the writer was certain that "if there is one lawyer in the state more than another who is bigger than his employment or employers, that man is Harmon. . . . " True to his word, Johnson did bury the hatchet when he met the party nominee in Columbus a week later. Johnson promised to support him in the campaign; Harmon agreed to back the platform.[18]

Not all the reformers, however, were so easily assuaged. Negley Cochran condemned the candidate and the convention as being as much boss-controlled as their Republican counterparts. Peter Witt unleashed his sarcasm in a letter of May 7 to Brand Whitlock, which was published two days later in the *Enquirer*: "With the stamp of Clevelandism on his back, sitting astride a barrel of whiskey Judson Harmon is the candidate of the system for Governor of Ohio, yelling like a Comanshe indian [sic] for 'personal liberty.' But for its sadness it would be amusing. An agent of booze, the product of bosses, the representative of predatory wealth as the champion of 'personal liberty' (whatever that may mean), is a sight for gods and men to behold." Since no self-respecting man could vote for either him or the Republican candidate, Witt pleaded for a third party with Whitlock at the head of the ticket, a proposal that came to naught.[19]

It was characteristic of Johnson to bounce back from defeat and turn with unflagging optimism to the next matter at hand. By the end of June he was looking forward to the Democratic national convention with the same high hopes that he had felt before the state conference. A national committeeman and intimate of Bryan, the party favorite, Johnson had reason to believe he might play an effective role at the convention to be held in Denver. He left on July 2, several days early, to confer en route with Bryan in Lincoln, Nebraska. The Mayor was eager to persuade the candidate to commit himself in advance to platform planks endorsing the initiative and referendum and public owner- ship of all utilities and denouncing the use of injunctions in labor disputes.[20]

Bryan, who had previously endorsed these three reforms, was now more interested in creating a public image of himself as a moderate than as a champion of radical change. Having listened to the voice of the people and concluded that the majority were opposed to government ownership, he had changed his mind on this reform and dropped it as a practical measure. He con- tinued to favor changes that would make democracy more direct, including the initiative and referendum, yet he preferred to ignore this particular reform in the platform because it was the most controversial of all. The one of the three reforms he did agree to support was the anti-injunction resolution, but only to please Samuel Gompers and the labor unions, not the Cleve- land mayor.[21]

Rebuffed by the candidate, Johnson was further humiliated by the Ohio delegation at Denver. He was defeated for re- election to the national committee, an honor that was conferred upon his archenemy, Harvey Garber, to make the gall more bitter. Anti-Johnson men were placed on the several committees. All these selections were made at the Ohio delegation caucus before the arrival of Johnson's friends, who had been stranded on the "Cleveland Special" outside of Denver. Yet even had the full Johnson strength been present, it would not have been sufficient to alter the results. Conservatives rejoiced at his humil- iation and hoped that he had been eliminated forever. Their hopes were gratified as far as Johnson personally was concerned. A year later he was defeated for mayor and left office mortally ill, never again to direct a convention fight.[22] Nevertheless, his opponents had only given a political burial to the man, not to his ideas or spirit, which were to triumph four years later.

The Democratic national convention on July 10 nominated Bryan for President and endorsed his choice for vice-president, John W. Kern of Indiana, to run on a platform that was hand- tailored to suit the Commoner and avoided controversial issues. It was scarcely distinguishable from the one the Republicans had adopted at their national convention in June. Nor did the cautious Bryan of 1908 seem to be very far apart in the political spectrum from the Republican nominee, William Howard Taft.[23]

Although this son of Ohio had received the powerful endorsement of Roosevelt as the presidential heir apparent and might
have coasted into the nomination on that asset alone, he had
not been idle in building his own political fences. His efforts
had been especially strenuous in his native state, where he was
faced with another contender for the highest honor in the nation,
Joseph B. Foraker, then completing his second term as United
States senator. In the Ohio preliminaries Taft revealed that he
was no political tyro, even though he had only run for one
elective political office, judge of the Superior Court of Cincinnati. Through federal patronage Taft gained control of the state
central committeemen, who issued a call on January 2, 1908,
for state primaries to elect delegates to the state convention
pledged to support a presidential candidate. This was a victory
for the Taft forces, since they favored, while Foraker opposed,
a clear expression by the people. Taft swept the primaries, and
his faction was in complete control of the Republican state
convention which assembled in Columbus on March 3.

The Taft partisans included, on the one hand, such independent Republicans as James R. Garfield and Arthur L. Garford, who were to be leaders in the Roosevelt Progressive Movement of 1912, Congressman Theodore Burton, and Arthur I.
Vorys, Taft's manager in the state; and on the other hand, such
regulars as Malcolm Karshner of Columbus, Maurice Maschke,
the rising star in Cleveland, Walter F. Brown of Toledo, Boss
Cox, back in the saddle after his Cincinnati victory in November
1907, and, finally, Harry M. Daugherty, Warren G. Harding,
and State Auditor Walter D. Guilbert.[24]

The convention proceedings were conducted with smoothness
and precision. The Roosevelt policies were praised, Taft was
endorsed for the Presidency and his candidacy urged upon the
nation, and the important leaders were given an opportunity
to select the slate of candidates. Burton nominated Francis W.
Treadway for lieutenant-governor; Brown chose Ulysses G. Denman for attorney-general; Guilbert and Cox named Edward M.
Fullington for state auditor and Charles C. Green for state treasurer. The ticket, headed by Andrew L. Harris, who had been
renominated for governor, was ratified by the delegates without a contest. The platform adopted was half devoted to na-

tional issues, half to state, and recommended extension of the merit system, competitive bidding for state purchases, abolition of child labor, protection of employees against loss from injuries, an effective primary law, control of public-service corporations, a referendum on franchises, and taxation of franchises, stocks, bonds, and other intangibles. Everyone was satisfied with the work of the convention except Senators Foraker and Dick, who had been ignored.[25]

In an interview after the Republicans had adjourned, Tom Johnson pointed out how their platform had progressed, now incorporating items that were considered "fads and fancies" a few years ago. But, he added, the executive departments of the state and particularly the tax machinery were still, and would remain, in the hands of the bosses in league with the public utilities, if the Republican slate of candidates was elected. It behooved his own party, he continued, to defeat this ticket and elect candidates who would dissolve the partnership between privileged business and the state Republican machine. His plea became the central theme of the state Democratic campaign.[26]

Early in the fall the Democrats were aided in their line of attack from an unexpected quarter. William Randolph Hearst, who had left the party to stump the country for Thomas L. Hisgen, presidential candidate of the Independent League, arrived in Columbus to speak on the night of September 17. A large audience, which had assembled out of idle curiousity to see the extraordinary journalist, was suddenly startled as he began reading the first of a series of letters from John D. Archbold, vice-president of the Standard Oil Company, to Ohio's senior senator, Joseph B. Foraker. The correspondence, dating from 1900 to 1903, indicated that Foraker had been the Standard's legislative agent at the same time that he was a member of the Ohio legislature and of the United States Senate and that in return for his services he had received known fees of $29,500. Such damning evidence dumfounded the public. Nor was their amazement dispelled when Foraker admitted his employment as counsel for the unpopular oil trust in Ohio and expressed the belief that his connection was common knowledge, since he was pleased to have people know he had such clients.[27] The following night in St. Louis, Hearst read two more letters, one enclosing a draft for $50,000, the other discussing an antitrust bill before the United States Senate which the Standard wanted killed. Foraker managed to explain the reason for the $50,000, which he had actually returned, and he denied that he had ever been compensated or rewarded for supporting or opposing any bill. Nevertheless, the effect of the disclosures was to force the senator from Cincinnati to bow out of the campaign.[28]

These revelations reflected not only on the personal probity of Foraker but also on the judgment of the party that had supported him. Certainly, when the Republican electorate went to the polls on November 3, they scanned the party ticket even more closely than they had in 1905. Taft received a comfortable plurality of 69,591 for President, but enough Republicans scratched their ballots to defeat the colorless Harris for governor and Charles Green, a henchman of the notorious Cox-Guilbert state machine, for state treasurer. The party, however, elected the rest of its slate, a substantial majority of the legislature, and thirteen of the twenty-one congressmen. In the contest for seats in the General Assembly the Cuyahoga Democratic delegation lost, and the representation of the Toledo Independents was reduced to one, namely, Cornell Schreiber. Nevertheless the Democrats were heartened by the victory of Harmon for governor, Creamer for state treasurer, and four more congressmen than in 1906. Bryan's return as the national standard bearer had inspired more partisans to vote than had gone to the polls in 1904. It was generally conceded that Harmon had made a remarkable race, even though his plurality of 19,372 was substantially less than Pattison's 42,647, because the Republican tendency to vote for Taft and the straight ticket gave an obvious advantage to Harmon's opponent.[29]

The bright spot for the Democratic party was Montgomery County, which reversed its traditional pattern and went solidly Democratic, giving even Bryan a plurality. The election marked the advent of a new figure in the Democratic party of Ohio, James Middleton Cox, the Dayton newspaper publisher, who was the successful candidate for Congress from the Third District. He had been urged to make the race two years before, but then he pleaded that he could not afford to leave journalism. In 1908, however, when a row among the local Republicans made the prospect bright for a Democratic candidate, he dropped a hint to his friends that he was available. He entered the contest with two strong advantages: a reputation for integrity as a journalist and a known preference for a low tariff, a view that was popular in this exporting district. In a three-cornered race he won with an actual majority over his two rivals. Still to the reformers he was an unknown quantity in 1908. Although his newspapers had backed some of their principles, he was associated with Edward W. Hanley, officer of various Dayton utilities and leader of the conservative local Democratic organization.[30]

The election of a majority to the General Assembly assured the Republicans of the United States Senate seat, but there was no party unanimity on a candidate. Foraker made it clear that he was still in the race to succeed himself. Roosevelt's choice was Theodore Burton. A third contender was the half brother of the President-elect, Charles P. Taft, a dark horse, whose intentions were a source of embarrassment to the administration in Washington. At the eleventh hour Charles Taft was persuaded to withdraw in the interest of party harmony, and Foraker, seeing that his own chances were hopeless, voluntarily retired. Burton received the vote of the Republican caucus for senator on January 2, an action that was ratified at the formal election in the General Assembly on January 12, 1909.[31]

The Republicans, who dominated the legislature, had shown a certain independence of the bosses in choosing Theodore Burton. The question remained in the minds of many how much further they would go. Would they support the Democratic governor-elect in cleaning up the state administration? Would they enact any of the reform legislation that had failed in the previous sessions? Another question of equal concern was the kind of leadership that the new governor would exercise. Would he go beyond his promise to clean house? Would he meet the reformers part way in carrying forward their program?

In his inaugural address Governor Judson Harmon announced the aims of his administration. He was to be guided by "the respect for law because it is the law, the spirit of fairness to all men under all conditions, the singleness in devotion to the common good, which gives a touch of sacredness to public duty." Voicing his opposition to the encroachment of federal power, he declared his intent to make the state government "more broadly useful," yet at the same time more efficient and economical. The people, he continued, were now aroused by the mounting expenses of government and were demanding reform. To this problem he would address himself by continuing the investigations of past betrayals of public confidence and by selecting men worthy of the people's trust.[32]

Harmon's official correspondence during his first three months in office bears witness to the sincerity of his efforts to appoint good men. Hundreds of letters poured in recommending applicants, whom he screened with painstaking care to determine their fitness for the positions to be filled. Furthermore, he refused to fire competent Republicans from office. So strictly did he apply the merit principle in making appointments that he incurred the wrath of Harvey Garber, who broke with the Governor over control of party patronage.[33]

In addition, Harmon proposed to the General Assembly in mid-January, 1909, that the investigation of affairs in Cincinnati, Cleveland, and the state treasurer's office begun in the preceding administration "be promptly and thoroughly completed." "The persons affected by the investigation," he reminded them, "had sufficient interest to go to the expense of litigation to stop it, so the public certainly has an equal interest in having it go on."[34]

The legislators responded, two Republicans and one Democrat introducing the necessary bills. Although the enthusiasm for the Cincinnati and Cleveland probes quickly died, the Republican-controlled Assembly did adopt a proposal to create a two-man, bipartisan commission to investigate the state offices. Harmon, never afraid to use his veto power, killed the measure on the grounds that it gave the governor no authority to participate and favored the interests of the officials instead of those of the state. He proceeded to conduct his own inquiries with the aid of the Democratic state treasurer, David S. Creamer.[35]

The fact that the Democrats controlled the office where the alleged evils had been the worst removed one of the obstacles confronting the earlier investigators. Although no more successful than Howe in obtaining the co-operation of banks that were going concerns, Harmon and Creamer did gain access to the books of certain financial institutions which had gone bankrupt in the intervening period. After a year's investigation they unearthed a major scandal of graft and corruption: no records had been kept of the deposits of state funds; deposits had been made by former treasurers in banks in which they had stock-holdings, and the interest rates set for the state funds had been lower than those paid on other deposits; the enormous amounts of cash reported in the state vaults, a daily average of $800,000, had actually been on hand only during the quarterly audits, and during the rest of the year they had been on deposit in banks which paid the interest directly to the state treasurers. More-over, large sums of interest had been lost to the state by the failure of other officers to turn over tax revenues promptly to the treasury. It had been the practice to deposit tax-money drafts and checks "for collection" in favored banks for long pe-riods, the interest being paid to the individual officers. Among the offending institutions were: the Euclid Avenue Trust Company in Cleveland, whose president was an intimate of William S. McKinnon; Boss Cox's Cincinnati Trust; and the Columbus Savings and Trust, of which Isaac B. Cameron, former Repub-lican state treasurer, was president.[36]

Harmon pursued two courses of action. On December 6, 1909, he directed Ulysses G. Denman, the Republican attorney-general, to bring suit against those who had betrayed their public trust. Proceedings were begun to collect $211,721 of interest on state funds illegally pocketed by Cameron, and $114,506 from the estate of the deceased McKinnon. After a delay of several years Cameron and Charles Green, McKinnon's deputy, were indicted for embezzlement by the Franklin County Grand Jury for lending state funds without authority, an indictment sustained by the Ohio Supreme Court.[37] Secondly, the Gov-ernor urged the legislature in his message of January 3, 1910, to make mandatory the reforms which Creamer had voluntarily introduced: a daily report of cash in the treasury to the gov-ernor and the auditor, weekly collection of funds by all depart-ment heads and immediate payment to the treasurer, and the allotment of state funds to depositories on the basis of competi-tive bids. Such a bill passed the Senate but failed in the House. Not until the 1911 session was the requisite legislation adopted.[38]

Not to be outdone by the executive department, the General Assembly sought to conduct its own investigations of state of-fices. Four days after the opening of the 1910 session, Democratic Senator Richard Beatty introduced, and the Republican majority approved, a joint resolution to create a bipartisan committee of four, half to be appointed by the speaker, half by the lieutenant-governor. Their probe was to supplement but not to interfere with the work of the executive department in the treasury. Although it was rumored that Harmon was offended, he dispelled the idle talk by promptly co-operating with the commission, handing to them all the pertinent material he had collected. The Beatty committee uncovered graft of the crassest sort committed by the state printer, Mark Slater, a lieutenant of Dayton's former Republican boss, Joseph E. Lowes. Supply bills had been padded by thousands of dollars. In one instance goods which had been purchased for $1,647.10 were billed at $16,455.90. Further investigation revealed that this evil had been widespread, practiced by clerks in the offices of the state fire marshal, the railroad commission, and the secretary of state. The evidence was turned over to the Franklin County Grand Jury, which indicted Slater, two former state department and railroad commission clerks, and their accomplices.[39]

Nor was this all. Harmon conducted inquiries into the management of the state penal and charitable institutions, discovering waste, incompetence, payrolls padded with unnecessary jobs awarded as political plums, and working agreements between the stewards and favored merchants. In some instances there were political ramifications. One merchant, for example, controlled the legislative delegation from a senatorial district, all of whom were pledged to prevent any meddling with state institutions.[40]

Although some took alarm at the conditions revealed by these exposures, others recognized in the investigations themselves the signs of a "moral renaissance" of the people. In one of his Sunday night sermons Washington Gladden took this subject as his theme. He applauded the spirit prompting such inquiries. "The improved ethical sentiment of the people," he declared, "is now seen to be reflected in the character of their representatives in office, and this explains the new activity of officials in ferreting out graft and punishing crimes. These evils, lately exposed, are of long standing; they afford no evidence that things are growing worse. . . ."[41]

Exposing fraud and waste, cleaning up the management of

state affairs, elevating the tone of government — these were Harmon's distinctive contributions to reform. Conservatives and reformers alike applauded his activities. Yet, whereas the former considered such goals the ultimate in reform, the latter counted them only on the negative side and insisted in addition on a positive, aggressive program to extend democracy and economic equality. Harmon, despite his conservative tendencies, was willing to go part way with the reformers. He accepted, for example, the need for tax reform to eliminate unjust discriminations and restore fair treatment of all interests. He believed in applying the same standards to business as to government and in the right of the state to enforce proper rules of conduct. But beyond that he would not go, and toward several of the key proposals of the reformers he was either indifferent or hostile.[42]

The Governor was not the only impediment in the path of thoroughgoing reform. The Republican-dominated legislature threatened to obstruct even the limited measures of change which the administration was willing to sponsor.[43] Democratic newspapers saw the specter of George Cox, who dominated the large Hamilton County delegation, behind these moves. It was alleged that the Cincinnati boss would try to repeal the amendments to the municipal and election codes passed in the previous session. Actually, however, progressive Republicans controlled the organization of the House of Representatives, selecting as speaker Granville W. Mooney, a teacher from Ashtabula County, who appointed able, high-minded chairmen to the important committees. Forming a coalition with like-minded Democrats, this Republican group proposed legislation that was more sweeping than Harmon's program.[44]

In the Senate the reverse was true: reactionary Republicans in league with Democrats of similar stamp organized the chamber and acted as a brake on reform proposals. The reformers were infuriated when eleven Democrats joined a minority of eight Republicans to elect Thorne Baker, a "Cox senator" from Cincinnati, chairman of the important finance committee. Negley Cochran's New-Bee declared: "The spectacle afforded by the Democratic senators at Columbus is one to make God weep and the decent people of Ohio hold their noses." Harmon and William Finley made a personal investigation of the vote to see if it reflected a conspiracy between these Democrats and the Cox Republicans as was alleged. Their findings, however, indicated that the alliance was a temporary one and represented nothing more than an indulgence in obstructionist tactics. Nevertheless, the reactionary character of five of the Democrats who were a party to the vote was not to be denied.[45]

The legislature met in special session in 1909 principally to elect a United States senator and pass an appropriation bill, but a host of other proposals were offered, most of which were carried over to the regular session of 1910. During its first year the press characterized the legislature as a "do-nothing" body; however, reaction to its second session was somewhat less harsh as a result of the improved record.[46]

From the point of view of the Johnson reformers the Seventy-eighth General Assembly achieved one great triumph, the enactment of a broad program of tax reform. The educational work begun by the Cleveland Mayor in 1901 and carried forward by the Tax Commission of 1908 had slowly converted a majority to the necessity of overhauling the tax machinery. So thoroughly had the radical program permeated the thinking of the legislators that progressive Republicans were as eager to sponsor this reform as the Democrats.

In his inaugural address Harmon had asked the legislature for "fairer and more effective rules and methods for the taxation of both real and personal property, private and corporate." Although that body responded by initiating bills to achieve this end, the only one to pass in 1909 was the Quadrennial Assesment Act. Introduced by two Republican senators, Milton E. Rathburn of Meigs County and Albert Mendelson of Cuyahoga County, it passed the upper chamber without a dissenting vote, and six days later the lower house concurred. In addition to shortening the period between the appraisements of real estate from ten to four years, it introduced even more revolutionary features. Each township and village was to elect one appraiser, each city a board of five assessors on a nonpartisan ballot to conduct the valuation work, and each board was empowered to hire such clerical assistants and experts as were necessary. Most important, their valuation figures were to be printed in pamphlet form and distributed to every taxpayer. The act embodied most of the reforms which the Cleveland Tax School had first introduced in 1901 and brought Ohio in line with the best practices in other states.[47]

Because of the failure to enact any further part of the program, Governor Harmon opened the regular session of 1910 with a message listing a set of proposals for additional tax reforms. He recommended the creation of a state tax commission to replace the numerous ex officio state boards, which had been urged by the tax probe in 1908; he endorsed two changes long supported by the municipal reformers: to apply the unit rule of the Nichols Law to all utility corporations and to allow cities to appoint their tax boards of review. Also he included two measures which had had conservative backing: to abolish the state tax on property and to place a 1 per cent limit on tax levies.[48]

Particularly dear to the Governor was the proposal for a tax ceiling. He correctly anticipated that the limitation would aid the quadrennial assessors in appraising real property at its true value, as described below. Furthermore, he believed a low rate would encourage public-spirited persons, who regarded the existing levies of 3 to 4 per cent as confiscatory, to declare their intangible property. An administration bill placing a ceiling on the tax rate of 1 per cent of the assessed valuation was introduced in the Senate by Senator Walter A. Alsdorf of Licking County. Cries of protest from the Cleveland and Cincinnati senators, who declared their cities could not operate under such a limit, led to an amendment before passage to permit the figure to be increased by a referendum vote. In its final form, as approved by both houses, the measure raised the maximum to 1.5 per cent exclusive of sinking fund and interest, required a 60 per cent vote to approve an increase above the maximum, and placed a limit on bonded indebtedness.[49]

By the end of January, 1910, a second recommendation of the governor, namely, to establish a state tax commission, had been reintroduced in two separate bills. One, the so-called administration measure, was placed before the Senate by Alsdorf; another, more radical one, was presented to the House by a progressive Republican, Lawrence K. Langdon of Warren County. Langdon's proposal extended the basis of valuation of the Nichols Law to all utilities, while this recommendation of Harmon's had been deleted from Alsdorf's. Before either bill came to a vote, advocates of this reform were aided by a fortuitous law suit. A Standard Oil subsidiary, the Buckeye Pipe Line Company, challenged the constitutionality of the Cole Law excise levy on gross receipts because it taxed business done outside the state. Attorney-General Denman, fearing that the courts would sustain the company's contention, urged that the principle of the Nichols Law be applied to all utilities. A few days later, on March 16, the House passed the Langdon bill with near unanimity, 101 to 2.

Although losing the battle in the lower chamber, the utilities still had hopes of emasculating the bill by amendments in the conservative Senate. Their attorneys were endeavoring to persuade the committee in charge to substitute a vague clause for the clear language of the Langdon measure extending the unit rule. It was reported that the railroads were exerting pressure on the Buckeye Pipe Line to drop its suit, but the company refused. On April 29 the Senate passed the Langdon bill unanimously, its essential provisions intact.[50]

By this legislation Ohio moved from its position among the backward states to the ranks of those that had been most progressive in tax reform, such as Pennsylvania, Illinois, New York, Connecticut, Michigan, and Wisconsin. The new act swept away the sprawling number of ex officio state boards, as well as the boards of county auditors for assessing railroads, and concentrated their authority in a three-man commission. It was empowered to tax all utilities at their true value in money, including franchises, good will and other intangible assets; to equalize the basis on which excise taxes and taxes on bank shares were paid; and to sit as a state board of equalization for the appraisement of real estate which was then being made under the previously described Quadrennial Assessment Act.[51]

Governor Harmon helped to implement the law by staffing the tax commission with able appointees, namely, Judge Robert M. Ditty, an expert on the legal aspects of taxation and a student of European tax methods, who had helped frame the tax commission bill; Francis E. Munn, a Wood County banker and farmer, who had had wide experience in land appraisal; and Christian Pabst, who had served as auditor of Butler County and as a member of the board of public service of the city of Hamilton. Although the commissioners took office on July 1, 1910, their important work did not begin until the first of January 1, 1911.

By then the commission had prepared new forms on which each utility in the state had to report its capitalization, income, and property to the smallest detail. The result was a thorough revaluation of every utility company in Ohio and a remarkable increase in their assessment.[52]

The extent of the increases was a measure of the astonishing inefficiency of the old state and county boards of assessors. Tom Johnson's pioneer investigations were being substantiated many fold. Even the telegraph and telephone companies assessed before under the unit-rule principle of the Nichols Law had their valuations doubled and trebled respectively. Much more extraordinary were the increases in the valuations of the other utilities which had escaped the application of the unit rule. Abandoning the principles and practices of the previous boards, the commission arrived at the valuations of these companies by using the market value of their stock as a guide—the principle of the Nichols Law—and combined it with another method of valuation based on the capitalization of net earnings. Under this scientific system of assessment, the valuation of steam railroads was raised over 300 per cent, street and interurban railways 400 per cent, electric-light companies nearly 500 per cent, natural-gas corporations 250 per cent, and all utilities 370 per cent. The total dollar increase was from about $263,000,000 to nearly $913,000,000.[53]

If such results definitely established the worth of centralized assessment for public utilities, the success of the commission in co-ordinating the work of the quadrennial appraisers of real property was further corroboration. The reappraisal begun in 1910 and completed in 1911 was the most satisfactory assessment of real estate that had ever been achieved in the state. Each county and city elected its own board of assessors to initiate the work of establishing property values. The model community was Cleveland, where the board, which included Frederick Howe and other Johnson men, applied the scientific Somers system of unit valuation to every city lot and building, with the direct assistance of W. A. Somers himself, who served as chief clerk. In most of the other major cities and in a majority of the counties the work was also effectively done. The exceptions were Cincinnati, where the George Cox machine controlled the board, thirty-two other small cities, and twenty-nine counties. However, their initial effort to perpetuate the existing undervaluations and inequities was not allowed to stand. The state tax commission was empowered to act as an agency to review and equalize the returns from the local boards. It ordered the recalcitrant communities and counties to redo their work and assisted them by sending experts into the field to collect data from sales abstracts and to discuss relative property values. The final figures revealed that the assessment of Ohio real estate had been increased 154 per cent, from about $1,662,000,000 to nearly $4,250,000,000. For the first time the constitutional requirement of valuing tangible property at its true value had been nearly met.[54]

Several factors contributed to this result. The tax-limitation law, already described, made the increased values palatable to small homeowners and, at the same time, forced many communities to raise their assessments in order to obtain needed operating revenues. The virtual elimination of the direct state tax on real estate removed what had been a source before of competitive undervaluation by local governments. Popular dissatisfaction with the existing tax conditions was another contributing element. Finally, the tax commission itself deserves the major credit for the overall results because of its enforcement of an upward revision in every county and city.[55]

In the interest of efficiency and economy, Governor Harmon proposed to centralize other branches of the state administration. During his campaign it had been brought to his attention that there was general dissatisfaction with the management of the state's benevolent, reformatory, and penal institutions. As previously noted, he investigated and found that the charges of waste in purchasing and political interference in the selection of personnel were not idle suspicions but facts. He became convinced that the defect was in the system itself, which needed radical overhauling, not merely tinkering.[56]

In response to the needs of population growth and urban-industrial expansion, the state had established nineteen such institutions and was constructing a new hospital for the criminal insane at Lima. Although the long-established Ohio Board of State Charities exercised a general supervision over the several institutions, each unit was in fact a separate entity, controlled by its own board of trustees serving part time without compensation. They appointed the superintendent, the steward, and the entire staff, approved of all contracts, and set the standards for their particular institution. The inmates of all the institutions totaled fifty thousand, and expenses had nearly doubled in the last twenty years. It was this spiraling rise in cost that alarmed the economy-minded governor. Certain that large savings would accrue from centralization, he advocated that the responsibility for managing all these institutions be removed from the separate trustee boards and entrusted to a commission of four experts paid to devote their whole time to these affairs.[57]

Senator Alsdorf introduced Harmon's bill in the Senate, calling for a central board of administration, the merit system, joint purchasing, and a renovated bookkeeping system. Publicly endorsed by Theodore Burton, it received enough Republican support to pass the upper chamber twenty to thirteen. The House finance committee, however, was willing to experiment in only a tentative way, amending the bill to limit its application to the state's penitentiary and three reformatories and excluding the civil service provision. In this form it passed the House and was accepted by the Senate unanimously, only to be vetoed by Harmon, who refused to countenance "the mangled remains of a carefully drawn measure." A board thus restricted, he argued, could not make a fair showing and the results would cast further discredit on the plan.[58]

In still other ways Harmon recommended that the state tighten the administration of its penal and charitable institutions. Since the passage of the Wertz Law prohibited the use of convict labor by private industry, he proposed that the inmates of the penitentiary be employed to manufacture goods for political subdivisions as well as the state itself. In his inaugural he said, "The inmates cannot be left idle, and the taxpayers of the state will hold us responsible if our prison labor is not made at least self-supporting. . . ." Instead of introducing any legislation, however, the General Assembly appointed a committee to investigate the matter. Nor did it take any action on Harmon's recommendation that the expense of caring for the insane be partially reduced by requiring those who could afford it to pay for their keep.[59]

Throughout the discussion of the subject Harmon showed no awareness of the humanitarian gospel which inspired the work of Johnson and Cooley in Cleveland, Jones and Whitlock in Toledo. The taxpayer, not the convict or ward, was foremost in his mind. Although he accepted the Christian duty of caring for the afflicted, he insisted that it must be accomplished without selfish waste or sentimental extravagance and indulgence.[60] This was evidence again of his essential conservatism.

Another sign was his indifference toward the expansion of state regulation over public-service corporations through the creation of a commission with broad powers. Although he approved of the centralization of existing machinery and authority, if he were satisfied that it would mean greater efficiency and economy, he was reluctant to substantially extend state control into new economic and social areas. The initiative in advocating such regulatory legislation was taken by a progressive Republican member of the House, Frank W. Woods of Medina. Drawing heavily upon the experience of New York and Wisconsin, pioneers in this field, he proposed a three-man commission with power to regulate the services, rates, and charges of all public-service corporations, to require the return of full financial information on which to base actual valuation, to prescribe a uniform accounting system, and to control the issuance of stocks and bonds. Under Wood's bill the cities retained home rule over local utilities, but the state board could step in whenever the council failed or lacked the power to insure adequate service. Introduced first in the 1909 session, when it passed the House only to fail in the Senate, it was dropped into the legislative mill again the following year.[61]

On February 26, 1910, a counterproposal was sponsored by the Democratic floor leader, Cyrus B. Winters of Erie County, whose bill offered to extend the authority of the existing railroad commission, without enlarging its powers, to all utilities except those operating in municipalities. The effect of this version was to draw the teeth of the Woods proposal. Though there was much speculation that Harmon would make the Winters bill an administration measure, he preferred to remain silent.[62]

Threatened with effective regulation, the utilities, through their attorneys and lobbyists, painted a dire picture of the industrial disaster that would occur were the Woods bill to pass. A Republican delegation made a pilgrimage to Washington to persuade President Taft to openly oppose the proposal. Wisely he declined to comment, maintaining that the members of the General Assembly should make their own decision. In the final House debate Frank Woods defended his measure in these words:

> I have heard it said there is no demand for the regulation of public service corporations. I do not think any well posted man thinks so. States all around us have gone further than Ohio. Rich and poor alike say the New York Commission law is good. Wisconsin is satisfied with its iron-clad law. In this state we hardly regulate utilities at all. . . .
> I have been called an anarchist. I hope I am not. I believe the big corporations for their own salvation had better ask for regulation. If they knew what was good for them, they would have done so instead of placing every block in the way they could. They will have to accept some regulation either this year or later and the longer it is deferred, the more stringent will be the regulation imposed.

On March 30 the lower chamber passed the Woods bill by the overwhelming vote of ninety-one to sixteen. Credit for the victory belonged to the author, whose sincerity was persuasive, Speaker Granville Mooney, and William E. Bense of Ottawa County, an enthusiastic advocate who had lined up thirty-nine of his Democratic colleagues in support of the measure, declaring that since it exemplified "simon pure Democratic doctrine," they could not afford to oppose it merely because it was Republican-inspired. Harmon's only part in the proceedings was to let it be known through the speaker that he was not hostile to the bill.[63]

After their defeat in the House the utilities stepped up their opposition, bombarding senators with letters and petitions to prevent final passage. Under pressure from the railroads, manufacturers of their supplies jammed the Senate mailboxes with letters, all similar in tone and phrasing, describing the peril to the transportation companies if the bill were to be adopted. The lines, they argued, would not have enough money left after taxes to buy supplies, and the commission would prohibit further rail extensions in the state. As the *Ohio State Journal* dryly remarked, the railroads seemed to be talking nonsense to the suppliers. Nevertheless such propaganda and other pressure were successful. On April 25 the Woods bill, mutilated by six hundred amendments but still providing for a skeleton of regulation, was reported out of committee; three days later, even in this truncated form, the Senate killed it by an adverse vote of ten to twenty-two, the Republicans splitting nine to nine, while all the Democrats save one were on the negative side. Although the Cuyahoga Republican senators, backed by Theodore Burton, pleaded for favorable action, pointing out that the committee had amended the measure to meet most of the demands of the corporations, they failed to alter the opposition of either one of their party leaders in the upper chamber, Frank N. Patterson and Nation O. Mather, or the partisan hostility of the Democrats.[64]

The press promptly blamed Harmon for the defeat of the measure. The *Toledo News-Bee* took him to task for his lack of interest and his weak explanation that he had not read the amended bill before the vote. Was the real Harmon a reactionary, they queried? Had he been too long out of public life to recognize the great progressive movement sweeping the country? Harmon's negative virtues of honesty and Democratic simplicity were not enough. "A few more Woods bill episodes," the paper concluded, "and the political future of Ohio's honest, rugged governor will be about as dark as that of another distinguished citizen of Cincinnati at present residing in Washington [President Taft]." The Republican *Ohio State Journal* urged its party to make a campaign issue of the charge that Harmon was responsible for the bill's defeat.[65]

To make amends for killing the Woods proposal the Senate on April 30 did approve a bill passed by the House strengthening the powers of the railroad commission and making definite its authority to regulate rates and services, which had been attacked in the circuit court. Although opposed by the railroads it had the powerful backing of the Ohio Shippers' Association.[66]

While the lobby had been strenuous in its exertions against these utility regulation measures, no breath of scandal touched its activity. Such was not the case, however, in the fight over a third bill introduced by Asa W. Elson, a rural Democrat from Tuscarawas County, to permit the merger of every telephone company in Ohio without state control over their security issues. Since it ran counter to the Woods bill and since there was the obvious threat of watered stock being issued by the consolidated companies, many legislators were hostile to it from the start. Despite the opposition, it passed the House by the narrow margin of fifty-nine to fifty. No sooner had the vote been taken than charges were made by the members that the telephone lobby had resorted to corrupt practices to insure its passage. At the investigation which was ordered by the House, one Democrat, Howard W. Pears, testified that he had been offered a bribe of $100 for his vote; another, Cyrus Winters, was told he could have anything he wanted if he would support the bill. Under this cloud of bribery charges, the bill reached the Senate. Although its friends managed to postpone consideration for a week to enable the telephone interests to work on the members, it was voted down fourteen to nineteen, only five Republicans and nine Democrats willing to support it.[67]

Following the exposé of the lobbyists' methods in this instance, Harmon sent a special message to the General Assembly, urging the adoption of a measure patterned after a New York law which required the registration of all legislative agents, a listing of the clients whom they represented, and a declaration of the measures in which they were interested. The House promptly passed such a bill under suspension of the rules and reported it to the Senate, where it was tabled by voice vote. This unceremonious course was defended on the ground that the Governor's interference in legislative matters was unwarranted.[68]

On other reform legislation the record of the General Assembly was none too impressive. The initiative and referendum bills for which Herbert Bigelow continued to find legislative sponsors were defeated in both sessions. Election reform fared little better. Efforts to promote a state woman-suffrage amendment were abortive. A bill to make the judicial ballot nonpartisan was also defeated. Except for one law making mandatory direct-primary elections for congressional candidates and delegates to national party conventions, the legislative action was mainly directed at beating down attempts to destroy the structure already built. One defeated bill would have re-enacted the old Dana Law prohibiting a candidate's name from appearing more than once on a ballot; another would have dispensed with the compulsory direct primary in villages, townships, and municipalities not having a registration of voters.[69] Cities received some minor favors but no major benefits.[70]

Moral reform continued to command the attention of the legislators. Although no new advances were made toward state-wide prohibition, the Anti-Saloon League was successful in forestalling any tampering with the existing county local-option law. The League's backing of a measure to permit the governor to remove a mayor for refusal to enforce the laws, however, proved the bill's undoing. The health and morals of Ohio minors were protected against that "little giant of evil," that "character destroyer," the cigarette, by raising the legal age for smoking from sixteen to twenty-one. In answer to the pleas of the workingmen an optional Sunday-baseball law was adopted, only to be vetoed by the Governor as special legislation in violation of the constitution.[71]

Increased recognition of labor's interests was manifested in other ways. Although spurning the demand for a nine-hour law for women the legislature did pass three other important labor bills. One radically modified the common-law defenses in industrial accident suits and took the first step in establishing employers' liability in Ohio. In damage claims for injury or death occurring in industry the existing laws stacked the cards markedly in favor of the employer, who could claim three defenses—the fellow-servant rule, contributory negligence, or assumption of risk. The new statute ruled out the negligence of a fellow servant as a defense, declared that slight contributory negligence was no bar to recovery, and stated that an employee was assuming no risk when carrying out the instructions of his employer or "superior." Limits were set on the amount of damage claims which could be recovered by heirs or dependents in the event of death.[72] A second act was a corollary of the first one, and established a five-man commission to study employers' liability statutes in other states. A third adopted a comprehensive revision of the Mining Code, stiffening the safety rules and permitting the chief mine inspector to enjoin a mine owner who violated them from further operation until the standards were met.[73]

Although there was grudging admission that the General Assembly had done some good things, the tone of the press was one of disappointment. The *Cleveland Plain Dealer* dwelt on the work undone, particularly the defeat of the Woods bill and the emasculation of the central-board measure. In praising the House for its independence of corporate interests and condemning the Senate for its subserviency, the newspapers tacitly recognized the division over reform.[74] It was not between one set of men wearing the Republican label and another the Democratic; rather it was between progressives, as the reformers were now called, and conservatives within each party. Scrutiny of the record of the past session would support the claim that more friends of reform were Republicans than Democrats. What did the future hold? Would the party of Mark Hanna become once again the party of Lincoln in Ohio? Had the Johnson reformers, with the retirement of their leader, become impotent in the councils of the Democratic party? These were questions which the political events in the summer and fall of 1910 were to answer.

1. *Canton* (Ohio) *Repository,* February 20, 28, 1908; *Ohio State Journal* (Columbus), February 29, 1908; F. M. Vanover and Others to Atlee Pomerene, February 27, 1908, in the Papers of Atlee Pomerene (MSS in the Kent State University Library, Kent, Ohio [herefater referred to as Pomerene Papers]).

2. The biographical data on Pomerene are drawn from articles in the *Canton* (Ohio) *News-Democrat,* October 28, 1893, and the *Ohio State Journal,* May 6, 1908.

3. Pomerene's support of Johnson was reported in the *Canton News-Democrat,* October 21, 1903, his support of Pattison in the *Cleveland Plain Dealer,* October 18, 1905. In a letter, the tone of which indicated a degree of intimacy and fondness for the younger man, Pattison chided Pomerene for making so little effort to become elected (John M. Pattison to Atlee Pomerene, November 20, 1905, Pomerene Papers).

4. Johnson's accusations were quoted in the *Cincinnati Enquirer,* February 26, 1908; the maneuvers and exchanges between the two men were reported in the *Ohio State Journal,* February 26, March 8, 13, 1908, the harmony meeting in *ibid.,* March 26, 1908.

5. *Cleveland News,* February 29, 1908; *Columbus Evening Dispatch,* April 19, 1908; Charles P. Salen, "The Democratic Opportunity," *Ohio Magazine,* IV (March, 1908), 226–28.

6. *Ohio State Journal,* April 5, 1908.

7. The physical description and accounts of Harmon's early life are drawn from William B. Hale, "Judson Harmon and the Presidency," *World's Work,* XXII (June, 1911), 14,446; Robert M. Ditty, *Judson Harmon of Ohio, a Man of Deeds, not Words* (Columbus [1912?]), 1–2; Arthur C. Cole, "Judson Harmon," *Dictionary of American Biography,* VIII, 277; and Hugh L. Nichols, "Judson Harmon," *Ohio Archaeological and Historical Quarterly,* XLI (1932), 141–42.

8. Judson Harmon and Frederick N. Judson to W. H. Moody, Attorney-General, June 5, 1905, printed in the *Cincinnati Enquirer,* June 22, 1905.

The whole dispute was well aired in the press (*ibid.*, June 17, 22, 1905). It is discussed in Nichols, "Harmon," 141–42. Morton resigned but Theodore Roosevelt's confidence in him remained undisturbed (Salen, "The Democratic Opportunity," 230).

9. The most sympathetic portrait of Harmon is in Nichols, "Harmon," 142–43, 149. Critical analyses, especially on the point of his progressivism, are in Hale, "Judson Harmon and the Presidency," 14,456–59; Burton J. Hendrick, "Judson Harmon: Progressive Candidate," *McClure's Magazine*, XXXVIII (April, 1912), 619–24; and Harry B. Mackoy, "Judson Harmon," *Independent*, LXIX (September 29, 1910), 698–99.

10. *A Story of Progress in Ohio during Governor Judson Harmon's Administration* (Columbus [1911]), 1–2; James K. Mercer, ed. and compiler, *Ohio Legislative History* (6 vols.; Columbus [1914] - 1926) [I], 14, 125–28.

11. On the eve of the convention Johnson issued a signed statement attacking Harmon (*Toledo News-Bee,* May 5, 1908). The Finley-Garber support and the widespread backing for Harmon were reported in the *Ohio State Journal,* March 26, April 5, 1908, and in Powell, *The Democratic Party of the State of Ohio,* I, 419–20.

12. *Ohio State Journal,* May 6–7, 1908; *Cleveland Plain Dealer,* May 6, 1908. The split in the delegation from Hamilton County was between the Bernard-Harmon forces and the pro-Bryan wing, which favored Pomerene. None of the Vine Street radicals, such as Bigelow, Kiefer, or Lawson, were members of the delegation. (*Cincinnati Enquirer,* May 4, 1908.)

13. *Cleveland Plain Dealer,* May 7, 1908.

14. The two Johnson speeches were reported in *ibid.,* May 6–7, 1908, his nominating speech for Pomerene in the *Canton Repository,* May 6, 1908. Attacks against Johnson were made in the *Cincinnati Enquirer,* May 7, 1908, and in the author's interview on September 28, 1949, with Graham P. Hunt, then the leader of the Harmon forces in the Hamilton County delegation. Why Johnson delivered such a tirade against Harmon is a question not easily answered. Certainly it was not warranted by the character of the man, who was honest, forthright, and not a tool of the interests. In part, Johnson may have been led astray by the Vine Street radicals as well as by members of his own circle, like Peter Witt, who were bitter in their denunciations of Harmon. It was hard for Johnson to forgive a member of his party who differed with him on principle, as did Harmon. At the time of the convention Johnson was under a great strain because the strike against the Municipal Traction Company was still in progress. Finally, his own ill health tended to mar his judgment during these days. For all or part of these reasons he gave a performance that was as uncharacteristic as it was unworthy of him.

15. On the first ballot Harmon received 463 votes, Pomerene 381; on the second, Harmon was nominated with 512 votes. Pomerene's total dropped to 363. (*Ohio State Journal,* May 7, 1908; Powell, ed., *The Democratic Party of the State of Ohio,* I ,420)

16. *Ohio State Journal,* May 7, 1908.

17. *Ibid.,* May 7, 1908. The nominees for other offices were: Hugh T. Mathers and George B. Okey, justices of the supreme court; Henry W. Newman, secretary of state; William W. Durbin, auditor of state; Bernard Doran and Joseph A. Slates, members of the board of public works; David Eley, dairy and food commissioner; and John A. McDowel, state school commis-

sioner (Powell, ed., *The Democratic Party of the State of Ohio*, I, 420–21). The other three delegates-at-large to the Democratic national convention were pro-Bryan but anti-Johnson men, Matthew R. Denver, Edward W. Hanley, and Will S. Thomas (*Cleveland Plain Dealer*, May 7, 1908).

18. The editorial appeared in the *Youngstown Vindicator*, May 7, 1908. Clarke, although he lived and practiced law in Cleveland, continued to write regularly for the *Vindicator*, in which he had a part interest (Warner, *The Life of Justice Clarke*, 10, 52). The Johnson-Harmon reconciliation was reported in the *Cleveland Plain Dealer*, May 16, 1908.

19. *Toledo News-Bee*, May 7, 1908; Peter Witt to Brand Whitlock, May 7, 1908, Whitlock Papers; reprinted in the *Cincinnati Enquirer*, May 9, 1908. Whitlock himself did not share Witt's bitterness. After the election Whitlock sent a congratulatory letter to Harmon expressing his pleasure in the latter's victory because he was a city man and interested in penitentiary reform. (Brand Whitlock to Judson Harmon, November 13, 1908, Whitlock Papers) Newton Baker, although unsympathetic to the Governor-elect, could "see no particular good" in the controversy that Witt was seeking to have with Harmon (N. D. Baker to Daniel Kiefer, June 17, 1908, Baker Papers, CCH).

20. *Cleveland Plain Dealer*, July 3, 1908.

21. A discerning and sympathetic discussion of Bryan's views in 1908 is in Glad, *The Trumpet Soundeth*, 94, 97, 103–5, 136–37, 162–63.

22. Baker thought Bryan's treatment of Johnson was unforgivable (N. D. Baker to Daniel Kiefer, January 8, 1912, Baker Papers, CCH). *Cleveland Plain Dealer*, July 8, 1908; *Cincinnati Enquirer*, July 8, 1908. An editorial in the *Ohio State Journal* reported that "all the people" were gratified that Johnson had been eliminated as the chieftain of Ohio Democracy, but it expressed doubt that he had been buried for good (*ibid.*, July 8, 1908). Johnson's defeat as mayor and his retirement are reported above on Chap. III, p. 73.

23. The Democratic national convention was reported in the *Cleveland Plain Dealer*, July 10–11, 1908, the Republican in the *Ohio State Journal*, June 18–19, 1908. At Denver there was an incipient boom for Harmon as a vice-presidential candidate, which had support from Southern delegates and, surprisingly enough, the approval of the Johnson crowd, probably in the hope that such a nomination would remove Harmon from the gubernatorial race and give Pomerene a second chance (*Cincinnati Enquirer*, July 11, 1908).

24. *Ohio State Journal*, January 3, February 12, 1908. *Cleveland Plain Dealer*, February 12, March 4, 1908. Walters, *Foraker*, 258–68. Morison and Blum, eds., *The Letters of Theodore Roosevelt*; V. 670, n. 2; 720, n. 1; VI, 1149, n. 1. Robert F. Wolfe to T. E. Burton, January 23, 1908; Datus R. Jones to T. E. Burton, November 28, 1908, Burton Papers.

25. *Ohio State Journal*, March 5, 1908; *Cleveland Plain Dealer*, March 5, 1908; Walters, *Foraker*, 267–68; T. E. Burton to Nat C. Wright, February 27, 1908, Burton Papers.

26. Johnson was quoted in the *Ohio State Journal*, March 6, 1908. Campaign speeches which heeded his plea were reported in the *Cleveland Plain Dealer*, September 27, October 2, 1908, and the *Dayton Daily News*, October 28, 30, 1908. Johnson's criticisms of the Republican slate was privately shared by Congressman Burton, who regarded the selection of Green as "a mistake" and thought the party had "enough to carry" in Fullington and Denman (T. E. Burton to William S. Fitzgerald, March 23,

1908, Burton Papers). According to the Congressman, the ticket had been poorly chosen because of the priority given to other demands: Taft's endorsement, a strong platform, and a desire to avoid the charge of "bossism" in making up the slate (T. E. Burton to Dataus R. Jones, April 9, 1908, Burton Papers).

27. *Ohio State Journal,* September 18, 1908; the letters are quoted in Walters, *Foraker,* 273–74. They had been rifled from the company files by two employees and sold to Hearst (*ibid.,* 282). Foraker replied in an open letter printed in the *Ohio State Journal,* September 19, 1908.

28. *Ohio State Journal,* September 19, 1908. The $50,000 draft was a loan advanced to Foraker to assist him in the purchase of the *Ohio State Journal,* which was on the market in January, 1902, for $135,000. The deal fell through when Robert F. Wolfe, with the aid of the Hanna-Herrick faction, bought the paper, and Foraker returned the money, a fact that Hearst had deliberately omitted (*ibid.,* September 20, 1908; Walters, *Foraker,* 276–80). There is an excellent analysis of the reaction to the Foraker disclosures in the national press in *ibid.,* 281–82.

29. *Cleveland Plain Dealer,* November 4–6, 1908; *Cincinnati Enquirer,* November 5–6, 1908; *Toledo News-Bee,* November 4–6, 1908. The Ohio election returns were as follows: for President, Taft (Republican) 573,312; Bryan (Democrat) 502,271; Eugene V. Debs (Socialist) 33,795; Eugene Chafin (Prohibition) 11,402; Thomas Hisgen (Independent) 439; Thomas E. Watson (People's) 162; August Gilhaus (Socialist Labor) 721; for governor, Harmon (Democrat) 552,569; Harris (Republican) 533,197; Robert Bandlow (Socialist) 28,573; John B. Martin (Prohibition) 7,665; Andrew F. Otte (Independent) 397; John Kircher (Socialist Labor) 797 (*Report of the Secretary of State of Ohio* [1908], 134, 138). Creamer's defeat of Green was not verified until the official tabulation had been made several days after the election. His plurality was 1,431. The rest of the Republicans won by pluralities ranging from 19,000 to 54,000. (Mercer, ed., *Ohio Legislative History* [I], 16). In Cuyahoga County the only Democrat elected was Charles Salen, whom Peter Witt accused of selling out the rest of the ticket in order to get Republican votes for himself (*Cleveland Plain Dealer,* November 4, 1908). In Toledo the Republicans were able to do so well because the opposition was split among the Independent Voters, Democrats, and workingmen who supported the Socialist ticket (*Toledo News-Bee,* November 4–6, 1908).

30. The election results were reported in the *Dayton Daily News,* November 4–6, 1908. Cox's campaign is described in *ibid.,* October 20, 23, 1908, and in Cox, *Journey through My Years,* 57–58. Cox stated that Edward W. Hanley, chairman of the Montgomery County Democratic Executive Committee, was the most important influence in overcoming his reluctance to enter politics. The vote in the Third Congressional District was Cox (Democrat) 32,324; William G. Frizell (Republican) 12,593; John E. Harding (Independent) 19,306 (*Report of the Secretary of State of Ohio* [1908], 193–203).

31. *Cleveland Plain Dealer,* January 1, 1909; Walters, *Foraker,* 283–84; Crissey, *Burton,* 161–79. In addition, J. Warren Kiefer, Harry M. Daugherty, Dr. Charles A. Reed, and Warren G. Harding were also potential candidates. The vote for senator in the General Assembly divided on strictly partisan lines: Burton (Republican) 89; Campbell (Democrat) 57; Harmon (Demo-

crat) 1 (*Ohio State Journal*, January 13, 1909). Burton, who felt that he was entitled in 1908 to the Republican nomination for senator because he had been ignored after Hanna's death in 1904, announced his candidacy early. Then he was persuaded to withdraw in the interest of party harmony in order that Foraker might run unopposed for re-election to the Senate instead of challenging Taft in the presidential race, as the Cincinnati senator threatened to do. After the Senator had been exposed by Hearst, Burton re-entered the senatorial contest, only to find himself threatened a second time by an unexpected foe, the President-elect's half brother, Charles P. Taft. An effort was made to buy off the Cleveland congressman with a cabinet post, but he remained adamant. In the end it was not Burton but C. P. Taft and Foraker who were forced to withdraw "in the interest of party harmony." In addition to Roosevelt's endorsement the Clevelander had strong newspaper backing, including that of the Scripps-McRae papers (Crissey, *Burton*, 161, 164–65, 171–79; Negley D. Cochran to T. E. Burton, January 6, 1908; R. F. Wolfe to T. E. Burton, January 23, 1908, Burton Papers).

32. Harmon's inaugural address, January 11, 1909, is printed in Mercer, ed., *Ohio Legislative History* [I], 21–26.

33. Executive Documents–Correspondence of Judson Harmon, January– March, 1909 (MSS in the Ohio Historical Society, Columbus [hereafter referred to as Harmon, Exec. Docs.]). His patronage problems and break with Garber were reported in the *Cleveland Plain Dealer*, October 19, 1909, and in Powell, ed., *The Democratic Party of the State of Ohio*, I, 423.

34. Special message to the General Assembly, January 19, 1909, printed in Mercer, ed., *Ohio Legislative History* [I], 43.

35. A bill to investigate Cincinnati was introduced by Senator James E. Mathews, Cuyahoga County Republican; one to probe Cleveland by Senator H. L. Yount, Democrat from Darke County; a third to investigate the state offices by a Republican representative from Medina County, Frank W. Woods (*Ohio State Journal*, January 21, 1909; *Cleveland Plain Dealer*, January 22, 1909). The bill to probe the state offices was adopted March 9, while those pertaining to Cincinnati and Cleveland were rejected two days later (*Ohio State Journal*, March 10, 12, 1909). Harmon's veto message of March 20, 1909, is printed in Mercer, ed., *Ohio Legislative History* [I], 46–48.

36. The exposures were reported in the *Cleveland Plain Dealer*, December 5–7, 1909, the *Ohio State Journal*, December 5–8, 1909, and the Governor's message to the Seventy-eighth General Assembly, January 3, 1910, printed in Mercer, ed., *Ohio Legislative History* [I], 27–28. The suspicions against the Columbus Savings and Trust Company were not proven until 1913 when it went bankrupt, thus permitting an examination of its books. Its records were found multilated by erasures and blottings; nevertheless, through the disclosures of a former secretary-treasurer of the bank and the confessions of Charles C. Green, the story of Cameron's and McKinnon's peculations were reconstructed. (*Ohio State Journal*, March 11–14, 19, 21, 25–26, April 2, 1913)

37. Judson Harmon to U. G. Denman, December 6, 1909, Harmon, Exec. Docs., also printed in the *Ohio State Journal*, December 7, 1909. On January 20, 1910, the attorney-general filed suit against the McKinnon estate and two days later against Cameron (*ibid.*, January 21, 23, 1910). These sums had to be recovered from the bondsmen of the two treasurers. At first the court decisions were adverse, but Timothy Hogan, Denman's successor,

finally established the right to recover these unlawful gains from the bonds-men. (Harmon's message to the Eightieth General Assembly, January 6, 1913, printed in Mercer, ed., *Ohio Legislative History* [I], 116) The grand-jury indictments against Cameron and Green were reported in the *Ohio State Journal*, April 18–20, May 30, 1913. These indictments, the *Cincinnati Enquirer* pointed out, were the first ones brought against a state official in a half-century (issue for April 18, 1913).

38. Creamer's reforms are described in Powell, ed., *The Democratic Party of the State of Ohio*, I, 426–28. Harmon's recommendations in his speech are printed in Mercer, ed., *Ohio Legislative History* [I], 28. The legislative history of the bill is in the *Ohio State Journal*, March 30, 1910; the text of the act is in 102 O.L. 33 (1911).

39. The formation of the Beatty committee was reported in the *Ohio State Journal*, January 4–6, 1910. The text of the joint resolution is in 101 O.L. 438 (1910). The probe itself is reported in the *Cleveland Plain Dealer*, February, 6, 8, 16, 1910, and *Ohio State Journal*, February 15, 1910. Slater was tried and convicted (*ibid.*, February 17, March 17, 25, 30, 1910). The investigation of the affairs of past incumbents of the office of state fire marshal spared neither Democrats nor Republicans. The facts disclosed that State Treasurer David Creamer, when he occupied the office, had charged to state expense two pleasure trips to his home in St. Clairsville and to two Democratic conventions. He confessed and returned $300 to the state. (*Ibid.*, October 8, 1910)

40. *Cleveland Plain Dealer*, November 9, 1909; September 14, 1910. The legislature appointed its own committee also to investigate the canals. The text of the resolution is in 101 O.L. 444 (1910).

41. Quoted in the *Ohio State Journal*, April 18, 1910.

42. His acceptance of tax reform was expressed in his inaugural address, January 11, 1909, printed in Mercer, ed., *Ohio Legislative History* [I], 25. His official correspondence as governor reveals that he relied on the conserva-tive wing of the party for advice, such men as: Charles Salen, the trimmer from Cleveland; John McMahon, a conservative elder statesman from Dayton; and his law partners in Cincinnati. He only consulted Newton Baker on minor municipal problems and remained even more aloof from Brand Whitlock. There was no correspondence with Herbert Bigelow and only two inconsequential letters from Daniel Kiefer. (Harmon, Exec. Docs., Jan-uary 1, 1909–December 31, 1912) The attitude of the Johnson group toward the Governor was expressed by Newton Baker when he characterized Harmon's point of view as "archaic."–N. D. Baker to Frank H. Baker, Novem-ber 23, 1908, Baker Papers, CCH.

43. The composition of the General Assembly was as follows: the Senate, twenty Republicans, fourteen Democrats; the House, seventy-one Republicans, forty-three Democrats, one Independent (*Report of the Secretary of State of Ohio* [1908], 35–37).

44. Fears of Cox were expressed in the *Cleveland Plain Dealer*, January 6, 1909, and in the Republican *Ohio State Journal*, January 16, 1909. The organization of the House was reported in *ibid.*, February 27, 1910, and in the *Cleveland Plain Dealer*, January 7, 1909.

45. The organization of the Senate were reported in the *Cleveland Plain Dealer*, January 13–15, 1909, and in the *Ohio State Journal*, April 4, 1910. Cochran's criticisms were printed in the *Toledo News-Bee*, January 21, 1909. The investigations of Harmon and Finley were described in the *Cleveland*

Plain Dealer, January 17, 1909. A few days later the finance committee was enlarged and filled with anti-Cox members to nullify the threat of Baker's chairmanship (*ibid.,* January 22, 1909). The five Democratic reactionaries were Senators H. L. Yount of Darke, Thomas A. Dean of Fremont, George K. Cetone of Montgomery, Richard A. Beatty of Wood, and Isaac E. Huffman of Butler.

46. *Cleveland Plain Dealer,* February 28, 1909; *Toledo News-Bee,* March 10, 1909; *Ohio State Journal,* March 12, 1909.

47. Harmon's recommendation is recorded in his inaugural address, January 11, 1909, printed in Mercer, ed., *Ohio Legislative History* [I], 25. The Quadrennial Assessment Act is in the *Cleveland Plain Dealer,* March 4, 10, 1909; its text is in 100 O.L. 81 (1909); its significance is stressed in Johnson, *My Story,* 130.

48. Governor's message to the Seventy-eighth General Assembly, January 3, 1910, printed in Mercer, ed., *Ohio Legislative History* [I], 28–32.

49. Harmon's recommendations are in *ibid.* [I], 29–30. The legislative history of the bill is in the *Ohio State Journal,* March 11, April 30, May 1, 1910, and the *Cleveland Plain Dealer,* March 23–24, April 30, May 1, 1910; the text is in 101 O.L. 430 (1910). The statute also stated that the total taxes could not exceed the 1909 returns by more than 6 per cent in 1911, 9 per cent in 1912, 13 per cent in 1913; the limit on bonded indebtedness was 2.5 per cent of the grand duplicate without a vote, 5 per cent with a vote. The aid of this legislation in the work of the quadrennial assessors was explained by the president of the Columbus board in the *Ohio State Journal,* March 24, 1910.

50. The bill's legislative history was reported in the *Cleveland Plain Dealer,* January 23, 25, March 17, 1910, and the *Ohio State Journal,* March 17, April 19–20, 23, 28, 30, May 1, 11, 1910. Minor differences between the House and Senate bills were ironed out by a conference committee, and the measure in its final form passed with only one dissenting vote. The suit of the Buckeye Pipe Line Company was reported in *ibid.,* March 9, 1910.

51. The significance of the legislation is discussed in Ernest L. Bogart, "Recent Tax Reforms in Ohio," *American Economic Review,* I (September, 1911), 510, and Bogart, *Financial History of Ohio,* 251–52. The text is in 101 O.L. 399 (1910). The new law retained the excise taxes levied under the Willis and Cole laws but assessed them on a new basis. The change was forced by a decision of the United States Supreme Court holding unconstitutional a tax on *gross* receipts because it affected interstate commerce. (*Galveston, Harrisburg and San Antonio Railway Co. v. State of Texas,* 210 U.S. 217 [1908]). To meet this objection the Ohio law was rewritten to specify an excise tax on gross earnings *excluding* interstate and federal business, but instead of the rate being 1 per cent for railroads it was raised to 4 per cent. The rates on other utilities having interstate as well as intrastate business were correspondingly increased. The constitutionality of this levy was sustained by the United States Supreme Court as a proper tax on the privilege of doing busniess in Ohio. It was not, said the court, double taxation, nor an undue burden on interstate commerce, nor discriminatory, as the carriers contended. (*Ohio Tax Cases,* 232 U.S. 577 [1914])

The one vestige of the old machinery left was the Ohio State Board of Appraisers and Assessors retained to name the city boards of review. Harmon had recommended that such appointing power be vested in the new commission or preferably the mayors, but the Republican majority refused to yield. The existing arrangement had greatly benefited the Republicans, for, even after Harmon became governor in 1909, they continued to dominate the state board of assessors, which was composed of the state treasurer, state auditor, and secretary of state, and, thus, to control the city boards of review. In reality this meant that these officers merely rubber-stamped appointments made by Myron T. Herrick and Willard J. Crawford in Cleveland, Walter Brown in Toledo, Malcolm A. Karshner in Columbus, and George B. Cox in Cincinnati. The only Democrats appointed were nominal ones who were under the thumb of the Republican politicians. (William Gordon to Judson Harmon, November 17, 1909, Harmon, Exec. Docs., *Cleveland Plain Dealer,* February 4, 1910; March 17, 1910)

52. Ditty and Munn took office on July 1, 1910; Christian Pabst was appointed on January 1, 1911, when William B. Poland, one of the three original appointees, resigned because of a disagreement with his other two colleagues over the details of valuation methods. (*Ohio State Journal,* June 25, September 7, 1910; January 1, 8, 1911; Mercer, ed., *Ohio Legislative History* [I], 238–39)

53. Between 1910 and 1911 the valuation of telegraph companies was increased from $2,734,725 to $4,847,260, telephone companies from $21,-654,529 to $61,116,110, steam railroads from $167,453,818 to $571,281,620, street and interurban railways from $32,693,904 to $123,044,180, electric light companies from $6,387,934 to $29,373,430, natural-gas corporations from $20,881,531 to $78,486,270, and all utilities from $263,191,480 to $912,862,833 (*Second Annual Report of the Tax Commission of Ohio* [1911], 29). The methods and achievements of the tax commission are assessed in Lutz, *The State Tax Commission,* 495–96; James C. Dockeray, *Public Utility Taxation in Ohio* "(Ohio State University Studies, Contributions in Economics," No. 2 [Columbus, 1938]), 74–81.

54. The success of the appraisals in every major city except Cincinnati was noted in the *Second Annual Report of the Tax Commission of Ohio* (1911), 23. The election of the board controlled by the Cincinnati boss was reported in the *Cleveland Plain Dealer,* November 3, 1909. The work of the Cleveland board was described in *First Quadrennial Report of the Board of Assessors of Real Property of Cleveland, Ohio* (Cleveland, 1910), 8–10, which was dedicated to Tom L. Johnson. The Cleveland mayor had made the election of an honest board of tax assessors one of the leading issues in his last mayoralty campaign in 1909. Four of the five candidates elected had received his endorsement. They included, in addition to Howe, Arthur F. May, Joseph F. McKenna, and John A. Zangerle. The fifth member of the board was a Republican, Theodore M. Bates, who had been endorsed by the Municipal Association and the Cleveland Real Estate Board. Johnson took a great interest in the work of the assessors and was instrumental in obtaining the services of W. A. Somers to aid in the application of his system. (Johnson, *My Story,* 291–92; *Cleveland Plain Dealer,* September 2, 9, October 14, 16, 20, 24, November 6–7, 17, 21, 23, 1909)

The criticism of the rural boards and the assignment of the task of equalization work to the commission are all reported in the *Second Annual Report of the Ohio Tax Commission* (1911), 23, 49–50, 66–68; Table I, 70–217. The law making the commission a review board is in 102 O.L. 224 (1911).

55. Lutz, *The State Tax Commission,* 486–88.

56. Inaugural address, January 11, 1909, printed in Mercer, ed., *Ohio Legislative History* [I], 25; *Cleveland Plain Dealer*, November 9, 1909.

57. Governor's message, January 3, 1910, printed in Mercer, ed., *Ohio Legislative History* [I], 34; Nichols, "Harmon," 146. The Ohio Board of State Charities was established in 1867. Boards to supervise state charities had been created in eighteen other states by 1893. However, the idea of the central administration of charities was new. See Arthur M. Schlesinger, *The Rise of the City* (*A History of American Life*, eds. A. M. Schlesinger and D. R. Fox, Vol. X [13 vols.; New York, 1927–48]), 350; Mercer, ed., *Ohio Legislative History* [II], 413–14.

58. The legislative history of the bill was reported in the *Cleveland Plain Dealer*, April 15, 1910, and the *Ohio State Journal*, April 15, 19, May 1, 1910. Harmon's veto message, May 18, 1910, is printed in Mercer ed., *Ohio Legislative History* [I], 58–59.

59. Inaugural address, January 11, 1909, printed in Mercer, ed., *Ohio Legislative History* [I], 25. Harmon's other recommendations were contained in his message of January 3, 1910, printed in *ibid.* [I], 34–35. The joint resolution setting up the investigating committee is in 100 O.L. 120 (1909).

60. Harmon expressed his views in his message to the Eightieth General Assembly, January 6, 1913, printed in Mercer, ed., *Ohio Legislative History* [I], 113.

61. Although in his inaugural address Harmon had mentioned the need to "supervise the creation and extension of corporate rights," he was silent on the issue in his message of January 3, 1910. (*Ibid.*, *[I]*, 23, 27–37) The fate of the Woods bill in the 1909 session was reported in the *Ohio State Journal*, January 21, February 2, 19, March 3, 10, 1909, its reintroduction in 1910 in *ibid.*, February 27, 1910. The pioneer work of New York and Wisconsin, as well as the action of other states in adopting such commissions, is discussed in Huebner, "Five Years of Railroad Regulation by the States," 140–41, and in John A. Lapp, "Public Utilities," *American Political Science Review*, VI (November, 1912), 576.

62. *Ohio State Journal*, February 27, March 1, 1910. The Winters bill, for example, did not give the commission authority to determine the value of the property of utilities.

63. The lobby's opposition was reported in *ibid.*, March 3, 1910, Taft's remarks in *ibid.*, March 25, 1910, Wood's defense in *ibid.*, March 30, 1910, Bense's statement and the bill's passage in *ibid.*, March 31, 1910.

64. The activity of the lobby in the Senate was reported in *ibid.*, April 12, 23, 1910, the history of the bill and the vote in the upper chamber in *ibid.*, April 4, 26, 29, 1910.

65. *Toledo News-Bee*, April 29, 1910; *Ohio State Journal*, April 29, 1910. In the 1910 campaign Frank Woods did follow the *Ohio State Journal's* suggestion and charged Harmon with the responsibility for the failure. The Republican representative claimed that the Governor had first asked him to remove everything from his bill except the creation of a commission. When the former refused to make the changes and the bill passed the House, Harmon, according to Woods, tried then to smother it in committee in the Senate. (*Ibid.*, October 26, 1910)

66. *Cincinnati Enquirer*, May 1, 1910; *Ohio State Journal*, May 1, 1910.

67. The vote in the House was reported in *Ohio State Journal*, March 17, 1910, the bribery testimony in *ibid.*, March 17, 20, 22, 24, April 1, 8, 1910. The evidence indicated that the bribe giver was Simon Cronin, agent of the Central Union Telephone Company. The House voted to turn over the testimony gathered by the Langdon probe committee to the Franklin County Grand Jury, but the Senate allowed the resolution to die. (*Ibid.*, April 17, 1910; *Cleveland Plain Dealer*, May 1, 1910) The vote in the Senate was reported in *ibid.*, April 21, 1910, and the *Ohio State Journal*, April 13, 21, 1910.

68. Governor's special message, March 17, 1910, printed in Mercer, ed., *Ohio Legislative History* [I], 49–50; *Ohio State Journal*, March 18, 1910.

69. The unsuccessful efforts for direct legislation were reported in *Ohio State Journal*, March 4, 10, 1909, and March 2, April 23, 1910, the failure of the woman-suffrage amendment and the nonpartisan judicial ballot, in *ibid.*, April 14, 19, 1910, the passage of the direct-primary law for congressional candidates and delegates to national party conventions, in the *Cleveland Plain Dealer*, April 1, 1910. The text is in 101 O.L. 41 (1910). The two election bills defeated are in the *Ohio State Journal*, April 13, 20, 1910.

70. For example, one enactment established a municipal court for Cleveland of a chief justice and four judges to perform the duties of the justices of the peace and the police court judge. Another extended the merit system to schools. A third permitted cities to improve rivers and water courses and charge the expense to abutting property owners. A fourth increased from 50 per cent to 65 per cent the share railroads had to pay in eliminating grade crossings, and a fifth permitted cities to issue bonds in excess of the statutory authority limitations for that purpose. The texts are in 101 O.L. 364, 154, 134, 377 (1910), respectively. Harmon vetoed the last one (Veto message, May 23, 1910, printed in Mercer, ed., *Ohio Legislative History* [I], 63).

71. The activity of the Anti-Saloon League in relation to legislation was reported in the *Ohio State Journal*, February 16, 23, March 23, 1910, and *Cleveland Plain Dealer*, February 25, 1910. The cigarette law is in the *Ohio State Journal*, March 2, 1910, the Sunday-baseball law in *ibid.*, April 22, 1910. The Governor's veto message, April 21, 1910, is printed in Mercer, ed., *Ohio Legislative History* [I], 51–53.

72. The bill was sponsored by two Cleveland Republicans, W. W. Norris in the House and James E. Mathews in the Senate (*Ohio State Journal*, March 31, April 27–28, 1910). The text is in 101 O.L. 195 (1910). Under the fellow servant rule, if injury or death occurred because of the carelessness of a fellow worker, then no damages could be awarded. Secondly, if an employee was caught in the machinery through his own negligence and injured or killed, his claim for compensation was denied on the grounds of contributory negligence. Thirdly, if a workman was injured or killed as a result of the hazards of normal employment, again the employer would be relieved of payment on the theory of assumption of risk. (Cox, *Journey through My Years*, 139) Prior efforts to change the rules and the opposition they aroused are discussed in Herbert R. Mengert, "The Ohio Workmen's Compensation Law," *Ohio Archaeological and Historical Quarterly*, XXX (1921), 5–6.

73. The passage of the acts was reported in the *Ohio State Journal*, April 29–30, May 1, 1910; the texts are in 101 O.L. 231 and 52 (1910), respectively. Another noteworthy revision was that of the General Code of

Laws adopted in the 1910 session after consideration by seven different committees (Walter J. Shepard, "The Legislative Session in Ohio," *American Political Science Review*. IV (May, 1910), 231–32).

74. *Cleveland Plain Dealer*, May 1, 3, 12, 1910; *Toledo News-Bee*, May 2, 1910. Washington Gladden was convinced that the intellectual and moral average of the whole body had improved perceptibly over the legislatures of twenty years before (statement in the *Ohio State Journal*, April 18, 1910).

CHAPTER TEN

THE ONWARD MARCH
OF REFORM
1910■1911

On the eve of the 1910 campaign there were few guides by which an observer might foretell the strength of the progressive and conservative factions within each party. The constitutional amendment which shifted state elections from odd to even years also eliminated the off-year ones by making the terms of the secretary of state and other state officers coterminous. In the intervening period since the 1908 contest the only polls of Ohio opinion were the local and municipal elections of 1909, which gave an imperfect answer.

In Cincinnati George B. Cox and his gang had regained their ironclad control of the local Republican party with the tacit consent of the administration in Washington. The Taft family had made its peace with the Cincinnati boss when Charles, the President's half brother, nominated Cox chairman of the Hamilton County delegation to the state convention in 1908. Theodore Roosevelt, who attacked machine politicians and reactionaries elsewhere, had nothing to say against the boss of Cincinnati, whose support was vital to his protégé, William Howard Taft, and to Roosevelt's son-in-law, Nicholas Longworth. In the fall of 1909 Cox nominated his entire ticket, headed by the affable, popular physician, Dr. Louis Schwab.[1]

Since the Republicans were committed to reaction, it might be supposed that the Cincinnati Democrats would take a militant position on the other side. The radical wing, however, was rendered powerless by a split between the Bigelow-Kiefer faction and the Dempsey partisans. The largest and best-knit group were the Harmon supporters, who succeeded in nominating their candidate for mayor, John Weld Peck, an attorney for the liquor interests and utilities. As hostile as a conservative Republican to the Tom Johnson program of reform, Peck campaigned for "personal liberty" and honest government. On election day many Democrats remained away from the polls, and the Cox candidates swept into office, Schwab leading with a plurality of fifteen thousand.[2]

Although the Cincinnati campaign had disclosed that conservatives were in the ascendency in both parties, the reverse appeared to be true in Cleveland. The Republicans nominated for mayor Herman C. Baehr, a popular German with a fine record as county recorder, to oppose Tom Johnson, who was running for the fifth time. Although accused by the opposition press of being secretly in league with the political agents of the utilities, Baehr was popularly believed to represent the progressive wing of his party. Senator Theodore Burton, who was enjoying a short-lived reputation for insurgency because of his opposition to the Old Guard in Congress, rushed home from Europe to campaign for the party nominee. The Republican strategy was to berate Johnson as an unscrupulous boss, yet to promise settlement of the street-railway issue on his terms or better and to support the humanitarian reforms already begun. After a campaign described by the press as the most apathetic in ten years, the Republicans were victorious. City Solicitor Baker and four members of the board of assessors were the only Democrats to survive.[3]

Still the defeat of Johnson did not mean the triumph of conservatism. A substantial part of the Cleveland electorate, weary of having one man occupy the limelight, believed they were exchanging one progressive leader for another.[4] Only the future could tell whether the voters were right or not. Moreover, the returns did not signify the elimination of the Johnson leadership from the Democratic party. At a meeting of the Tilden Club in Cleveland a month after the election, the defeated Mayor threw down the gauntlet to the conservative faction, who were hopeful of deposing him, and announced that he would be as active in the party as a citizen as he had been as chief executive.[5] Although ill-health forced him to delegate leadership, his lieutenants continued to keep the Cuyahoga Democracy true to his ideals. Thus it appeared that the progressives of both parties held the balance of power in Cleveland.

In Columbus the conservatives were routed in the Republican primaries when their candidate for mayor was defeated for nomination by George S. Marshall, the crusading city solicitor. On the other hand, the reactionary Democratic machine was successful in selecting Frank R. Vance as their nominee. Marshall, who campaigned on the issues of better government, tax increases on public-utility properties, and reduction of street-railway fares, won with the aid of progressives of both parties.[6]

Brand Whitlock was nominated by the Independent Voters for a third time in Toledo on a platform attacking bossism and promising a settlement of the traction question in the people's interest. The Democratic nominee was Joseph Eger, described as "a Weber and Fields character"; the Republican was David T. Davies, whom Whitlock characterized as "a typical ward-heeling, saloon-campaigning, gang politician who walks 'gallus 'and talks tough." After a campaign of vilification and abuse Whitlock and the Independent Voters' slate of candidates were returned to office by large pluralities. Their supporters consisted of the progressive elements of both parties, Republicans in revolt against the dominance of Walter Brown and Democrats who had broken with their unprincipled local leaders.[7]

Elsewhere the results were not so clearly defined. In Dayton and Youngstown, Democrats who were hard to classify were reelected over conservative Republicans. Behind Mayor Edward E. Burkhardt, returned to office in Dayton on a record of sound, honest government, loomed the shadow of Edward Hanley, a public-utility officer who controlled the local Democratic machine. Alvin W. Craver, who succeeded himself in Youngstown, was a very mild progresive. This lack of a clear-cut division between candidates in both the primary and general elections was characteristic of other municipal campaigns.[8]

In the months since the fall of 1909, however, there had been a sharpening of alignment between progressive and conservative Ohioans. The legislative session of 1910 had revealed the cleavage between the two factions on utility regulation, administrative reform, and direct legislation. The debates which rang through the halls of Congress on the Payne-Aldrich tariff, the power of Speaker Cannon, and the Ballinger-Pinchot conservation controversy were forcing Ohioans to ponder the larger underlying issues and to take sides. An informal canvass of political opinion conducted by the *Cincinnati Enquirer* in June, 1910, disclosed that the majority of those polled were dissatisfied with the Taft administration in general, and a larger number with the Payne-Aldrich tariff in particular. They were also opposed to the re-election of Senator Charles Dick, who had allied himself with the Old Guard. There were many demands for a realignment of progressive Republicans and progressive Democrats. Yet, barring such a shift, a majority believed that the political trend favored the latter party in the state.[9]

When the Democrats assembled in Dayton on June 20, 1910, for their state convention, the renomination of the middle-of-the-road Harmon for governor was a foregone conclusion. An overwhelming number of those answering the *Cincinnati Enquirer* poll agreed that his administration had been a popular success. The Cuyahoga Democrats, having approved his renomination late in March, intended to center their fight on the platform and the endorsement of a progressive for United States senator. Although at first they were treated with "suspicion and distrust" because of the ludicrous fear that Tom Johnson might once again appear "at the psychological moment and 'raise hell,'" they were agreeably surprised by the solicitous attention shown to them as the convention proceeded. Newton Baker, who inherited the mantle of leadership from the ailing Johnson, was offered the attorney-generalship, which he declined. Many delegates expressed sympathy for a senatorial endorsement, even though they were reluctant to make an issue of it in the face of Harmon's known opposition.

While the popular Governor dominated the convention and might have dictated the platform and slate of candidates, he had no intention of using his power to muzzle all opposition. The planks prepared by the resolutions committee, for example, were a compromise between his ideas and those of the radical wing. The stress placed on government efficiency and economy, the demand for a ten-mill tax limit, ratification of the federal income tax amendment, and a nonpartisan judicial ballot were written at his behest. On the other hand, he was known to be indifferent, if not opposed, to such radical planks as those endorsing the principle of the initiative and referendum, fair and just regulation of all public utilities, direct election of United States senators, and, pending such an amendment, the adoption of a plan for the nomination of senators by popular vote. Nevertheless there was one resolution on which Harmon refused to yield: the convention endorsement of a senatorial candidate. Baker, who had led an unsuccessful fight for its adoption by the committee, determined to carry the issue before the whole body in a minority report. His hopes for its acceptance were blasted, however, by a political stratagem.

Two of the Harmon floor managers, William Finley and Edward Hanley, arranged to shift the order of business to forestall a stampede for Baker's demand. Instead of adopting the platform before the nomination of candidates, the convention proceeded to the selection of Harmon, who was renominated by unanimous acclaim. The chairman of the resolutions committee then read the platform, followed by Baker, who presented the minority report favoring a senatorial endorsement. As he concluded his moving speech, the Cuyahoga delegation broke into cheers which showed signs of spreading. At that instant Harmon was escorted into the hall to make his acceptance speech. Baker smiled, knowing that his own plan had been foiled by the managers. When the minority report was put to a vote, the endorsement plank failed 254 to 840.[10]

Despite the sharp tactics no friction developed between Baker and Harmon. When the convention continued with the nomination of other candidates, the Johnson men were conciliated by the selection of Atlee Pomerene for lieutenant-governor, Timothy Hogan for attorney-general, and David Creamer for state treasurer. A determined opposition to Creamer developed among the conservative Hamilton and Montgomery county delegations because he was a Johnson man, but largely through the influential backing of the Cuyahoga delegation his renomination carried by a vote of 618 to 472.[11]

Within a few days after the convention adjourned, the Democratic State Central Committee met to select the executive board to manage the Harmon campaign. Notably absent was Lewis Bernard, who had failed of election after serving on this body for many years. The committee unanimously voted for Harmon's hand-picked nominees: Hugh L. Nichols, a progressive, chairman; Charles C. Marshall, secretary; and Fred J. Heer, treasurer. Without a suggestion from the Cleveland group, none of whom were present, Baker was also placed on the executive board.[12]

An appraisal of the work of the Democrats indicated that while the progressives had failed to get all they wanted, they had made headway. Most of their principles were embodied in the platform, and though they had to accept Harmon as the party standard-bearer, they did succeed in nominating several of their own for the other offices. Certainly they had fared better than such former party bosses as Bernard and Harvey Garber, who had been shoved into the discard.

When the Democrats disbanded in June, the Republican state convention was still a month away. For some time there had been much preliminary sparring between the progressive and conservative factions of that party, some of it in the open, most of it under cover. One of the great uncertainties was President Taft. Where did he stand, which faction did he favor? During the fight to clip Speaker Joseph Cannon's power in the national House of Representatives, the influential editor of the *Cleveland Leader,* Nathaniel C. Wright, wrote to a political confidant that newspapers and politicians from everywhere in the state were telephoning him to ask whether it was true that Taft was going to fight for Cannon. Although Wright believed that the President was only after the anti-Taft insurgents, many were convinced that he had declared war on everyone who dared to oppose Cannon. If this continued, the *Leader* editor added, "there won't be enough Taft sentiment in Ohio to address a souvenir post card to."[13] Certainly, if the administration in Washington became stamped with conservatism, that would adversely affect the party in Ohio, since it would repel the independent-progressive vote.

While the conservative leaders kept their plans to themselves, as was their custom, Republican progressives proceeded to make open appeals for their cause. Members of that faction in the state legislature announced in May that they would battle to control the party.[14] As the time for the convention approached in July, a new figure emerged to take command of the progressive wing, James Rudolph Garfield.

A son of the martyred President, he had retrod his father's

footsteps, first entering the law, then politics. Together with his brother Harry, he formed a law partnership in Cleveland, to which Fred C. Howe was added when James entered the Ohio Senate in 1896. Howe described his two associates as "tolerant, kindly, scrupulous" men, who looked upon him as a radical when he deserted the Republican party for Tom Johnson's brand of Democracy, yet never attempted to alter his decision. During his two terms in the state Senate, James Garfield traveled an independent course, opposing ripper legislation and writing a corrupt-practices law to limit campaign expenditures, his most notable achievement. Because of his independence he incurred the enmity of Mark Hanna, who accused him of practicing "heavenly politics." Hanna's opposition had threatened to end Garfield's political career in 1900, when he was denied the organization backing as a candidate for Congress.

It was Theodore Roosevelt who readmitted him to political life by appointing him a federal civil service commissioner in 1902, head of the bureau of corporations the next year, and secretary of the interior in 1907. As head of the department of the interior, where he could see "the very inmost working of special privilege—of political influence metamorphosed into greed and chicanery," he received a rare schooling in progressive Republicanism and gained a reputation as an honest, efficient administrator. As a member of the "lawn tennis cabinet," he was considered to be one of the President's close advisers. When Roosevelt left office, Garfield retired with him and was ever afterwards first and foremost a Roosevelt Republican.[15]

This second taste of politics whetted Garfield's appetite for higher honors. Early in 1910 his friends staged a boom for him for governor, which died out in the spring but revived in the summer. In July he opened war on the reactionaries in his own as well as the Democratic party, leveling at them this shaft:

> Today political liberty is at stake and the life of the nation is threatened by special interests who would control our political activities for their own benefit, regardless of the common good. There is no half-way ground in the fight today. The special interests must be driven out of politics and kept out. The progressives of today will win the battle.

The reaction from Boss Cox was immediate. He stated flatly

that the Hamilton County delegation would walk out of the convention if Garfield was nominated. Neither Taft nor Roosevelt, who had just returned from his African safari, chose to be drawn into the fight. The most the former President would do was to express the hope that a progressive platform would be adopted.[16]

In spite of favorable press support from the *Cleveland Leader, Toledo Blade, Ohio State Journal,* and the Scripps-McRae papers, endorsing progressives of both parties, the Garfield wing had run behind in the primaries. Frank Woods had been defeated for renomination to the state Assembly, and conservatives had won in the congressional districts. On the eve of the convention the Scripps-McRae League released the results of a poll of Republican sentiment throughout the state, which proved to be a remarkable prognostication of events. Although a majority of Ohio Republicans, they reported, were progressive, favoring Theodore Roosevelt's policies and Garfield for governor, the boss-dominated delegates would control the state conclave and vote for anyone except Garfield. Cox, Dick, Brown, Ellis, and Burton, with Taft's consent, would pick the gubernatorial nominee and write the platform.[17]

When the Republicans gathered for their state convention on July 26, Garfield, in an attempt to seize the initiative, published his own statement of principles. He expressed confidence in the patriotism and sincerity of President Taft without mentioning the deeds or misdeeds of the administration, renewed the attack on special interests, and outlined a program of state legislation which embodied most of the progressive planks: commissions with power to regulate utilities and other corporations, stricter election laws to prevent the misuse of corporation funds for political purposes, the short ballot, a commission form of government for cities, the recall of legislative and executive officers, workmen's compensation, the extension of child labor reform, and maximum working hours for women.

This effort to stampede the body into acceptance of such a declaration, however, misfired. The resolutions committee was packed with conservatives, and Senator Dick was chosen its chairman in place of Congressman Paul Howland, Garfield's choice. Working through the night, the committee did not release its handiwork until the early hours of the following morning. The platform lauded Taft, endorsed his renomination in 1912, defended the Payne-Aldrich tariff, favored generous pensions to Civil War veterans, and tacked on a watered-down version of Garfield's progressive state planks.

When the Cleveland lawyer read it, he stated flatly that he could not run on such a platform. "It was at this point," wrote a correspondent of the *Toledo News-Bee*, "that Garfield displayed the hesitation, indecision and lack of insight and experience in politics and the ways of conventions that turned what would have been a splendid fight into a ridiculous fiasco." From the moment the resolutions committee was selected it was obvious that a fight for a minority report would have to be made on the floor, yet Garfield had not prepared one. Although a loyal band of progressives stood over him demanding action, he vacillated and finally declined to make a contest. He sat outside the convention hall minutely scrutinizing the platform adopted to see how many or how few of his planks it contained. At the critical hour this leader of the progressive uprising abandoned his men.[18]

On the following day, when the balloting for offices began, Garfield again refused to appear at the convention. He received seventy-three votes for governor on the first ballot, scattered among a number of county delegations, even though no one had officially proposed his name. George Cox was asked what he thought of Garfield's chances. "These are a mad set of men," replied the Cincinnati boss. "You can't tell what they might do." But Cox and the party regulars were still firmly in control of the delegates and could thwart the nomination of Garfield or any other progressive.[19]

They were unable, however, to agree among themselves. The Taft lieutenants, "Jake" Vorys and Wade Ellis, with the President's blessing, were prepared to back Judge Reynolds R. Kinkade of Toledo. Senators Burton and Dick were agreeable, but Kinkade for personal reasons refused to run, leaving these party conservatives without a candidate.[20]

Cox's choice was O. Britt Brown, for whom the Cincinnati boss had mustered an estimated 450 votes—only 84 short of the number required for nomination. To the other leaders the open backing of Cox seemed to carry a stigma that would effectively destroy Brown's chance of election. Indicative of this hostile public attitude were "the hoots, cat calls, and hisses" which greeted Cox's name whenever it was mentioned in the convention itself. Still the Taft lieutenants and the two senators could not agree on a candidate to beat Brown. Senator Dick preferred Carmi Thompson. Burton was indecisive; he objected to Warren G. Harding, the candidate of the Forakerites, because of the Marion publisher's straddle on the liquor question, and he would not agree to Nicholas Longworth, the alternate choice of the Taft men, convinced that the Cincinnati congressman would be no match for Governor Harmon.[21]

When the voting opened, no agreement had been reached among these various factions. The results on the first two ballots were indecisive. On the third round the Cuyahoga delegation, contrary to Burton's desires, cast its entire vote for Longworth. Cox, seizing upon this as a betrayal of Burton's promise to keep the Cuyahoga vote divided among the candidates, "double-crossed" his own supporters and shifted the Hamilton County vote from Brown to Harding—a move that assured the victory of the Marion candidate.[22] No contest developed over the other officers. Francis W. Treadway was renominated for lieutenant-governor and U. G. Denman for attorney-general; the former speaker of the Ohio House, Granville W. Mooney, was chosen as secretary of state and Randolph W. Archer as state treasurer. Cox did not hide his chagrin at failing to nominate his man for governor; he publicly denounced Burton as a traitor after the convention disbanded.[23]

Even more dissatisfield were the progressives. Theodore Roosevelt lamented to Garfield that the regulars had made "the average politician's platform and put on it the average politician's candidate." The *Ohio State Journal* dismissed the platform as a "standpat declaration," twisting into a derogation the phrase Hanna had coined originally to express Republican virtue. Though the *Cleveland Leader* did its best to ignore the national planks and underscore the state ones, it admitted that "the strong reactionary alignment of the resolutions committee and the illogical and absurd selection of Senator Dick as its chairman rob[bed] the progressive declarations of much of the force they would otherwise have had."[24]

The dissatisfaction of the progressives was indication enough that the Old Guard leaders had once again had their way. They had saddled the party with a candidate for governor who was a former Foraker partisan and a platform consisting of a hodge-podge of conservative and progressive planks which seemed to cancel each other.

At the launching of the Republican campaign in September conservatism seemed even more intrenched. Senator Dick opened with a standpat speech at Kenton, followed by Harding, who attempted to ape Hanna as a phrasemaker with the slogan, "Let us go on." Goaded by the Democrats, who again made Coxism an issue, the Republican candidate was soon expressing his "deference and devotion" to the Cincinnati boss. Although the party progressives were prepared to bury the hatchet, they were slow to make public their support, thereby adding to the impression that Harding had the endorsement only of the Old Guard.[25]

Foraker, who emerged from retirement to stump for the ticket, again created the chief excitement. In a speech at Marysville on October 22 he assailed the New Nationalism which Theodore Roosevelt had expounded at Osawatomie, Kansas, at the end of August. "Such a preachment," Foraker shouted, "is not nationalism, either new or old, but imperialism pure and simple. It is, in spirit at least, as treasonable as secession itself." Then he added with sharp-edged sarcasm, "It has one saving feature, however. There is about it such a preposterous absurdity and such an insufferable egotism as to excite not only condemnation but ridicule. It is another case of vaulting ambition o'erleaping itself."

In his first speech of the campaign James Garfield answered Foraker's assault:

> If his charge be true, then for six years the Republican party has been going on the wrong track. . . . If it is secession to insist on strong governmental policies in the regulation of great combinations of wealth, then I am a secessionist, as are millions of my countrymen.
>
> If it be treason to say that special interest must be driven from politics and treason to say that the federal government must protect the remaining natural resources in the public domain, then I say let Foraker and those who are with him make the most of such treason. The prosperity of this country is not to be judged from the stand point of dollars and giant corporations.[26]

The Democrats observed the family row in high glee. Harmon suggested a debate between the former senator and Colonel Roosevelt. Thoroughly disturbed and embarrassed, the Republican leaders tried to smooth the ruffled tempers and personal animosities of the two combatants. Foraker, after being openly rebuked, canceled all his speaking engagements in a huff, but two days later was persuaded to resume his tour. Harding tried to divert attention from the feud by launching a personal attack on Harmon, condemning him as a tax dodger, rebate giver, and political manipulator while receiver of the Cincinnati, Hamilton, and Dayton Railroad. This theme was picked up by Theodore Roosevelt in two speeches delivered at Cleveland and Toledo on the closing day of the campaign.[27]

Such attempts as these to steal the Democratic thunder and turn it against them came too late. From the very outset of the campaign, a month before the rift in the Republican ranks was blazoned before the public, it was apparent the Democrats had the edge. At the Canton opening on September 24 party orators struck the two themes at which they persistently hammered until election day: Harmon's clean record, on the one hand, and the graft exposures of past Republican administrations, on the other. The Governor's unvarnished, blunt speeches were easily assimilated by rural audiences. His invasion of his home city was a great success when he swung both fists at Cox, denouncing the Boss's graft in city, county, and state. Harmon proved himself a match for Roosevelt, tearing to shreds the Colonel's charges and raking up the Santa Fe affair in rebuttal.[28]

In Cleveland his tent rally became a moving occasion when Tom Johnson appeared unexpectedly as Harmon was about to speak. There was a hush, then a murmur, at seeing the ailing former Mayor, followed by applause that rocked the tent as the two men clasped hands. Chairman John H. Clarke announced that Johnson, in defiance of his physician's advice, had insisted on being present and wanted to say a few words. Inspired by the crowd and the old tent, he summoned forth for a few moments his old-time vigor. "I am here," he remarked, "to greet Governor Harmon and to express my deep conviction that the people of Ohio are going to honor themselves by re-electing a man who has made the record of governor that he has rather than a man who boasts of his loyalty to George B. Cox and his unspeakable organization."

After the Mayor sat down, Harmon gave a touching tribute:

> The demonstration we have just witnessed has stirred me to the depths of my soul. I can only say that if at any time after my service as governor has expired and I appear before a body of citizens of my State and there, without the powers of office, without the possibility of bestowing favors, I shall receive such a testimonial as you to-night have given your old fighting leader, I will consider that life certainly has been well worth living.[29]

Not only did Harmon's rallies arouse more enthusiasm, but he also had a more favorable press in the metropolitan centers than did his opponent. In addition to such loyal Democratic journals as the *Cleveland Plain Dealer, Dayton Daily News,* and *Youngstown Vindicator,* he won the support of the *Cincinnati Enquirer* and the powerful Scripps-McRae chain. One of the papers in the chain, the *Toledo News-Bee,* explained that it was backing Harmon, not because he was the ideal candidate, but because a vote for him was a vote against special privilege and the bosses in control of the Republican party.[30]

On election day the returns vindicated these bellwethers of opinion. The Democrats achieved their most sweeping triumph in two decades, electing Harmon, their entire state ticket, a majority of the legislature, and sixteen of the twenty-one congressmen. Harmon's plurality of 100,377 was an indication of how the tide had turned against the once powerful Republicans. He carried sixty-five counties—all those containing large urban concentrations and a number of rural ones along the Ohio River, in the Western Reserve, and in the northwest corner of the state which had seldom deviated in their Republican loyalty. The pluralities of the other state officers, however, were substanially short of the popular Governor's, ranging from Lieutenant-Governor Pomerene's 45,531 to Attorney-General Hogan's 8,000. Credit for this surprising overturn belonged not only to the independent progressives but also to thousands of middle-of-the-road Republicans who boycotted the elections.[31]

Clearly the election was a rebuke, a more thoroughgoing one than that delivered in either 1905 or 1908, to the Republican leaders who persisted in identifying the party with the bosses and the Old Guard. Even Harding frankly attributed his defeat to Coxism, graft charges, and dissatisfaction in the country. The progressive wing was not inclined to waste much time in sorrow. Their sentiment was expressed by Arthur L. Garford in a letter to one of the defeated candidates:

> I agree with you that the political disappointment is not very great, that as compensation for it, we are now afforded an opportunity of re-organization that could not have existed except for the house cleaning which has occurred in the Republican party and because of which the political parasites that have been sapping the life blood of the organization for years will be relegated to the scrap heap in the back yard.[32]

The Ohio results were symptomatic of a national trend. Voters in other states showed the same willingness to relegate their "political parasites" to the "scrap heap in the back yard." Republicans were turned out of office in Maine, New York, Massachusetts, Connecticut, and Indiana. New Jersey chose a Democratic governor from outside the political ranks, Woodrow Wilson, president of Princeton University. In California the electorate selected Hiram Johnson, a Republican, but one dedicated to the destruction of the bosses. The political complexion of the national House of Representatives was changed when the Democrats gained sixty-three seats to win a majority of thirty-one over their opponents.[33]

Nevertheless, neither in Ohio nor in many of the other states was it clear how the popular mandate should be interpreted. Was it a vote of confidence in the Democrats, no matter what their convictions might be on the issues of the day, or was it an endorsement of those committed to progressive Democracy? Shortly after the election the issue came to the fore in Ohio as the several candidates entered the lists to contend for the seat in the United States Senate occupied by Charles Dick. Because of the Democratic majority in the General Assembly of eighty-eight to sixty-three, a candidate of that party was assured of election.

Since this was the first time in two decades that the senatorship was within the grasp of a Democrat, the secret ambitions of many for that honor were marched into the open. John R.

McLean reappeared on the Ohio scene to promote his own candidacy. He returned to vote in Cincinnati for the first time in nine years and donated generously to the party campaign funds. His two Cincinnati newspapers, the *Enquirer* and *Commercial-Tribune,* backed Harmon and the state ticket with uncustomary vigor. After the election his agents flooded the state Democratic press with clippings and newsletters favorable to him. Still McLean was devoid of popular appeal, and the times had changed from those when a legislature could be bought. Another candidate was Congressman Carl C. Anderson, who claimed to be backed by Samuel Gompers and organized labor. Scattered support existed for a number of other men long prominent in party councils: former Governor James E. Campbell, Colonel James Kilbourne, John J. Lentz, and M. A. Daugherty.[34] The two contenders with the strongest prospects for success, however, were Edward W. Hanley and Atlee Pomerene.

Hanley had been born in Dayton, the son of an Irish laborer, and was a self-made man. He had worked his way through commercial college, then entered politics in the 1880's, first as deputy county clerk, later as assistant postmaster in Grover Cleveland's first administration. Shortly thereafter he met Calvin S. Brice, then United States senator from Ohio, who made the Dayton man a protégé in his business enterprises, and in time Hanley became the secretary-treasurer and Ohio manager of the Brice-Thomas gas and electric interests. Having made a success in the business world, he yielded to his Irish love of politics and became a power in the Democratic organization of his native city by reorganizing its machinery and personnel. By 1910 he not only ruled Dayton and the county, but he was a major figure on the Democratic State Central Committee. His senatorial candidacy was launched by the Montgomery County legislative delegation a week after the election, and Congressman James M. Cox took charge of his campaign. But because he represented the utility interests and was more conservative than Harmon, Hanley was anathema to the progressive Democrats.[35]

The preferred candidate of the Johnson men and the Scripps-McRae papers was Brand Whitlock. Yet when it became apparent that Hanley could not be defeated unless all the opposition concentrated on one man, they declared for Atlee Pomerene, who had made such a fine showing in the race for lieutenant-governor and who certainly possessed the strongest following.[36]

Pomerene made an ideal candidate. Nearly six feet tall, erect in bearing, with a lofty brow heightened by receding hair, he looked the part of a Roman senator. A lawyer without utility connections, he had supported most of the reforms of the day. Since the time Tom Johnson had first lifted him from relative obscurity to back him for governor in 1908, Pomerene had become increasingly well known throughout the state. A progressive, however, more by political accident than inward conviction, he was a good deal more conciliatory toward men of other opinions than his mentor, and he had won adherents outside the Johnson faction.[37]

During November the contest between Pomerene and Hanley was confined to the newspapers, but in December the two men took to the stump to appeal to the people to dictate their choice to their representatives. A superb orator, Pomerene challenged his opponent to a series of joint debates, six of which were held in the week beginning December 14. The Canton lawyer concentrated his attack on Hanley's most vulnerable point, upbraiding him for being "the very embodiment of the public service corporation man" and denying that there was any need for more representatives of special interests in the Senate. Hanley flung back the charge that Pomerene was unsuitable for the office because of the character of his associates, contending that his principal backers were that "vicious and unscrupulous combine" the Scripps-McRae League and the Johnson reformers, who had denounced Harmon in 1908.[38]

As the time approached for the legislature to cast its ballot, it was apparent that Pomerene was the public favorite. Yet it was something else again to make the representatives responsive to the popular will. It was announced that the Democratic legislators would caucus on January 5 to select a party nominee. At first the Cuyahoga delegation of eleven, pledged to Pomerene, hesitated to enter the conference, knowing they would have to abide by the majority decision should Hanley be chosen. Assured, however, by Pomerene's manager that with their votes the Canton lawyer would win on the first ballot and convinced of the hopelessness of trying to elect him on the floor, they yielded. On their way to the caucus meeting in the Statehouse the Cuyahoga delegation rapidly circulated their decision in order to catch a few who were wavering but might eagerly climb on the bandwagon for Pomerene, if convinced that one existed.

After the eighty-eight members assembled in the Hall of Representatives, the room was cleared of everyone except the legislators and accredited newspaper correspondents. Eleven candidates were nominated, and the voting began. On the first ballot Pomerene received forty-five votes, the exact number necessary for nomination, and the motion was then carried to make the election unanimous. A week later the General Assembly went through the official formality of ratifying the caucus choice.[39]

Although Hanley took the defeat with ill grace, James Cox, his manager, offered his good will and support to Pomerene, who, he said, "will make a good Senator and will be a credit to the state." The Dayton congressman was paying the victor more than lip service, for ideologically he was much closer to the Canton man than to the conservative whose campaign he had managed.[40] Among the party progressives there was great jubilation over the Pomerene triumph. "[It was] a blow at the machine politicians in Columbus," Newton Baker declared, "and a credit to Cuyahoga County and clean politics all over the state and country." He especially rejoiced at the vindication of his beloved master, since Pomerene's selection proved that Tom Johnson's endorsement was no longer an effective curse upon a man in public life.[41] As the first important act of the new legislature, it was a hopeful portent that the Democratic progressives, with support from like-minded Republicans, were powerful enough to enact the reform legislation both parties had endorsed. The *Toledo News-Bee* prophesied "a new deal in Democratic politics in Ohio."[42]

This flush of optimism, however, proved short-lived. As soon as the two houses of the Seventy-ninth General Assembly had organized, it was evident that the conservative faction was powerful enough to endanger the fulfillment of the reform platform to which the Democrats were pledged. In the Senate the reactionaries controlled the Democratic committee on committees and assigned the chairmanships of the four most important to men who became the leading obstructionists of the session: George

K. Cetone, municipal affairs; Thomas A. Dean, railroads and telegraphs; Frank T. Dore, taxation; Isaac E. Huffman, judiciary. It was noteworthy that two of them, Cetone and Huffman, came from Edward Hanley's district. Only one member of the three-man Cuyahoga delegation received such an appointment: James Reynolds to head the labor committee. A Welsh-born, union-labor man, he had served in the House during the 1906 and 1908 sessions and was a devoted follower of Tom Johnson. Another protégé of the Cleveland mayor in the Senate, John N. Stockwell, aspired to the office of president pro tempore. His candidacy was anathema to the ruling conservative clique, who proposed Huffman. However, when they could not muster sufficient votes for their choice, they shifted to William Green, a political unknown from Coshocton who had been president of the Ohio Mine Workers. But his selection proved to be no better for them, because he worked closely with the defeated Stockwell and the reform element.

In the Senate the Democrats numbered nineteen, the Republicans fifteen, but the progressives could count on only eleven certain votes, nine Democratic and two Republican, while the conservatives' strength totaled seventeen, five from the majority party and twelve from the minority. The remaining five Democrats and one Republican took a middle-of-the-road position.[43]

In the House the picture was not so bleak. There the division by parties was sixty-eight Democrats, forty-eight Republicans, and one Independent. Forty-four of the Democrats were progressives and were joined by the one Toledo Independent and ten Republicans. Nevertheless, they lacked control, for their combined vote was four short of a majority. Opposed to them were forty-three conservatives, divided twelve to thirty-one between the majority and minority parties. The balance of power was held by the remaining twelve Democrats and seven Republicans, affiliated with neither wing.

A three-cornered contest developed for the speakership between: Cyrus Winters of Erie County, the conservative contender; William T. Smith of Marion County, the progressives' choice; and Samuel J. Vining of Mercer County, a compromise candidate. Vining won on the first ballot. In making committee appointments Vining listened to one side then the other and was accused by the progressives of lacking a backbone. He inclined toward the recommendations of Hanley and Garber, appointing conservatives to head some of the important committees. On the other hand, the progressives were not ignored in such assignments, and throughout most of the session Vining worked in harmony with them to redeem platform pledges.

Reformers were able to elect their nominee, Price Russell of Wayne County, majority floor leader. Furthermore, they were fortunate in having on their side a group of able young men serving their first term in the House. Among them were two Clevelanders, Robert Crosser and Carl D. Friebolin, who played a much more aggressive part in proposing and guiding legislation than their years or experience seemed to warrant.[44]

Despite their partial success in organizing the House, the problem of achieving effective leadership continued to plague the progressives. Tom Johnson, who had given direction in earlier sessions, was mortally ill at the beginning of 1911 and died on April 10.[45] The middle-of-the-road Harmon was reluctant to interfere with the legislative branch, because that violated his sense of constitutional propriety. Although as party leader he finally did consent to intervene to secure the enactment of party pledges, in the early stages of the session he left the burden to the individual members.[46]

His first message to the General Assembly was in no sense a manifesto of reform. He confined his legislative requests to a few topics: a more rigid limitation on tax levies than had been prescribed in the 1910 law, economy in the management of the canals and the completion of improvements already underway, caution in expenditures, the consolidation of the management of the state penal and charitable institutions in a single board, and a corrupt-practices act to guard the purity of the ballot.[47]

The need for increased statutory protection of the election process, which the fraudulent methods of the Cox machine had first illuminated, was suddenly dramatized by exposures of vote buying in Adams County. During Christmas week, 1910, Judge Albion Z. Blair and a grand jury revealed a state of affairs in this Ohio River county which shocked Ohio and the nation. For thirty years, the testimony disclosed, voters of every class and political affiliation — clergymen, physicians, prominent businessmen, as well as humble farm hands and the village poor—

had been selling their votes to candidates for office of either party, whichever was willing to pay the price. When the grand jury completed its work in mid-January, 1911, 1,690 persons—all vote sellers—were indicted and pleaded guilty before Judge Blair. Since his purpose in initiating the probe had been to stop the practice rather than to exact a heavy punishment, his penalties were light. A typical sentence was a fine of twenty-five dollars, with all but five dollars remitted, a prison sentence of six months, at once suspended, and loss of voting rights for five years, which was absolute. The number disenfranchised totaled nearly a third of the voting population.[48]

What was especially disturbing was that this practice, so open and widespread as to have become an accepted custom, had occurred in an area populated almost entirely by white native stock whose chief source of livelihood was farming. No recent immigrants were convicted and only a handful of Negroes. Rural districts heretofore had been placed before the public as models of integrity. One writer found the explanation in a familiar historical pattern. Once a vigorous pioneer community, Adams County had declined because its soils were no match for the rich lands opened on the prairies. As competition cut the region out of its markets, the strongest and ablest men departed for better farm country, leaving behind the weakest, who eked out a poor living. In support of this thesis the record revealed that the vote-selling evil was at its worst in the eroded hill-country townships. It was alleged that this malpractice extended to a half dozen other rural communities. Actual probes in Scioto and Pike counties, however, did not substantiate comparable conditions, although some indictments were returned.[49]

Since vote purchasing had already been outlawed by statute in 1889, the need was to add further safeguards to forestall violations of the law. Appropriately, it was the Democratic representative from Adams County, B. F. Kimble, who sponsored a corrupt-practices act embodying the Governor's recommendations; after some prodding the General Assembly adopted it near the end of the session. It sought to strike at the source of the evil, the vote buyers, by demanding full publicity from candidates of their campaign expenditures, by specifying the purposes for which funds might be used, and by placing ceilings on the total any nominee might spend. The use of force to threaten, abduct, or delay a voter was also proscribed by the new law.[50]

Under the auspices of the Governor, bills were drafted incorporating two more of his recommendations: one to establish a central board of administration for the state penal and eleemosynary institutions, and another to place limitations on the tax rate. The majority floor leader, Price Russell, introduced the central-board measure, which passed the House on February 9 by a vote of seventy to thirty-eight. Only two Democrats were on the negative side, William E. Donson and Christian Roth, both, significantly, from Hanley's district. The Republicans, treating it as a partisan measure, first tried to emasculate it with amendments, and, when defeated, opposed it on passage.

As passed by the House it established a bipartisan central board of four to administer all of the state penal and charitable institutions except the State Soldiers' and Sailors' Orphans Home and the Lima State Hospital. The board was to appoint all superintendents, centralize purchasing in one agent, institute the merit system, and promote the education and training of inmates, as well as study the causes and cure of dependency and delinquency. In addition, the board was to encourage the production of goods in the prisons and homes, which the state and its political subdivisions were required to buy.

Although the bill had survived the onslaught of its enemies in the House, Democratic obstructionists combined with Republican opponents in the Senate to alter it by crippling amendments which eliminated the provisions requiring bulk buying and the purchase by political subdivisions of convict-made goods. Passed in this form by the upper chamber on April 4, it was sent to a conference committee of the two houses.[51]

So powerful was this combination of reactionary Democrats and Republicans that the Senate in this session came to be known as the "graveyard of progressive legislation."[52] The fate of the tax-limitation bill was somewhat similar, though instead of being weakened by amendment it was buried in committee. On March 7 the House passed and sent to the Senate the administration bill sponsored by William T. Smith to limit the aggregate tax levy to ten mills. There it reposed in the taxation committee until an explosion over graft and bribery charges jarred it loose.[53]

Harmon's program was not the only one to suffer in the Senate. Three bills demanded by progressives and pledged in the party platforms were likewise locked away in the fastnesses of hostile committees in the upper chamber. The first to pass the House was a municipal initiative and referendum bill introduced by Robert Crosser. Partisans of this reform decided to concentrate on this limited application because the Ohio Constitution at that time only permitted direct legislation in the cities and the proponents were eager for a trial. They were willing to postpone consideration of their demand for an amendment to permit the state-wide adoption of such legislation until the forthcoming constitutional convention.

When the Crosser bill reached the Senate, it was assigned to the municipal affairs committee headed by the Dayton reactionary, George Cetone, whose tactic was to postpone consideration for four weeks. Impatient of further delay, five progressive members, four Democrats and one Republican, presented a majority report on April 6, recommending passage. This attempt to force action, however, was defeated on a point of order raised by another Democratic obstructionist, Frank Dore.

Nevertheless, this evidence of the progressives' determination did convince the conservatives that such legislation would pass in some form, and their only hope was to draw its teeth by amendment. This they succeeded in doing by increasing the percentage of electors required to sign petitions from the 8 per cent specified in the House bill to 30 per cent for initiative petitions and 15 per cent for referendums, and limiting the submission of direct legislation to general elections instead of permitting special ones, as the Crosser measure had done. Even in this amended form the proposal was not acted upon by the Senate for another six weeks.[54]

A second bill high on the progressives' program was one to apply in Ohio the Oregon Plan for the direct election of United States senators. This scheme provided that the names of senatorial candidates would appear on the party ballots, and that legislative candidates would file with their primary petitions either a pledge to accept the popular verdict as binding or a declaration that they would consider it a mere recommendation. The sponsors believed that public opinion in Ohio would force legislators to make a binding pledge, as had happened in Oregon. Introduced in the Senate on January 10 by John Stockwell, the bill was referred to the committee on privileges and elections, which two weeks later voted five to three to postpone indefinitely its consideration, the Democrats dividing three to two. When Stockwell reminded the three party renegades of the platform pledge, one of them, George Cetone, scornfully replied, "What the Hades do the people care about platforms. Half the people never read them." Dore, another one of the three, accused the Cleveland delegation of advocating the measure to pave the way for the election to the United States Senate of "that socialist," Brand Whitlock.

In the fight for this bill the progressives had the advantage of having the Governor on their side. Harmon, who was at first inclined to oppose such a reform, had become convinced that it was necessary, and for the first time in his administration began to exert leadership among the legislators of his party in its be-half. He conferred not only with Democratic members of the committee but with each Democratic senator to urge support for the proposal. Nevertheless, even after Harmon's intervention, a second motion from the floor to relieve the committee of the bill was defeated on March 7.

Since it was believed that some of the opposition was inspired by the personality of Stockwell, the sponsor, who was very able but also argumentative, the progressives introduced in the House a duplicate fathered by Charles M. Wyman of Shelby County. By a thumping margin of eighty-nine to thirteen, the bill passed that chamber on March 30. Party lines were disregarded; only ten Republicans and the three Democrats from Montgomery County were in opposition. Still, this House action did not seem to shake the imperturbability of the obstructionists in the Senate.[55]

The third measure of primary importance to progressives was a public-utility bill defeated in the previous session. Identical proposals were introduced in the House by Cyrus Winters and in the Senate by S. B. McGuire of Tuscarawas County. When public hearings were begun before the House committee in March, criticism from the corporations affected did not seem severe. The strongest objections were raised by shippers who feared that to lump together in one commission the regulation of railroads with other utilities would delay consideration of their complaints against the carriers. However, the measure as reported out of the committee bore evidence of utility pressure on the members. So favorable was it to the public-service corporations that the *Toledo News-Bee* called it worse than no bill at all, and the *Ohio State Journal* described it as a "travesty" on real regulation, "a gold brick." Nevertheless, on the floor, mainly through the skill and zeal of the Republican floor leader, Lawrence K. Langdon, bone and sinew were restored to the bill. With the Langdon amendments, which made it even stronger than the Woods proposal of 1910, it passed the House on April 5 by a vote of ninety to fourteen, opposed by seven Republicans and seven Cuyahoga Democrats, the latter all ultra-progressives, who refused to accept it because it violated the home-rule principle of utility regulation. As approved, it provided for a three-man commission empowered to control stock and bond issues; to regulate rates which were to be based on physical valuations; to supervise mergers which had to be complete, not mere stock purchases; and to review the rates and regulations established by city councils over utilities, the offensive provision to the Cleveland Democrats.

The lobby, repeating its tactics of 1910, abandoned its fight against the bill in the House in order to concentrate its attack in the Senate. It was reported that the docile committee on railroads and telegraphs, to which the proposal had been referred, was concocting a "futilities bill" out of amendments prepared by the corporations, a task that occupied all of the committee's time for the remainder of April.[56]

For some weeks the progressives had grown increasingly restive over the treatment accorded their measures by the obstructionist senators. During the first four months of the session only two platform pledges had been redeemed: ratification of the federal income tax amendment and provision for a nonpartisan judicial ballot in general elections. The only other source of mild satisfaction was that the troublesome and disruptive liquor question had been laid to rest for the session by the defeat in February of a bill to amend the existing County Option Law.[57] Still, such a record gave no cause for real rejoicing.

As March gave way to April, the progressive press began to increase the tempo of its attacks on the recreant senators. Negley Cochran exposed the bipartisan senatorial alliance between five reactionary Democrats, whom he named, and all the Republicans with two exceptions—an alliance that was determined to oppose all reform legislation. The *Toledo News-Bee* editor accused the combination of playing "peanut politics" and of "making representative government a joke." The same theme was amplified in an *Ohio State Journal* editorial: "It is very disgusting and humiliating to high minded Republicans to note the subserviency of so many state senators bearing the party name to the inner ring of the Democratic party."[58]

An attempt was made to shame the renegades into mending their ways by praising the conduct of the House and publicizing the accomplishments of legislatures in other states. On March 28 the Scripps-McRae papers printed a United Press release on the legislative achievements of Hiram Johnson's administration in California, which had adopted a constitutional amendment for the initiative, referendum, and recall; extended the power of the railroad commission to all utilities; limited the hours of working women to an eight-hour day; abolished the party circle on the ballot; provided for the nonpartisan election of judges; and established a state superintendent of instruction. The article reminded the public that this was what a real legislature had done in California, but not in Ohio.[59]

Nor did the press fail to draw the moral between the effective leadership Hiram Johnson had given in behalf of reform in his state and Harmon's reluctance to provide similar guidance at home. Negley Cochran lectured the Governor on the value of publicity. On April 6 Harmon responded to such promptings by sending a special message to the Senate asking for the passage of a few pending bills. There was much disappointment, however, at its "mildness of tone," its lack of punch. He was most insistent on the approval of the Smith 1 per cent proposal and, in addition, urged the adoption of a number of election and ballot reform measures, including a state-wide direct-primary system and the Oregon Plan for the selection of senators. The press was quick to point out the omissions in the message—its silence on legislation to create a central board of administration and a utility commission and its failure to mention bills demanded by labor.[60]

When this limited appeal failed to produce action, some of the Governor's closest associates, concerned over his political future, persuaded him to take more aggressive steps. On April

26 he called a caucus of all the Democrats in the General Assembly to confer with him on a seventeen-point program which he believed was minimum. It was his purpose, he said, not to dictate to them as governor but to share with them as a party associate his personal opinions and information he had gathered from independent study and from governors of other states. He asked the legislators to endorse each point by majority vote and exhorted the minority to stifle their differences and support the majority decision for the good of the party. Although many of the items were part of the platform, others had been held over from his previous administration. He appealed to their sense of duty and responsibility, stressing the public's impatience with their inaction and undue prolongation of the session.

Having stated his reasons for calling the caucus, he then proceeded to brief the members on each point or bill. His first three recommendations covering tax limitations and changes in the methods of assessment, he considered to be "great reforms." His fourth recommendation, the central-board bill, he foresaw, would bring substantial economies. The next eight bills he described briefly. One proposed to make the chief engineer of the state executive head of the canals; the other seven dealt with the following election and ballot reforms: a nonpartisan ballot for the election of delegates to the constitutional convention, corrupt-practices legislation, registration of voters in lodging houses, the Oregon Plan for electing senators, statewide direct primaries, elimination of party emblems on city tickets, and nonpartisan nomination of judges. He confessed he did not know much about the next proposals, to establish a public-utility commission and to introduce the initiative and referendum into cities, but they were platform pledges to be redeemed. An employers' liability proposal he considered very important, and the last two bills, to establish a women's reformatory and head the Girls' Home with a woman, he acknowledged, had more personal interest to him than any others.

Harmon was followed by Hugh L. Nichols, "a fearless progressive," who had been appointed lieutenant-governor in Pomerene's place. He made an even more vigorous plea, baldly stating, "There are many things in the legislative halls that are not right or honest." If they were not stopped, and if the Demo-

crats failed to meet their responsibilities, he concluded, the legislators would return home disgraced. Although the caucus did
not bind the members to the program, as the Governor had
recommended, and although three of the recreant senators and
two representatives voiced their continued opposition to specific
points, Harmon felt the conference had accomplished some
good.[61]

Three days after the caucus Harmon and the progressives
were aided by a fortuitous event which had a decisive effect in
breaking the legislative log jam in the Senate. Several of its
worst obstructionists, as well as some of the most conservative
members in the House, became implicated in bribery charges.
For some time there had been suspicions of corruption. Lieutenant-Governor Nichols was not the first to mention them, for
there had been earlier veiled accusations in the press. The graft
exposures broke when a Democratic representative from Pike
County, George B. Nye, asked for the arrest of three Burns
detectives, who had been posing as lobbyists, on the charge of
attempting to bribe him to influence legislation. Soon, however,
the shoe was on the other foot as the detectives countered with
startling allegations against various members of the Assembly
as bribetakers.

The private operatives disclosed that they had been hired by
a group of Columbus businessmen who were disgusted with the
frequent demands for money from boodlers and determined to
expose the crooks in the legislature. In the guise of lobbyists the
detectives had lured various suspect members to a hotel room,
where the bribery deals were transacted. A dictagraph concealed
behind a piece of furniture permitted a stenographer in an adjacent suite to transcribe the conversation word for word. The
entire proceedings had been conducted in collaboration with the
Franklin County prosecuting attorney, Edward C. Turner, who
had supplied the stenographer and to whom the testimony was
given for legal action.

Those indicted by the Franklin County Grand Jury on May 3
were George Nye, Senator LaForrest R. Andrews, Republican
from Ironton, Senator George Cetone, and Senator Isaac Huffman, all of whom were charged with soliciting bribes to vote for
an insurance bill. Also the Senate sergeant-at-arms, Rodney J.
Diegel, was charged with acting as a go-between. The insur-

ance measure was known as a "milker" bill, a type of nuisance legislation introduced for the purpose of extracting money from the corporations affected. In addition, Nye and A. Clark Lowry, Republican representative from Ironton, were indicted for soliciting bribes to defeat a maximum-hour bill for women.[62]

Both Attorney-General Hogan and the Governor promised to back the grand-jury investigations to the hilt and announced they would do all in their power to send the guilty men to prison. "Although we are Democrats," said Harmon, "we will not protect dishonest Democratic legislators." In Dayton, the home of George Cetone, the *Dayton Daily News* adopted the same stern attitude. While first cautioning its readers not to condemn the accused until the evidence had been presented, its editorial concluded, "If a Democrat is shown to be guilty, he should be cast out of the party as a leper would be cast out. He should be condemned from every angle. . . . The Democratic party in Ohio is on trial; it came into power for a purpose. It must make good." On the other hand, Edward Hanley telegraphed Cetone that Dayton friends believed him innocent and would stand by him to the end.[63]

The Senate, over the Governor's protests, voted on May 9 to conduct its own investigation, naming five Democrats and five Republicans to take charge. Since the lieutenant-governor had been by-passed in the selection of the probe committee and since its composition was heavily weighted with sympathetic reactionaries, there was a public suspicion that the real intent was to whitewash those implicated. The only two Democratic progressives appointed, William Green and John Krause from Cleveland, refused to serve. The other committee members accused them of yielding to newspaper pressure, and the Senate rejected their resignations. After meeting for three weeks the committee lamely reported that they could accomplish nothing because witnesses refused to testify.[64]

Meanwhile the grand jury had continued its investigations, adding to the list of indictments Senator Edgar T. Crawford, Republican from Stark County, and Senator Thomas A. Dean, Democrat from Fremont; and Representative Owen J. Evans, Democrat from Canton, and Representative Frank M. Calvey, Republican from Cleveland. All were indicted for soliciting bribes for their votes on a variety of bills.[65] Although this was not the first time in Ohio history that legislators had been indicted on such charges, never had the number of accused been so great nor the evidence so well substantiated.[66] Diegel, the first to be tried, was convicted and punished with a penitentiary sentence. Many months later Cetone, Andrews, and Huffman were brought to trial and received a similar punishment. Evans confessed and likewise did Nye. The Pike County legislator's statements were the most astounding. This one-time school teacher, practicing physician, and political boss admitted being the legislative agent for a public utility which absolutely dominated certain members of the Assembly and declared that his annual take from bribes was as high as ten thousand dollars.[67]

The prison terms which four of the men were eventually sentenced to serve constituted a new penalty established by a bill which had been introduced by Senator David Tod, a Republican from Mahoning County, and passed on May 3, just in time to apply to these cases. Previous legislation had merely required the guilty person to pay a fine.[68] This was only one of the legislative results of the grand-jury investigation. Another was to curb the power of the offenders in the Assembly, even though they were allowed to serve through the rest of the session. The House disbanded the calendar committee, of which Lowry, Nye, and Evans had been members, and replaced it with a new steering committee controlled by progressives of both parties. In the Senate, however, no reorganization took place. Still there was a remarkable change in spirit. The intense partisanship declined and the Democratic recreants were greatly subdued. Harmon promptly capitalized on the situation, soliciting the co-operation of two Republican progressives, Langdon in the House and Tod in the Senate, to push the administration program.[69]

On May 2 the central-board bill, with its original provisions restored, was reported out of the conference committee and passed by both chambers, only one Democrat dissenting in the House and none in the Senate. On the same day the upper body approved the Wyman bill for the direct election of United States senators by the narrow margin of eighteen to sixteen. The victory was achieved through the support of three Republicans and Dean's shift to the affirmative side. However, the other Democratic reactionaries, Senators Dore, Cetone, Cahill, and

Huffman, though reduced to silence, cast their ballots against the proposal.[70]

Nevertheless, no such easy victory was in store for the House-approved utility bill. On May 4 the Senate committee on railways and telegraphs reported out the measure with a long queue of amendments, as important as the bill itself, which had been drafted by a subcommittee of five. Two changes which were particularly obnoxious to progressives permitted rates for public service to be based on capitalized values plus cash investments instead of physical valuation and placed the granting of new franchises in the hands of the public-utility commission, thus violating home rule.

John Stockwell, aided by William Green, led the opposition to the amendments. As the Cleveland senator queried the subcommittee of five on the deletion of the physical-valuation provision, the chamber took on the air of a courtroom, with Stockwell in the role of prosecuting attorney and the five committeemen as silent, reluctant witnesses. Three times he asked them whether this provision had been stricken out in the interest of the public or the corporations; three times he was rebuffed by silence. After more pauses Senator Sherman Deaton, a Republican conservative from Urbana, half rose from his seat to demand that the senator explain why the amended clause would not benefit the public. And Stockwell replied:

> Yes, I will tell you. The change you made will allow public service concerns to charge the people of this state, you and me and our children and grandchildren, rates for their service that will pay dividends on fictitious values in the form of watered stock. Your change will allow them to milk the public to the end of time. That's why it won't benefit the public and that's why I ask you again why you made the change.

Still neither his interlocutor nor any other members of the subcommittee deigned to answer, secure in the knowledge that they had the votes without entering into debate.

Stockwell, Green, and Nichols tried to fend off a motion to consider the amendments as a whole. Green asked for a week's postponement of the vote, declaring, "This fear of the real nature of the amendments has been greatly increased this afternoon by the persistent and stubborn efforts of Senator [John E.]

Todd to have it crowded through." The "fear" to which he referred was a charge circulated by the Scripps-McRae papers that a $100,000 jackpot had been distributed among the subcommittee, of which John Todd, a Republican reactionary and law partner of Harry M. Daugherty, was the leading spirit. Senator Deaton rose to the defense, vociferously denying the alleged boodle. Todd turned the attack on Stockwell, charging him with opposing the amended bill because he represented the East Ohio Gas Company, which wanted no regulation at all. Nevertheless, the efforts to delay consideration failed, the motion carrying eighteen to sixteen through a combination of the five Democratic recreants with all of the Republicans except David Tod of Mahoning County and S. F. Macdonald of Ashtabula County. This was the decisive vote; the division in favor of the amendments was twenty to twelve. A last-ditch attempt of the progressives to restore the physical-valuation and home-rule provisions on the final passage was beaten down.[71]

The *Cleveland Plain Dealer* castigated the Senate action as a "brazen defiance of public opinion," a viewpoint shared by the House majority, which voted decisively to demand a conference committee rather than accept the changes made by the upper chamber. Speaker Vining appointed Winters, William B. Kilpatrick, a Trumbull County Democrat, and Langdon; Lieutenant-Governor Nichols selected McGuire, Stockwell, and Fred Bader, a Cincinnati Republican. Those who had engineered and led the movement for the Senate amendments were furious at being ignored in the appointments.

Despite the unremitting efforts of the utility lobbyists, the conference committee was successful in revamping the public-service bill by discarding many of the Senate changes. The public was given full protection in the event of any telephone merger, physical valuation as a basis for rate-making was restored, and city councils were permitted to grant franchises, subject to the review of the commission. On the last day of May the report of the conference committee was submitted to the two chambers, the Senate approving it nineteen to six, the House, eighty-two to five. Stockwell and five Cleveland representatives voted no on final pasage because of its insufficient protection of the home-rule principle. Governor Harmon allowed the bill to become a law on June 14 without his signature, making Ohio the tenth state to establish a public-service commission.[72]

Several factors contributed to this ultimate triumph. Among the major utilities, the telephone companies were willing to accept real regulation for the right to merge their properties and had thrown their influence behind the bill. But the measure might never have been adopted by the Assembly had it not been for the tenacity and zeal of the progressive minority. In turn, they might have been helpless without the powerful support of such journals as the *Cleveland Plain Dealer* and the Scripps-McRae papers. The newspapers were the ones that kept before the public the nature of the utilities' opposition, exposed John Todd and others as lobbyists of the public-service corporations instead of true representatives of the people, and insisted on a strong measure. That their biting criticism was successful was evidenced by a motion of the Senate obstructionists to bar the Scripps-McRae correspondents from the Senate floor because they were "assassins of character." Although Stockwell and Green protested against muzzling the press, the motion carried twenty-four to eight, an indication of the number who felt offended by these papers.[73]

During the course of the protracted fight on the utilities measure, other bills singled out by Harmon in his caucus speech received consideration. The Democratic opponents buried the hatchet on the popular Smith proposal to limit taxes to 1 per cent, and it passed on May 10 with solid Democratic support plus the vote of three Republicans. As finally approved, it provided that the aggregate levy of all tax districts, exclusive of bond interest and sinking funds, should not exceed ten mills without a popular referendum, which might raise it to a maximum of fifteen mills; placed a ceiling on each taxing unit (for example, five mills for municipal corporations); and further limited the total of the 1911 levy to the amount raised in 1910, to be increased in succeeding years only by specific percentages. The act established a budget commission composed of the auditor, prosecuting attorney, and the mayor of the largest city of the county to check the levies requested and make them conform to the law. The low rate was predicated on the revaluations which were then being made by the quadrennial boards of assessors and the tax commission of tangible property at 100 per cent of its true value in money. It was hoped and believed by its friends that this measure would bring intangible property out of hiding and on to the duplicate.[74]

Although Harmon rejoiced at the passage of this tax reform he had backed so insistently, the municipal progressives did not welcome it because it threatened their plans to extend city services.[75] Much more to their liking was a bill introduced by Ralph W. Edwards, a Cleveland Democrat, to restore home rule in the selection of urban tax boards by making the memberships elective, rather than appointive by the state board of assessors. In committee the proposal was altered to provide for a deputy commissioner in each county, appointed by the state tax commission, to take charge of appraisals. Vehemently attacked by lobbyists for the existing boards, it was first defeated in the House, then reconsidered and passed. Instead of the state tax commission's making the appointments, however, the job was assigned to a board composed of the governor, secretary of state, and state auditor. Though the municipal progressives were disappointed at the defeat of the home-rule principle, they accepted the amended measure because it would rid the cities of the boss-controlled tax bodies. Changes in the Senate forced the selection of a conference committee. The hostile reactionaries in the upper chamber, taking no chances on the kind of men Nichols might appoint, named their own committee of Dore, Cetone, and John Todd. They made short work of the bill by loading it down with unacceptable amendments.[76] Thus, the Edwards bill failed, and the existing local machinery for making appraisals remained intact.

The only other tax legislation of the session was a revision of the tax-commission measure passed in the previous session. The tenure of the commissioners was lengthened from three to six years, as the Governor had recommended, the correlation between their work and that of existing boards was clarified, the types of public utilities subject to the act were listed by name, and the language was made more precise where ambiguities had been discovered.[77]

The Crosser initiative and referendum bill, a cardinal point in the progressive program, was finally brought to a vote in the Senate on May 19. All efforts to restore the low percentages specified in the House version proved unavailing, however, and the measure passed by a vote of twenty-three to eight as amended in committee. The House concurred, and it became a law on June 14 without Harmon's approval.[78] Still the victory was a mixed one; the act established the principle of the initiative and referendum, but the high number of signatures required made its practical application almost an impossibility.

A more convincing triumph for the progresives was the adoption of the Green bill, which provided for the election of delegates to the constitutional convention on a ticket without party labels. The final effort to make the nominations of judges non-partisan, however, failed. Likewise, state-wide direct-primary bills were defeated, that of Stockwell in the Senate through the vote of six recreant Democrats, and an identical one in the House by the action of twelve party members who broke ranks. A Stockwell substitute to limit direct nominations to the governor and lieutenant-governor met a similar fate, but his bill to nominate congressmen in primary elections and to permit voters to express their preferences for presidential candidates was approved. Statutory regulations for registering voters were tightened to eliminate the frauds practiced by the political machines in Cincinnati. The support for these proposals came from the progressives of both parties, the Democrats being far from unanimous in backing such legislation.[79]

Other reforms of the political machinery desired by radicals which failed of adoption were ones permitting popular recall of elected officials, establishing a state civil service system, allowing cities to adopt either the federal or commission plan, and authorizing the municipal ownership of street railways. The only legislation to pass which affected urban communities directly was the Friebolin bill providing for small councils.[80]

No real resistance, however, was encountered by a labor measure to establish an optional system of workmen's compensation. In the previous session the first tentative steps had been taken to protect the rights of workers in recovering indemnities for losses due to industrial accidents, and a commission had been appointed to study the problem. Despite the failure of the legislature to provide funds for the investigation, the commission was able to proceed, through the personal donation of $5,000 by Governor Harmon. Its report was ready by the time the session opened in 1911. Although three bills were introduced, each based on the commission's study, the one that received attention was William Green's. It passed the Senate on March 22 and was engineered through the House a month later by Raymond Ratliff, a Republican lawyer from Cincinnati. Slight differences in the two versions required adjustment by a conference committee, whose report was unanimously adopted by both chambers on May 16.

The act created a three-member state liability board of awards to set up an insurance fund from premiums, of which 90 per cent were to be paid by employers and 10 per cent by employees and outlined the basis for awards. It relieved a contributing employer of liability, either under common law or statutory law, for the injury or death of his employees, unless the cause was the failure to comply with state safety codes. In that event the employee could seek in court greater damages than the law allowed. On the other hand, it denied to those who did not contribute the common-law defenses of the fellow-servant rule, assumption of risk, and contributory negligence. A landmark in Ohio labor reform, it was considered one of the best among the states.[81]

Senator Green sponsored two other bills in the interest of the working class. One was a proposal for a maximum eight-hour day for women in industrial and commercial occupations. It was first amended by the Senate to raise the hours to nine; the House later increased the hours to ten and a total of fifty-four per week. In this form it was accepted and sent to the Governor. Green's other measure, a bill to remedy a grievance of the Ohio coal miners, failed. This would have required operators to pay the men for run-of-the-mine coal instead of only for two-inch lump, the customary practice in the Ohio field. After a filibuster in which there was much horseplay, the Senate voted the proposal down.[82]

In appraising this session of the Seventy-ninth General Assembly, the *Cleveland Plain Dealer* spoke of it as one of contrasts. The *Toledo News-Bee* elaborated on this theme, declaring that it "both passed and killed more progressive legislation than any of its predecessors." One reason for this anomaly was that more reform measures had been introduced than ever before. Another was the strength of the obstructionists in the Senate, who "seemed to be constantly in some selfish scramble and to be beyond the respectable influence even of their own party," in the opinion of the *Ohio State Journal*. The credit for rescuing so many good bills was bestowed equally upon the press for exposing the machinations of the recreant senators, upon Governor Harmon for his determination to carry out the platform pledges, and upon the progressive legislators of both parties for their persistent efforts for the reform program.[83]

One aspect of the session which passed by without press comment was the preoccupation of the Assembly with election and ballot reforms rather than with economic and humanitarian changes. The shift in emphasis was particularly noticeable within the Tom Johnson group. To be sure, the progressives had labored hard for the utility-commission act and backed whole-heartedly the optional workmen's compensation and women's maximum-hour laws. Furthermore, tax reforms had not been ignored. Nevertheless, their primary insistence had been on changes in the machinery of government. John Stockwell explained this new viewpoint when he said in an interview, "Political reform must be distinguished from economic reform before we can secure progressive legislation along economic lines." The central problem, he continued, was to make the government "responsive and responsible to the popular will." True democracy could not be achieved until the people, not the bosses, controlled the system of nominations and elections and were able to hold their representatives in check through the initiative, referendum, and recall.[84]

Though the progressives' faith in the efficacy of mechanical governmental changes appears excessive in the light of history, there were few doubters at the time. Stockwell and his Ohio brethren were merely subscribing to tenets that were part of the climate of opinion of that day. What they failed to achieve one year, they were certain would be accomplished the next. The ultimate victory belonged to them. It was with confidence, therefore, that the Ohio reformers faced the important election of 1911, in which they hoped not only to win control of the cities of the state, but also to secure a majority of the delegates to the constitutional convention of 1912 and rewrite Ohio's fundamental law in the light of their democratic faith.

1. The Taft-Roosevelt relations with Cox are treated critically in Turner,

"The Thing above the Law," 588–91. During the 1910 campaign, when Longworth was running for re-election to Congress, Roosevelt stopped off in Cincinnati to attend a reception at his son-in-law's house. There he grasped the hand of George Cox and talked with his lieutenants. Cincinnati reformers could not help but view this act of Roosevelt's with some cynicism because only the night before in Chicago he had refused to sit at dinner with Senator Lorimer and the next day made an eloquent plea for independence from the bosses in Pittsburgh. Roosevelt defended his meeting with Cox by declaring that he would have made himself "utterly ridiculous" if he "had proceeded to set [himself] up as a censor and had declined to shake hands with anyone whom popular report accused of being a boss."—Theodore Roosevelt to Alfred Borden, November 2, 1910, in Morison and Blum, eds., *The Letters of Theodore Roosevelt,* VII, 153. The nomination of the Republican slate by Cox was reported in the *Cleveland Plain Dealer,* September 8, 1909.

2. *Cincinnati Enquirer,* May 4, 1908; *Cleveland Plain Dealer,* September 8, October 24, November 3, 1909. The *Enquirer* virtually ignored the local campaign and election. There was not a line of editorial comment and only one or two news stories prior to election day.

3. The nomination of Baehr was reported in the *Cleveland Plain Dealer,* September 1, 8–9, 1909, the charges and countercharges in *ibid.,* October 19–22, 1909. The note of apathy was commented on in *ibid.,* October 25, 1909, in an article by James W. Faulkner in the *Cincinnati Enquirer,* October 26, 1909, and in N. D. Baker to Leon P. Lewis, November 26, 1909, Baker Papers, CCH. The election returns are in the *Cleveland Plain Dealer,* November 3, 1909, and the *Cleveland Leader,* November 3, 1909.

4. *Cleveland Leader,* November 3, 1909.

5. *Cleveland Plain Dealer,* December 8, 1909.

6. *Ibid.,* September 8, October 10, 31, November 3, 1909; *Ohio State Journal* (Columbus), September 8, October 15, November 3, 1909.

7. Whitlock's characterizations of his opponents and recation to the campaign appeared in letters to his friends: Brand Whitlock to Lincoln Steffens, September 23, 1909, and Brand Whitlock to Octavia Roberts, November 8, 1909, in Nevins, ed., *The Letters and Journal of Brand Whitlock,* I, 118–19 and 121, respectively. The campaign and election were reported in the *Toledo News-Bee,* October 15–30, November 3, 1909, the *Toledo Blade,* November 3, 1909, and in an article by James W. Faulkner in the *Cincinnati Enquirer,* October 28, 1909.

8. The Dayton campaign was reported in the *Dayton Daily News,* September 8, October 16, 18, 23, November 3, 1909, the Youngstown campaign in the *Youngstown Vindicator,* October 25, 30, November 3, 1909. James W. Faulkner, the roving correspondent for the *Cincinnati Enquirer,* investigated the mayoralty campaigns in a number of cities of the state and observed in general a lack of leading issues (*Cincinnati Enquirer,* October 31, 1909).

9. *Cincinnati Enquirer,* June 19, 1910.

10. The poll on Harmon was reported in *ibid.,* June 19, 1910. The treatment of the Cuyahoga Democrats was described in N. D. Baker to Tom L. Johnson, June 24, 1910, Baker Papers, CCH; *Cleveland Plain Dealer,* June 21, 1910; *Toledo News-Bee,* June 21, 1910. Harmon's moderation was described in the *Cleveland Plain Dealer,* June 21, 1910, and *Ohio State Journal,* June 22, 1910. The platform and the contest over Baker's minority resolution are reported in *ibid.,* June 22–23, 1910, and *Cleveland Plain Dealer,*

June 22–23, 1910. Baker had hoped to outwit the managers on this issue by moving for the endorsement of Atlee Pomerene for United States senator shortly after the latter's keynote address in order to gain the full advantage of the enthusiasm and personal popularity the speech might generate. But the scheme failed because the speech was a flat failure and Pomerene refused to consent to such a use of his name—a wise refusal in the face of his dull speech. (N. D. Baker to Tom L. Johnson, June 24, 1910, Baker Papers, CCH) The platform also contained two other state planks recommending a uniform schoolbook law and extension of agricultural instruction as well as several planks touching national affairs (Mercer, ed., *Ohio Legislative History* [I], 65–67).

11. *Ohio State Journal,* June 22–23, 1910; David S. Creamer to Brand Whitlock, October 31, 1910, Whitlock Papers; N. D. Baker to Tom L. Johnson, June 24, 1910, Baker Papers, CCH. Other candidates nominated were: Charles S. Graves for secretary of state; Sylvanus E. Strode, dairy and food commissioner; Frank W. Miller, commissioner of common schools; Joseph A. Slates, member of the board of public works; James G. Johnson and Maurice H. Donahue, justices of the supreme court (Powell, ed., *The Democratic Party of the State of Ohio,* I, 423–24.

12. *Cleveland Plain Dealer,* June 23, 1910; *Ohio State Journal,* June 30, 1910.

13. Nathaniel C. Wright to A. L. Garford, January 5, 1910, Garford Papers.

14. *Cleveland Plain Dealer,* May 11, 1910.

15. The description of Garfield's political career and his relations with Hanna and Roosevelt are drawn from the *Cleveland Press,* February 3, 1900, the *Toledo Blade,* October 28, 1910, and the obituary in the *New York Times,* March 25, 1950. Howe's commentary is taken from Howe, *The Confessions of a Reformer,* 198.

16. The boom for Garfield was reported in the *Ohio State Jounral,* July 3, 1910. The quotation is from an open letter, printed in *ibid.,* July 2, 1910. The reaction of Cox, Taft, and Roosevelt is in *ibid.,* July 3, 20, 1910.

17. The primary results were reported in *ibid.,* May 18, 1910, and *Cleveland Plain Dealer,* May 18–19, 1910, the Scripps-McRae poll in the *Toledo News-Bee,* July 23, 1910.

18. Garfield's platform was printed on the front page of the *Toledo Blade,* July 26, 1910. The action of the resolutions committee was reported in the *Ohio State Journal,* July 27, 1910, and the *Cleveland Leader,* July 28, 1910. Garfield's reaction is in *ibid.,* July 28, 1910, the quotation in the *Toledo News-Bee,* July 27, 1910. Negley Cochran, who had been diligently boosting Garfield, was particularly bitter. The volatile Toledo editor told a fellow newsman that neither the *News-Bee* nor any other Scripps-McRae paper, as long as he had anything to do with them, would ever support Garfield in any future undertaking. See Joseph Garretson to W. H. Taft, July 28, 1910, in the Charles Dewey Hilles Papers (MSS in the Yale University Library [hereafter referred to as Hilles Papers]). The *Cleveland Leader* and *Ohio State Journal,* while not bitter toward Garfield, were sadly disappointed in his failure to act (*Cleveland Leader,* July 28, 1910; *Ohio State Journal,* July 28, 1910).

19. The vote for Garfield and Cox's comment were reported in the *Cleveland Leader,* July 28, 1910.

20. A. I. Vorys to W. H. Taft, July 21, 22, 1910; Wade H. Ellis to W. H. Taft, telegrams, July 23, 1910, Hilles Papers. Several years before, Judge

Kinkade had gained a reputation for independence, when, for the first time in a case involving an infraction of the Ohio Antitrust Law, he had imposed a jail term as well as a stiff fine on five prominent businessmen indicted for organizing an ice monopoly in Toledo and fixing the price of ice (Robert H. Bremner, "The Civic Revival in Ohio: Gas and Ice Monopolies in Toledo," 426).

21. Joseph Garretson to W. H. Taft, telegram, July 25, 1910, July 28, 1910, Hilles Papers. Garretson was an editorial writer on the *Cincinnati Times-Star*, owned by the President's half brother, and reported on the backstage maneuverings during the convention in a typewritten letter six and one-half pages long.

22. Joseph Garretson to W. H. Taft, July 28, 1910, Hilles Papers. Cox circulated the statement that he had Burton's promise to swing the Cuyahoga delegation behind Brown, but Garretson, who was present at the conference between the two men, recorded that the Cleveland senator's pledge was only to keep the vote of the Cuyahoga delegates split among the several candidates. The Cox statement was reported in the *Cincinnati Enquirer*, May 21, 1916. President Taft received assurances of Harding's loyalty to him, first from Garretson, later from the candidate himself, and was pleased by the convention's choice. See Joseph Garretson to W. H. Taft, July 28, 1910, and W. G. Harding to W. H. Taft, August 2, 1910, Hilles Papers, and the *Ohio State Journal*, July 28, 1910.

23. Wade H. Ellis to W. H. Taft, July 30, 1910; A. I. Vorys to W. H. Taft, August 3, 1910, Hilles Papers.

24. Roosevelt's comment was in Theodore Roosevelt to J. R. Garfield, August 6, 1910, in the Papers of Theodore Roosevelt, (MSS in the Library of Congress [hereafter referred to as T. Roosevelt Papers]); also quoted in George E. Mowry, *Theodore Roosevelt and the Progressive Movement* (Madison, Wis., 1946), 134. Roosevelt repeated the same phrase to Nicholas Longworth (Theodore Roosevelt to Nicholas Longworth, August 6, 1910, in Morison and Blum, eds., *The Letters of Theodore Roosevelt*, VII, 106). The criticism by the *Ohio State Journal* appeared in the issue for July 28, 1910, and that by the *Cleveland Leader* in the issue for the same date.

25. *Cleveland Leader*, Setpember 18, 1910. Privately the progressive Republicans considered Harding's eulogy of Cox a blunder. See A. L. Garford to Dr. Clarence Maris, September 28, 1910, Garford Papers. Dr. Maris was secretary of the Ohio Republican League. The lagging character of progressive support is illustrated by Garfield, who announced on September 26 that he would stump for Harding, but made no speeches until October 24, 1910 (*Ohio State Journal*, September 26, 1910; *Cleveland Leader*, October 25, 1910).

26. Foraker's speech was reported in the *Ohio State Journal*, October 23, 1910, Garfield's rebuttal in *ibid.*, October 25, 1910.

27. The Democratic reaction was reported in the *Cleveland Plain Dealer*, October 25, 1910, the Republican effort to smooth tempers in the *Ohio State Journal*, October 26–28, 1910, and in Walters, *Foraker*, 289. The Harding and Roosevelt attacks on Harmon are in the *Ohio State Journal*, October 28, November 6, 1910. On election night Hugh L. Nichols, the Democratic campaign manager, telegraphed Roosevelt: "Lucas County and Cuyahoga County, the two counties where you defamed Harmon show a net Democratic gain of 9,000. Come again."—*A Story of Progress in Ohio during Harmon's Administration*, 104.

28. Examples of Harmon's campaign speeches are found in: *Cleveland*

Plain Dealer, September 25, October 16, 1910; *Ohio State Journal,* September 25, October 9, 29, 1910; *Toledo News-Bee,* September 26, 1910. His reply to Roosevelt is in Mercer, ed., *Ohio Legislative History* [I], 122–24.

29. The speeches of the two men were reported in the *Cleveland Plain Dealer,* November 2, 1910; the rally was described in Johnson, *My Story,* 305–6. Amicable relations between the two men had been restored soon after the election of 1908. The first move had been made by Harmon, but Johnson responded warmly. (Tom L. Johnson to Judson Harmon, December 17, 1908, in the Tom L. Johnson Papers [MSS in the Cleveland City Hall, Cleveland, Ohio])

30. *Toledo News-Bee,* September 28, 1910.

31. *Ohio State Journal,* November 9–10, 30, 1910. The vote for governor was as follows: Harmon (Democrat) 477,077; Harding (Republican) 376,700; Tom Clifford (Socialist) 60,637; Henry A. Thompson (Prohibition) 7,129; J. R. Mailey (Socialist Labor) 2,920 (*Report of the Secretary of State of Ohio* [1910], 137).

32. Harding's comment was quoted in the *Ohio State Journal,* November 10, 1910, Garford's in A. L. Garford to Granville W. Mooney, November 14, 1910, Garford Papers. Garford repeated the sentiment in A. L. Garford to Myron T. Herrick, November 17, 1910, Garford Papers.

33. *Ohio State Journal,* November 9–10, 1910; Mowry, *Theodore Roosevelt and the Progressive Movement,* 155–56.

34. McLean's promotion of his own candidacy was reported in the *Ohio State Journal,* November 10, 1910, and the *Toledo News-Bee,* December 3, 1910, the support the others received in the *Ohio State Journal,* December 29, 1910. Three others were also placed in nomination at the party caucus on January 5, 1911: Thomas Powell, Oliver H. Hughes, and Will S. Thomas (*ibid.,* January 6, 1911). Not until the 1910 campaign was it known that McLean owned a controlling interest in the *Commercial-Tribune,* heretofore a staunchly Republican paper. "The whole, horrible truth came out" when the supposed owner directed the editor on McLean's order to back Harmon to the hilt.–B. E. Williamson to N. C. Wright, July 15, 1910, Garford Papers.

35. The biographical sketch of Hanley is drawn from the *Dayton Daily News,* November 6, 1907, from Powell, ed., *The Democratic Party of the State of Ohio,* II, 206, and from the author's interview with James M. Cox, June 29, 1949. The launching of his senatorial campaign and the opposition of the progressive Democrats were reported in the *Dayton Daily News,* November 14, 1910, the *Ohio State Journal,* November 27, 1910, and the *Toledo News-Bee,* November 28, 1910.

36. N. D. Baker to Tom L. Johnson, August 12, 1910, Baker Papers, CCH; N. D. Baker to Brand Whitlock, November 17, 1910; Harry N. Rickey to Brand Whitlock, June 4, 1910; Whitlock Papers. Rickey was editor-in-chief of the Scripps-McRae papers in Ohio.

37. The description of Pomerene's physique and political views is drawn from the author's interview with Carl D. Friebolin, August 1, 1949, the *Toledo News-Bee,* January 6, 1911, and N. D. Baker to Carl N. Osborne, December 9, 1910, Baker Papers, CCH.

38. Their joint debates were reported in the *Ohio State Journal* and *Cleveland Plain Dealer,* December 9–10, 14–20, 1910,

39. Pomerene was the favorite in a poll of editors of the Democratic papers

THE ONWARD MARCH OF REFORM

in Ohio taken by the Scripps-McRae League (*Toledo News-Bee,* December 23, 1910). Baker explained the reluctance of the Cleveland delegates to join the caucus in N. D. Baker to Atlee Pomerene, January 3, 1911, Baker Papers, CCH. The maneuvers of the Cuyahoga County delegation were reported in the *Toledo News-Bee,* January 5, 1911, the *Cleveland Leader,* January 6, 1911, and the author's interview with Carl D. Friebolin, who was a member, August 1, 1949. The Democratic caucus and the vote were reported in the *Ohio State Journal,* January 6, 11, 1911. Pomerene received all of the Democratic votes in the General Assembly; Whitlock received one vote from the Toledo Independent, Frank Hillenkamp; the Republican vote was scattered among fourteen candidates, Harry M. Daugherty leading with seventeen, Dick receiving only nine.

40. *Ohio State Journal,* January 6, 1911; *Dayton Daily News,* January 6, 1911. Cox had respect for Hanley's personality and ability and was deeply offended by what he called "the brutal assassination" of his candidate's character in the senatorial campaign. Yet in their political views they were widely apart. Later Hanley joined Harvey Garber in opposing Cox's program of progressive legislation in the 1913–14 sessions. (James M. Cox to the author, September 16, 1949)

41. Statement of Baker, printed in the *Cleveland Leader,* January 6, 1911.

42. *Toledo News-Bee,* January 6, 1911.

43. The organization of the Senate was reported in the *Ohio State Journal,* January 11, 1911, the facts on Reynolds in *Cleveland Plain Dealer,* March 12, 1911. The contest over the presidency pro tempore was reported in the *Ohio State Journal,* November 10, December 8, 1910; January 11, 1911. The appraisal of Green is in the *Cleveland Plain Dealer,* April 2, 1911. The division of political strength in the Senate is based on the voting record of the senators throughout the session, compiled by the Scripps-McRae League (*Toledo News-Bee,* June 1, 1911).

44. The ideological makeup of the House is based on the voting record of the representatives during the session as compiled by the Scripps-McRae League (*Toledo News-Bee,* June 1, 1911). The contest over the speakership was reported in the *Ohio State Journal,* December 23, 1910, the organization of the House in *ibid.,* January 11, 1911. Some of the conservatives appointed to committee chairmanships were: Cyrus Winters, cities; George Nye, corporations; Harry L. Goodbread, finance; Mahlon Gebhart, judiciary. On the other hand, the following progressives received such assignments: Charles M. Wyman, elections; William T. Smith, taxation; Bernard Bell, labor. The appraisal of Vining is drawn from the *Cleveland Press,* June 2, 1911.

45. Johnson, *My Story,* 312–13. Shortly after his death the General Assembly passed a memorial resolution, introduced by his friends, which was a moving tribute to this "champion of the rights of men . . . [who] ever sought to exalt the ideals of citizenship and of government." The text is in 102 O.L. 743 (1911).

46. Harmon expressed his views on the role of the governor with respect to legislative leadership to William Bayard Hale (Hale, "Judson Harmon and the Presidency," 14,449–50).

47. Governor's message, January 2, 1911, printed in Mercer, ed., *Ohio Legislative History* [I], 82–93.

48. The fraud exposures received widespread coverage in the newspapers of the time. One of the fullest running accounts is in the *Ohio State Journal,*

December 22, 24, 29–31, 1910; January 3, 15, 31, 1911. Judge Blair reviewed his part in the investigations, defended his leniency, and confessed that he had been a vote buyer himself when he first entered politics, in A. Z. Blair, "Seventeen Hundred Rural Vote Sellers: How We Disfranchised Voters in Adams County," *McClure's Magazine*, XXXVIII (November, 1911), 28–40. A detailed review of the case has recently appeared: Genevieve B. Gist, "Progressive Reform in a Rural Community: The Adams County Vote-Fraud Case," *Mississippi Valley Historical Review*, XLVII (June, 1961), 60–78. In the 1913 legislative session the representative from Adams County, James R. B. Kessler, introduced a bill to restore the franchise to those who had lost their voting privilege. It passed the Assembly but was vetoed by Governor James Cox, who declared the bill unconstitutional since the pardoning power was vested exclusively in the chief executive. (*Ohio State Journal*, March 6, April 12, May 4, 1913)

49. A typical example of press reaction is the editorial in the *Cleveland Plain Dealer*, December 28, 1910. The suggested explanation of the underlying causes is in Albert Shaw, "A National Lesson from Adams County," *Review of Reviews*, XLIII (February, 1911) 173–74, 179. The probes in other counties are described in the *Cleveland Plain Dealer*, December 27, 1910, the *Ohio State Journal*, January 18, May 8, 1911, and in Gist, "Progressive Reform in a Rural Community," 73–78. In an article on the city which Brand Whitlock wrote shortly after the vote-selling exposures, he noted that similar venality had been uncovered in Putnam County, New York, and Vermillion County, Illinois. In a city, he concluded, corruption of voters never approached such a scale; the highest estimate of municipal vote bribery was 5 per cent. (Brand Whitlock, "The City and Civilization," *Scribner's Magazine*, LII [November, 1912], 627)

50. This legislation replaced the Garfield Corrupt Practices Act, which had been passed in 1896 and then repealed in 1902. See *Ohio State Journal*, May 18, 1911; *Cleveland Plain Dealer*, June 1, 1911. The text is in 102 O.L. 321 (1911).

51. The passage in the House was reported in the *Ohio State Journal*, February 10, 1911, its fate in the Senate in the *Cincinnati Enquirer*, April 5, 1911.

52. *Ohio State Journal*, April 6, 1911.

53. *Ibid.*, March 8, 1911.

54. The Crosser bill passed the House by a vote of seventy-nine to sixteen (*Cleveland Plain Dealer*, March 9, 1911). Its treatment by the Senate was reported in the *Cincinnati Enquirer*, April 6, 1911, and *Cleveland Leader*, April 7, 12, 1911. Dore's point of order was that the report was not accompanied by the bill, which Cetone had purposely kept in his possession.

55. The fate of the bill in the Senate and Cetone's and Dore's reactions are reported in the *Cleveland Plain Dealer*, January 11, 1911, and *Ohio State Journal*, January 26, March 10, 1911, Harmon's intervention in the *Cleveland Plain Dealer*, January 11, 31, February 8, 1911, and in "Judson Harmon—His Record and His Views," *Outlook*, C (January 27, 1912), 180–81, described as "an authorized interview," although the author's name was not revealed. The House action is reported in the *Ohio State Journal*, March 11, 31, 1911. John Stockwell admitted that a bill with his name attached was self-condemned (the author's interview with Carl D. Friebolin, August 1, 1949).

56. The introduction of the bill was reported in the *Ohio State Journal*,

THE ONWARD MARCH OF REFORM

February 16, 1911, the complaint of the shippers in *ibid.*, March 9, 1911, the press criticism in the *Toledo News-Bee*, March 28, 1911, and *Ohio State Journal*, April 4, 1911. The acceptance by the House is in *ibid.*, April 6, 1911, the treatment by the Senate in *ibid.*, April 23, 1911.

57. Ohio became the tenth state to ratify the federal Income Tax Amendment (*Ohio State Journal*, January 20, 1911). The text is in 102 O.L. 732 (1911). The adoption of the nonpartisan judicial ballot bill was reported in the *Ohio State Journal*, January 19, February 2, 1911; the text is in 102 O.L. 5 (1911). A companion piece to make the nomination of judges non-partisan was killed in the Senate (*Ohio State Journal*, March 2, 1911). The defeat of the liquor bill was reported in *ibid.*, January 24, February 2, 10, 22, 1911.

58. Editorials in the *Toledo News-Bee*, April 6, 1911, *Ohio State Journal*, April 7, 1911. The five Democratic reactionaries named by Cochran were: Thomas Dean of Fremont, Frank T. Dore of Tiffin, George Cetone of Dayton, Michael Cahill of Eaton, and Isaac Huffman of Oxford. The last three were from the region controlled by Hanley. Moreover, Dean, Cetone, and Huffman had been obstructionists in the legislative sessions of 1909–10. See chap. x, n. 45.

59. *Cleveland Press*, March 28, 1911; *Toledo News-Bee*, March 28, 1911.

60. Cochran's "lecture" was in the *Toledo News-Bee*, March 10, 1911. The Governor's special message, April 6, 1911, is in Mercer, ed., *Ohio Legislative History* [I], 141–42. The press criticism was in the *Cleveland Plain Dealer*, April 7, 1911, and the *Ohio State Journal*, April 7, 1911.

61. Persuasion to act came from various Democratic leaders: Charles P. Salen to Judson Harmon, April 10, 1911; Henry T. Hunt to Judson Harmon, April 21, 1911, in Harmon, Exec. Docs.; see also Hendrick, "Judson Harmon," 623–24. The text of Harmon's speech to the Democratic caucus is in Mercer, ed., *Ohio Legislative History* [I], 130–37. Nichols' remarks are in the *Cleveland Plain Dealer* and *Ohio State Journal*, April 27, 1911, Harmon's reaction in *ibid.*, April 27, 1911. The characterization of Nichols was made by Cochran in the *Toledo News-Bee*, March 10, 1911.

62. Suspicions of bribery had been expressed in the *Cleveland Press*, April 25, 1911. The graft exposures were reported in the *Ohio State Journal*, April 30, May 1–4, 1911, and the *Toledo News-Bee*, May 1–3, 1911. The initiative in organizing the investigation came from Opha Moore, secretary of the Ohio Manufacturers' Association. He hired Rodney Diegel to report on the legislators who could easily be approached and were responsible for the nuisance or "milker" bills. Diegel created the web which finally caught him as well, for he, too, accepted money from the detectives hired by Moore. (George Creel and Sloane Gordon, "What Are You Going to Do About It— The Shame of Ohio," *Cosmopolitan*, LI [October, 1911], 599–610). Long before their indictment Nye and Lowry had had an unsavory reputation. Carl Friebolin, a new member, had only been in the legislature a short time when a seasoned colleague took him aside and pointed first to Dr. Lowry, saying, "There is the paymaster of the Republican party," then to Dr. Nye, "And there is the paymaster of the Democrats."—the author's interview with Carl D. Friebolin, August 1, 1949.

63. Harmon was quoted in the *Toledo News-Bee*, May 2, 1911; the editorial in the *Daily News* and Hanley's telegram were in the *Dayton Daily News*, May 2, 1911.

64. *Cincinnati Enquirer,* May 10–11, 1911; *Cleveland Plain Dealer,* May 10–11, 31, 1911.

65. Crawford was indicted for soliciting a bribe on a trading-stamp bill, Evans for his vote to amend the County Local Option Liquor Law (*Cleveland Plain Dealer,* May 17, 1911). Dean, together with an ex-mayor of Columbus, Anson Bond, was charged with offering a bribe to two legislators in the 1908 session to defeat a county local-option liquor bill. Calvey was charged with soliciting a bribe on a Cleveland subway bill. (*Ohio State Journal,* June 10, 1911).

66. Five legislators were indicted for bribery by a grand jury in 1896. Only one was convicted, and he appealed his case on error to the circuit court, which reversed the decision of the lower court. (*Ohio State Journal,* May 7, 1911).

67. Diegel was convicted on July 3 in the Franklin County Court of Common Pleas and appealed the decision on error through the circuit court to the Ohio Supreme Court, which upheld the lower courts on all points. He was sentenced to three years in the penitentiary. (*Ohio State Journal,* July 2–4, 1911; November 18, 1912). Andrews and Huffman were not tried until the spring of 1912; both were convicted, and both appealed and lost. Andrews was sentenced to nine months, Huffman to three years, in the penitentiary. (*Ibid.,* March 14, 19, November 18, December 18, 1912). Because of his ill health Cetone's trial was postponed from the spring until November, 1912, when he was convicted and sentenced to serve three years in the penitentiary (*Ibid.,* November 26, 30, December 5, 25, 1912). Lowry was a very sick man and apparently died before standing trial (*ibid.,* October 12, 1912). Dean was tried, but the jury could not reach an agreement and he was freed (*ibid.,* February 4, 12, 1913). The charges against Crawford and Calvey were dropped (Mercer, ed., *Ohio Legislative History* [I], 287). Evans, because of his confession, was let off with a $500 fine. He was also barred from his seat in the legislature and from ever holding public office again in Ohio. (*Ohio State Journal,* June 6, 1911). Nye had been indicted for bribery on four separate counts. Of the charge of soliciting a bribe from the state printer on a gerrymander bill, he was acquitted by the jury on June 1, 1911. (*Ibid.,* May 23, 25, June 2, 1911). But a year and a half later he pleaded guilty to soliciting a bribe from B. F. Kimble on the same bill. It was in this confession that he made his startling statements. The press believed that numerous indictments would follow Nye's testimony to the judge, but no new ones were made. Nye turned state's witness in the Cetone case and no doubt helped to convict the Dayton senator. For confessing Nye escaped a penitentiary sentence. (*Ibid.,* October 10, 11, November 30, 1912).

68. *Cleveland Plain Dealer,* May 4, 1911.

69. The committee changes in the House were reported in the *Toledo News-Bee,* May 3–4, 1911. The new steering committee was composed of Price Russell, J. S. Combs, Carl D. Friebolin, Samuel R. Gotshall, and Harry W. Crist, Democrats; Lawrence Langdon, and Earl N. Gibbs, Republicans. Harmon's solicitation was reported in *Cincinnati Enquirer,* May 3, 1911, and *Cleveland Plain Dealer,* May 3, 1911.

70. *Cleveland Plain Dealer,* May 3, 1911; *Cincinnati Enquirer,* May 3, 1911; *Ohio State Journal,* May 3, 1911. The texts of the acts are in 102 O.L. 211 and 119 (1911), respectively. In addition Harmon's other pet reform, a women's reformatory, was approved, the text of which is in 102 O.L. 207 (1911).

71. The debate in the Senate on the utility bill was reported at length in the *Cincinnati Enquirer,* May 5, 1911, the charge against Todd in the *Toledo News-Bee,* April 29, 1911, the Senate vote in *Ohio State Journal,* May 5, 1911, and *Cleveland Press,* May 5, 1911.

72. The *Cleveland Plain Dealer* reaction appeared in the issue for May 8, 1911. The appointment and work of the conference committee were reported in the *Cincinnati Enquirer,* May 12, 1911, the final passage in *ibid.,* June 1, 1911, and the *Cleveland Plain Dealer,* June 1, 1911. New York and Wisconsin pioneered in the adoption of public-utility commissions in 1907. Vermont adopted such a law in 1908, Maryland in 1910, Washington, Kansas, Nevada, New Jersey, Connecticut, and Ohio in 1911. (Lapp, "Public Utilities," 576)

73. The utility corporations were split over the bill. It was reported that the Standard Oil Company and the telephone companies had accepted a regulatory commission with real power, while the railroads and the express and electric companies were opposed. (*Ohio State Journal,* April 23, 1911; *Cleveland Plain Dealer,* June 1, 1911). Had the utility bill failed, the telephone companies were prepared to obtain authority for their desired mergers through separate legislation. Such a bill passed the Senate. (*Ohio State Journal,* May 17, 1911) The legislators, singled out for special praise by the Scripps-McRae papers, were Langdon, Kilpatrick, and Stockwell (*Cleveland Press,* June 4, 1911). An example of the assistance given by the newspapers is the article in the *Cleveland Press,* exposing Todd's utility connections (issue for May 26, 1911). The motion to debar was reported in the *Toledo News-Bee,* May 31, 1911, and *Cleveland Plain Dealer,* June 1, 1911.

74. *Cleveland Plain Dealer,* May 11, 1911. The text is in 102 O.L. 266 (1911). Harmon elaborated on the potential effect of the measure in urging its adoption in his message of January 2, 1911 (Mercer, ed., *Ohio Legislative History* [I], 82–86).

75. This reaction was expressed in Brand Whitlock to Henry T. Hunt, October 14, 1911, Whitlock Papers. Three years later Newton Baker wrote Whitlock that he was going to attend a meeting of Ohio mayors in Columbus to ask the special session of the legislature "for some relief from the famine caused by the Smith–1% tax law–who the devil was Smith anyhow?–I never realized before how inconveniently–that law is named."–Newton D. Baker to Brand Whitlock, January 17, 1914, Whitlock Papers. Objections were also raised that the bill would cripple school financing (Junior Order United American Mechanics to Judson Harmon, April 5, 1911; Dr. Dan Miliken to Judson Harmon, January 31, 1911, Harmon, Exec. Docs.).

76. *Cleveland Plain Dealer,* January 19, April 27, 1911; *Ohio State Journal,* April 28, 1911; *Cleveland Press,* June 2, 1911.

77. The text is in 102 O.L. 224 (1911).

78. *Ohio State Journal,* May 19, 1911; *Cleveland Plain Dealer,* June 1, 15, 1911. Although he refused to sign the bill, Harmon was not opposed to this limited experiment with the initiative and referendum. Nevertheless, he continued to have grave doubts about the practicability of making such a change general. "Judson Harmon–His Record and His Views," 181.

79. The Green bill was reported in the *Ohio State Journal,* April 12, May 17, 1911; the text is in 102 O.L. 298 (1911). The act also provided that the delegate, if he wished, could indicate whether he favored or opposed the submission of a separate amendment on the question of licensing the liquor traffic. The failure of the judges' bill was reported in the *Ohio State Journal,*

March 2, 1911, the defeat of the Stockwell proposals in *ibid.*, May 11, 1911, the *Toledo News-Bee,* April 5, 1911, and the *Cincinnati Enquirer,* April 5, *May* 11, 1911. The vote in the Senate was fourteen to nineteen; the six Democratic senators in opposition were Cetone, Huffman, Cahill, Dean, Dore, and Rufus H. Finnefrock, "the human jelly-fish from Marion County." The adoption of the congressional direct-primary and presidential-preference bill was reported in *ibid.*, May 11, 1911; the text is in 102 O.L. 414 (1911). The new registration act required lodging-house keepers to maintain daily registers of all their guests, which were to be available to official inspection. The text is in 102 O.L. 181 (1911). The progressive support was noted in the *Ohio State Journal,* May 11, 1911.

80. Carl D. Friebolin introduced bills for the recall of officials and a state-wide merit system. The civil service proposal had been drawn by Mayo Fesler, secretary of the Municipal Association of Cleveland, in consultation with Newton Baker and other experts. An identical bill was placed before the Senate by John Krause of Cleveland. (*Cleveland Plain Dealer,* January 19, 1911; *The Municipal Bulletin* [Municipal Association of Cleveland], XV [May, 1911], 11–12). James Reynolds and Carl Friebolin introduced the two measures to permit cities to adopt the federal or commission plan (*Ohio State Journal,* January 17, 1911). Meyer Geleerd, a Toledo Republican, was the sponsor to the municipal-ownership bill (*ibid.*, February 1, March 15, 1911). The Friebolin bill for smaller councils was reported in the *Cleveland Leader,* April 7, 1911.

81. Harmon's donation was reported in Nichols, "Harmon," 144–46. The legislative history of the bill was carried in the *Ohio State Journal,* December 20, 1910; January 2, February 23, March 23, April 28, May 17, 1911. The text is in 102 O.L. 524 (1911). The law was validated by the Ohio Supreme Court in January 1912 (*Ohio State Journal,* January 21, 1912).

82. The Green maximum-hour bill for women was reported in *ibid.*, February 16, May 17, 1911; the text in 102 O.L. 488 (1911). The defeat of the coal miners' bill was reported in the *Ohio State Journal,* February 7, 15, 24–25, 28, 1911.

83. Editorial opinion was expressed in the *Cleveland Plain Dealer,* June 2, 1911, the *Toledo News-Bee,* June 1, 1911, and the *Ohio State Journal,* June 2, 1911. Of the seventeen bills enumerated by Harmon in his speech to the Democratic caucus, all but five were adopted. His list, however, did not include all the bills desired by progressives, and contained some in which they had little interest. The *Toledo News-Bee* listed fourteen progressive measures which failed to pass. See the issue for June 1, 1911.

84. Interview in the *Cleveland Plain Dealer,* May 13, 1911.

CHAPTER ELEVEN

VICTORY FOR PROGRESS
1911

THE OHIO CONSTITUTION OF 1851 had embodied the Jeffersonian principle that each generation should have the opportunity to review the state's fundamental law and provided for the mandatory submission to the voters of a call for a constitutional convention every twenty years.[1] Had the constitutional calendar been followed, the call would have been issued in 1911; yet so eager were the advocates of change that the date was advanced twelve months.

Never before in the sixty-year span had this date fallen at such a psychologically favorable time. There was a pent-up demand among various groups for such reforms as municipal home rule, legal protection of workers, improvements in court procedure, and woman suffrage. Still the most insistent pleas for a constitutional convention came from three well-organized groups dedicated to their own particular reform: the Ohio State Board of Commerce, desiring a tax amendment to abolish the uniform rule and permit the classification of property; the liquor interests, wanting to license saloons; and Herbert Bigelow and the Direct Legislation League, eager for the enactment of the initiative and referendum.[2]

Bigelow, it will be recalled, had pressed unsuccessfully for an initiative and referendum amendment in the legislative sessions of 1908 and 1910. Disheartened by his defeats, he had decided in the spring of 1910 to abandon political action for educational work, hoping to create such an overwhelming popular sentiment for this reform that a later legislature would find its adoption irresistible. Although financing such a program presented many difficulties, Bigelow was able to solve them in two ways. He was, first of all, fortunate in receiving outside aid from the Joseph Fels Fund of America, established in 1909 by the wealthy manufacturer of naphtha soap, to promote the single tax. The chairman of the Fund was Bigelow's closest associate, Daniel Kiefer; the first treasurer was Tom Johnson. As previously noted, single taxers regarded the initiative and referendum as the key to the introduction of their tax reform. Secondly, Bigelow persuaded his congregation to sell their valuable church site on Vine Street and with the money from the sale both pay his modest salary and contribute toward the educational campaign. The name, People's Church and Town Meeting Society, was substituted for the Vine Street Congregational Church; the stage of the Grand Opera House became Bigelow's new pulpit.

The heart of the radical pastor's new scheme was to establish social centers for the discussion of public affairs in the city's school buildings along the lines of a similar experiment in Rochester, New York. When the Town Meeting Society presented its plan to the Cincinnati School Board, however, it received a peremptory rebuff, for the board was an adjunct of the Cox machine. This repulse changed Bigelow's mind, and he decided to pursue again a program of state-wide political action, joining his voice to the chorus of those demanding a constitutional convention to achieve their particular reforms.[3]

The form of the call was a victory for these partisans. It provided for an endorsement by political parties, since such an official certification of approval would automatically invoke a provision of the Ohio electoral law which declared that a straight party vote would constitute a vote for a constitutional convention. Both the Republicans and the Democrats took the required action. The results were overwhelmingly in favor of calling a convention—693,263 to 67,718. After the election conservatives decided the arrangement had been a fraud and claimed that political leaders had been beguiled into an endorsement by the "siren voices" of a minority group of "labor leaders, Socialists, single-taxers and other reformers" in defiance of the majority opposed to any revision. Although this estimate of state senti-

ment was highly questionable, it is true that the vote of ten to
one was also suspect. No doubt many who voted a straight
ticket gave only perfunctory attention to the question. Still, the
militant opposition as reflected in the negative vote was surprisingly small.[4]

With this hurdle behind them partisans began organizing a
campaign to elect delegates to their particular reforms. None
were more active than Bigelow, who in June, 1911, formed a
new organization, the Progressive Constitutional League. Brand
Whitlock accepted the presidency; a professor, an editor of a labor
journal, and an officer of the Ohio State Grange were made vice-
presidents; the treasurer of the Grange was named to the same
League office; and Bigelow was appointed secretary. The League
concentrated its attention on three issues: municipal home rule,
the recall, and the initiative and referendum. To eradicate any
doubt about what they meant by the last proposal, they spelled
out the details, specifying the exact percentages of voters required to set the wheels in motion for direct legislation, insisting
on its application to all political subdivisions of the state, and
stipulating decisions by majority vote on the measure itself
rather than by a majority of the total votes cast in the election.[5]

Throughout the summer, Bigelow and other field workers
stumped Ohio, winning endorsements of the initiative and referendum from hundreds of organizations—from chambers of
commerce to the smallest local granges and labor unions—and
seeking pledges from candidates to the convention. Financially
aided by the Fels Fund, the League was further helped by the
spirited campaign conducted by the Scripps-McRae papers,
whose reporters circulated through the counties to assist in
securing public commitments from candidates to vote for an
effective initiative and referendum amendment. As the *Cincinnati Post* explained, Ohio progressives must profit from the lesson
of the Michigan constitutional convention of 1907, which
adopted an emasculated direct-legislation provision because the
delegates were not publicly pledged beforehand.[6]

When it became apparent that support for this movement
was rolling up like a snowball, alarmed conservatives began a
counterattack. The chief opposition came from the Ohio State
Board of Commerce, which was under the personal direction
of Allen Ripley Foote, "a shrewd political and legislative mana-

ger for special privilege," according to a progressive journal. He persuaded big business to contribute money, dispatched boiler plate attacking the proposal as communistic to the rural press, and organized support for conservative candidates.

Nevertheless, Foote failed to enlist all of the industrial and commercial class for his cause. The Ohio Manufacturers' Association took a neutral position. Bigelow, furthermore, had already succeeded in creating enthusiasm for the initiative and referendum among the liquor interests, to whom he had easy access, since their headquarters was also in Cincinnati. While the legislature, he pointed out, tended to favor the "drys" because of the preponderant strength of the prohibition-minded rural counties in the lower house, a popular referendum would give full weight to the "wet" urban electorate underrepresented in the Assembly. This piece of political opportunism did not, however, signify a real alliance between the opponents of prohibition and the advocates of the initiative and referendum. Not all wets were for direct legislation, nor all drys opposed. In the rural counties, where the League concentrated its efforts, Bigelow and his fellow partisans endorsed any candidate who would support the initiative and referendum, regardless of his stand on the chief emotional issue of the day.[7]

Strong sentiment already existed for their program in the cities. In Cleveland and Cuyahoga County a branch of the League, representing 150 civic and labor organizations, nominated a slate of ten candidates pledged exclusively to this issue. Although three other groups—the Muncipal Conference, the Socialists, and the Democrats—prepared separate tickets, all of their nominees were likewise committed to the principle of the initiative and referendum. Further publicity was given the cause when a week before the election Senator Moses E. Clapp of Minnesota addressed an audience of two thousand in Grays' Armory in support of direct democracy. Since the Cleveland advocates of this reform believed that with its adoption other ills, such as taxation evils and the lack of municipal freedom, could be cured, their tendency was to concentrate on it alone.[8]

In Columbus a different plan for the selection of candidates led to less emphasis on direct legislation, though an endorsement was not neglected. At a meeting on July 25, presided over by Washington Gladden, the representatives of more than a hundred civic, professional, farm, and labor organizations formed the United Constitution Committee of Franklin County. The assembled group listened to an address by Bigelow, voted to allow labor, agriculture, and business groups each to select one candidate to the constitutional convention, and planned public forums on a variety of subjects: the commission government for cities, taxation, the initiative and referendum, reform of judicial procedure, and nonpartisan elections. The best organized of all the pre-convention movements in the cities, the United Constitution Committee held open discussions at regular intervals, nominated candidates representing each of the three major economic classes, and committed them to a platform of direct legislation, municipal home rule, and reform in judicial procedure. The progressives also received aid from Senator Clapp, who spoke in Columbus the night before his address in Cleveland.[9]

In Cincinnati an organization bearing the same title as that in Columbus was formed to name a slate of candidates and adopt a platform. Representing almost every civic, social, and business organization in the city, it selected a panel of nine, including union-labor, business, and professional men and Herbert Bigelow, and pledged them to the initiative and referendum as well as three other reforms. The Personal Liberty League, an organization of wets, also endorsed a ticket of candidates, four of whom had also been sponsored by the United Constitution Committee.[10]

Not in every city, however, was there the same well-developed support and interest in the selection of delegates to the constitutional convention. Candidates in Toledo had to depend mainly on newspaper backing. Walter F. Brown, who had become a sudden convert to progressive principles, including a moderate form of the initiative and referendum, was a favorite of the *Toledo Blade*. In turn, the *Toledo News-Bee* gave strong editorial support to three candidates pledged to the Progressive Constitutional League's initiative and referendum plank. In Dayton, on the other hand, the *Dayton Daily News* failed to endorse anyone, even though in editorials it praised direct legislation, to which the three victorious delegates from Montgomery County were committed. In Youngstown, where the interest was as slight as in Dayton, the *Youngstown Vindicator* tried to drum up some enthusiasm to promote the candidacy of the publisher's son, William F. Maag, Jr., a progressive Democrat.[11]

When the nominations were completed, the *Toledo News-Bee* reported that, of the 419 candidates, 286 were declared progressives, 120 were known conservatives, and 13 had not expressed their opinions. Despite this substantial majority there was still danger in the situation, the editor believed, for the opponents under the leadership of the Ohio State Board of Commerce were centering their efforts on the smallest number of candidates in the hope of electing their men by taking advantage of a possible split in the progressive vote.[12]

Another difficulty which disturbed the constitutional reformers was the competing interest of the electorate in the municipal elections taking place simultaneously. There was the danger that the electorate would become absorbed in city issues and candidates to the exclusion of those of the constitutional convention. Only a few progressives, like Bigelow and Gladden, devoted their whole attention to the latter. Furthermore, the fact that the delegates were to be elected on a nonpartisan ballot meant that party organizations would not be inclined to work for a slate of candidates. The Democrats in Cleveland were the exception, and even they included nominal Republicans on the list for which they campaigned.[13] In most places the nominees had to depend upon the support of nonpartisan groups, such as those in Columbus, Cleveland, and Cincinnati, and friendly newspaper editors.

There was little evidence that the municipal and constitutional campaigns dovetailed in any significant way. In Toledo, fusion of the two movements seemed promising when Brand Whitlock, president of the Progressive Constitutional League, was renominated for mayor by the Independent Voters. However, his party failed to endorse a panel of delegates, and the mayoralty battle was fought entirely on local issues and personalities. Three other candidates opposed Whitlock: Carl H. Keller, Republican, whose record as a state senator in the past session had been conservative; Charles S. Ashley, Democrat; and William F. Ries, Socialist, who drew away from the Independents much of their former strength among the workingmen.[14]

Settlement of the street-railway problem was the principal issue in Toledo. The situation had reached a critical stage on

November 10, 1910, when franchises embracing the heart of the transportation system had expired. Though Whitlock had promptly notified the Toledo Rail and Light Company that they were trespassers in the streets, he had allowed them to continue operations as a matter of public convenience. During the spring of 1911 he held daily conferences with the president of the company in the council chambers after the manner of Tom Johnson. Not only did he borrow the Johnson methods, but the Toledo mayor also received direct support from other members of the Cleveland group. Throughout the prolonged negotiations he leaned heavily upon them, turning to Newton Baker for legal advice, to Carl Nau's firm to examine the company's books, and to Edward Bemis to appraise the street-railway property. Whitlock proposed an immediate settlement on the basis of a three-cent fare and provision for municipal ownership whenever the law permitted. The company balked, and the city prepared a law suit to collect $250 per day rental for the use of the streets. By fall negotiations had reached a stalemate pending the outcome of the election.[15]

The Mayor's opponents seized upon this state of affairs to charge him with lack of backbone in settling the dispute. They raised again the issue of law and order, accusing him of retarding the growth of the city because of his leniency toward the criminal elements. These attacks, however, could not destroy the great popularity Whitlock had won among all classes in the city. It was noteworthy that the *Toledo Blade* had dropped its hostility; the *Toledo News-Bee* was as ardent a supporter of the Mayor as before. Negley Cochran answered Whitlock's critics, pointing to the expansion and material progress of Toledo during his administration, stressing the additional park facilities and the plan for a civic center, and daily reminding his readers that the Mayor's re-election was the only guarantee of a street-railway franchise settlement in the people's favor.[16]

The Cleveland mayoralty campaign was of a similar nature, dominated altogether by local issues. In the Democratic primaries Newton Baker handily defeated Charles P. Salen, a very stimulating victory to the Johnson coterie, since it would, as the nominee wrote to Whitlock, "increase the respect felt by the down-state politicians for our kind of democracy, and particularly for the strength and solidity of our movement here." The

Republican incumbent, Herman Baehr, who had proved to be neither a progressive nor an able administrator, declined to run, and that party's nomination was given to the director of public safety, Frank C. Hogen. A third candidate was the Socialist, Charles E. Ruthenberg.

Baker was attacked as a dreamer, absorbed only in fads and fancies, although the *Cleveland Plain Dealer* and the *Cleveland Press* hardly thought that his program—to strengthen the Tayler franchise, continue the work at Cooley Farms, expand the park system, extend home rule, and provide cheap electricity —was visionary. Eschewing personalities, Baker made the chief issue of the campaign the approval of the proposed $2-million bond issue to expand the municipal electric plant and thereby to cut the electric-light rate to three cents. His meetings were strongly reminiscent of those of the Johnson days, not only in their physical trappings of the big tent, but also in their educational, uplifting character as forums on public affairs.

His most moving effort was a debate with Samuel Scovil, president of the Cleveland Electric Illuminating Company, in the auditorium of the Cleveland Chamber of Commerce. Gathered before the two debaters were the leading businessmen of the city. Without mincing words Baker told them that the public-service corporations of the country had "consistently corrupted and depraved the government" for the last fifty years, that public regulation had proved inadequate, and that, therefore, municipal ownership was inevitable for the purification of municipal politics. Furthermore, he continued, competition was the way to reduce rates, as had been proven in the street-railway battle. He concluded with a characteristic dramatic touch, "I am in the house of have. I appeal on behalf of the house of want—for justice."[17]

The most strenuous mayoralty campaign took place in Cincinnati, where another revolt against the Cox machine was brewing. The Democratic nominee was Henry T. Hunt, who, in the tradition of Joseph W. Folk of Missouri and William Travers Jerome of New York, had made his reputation as an aggressive prosecuting attorney. Hunt came from a respected, well-to-do Cincinnati family, conservative politically except for an eccentric uncle who was a Henry George disciple. His father, as a trustee of the Cincinnati Southern Railroad, had helped to prevent the theft of this municipally owned line by a New York syndicate aided by the Cox gang. Young Harry went to Yale, returned to Cincinnati after graduating to study law, and was admitted to the bar in 1903. He served as a member of the Honest Election Committee in the Dempsey campaign of 1905 and was elected in the same year to the legislature, where his record tended to be conservative.[18]

In 1908, after the second legislative probe of Cincinnati had been held illegal, he was persuaded by his friend, Graham P. Hunt, to run for prosecuting attorney in order to carry on the investigation through the only channel which the courts had left open, namely, inquest by grand jury. Henry Hunt was nominated and elected at the same time as a Democratic judge, Frank M. Gorman. George Cox, who had treated their nominations as a joke, was greatly disturbed by their election and sought to protect himself against these intruders. The calendar of the Hamilton County Court of Common Pleas was so arranged that Gorman would not serve on the criminal bench for two years. Hunt was hampered at every turn. He was shadowed by detectives; corrupt and docile clerks turned over his correspondence and data to the Cox gang; and attorneys were hired to harass him. Nevertheless, he showed he had the nerve and tenacity for the job, shutting down gambling rooms and driving out the slot machines and bucket shops from the county.[19]

Re-elected in 1910 by double the plurality of the previous election, he took office on the day Gorman occupied the chair of the presiding judge of the criminal branch of the Hamilton County Common Pleas Court, the very contingency Cox had feared. Under a little-used law Judge Gorman issued a special venire for a grand-jury panel, selecting prominent businessmen, many of whom were members of the City Club, the principal good-government organization of Cincinnati.

This jury indicted Joseph Baschang, henchman of Cox and deputy collector of liquor licenses, for taking bribes from disorderly houses and saloons to keep them off the tax list; the director of public service and the chief engineer of the city for accepting inferior cement on a contract paving job; and, finally, George B. Cox himself for perjury on the charge that he had lied when he told the grand jury in 1906 that he had never received any portion of the moneys paid by the banks to the county treasurer as interest on the deposit of public funds.

Hurt and angered, Cox fought back, obtaining a writ to enjoin Gorman from trying the case because of bias and prejudice. Hunt countered with a motion to change the venue to Clermont County, alleging the impossibility of conducting a fair and impartial trial of Cox in his home county. Although Gorman granted the prosecuting attorney's request, the decision was overruled on technicalities. The case remained in Hamilton County and a Republican judge friendly to Cox quashed the indictment. Such a smokescreen had been raised by the legal maneuvers of both sides that the public tended to lose sight of the real issues, namely, Cox's peculation of public funds, his perjured testimony, and his control of the courts.[20]

Even though Cox avoided trial, he felt obliged, on the very day he was legally absolved, to announce his political retirement for the good of the party. His opponents, however, remained properly skeptical of the genuineness of his decision, for not only had he twice before announced his withdrawal and then returned, but just seventeen days before his announcement he had stated in an interview that his boss-ship, though none of his making, was so much a part of him that he could not voluntarily renounce it. "In fact," he added, "the question of retiring has never entered my mind." Nevertheless, this time such factors as ill health, the pleading of his wife, and the demands of his extensive business affairs did make his choice a final one. But the machine he had built was held together by his lieutenant, Rudolph Hynicka.[21]

Because of this background, the Cincinnati mayoralty campaign of 1911 was one of unprecedented bitterness. The Cox Republicans were grimly determined to defeat Hunt, who had dared to traduce the boss. The Democratic nominee, who had a quiet manner and a boyish smile, scarcely appeared a match for his seasoned opponents; only an obstinate jaw revealed his fighting character. He proved a forceful campaigner, fearless in invading the gang's bailiwicks. Coxism he made the main issue. The Republican candidate, Louis Schwab, who was seeking re-election, was ignored as a mere frontispiece. Although the *Cincinnati Enquirer* endorsed Hunt and the Democratic ticket in one of its periodic fits of virtue, his major support came from the *Cincinnati Post,* which exposed the machinations and mal-administration of the Cox machine in a series of articles and editorials. They disclosed the purchasing methods of the public-service department, by which the administration kept within the letter of the law yet violated its spirit; they published a study of the way in which three slum wards had been converted by illicit means from a Democratic to a Republican majority; they ripped apart the fiscal schemes of Cox's government to show that the tax rate was kept low by deferring part of the cost of administration through deficit financing.

Such disclosures, together with the apparent failure of their own party to clean house, persuaded a number of Republicans to switch to the Democratic side. A naïve and ineffectual attempt had been made by Julius Fleischman to inaugurate a new order by trying to induce a prominent attorney or merchant to run for mayor, but Fleischman was prepared to let Cox's lieutenants continue in power as long as Cox himself remained in retirement. The assurance from Fleischmann that he and his fellow workers were "honest in their effort to get out of the old rut" was enough to convince Cincinnati's most prominent Republican that conditions had changed since his Akron speech. On the Saturday night before election, President William Howard Taft arrived in his native city and announced that he would vote the straight Republican ticket. It seemed apparent to many that Coxism was still in the saddle and that, in accepting the wish for the deed, Taft was swayed by the political expediency of holding the support of the party regulars for his candidacy in the presidential campaign only a few months away. Perhaps for that reason the President's announcement had little effect in halting the swing of independent Republican voters to Hunt.[22]

Although Republican conservatives had captured the mayoralty nominations in Toledo, Cleveland, and Cincinnati, there was an exception to this pattern in Columbus, where the progressive Republican incumbent, George S. Marshall, was renominated. Running on a platform of park expansion, municipal ownership of all utilities, and more direct democracy, he had the support of such leading reformers as Washington Gladden and Judge David Pugh. Unfortunately he had made many enemies as a result of a violent street-railway strike during the spring and summer of 1910. Many blamed him for failing to prevent

305

violence; labor groups were hostile because he had called in the National Guard to restore order, even though he had done his best to respect their rights. The striking car men had been left in a sulky mood because they had not gained one concession when their resistance was broken. Furthermore, Marshall had alienated some of the German groups by his strict enforcement of the Sunday-closing laws for saloons. The Democratic candidate was the affable, dapper George J. Karb, a conservative on economic issues but a "liberal" on the liquor question. A third contender was the Socialist Alvah Eby, who won a large following among the workingmen, principally as a result of the strike.[23]

Throughout the cities of Ohio the Socialists made an active and effective campaign, especially wherever the two major parties presented colorless candidates and indulged in shadowboxing without striking at the main issues of the day. Such speakers as Eugene V. Debs, William Haywood, Ben Wilson, Charles Russell, and Mother Ella Bloor invaded the state to preach the cause.[24] Had their announced program not already been adopted by the progressives of both parties, their campaign might have been more successful than it was in capturing the protest vote.

The election results generally throughout the state were a victory for progress, in the selection of both municipal officers and delegates to the constitutional convention. Toledo returned Whitlock to the mayor's chair for a fourth time, evidence, said the *Toledo Blade,* of the people's warm admiration and faith in his integrity and good purpose. The Independents there also won the other municipal offices and half the council. Baker and the Democratic ticket swept into power in Cleveland with impressive pluralities. "The vote," said the mayor-elect, "is a tribute to the late Tom Johnson and a vindication of the principles for which he labored." In Cincinnati, Hunt, the third of the "Holy Trinity," as these three mayors came to be known, was elected by a comfortable margin and carried the rest of the Democratic slate. His election, declared the *Cleveland Plain Dealer,* "will be heralded far and wide as a long delayed triumph for decency in a community considered all but impotent to reform."

To be sure, the verdict for progress was not unanimous. The reform candidate, George Marshall, was defeated in Columbus by "Gentleman George" Karb, and Dayton and Youngstown gave pluralities to Republican mayors of a conservative hue.

Nevertheless the progressive tenor of the times was further revealed by the sizeable Socialist vote. That party elected mayors in twelve cities, and four councilmen in Columbus, two in Dayton, and one in Toledo. Although some of the Socialist strength came from genuine believers, most of it was a protest by non-Socialists against the complacent candidates and the factional bickerings of the two major parties.[25]

An even more convincing measure of the progressive swing in Ohio was the vote for delegates to the constitutional convention. The newspapers, by dramatizing the epochal nature of the occasion, had generated a strong interest in the constitution among the electorate. Three counties polled a bigger vote for convention delegates than they did the year before for governor, and the count was almost as large in several others, though in the state as a whole it was smaller. The ten Cuyahoga delegates, the three each from Franklin, Lucas, and Montgomery, and all but one of the nine from Hamilton were progressive. It was estimated that only 25 per cent of the 119 members elected were conservatives, nearly all from the rural districts.[26]

Although this triumph of progressivism was the work of many men, no single person deserved more credit for its achievement than Herbert Bigelow. A voice crying in the wilderness for many years, he at last had won broad public support for the reform he had so long championed. Not only was he one of the delegates himself, but sixty others of those chosen were pledged to his kind of an initiative and referendum amendment. In addition, twenty-six more had spoken in favor of the principle of this reform. Since the attitude toward direct legislation was the popular norm for judging the political temper of a state, Ohio, it was declared, had gone radical. Progressives expected great accomplishments from the convention which was about to take place; conservatives feared the worst.[27]

1. A call in 1871 had been approved, one in 1891 voted down.

2. Cox, *Journey through My Years*, 121–22; Edmund B. King to James K. Mercer, November 1, 1913, in Mercer, ed., *Ohio Legislative History* [I], 412; Henry W. Elson, "Making a New Constitution for Ohio," *Review of Reviews*, XLVI (July, 1912), 86; Ernest I. Antrim, "The Ohio Constitutional Convention," *Independent*, LXXII (June 27, 1912), 1423.

3. Bigelow's earlier work for the adoption of the initiative and referendum is told above, Chap. VIII, pp. 195–96. His educational work for the cause in

Cincinnati and his switchback to political action is recounted in Stockbridge, "Ohio Wide Awake," 706–7. The Fels Fund spent more than $3,000 in Ohio in 1909 to promote the initiative and referendum. The Fund also supported similar campaigns in New Mexico, Arizona, Colorado, Arkansas, and Minnesota. Some of the orthodox single taxers criticized the diversion of the Fund for this purpose, but the Ohio disciples of Henry George were strongly committed to this approach. (Arthur Nichols Young, *The Single Tax Movement in the United States* [Princeton, N. J., 1916], 163–66, 10, p. 166).

4. The first act providing for the call did not include the endorsement by political parties; this was added by separate legislation at the next session. The texts of the acts are in 100 O.L. 18 (1909) and 101 O.L. 169 (1910). The official returns are listed in *Ohio Election Statistics* (1910), 32–33. An example of conservative reaction is found in Daniel J. Ryan, "The Influence of Socialism on the Ohio Constitution," *North American Review,* CXCVI (November, 1912), 665–66. Of those who went to the polls, 23 per cent failed to vote on the issue. The significance of the vote is discussed in Robert E. Cushman, "Voting Organic Laws: Action of the Ohio Electorate in the Revision of the State Constitution in 1912," *Political Science Quarterly,* XXVIII (June, 1913), 208–9.

5. The vice-presidents were, respectively, Joseph V. Denney, John Frey, and L. G. Spencer; the treasurer, O. J. Demuth. Bigelow had been first elected vice-president, but when Charles B. Galbreath, the former state librarian, resigned as secretary, the Cincinnati minister took that post. (Herbert S. Bigelow to Brand Whitlock, June 7, 1911, Whitlock Papers; *The Public,* XIV [June 9, 1911], 537). The League's proposals on the percentages of signatures were: 12 per cent or less for the submission of constitutional amendments, 10 per cent on initiated legislation, and 8 per cent on referendums (Herbert S. Bigelow to Brand Whitlock, August 12, 1911, Whitlock Papers).

6. The work of Bigelow and the League is described in Stockbridge, "Ohio Wide Awake," 707, and in the *Ohio State Journal* (Columbus), November 15, 1911. The commentary of the *Cincinnati Post* is in the issue for October 26, 1911. During October the *Post* published statements endorsing the initiative and referendum by James Bryce, Woodrow Wilson, Theodore Roosevelt, Robert La Follette, and Atlee Pomerene. See the issues for October 18, 20–21, 24–25, 1911.

7. The opposition is rescribed in Stockbridge, "Ohio Wide Awake," 707. The quoted characterization of Foote appeared in "Ohio Constitutional Convention," *The Public,* XIV (July 7, 1911), 632. A penetrating analysis of Foote's conservatism and methods of pontificating in his writings is in Robert H. Bremner, "The Fight for Home Rule," *American Journal of Economics and Sociology,* XI (October, 1951), 107–9. The courting of the liquor interests was described in the *Ohio State Journal,* August 6, 1911, in the author's interview with Herbert S. Bigelow, September 26, 1949.

8. *Cleveland Plain Dealer,* October 21, November 4, 1911; *The Municipal Bulletin* (Municipal Association of Cleveland), XV (November, 1911), 1–6. There were many duplications of names on the four lists. For example, the Progressive Constitutional League and the Democrats both nominated Robert Crosser, Edward Doty, John Fackler, Daniel E. Leslie, Aaron Hahn, and Thomas Fitzsimmons; Democrats and Socialists, Harry Thomas; Municipal Conference and Democrats, Frank Cullitan and Augustus R. Hatton. John Fackler was also a nominee of the Municipal Conference. Baker thought the

multiple slates left the situation in a muddle (N. D. Baker to F. C. Howe, August 28, 1911, Baker Papers, CCH).

9. *Ohio State Journal,* July 26, September 2, 9, October 15, November 3, 1911. The candidates were James W. Harbarger, representative of labor; Edward A. Peters, representative of the farmers; and Professor George W. Knight, selected by the business and professional groups. Three planks proposed for inclusion in the platform were voted down; they were home rule in taxation, the recall, and equal suffrage.

10. *Cincinnati Enquirer,* November 4–5, 1911; Charles Sawyer, "The Ohio Constitution: A Reply and a Rejoinder," *North American Review,* CXCVII (February, 1913), 276–77. The three other planks were municipal home rule, licensing of saloons, and classification in taxation (Edmund B. King to James K. Mercer, November 5, 1913, in Mercer, ed. *Ohio Legislative History* [I], 421). The four who were jointly endorsed were Herbert Bigelow, George W. Harris, Hiram D. Peck, and William Worthington.

11. The nominations in Toledo were reported in the *Toledo Blade,* October 21, 27, 1911, and the *Toledo News-Bee,* October 30, 1911. The candidates endorsed by the *News-Bee* were John Ullmer, Thomas Rumsey, and James Nye. The *Dayton Daily News* did not run any pre-election editorials or articles on the candidates for the constitutional convention. This seems strange because the three elected were Democrats and considered progressive; furthermore, the *News* actively supported the initiative and referendum—the only paper to do so other than those "catering to class interests" (i.e. the Scripps-McRae papers), according to the *Ohio State Journal,* August 6, 1911. The nominations in Youngstown were reported in the *Youngstown Vindicator,* November 2–4, 1911.

12. *Toledo News-Bee,* October 11, 1911.

13. The Democrats endorsed two Republicans, John Fackler and Daniel E. Leslie, and one Socialist, Harry Thomas.

14. *Toledo News-Bee,* September 6, October 18, 1911; *Toledo Blade,* September 6, 1911. Brand Whitlock to Nicholas Roberts, October 31, 1911; Brand Whitlock to Joseph R. W. Cooper, November 29, 1911, in Nevins, ed., *The Letters and Journal of Brand Whitlock,* I, 144 and 145, respectively.

15. The street-railway situation was reported in detail in the press and mentioned frequently in Whitlock's letters to his friends. As a campaign issue it was reported in the *Toledo News-Bee,* October 27, 1911. Examples in the Whitlock correspondence are: Brand Whitlock to Louis F. Post, November 15, 1910; to Lincoln Steffens, May 12, 1911, Whitlock Papers. His dependence on the Cleveland groups is well documented in the substantial exchange of letters, too numerous to cite, between Whitlock and Carl Nau and Edward W. Bemis during the years 1910 and 1911, in the Whitlock Papers. An able review of the street-railway problem is in Nevins, ed., "Biographical Introduction," *The Letters and Journal of Brand Whitlock,* I, xxxiii–xxxix. At the end of Whitlock's last term the situation was brought to a head by the adoption of a drastic ordinance prepared by Cornell Schreiber requiring the company to accept a three-cent fare and other conditions and to pay the city $250 per day for the use of the streets. The city's case had been strengthened by a court decision upholding the rent charge. This brought the company to terms and it agreed to a compromise which provided for a three-cent fare during the rush hours and a five-cent fare (six tickets for a quarter) at all other times. The city was also given the right to examine the company's books. This settlement remained in effect until

1916. (Brand Whitlock to Edward W. Bemis, February 13, 1912, in *ibid.*, I, 150–51; Killits, ed., *Toledo and Lucas County*, I, 582–84.)

16. The criticisms of Whitlock were reported in the *Toledo Blade*, October 20, 25, November 1, 1911, the defense in the *Toledo News-Bee*, October 26, 27, November 1, 1911.

17. The nominations were reported in the *Cleveland Plain Dealer*, September 6, 1911. The Baker quotation is taken from N. D. Baker to Brand Whitlock, September 7, 1911, Whitlock Papers. The weaknesses of the Baehr administration are discussed in the *Cleveland Press*, October 17, 1911, and in *The Municipal Bulletin* (Municipal Association of Cleveland), XV (February, 1911), 4–7. The campaign is reported in the *Cleveland Plain Dealer*, October 28, 30, 1911, and the *Cleveland Press*, October 11, 1911; Baker's debate with Scovil in the *Cleveland Plain Dealer*, November 1, 1911.

18. This biographical account of Hunt is drawn from Brand Whitlock, "Henry T. Hunt," *American Magazine*, LXXIV (July, 1912), 297, from Powell, ed., *The Democratic Party of the State of Ohio*, II, 207–8, and from the author's interview with Graham P. Hunt, September 28, 1949.

19. Koch, "An Ohio Warwick," 33; Stockbridge, "The Biggest Boss of Them All," 627; Whitlock, "Hunt," 297.

20. Hunt's re-election, the convening of the grand jury by Judge Gorman, and the indictments are related in Stockridge, "The Biggest Boss of Them All," 627–29, and the *Ohio State Journal*, February 22, March 2, 18, 1911. The Cox trial was reported in *ibid.*, March 21, April 4, 19, May 21, 1911, and in *State of Ohio v. George B. Cox*, Record of Case No. 16466, Court of Common Pleas of Hamilton County, Ohio (March 31, 1911). According to his son, Judge Gorman later regretted that he had granted Hunt's motion for a change of venue because in the state of public confusion over the issues it would have been better to concentrate on Cox's control of the courts rather than to maneuver for an impartial trial of the Boss in another county (the author's interview with Robert N. Gorman, October 18, 1959).

21. Cox's retirement was announced in the *Cincinnati Enquirer*, May 21, 1911; the Cox quotation appeared in *ibid.*, November 5, 1911, and was taken from an interview with Cox printed in the *New York World*, May 4, 1911. Rudolph Hynicka continued his control until 1925.

22. The bitterness of the campaign was noted in the *Ohio State Journal*, November 5, 1911, Hunt's role in Turner, "The Thing above the Law," 588, and in Whitlock, "Hunt," 296. The *Cincinnati Enquirer's* endorsement of Hunt is in the issues for November 4–5, 1911, the *Cincinnati Post's* support in issues for October, 1911, *passim*. The efforts of Fleischmann to inaugurate a new order are described in Julius Fleischmann to Charles D. Hilles, July 25, 29, 1911, and Gus J. Karger, Memorandum for President Taft, June 7, 1911, Hilles Papers, and in the *Cincinnati Post*, November 1, 1911, and *Cincinnati Enquirer*, November 5, 1911. Taft's return to vote for the Republican ticket is reported in *ibid.*, November 4, 1911, the reaction of independent Republicans in L. C. Black and Others to W. H. Taft, telegram, November 4, 1911, Hilles Papers.

23. *Ohio State Journal*, September 6, November 4–5, 1911. The strike against the street-railway company began April 30, 1910, in a dispute over union recognition and wages. The situation was complicated by the feud between the Mayor and the company as a result of the previous campaign. Marshall forced a settlement of the strike on May 4, when he agreed to find city jobs for four union men the company refused to rehire. The strike

broke out once again after both sides rejected the verdict of the State Board of Arbitration. So serious was the violence this time that the Mayor had to call upon the National Guard to restore order. But the troops were disbanded prematurely, and when violence was resumed, Governor Harmon ordered the troops to duty again. Finally, on October 18, 1910, the unionists voted, ninety to thirty-two to end the strike, even though none of their demands had been granted. (*Ibid.*, May 1–5, July 24, August 5, 12–16, 31, September 3–4, October 19, 1910; *Cleveland Plain Dealer*, May 4–5, September 13, 1910)

24. *Ohio State Journal*, October 2, 1911.

25. The election results in Toledo were reported in the *Toledo Blade* and *Toledo News-Bee*, November 8, 1911, those in Cleveland in the *Cleveland Leader* and *Cleveland Plain Dealer*, November 8, 1911. Baker's comment was quoted in *ibid.*, November 8, 1911. The $2,000,000 bond issue for the municipal electric-light plant in Cleveland also carried. The results in Cincinnati were reported in the *Cincinnati Enquirer*, November 8, 1911, and the *Cleveland Plain Dealer*, November 9, 1911. A venerable lady in Pittsburgh told Baker that the three were known as "The Holy Trinity" (N. D. Baker to Brand Whitlock, January 21, 1913, Whitlock Papers). The election results in the other cities were reported in the *Ohio State Journal*, *Dayton Daily News*, and *Youngstown Vindicator*, November 8, 1911. The Socialists elected mayors in Canton, Lima, Lorain, Barberton, Mt. Vernon, Martins Ferry, Conneaut, Fostoria, Salem, and Dillonvale, as well as four smaller towns. The Socialist vote was discussed in the *Dayton Daily News*, *Cleveland Plain Dealer*, November 8, 1911, and in A. L. Garford to Charles Frank, May 7, 1912, Garford Papers.

26. The vote for delegates to the constitutional convention was reported in the *Cleveland Plain Dealer*, November 9, 1911, the *Ohio State Journal*, November 9, 1911, the *Toledo News-Bee*, November 8–9, 1911, the *Dayton Daily News*, November 8, 1911, the *Cincinnati Enquirer*, November 9, and the *Youngstown Vindicator*, November 8, 1911. The size of the vote is examined in Cushman, "Voting Organic Laws," 209–10. There were some unforeseen results in the election. In Mahoning County, where the vote was unusually light, William F. Maag, Jr., lost to David F. Anderson, a Republican dry, who did favor, however, the initiative and referendum. The most suprising upset was the defeat of James R. Garfield by a progressive Democrat in rural Lake County.

27. The recognition of Bigelow's work was noted in the *Toledo News-Bee*, November 9, 1911; the number of those in favor of the initiative and referendum was reported in *ibid.*, Noverber 9, 1911; the characterization of the temper of the state as radical was made in an editorial in the *Cleveland Plain Dealer*, November 10, 1911.

CHAPTER TWELVE

WRITING A
TWENTIETH-CENTURY CHARTER
1912

ON THE MORNING of January 9, 1912, the fourth Ohio Constitutional Convention assembled in the Hall of Representatives at the Capitol, dedicated to the task of framing a new charter which would reflect "the improved and progressive conditions" of a twentieth-century world. The honor of serving as temporary chairman was bestowed upon the oldest member, eighty-two-year-old Judge Dennis Dwyer of Dayton; other temporary offices were filled; the roll was called, all but 4 of the 119 members answering; and the delegates were sworn in by the chief justice. In the opinion of a veteran newspaper correspondent, it was "the most inspiring body" that he had observed in his forty years' experience with Ohio legislative assemblies.[1]

Included among the delegates were many able and experienced men representing most of the major occupations. Lawyers predominated with forty-six members, several of whom were outstanding in the convention. In addition to Dwyer there were two Cincinnati judges, Hiram D. Peck and William Worthington; two Cleveland attorneys, John D. Fackler and Robert Crosser; Stanley Bowdle of Cincinnati, leader of the "wets"; and David F. Anderson of Youngstown, leader of the "drys" and a labor champion. Farmers were the next largest occupational group, with twenty-five. Bankers and businessmen numbered fourteen. Ten delegates were drawn from the ranks of labor, four of whom played a prominent part throughout the proceedings: Harry Thomas and Stephen S. Stilwell of Cleveland,

Percy Tetlow of Columbiana County, and William P. Halen-kamp of Cincinnati, aged twenty-seven, the youngest member of the convention. Six educators, two newspaper editors, four ministers, and four physicians represented the professions other than the law. Particularly influential in this group were Presidents Simeon D. Fess of Antioch College and George H. Colton of Hiram; Professors George W. Knight of Ohio State University and Henry W. Elson of Ohio University; J. W. Tannehill and A. Ross Read, editors; and Herbert Bigelow. The nine remaining members represented miscellaneous occupations.[2]

By national affiliation, the Democrats predominated with sixty-five, followed by forty-eight Republicans, three Independents, and three Socialists, but party alignments were obliterated on roll calls. The real division was between conservatives and progressives, between "those who," in the words of Thomas Babbington Macauley, "cling to the past, distrusting change; and those who instinctively challenge precedent." Progressives were in the ascendency. "An enthusiastic reformer with a brand new banner of many colors always got a hearing," wrote a conservative, in retrospect, "and a loyal veteran with the 'old flag' did well to keep it still afloat." Another delegate described the convention as "a body of progressives possessing some conservative tendencies."[3] Among "the enthusiastic reformers" who played a role far out of proportion to their numbers were seven single taxers: Bigelow, Halenkamp, Read, Crosser, Fackler, Stilwell, and Edward W. Doty of Cleveland.

Although the numerical superiority of the progressives left little doubt of the outcome, the conservatives put up a stiff fight in the contest for the presidency of the convention. The most publicized candidate for the post was the Cincinnati radical single taxer, Herbert Bigelow. Endorsed first by the *Dayton Daily News* the day after the November elections, he received almost simultaneously the backing of the Scripps-McRae papers, who not only gave him their editorial blessing but directed their Columbus correspondents to form an active lobby for his election at the convention. More important, he won the support of the state Democratic organization and had a solid core of nineteen votes from the combined Hamilton and Cuyahoga County delegations.[4]

Alarmed by the strength rallying behind the radical preacher, opponents began preparing a countermove, initiated by, though not confined to, Republicans. Frank Woods, delegate from Medina, wrote a friend, "I think I am Progressive enough, but Bigelow is nothing but a Socialist if not an Anarchist. I can't stand that much." Undercover work was pursued by Walter F. Brown, elected from Toledo, whose long experience in political conventions made him an expert wirepuller. His candidate was the conservative Judge Caleb H. Norris of Marion. Two other strong contenders were D. F. Anderson, backed by the Anti-Saloon League, and Henry W. Elson, who appealed to the moderates.[5]

The contest for the presidency was one of the sharpest fights of the convention. Several days before the doors were opened, headquarters were established in Columbus for the several contestants; managers buttonholed uncommitted delegates; the buzz of political activity in the hotel corridors was much the same as that preceding organization of the General Assembly. It boded ill for the serious work which lay ahead. Fortunately the issue was disposed of on the first day. The four candidates were placed in nomination, and Bigelow led on the first vote with fifty-four, six short of a majority. As the balloting proceeded, Norris and Elson began to lose strength to Anderson. The wets, alarmed by this concentration on the Anti-Saloon candidate, persuaded enough men to shift to Bigelow to enable him to win on the eleventh ballot with sixty-two votes, a decision that was then made unanimous. He triumphed because of the stamina of his followers, who loyally clung to him throughout the balloting.[6]

The press reaction to Bigelow's election ran the gamut of criticism and praise. "The most self-advertised-man-without-a-collar," sneered the *Toledo Blade,* was "wearing the collar of the brewers superimposed by the collar of Oil Inspector Finley." The *Dayton Daily News,* on the other hand, basked in the success of the candidate whom it had been first to support, and the *Toledo News-Bee* vented its enthusiasm, claiming that Bigelow's election was a sign to the nation "that Ohio has swung her mighty forces into line for better government and better conditions for all the people."[7]

To Frank Parker Stockbridge, writing for *Everybody's Magazine,* it seemed fair to say that Tom Johnson had won, "for Johnson was the first great leader in Ohio to trace the political wrongs back to the constitution itself." Stockbridge recounted an incident which had occurred one August morning in 1902 when August Lewis and Bigelow stood on the veranda of Johnson's house in Cleveland. Throwing his arm affectionately around the shoulder of the young preacher, the Mayor said, "Lewis, some day Bigelow and I are going to rewrite the constitution of the state of Ohio."[8] Though Johnson did not live to see his prophecy fulfilled, his protégé's election as president of the convention and the progressive victory were in large measure the direct heritage of his pioneer work for reform.

In the selection of other officers there was a contest for each post, though with no such intensity of feeling. The victor among the three candidates for secretary was Charles B. Galbreath, a Republican and former state librarian. Not until a week later did the convention decide to select a vice-president to serve in the absence of the chief officer. The three nominees were: D. F. Anderson; Edward W. Doty, a Republican single taxer and clerk of the Ohio Senate for many years and an intimate of both Mark Hanna and Tom Johnson; and Simeon D. Fess, a moderate reformer and compromiser. Although Fess won, Doty scarcely suffered in defeat. Direct and quick, trustworthy and fair, the Cleveland delegate was recognized as the expert parliamentarian of the convention, who exercised a control over debate second only to that of the president. Moreover, as Bigelow's confidant and right bower, Doty was very able in interpreting the chair to the other delegates, smoothing over ill-advised decisions which the preacher's inexperience led him to pronounce.[9]

The tense atmosphere which had marked the first day of the convention continued into the next in a dispute over the method of appointing committees. The progressives proposed that they be selected by Bigelow; the conservatives countered with a recommendation that they be chosen by a committee-on-committees composed of one delegate from each congressional district. In the topsy-turvy debate that followed, each side seemed to be stealing the other's argument, for the conservatives urged their proposal because it was *democratic* and the progressives theirs because it was *efficient*. Bigelow, after he had been accused of Cannonism and suspicion had been cast on his fairness, left the chair to answer his critics. He charged that their proposal would lead to blind geographical determination and would increase partisan rancor. He appealed to them to trust him and grant him the power to appoint the committees, so that they might not lose the golden moment to bring "order out of chaos and friendship and unity out of strife." The conciliatory Fess rose to support Bigelow, asking the convention to take the president at his word; if he failed them, they could take up the cudgels later. With that the opposition gave way.[10]

The convention adjourned for a week to give Bigelow and the rules committee time to complete the organization. There was some initial resentment at the number and scope of the standing committees proposed, since they reflected a narrow interest in specific amendments rather than in a general overhaul of the fundamental law. Nevertheless, an anticipated third fight on the floor over these differences was circumvented by hearings before the committee. The persuasive arguments of Fess, Knight, and Henry Eby of Preble County were successful in enlarging the titles and implied scopes of several committees and in increasing the number, by four, to a total of nineteen. Each was composed of seventeen to twenty-two members, each individual delegate serving on three. Though one member criticized their size as too unwieldy and the assignments to three of the committees as too arduous, the convention was moderate in both respects by comparison with any legislative body of the day. Not all the committees were of equal importance. Those with the greatest volume of work were the committees on education, equal suffrage and elective franchise, good roads, initiative and referendum, judiciary and bill of rights, labor, legislative and executive departments, liquor traffic, municipal government, and taxation.[11]

When the committee assignments were announced, there was general agreement that Bigelow had exonerated himself in dealing fairly with all the major interests. On the liquor traffic committee he placed eight wets, eight drys, and five not committed, an excellent discharge of a delicate duty; on the initiative and referendum committee he put some of its most militant opponents as well as its friends; on the municipal government committee he seated representatives of every large city; and he assigned all of the educators to the education committee and eight of the ten workingmen to the labor committee. The opposition was further mollified by the selection as committee chairmen of two conservatives—Elbert L. Lampson, good roads, and W. S. Harris of Ashtabula, legislative and executive departments —and of the moderate Fess, education. Friendly progressives, to be sure, received most of the important chairmanships; Robert Crosser, the initiative and referendum committee; Hiram D. Peck, the judiciary; William B. Kilpatrick, equal suffrage and elective franchise; Stephen S. Stilwell, labor; John D. Fackler, short ballot; George W. Harris of Cincinnati, municipal government; Edward W. Doty, taxation.[12]

Fears and suspicions of steam-roller tactics by the progressive majority were also quieted by the rules adopted. Committees were directed to announce schedules of weekly meetings, at which times they were to consider any proposition brought forward by a citizen of the state, thus guaranteeing everyone his day in court. Another rule destroyed the threat of committee despotism by authorizing originators of proposals to remove them from committees and place them on the calendar if two weeks had elapsed without action. Two provisions concerning debate and procedure on the floor were designed to protect minorities. One lightened the gag or previous-question rule by requiring ten instead of five delegates to initiate action and two-thirds of a quorum in place of a majority to stop debate. The other provided two opportunities for argument, after the second reading and again after the third. Finally, an anti-lobby rule, though not as severe as anticipated, eliminated the worst evils of minority pressure tactics. Lobbyists were denied the floor and smoking rooms and were required to register and name the group or organization they represented, and, upon demand of the chairman or any three members of a committee, to state the amount and source of any compensation received.[13]

For several weeks the important question of the manner in which the work of the convention should be submitted to the people hung in the balance. Not until March 11 was the point debated and a decision reached. Bigelow, as well as a number of other progressives, thought all along in terms of presenting separate amendments, but a substantial group clung to the idea of a general revision to be submitted as a whole. The memory of the defeat of the work of the Ohio Constitutional Convention of 1873–74, when the document was presented as a unit, and the prevailing popular sentiment in 1912 that the constitution of 1851 needed only tinkering, not radical revision, weighed in favor of the separate-amendment method. Moreover, only four days previously the convention had decided to present the woman-suffrage amendment separately. In the debate, the conservative Raymond G. McClelland of Knox County and the moderate Fess spoke on the same side as Bigelow. When the division was called, the resolution to submit the amendments individually carried sixty-eight to thirty-five.[14]

During the first two months the convention considered only four proposals; the bulk of each day was devoted to committee hearings, and many hours were spent listening to speeches by visiting dignitaries. Since it was a presidential election year, partisans insisted on inviting their favorite candidates to make addresses. Except for the omission of Champ Clark and Robert M. La Follette, the roster of those invited included the leading contestants of the two major parties: President William H. Taft, Theodore Roosevelt, Hiram Johnson, Governor Harmon, Woodrow Wilson, and William J. Bryan. In addition, Ben Lindsey, Joseph B. Foraker, the two Ohio senators, Theodore Burton and Atlee Pomerene, and Mayors Henry Hunt, Newton Baker, and Brand Whitlock received invitations. So long was the list that Judge Peck proposed that the official title of the convention be changed to the "oratorical assembly".[15]

Although Wilson failed to appear and Taft said little, the other presidential nominees used the occasion to make stump speeches. Bryan, in an effort to restore himself with the radical wing of his party, espoused every progressive principle, including the controversial recall of judges. In an address also intended for a national audience, Governor Hiram Johnson reviewed his administration in California and reiterated his faith in the major tenets of ultraprogressive doctrine. But the two speeches that were most momentous in their consequences were those by Harmon and Roosevelt. The Ohio governor, by voicing his conscientious scruples against the initiative and referendum, sacrificed his chances for progressive support in the Democratic presidential race. The former President, in proposing popular review of judicial decisions, strengthened the resolve of conservative Republicans to defeat his renomination, whatever the cost.[16]

Such speeches as these threw the spotlight on the convention, but they were not the only reason for the strong public interest in the proceedings. Both the county weeklies and metropolitan dailies of Ohio extensively reported the debates. Some towns held meetings each Saturday night, when people gathered to discuss the issues argued before the convention during the preceding week. Whatever else it accomplished, the constitutional assembly was of great educational value. Not only in the newspapers at home but also in the national weeklies and scholarly journals, the work of the convention was reported with absorbing interest. Special articles were penned by four delegates. Practical legislators and reformers were eager to observe how Ohio dealt with the leading progressive issues of the day.[17]

The convention, in due course, wrestled with all these issues. Yet before it could concentrate upon them, it had to deal with the "irrepressible conflict" over the liquor question. This discussion occupied two weeks—more of the members' time than any other amendment except the initiative and referendum. Fortunately it was disposed of early in the session. The central problem was whether or not to change the existing constitutional prohibition against the licensing of saloons.[18]

In 1912 the wets were determined to repeal this prohibition in the hope that, if constitutional authority was obtained for licensing saloons, the question of state-wide prohibition would be removed from the hands of the legislature. In the end these partisans won the right to submit the license question, but the drys hedged the amendment with so many restrictions that the wets were unhappy about the results. Under the drys' limitations, breweries were to be prohibited from owning and operating saloons; saloonkeepers had to prove good moral character; licensed establishments were to be limited to one for every five hundred population; and temperance laws were to be safeguarded. The crucial vote after second reading was taken March 5, when the amendment was approved ninety to eighteen.[19] Although the main liquor issue had been laid to rest, its ghost kept rising to plague the friends of woman suffrage and municipal home rule, distracting attention from a discussion of these questions on their own merits.

During the time that the liquor question was preoccupying the interest of the wets and the drys on the convention floor, progressives, inclined to ignore the chief emotional question of the day as a side issue, were busy outside the hall drafting an initiative and referendum amendment. Some enthusiasts for this reform believed the victory at the polls had been so decisive that there would be no fight. Clearly the proposal was no novelty. Adopted first on a state-wide scale in South Dakota in 1898, it became popular after 1902, the year William S. U'Ren succeeded in introducing the experiment in Oregon. Largely through the publicity he gave the movement, it spread until eleven states had the initiative and referendum by 1912. In addition, such speakers as Bryan, Hiram Johnson, and Theodore Roosevelt had advocated the reform directly in their addresses to the convention itself. On the other hand, Theodore Burton had given it only qualified support, and Judson Harmon and J. B. Foraker had opposed it in their speeches.

Even before the latter two spoke against the proposal, it was evident that the hostile delegates had not renounced their determination to fight. Convinced that they lacked the votes to defeat the initiative and referendum outright, opponents sought to surround these processes with "safeguards" to make them as innocuous as possible. This appeal for proper protective devices was also attractive to the moderates. Therefore, the task of the enthusiastic believers in the principle was to frame a measure which met these demands without destroying an effective direct-legislation system.[20]

In the expectation of compromise, the progressives advanced their most radical proposal first: a fixed number of signatures on petitions, with no requirement for geographical distribution over the state, and the direct as well as the indirect initiative. Introduced by Crosser, it was referred to the committee on the initiative and referendum, which he headed. As the murmurings against the Crosser amendment increased, the discussions were removed from the committee to a caucus of sixty delegates friendly to the principle. Although opponents condemned this method as "steam-roller tactics" and unsuccessfully tried to outlaw caucuses by vote of the convention, Bigelow defended the procedure on the ground that a majority had been sent to the convention to pass such an amendment, and that they had the right to iron out differences in detail among themselves before they debated with their opponents.

Weekly caucuses held during February revealed that support

for the initial proposal, even among sympathizers, was divided, with a narrow majority in its favor. The principal points of controversy arose over whether the number of signatures to petitions should be fixed or a percentage, and over whether the initiative should be indirect or direct. At the third caucus, on February 23, harmony was restored by the adoption of a compromise agreement, approved fifty to one. It provided for the percentage system; 4 per cent of the electors could initiate legislation to be referred first to the General Assembly (the indirect initiative); 8 per cent could submit a measure directly to the people (the direct initiative); 12 per cent could propose an amendment to the constitution; and 6 per cent could hold a referendum vote on a law passed by the legislature. Roosevelt's speech advocating the indirect initiative, delivered two days before, was alleged to have swayed the caucus in favor of the compromise plan. The initiative and referendum committee added another change specifying that in each case half of the required percentage of signatures had to be obtained from half of the counties of the state. In this form the amendment was given its second reading on March 12.[21]

The debate occupied most of the remainder of the month. Friends of the reform argued that the people of Ohio had lost faith in representative government because of the corruption and irresponsibility of the legislature and were determined to have a larger direct share in policy-making through the initiative and referendum. Opponents, in addition to making frontal attacks, raised the bogy of the single tax, seeking to discredit the proposal by linking it with this radical doctrine. This was easy to do because of the publicized activities of the Fels Fund in financing campaigns for the initiative as a device to introduce the single tax. One of the conservatives, E. L. Lampson, proposed to prohibit its use to initiate either a law or a constitutional amendment imposing Henry George's reform in Ohio. "I'll stand here," he declared, "and defend the home owners and the farmers . . . of Ohio against this monstrous single tax . . . until my tongue is palsied and clings to the roof of my mouth." The presentation of the Lampson proposal created a near crisis when Bigelow tried to shut off debate by ruling that a motion had carried to recess the convention, despite the clamor to "vote" on the question. As the president left the chair, shouts for "Vice-President Fess" brought that officer to the rostrum. Bigelow's ruling on the recess motion was then overruled, and the hostile amendment was submitted for discussion. Although Bigelow apologized the next day, the episode continued to rankle with his opponents.[22]

As the debate dragged on, it became apparent that general sentiment was not sympathetic to the low percentages proposed or to the direct initiative. On March 26 Bigelow appointed a special committee to redraft the work of the caucus in order to meet many of the objections raised in debate. The following day this revision was presented and ably explained by John R. Cassidy of Bellefontaine.

In his major oratorical effort at the convention Bigelow supported the work of the committee. His speech had the quality of a sermon. Garnishing his argument with vivid, emotional language, parables, and biblical quotations, he insisted that the initiative and referendum was necessary, first, for the sake of the representative, to protect him from temptation, and secondly, for the good of the people and for their education in democracy. "Oh, my friends," he concluded, "we are striking down tyranny. We are forging the greatest tools democracy ever had. We are building grander institutions for freedom and for humanity than the world has ever known. We are engaged not only in an important civic work. Our task is a profoundly religious one."

This burst of oratory held the middle-of-the-road supporters in line for the initiative and referendum, and the convention voted ninety-seven to fifteen to accept the Cassidy amendment. Although Bigelow rejoiced at the culmination of a fifteen-year fight, Crosser was disgruntled by the results, for the radicals had had to give ground on every controversial point: the direct initiative was eliminated for laws and retained only for constitutional amendments; the percentage for indirect-initiative petitions for laws was increased from four to six; and the use of the device was prohibited for proposing laws enacting classification of property or the single tax. Bigelow defended the last proposition to his friends, assuring them that it would not interfere with the adoption of land-tax reform whenever public opinion was ripe, since the prohibition applied only to initiated *laws* and not to initiated *constitutional amendments*. The latter procedure could be used at some later time to remove the reservation against the single tax.[23]

On the third reading, March 28, Crosser reopened the issues of the high percentages and the failure to provide for the direct initiation of laws. To shorten debate the amendment was again referred to a special committee. It recommended that the percentage on petitions to initiate directly a constitutional amendment be cut from twelve to ten, and it proposed a compromise on the procedure to be used in initiating laws. The indirect initiative was to be made only the first, not the final, step in the process of lawmaking by the people, and the percentage of electors required to invoke this procedure was reduced from six to three. Then, if the legislature failed to enact the bill in the form proposed, and the sponsors, thereafter, obtained the signatures of another 3 per cent of the electors, making a total of 6 per cent, the proposed law could be submitted directly to the people. The effect was to reinstate the direct initiative but to restrict its use to the second step after the indirect initiative had been tried and had failed. These changes were accepted and incorporated into the final version, which was approved by the convention, eighty-five to fourteen on May 29.[24]

A complementary measure designed to make less difficult the regular process of amending the constitution was adopted without protest. Introduced by Starbuck Smith of Cincinnati, this reduced the necessary majority in each house from two-thirds to three-fifths for proposing amendments, and required only a majority of the popular vote on the amendment, instead of a majority of those voting at the election for ratification. Other sections of the measure provided that the Assembly by a two-thirds vote might submit to the people at any time the question of holding a constitutional convention, and required such submission every twenty years without a vote of the legislature. In each case a majority voting thereon was sufficient for adoption, and the delegates were to be nominated only by petition and elected on a nonpartisan ballot. The change in the majority requirement reflected a general trend in the country. It struck at the electors who were too indifferent to vote, but who had been able to block desirable reforms under the old system.[25]

Another procedure closely associated with the initiative and referendum and pressed by ultraprogressives was the recall of elective officials. First tried in Los Angeles in 1903, it had been adopted by two states before 1912 and five more approved it that year. Five such proposals were presented to the Ohio convention; four were bottled up in the judiciary committee; the fifth, referred to the committee on the initiative and referendum, was favorably reported on April 15. The report of the committee majority specified that petitions for recall must be signed by 20 per cent of the electors to remove state officers and 25 per cent to remove local officials. The minority of the committee, however, submitted a report condemning the recall as "obnoxious to the spirit of our institutions and . . . a supplemental blow aimed at the integrity of representative government." Its recommendation that consideration of the proposed amendment be postponed indefinitely carried fifty-seven to forty-five. Though support for the recall came from individual conservatives as well as progressives, it was defeated by the opposition of two groups: those sympathetic to the point of view of office-holders who felt that every two years was often enough to face the electorate, and those who violently reacted against the recall of judges as destructive of the sanctity of the law.[26]

In place of the radical recall, the convention did adopt a partial substitute providing for another method of removing officers in addition to the cumbersome one of impeachment. This amendment directed the legislature to enact appropriate laws to remove state and local officers found guilty of misconduct involving moral turpitude or other causes.[27]

A reform considered by progressives only second in importance to the initiative and referendum was the direct-primary system of nominating elective officers. If the one was intended to give the people a more direct share in the legislative process, the other was designed to give them a more immediate control over the selection of officials. So widespread had become the distrust of the familiar delegate-convention system of nominating candidates, that twenty-one states had already adopted this reform. While Ohio had followed the general trend in piecemeal fashion, it still lacked a state-wide direct-primary system.

It was to correct this situation that an amendment to make the procedure mandatory was introduced by a Morgan County editor, J. W. Tannehill. The principal argument against the measure, attacked it as being a legislative and not properly a constitutional matter, was disposed of by Richard A. Beatty, who pointed to the several failures of the General Assembly to enact a direct-primary law affecting its members. Sentiment in favor of the principle was overwhelming; the only difference of opinion was over detail. In the debate on second reading, the original proposal was amended to include provisions for a preferential vote for United States senators and an expression of presidential preferences by delegates to the national conventions. Efforts in the final debate after the third reading to place all primary tickets on one ballot (the open primary) and to introduce the office-type ballot in general elections, however, failed. A comparison of the two decisive votes, taken six weeks apart, indicated that some delegates weakened in their resolve to support the proposal, yet the defections were not enough to seriously threaten its defeat.[28]

A supplementary reform to protect the purity of elections by permitting the use of voting machines was approved. In this case constitutional sanction was necessary for a seemingly legislative matter because of an adverse decision of the Ohio Supreme Court voiding an 1898 statute on the subject.[29]

Another reform of major interest to progressives was that to broaden the suffrage provisions of the state constitution of 1851, which limited the vote to "white male citizens of the United States," twenty-one years of age or older, who had been residents of the state for a year. Since the Fifteenth Amendment to the United States Constitution had annulled this limitation to "white" males, the Ohio convention approved a proposal to eliminate the obsolete adjective entirely.[30]

While this passed without debate and with near unanimity, an amendment to extend the suffrage to women met stiff opposition. This was not surprising in view of the resistance to this reform found everywhere except in the states of the Pacific slope and Far West. In Ohio, as in many other states, women had been granted partial suffrage in the privilege of voting in school elections. But further extension required a constitutional amendment. For many years the Ohio Woman Suffrage Association had been agitating for full voting equality, receiving encouragement from such male partisans as Tom Johnson, Frederic Howe, Brand Whitlock, and Newton Baker. The association had also won endorsements for woman suffrage from the Ohio State Grange and the Ohio Federation of Labor.[31] Nevertheless, they had made scant headway with the legislature in getting the necessary amendment initiated.

In the convention the issue was assured its full measure of attention by the deliberate creation of a separate equal-suffrage committee and the appointment of an enthusiastic advocate as chairman, William B. Kilpatrick, as well as a majority favorable to the amendment. In the debate on the floor the chief defenders were progressives, the principal opponents conservatives, though the pattern was not a rigid one. For some delegates the liquor issue, with which woman suffrage seemed inextricably intertwined, outweighed any other considerations. Stanley Bowdle, chieftain of the wets and a progressive on other points, led the opposition. A diatribe, occupying five pages of the record and inveighing against the proposal as counter to biblical injunctions and the will of God, was delivered by a "dry" farmer from Coshocton County, Allen M. Marshall. What carried the amendment was the general sentiment that the only fair and democratic procedure was to resolve all doubts by letting the electorate decide by its vote on the proposed amendment. Amidst cheers from the women who filled the galleries, the Kilpatrick proposal passed on March 7 by a vote of seventy-six to thirty-four.[32]

One other amendment directly affecting women by making them eligible to hold certain appointive offices was accepted with only one dissenting vote. Introduced at the request of the Ohio Federation of Women's Clubs, it allowed women to be notaries public and members of boards or officers of institutions for the care of women or children. Though an effort was made to enlarge the scope of the original proposal to permit women to occupy any appointive office, this was as far as the majority was willing to go.[33]

Progressives were not only interested in promoting reforms to broaden popular participation in government, but they were also concerned with changes which would increase the efficiency of administration. The failure of the General Assembly to enact civil service legislation for the state was responsible for an amendment making such a service mandatory. The debate was brief, only one delegate, who branded it as the "snivil service," voicing opposition. Although this was deceptive of the extent of the resistance, the measure passed eighty-four to twenty-one. Most opponents were afraid to speak against this popular reform.[34]

A much more controversial proposal for improving governmental efficiency was one for a short ballot. As with woman suffrage, a separate standing committee was established, and an ardent partisan, John Fackler, put in charge. Professor Henry W. Elson presented the majority report proposing to limit the elective state officers to the governor and lieutenant-governor. Friends of the change argued that the short ballot would enable the electorate to vote more intelligently, and, by concentrating responsibility in the governor, would eliminate the inefficiency, waste, and corruption promoted through divided authority. Opponents accused them of inconsistency in advocating the initiative and referendum, on the one hand, and the short ballot, on the other. They insisted that the proposal was undemocratic because it made state officials less responsive to the people. Finally, they stressed the potential opportunity it presented to a governor to build up a political machine. Although amendments were accepted on the floor to make it more palatable by adding the state auditor and attorney-general to the elective officers, the proposal was voted down, fifty-seven to forty-seven. The hostility of office-holders, supplemented by the opposition of farm and labor representatives, was too strong to be overcome.[35]

Despite this defeat of the effort to shorten the ballot drastically, the convention later did take two steps in that direction: the elective statutory office of commissioner of schools was replaced by a superintendent of education appointed by the governor, and a superintendent of public works chosen by the chief executive was substituted for the existing elective board.[36]

Several other miscellaneous changes affecting the governor and legislature were made by the convention. One amendment increased the chief executive's power by permitting him to limit the agenda for extraordinary sessions of the legislature; another reduced it by lowering the majority required to override his veto from two-thirds to three-fifths of each house. Although the ultraprogressives proposed to go even further and return to the status before 1903, when the governor of Ohio had no veto, they were defeated. A third proposal—to correct the principle of a court decision which had stopped the Drake investigation of

Cincinnati in 1908 because it had been authorized by only one house—was unanimously approved. A fourth removed a constitutional prohibition against the state's doing its own printing.[37]

One of the issues prominent in pre-convention discussions was judicial reform. Members of the Ohio Bar, progressives, and labor groups were all interested in revamping the court structure and certain court procedures, though not always in the same fashion or for the same reasons. Judge Hiram Peck took charge of the major proposal to reconstruct the state courts. He was a happy choice from the progressives' standpoint, for he possessed an intimate knowledge of the faults and virtues of the existing system and favored radical change.

It was widely recognized among informed persons that the Ohio judicial organization was "antiquated and cumbersome." Modeled after the federal system, it consisted of courts of common pleas in the counties, circuit courts, and a supreme court. There were few restrictions on appeals; the circuit bench was a kind of sieve through which cases passed from the lower to the supreme courts. As a result, suits had piled up on the dockets of the highest bench until it was one to three years behind in its work. The Peck amendment proposed to replace the circuit branch with courts of appeal which would have power of final review in all cases except felonies and those involving questions of constitutionality or major public interest. This change would shorten judicial proceedings in most cases to one trial and one review, eliminating the expense of long delays and two appeals and the overcrowding of the docket of the supreme court.[38]

While most delegates conceded the necessity for this reform, conservatives spiritedly protested a second part of the Peck proposal, which would require a unanimous vote of the supreme court to declare an act of the legislature unconstitutional, except in affirming a decision of the court of appeal holding a law void, in which case a majority was sufficient. This proposal was attacked by Judge William Worthington, a fellow delegate from Cincinnati, as a revolutionary reversal of a historic American judicial tradition; others who clung to the old ways shared his resentment. Yet the feeling was strong among the majority that some curb should be placed on the power of the courts to interfere with the legislature. This sentiment had been encouraged by the speeches of Theodore Roosevelt and Ben Lindsey. Wisely, the former President's plan of the recall of judicial decisions was rejected, and the Peck substitute, which the Denver judge had endorsed, was proposed. Although one extremist would have gone farther than Peck—and abolish judicial review alto- gether—others regarded the unanimity requirement as too exact- ing. On April 10, at the end of a week of debate, John Fackler offered an amendment to require the concurrence of all but one judge. This was accepted. One other change was adopted— to add a chief justice as a seventh member of the court—before the measure passed the crucial vote on second reading, seventy- eight to twenty-eight. By the time of the third reading, a month later, the opposition had melted away, only five die-hards casting their ballots against it.[39]

Two other proposals affecting the judicial structure were adopted with little protest. One was designed to speed litigation in the common pleas courts by providing for a judge in each county and permitting populous counties to have more than three, the maximum under the existing constitution. Since this would add expense, another clause permitted counties with a population of less than sixty thousand to combine their com- mon pleas and probate courts by referendum vote. The other eliminated justices of the peace in cities where municipal courts had been established. As this only applied to Cleveland at the time, it scarcely aroused a ripple of interest.[40]

Certain procedural changes also met the opposition of con- servatives who resented tampering with the traditional common- law processes. One proposed to alter the jury system in civil cases by authorizing a three-fourths vote instead of a unanimous verdict of the jurors; another directed the legislature to prescribe the size of the grand jury and the number necessary to concur in an indictment, and modified criminal procedure in other respects; a third empowered the General Assembly to regulate the use of expert witnesses in criminal trials, especially in the presentation of medical testimony. All three ultimately passed.[41]

A modification in equity procedure, long demanded by labor, was approved with surprisingly little opposition. Its purpose was to curb the use of the writ of injunction in labor disputes and to provide for a jury trial for contempt committed elsewhere than before the court. William P. Halenkamp, who introduced the amendment, fulminated against the perverted use of this "beneficent writ" as a powerful weapon of the "industrial tories" to crush trade unionism. Although conservatives attacked the measure as being of a statutory nature, Judge Peck replied to these critics that a matter of such great importance rightfully belonged in the constitution.[42]

No excitement was aroused over an amendment authorizing the legislature to provide by general law for suits against the state.[43] A proposal to abolish capital punishment, however, met stubborn opposition. The debaters concentrated upon the purpose of the death penalty and the experience of states where it had already been prohibited. Backed by progressives from the northern part of the state, particularly Cleveland, and most of the labor representatives, the amendment received enough conservative support to counterbalance the negative vote of those who were usually on the side of reform and passed, sixty-nine to thirty-five.[44]

It was not surprising that Cleveland progressives took the lead in drafting and sponsoring an amendment to grant municipal home rule. Tom Johnson and his followers had been championing this reform since 1901, for to them it was the key to the realization of urban democracy. In 1902, when the Ohio Municipal Code was rewritten, they had lost because reactionaries had the upper hand, but in 1912, with the situation reversed, city progressives were confident victory would not again be snatched from them.

The initiative in drafting a home-rule amendment was taken by the Municipal Association of Cleveland. As early as 1910 it had appointed a committee with Augustus R. Hatton as chairman and Newton D. Baker as one of its nine members, to make a state-wide canvass to ascertain the sentiment for this reform in Ohio. As the constitutional convention assembled in January, 1912, the committee issued its report, which was distributed among the members and city officials throughout the state. The committee was also authorized to call a conference of mayors and representatives from the eighty-three Ohio municipalities, which met in Columbus from January 23 to 25, 1912.

Some 150 delegates attended, representing 53 cities, and elected Newton Baker chairman. Two drafts of a proposed home-rule amendment were presented, one by Augustus R. Hatton, the other by A. Julius Freiberg of Cincinnati; the principal difference between the two plans was the degree of freedom from state control. Although both would grant cities the right to frame their own charters, the Hatton formula guaranteed a maximum of municipal sovereignty by spelling out the powers reserved to the cities; the Freiberg proposal was couched in broad terms and left intact the authority of the General Assembly to control cities by general law. After a lengthy debate, the Cleveland draft was adopted together with appropriate resolutions to present it to the constitutional convention.

A second move of the conference was to organize itself formally as the Ohio Municipal League, electing Baker as its first president and Mayo Fesler of the Cleveland Municipal Association as secretary-treasurer, in recognition of the leadership taken by the Cleveland group. The immediate objective of the League was to campaign for the adoption of a home-rule amendment; its larger purpose was to promote beneficial legislation, collect and disseminate data on municipal problems, and create a common forum for the discussion of city affairs. Before adjourning, the conference was addressed by Washington Gladden, the mayors of Cleveland, Toledo, and Cincinnati, and Herbert Bigelow, who drew cheers from the gathering when he paid tribute to the memory of Tom Johnson.[45]

The preliminary fight before the municipal conference was only the beginning of the struggle for the friends of a strong home-rule amendment in the constitutional convention. The chairman of the committee on municipal government, George W. Harris of Cincinnati, was hostile to the Cleveland draft. Lobbyists of the public-service corporations tried to impair the ability of cities to finance municipal utilities. Baker, who was frequently called to Columbus, did his most effective work in the hearings before this committee in preserving as much of the original plan as possible. Through his knowledge of the subject and his tact in presenting his arguments, he won confidence in his ideas. Still, he had to yield on freedom in financial affairs, conceding the authority of the General Assembly to limit the power of municipalities to tax and incur debts.

Late in April the convention began a two-day debate on the amendment. Professor George Knight, a member of the committee, expressed the three aims of the proposal: to allow a diversity of charters, and thus enable each Ohio city to have the form of government it desired; to give municipalities all powers not specifically denied them, reversing the existing situation, in which they possessed only such authority as the legislature granted them; and to permit cities to construct, own, and operate all public utilities serving the municipality. Opposition stemmed from four sources. Rural members looked askance at the measure as being a plot by the cities to free themselves from all state regulations. The drys, on the one hand, were suspicious because it tended to break down state liquor control, while the wets, on the other, were annoyed because it did not give cities complete freedom in the matter. But the chief assault came from spokesmen for the public-service corporations, who argued that the amendment threatened to destroy their interests by failing to restrain unfair competition by municipally-owned utilities. Their argument carried some weight until they overplayed their hand by proposing an amendment which would practically have nullified the municipal-ownership provisions. This the convention rejected by a large majority and refused to reconsider. The home-rule proposal passed the critical test on second reading, 104 to 6. The surprisingly small negative vote, however, did not indicate the extent of the opposition. Before the division, supporters polled the delegates and found they had the necessary votes. After word of this was spread around, many doubtful members switched to the majority side.[46]

On the heels of the debate over home rule came discussion of the controversial taxation issue. Urban progressives, who had failed to write a local-option tax provision into the municipal-government amendment, hoped to incorporate such a clause in the revision of the constitutional tax article. Edward Doty, a champion of this reform, was chairman of the taxation committee, which contained a majority initially committed to change. The hope of tax reformers was to strike out the uniform rule and adopt a system of classification of property, either state-wide, or on a county-option basis. The issue led to some strange combinations: conservatives such as James Halfhill, Nelson W. Evans, and Judge William Worthington, who attacked every other part of the program of the progressives, joined the latter in the battle for classification.

332

As the hearings before the committee wore on, however, it became apparent that the reformers were losing ground. Only eleven members signed the majority report recommending classification on a local-option basis, while nine submitted a minority proposal to continue the uniform rule, but with additional provisions to permit graduated inheritance and income taxes, to place limitations on levies and indebtedness, and to remove the exemptions on state and local bonds.[47]

After the first two days of debate it was abundantly clear that majority sentiment favored retention of the uniform rule. Under the application of the Smith 1 Per Cent Law, farmers had become attached again to the existing system. More important, classification had become suspect to them because of its friends among the single taxers. The rural delegates were haunted by the fear that classification would open the door to the dreaded single tax, which would make land carry the whole burden. For the second time this specter threatened to destroy clear debate and rational judgment. Recognizing the majority temper, John Fackler on May 6 proposed a substitute which gave way on the uniform-rule issue but tried to salvage as many progressive points as possible. His amendment followed the minority report by providing for income and inheritance taxes and the removal of the exemption on state and local bonds, but it deleted the clause on tax and debt limitations and provided for excise and franchise taxes on coal, oil, gas, and minerals. Although the farmers favored the retention of a limit on debts and taxes, the convention voted down repeated efforts to include it, and the Fackler substitute was accepted intact by a vote of seventy-seven to thirty-one.

On the third reading, opponents made a final attempt to carry a compromise offered by Doty which had been defeated in the first debate. This proposed to submit to the electorate simultaneously with the Fackler amendment an alternate amendment calling for classification and the exemption of state and local bonds from taxation, but the maneuver failed by two votes. With minor changes the Fackler measure was approved finally, seventy-three to thirty-two.[48]

This action of the convention aroused more resentment among the minority than any other. Conservative Judge Edmund King castigated the amendment as reactionary; Worthington condemned it for continuing the faults of the old system and adding new evils; Professor Knight lamented the failure to seize the opportunity to adopt a modern, scientific, equitable taxing program which would tap the hidden wealth in intangible personal property. Urban progressives were disturbed not only by the failure of classification by local option but also by the restoration of state and local bonds to the duplicate, an action that would impair the market for municipal utility bonds. On the other hand, they took some comfort from their success in making explicit the power to tax franchises and the mineral products of the earth, thus striking at two bases of monopoly.[49]

The taxation amendment was not the only one affecting the business community. Bryan in his speech had raised the issue of banking reform, recommending that the state guarantee all bank deposits to a certain maximum. Although this was considered too radical, the convention did adopt a proposal to give depositors additional protection by imposing a double liability on bank stockholders. The same measure also extended state inspection to private banks. Control over corporations and the sale of securities by foreign and domestic concerns was strengthened by another amendment. A third granted the legislature the constitutional right to regulate insurance rates and allowed the state to insure public property in mutual insurance companies and associations. One delegate recommended that Ohio go even further and enter the insurance business itself, but this found little support. At the request of a number of social and business clubs, Judge Peck introduced a measure to permit the legislature to prohibit outdoor advertising. This worthy effort to prevent the defacement of the countryside was approved without debate, sixty-eight to twenty-eight, the opposition being divided between conservatives and farmers. A final amendment was necessitated by an adverse decision of the Ohio Supreme Court. It proposed to clear the way for the adoption of the Torrens system for registering land titles.[50]

Labor was generously treated by the convention. Many who were conservative on political reforms were enthusiastic for radical measures to ameliorate conditions for the workingman in industry. Though there was little debate on any of the labor proposals, what opposition there was came from a few die-hard conservatives joined by a sprinkling of doctrinaire progressives whose sympathy for reform was limited to specific changes in the political mechanism. A number of the measures were introduced either because of past adverse court decisions or in anticipation of unfavorable judicial action.

The nature and scope of the proposals presented by the labor delegates marked an important shift in policy. Heretofore this economic class had distrusted political action, placing its chief reliance on the trade-union tactics of collective bargaining, the boycott, and the strike. But the unequal nature of their struggle with capital, the application of the injunction after 1895 to labor disputes, and the consequent restrictions placed on their chief economic weapons forced labor to turn to the state for protection. Not all of labor's demands were acceptable to the convention. Prohibitions against the black-listing of union men and the employment of strikebreakers and a specific guarantee of the right to organize and strike were tabled. The only aid in this direction labor received was the amendment to correct the worse abuses of the injunction in industrial disputes.[51] Though the delegates were unwilling to buttress such supports for trade unionism, they showed strong sympathy for measures which would protect labor from the worst evils of the industrial order.

The most radical proposal adopted was one to permit the General Assembly to fix minimum wages as well as set maximum hours and provide for the health, safety, and general welfare of all employees. Originating in 1897 in Australia, "the experiment station of the world," minimum-wage legislation was introduced in Great Britain in 1909 and came to these shores three years later when Massachusetts adopted such a law for women. Thomas S. Farrell, a Cleveland trade unionist who introduced the measure, declared that he had once opposed such legislation but that he had been converted to the legislative approach by the failure of labor-union methods to establish minimums and by the writings of the English Fabian Socialists, Sidney and Beatrice Webb. The most forceful defense of the proposal came from the moderate conservative Judge Dennis Dwyer, who stated that this was a proper exercise of the state's police power and was as socially desirable as fixing maximum interest rates. When questioned as to the necessity of the amendment, he insisted on a positive grant of power to forestall an unfavorable court decision. Another delegate pointed to an Ohio

335

minimum-wage law for teachers, which had been held unconstitutional. Although a conservative manufacturer argued that
a minimum wage would be ruinous to Ohio industry, and
although the progressive George W. Harris branded it "economic
insanity," the amendment passed eighty to thirteen on second
reading, and the opposition dropped to five on the final vote.[52]

This grant of power was broad enough to encompass two
other proposals, but labor demanded and won their separate treatment. Miners had long protested against the practice of Ohio coal
operators of paying only for screened coal instead of for run-of-
the mine. Having failed to eliminate this grievance through
collective bargaining, the miners' representative, William Green,
had tried unsuccessfully to abolish it by legislative decree in
1911. Since, however, there was doubt about the General Assembly's power to act, a clause was now written into the conservation amendment conferring upon that body the authority
to regulate mining, weighing, measuring, and marketing of coal,
oil, gas, and other minerals.[53]

The other measure was to make secure workmen's compensation legislation. Even though the optional law passed by the
legislature in 1911 had been upheld by the Ohio Supreme
Court in a four-to-two decision, labor insisted on specific constitutional authority for a compulsory law. Sentiment in favor
of the proposal was overwhelming. Judge Lindsey, Roosevelt,
and Bryan had given it unqualified endorsement in their addresses. The Scripps-McRae League not only crusaded for it
in their papers, but J. Chandler Harper, the organization's attorney, and their correspondents covering the convention actively
lobbied for its passage among the few doubting members. The
country-wide campaign by the National Civic Federation for
this reform also helped to win adherents. On the votes after
both second and third readings not a single ballot was registered against it.[54] Also adopted was a supplementary amendment relating to compensation, which prohibited any limit on
damages recoverable in a civil action for wrongful death.[55]

Two other proposals, seemingly of a statutory nature, had
been made necesary because the courts had annulled previous
laws on the subject. One was to permit the General Assembly
to write mechanics' and builders' lien legislation, and the other
to establish an eight-hour day on public works. When the latter

was challenged as superfluous because of the broad wage-and-hour amendment, Walter Brown supported labor's plea that this policy was important enough to be declared expressly in the fundamental law.[56]

Workingmen again found a friend in Walter Brown when he made an earnest, persuasive speech for an amendment to prohibit prison contract labor, proscribing such employment as a form of peonage. On the narrow grounds that the convicts would then be used to raise a food supply for the state institutions and thus deny the farmers this market, the rural delegates opposed it, but they were outvoted sixty-eight to thirty-five. This was the only labor measure encountering serious resistance.[57]

Three amendments affecting the general welfare of all classes were passed. George Knight introduced a comprehensive proposal on education, vesting in the General Assembly power over the organization, administration, and control of schools, yet permitting each school district by referendum vote to determine the size and organization of its own board of education. In view of the municipal home-rule amendment, it was believed necessary to declare the supremacy of the state over the educational system, at the same time preserving some discretionary power among local units, which urban reformers had demanded. Since many felt it unwise to grant even this much freedom to rural school boards, an amendment was offered and adopted limiting such discretion to cities.[58]

Closely linked to the hope for school reform through a state program was the demand for a proposal to finance good roads. This plan recommended a state bond issue of $50 millions over the next five years to build a system of intercounty highways. While a spirit of local jealousy was displayed by some delegates from counties where a good-roads program had already been initiated, the main opposition came from those who preferred a pay-as-you-go method by taxation to saddling the state with an enormous debt. Provision for a sinking fund partially answered these critics, and enough were satisfied to pass the proposal seventy-two to forty.[59] This was the heaviest opposition recorded against any amendment.

The third in the general-welfare category was the conservation measure. First proposed in three separate parts, it was consolidated into one article and adopted ninety-one to twelve. It

337

conferred on the legislature the power to: encourage forestry by exempting timber lands from taxation and by establishing state forest reserves by gift or purchase; protect streams and lakes, drain swamps, and control water power; and regulate the mining, weighing, measuring, and marketing of coal, oil, gas, and other minerals. This enlightened amendment met the demands of the leading conservationists of the day.[60]

The final task of the convention was to determine a schedule for the effective date of the amendments, the form of the ballot, and the method of publicizing its work. Agreement was quickly reached on the schedule: all amendments were to become effective, if ratified, on January 1, 1913, unless specifically provided otherwise. In the event of any conflict between the amendments adopted and the existing constitution, the former were to prevail. There was less harmony displayed in deciding on the form of the ballot. Some advocated a circle above the column of amendments to permit a straight vote for all the proposals. One delegate queried with tongue in cheek, "Is the circle square?" The majority felt not and provided for a separate vote on each amendment, a majority of the ballots cast being sufficient for its adoption.

The question of publicizing the convention's work aroused the sharpest controversy. There were altogether forty-two amendments for the voters to review, and it was important to devise the proper means to inform the people about such a formidable number of constitutional changes. Harry Thomas proposed the preparation of brief statements, pamphlets and newspaper boiler plate on each of the amendments. His recommendation was branded by its opponents as extravagant, egotistical, illegal, and vicious, and was defeated in a close vote. The next day, when calmer heads prevailed, a more modest compromise resolution was adopted. This directed the president to appoint a committee to prepare a single pamphlet to be mailed to every voter in the state, in which would be listed the short title and full text of each amendment, followed by a brief explanation of its purport. Although this publication had wide distribution, no systematic effort was made to see that a copy reached the hands of each elector. The convention's main reliance was on newspaper publicity.[61]

Friends of the amendments possessed a number of assets in their campaign for ratification. They were, to begin with, better organized than their opponents. In January, 1912, they had founded the New Constitution League of Ohio, with Bigelow as president and John Stockwell as treasurer. Representatives from five of the major cities sat on its executive committee, and progressives from each of the twenty-one congressional districts composed an advisory board. Its purpose was to educate the public to the vital need for the initiative and referendum as well as to urge the adoption of all the amendments submitted.[62]

With certain exceptions the delegates favored the work they had done and spoke on behalf of the proposals. The convention's handiwork received the blanket endorsement of the Democratic state convention and of the Roosevelt Progressives. Because of the generous treatment granted workingmen, union labor leaders and Socialists were enthusiastic advocates. The character of the men who stumped the state endorsing the amendments inspired confidence. They included James M. Cox, the Democratic nominee for governor; Mayors Baker, Hunt, and Whitlock; and Herbert Bigelow, then at the height of his popularity. Important work for the cause was done locally by several of the Roosevelt Progressives, among whom were John Fackler in Cleveland, Judge Robert M. Wanamaker in Akron, and Washington Gladden in Columbus.[63]

Equally important was the generally favorable press given the amendments. During August the *Toledo News-Bee* discussed each proposal individually, endorsing all but three or four, underscoring the initiative and referendum, municipal home rule, and labor amendments with front-page articles. The other Scripps-McRae papers in Ohio and the *Cleveland Plain Dealer* matched this service to their readers; not far behind were the *Toledo Blade, Cleveland Leader,* and *Dayton Daily News.* Some papers preferred to concentrate on a few amendments. Not all the metropolitan press, however, was favorable. The Wolfe family papers in Columbus adopted a cautiously hostile tone, as did the *Enquirer* and *Times-Star* in Cincinnati.[64]

Overt opposition did not arise until late in the campaign. Appearing under an anonymous guise, it was led by Allen Ripley Foote, president of the Ohio State Board of Commerce, and supported by the public utilities. Hostile to the initiative and referendum and labor reforms, Foote was further embittered by the failure of the tax-classification amendment to carry in the convention. His method was to deluge the rural press with boiler plate crassly attacking the work of the convention. When the editors refused to publish this material because it was so highly colored and factually false that their readers balked, the opposition turned as a final resort to pamphlets and dodgers, tons of which were circulated. One of the opposition canards was the statement spread among small shopkeepers and farmers that the office of justice of the peace had been destroyed throughout the state. Such wide currency did this gain that the convention at its one-day meeting in August issued a special statement to spike this falsehood.[65]

General public interest centered on not more than nine of the proposed amendments: liquor license, woman suffrage, initiative and referendum, welfare of employees, changes in the judicial system, primary elections, good roads, and municipal home rule. Woman suffrage was the most widely discussed. The campaign for the initiative and referendum and municipal home rule was particularly heated, for the more the progressives shoved them to the forefront, the harder the opposition fought to defeat them by distorting their purpose to the rural voters. The labor welfare amendment was defended and attacked with vehemence. Taxation failed to arouse the same rancor because many progressive and conservative classificationists were on the same side in opposition to the proposed measure.[66]

As the campaign came to a close, the Ohio State Board of Commerce spread the word, "When in doubt, vote no." This slogan turned into a boomerang when friends of constitutional change urged everyone, "When in doubt, vote yes." The question then became, as a *Cleveland Leader* correspondent wrote, whether those in doubt should follow the advice of Allen Ripley Foote, the voice of the special interests, or that of such men as Washington Gladden and President William O. Thompson of Ohio State University, who pointed out that the amendments were the product of five months of diligent work by a nonpartisan body and merited the confidence of the voters.[67]

The day after Labor Day, September 3, was selected for the election in order to give labor orators the opportunity to make a last-minute appeal to workingmen to get to the polls and vote.

The warm, sunny weather seemed favorable for a record vote; yet no one expected such a result, because observers had already reported that the citizens had become absorbed in the Taft-Roosevelt-Wilson presidential campaign and were apathetic to the constitutional changes. The predicted light vote was realized.[68]

Woman suffrage polled the highest number, 586,295, or 63.4 per cent of the vote for governor in 1910; the liquor-license proposal, which had apparently been overlooked by many electors because of its isolated position on the ballot, polled the fewest, 462,186, or 50 per cent. These totals compared unfavorably with the vote on the constitution of 1851, which was 83 per cent of that for governor; they were slightly below the poll on the defeated constitution of 1874, which was 60 per cent. There was no marked difference between urban and rural areas in the percentages. In the twelve largest urban counties 67.5 per cent of the vote for governor in 1910 was cast for the amendments; in thirty typical rural counties the percentage was 63. The variation in city counties ran between Hamilton's 56.2 per cent and Cuyahoga's 80.6 per cent; in rural ones, it ran from a low in Adams County of 36.7 per cent to a high in Lake County of 87.2 per cent.[69]

But geography was significant in the distribution of the vote for and against the amendments. In the twelve principal urban counties the city population favored almost every amendment, and, in the aggregate, approved of all except those for woman suffrage and voting machines. Columbiana, Lucas, and Summit counties actually supported every amendment.[70] The northern cities were more consistently and decisively committed to change than the southern, partly as a result of the greater power of organized labor in the north, but mainly because the need for these reforms had been made familiar through the pioneer work of Sam Jones and Tom Johnson and the continuing educational program they had inspired.

The influence of the cities in the northeastern area spread to adjacent counties, where the rural population voted generally the same. The old New England stock of this region was once again in revolt against established political traditions, turning its back on Old Guard Republicanism for Theodore Roosevelt's brand of progressivism. The vote in the rural counties farthest away from the influence of the northern progressive cities is in striking contrast. Seven voted no on every amendment, nine others defeated all except that on liquor-licensing. Had it not been for the heavy favorable vote in the twelve urban counties, nineteen of the thirty-four amendments which passed would have failed.[71]

Despite the rural opposition, all save two of the proposed amendments adopted were ratified by substantial majorities. The closest votes occurred on those that were rejected. Among the eight which failed of endorsement were some surprises. Four had been strongly favored by the convention: elimination of the word "white," which was defeated by the strength of racial prejudice in Ohio; voting machines, opposed by rural and urban voters alike; modification of injunction proceedings; and the eligibility of women for certain offices. The other four defeated measures, however, were known to be controversial from the size of the opposition in the convention itself: woman suffrage, good roads, regulation of outdoor advertising, and abolition of capital punishment. In defeating both of the amendments affecting women, Ohio males were apparently determined to keep the opposite sex out of political life entirely, a decision ascribed to lack of public education and the hostility of the liquor interests. The bond issue for intercounty highways was the victim of Ohio's conservatism on money expenditures and the narrow selfishness of voters in counties already equipped with good roads. Propaganda of the billboard companies proved effective against state regulation of outdoor advertising. Old Testament farmers who believed in an eye for an eye voted down the prohibition of the death penalty.[72]

Since only three of the eight defeated amendments had been forcefully espoused by the progressives, these casualties at the polls scarcely affected the belief that the election results were a victory for radical progressivism. Clearly the tone of conservative criticism confirmed this. An outraged conservative, Daniel J. Ryan, wrote: "The amendments submitted ranged in merit from the unnecessary and harmless to the vicious and revolutionary." In the latter category he placed the direct-legislation measure and labor welfare measure, which he gloomily prophesied were "part of a plan adroitly consummated . . . to strike a fatal blow at the stable property and business interests of

Ohio." Furthermore, he alleged that these "Socialistic" amendments had been railroaded through, and that the vote did not reflect the sensible, mature judgment of a naturally conservative state.[73]

Despite such allegations, Ohio's decision to go radical was hardly the result of any sinister plot. The amendments had been ably discussed in the press and by speakers in public forums. All of the electorate had had an opportunity to be informed, and in the opinion of many observers were well briefed in those amendments which conservatives found most objectionable.[74] Moreover, the contention that the conservative, propertied element stayed away from the polls in greater numbers than the radical, propertyless masses is not borne out by the press reports. Instead of the expected large labor-Socialist vote, there were light returns from these groups in Columbus, Cincinnati, Dayton, Springfield, and Toledo. And in the capital city it was pointed out that the heaviest balloting occurred in the conservative, well-to-do wards.[75] The leftward swing of the pendulum was a product of the times, a product of the same forces which had produced the victory of the progressive wing in the Democratic party and the split in the Republican when the Roosevelt faction failed to gain control. The psychological climate in 1912 was ripe for change. Had the Ohio Constitutional Convention been held two years before or two years later, the results might have been substantially different.

None were more aware of their good fortune than the reformers themselves. It was a moment of triumph for Bigelow, Whitlock, Baker, and a host of other men who had long been tilling the Ohio vineyard in the hopes of such a harvest. They counted as their principal fruits the initiative and referendum, the direct primary, judicial reform, municipal home rule, and benefits for labor.. These were the changes which would make Ohio "a free state."[76] The only step remaining was to adopt the necessary legislation to make the amendments effective. The manner in which this should be accomplished and the party to whom this important task should be entrusted became the central issues of the Ohio campaign and election of 1912.

1. The principal source on the organization and proceedings of the convention is the *Proceedings and Debates of the Constitutional Convention*

of Ohio, 1912 (2 vols.; Columbus, 1912), (hereafter referred to as *Proceedings and Debates*). The first quotation is from a speech of Judge Dwyer in *ibid.*, I, 24; the organization was reported in *ibid.*, I, 21–25; the veteran correspondent was Herbert R. Mengert of the *Cincinnati Enquirer*, quoted in Cox, *Journey through My Years*, 123.

2. The name, address, and occupation of each delegate is listed in the *Journal of the Constitutional Convention of the State of Ohio, 1912* (Columbus, 1912), 921–22.

3. The absence of party alignment in votes was noted by Henry W. Elson, "The Fourth Constitutional Convention of Ohio," *Review of Reviews*, XLV (March, 1912), 338. The quotations are to be found, respectively, in remarks on the constitutional convention by Herbert Bigelow and Elbert L. Lampson in Mercer, ed., *Ohio Legislative History* [1], 410, 420, and in Antrim, "Ohio Constitutional Convention," 1426.

4. *Dayton Daily News*, November 9, 1911; *Cincinnati Post*, November 9, 1911. His other support was reported in the *Ohio State Journal* (Columbus), January 5, 1912. Correspondents of the Scripps-McRae press were active not only in promoting Bigelow but also in lobbying for the initiative and referendum and labor amendments. This information is from the author's interview with Henry P. Boynton, October 3, 1949. Boynton was a correspondent of the *Cleveland Press* at the convention. Conservatives recognized and feared the influence of these papers. See Clarence Maris to A. L. Garford, November 16, 1911, Garford Papers. Maris was the head of the Ohio Republican Press Bureau.

5. The Woods quotation is in Frank W. Woods to A. L. Garford, November 11, 1911, Garford Papers. Garford, who was the gubernatorial candidate of the Progressive party in Ohio in 1912, shared this opinion of Bigelow (A. L. Garford to Clarence Maris, November 17, 1911, Garford Papers). Brown's activity for Norris was related in Walter F. Brown to A. L. Garford, November 9, 1911, Garford Papers, and in the author's interview with Herbert S. Bigelow, Setpember 26, 1949. Immediately after his election Brown began collecting data on his fellow delegates, their politics, religion, and business or profession. During the organizational stage he was very active on behalf of his candidate, but once the organization was completed, he was very quiet.

6. The contest over the presidency was described in the remarks of Charles B. Galbreath on the constitutional convention in Mercer, *Ohio Legislative Histroy* [I], 444, and in the author's interview with Herbert Bigelow, September 26, 1949. Simeon Fess, although never formally nominated, began receiving votes on the fifth ballot in an unsuccessful move to swing the moderates to his standard. The vote on the decisive eleventh ballot was: Bigelow, sixty-two; Norris, three; Anderson, forty-eight; Thomas, one. Under instructions from the Socialist party, Thomas voted for himself throughout (*Journal of the Constitutional Convention, 7–15*).

7. *Toledo Blade, Dayton Daily News, Toledo News-Bee*, January 10, 1912.

8. Stockbridge, "Ohio Wide Awake," 698.

9. Galbreath won the secretaryship on the second ballot. The votes: Galbreath, seventy-two; Walter F. Pollock, thirty-two; and Leander L. Faris, eleven. (*Proceedings and Debates*, I, 33–34) On the balloting for vice-president the vote on the first ballot was: Doty, forty-seven; Anderson, thirty-six; and Fess, thirty-one. Then Anderson withdrew, and on the second

ballot Fess received sixty-one, and Doty, fifty-three (*Journal of the Constitutional Convention*, 51–52). The biographical data on Doty is drawn from the author's interview with Henry P. Boynton, October 3, 1949, and Hal C. DeRan to the author, October 5, 1949. Examples of Doty's aid to Bigelow are cited below in footnote 22.

10. *Proceedings and Debates*, I, 38–51. The Bigelow quotation is in *ibid.*, 49–50.

11. Bigelow appointed to the rules committee himself, Samuel A. Hoskins, Edward W. Doty, Stanley Shaffer, and Fred G. Leete, progressives; and Elbert L. Lampson and John W. Winn, conservatives. Hearings before the committee were reported in the *Ohio State Journal*, January 17, 1912. Criticism of the work of the committee was made by Worthington in remarks on the constitutional convention in Mercer, ed., *Ohio Legislative History* [I], 424. The other nine less important committees were: agriculture, banks and banking, corporations other than municipal, county and township organization, methods of amending the constitution, miscellaneous subjects, public works, schedule, and short ballot. In addition there were various committees concerned with the administrative aspects of the convention: claims, employees, printing and publication of proceedings, and submission and address to the people. After the initial organization was completed, the rules committee had few functions to perform. A final committee which played an important part was the one on arrangement and phraseology, which reviewed and revised every amendment for clarity of language and accuracy (*Journal of the Constitutional Convention*, 57–62).

12. The committee assignments and chairmanships are listed in *Journal of the Constitutional Convention*, 57–62; praise for the work of Bigelow and the rules committee came from the *Ohio State Journal*, January 18–19, 1912.

13. The favorable reception of the rules was reported in *Ohio State Journal*, January 21, 1912. The rules mentioned were, respectively, 105, 82, 62, 94, and 105 again (*Proceedings and Debates*, I, 79–80, 76–77, 73–75, 78).

14. *Proceedings and Debates*, I, 650–62.

15. Motions to invite La Follette and Clark as well as Eugene V. Debs were tabled (*ibid.*, I, 230, 410, 867). Peck's remark was quoted in *ibid.*, I, 416, and in the *Ohio State Journal*, February 23, 1912.

16. The speeches of Taft, Bryan, Johnson, Harmon, and Roosevelt are reported, respectively, in *Proceedings and Debates*, I, 145, 663–70, 544–49, 236–38, 378–87. Commentary on Harmon's speech is found in Nichols, "Harmon," 148–49, and in Cox, *Journey through My Years*, 133. One of Roosevelt's biographers calls his speech "the most sincere and the most disastrous of Roosevelt's public addresses."—Mowry, *Theodore Roosevelt and the Progressive Movement*, 212. The speeches of the mayors of Cleveland, Cincinnati, and Toledo, who spoke on the same day, and of Joseph B. Foraker and Theodore Burton are reported, respectively, in *Proceedings and Debates*, I, 119, 717–24, and 748–54. Pomerene declined to speak (*Ohio State Journal*, March 26, 1912).

17. Descriptions of the town meetings to discuss the work of the convention are in Elson, "The Fourth Constitutional Convention of Ohio," 338. Such national magazines as the *Literary Digest, Outlook,* and *Chautauquan* carried general articles on the proposed Ohio constitutional revisions. Special articles on particular phases of the convention's work were written by Mayo Fesler, Oliver C. Lockhart, and Robert M. Ditty, the exact titles of which are given in the Bibliography. A debate was conducted in the pages

of the *North American Review* between two Ohioans, Daniel J. Ryan, conservative, and Charles Sawyer, progressive, on the character of the constitutional changes. See the Bibliography. The four delegates to write about the convention were Antrim, Elson, Crosser, and Galbreath, whose articles are listed in the Bibliography.

18. The debate began on February 12, was dropped, then resumed from February 20 to 29, and continued on March 4 and 5 when the proposal finally passed after second reading (*Proceedings and Debates*, I, 257, 354–76, 387–404, 413–33, 448–54, 571–97).

19. *Ibid.*, I, 597–98. The amendment passed on third reading on May 24 by a vote of ninety-one to eighteen (*ibid.*, II, 1807). The attitude of both drys and wets toward the proposed is discussed in Elson, "Making a New Constitution for Ohio," 83–84.

20. The enthusiasm for this reform and the strategy of its partisans are reported in Robert Crosser, "The Initiative and Referendum Amendment in the Proposed Ohio Constitution," *Annals of the American Academy of Political and Social Science*, XLIII (September, 1912), 191–93. The speeches of Bryan, Johnson, Roosevelt, Burton, Harmon, and Foraker are cited above in footnote 16. The nine other states to adopt the initiative and referendum after South Dakota and Oregon were Nevada (referendum, 1905, initiative and recall, 1912), Montana (1906), Oklahoma (1907), Missouri (1908), Maine (1908), Arkansas (1910), Colorado (1910), Arizona (1911), and California (1911). See Judson King, "Safeguarding Petitions," *Bulletin of the National Popular Government League*, No. 4.

21. The proceedings of the caucus were reported in the *Ohio State Journal*, February 8–9, 15, 21, 24, 1912. The changes made in the proposal reported by the caucus are noted in *Proceedings and Debates*, I, 671. Crosser's explanation and analysis of the amendments are in *ibid.*, I, 674–75.

22. Typical speeches in favor of the initiative and referendum are those of Samuel A. Hoskins and Stephen S. Stilwell (*Proceedings and Debates*, I, 901, 933, respectively). Foraker raised the single-tax bogy, which was repeated by various conservatives. The Lampson quotation is from his speech reported in *ibid.*, I, 713. The relation of this reform to the introduction of the single tax is discussed above (Chap. VIII, p. 195). The Bigelow contretemps over the motion to amend is recorded in *Proceedings and Debates*, I, 807–8. Five days later, when one of the conservatives renewed the criticism of Bigelow's action, Doty assured the convention that it would not happen again, and, in addition, apologized for the mistake the president had made in appointing himself to a vacancy on the liquor traffic committee (*ibid.*, I, 810, 912).

23. The low percentages were criticized by Judge Peck and George W. Knight (*ibid.*, I, 776–82, 789–96). Washington Gladden expressed a similar objection (*Ohio State Journal*, March 18, 1912). The presentation of the Cassidy amendment is recorded in *Proceedings and Debates*, I, 942–46. Bigelow's speech for the amendment is in *ibid.*, 937–42; his defense of the prohibition against the use of the initiative to introduce the single tax is drawn from the author's interview with Herbert S. Bigelow, September 26, 1949. Crosser's dissatisfaction was reported in the *Ohio State Journal*, March 29, 1912. The text of the amendment and the vote after second reading is in *Proceedings and Debates*, I, 951–54.

24. *Proceedings and Debates*, II, 1882–1902, 1906–9, 1934–43. The text of the amendment in its final form is in *ibid.*, II, 1941-43.

25. It was approved on second reading 102 to 0 and adopted after third reading 105 to 1 (*ibid.*, II, 1365–71, 1913–14). The significance of the amendment was commented upon by George H. Colton in his remarks on the constitutional convention in Mercer, ed., *Ohio Legislative History* [I], 428.

26. *Proceedings and Debates,* I, 639, 746; II, 1217, 2239, 1345–46. The quotation from the minority report is in *ibid.*, II, 1291. Two conservatives, John W. Winn and George W. Pettit, spoke in support of the recall, as did the progressives John Fackler and Thomas Fitzsimmons. On the other hand, the conservative James Halfhill was violently opposed to the recall of judges and the progressive Hiram Peck thought the recall in general unnecessary. (*Ibid.*, II, 1292–94, 1301–8) The states which had adopted the recall were Oregon (1908) and California (1911), and the five that approved it in 1912 were Arizona, Colorado, Idaho, Nevada, and Washington. See Benjamin P. DeWitt, *The Progressive Movement* (New York, 1915), p. 233, n. 2.

27. Proposed by Judge Peck, it was not debated until the recall proposal had been defeated. It passed on second reading by vote of 93 to 2 and was approved after third reading 107 to 0. (*Proceedings and Debates,* II, 1309–11, 1347–49, 1381–84, 1406, 1773–76)

28. *Ibid.*, II, 1240, 1242–43, 1247, 1923–27. The amendment passed on second reading ninety to two, on third reading seventy-eight to twenty-three. The sponsor, J. W. Tannehill, in his speech presenting this amendment, listed the states in which the reform had already been adopted: in the Far West, Oregon, Washington, California, Nevada, and Idaho; in the Middle West, Michigan, Wisconsin, Illinois, Minnesota, North Dakota, South Dakota, Nebraska, Kansas, Missouri, and Iowa; in the South, Louisiana, Mississippi, Texas, and Oklahoma; and in New England, New Hampshire and Massachusetts. (*Ibid.*, II, 1240)

29. *Ibid.*, II, 1317–21, 1860. The bill passed on second reading sixty-nine to eighteen, on third reading ninety-seven to eight. The adverse Ohio Supreme Court decision was in *Karlinger* v. *Board of Control* (Cleveland), 60 Ohio 489 (1898).

30. The suffrage provisions are found in Art. V, sec. 1, Ohio Constitution of 1851. The amendment passed on second reading by a vote of one hundred to two, on third reading by ninety-seven to none (*Proceedings and Debates,* II, 1233, 1792).

31. Only six states had adopted statewide woman suffrage prior to 1912: Wyoming, Colorado, Utah, Idaho, Washington, and California. The issue was pending in six states in that year: Oregon, Kansas, and Arizona, where it was approved; Michigan, Wisconsin, and Ohio, where it was defeated. See Harold U. Faulkner, *The Quest for Social Justice* (*A History of American Life,* ed. A. M. Schlesinger and D. R. Fox, Vol. XI [13 vols.; New York, 1927–48]), 172–74, and Ida H. Harper, ed., *The History of Woman Suffrage* (6 vols.; New York, 1922), V, 339. The history of woman suffrage in Ohio and the men who supported it are discussed in Elizabeth J. Hauser, "The Woman Suffrage Movement in Ohio," *Ohio Magazine,* IV (February, 1908), 91–92.

32. *Proceedings and Debates,* I, 605–10, 634–39; II, 1857; *Ohio State Journal,* March 8, 1912. The amendment was approved on third reading by a vote of seventy-four to thirty-seven.

33. *Proceedings and Debates,* II, 1219–28, 1792. The vote after second reading was ninety to one, after third reading, one hundred to none.

34. *Ibid.*, II, 1380, 1793. The vote on third reading was eighty-four to sixteen. The sarcastic comemnt was made by George W. Pettit (*ibid.*, II, 1380).

35. *Ibid.*, I, 955–74, 993–1014; II, 1692–96; The author's interview with John Fackler, October 7, 1949; *Ohio State Journal*, March 29, May 9, 1912.

36. *Proceedings and Debates*, II, 1733, 1814; II, 1714, 1859, respectively.

37. The debate and vote on these amendments are recorded, respectively, in *ibid.*, II, 1349–54, 1793; II, 1198–1204, 1816; II, 1164, 1770; II, 1356, 1910.

38. The Ohio judicial organization was critically appraised by Henry W. Elson in his remarks on the constitutional convention in Mercer, ed., *Ohio Legislative History* [I], 430. The text of the Peck amendment is in the *Proceedings and Debates*, I, 1025–26.

39. In addition to Worthington, Judge Edmund B. King of Sandusky and George W. Harris, a single taxer from Cincinnati, opposed the amendment (*Proceedings and Debates*, II, 1107–13). Speeches in favor of the change were made by moderates David F. Anderson and Simeon Fess as well as by progressives George Knight and Samuel A. Hoskins (*ibid.*, II, 1088–1130). Roosevelt's statement is in *ibid.*, I, 378; Ben Lindsey's was reported in the *Ohio State Journal*, January 19, 1912, but not in the official record. The change in the amendment and the votes were recorded in *Proceedings and Debates*, II, 1117–18, 1147, 1163, 1825. The vote on third reading was ninety-seven to five. Some years later the amendment was challenged in a suit that went to the United States Supreme Court and was upheld (*Bryant v. Akron Metropolitan Park District*, 281 U.S. 74 [1930]). The effect of the amendment and the problems it has raised are discussed in Francis R. Auman, "The Course of Judicial Review in the State of Ohio," *American Political Science Review*, XXV (1931), 374–75.

40. The debates and votes are recorded, respectively, in the *Proceedings and Debates*, II, 1402, 1922; I, 552, II, 1772.

41. The debates and votes are recorded, respectively, in *ibid.*, I, 198, II, 1767; II, 1700, 1815; II, 1422, 1837. Although there was little debate on the last two amendments, the size of the negative vote indicated the determined resistance of conservatives to any changes in traditional procedures. The votes on the crucial second readings were, respectively, sixty-six to thirty-three and sixty-five to thirty-seven.

42. The debates and votes are recorded in *ibid.*, II, 1676–82, 1839. The vote on second reading was eighty to thirteen, on third, ninety-four to nine.

43. The debates and votes are recorded in ibid., II, 1432, 1919.

44. The debates and votes are recorded in *ibid.*, II, 1247–62, 1268–79, 1823. The death penalty had been abolished in Wisconsin, Michigan, and Kansas. Speakers in favor of the amendment included Doty, Aaron Hahn, H. G. Redington of Elyria, W. W. Farnsworth of Toledo, Richard A. Beatty of Wood County, Ernest I. Antrim, George Knight, and James Halfhill; among those opposed were the progressives Frank Woods and Starbuck Smith.

45. The preliminary activities of the Municipal Association are described in "Twenty-five Years of Home Rule," *Greater Cleveland*, XIII (December 30, 1937), 74–75. The conference of representatives of Ohio cities and the formation of the Ohio Municipal League were reported by Mayo Fesler, "Municipal Home Rule," *National Municipal Review*, I (July, 1912), 285; "The Ohio Municipal Conference," *Ibid.*, I, 302; *Ohio State Journal*, Jan-

uary 24–26, 1912; *Cleveland Leader*, January 24, 1912. Elliott H. Pendleton was one of the vice-presidents of the League, and Brand Whitlock was a member of the executive board.

46. The hearings before the committee were reported in "Twenty-five Year of Home Rule," 73–75, and in the *Ohio State Journal*, February 22, 1912. Harris' opposition to the Cleveland draft is in his speech in *Proceedings and Debates*, II, 1456–57, The debates and votes are recorded in *ibid.*, II, 1433, 1463–74, 1491–96, 1862–67, 1960. The vote after third reading was ninety-five to eight.

47. The committee hearings were reported in the *Ohio State Journal*, February 28, 1912. Robert M. Ditty, chairman of the state tax commission, defended the uniform rule at the hearings. He was believed to represent the views of the Harmon administration. The majority and minority reports are in *Proceedings and Debates, II,* 1326–27. The speeches of Worthington, Evans, and Halfhill in favor of classification are recorded, respectively, in *ibid.*, II, 1326, 1548, 1609–14.

48. The rural opposition and the single-tax bogy are discussed in the *Ohio State Journal*, May 2, 3, 7, 1912, in Antrim, "Ohio Constitutional Convention," 1423, and in Oliver C. Lockhart, "Taxation in Ohio," *American Economic Review* II (Setpember, 1912), 730. Typical of the reaction of rural delegates was the speech of Solomon Johnson, a farmer from Williams County. He told the convention that he personally favored classification but that nine-tenths of his constituents favored retention of the uniform rule and that is the way he would vote. (*Proceedings and Debates*, II, 1632) The vote on the Fackler substitute (second reading) was recorded in *ibid.*, 1674, the debate and vote on third reading in *ibid.*, 1876–82, 1957.

49. The criticisms of King, Worthington, and Knight are contained in their remarks on the constitutional convention in Mercer, ed., *Ohio Legislative History* [I], 413, 424, and 439, respectively. During the campaign for ratification both Baker and Whitlock denounced the provision to restore state and local bonds to the tax duplicate (*Cleveland Plain Dealer*, August 31, 1912).

50. The debates and votes on these several amendments are recorded, respectively, in *Proceedings and Debates*, II, 1186, 1850; II, 1388, 1768; II, 1731, 1825; II, 1715, 1799–1800; II, 1715–16, 1719, 1871–73, 1905. The Torrens system provided that land titles had to be warranted by a court prior to registry. It had been adopted in seven states, including Ohio, where it had been held unconstitutional by the state supreme court. The chief criticism against the system was the expense to the landowner of registering title.

51. The tabling of these demands of union labor is recorded in *ibid.*, II, 1404. Another proposal—to make arbitration of labor disputes compulsory—was also tabled. However, this was opposed by most laboring men. (*Ibid.*, I, 640; II, 1404). The limitationes on the use of injunctions in labor disputes are discussed on pages 9–30, above.

52. The history of such legislation was reported in the *Ohio State Journal*, September 8, 1912. The speeches of Farrell, Dwyer, and Harris are recorded in *Proceedings and Debates, II,* 1328–32, 1332–36, 1336–38, the vote in *ibid.*, II, 1338.

53. *Proceedings and Debates*, II, 1280–82. Percy Tetlow, a miner from Columbiana County, championed this reform.

54. The debates and votes are recorded in *ibid.*, II, 1346–37, 1769. The support of Roosevelt and Bryan is found in their speeches in *ibid.*, I, 378–87,

663–70, respectively. Lindsey's endorsement was quoted by Henry Cordes in *ibid.*, II, 1346–47. The backing of Harper and the Scripps-McRae correspondents was described in the author's interviews with Herbert S. Bigelow and Henry P. Boynton, September 26, 1949 and October 3, 1949. The campaign of the National Civic Federation is reported in O. M. Eidlitz to A. L. Garford, August 1, 1912, Garford Papers. Eidlitz was chairman of the finance committee of the Federation.

55. The votes are recorded in *Proceedings and Debates*, II, 1713, 1793.

56. The debates and votes are recorded, respectively, in *ibid.*, II, 1412–18, 1787; II, 1339–45, 1769. Brown's plea is in *ibid.*, II, 1343. An eight-hour-day law adopted by the Ohio legislature in 1900 (94 O.L. 357) had been held unconstitutional in *Clements Construction Company* v. *City of Cleveland*, 67 Ohio 197 (1903). Eight-hour-day laws had been adopted in Arizona, Oklahoma, New Mexico, California, Idaho, Wyoming, New York, and Massachusetts.

57. The debates, including Brown's speech, and the votes are recorded in *Proceedings and Debates*, II, 1389–97, 1704, 1842.

58. The debates and votes are recorded in *ibid.*, II, 1499–1505, 1928–33.

59. The debates and votes are recorded in *ibid.*, I, 208–23, 259–89, 295–317, 343–53; II, 1783. Such an amendment was necessary because the state debt was limited by the constitution to $750,000.

60. The debates and votes are recorded in *ibid.*, II, 1234–39, 1280–91, 1839.

61. The debates and votes on these three items are recorded, respectively, in *ibid.*, II, 1923, 1981–84, 1998; II, 2006–11; II, 1999–2006, 2019–20, 2056–61, 2073. The convention voted to print the entire pamphlet, known as "The Address to the People," as an advertisement in at least two newspapers of opposite politics in each county of the state once a week for five weeks preceding the special election. Contracts were made with 492 papers for this advertising.

62. *Ohio State Journal*, January 24, 1912. The executive committee was composed of Bigelow, chairman; John Daily of Toledo, Whitlock's secretary; Peter Witt; George F. Burba of Dayton, later secretary to Governor Cox; and Charles E. Mason of Hamilton. See J. M. Eilers to Brand Whitlock, April 2, 1912, Whitlock Papers. Eilers was secretary of the New Constitution League.

63. Support by the delegates themselves is stressed in Mercer, ed., *Ohio Legislative History* [I],447, and in the *Cleveland Plain Dealer*, September 1, 1912. The endorsement by the Democrats and Progressives was reported in the *Ohio State Journal*, September 2, 1912, support by labor and Socialists in *ibid.*, July 15, 1912. Endorsement by Cox and others was noted in the *Toledo News-Bee*, August 13, 20, 1912, the *Cleveland Plain Dealer*, September 1, 1912, the *Dayton Daily News* August 27–28, 1912, and in Cox, *Journey through My Years*, 126. Washington Gladden's open letter and Sunday-evening sermon were printed in the *Ohio State Journal*, August 26 and September 2, 1912, respectively.

64. *Toledo News-Bee, Cleveland Press, Cincinnati Post, Columbus Citizen, Akron Press*, August 1–30, 1912, *passim; Cleveland Plain Dealer*, June 6–August 30, 1912; *Toledo Blade*, August 31, 1912; *Cleveland Leader*, August 22–30, 1912; *Dayton Daily News*, August 1–30, 1912. The *Vindicator*, for example, concentrated on six amendments it considered necessary to bring Ohio "forward in the van of progress": the initiative and referendum, woman

suffrage, good roads, civil service, municipal home rule, and the licensing of saloons (*Youngstown Vindicator*, August 31, 1912. The *Ohio State Journal* maintained a running attack on the initiative and referendum and urged the voters to vote no when in doubt on the assortment of "legislative whimsicalities" (issues for August 15–31, September 2–3, 1912). The *Columbus Dispatch* supported municipal home rule and civil service, but on the eve of the election advised those in doubt to vote no (issues for August 21–30, September 2, 1912). The *Cincinnati Enquirer* issued the same advice to its readers (issue for September 1, 1912).

65. The shifting tactics of the opposition were publicized in the progressive newspapers: *Toledo News-Bee*, August 15, 1912; *Cleveland Leader*, August 15, 1912; *Cleveland Plain Dealer*, August 29–30, 1912; *Toledo Blade*, September 4, 1912; *Dayton Daily News*, August 30, 1912. They were also remarked upon in C. B. Galbreath, "Vote on the Ohio Constitution," *Independent*, LXXIII (December 19, 1912), 1407, and in Clarence Maris to Carmi A. Thompson, July 30, 1912, Hilles Papers. Foote urged businessmen to contribute at the rate of one-tenth of a mill of their capital investment to a fund for educating the people in the constitution, in order to defeat these "radical and socialistic amendments" (Allen R. Foote to members of the Ohio State Board of Commerce, August 1, 12, 1912, in uncatalogued material on the Ohio Constitutional Convention, 1912, Western Reserve Historical Society Library). Foote's tactics in opposing the amendments are further analyzed in Robert H. Bremner, "The Fight for Home Rule," *American Journal of Economics and Sociology*, XI (October, 1951), 107–9.

The convention sought to dispel the false rumor about the justices of the peace by appointing Judges Peck, King, and James Nye to prepare an appropriate statement explaining that only in cities where municipal courts had been established was the office of justice of the peace abolished (*Proceedings and Debates*, II, 2086–92; *Toledo News-Bee*, August 15, 1912; *Cleveland Leader*, August 27, 1912).

66. *Cleveland Plain Dealer*, August 29–September 1, 1912; *Cleveland Leader*, August 15, September 1, 1912. The opposition of the utilities to the municipal home rule amendment is discussed in Mayo Fesler, "Home Rule for Ohio Cities," *National Municipal Review*, I (October, 1912), 714.

67. Allen R. Foote to the members of the Ohio State Board of Commerce, August 20, 1912, in uncatalogued material on the Ohio Constitutional Convention, 1912, Western Reserve Historical Society Library. The United Constitution Committee of Franklin County was one organization to institute a countercampaign. It issued an open letter, containing the motto, "When in doubt, vote yes," signed by Gladden and Thompson. (*Ohio State Journal*, August 15, 1912) The remarks of the correspondent of the *Cleveland Leader* are in the issue of September 1, 1912.

68. Galbreath, "Vote on the Ohio Constitution," 1407.

69. The official tabulation of the vote on each amendment is in the *Report of the Secretary of State of Ohio*, (1912), 668–69. The vote on the amendments has been intensively analyzed in Cushman, "Voting Organic Laws," 214, 222–23. This article is the basis of much of the statistical data which follows. However, this author does not endorse all of Cushman's conclusions. The low vote in Adams County is explained by the disfranchisement, for vote selling of two-thirds of the voters two months after the 1910 election.

70. The twelve counties were Cuyahoga, Hamilton, Franklin, Lorain, Butler, Montgomery, Lucas, Columbiana, Summit, Mahoning, Stark, and

Clark, in which 55 to 85 per cent of the population live in large cities. Half the population of the state was contained in these twelve counties (Cushman, "Voting Organic Laws," 219–20. Cuyahoga County approved all of the amendments except the two mentioned in the text; Franklin and Hamilton each turned down four, Montgomery seven, Stark and Mahoning two, Lorain one, Butler five, and Clark seventeen. In addition to the two proposals which were defeated, the amendments to abolish capital punishment, increase the state indebtedness for good roads, and to modify the tax system received heavy opposition in the urban counties. (*Cleveland Plain Dealer,* September 4, 1912; *Cincinnati Enquirer,* September 4–5, 1912; *Ohio State Journal,* September 6, 1912; *Dayton Daily News,* September 4, 1912; *Youngstown Vindicator,* September 4, 1912)

71. Cushman, "Voting Organic Laws," 220–21.

72. The two amendments adopted by narrow margins were those to make the office of state superintendent of education an appointive office (ratified by a majority of 4,669), and to abolish the justices of the peace in the cities (majority of 11,896). The amendments which had been the most controversial in the convention passed with comfortable to large majorities: change in the judicial system, 20,547; taxation, 19,175; the initiative and referendum, 81,280; home rule, 86,741; civil service, 102,187; direct-primary elections, 166,689; welfare of employees, 163,860; license, 84,536. The reasons for the failure of the four amendments strongly favored by the convention are discussed in Galbreath "Vote on the Ohio Constitution," 1409, and in Clement L. Martzolff, "Ohio: Changes in the Constitution," *American Political Science Review,* VII (November, 1913), 574. The defeat of the amendments affecting women is discussed in N. D. Baker to Brand Whitlock, September 5, 1912; Herbert Bigelow to Brand Whitlock, September 14, 1912, Whitlock Papers; in the *Dayton Daily News,* September 4, 1912; and in Harriet Taylor Upton, "Ohio," in Harper, ed., *The History of Woman Suffrage,* VI, 510–11. The defeat of the good-roads and billboard amendments is discussed in Galbreath, "Vote on the Ohio Constitution," 1409, the prohibition of the death penalty in Baker to Whitlock, Sepember 5, 1912.

73. Ryan, "The Influence of Socialism on the Ohio Constitution," 667. Martzolff echoed the same sentiment in Martzolff, "Ohio: Changes in the Constitution," 573.

74. This was the opinion of leading newspaper correspondents and also of Charles Sawyer, who stated it in his rebuttal to the charges of Ryan (Sawyer, "The Ohio Constitution," 275–79). Robert Cushman, however, in his study, while admitting that those with any desire to be informed had ample opportunity, concluded that the people of Ohio had not been "adequately aroused or sufficiently instructed," and that "thousands based their decisions on snap judgments and ignorance." He claimed that the greatest hindrance to intelligent voting was the form of the constitutional ballot and the misleading titles of some of the amendments. Examples he cited were "Welfare of Employees," the innocuous title given to the radical minimum-wage amendment; and "Eligibility of Women for Certain Offices," which actually provided for limited office-holding, but which ignorant voters may have supposed permitted women to become legislators or even governor. The most glaring instance was the way in which the electorate voted on amendment forty-one, "The Schedule." Anyone favoring one or more amendments should have voted for the schedule setting the effective date for them, but it was defeated in twenty-six counties where the voters approved one to

twenty-five amendments. The title failed to convey its true purpose. (Cushman, "Voting Organic Laws," 226–29) On the other hand, and contrary to Cushman's view, there can be no doubt about the clarity of either the title or the official explanation of some of the most controversial amendments, e.g., the "Initiative and Referendum," "Abolition of Capital Punishment," "Woman Suffrage," "Primary Elections," "Civil Service," "Municipal Home Rule," and "Licensing of Saloons." These were all subjects of special editorial comment and discusson by those opposed as well as by those in favor. The fact that some were defeated and others approved by large majorities adds further support to the view that the voters were exercising a thoughtful, discriminating judgment.

75. *Dayton Daily News,* September 5, 1912; *Toledo News-Bee,* September 4, 1912; *Columbus Dispatch,* September 3, 1912. A recent study of the non-voter throws further light on this subject. This analysis indicates that those with the most education and economic security (i.e., conservatives) provide a greater percentage of the vote in elections than any other group. (Gordon M. Connelly and Harry H. Field, "The Non-Voter—Who He is, What He Thinks," *Public Opinion Quarterly,* VIII [1944], 175–87).

76. These, with the addition of two defeated amendments, woman suffrage and the abolition of capital punishment, were the proposals for which they had campaigned intensively. (Stockbridge, "Ohio Wide Awake," 696; the author's interview with Herbert S. Bigelow, September 26, 1949)

CHAPTER THIRTEEN

THE ELECTION OF 1912

THE POLITICAL CALENDAR for 1912 was unquestionably one of the most crowded in the annals of Ohio. The voters were asked not only to follow the debates in the constitutional convention and to vote upon its work but also to participate in a series of political contests rare in excitement and drama. The normal interest which the bracketing of a presidential election with that of a governor aroused was heightened by the avowed aspirations of two native sons for the highest office in the land—William Howard Taft, seeking a second term, and Judson Harmon, a first—and by the entry into the race of Theodore Roosevelt, whose candidacy Ohio men did much to promote. The contests began before the year was born and continued with little abatement until the polls closed in November.

The two contending hosts in the political arena were much the same as those in the constitutional convention: progressives on one side, conservatives on the other. But whereas the progressives controlled the constitution-making body, conservatives dominated the machinery of the two major parties in Ohio. The task of militant reformers was to push out the Old Guard, remold the party organization to reflect the spirit of the times, and drive to victory. Having achieved a partial triumph in reframing the fundamental law, progressives were reinforced in their determination to win success in full measure.

In such an organizational struggle the odds were against the reformers. They were long on enthusiasm and earnestness, but short on political skill and shrewdness. Furthermore, the conservatives had a strong advantage in their control of both the party machinery and patronage. President Taft had followed the time-honored rule of his predecessors, using federal appointments to build a personal following and to insure a favorable press at home. His conservative faction dominated the Republican state central committee. He enjoyed the favor of the men who had led the party for the past half-dozen years: Senator Theodore E. Burton, Charles Dick, Warren G. Harding, and George B. Cox's successor, Rudolph Hynicka. "Federal nephews," such as Maurice Maschke in Cleveland, kept city organizations loyal. Arthur I. Vorys, an old personal friend, whose one public office had been state insurance superintendent, acted as state manager for the President.[1] The Taft movement, geared as it primarily was to the promotion of his candidacy, was to prove very embarrassing to the party in Ohio. Since no move could be made without considering its effect on the presidential aspirant, state Republican leaders frequently found their hands tied and compromise impossible with the anti-Taft, progressive wing.

On the Democratic side conditions were comparable. Governor Harmon controlled both the state executive and central committees; and he had rewarded the faithful with state jobs. Senator Atlee Pomerene, once an opponent, now a friend, distributed what few federal crumbs he received in a manner that would not embarrass the Governor. Since 1910 Harmon had been pointing toward the presidency. A proven vote getter, an able administrator, and governor of a key state, he was a highly "available" candidate. Yet the radical wing had tolerated but never accepted him as one of them. It had become all the more apparent since he had been governor that his fixed convictions were at odds with their own thinking and aims. He seemed to them to be another Taft in the conservative bent of his temperament and outlook.[2] Many Democratic progressives now felt Harmon's usefulness had passed and were ready to aid in the eclipse of his political fortunes. Again this struggle, which was pitched principally at the national level, had strong repercussions on the state's internal politics.

The first to organize against the conservatives were progressive Republicans in the old Western Reserve, the party's chief center of discontent. At a dinner meeting in Cleveland on November

3, 1911, attended by three hundred insurgents, a temporary organization called the Ohio Progressive Republican League was established; it was soon expanded with branches in twenty-four counties and headquarters in Columbus. United in their hostility to Taft, the members were divided on whom to support as an alternate. One faction, committed to Robert M. La Follette, had the initial advantage, for the Wisconsin senator was an avowed candidate, and his leading Ohio champions, Judge Robert M. Wanamaker of Akron and John D. Fackler, took charge of the League's early organization.[3] Both were honest, sincere progressives, but neither was politically well known.

Wanamaker had a high reputation on the bench locally. Fackler had gained some prominence in campaigning as a delegate to the constitutional convention, where he received his first practical political as well as legislative experience. He had been converted to the progressive cause in 1905 following Charles E. Hughes's life insurance exposures in New York. Employed at the time as the Ohio supervisor of the Equitable Life Assurance Society, Fackler was appalled by the scandalous practices of the several companies, including his own, which the Hughes investigation disclosed. Not only did he resign his position, but he also sought to explore the basic causes of such evils. He turned to Henry George's *Progress and Poverty* and, like so many before him, became a convert to the single tax. Born and reared in the Republican fold, Fackler was impelled by old loyalties to remain there rather than ally himself with the other Cleveland single taxers in the Democratic party. By 1912 his private law practice and favorable investments had given him the independent means to pursue his latent political ambitions.[4]

The La Follette partisans were challenged by other insurgents rallying to the banner of Theodore Roosevelt. The latter faction were in an awkward position because their candidate was undeclared. Their tactics, therefore, were to work privately to persuade the reluctant former President to declare his candidacy openly and meanwhile to head off any endorsement of La Follette. They accused "the honorable judge from Summit County [Wanamaker] and the would-be lime-light performer by the name of Fackler" of supporting the Wisconsin reformer to feather their own political nests.[5]

It was not long before the pro-Roosevelt group, in an effort to solve their dilemma, were forcing the Colonel to make a decision. At a Garfield Club anniversary banquet in Youngstown on November 20, which Roosevelt had declined to attend, his name was presented as the next party nominee. Although the honor of making the speech was allotted to John J. Sullivan, James R. Garfield, who was present and also spoke, spearheaded the movement in behalf of his patron and hero. Roosevelt, while privately stating that such an endorsement made him uncomfortable, did nothing to stop it.

Open declarations for Roosevelt began to snowball. The *Cleveland Leader* ran a long front-page article on November 26 booming his candidacy and quoting favorable comments in the nation's press on the trial balloon launched at the Garfield Club dinner.[6] The political world took due note of this, since the owner of the *Cleveland Leader* was Dan R. Hanna, Mark's son, whose attachment was important, if only for his name and fortune.[7]

Why Dan Hanna strayed from the regular Republican reservation is a moot point. During the campaign Taft and other speakers openly accused him of turning against the administration because Attorney-General George W. Wickersham had pressed a law suit against him personally, as well as against his company, for violating the federal statute prohibiting rebates. A close friend is convinced that this suit had little to do with his decision. According to this source, Hanna was attracted by the Colonel's colorful personality and drive and his known record as a vote getter and fighter.[8] Mark's son was not the only large industrialist to be so enamored. Though unsympathetic to some of Roosevelt's stump pronouncements, these men concluded on the basis of his tariff and antitrust policies that he was "safe" as far as big business was concerned.[9]

The editor of the *Cleveland Leader*, Nathaniel C. Wright, also operated the *Toledo Blade* under a lease arrangement. For the past two years he had been privately critical of Taft and jumped at the opportunity to support the dynamic, popular Roosevelt. Thus another Ohio newspaper soon joined its voice to the clamor for the Colonel.[10]

As though it were not surprising enough to find Dan Hanna an insurgent, Ohioans really rubbed their eyes when they read

Walter Brown's announced preference for Roosevelt in a letter to John Fackler, printed in the *Cleveland Leader* on the morning of December 3, 1911. Chairman of the Republican State Central Committee, public-utility lawyer and lobbyist, foe of Jones and Whitlock, Brown had been tagged as the most regular of the regulars. His campaign and election to the constitutional convention on a mildly progressive program had furnished scarcely more than a hint of the action he took now.

Speculation was rife as to why this professional politician had swapped horses. It was alleged that he had been rebuffed by Taft on patronage matters and that he believed Roosevelt, a fighter with a large personal following and access to unlimited funds, would be the better candidate to help carry the local ticket. The *Toledo News-Bee* credited Brown's shift to his shrewdness and to the trend of election results which "convinced him that to stay in politics, a man must be a Progressive. So Brown, at the eleventh hour, apparently on his deathbed politically speaking, renounced standpattism and accepted the new life of progressivism." To sincere radicals in the Ohio Progressive Republican League, Brown's decision was something of an embarrassment; Fackler gave him a peremptory rebuff.[11]

Though the Ohio boom for Roosevelt enjoyed the distinction of being the first, it was soon repeated in state after state. These demonstrations were reinforced by a barrage of letters, pleading with him to become a candidate. On December 1 he yielded and told his friends to work for his nomination, but still he shied from a public announcement.[12] When, therefore, 150 delegates assembled in Columbus on New Year's Day, 1912, to launch formally the Ohio Progressive Republican League, his followers were still in a difficult position. Hanging over their heads was the threat of a La Follette endorsement, which they were as determined as before to prevent.

In the four days preceding the meeting, the Wisconsin senator had made a whirlwind tour of the state, accompanied by Judge Wanamaker and Fackler. Although La Follette confined his remarks to promoting the progressive cause in general, Senators Moses E. Clapp of Minnesota and John D. Works of California entered Ohio to urge his open endorsement by the League. The strategy of the Roosevelt forces, on the other hand, was to keep the door open so that the Colonel might enter at the propitious moment. Gifford Pinchot, who had been an early La Follette supporter but who was now hopeful that Roosevelt might soon declare his candidacy, came to Ohio to help assure the success of their maneuver.[13]

In this endeavor the pro-Roosevelt men were favored by the sentiment among the delegates that the League's task was to form a cohesive organization, not to divide its ranks at the outset by a rash decision. Though La Follette was the overwhelming choice of the members, they refused to commit the League to his candidacy. Instead, they adopted a resolution, prepared by Pinchot and Garfield, opposing Taft and pledging support of a progressive Republican for president, whether he be La Follette, Roosevelt, or someone else. Judge Wanamaker, who had been won over to this compromise, said in the closing speech before the vote, "You don't need a man when you have a principle. Be anti-Taft. That's enough to win on." Not all the La Follette men, however, were appeased; Edward Doty made the laconic comment, "Anti-Taft is our candidate now."

After the burning question of the endorsement was disposed of, the convention adopted a platform drafted by progressives from the Western Reserve, endorsing Roosevelt's planks on the tariffs and trusts: a downward revision of the tariff while preserving the protective principle, the measure of which was the differences in wages and raw material at home and abroad; the regulation but not the elimination of trusts and the prevention of recognized wrongs in corporate practices. In addition, the platform advocated the direct election of senators, the Pinchot-Roosevelt conservation policy, and a graduated income tax. On state issues it recommended direct primaries, the initiative and referendum, the short ballot, presidential-preference primaries, the supervision of all corporations in the state by a commission, and the elimination of delays in judicial procedure. It was silent on such controversial points as the recall, the commission plan of city government, and labor welfare legislation. Only in the platform did state affairs receive any attention, so concerned was the convention with the presidential question.[14]

Politicians and the press throughout the country interpreted the decision of the Ohio Progressive Republican League as a silent bid for Roosevelt. A *Cleveland Leader* editorial endeavored to eradicate any doubt on the point by declaring that

359

all the La Follette partisans had accomplished through their ill-advised effort to press his endorsement was to reveal the weakness of his support and "to give added evidence to the entire country of the tremendous hold that Theodore Roosevelt has on the minds, hearts, and hopes of Ohio Republicans."[15]

Despite the compromise adopted, the conference failed to close the rift between the two factions, which continued throughout January. Pro-Roosevelt men were reluctant to contribute financially to the League because the important officers were La Follette supporters; many of the latter were lukewarm to the organization because of the failure to endorse their candidate.[16] The dilemma was finally resolved by an unforeseen event.

On the night of February 3, in Philadelphia, La Follette suffered a nervous breakdown. Exhausted by incessant campaigning on top of his senatorial duties, he collapsed at the end of a long, rambling, repetitive address before the Periodical Publishers' Association in which he had denounced the newspaper and magazine publishers for failing to resist the lure of commercialism. The newspapers promptly interpreted the incident as the end of his campaign for the presidency, and many of his friends concurred. The feeling had been gaining ground among his Eastern supporters that he could never beat Taft, and they had been hoping for some time for his withdrawal. They wished to shift to Theodore Roosevelt, who appeared to be the only man capable of defeating the President. To them the occasion promised a means of escape from their uneasy situation. Hence they quickly accepted the release that La Follette's manager offered them from their commitment to the senator's candidacy, and never returned, even after the candidate himself later repudiated the action taken in his name.[17]

The Ohio La Follette men, in an endeavor to make their own estimate of the situation, sent John Fackler to Washington to interview the ailing candidate and try to persuade him to drop from the race and declare for Roosevelt. As "Old Bob" was beginning to weaken, according to the Cleveland lawyer, "Young Bob," then a boy of fifteen, entered the room and by a few words stiffened his father's spine. Nevertheless Fackler was convinced that the candidate was too exhausted to conduct the kind of vigorous campaign that might have a chance of success. Upon his return he issued from League headquarters a statement urging that Roosevelt be drafted and announcing that the organization would work toward the selection of delegates pledged to his nomination.[18]

The Colonel immeasurably strengthened himself with the Ohio progressive Republicans by his appearance in the state on February 21 to address the constitutional convention. His message was widely praised in the state newspapers. The conservative *Ohio State Journal* expressed hearty sympathy for the "square deal idea," which occupied so much of the speech. It also found his endorsement of the initiative and referendum guarded enough, and his invention of the recall of judicial decisions not "a startling proposition," though its practical application suggested many doubts. The partisan *Cleveland Leader* and *Toledo Blade* eulogized Roosevelt as "an evangel of justice, a crusader for human rights whose high mission was to kindle a finer enthusiasm for truth and equity, a surer devotion to ethical as well as material progress. . . . "[19]

As important as the speech itself was the opportunity the occasion afforded for "politicking." As the Colonel stood by grinning in the halls of the Capitol, a member of his entourage pinned "Roosevelt 1912" buttons on each newcomer. Meetings were arranged with key figures in the state progressive Republican movement. He lunched with Washington Gladden and entrained for Cleveland with Arthur L. Garford, Nat Wright, and "several other friends and associates," who had a chance "to go over all matters of interest with him." In high spirits the Colonel told these intimates that "on Monday next . . . [he intended to] 'throw his hat into the ring and continue the bout until he is either declared the winner or takes the count.'" On February 25 he publicly announced his candidacy.[20] Ohio progressive Republicans, now united save for a few recalcitrants, were jubilant that they had such a vigorous and compelling leader to guide them. They began preparing in earnest to organize the state for the selection of Roosevelt delegates to the national convention.

On the Democratic side a similar protest movement against party conservatism had been gaining momentum. The day after the Republican insurgents met in Columbus a group of Democratic malcontents assembled, and, not to be outdone by their opponents, even lifted their title, founding the Ohio Progressive

Democratic League. Led by such old Bryanites as John J. Lentz, Harvey Garber, and William W. Durbin, this rump organization boomed the Great Commoner for president in place of Ohio's favorite son, Judson Harmon. Even though their hostility to the Governor arose over narrow, selfish points of patronage, and their progressivism was suspect, they proved an important force in shifting party control from conservatives to sincere reformers.[21]

At first, however, the anti-Harmon movement could make little headway. Although journalists and radicals might charge the Governor with conservatism, it was difficult to convince the rank and file of this because the legislative record was such as to conceal his real nature. On the face of it his administration seemed sanely progressive. As his opponents were searching about for a point of attack, the Governor made one for them. On February 8 he delivered his fateful address to the constitutional convention, opposing the initiative and referendum and other innovations. Admirable as it was to place personal conviction above political expediency, he nevertheless openly revealed that he was out of tune with the progressive thinking of the day. From that hour Harmon's chances for the presidential nomination and continued leadership of the Ohio Democracy were doomed.[22]

Pseudo-progressives were now joined by sincere reformers who could attack the Governor on principle. Newton Baker accused him of betraying the party platform, which had twice endorsed direct legislation. Others attacked him as a minion of Wall Street, an ultra-reactionary. The report was broadcast that Harmon, contrary to the statement of his managers, had taken little part in either promoting or guiding to passage the progressive measures adopted during his administration.[23]

Still, it was one thing to cast Harmon aside and another to agree on an alternate. Bryan had lost favor with many of the urban reformers, especially the Cleveland group. Baker's favorite was the scholar-in-politics, Woodrow Wilson, his former teacher at Johns Hopkins, who had moved from the presidency of Princeton University to the governorship of New Jersey in 1910. Although he had belonged to the conservative, anti-Bryan wing of the party and had been elected with the backing of the Democratic machine, Wilson as governor experienced a political transformation, turned on the bosses, and made an enviable record in pushing progressive legislation through the state legislature. By the end of February the Scripps-McRae papers were encouraging the Wilson candidacy. Although the same division threatened the Democratic insurgents as split their Republican counterpart, a rift was avoided by Bryan's refusal to run and the voluntary decision of his Ohio followers to back Wilson.[24] As the Democrats approached the primaries, the Harmon forces, once confident of an easy victory, were aware they had a severe challenge to meet from the combined Wilson-Bryan faction.

Because of the familiar political maxim that a contender for a presidential nomination must carry his home state, the pre-primary campaigns in Ohio attracted national interest. The Republican contest, in particular, caught the public imagination. A President challenged by an ex-President in itself made good copy, but it was the bitter, emotionally overcharged character of the campaign which made it sensational.

Taft was determined to show the nation that his prestige in his home state was as great in 1912 as it had been in 1908. Roosevelt was equally determined to shatter the illusion. Making two separate tours, Taft traveled 3,000 miles in the state and spoke to more than a hundred audiences, who were too often stolid and unfriendly. Roosevelt covered 1,750 miles of Ohio terrain, delivering seventy-five talks. The presidential reserve was laid aside as Taft cuffed his opponent with verbal blows, anathematizing him as a "flatterer," "demagog," "honey-fugler," "egoist," and "bolter." Roosevelt, who had proposed "to make the issue one of principle, and not of personal abuse," was soon answering in kind, branding Taft as a "standpatter" who was "boss-controlled." La Follette, who also made a two-day tour, added his word of derision. After attacking both his rivals for their failure to cut out the parasitic trusts, he concluded that the task was beyond the skill of "a rough rider or an amiable, easy going fat man."[25]

The primary-election returns were a blow to Taft and a disappointment to La Follette. Roosevelt won thirty-four of the district delegates, Taft only eight, and La Follette none. The President's native county, Hamilton, accounted for four of the eight that he received; the remaining delegates were scattered.[26] With such overwhelming popular sentiment in the Colonel's favor, the Roosevelt forces fully expected to capture the six delegates-at-large to be selected at the Republican state convention called for this purpose on June 3. But the party professionals remained loyal to President Taft, and, though they could not control the primary election, they could dictate to the convention.

On the eve of the meeting the delegates were divided: 349 for Taft, 335 for Roosevelt, and 74 uninstructed, 53 of whom were from Cuyahoga County. Although local leaders on both sides would have preferred a compromise to promote harmony, both of the candidates turned a deaf ear to such overtures. To salvage some remnant of his prestige, the President had warned his friends "not [to] consider for a moment the suggestion of a compromise," for "the principles that we represent are too important to the country to lose anything by our voluntary concessions." With equal emphasis the Colonel declared, "Any attempt to give Mr. Taft a single delegate-at-large would mean to sanction a deliberate effort to defraud the people and by a trick to nullify their expressed will."[27]

When the crucial vote was taken, the six Taft candidates were elected, 390½ to 362½. In defiance of the expressed sentiment of Cleveland Republicans, Maurice Maschke, the local boss, had delivered to Taft 48 of the 53 Cuyahoga County delegates.[28] The first betrayal of the Roosevelt forces had been committed. The only crumb of satisfaction to the Colonel's partisans was Walter Brown's re-election as chairman of the Republican State Central Committee.[29] Still the outcome left scant hope that the progressive wing could control the nominations in the second state convention that was to meet in July, after the national party conclave in Chicago.

The Democratic pre-primary campaign was less of a personal vendetta than that of the Republicans, for Wilson made no tour himself. The one major out-of-state speaker was Bryan, who made a two-day swing to support Wilson, flaying Harmon as "the prince of reactionaries," "friend of Wall Street," and a man who "might do in a stone age; [but] he won't do now." In the final week Harmon stumped the state, cracking back at Bryan, as well as publicizing his own role as a trust buster when he was President Cleveland's attorney-general.[30]

At the May primary elections the Democratic voters were given a separate ballot on which to express their presidential preference, the popular choice to bind the delegates-at-large elected by the state convention. Also in many congressional districts they had an opportunity to choose between delegates pledged to Harmon and those to Wilson. However, in the two Cleveland congressional districts the Wilson candidates were unopposed; in the Cincinnati districts Harmon men were the only ones on the ticket; while in the Dayton congressional area the two delegates were undeclared. This makeshift arrangement produced some anomalies. Hamilton County (Cincinnati) gave Wilson a slight margin on the presidential-preference vote, while electing the four unchallenged Harmon men. Lucas County (Toledo) favored the New Jersey governor two to one; yet the two congressional district delegates were split between Harmon and Wilson.[31]

The vote gave cold comfort to Harmon and his backers. He had received a bare majority of 6,000 in the state preferential primary out of 194,000 ballots cast. Although he was thus assured of the six delegates-at-large, and, in addition, twenty-three of the delegates from the congressional districts, he had failed to show commanding strength in his native state, so necessary for the success of his presidential aspirations. The pro-Wilson wing, on the other hand, had demonstrated considerable power in winning nineteen of the district delegates for their candidate. The outcome for that faction was particularly propitious in Cuyahoga County, where a large preferential vote had been mustered for Wilson and four delegates pledged to him had been elected, including Newton Baker. Such success revealed that the Cleveland mayor was the heir, in fact as well as in name, of Tom Johnson, and had earned the right to direct the progressive forces which his predecessor had marshaled.[32]

The Democrats set the date of their state convention for June 3 and decided to complete their business in one session instead of resorting to the split-session plan adopted by their opponents. Since the first of the year the main interest of the party leaders had focused on the selection of a nominee for governor to succeed Harmon, who had ruled himself out in order to run for president. The Scripps-McRae papers began hinting that Herbert Bigelow was the man for the job, without arousing enthusiasm from any quarter. Baker's choice was Oliver E. Hughes, a militant member of the Ohio Public Service Commission, but politically weak. The strongest candidate was

James Middleton Cox, who had the support of Governor Harmon, Edward Hanley, and other state leaders. Such backing, however, made him distasteful to the Cuyahoga County organization.[33]

Cox's success as a vote getter in the Third Ohio Congressional District in 1908 and 1910 had made him an "available" gubernatorial candidate in the eyes of the party hierarchy. In the national House of Representatives his record revealed that he was an astute politician with strong progressive leanings. Also, through a parliamentary ruse he had pushed through appropriations for a new post office building in Dayton. He had succeeded in increasing the subsistence funds for the Soldiers' and Sailors' Home in Montgomery County by $250,000. As a result of his successes, this Republican stronghold cast a majority for him in every precinct in 1910. On national issues he supported a low tariff and the Canadian reciprocity treaty, followed La Follette's liberal views on railroad-rate legislation, and approved the Parcel Post Act. At the time of the House "revolution" he had voted to curb the speaker's powers. He later wrote that it was an exhilarating experience to be in Congress during these years which "witnessed the eclipse of the standpat conservatism represented by the Old Guard leaders about Taft, and the growth of great new progressive forces—a change which I heartily approved and so far as I could assisted."[34]

Though his House record was unimpeachably progressive, his close association with Edward Hanley made him suspect to reformers at home. The doubts that were raised then about the sincerity of Cox's attachment to the radical cause linger on to this day. By implication he has endeavored to answer his detractors in his autobiography, documenting his intellectual development as a progressive.

As early as 1896, when he was a young man of twenty-six, he classed himself as a dissenter in the conservative Republican environment of Ohio. Not only was he a Democrat, an allegiance he had inherited, but he was something more. His experiences as a farm boy, schoolteacher, printer's devil, newspaper reporter, and secretary to a congressman in Washington had made him "a Democrat aligned with the progressive tendencies of the time." He had begun to examine the forces underneath the surface which produced the Panic of 1893, and concluded that "there was a great deal to the Populist movement and the radical philosophy of the West that deserved support."[35]

After he entered the newspaper field in 1898 as the editor-publisher of the *Dayton Daily News* and later of the *Springfield* (Ohio) *News*, he had read all of the muckraking literature of Lincoln Steffens, Ida Tarbell, David Graham Phillips, Ray Stannard Baker, and others. His newspaper activities had made him familiar with Ohio reformers, whose work he watched with interest: Jones and Whitlock in regenerating Toledo, Johnson and his coterie in making Cleveland "a City on a Hill." Although he knew Johnson only slightly, he had praised his leadership and applauded his platform in 1903. When Johnson was defeated, however, his paper did no further crusading for the progressive cause. Always a "sensitive barometer of the political weather," he bided his time.[36]

No doubt it was his political association with the reactionary Hanley, the local Democratic boss, that stopped him from backing a real reform movement in Dayton such as Negley Cochran had nurtured in Toledo. It was Hanley who had backed Cox for Congress in 1908, and the latter had returned the political favor by managing the Dayton boss's senatorial contest in 1910–11. Still this is not to imply that the two men shared a common political viewpoint. Already the young congressman had revealed by his voting record that he leaned toward progressive ideas which were anathema to his old mentor.[37]

During 1911 Cox had continued to give voice to his burgeoning progressive sympathies. In July of that year he strongly endorsed the initiative and referendum and other forms of direct democracy. By fall he was booming the radical Bigelow for the presidency of the constitutional convention.[38] However, Cox's shift from the Hanley camp to that of the progressives had been so rapid that it was little wonder men questioned the sincerity of his conversion. Would he remain a true disciple or would he be a backslider if entrusted with high office?

This was the question uppermost in the minds of dedicated progressives when the Democratic convention met in Toledo on June 3. The Cox managers had organized strong support for their candidate, and it was apparent that he had the nomination unless he was drawn into a long, bitter fight over the unit rule. The Wilson delegates, led by Newton Baker, were prepared to break the traditional Democratic regulation that all delegations to the national convention must vote as a unit for the candidate receiving a majority vote of the group. The Harmon men were as determined to impose it. Though privately sympathetic to the position of the Wilson partisans, Cox held his tongue, resisting efforts by both sides to wheedle a declaration from him, and his managers did their best to prevent a fight from precipitating.

Although a contest did develop, it was not disruptive, partly because the decision was never in doubt, and partly because Baker, who led the minority protest, was not a vindictive man. The Cleveland mayor, after being turned down by the platform committee, carried the fight against the unit rule to the floor by a minority resolution. Despite his protests against the measure as illegal and immoral, the motion to impose it carried 597 to 355. But Baker hoped to reverse this decision by making a second appeal at the party's national convention.[39]

After this potentially explosive issue had been disposed of and harmony had been restored, the convention turned to the nomination of state officers. The honor of placing Cox's name before the convention was bestowed on a fellow townsman, Judge Benjamin F. McCann, and Bigelow made one of the seconding speeches. After the roll call showed that Cox was the unanimous choice, a motion to make the nomination by acclamation was carried. A mighty cheer greeted the proposal, and did not die down until Cox was brought forward to the platform. His ready smile, brisk manner, and youthful appearance made him immediately appealing, and he added to the favorable first impression by proclaiming his faith in a progressive charter and praising the recently completed work of the constitutional convention.

Proceeding to the selection of other candidates, the gathering drafted Hugh Nichols to serve again as lieutenant-governor, Charles Graves as secretary of state, and Timothy Hogan as attorney-general. John P. Brennan was named for the post of state treasurer, A. Victor Donahey for auditor, and Robert M. Crosser for congressman-at-large. Instead of six, twelve delegates-at-large to the national convention, each with half a vote, were hand-picked by Harmon.[40]

Cuyahoga County's support for Cox's nomination had been secured by the acceptance of a progressive platform. Expressing the general aims of restoring government to the people, abolishing privilege, and providing equal opportunity for all, the Democratic declaration advocated specifically the short ballot, direct election of United States senators, adoption of the proposed initiative and referendum amendment, home rule for cities (including municipal operation of all public utilities), ad valorem valuation of utilities in rate-making, reduction of hours of labor for women, restriction of child labor in industry, workmen's compensation, improvement of highways, reform of the state penal institutions, construction of a new penitentiary, and licensing of saloons.[41]

The first reaction of the powerful Scripps-McRae papers to the work of the Democratic state convention was hostile, and Cox was duly apprehensive. The editor of the *Dayton Daily News* echoed Cox's fear, insisting that "politicians are as afraid of them [the Scripps-McRae papers] as a steer is afraid of a gad-fly. They sting politicians very much as the gad-fly stings steers, too." The *Toledo News-Bee* hinted that Cox and the reactionary Harmon forces had pulled a deal on the unit-rule issue, and damned the platform with faint praise. Nevertheless, as a result of Bigelow's intercession and Cox's excellent performance in stumping for the constitutional amendments, this newspaper chain eventually supported him.

The usually noncommittal *Cincinnati Enquirer,* on the other hand, was immediately enthusiastic. It praised the convention for choosing "the brilliant young Congressman" and placing him "upon a platform which he truly represents and for the constituent elements of which he has stood manfully for all of his years of public life." At the same time the *Enquirer* applauded Baker for promising to carry the fight against the unit rule to the national convention.[42]

When the Democrats assembled in Baltimore at the end of June, the Ohio delegation restaged the Columbus contest over that issue. It was well understood that retention of the unit rule would favor the nomination of Judson Harmon and that its defeat would enhance the chances of Woodrow Wilson. The Wilsonian minority tried unsuccessfully to win release from the ironclad rule in the committee on rules. Failing there, they determined to wage a final fight before the whole convention by means of a minority resolution introduced by Wilson's floor manager, Robert L. Henry, and championed fervently by Baker. In a speech that Cox characterized as "one of the greatest efforts of Baker's career," the Cleveland mayor pleaded for the right to be allowed to fulfill his pledge to the people who had elected him to vote for Wilson—a pledge that ought to be inviolate and that no convention should force him to betray. John Weld Peck, a Harmon delegate from Cincinnati, arose to make the principal rejoinder, but he was soon silenced after he mentioned Wilson's name and touched off a demonstration for the New Jersey governor which roared on for a half-hour. When order was restored and the vote taken, the minority resolution passed by the close margin of 565½ to 492⅓. The Wilson faction won with support from Southern delegations pledged to Oscar W. Underwood and a scattering of others committed to Champ Clark. The victory added a much needed nineteen votes to the thin Wilson column. Newton Baker became the idol of the Wilsonians and a national figure overnight.[43] The victory virtually eliminated Harmon and paved the way for the ultimate choice of Wilson, who was nominated on the forty-sixth ballot. Baker was elated by the outcome, since it brought enhanced prestige both to himself and to the progressive Democrats in Ohio. Conversely, Harmon's eclipse at the convention foretold the decline of his own power and that of the conservative wing that he led.[44]

A few days before at Chicago the Republicans had renominated Ohio's other native son, William Howard Taft, for President, an action which precipitated the Roosevelt bolt. "I do not regard successful fraud and deliberate political theft," the Colonel expostulated, "as constituting a title to party regularity, or a claim to the support of any honest man of any party." Taft had received fourteen votes from the Ohio delegation, but the remaining thirty-four members abstained from the balloting in accordance with instructions from the Roosevelt high command. Though James Garfield remained behind in Chicago to assist in the organization of a new Roosevelt party, the rest returned home, noncommital about bolting.[45]

While shaken by the success of the Taft faction both at the first session of the state convention and at the national convention, the progressive Republicans still clung to the hope that they would write the platform and name the state officers at the second state meeting scheduled for July 1. Their nominee for chief executive was Arthur L. Garford, a successful industrialist and business promoter in Elyria who had been a rock-ribbed Republican all his life, serving on local and state committees and always contributing liberally to campaign chests. Ever since 1910 he had cherished an ambition to be governor, and had been encouraged by his intimate friend, Nat C. Wright, who gave him the support of the *Toledo Blade* and *Cleveland Leader*. Garford's business success and hostility to extreme radicalism, combined with his reputation as a public benefactor and friend of labor, made him a strong candidate. Nor did it hurt him with many of his party progressives that he was a favorite of the powerful Anti-Saloon League.[46]

His chances of nomination hung on the success of a compromise with the Taft partisans, who would control the second session as they had the first. The shrewd Walter Brown was made the negotiator for the progressives, Senator Theodore Burton for the conservatives. When the Senator demanded unqualified endorsement of Taft and the work of the Chicago convention as the price of support for Garford—impossible terms for the progressives—the deal fell through.[47]

The voting began on the second day of the Columbus convention, Garford leading on the first three ballots because the Taft men split their vote between two candidates. On the fourth ballot the conservatives swung to Judge Edmond B. Dillon, a dark horse, who won the nomination on the next round. The platform praised Taft and the proceedings at Chicago. The only bid made by the conservative majority to pacify the progressives in the party was to nominate John J. Sullivan, a charter member of the Ohio Progressive Republican League, for secretary of state. The rest of the slate included such stalwarts as Robert B. Brown, lieutenant-governor; Freeman T. Eagleson, attorney-general; and Edward M. Fullington, auditor—all identified with the Old Guard. The progressives departed, somewhat solaced by having forced the reactionaries to turn to the politically weak Judge Dillon, "who," in the opinion of Garford, "[could not] possibly command the strength of the party and very little, if any, of the progressive vote of the state."[48]

After this final defeat the Roosevelt partisans in Ohio had no plans for the future. Garford left for a sojourn in Europe, and

Walter Brown was as silent as a sphinx. Yet within six weeks events elsewhere had resolved the issue for them. The new Progressive party had been launched at Chicago on August 5 and had nominated Theodore Roosevelt for president and Hiram Johnson as his running mate. The reform wing now had a national organization and two inspired standard-bearers.[49]

Even before the new party had been formed, the Republican gubernatorial nominee, Judge Dillon, had concluded that his party was irreconcilably divided and formally withdrew his candidacy. The Taft men might have turned the awkward situation to their own advantage had they chosen as Dillon's replacement a man acceptable to the Roosevelt wing. Such a choice would have placed the Colonel's friends in a dilemma and might have divided their ranks. But the Taft majority on the Republican State Central Committee, to whom the selection was delegated, passed over the one man of their group who was also agreeable to the Roosevelt faction, Ulysses G. Denman, and instead nominated on August 10 Robert B. Brown, a Zanesville publisher, whose newspaper had been outspoken against the Colonel in the primary campaign. A separate Progressive party organization and campaign in Ohio was thus virtually assured.[50]

Walter Brown and seven other minority members resigned from the state central committee; ten days later he and Garford publicly left the Republican fold and declared their allegiance to the new Progressive party; and on August 20 Garfield issued a call for a convention of the Ohio Progressive party to meet in Columbus on September 4. All supporters of the national Progressive party ticket, whatever their former political affiliations, were invited to attend.[51]

The gathering in Memorial Hall, Columbus, was comparable to the Chicago convention which had nominated Roosevelt. There was the same spirit of mission among the rank and file of delegates. Many of those present had never officially attended a state convention before, and thought of themselves as soldiers on the firing line, battling for the Progressive party cause. The first session opened with a blessing pronounced by Washington Gladden, the reciting of the Lord's Prayer in unison, and the singing of "America." Walter Brown then welcomed the delegates, and James Garfield, temporary and later permanent chairman, delivered the keynote address.

On the following day, the convention, after listening to a two-hour speech by Hiram Johnson, nominated: Arthur L. Garford for governor by acclamation; L. J. Tabor, a Grange member also endorsed by labor, for lieutenant-governor; John L. Sullivan, who resigned from the Republican ticket, for secretary of state; William Kirtley, Jr., another renegade from the Republican slate, for treasurer; Robert R. Nevin, for attorney-general; Charles L. Allen, for auditor; and Robert M. Wanamaker, for justice of the supreme court. The entire panel was composed of former Republicans; Democrats were ignored because no prominent ones had joined the cause.[52] Brand Whitlock, whom the *Toledo News-Bee* in August had tried to boom as the Progressive nominee for governor, briefly flirted with the idea of associating himself with the new party, but after consulting friends held firm to his national and state Democratic allegiance.[53]

The platform was similar to the Democratic one on state planks, strongly emphasizing a number of labor reforms although omitting endorsement of either workmen's compensation or minimum-wage legislation. It supported the national Progressive party program, denounced the two old parties as "boss-ridden and machine controlled," and insisted that "twentieth century problems must be solved by a twentieth century party."[54]

In spite of the enthusiasm the Progressive state convention had generated, it was an ominous sign that so many of Ohio's most militant reformers were absent. To be sure, most were Democrats. But such Democratic converts as Bigelow and Whitlock were not tempted to throw in their lot with the new party; John Fackler, who had organized the anti-Taft revolt, had been brushed aside; Lawrence K. Langdon, radical legislator, had remained in the Republican party.

Not one of the major figures who were to guide the Ohio Progressive party had a strong intellectual commitment to the reform program; they were progressive in name only. Garfield's attachment to the Roosevelt cause was more personal than ideological; Garford and Brown were governed by political expediency, the one to satisfy a long-felt aspiration for high office, the other to recoup his prestige at home. So also, no deep-seated reforming zeal prompted the two principal financial backers, Dan Hanna and Henry H. Timken, a Canton manufacturer of roller bearings, to loosen their purse strings. They had become convinced that the Progressive party leaders were "safe" men, protectors of big business from the threatened onslaught of wild-eyed reformers who would rip down the tariff walls and wipe out the trusts. Such leadership was not peculiar to the Progressive party in Ohio. In Pennsylvania, Boss William Flinn, of Pittsburgh, was as important a Bull Moose organizer as Amos and Gifford Pinchot; in Indiana the standpat machine politician, Charles H. Campbell, was equal in significance to Albert J. Beveridge; and in Michigan the leading Roosevelt partisan was Truman Newberry, a conservative who was later involved in an election fraud.[55]

When the campaign opened on September 20, the gubernatorial candidates of all three parties had been abundantly publicized in the press, but the Democrat, James M. Cox, was the best known and most popular with the voters. He had spent the summer campaigning for the constitutional amendments, ingratiating himself with the progressive majority, and sincerely welcoming the opportunity to help in the regeneration of the state. Although he had not courted the support of conservatives, his success as a newspaper publisher tended to soften their hostility towards his advanced opinions. Furthermore, he had the strongest backing from the metropolitan dailies.[56]

It was auspicious for the Democrats that at their opener in Columbus, where Woodrow Wilson was the principal speaker, Judson Harmon presided as chairman, an indication that the Governor's faction was willing to overlook past differences and not knife the national or state ticket out of spite. Also on the program were Cox, Newton Baker, who performed yeoman service throughout the campaign, James Campbell, and Senator Thomas P. Gore of Oklahoma. The gubernatorial candidate devoted his address to state issues, endorsing the Toledo platform plank by plank and promising a compulsory workmen's compensation law. His major theme, repeated again and again in the campaign, was that human values should be raised above the dollar standard, that mankind deserved a greater measure of justice.[57]

Garford and other Progressive party orators, who had appropriated this same theme as their own, accused Cox of stealing their principles and of being an opportunist, and made the

374

most of his old association with Edward Hanley. The Democratic nominee retaliated, asking Garford why, if he was such a sincere reformer, he had spent the summer at a French spa, while he, Cox, was campaigning for the constitutional amendments? The Republican strategy was to attack Roosevelt, criticize the Democratic state platform, and praise Harmon for his conservatism.[58]

A major problem of all three parties was to keep alive the interest of a public satiated by the many campaigns within the past year. Not even the strategem of introducing big-name orators had aroused the electorate to a real pitch of enthusiasm. The chief effort of the Democrats was to get out their normal vote, which would insure them the victory, with the Republicans split two ways.[59]

When the polls closed on election day, November 5, it was evident that the citizenry was politically fatigued. The three-cornered race for the presidency might have been expected to draw a record vote, but actually the total fell behind the 1908 election figures by approximately 85,000. Since the stay-at-homes were about evenly divided among the major parties, the Democratic hopes were realized as they rode to victory with a large plurality over their divided foe. Wilson polled 424,834 votes, Taft, 278,168, and Roosevelt, 229,807—giving Wilson a margin of 146,666 over his nearest competitor. The results in the gubernatorial contest were slightly more advantageous for the Democrats: Cox's vote was 439,323, Robert B. Brown's, 272,500, and Garford's 217,903, with Cox's plurality 166,823.[60]

Whatever expectation the Bull Moose party had of drawing the progressive vote from the Democratic as well as the Republican fold proved ill-founded. While Wilson failed to get some of the independent support Bryan had received in 1908, and Cox's vote fell behind Harmon's in the latter's two campaigns, the overwhelming majority of Democrats, conservative and progressive alike, remained loyal to the party ticket. Cox had a plurality in sixty-nine counties, carrying all the major urban ones except two which went Progressive along with seven others. The once dominant Republicans could muster a plurality in only ten counties. The Democrats elected eighteen of the twenty-one district congressmen, the one congressman-at-large, and a large majority of the state senators and representatives.[61]

Although sorely disappointed at their failure to beat their Republican rivals, the Progressives took comfort from the election returns. For a new party with an incomplete organization and a short time for campaigning, they had made a remarkable race. Their strength was largely concentrated in the northern part of the state; all but one of the counties they carried were in that region. Garford won in Lorain, his home county, but missed by a narrow margin in Lucas, Walter Brown's county, though the Bull Moose party captured several county offices and two seats in the legislature in Lucas. In Cincinnati, Dayton, the city of Hamilton, and the southern rural counties the Republicans were much stronger than the Progressives because of the large personal following of Taft. Garford believed that, had not all the Taft supporters voted the straight ticket, thus making Robert B. Brown the beneficiary of the President's popularity, the gubernatorial returns would have shown a two-to-one margin in favor of the Progressive party's state candidates.[62]

After the election Roosevelt wrote Garfield in characteristic vein, "We have fought a good fight, we have kept the faith, and we have nothing to regret. Probably we have put the ideal a little higher than we can expect the people as a whole to take off-hand." Yet in the opinion of the *Toledo News-Bee* it was not excessive idealism that caused the Progressive party's failure. Its big mistake in Ohio was to place a reform platform in the hands of men who had been brazenly reactionary. If the Bull Moose party was to win in the future, "it must first lose Brown and Hanna and all of their kind." The Progressive party leaders, however, showed little inclination to dispense with the aid of these men. In a letter to Gifford Pinchot, Roosevelt declared that "almost every man of any prominence in this movement has been both a burden and an asset." He was receiving the bitterest attacks against Flinn and Hanna, he said, but, he added, "Our movement in Ohio came to a dead halt until Hanna decided to go with it." The Colonel wrote Walter Brown that Brown alone had made possible the partial success won in Ohio.[63]

The Ohio Progressive party leaders paraded their determination to continue the fight. Their announced immediate objective was to prepare bills embodying platform promises, introduce them in the legislature, and battle for them. If the Democratic majority failed to enact this humanitarian legislation, the Progressives could then turn to the initiative process.[64] The Democrats, however, gave their rivals no opening for complaint; if anything, the Progressives became alarmed by the sweeping extent of the changes the legislature introduced under the leadership of Governor Cox.

1. Arthur L. Garford estimated that there were 250 Republican and independent papers in Ohio, of which 135 to 140 were for Taft. As a partial explanation of the large number of pro-Taft papers, he noted that the President had appointed a large number of editors as postmasters. (A. L. Garford to E. W. Sims, March 7, 1912, Garford Papers) However, a Taft partisan complained that the Republican papers with a large metropolitan circulation were either knocking the President or only giving him lukewarm support (Malcolm Jennings to C. D. Hilles, August 1, 1911, Hilles Papers). On March 30 the Republican State Central Committee voted fifteen to six to endorse Taft (Ohio State Journal [Columbus], March 31, 1912). The President's support from Burton, Dick, and the others was reported in A. L. Garford to Pierre Depew, May 3, 1912, Garford Papers, and in the Cleveland Leader, June 5, 1912, and Ohio State Journal, February 25, 1912.

2. For example, William Finley, chairman of the state executive committee, had been appointed state oil inspector (ibid., March 20, 1912). Pomerene's support was revealed at a Jackson Day banquet on January 7, 1911, when he toasted Harmon as "the candidate of Ohio for the presidency." —ibid., January 8, 1911. In the Democratic state convention of 1910 Harmon had been endorsed as Ohio's favorite son for the presidency (Cleveland Plain Dealer, June 22, 1910). The radical wing's lack of enthusiasm for Harmon was noted in Hale, "Judson Harmon and the Presidency," 14,459, and in Mackoy, "Harmon," 698–99.

3. Wanamaker was chairman and Fackler was secretary of the temporary organization; Fackler also opened the headquarters in Columbus and later became president of the League (Cleveland Leader, November 4, 19–20, 24, December 10, 1911).

4. The author's interview with John D. Fackler, October 7, 1949.

5. A. L. Garford to Lawrence K. Langdon, November 15, 1911; Nathaniel C. Wright to A. L. Garford, November 11, 1911, Garford Papers.

6. John J. Sullivan, who presented Roosevelt's name, was a former district attorney of Cuyahoga County (Cleveland Leader, November 21, 1912). Roosevelt's reaction was stated in Theodore Roosevelt to James R. Garfield, November 24, 1911, in Morison, and Blum, eds., The Letters of Theodore Roosevelt, VII, 411 (also quoted in Mowry, Theodore Roosevelt and the Progressive Movement, 195). The trial balloon for Roosevelt appeared in the Cleveland Leader, November 26, 1911. The Cleveland Leader's quotes were drawn from papers in New York, Salt Lake City, and Akron, suggesting that national interest was not very intense.

7. Hanna purchased the Cleveland Leader in 1910 from Medill McCormick, his brother-in-law, who had owned the paper since 1905 (Shaw, The Plain Dealer, 299–303). The Cleveland capitalist gave further proof of his devotion by purchasing the Cleveland News when the owner refused

to back Colonel Roosevelt. Before buying, Hanna tried to persuade its proprietor, Charles A. Otis, to join the Roosevelt camp. But Otis declined to go along (the author's interview with Charles A. Otis, October 4, 1949).

8. Taft made the charge by implication in a speech at Peebles, Ohio, on May 8, 1912 (*Ohio State Journal,* May 9, 1912). Wickersham also reviewed the charges against Hanna in October during an Ohio tour (*Cleveland Leader,* October 29, 1912). Charles D. Hilles, Taft's campaign manager, in an open letter to John N. Willys, reviewed the whole case. On a report of the findings of the Interstate Commerce Commission, a federal grand jury had brought an indictment for consipracy to violate the rebate prohibitions of the interstate-commerce statute against the M. A. Hanna Company and two of its officers, Dan R. Hanna and Robert L. Ireland, and the Pennsylvania Railroad and its second vice-president, D. T. McCabe. Walter Brown intervened on behalf of Hanna, asking Hilles to see what he could do for the accused man, clearly insinuating that he wanted the indictment quashed. Brown pointed to the money Hanna was pouring into the *Cleveland Leader.* Hilles did investigate and found that the government had such a strong case that the suit could not be dropped. In the trial, Judge John M. Killits of the United States District Court dismissed the personal indictments, which both the attorney-general and the Interstate Commerce Commission stated formally had no merit, and fined the companies $20,000 each. (Charles D. Hilles to John N. Willys, May 12, 1912, Hilles Papers; also printed in the *Ohio State Journal,* May 14, 1912). The Taft partisans were convinced that had the indictment been quashed Hanna would have remained in the President's camp. The close friend who expressed the contrary opinion was Charles A. Otis (the author's interview with Otis, October 4, 1949).

9. Daniel Willard, the president of the Baltimore & Ohio Railroad, thought Roosevelt the safest of the so-called progressives. George W. Perkins, a Morgan partner and a director of United States Steel and the International Harvester corporations, was one of the Colonel's principal backers. (Mowry, *Theodore Roosevelt and the Progressive Movement,* 203–4). Anti-trust suits against these two corporations, begun by Attorney-General Wickersham, had been decisive in Perkins' rebellion against Taft and switch to Roosevelt (John A. Garraty, *Right-Hand Man: The Life of George W. Perkins* [New York, 1957], 243–59).

10. Wright and Harry S. Talmadge operated the *Toledo Blade* on a lease arrangement from 1908 until Wright's death in 1923. Dan Hanna never owned any interest in the *Blade.* (Grove Patterson to the author, March 20, 1950) Wright's critical view of Taft and preference for Roosevelt were revealed in N. C. Wright to A. L. Garford, January 5, March 6, 1910, Garford Papers, and in a memorandum to C. D. Hilles from Gus J. Karger, May 3, 1911, Hilles Papers. In December, 1911, Wright ran a poll among Republican voters, mostly in the northern part of the state, which purported to show that 71 per cent favored Roosevelt (*Cleveland Leader* and *Toledo Blade,* December 5, 1911).

11. To President Taft's half brother, Brown explained that in shifting his support to Roosevelt he had been motivated only by a consideration for "the welfare of the Republican party as I see it," and, further, that he believed the party could not hope to win with anyone other than the Colonel. See W. F. Brown to Charles P. Taft, January 27, 1912, in the Walter F. Brown Papers (MSS in the Ohio Historical Society, Columbus [hereafter referred to as W. F. Brown Papers]). The other explanations for Brown's

shift were first offered in the *Ohio State Journal,* December 4, 1911, and repeated in substance in the *Cleveland Plain Dealer,* August 20, 1912. Taft partisans also insisted that Brown was angry because the administration had refused to drop the Hanna indictment (*Ohio State Journal,* May 14, 1912). Brown had privately expressed his dissatisfaction with Taft a year previously (W. F. Brown to C. D. Hilles, November 26, 1910, Hilles Papers). *The Toledo News-Bee's* statement appeared in the issue for November 9, 1911. Sam Cohn, one of the Republican Old Guard leaders in Toledo, agreed with the *News-Bee's* explanation (memorandum to C. D. Hilles from Gus J. Karger, November 27, 1911, Hilles Papers). Fackler's rebuff was reported in the *Ohio State Journal,* December 28, 1911.

12. Mowry, *Theodore Roosevelt and the Progressive Movement,* 195–96.

13. *Ibid.,* 200–201; *Ohio State Journal,* December 27–31, 1911; January 2, 1912; *Cleveland Leader,* December 27, 1911. Pinchot's undercover work for Theodore Roosevelt during December is described in M. Nelson McGeary, *Gifford Pinchot: Forester-Politician* (Princeton, N.J., 1960), 219–20.

14. The convention was copiously reported in the *Toledo Blade,* January 2, 1912. The Wanamaker quotation was in *ibid.,* January 2, 1912, the Doty quotation in the *Ohio State Journal,* January 2, 1912. The full text of the platform was published in the *Cleveland Leader,* November 20, 1911. An off-the-record poll of the delegates indicated that sentiment for La Follette was strong among them, but they voted down a resolution to commit the convention to him, thirty-two to fifty-two, and, instead, supported almost unanimously the compromise resolution that was adopted on the endorsement question.

15. *Cleveland Leader,* January 3, 1912. The pro-Roosevelt interpretation also appeared in editorials in the *Boston Transcript, Pittsburgh Leader, Washington Star,* and *Washington Times,* reprinted in the *Cleveland Leader,* January 5, 1912.

16. The rift was reported in the *Ohio State Journal,* January 23, February 3, 1912.

17. *Ibid.,* February 4, 6, 1912. An eyewitness account of La Follette delivering his speech and the audience's hostile reaction is contained in Robert S. Maxwell, ed., "A Document on the Progressive Campaign of 1912 [Henry A. Cooper's memorandum], "*Mississippi Valley Historical Review,* XXXVI (June, 1949), 113–15. Amos Pinchot, William Flinn, Walter Weyl, and a number of others shifted their allegiance from La Follette to Roosevelt at this time. See Mowry, *Theodore Roosevelt and the Progressive Movement,* 207; Amos R. E. Pinchot, *History of the Progressive Party, 1912–1916,* Helene M. Hooker, ed. (New York, 1958), 131–39; Charles Forcey, *The Crossroads of Liberalism* (New York, 1961), 147–49; McGeary, *Gifford Pinchot,* 221–25.

18. The author's interview with John Fackler, October 7, 1949; *Ohio State Journal,* February 6, 1912.

19. Roosevelt's speech is reported in *Proceedings and Debates,* I, 378–87. The quotations of editorial opinion are from the *Ohio State Journal,* February 23, 1912, and from the *Toledo Blade* and *Cleveland Leader,* February 22, 1912. Outside Ohio, however, the conservative press singled out and bitterly assailed Roosevelt's proposal for the recall of judicial decisions. Even many of his supporters were hostile to this suggestion. Many conservative Republican leaders broke with the Colonel after his attack on the judiciary. George Mowry has presented the probable reasons for Roosevelt's advocacy

of this proposal and also has reviewed the conservative reaction in Mowry, *Theodore Roosevelt and the Progressive Movement,* 212–18.

20. *Ohio State Journal,* February 22, 26, 1912; Mowry, *Theodore Roosevelt and the Progressive Movement.* 219. The quotation is from A. L. Garford to E. W. Sims, February 22, 1912, Garford Papers.

21. The formation of the League was reported in the *Ohio State Journal,* January 3, 1912. Later the name was changed to the Pioneer Progressive League (*ibid.,* March 27, 1912). Garber explained that it was differences over patronage that had estranged him from Harmon (*ibid.,* April 7, 1912).

22. Harmon's speech is reported in *Proceedings and Debates,* I, 236–38. One admirer declared that Harmon never seemed so great as when he refused to barter the convictions of a lifetime for the presidential nomination (Nichols, "Harmon," 148–49).

23. These criticisms of Harmon appeared in: *Toledo News-Bee,* February 8, 1912; *Ohio State Journal,* February 15, 1912; Hendrick, "Judson Harmon," 619–24; and in Baker's correspondence (N. D. Baker to Atlee Pomerene, November 18, 1911, to John H. Clarke, March 18, 1912, Baker Papers, CCH). A few months earlier the *Independent* had asked James M. Cox to write an article on Harmon in a series they were running on the three most prominent Democratic presidential candidates, the other two being Woodrow Wilson and Champ Clark. Cox, without belaboring Harmon's progressivism, clearly implied that Harmon deserved credit for the progressive measures passed during his administration, thus following the line adopted by Harmon's managers. (James M. Cox, "Governor Judson Harmon," *Independent* LXXI [November 2, 1911], 959)

24. This thumbnail sketch of Wilson's political life is drawn from Arthur S. Link, *Wilson: The Road to the White House* (Princeton, N.J., 1947), 106–22, 126–27, 317, and from Link, *Woodrow Wilson and the Progressive Era, 1910–1917* (New York, 1954), 8–11. Baker's attraction to Wilson is enlarged upon in Hendrick, "Mayor Tom's Successor," 675, and in N. D. Baker to R. D. Lewis, August 24, 1911, and N. D. Baker to Daniel Kiefer, January 8, 1912, Baker Papers, CCH. The Scripps-McRae newspapers' support is discussed in the *Toledo News-Bee,* February 22, March 17, 1912. Bryan's reasons for not running are presented in Glad, *The Trumpet Soundeth,* 165–69. After Bryan decided not to run, his Ohio followers approached Champ Clark, but left the interview with the feeling that Clark, Harmon, and the Wall Street interests were plotting together. Subsequently they talked with Wilson, who made a favorable impression upon them, and they decided to back him. (William W. Durbin to Ray S. Baker, March 20, 1926, quoted in Link, *Wilson: The Road to the White House,* p. 418, n. 99) The Bryanites began circulating petitions to get Wilson's name on the Ohio Democratic primary ballot (*Ohio State Journal,* March 27, 1912).

25. The Taft campaign and Taft's bitter references to Roosevelt were reported in the *Cleveland Plain Dealer,* May 14, 16, 1912, and the *Ohio State Journal,* May 7–10, 14–21, and in Pringle, *Taft,* II, 784–85. Roosevelt's campaign and derision of Taft were reported in the *Ohio State Journal,* May 15–21, 1912. La Follette's jibe at his two rivals appeared in the *Toledo Blade,* May 20, 1912.

26. *Cleveland Leader,* May 22, 1912; *Ohio State Journal,* May 22, 24, 1912. Throughout the state Roosevelt delegates received 165,809 votes; Taft delegates, 118,362; La Follette delegates, 15,570. Roosvelt carried sixty-nine of the eighty-eight counties. At Roosevelt's personal request no contest was

made for the two delegates in the First Congressional District, President Taft's home district and also the one represented by the Colonel's son-in-law, Nicholas Longworth, who had already declared for Taft before Roosevelt had made up his mind to run (Theodore Roosevelt to Walter F. Brown, March 12, 1912, W. F. Brown Papers). One reason for the low La Follette vote was that he only challenged Taft and Roosevelt in seven congressional districts, elsewhere there was no chance for the electorate to cast a vote for the Wisconsin senator, (Ohio State Journal, April 17, June 1, 1912). Mowry is incorrect in stating that Roosevelt won all of the Ohio district delegates (Mowry,Theodore Roosevelt and the Progressive Movement, 235).

27. The division of strength between the two candidates was reported in the Ohio State Journal, May 24, 30, June 2, 1912, Taft's statement in W. H. Taft to A. I. Vorys, May 30, 1912, Hilles Papers, Roosevelt's statement in a telegram, Theodore Roosevelt to Walter Brown, quoted in the Ohio State Journal, June 1, 1912.

28. Ohio State Journal, June 3, 5, 1912; Cleveland Leader, June 5, 1912. Prior to the convention Maschke and Walter Brown, who were close friends, had worked out a deal: Maschke agreed to send Taft and Roosevelt delegates to the state conclave in proportion to the vote the two candidates received in the Cuyahoga County primaries. Since Roosevelt received 71 per cent of the vote, thirty-eight of the fifty-three county delegates should have been pledged to him, the remaining fifteen to Taft. In the Cuyahoga County convention, where the delegates to the state meeting were chosen, there had been no contest. The powerful Maschke had easily persuaded that body to elect five known Roosevelt supporters and forty-eight others who he knew would vote in the manner he dictated. At the state convention he cast the block of forty-eight votes for Taft. Had the deal been fulfilled, Roosevelt would have received thirty-eight instead of only five votes from the Cuyahoga delegation and would, thereby, have won the six delegates-at-large by a vote of 395½ to 357½.

Why was it that Maschke, who prided himself on a lifelong practice of keeping his word, failed to keep his promise to Brown? When he left Cleveland, he fully expected to carry through the agreement. But in Columbus he was collared by Senator Burton, who reported that the President had told him the night before that he was counting on him (Burton) to deliver the Ohio delegates-at-large. The senator told Maschke that he could not face the President again if the Cuyahoga delegation did not vote for Taft. He reminded the Cleveland boss of the favor that he had done him in persuading the President to disregard his own wishes and appoint Maschke the United States Collector of Customs in Cleveland. The latter capitulated. (George B. Harris, "The Ohio Republican State Convention of 1912 and Its Effect on United States History" [MS in the possession of George B. Harris, Cleveland, Ohio]).

29. The vote was thirteen to eight; Maschke was one of the Taft men on the state central committee who helped to re-elect Brown (Ohio State Journal, June 4, 1912).

30. The Bryan campaign and Bryan's derogatory remarks about Harmon were reported in ibid., April 16, 1912, Harmon's campaign in ibid., May 14–20, 1912.

31. The chief sponsors of the plan to hold a presidential-preferential primary election were the Harmon managers, confident of the popularity of their candidate. Garber and Durbin were opposed, but Baker supported it

wholeheartedly. Baker's course in attacking Harmon, yet voting with the Harmon managers on this question, tended to mystify the politicians. (*Ibid.*, March 20–21, 1913) The primary contests were reported in: *ibid.*, May 22– 24, 1912; *Cleveland Leader*, May 22, 1912; *Cincinnati Enquirer*, May 22–23, 1912; *Dayton Daily News*, May 22, 1912; *Toledo Blade*, May 22, 1912.

32. The primary election results are recapitulated in the *Ohio State Journal*, June 3, 1912. The delegates from the Cleveland area were: Herman Schmidt and Charles Lapp in the Twentieth Congressional District, Robert Bulkley and Baker in the Twenty-First. All were members of the Johnson circle. (*Cleveland Leader*, May 22, 1912). The favorable showing of Wilson and Baker's rise in prestige are noted in Link, *Wilson: The Road to the White House*, 418–19, and in Cramer, *Baker*, 64–66.

33. Baker expressed his doubts about Bigelow's candidacy in N. D. Baker to Brand Whitlock, May 1, 1912, Whitlock Papers. Baker's support of Hughes was reported in the *Dayton Daily News*, June 4, 1912, the Cleveland mayor's opposition to Cox in N. D. Baker to Atlee Pomerene, November 18, 1911, Baker Papers, CCH. Cox's candidacy was reported in the *Dayton Daily News*, January 10, May 15, 1912, and the *Ohio State Journal*, February 16, 1912.

34. Cox, *Journey through my Years*, 60–66, 115–17. The quotation is in *ibid.*, 115–16.

35. The quotations are in *ibid.*, 34–35, 36, respectively.

36. *Ibid.*, 116; the author's interview with James M. Cox, June 29, 1949. He supported Johnson in the editorial columns of his paper in 1903 (*Dayton Daily News*, August 27, 31, 1903). Cox's sensitivity to the political climate was commented upon by S. Gale Lowrie in an interview with the author, September 28, 1949.

37. By 1912 Cox had broken loose from Hanley's leading strings. The two were estranged after Cox became governor because Hanley opposed his program and joined Harvey Garber in opposition to the Cox administration (James M. Cox to the author, September 16, 1949).

38. *Ohio State Journal*, July 30, 1911; *Dayton Daily News*, November 9, 1911.

39. Cox's strength was reported in the *Ohio State Journal*, June 3, 1912. The fight over the unit rule was reported in: *ibid.*, June 5–6; *Dayton Daily News*, June 4, 1912; *Cincinnati Enquirer*, June 6, 1912; Cramer, *Baker*, 66; and N. D. Baker to Price Russell, May 29, 1912, N. D. Baker to Joseph Howley, June 7, 1912, Baker Papers, CCH. Cox privately favored Wilson over Harmon (Cox, *Journey through My Years*, 117).

40. *Ohio State Journal, Cincinnati Enquirer*, June 6, 1912; Powell, ed., *The Democratic Party of the State of Ohio*, I, 453–54; Cox, *Journey through my Years*, 126–27. The other officers nominated were: William Samse and Tobias Schott, members of the board of public works; Sylvanus E. Strode, dairy and food commissioner; Frank W. Miller, state school commissioner; Oscar W. Newman and William E. Schofield, justices of the supreme court.

41. Baker pledged Cox his support in N. D. Baker to J. M. Cox, June 6, 1912, Baker Papers, CCH. See the *Ohio State Journal*, June 5–6, 1912, and the *Toledo News-Bee*, June 5, 1912.

42. The quotation is from the *Dayton Daily News*, June 5, 1912. The reaction of the *Toledo News-Bee* is in the issue for June 6, 1912. (Bigelow spoke of his intercession in the author's interview with him, September 26, 1949) The response of the *Cincinnati Enquirer* is in the issue for June 6, 1912. The degree of enthusiasm displayed in the *Enquirer* no doubt reflected

the influence of James W. Faulkner, the paper's correspondent in Columbus and an intimate of Cox.

43. The contest over the unit rule is described in the *Cleveland Plain Dealer* and *Ohio State Journal*, June 27, 1912, and in Link, *Wilson: The Road to the White House*, 438–40, and Cramer, *Baker*, 66–68. The minority resolution declared that the unit rule did not apply when a state law provided for preferential primary elections. But the resolution did not affect the application of the unit rule to state delegations if such legislation was lacking. In supporting Baker, the Champ Clark supporters alienated the Harmon faction and destroyed any chance of later co-operation between the two, when Clark needed the Harmon votes (Cox, *Journey through my Years*, 133–34).

44. Harmon received 148 votes on the first ballot, his strength concentrated in 29 votes from Ohio and 90 from New York. On the tenth ballot New York left him. Although he then released the Ohio delegation, he received 10½ votes from its members on the final ballot. (*Ohio State Journal*, June 29-30, July 3, 1912) The fullest and most illuminating account of the Democratic national convention is in Link, *Wilson: The Road to the White House*, 431–65. The best interpretation of Bryan's role at the convention is in Glad, *The Trumpet Soundeth*, 170–72. Baker described his elation in N. D. Baker to Louis F. Post, July 3, 1912, Baker Papers, CCH.

45. The proceedings of the Republican national convention were reported in the *Cleveland Leader*, June 21–23, 1912; the quote is from a prepared statement of Roosevelt published in *ibid.*, June 21, 1912. Roosevelt's reaction is analyzed in Mowry, *Theodore Roosevelt and the Progressive Movement*, 237–55. Taft was nominated on the first ballot. The vote was: Taft 561, Roosevelt 107, La Follette 41, Senator Albert B. Cummins 13, with 344 abstaining.

46. The biographical data on Garford are drawn from: the *Cleveland Leader*, September 15, 1912; James H. Rodabaugh, "Arthur L. Garford," *Museum Echoes* (Ohio Historical Society, XXVIII (July, 1953), 51–54; Henry P. Boynton to the author, October 11, 1949. Boynton knew Garford intimately and served as the editor of a paper the latter owned, the *Elyria Telegram*. Garford's relations with Nat Wright are revealed in N. C. Wright to A. L. Garford, April 7, 1909, January 5, 1910, Garford Papers, and in an editorial in the *Toledo Blade*, October 28, 1910, Garford's prohibition leanings in Wayne B. Wheeler to A. L. Garford, June 24, 1912, Garford Papers.

47. *Cleveland Leader*, July 2, 1912.

48. The work of the convention was reported in *ibid.*, July 3, 1912, and in the *Cincinnati Enquirer*, July 2, 1912. The Garford quotation is from A. L. Garford to I. H. Griswold, July 3, 1912, Garford Papers.

49. The proceedings of the Progressive national convention in Chicago are ably covered in Mowry, *Theodore Roosevelt and the Progressive Movement*, 262–72, and in Garraty, *Right-Hand Man*, 264–70. A boom was launched for James R. Garfield for vice-president when it was rumored that Hiram Johnson would not accept the post, but it quickly expired after it was realized that the California governor was willing to run (*Cleveland Leader*, August 6, 1912).

50. Dillon's withdrawal was reported in the *Ohio State Journal*, July 28, 1912, and in C. D. Hilles to W. H. Taft, August 1, 1912, Hilles Papers. The selection of a successor by the state central committee is in the *Cleveland Leader*, August 10–11, 1912, and the *Cleveland Plain Dealer*, August 11–12, 1912.

51. *Cleveland Leader*, August 20–21, 1912.

52. The convention was minutely and enthusiastically reported in the *Cleveland Leader*, September 5–6, 1912, by the paper's able correspondent, John T. Bourke. Gladden explained his reasons for supporting the Progressive party thus: first, his old friends were a part of the national organization; second, he preferred the Progressive's plank on the trusts to that of the Democrats, for he favored government regulation and co-operation over a return to cutthroat competition (*Ohio State Journal*, October 24, 1912).

53. *Toledo News-Bee*, August 7, 1912. The files of the Whitlock Papers contain several communications on the subject. Whitlock was certain that he did not want the nomination for governor because he was determined to renounce politics for writing. But he was not so certain in August whether he would support Wilson or Roosevelt for President. However, such friends as Albert J. Nock and Peter Witt persuaded the Toledo mayor to remain loyal to the Democratic party. Later Whitlock disclaimed ever having had any wayward leanings toward the Bull Moose party. See: Brand Whitlock to Negley Cochran, August 7, 1912; Brand Whitlock to A. J. Nock, August 17, 1912, and Nock to Whitlock, August 29, 1912; Peter Witt to Brand Whitlock, August 6, 1912; Brand Whitlock to Newton D. Baker, September 22, 1912; Brand Whitlock to Woodrow Wilson, October 7, 1912 (Whitlock Papers).

54. *Cleveland Leader, Ohio State Journal*, September 6, 1912.

55. John Fackler and Henry P. Boynton both concurred in this estimate of the Progressive party leaders in Ohio (the author's interviews with Fackler and Boynton, October 7, 1949 and October 3, 1949). The ambivalence of Roosevelt himself and the Progressive party leaders in the nation and other states and the disparate nature of the leadership are stressed in: Mowry, *Theodore Roosevelt and the Progressive Movement*, 230–31, 263–64; Blum, *The Republican Roosevelt*, 149–50; Forcey, *The Crossroads of Liberalism*, 149, 193–94; Garraty, *Right-hand Man*, 265–73.

56. *Ohio State Journal*, July 22, September 2, 1912; Cox; *Journey through My Years*, 117.

57. *Ohio State Journal*, September 21, 1912; *Cleveland Plain Dealer*, October 29, 1912; Cox, *Journey through My Years*, 127–128.

58. The Progressive party's accusations against Cox appeared in the *Cleveland Leader*, October 6, 9, 17, 24–27, 1912; an example of Cox's retaliation is in the *Cleveland Plain Dealer*, October 29, 1912; and the Republican line of attack is exemplified in the *Ohio State Journal*, September 22, 1912.

59. The apathy was noted in the *Cleveland Plain Dealer*, October 27, 1912.

60. *Report of the Secretary of State of Ohio* (1912), 327, 329.

61. *Ibid.*, 328–29, 360–66, 350–51, 711–13. The congressman-at-large was Robert Crosser of Cleveland.

62. Appraisals of the Progressive party vote are found in A. L. Garford to George W. Perkins, November 18, 1912, Garford Papers, and in the *Toledo Blade*, November 6–7, 1912.

63. The quotations from Roosevelt are in, respectively, Theodore Roosevelt to James R. Garfield, November 8, 1912; to Gifford Pinchot, November 13, 1912; to Walter Brown, November 20, 1912, T. Roosevelt Papers. The quotation from the *Toledo News-Bee* is in the issue for November 8, 1912.

64. *Ohio State Journal*, November 7, 1912; *Cleveland Leader*, November 8, December 8, 1912.

CHAPTER FOURTEEN

GOVERNOR COX AS LEGISLATIVE LEADER
1912 ■ 1914

AT THE INAUGURAL CEREMONIES January 13, 1913, James M. Cox took the oath of office beneath the rotunda of the Capitol, a scene imbued with memories of the past. But the new chief executive found his inspiration in the present and the promise of things to come. In an address unprecedented for brevity, he voiced his beliefs with earnest simplicity: "We are entering upon a new day. The evolutions and processes of time are working great advances in every activity of man. The forces of human intelligence have carried us to a point of higher moral vision, and it would have been a distinct anomaly of history if government had not been carried on in the progress of the time. . . . I sense therefore the sublime responsibility of this hour!" [1]

The depth and genuineness of his emotion were transmitted to his audience. No doubt some of his fervor had been spontaneously generated by the great display of popular enthusiasm he had just witnessed. Crowds lined the approach to the Capitol, shouting, "Hello, Jimmy!" and waving flags and streamers. Bands in profusion marched in the parade, one from the Jefferson Club of his native Butler County, another from Dayton, followed by those from an Ohio regiment, the Army, and the Navy. Even the weather enhanced the gaiety, turning bright and crisp after a week of heavy skies and rain, and causing flags and bunting, sodden the day before, to flutter brightly. [2]

Still, it was more than the excitment of the moment that

385

had inspired his words. Cox was fired with a religious zeal for the progressive cause. Although he lacked the intellectual strength and dedicated spirit that possessed Jones and Johnson, his convictions were nonetheless real. Cox borrowed his ideas from them and from the Wisconsin reformers and other humanitarians, his quick, absorbent mind making their beliefs his own. Thus steeped in their philosophy, he looked upon the world with their "higher moral vision." Moreover, he was honestly convinced that the people of Ohio shared his faith. In the September referendum they had voted "every constitutional facility" to test "the principles of an enlarged social justice" through government. His decisive plurality in November he interpreted as a popular mandate to complete the work of regeneration.[3]

To this task he devoted his great energy and rare executive ability. The weeks between election and inauguration were consumed in preparing for the legislative session, mapping out the details of his program, assigning the work of bill-drafting, and selecting legislative leaders. He himself interviewed the department heads and the members of the boards and commissions of the Harmon administration to learn how each operated and what changes were needed. The principal state officers-elect he invited to a weekly round-table conference, tantamount to a cabinet meeting.

He had no intention, however, of limiting his counselors to his official family. He drew heavily on many sources for advice. Newton Baker was asked to draft legislation for the home rule of cities, Herbert Bigelow and John R. Cassidy, for election reforms, Carl Friebolin, for changes in the judiciary, and Robert M. Ditty of the tax commission, for centralization of the work of assessment. Labor measures were parceled out to a number of men: a compulsory workmen's compensation bill to the Cuyahoga delegation and Cleveland union leaders; child labor legislation to Alexander J. McKelway of the national child labor committee; a mothers' pension proposal to H. H. Shirer, secretary of the Ohio Board of State Charities; a minimum-wage bill for women to Judge Dennis Dwyer. Requisitions were made on the staff of Ohio State University to gather data for other legislation.[4]

Nor did Cox confine his circle of advisers to the state. Late in November he sent William L. Finley, chairman of the Democratic executive committee, and Oliver H. Hughes, of the Ohio Public Service Commission, to Madison to solicit the assistance of the Wisconsin group, as well as to convince Finley, the chief spoilsman of the party, of the worth of the "Wisconsin idea." In both endeavors Cox succeeded. Professors John R. Commons and Charles H. McCarthy came to Columbus to aid in the passage of a public-utility bill. Finley returned from his visit, impressed that the success of the Wisconsin idea depended not so much on the laws as on the men who administered them. Having observed the "great, big, brainy humanitarians" who served on the Wisconsin commissions, he solemnly vowed to make "no purely partisan recommendations" at home.[5] In addition to the Wisconsin reformers, Cox leaned on Henry R. Goddard, a research psychologist and persuasive writer from Vineland, New Jersey, for inspiration and guidance on penal reform and the handling of juvenile delinquents.[6]

The Governor-elect exercised a strong hand in the organization of the General Assembly before it convened on January 14, 1913. Although the large Democratic majorities of twenty-six to seven in the Senate and eighty-seven to thirty-six in the House assured complete party control, he defended his intervention on the ground that the people looked to him, not to the legislature, to fulfill the platform promises, and expected direct leadership from him. There was to be none of the halfhearted guidance Harmon had given. Cox's desire was to fill the chief offices with men who would not only be unyielding in devotion to reform principles, but who would also promote harmony and co-operation within the party.[7]

Acting on a generous first impulse, he offered the House speakership to Herbert Bigelow, an eager contender for the honor. When the proposal evoked opposition rather than enthusiasm from other Democrats, however, Cox retracted, and offered the Cincinnati preacher the floor leadership instead. At first Bigelow expressed willingness to accept the second honor, then rejected it in a huff, explaining in a newspaper interview that he wanted to see what the Hanley influence might be before he affiliated himself with the administration. "I am a Democrat," he added, "when the Democrats are right. When they are wrong, I am against them." He considered himself to be a free lance, at liberty to support or oppose, as he saw fit.[8]

Cox expressed apprehension at these remarks in a letter to Newton Baker, wondering what kind of obstructionist tactics might be expected. In reply the Cleveland mayor recounted some plain truths he had spoken to Bigelow—that the fulfillment of the progressive program was everything, the political advancement of individuals nothing. Though Baker was at a loss to explain the preacher's remarks, he did not anticipate trouble from that quarter so long as the legislature worked toward the goals on which they were all united.[9] Before the session ended, however, Bigelow became a thorn in Cox's side. The choice for speaker, after some deliberation, was Charles L. Swain, another member of the Hamilton County delegation, who was a progressive with previous parliamentary experience.

No further embarrassment arose over the selection of other officers. John H. Lowry of Henry County was named floor leader; Milton Warnes of Holmes County, whip; John R. Cassidy, who had won his spurs as a parliamentarian in the constitutional convention, clerk of the House. In the upper chamber the fair-minded progressive Hugh L. Nichols, lieutenant-governor, was automatically the presiding officer; William Green was the obvious choice to succeed himself as president pro tempore. Though serving without official title, Carl Friebolin of Cleveland acted as the administration's liaison man in the Senate, selected because of his quick mind, parliamentary skill, and thorough sympathy with the reform program.[10]

The practice of allowing the speaker to choose the committees in the House was continued, and a committee on committees, composed of four progressives and one conservative, was empowered to do the selecting in the Senate, thus insuring progressive chairmen of the most prominent ones. A tribute to the high standing of the Cuyahoga delegation was the assignment of its members to the chairmanships of six committees in the Senate and four in the House, several of which were important. Members of the Hamilton County delegation received the chairmanships of three major committees. Speaker Swain and Senator Green sat at the head of the powerful rules committees in their respective chambers.[11]

Although this tightly knit organization and concentration of power bore an unmistakable resemblance to the conditions in the national House of Representatives before the "revolution of 1909–11," reformers were never ones to wince at the adoption of the enemy's tactics, justifying their use as a means of routing intrenched privilege and fulfilling the popular will. By and large, the public and the press silently acquiesced.

Such preliminary preparations were only a part of Cox's total strategy. He wielded the club of patronage to hold recalcitrant party members in line, refusing to commit himself on appointments until the end of the regular session. Within the first two weeks he persuaded the legislature to pass the first Ohio law regulating lobbyists, which required them to register the name of the firm which employed them and to list the bills in which they were interested as well as their receipts and expenditures. Without a certificate a lobbyist could not appear before a committee of either house. Though the act was imperfectly enforced, the Capitol was no longer the rookery of paid agents that it had been in previous sessions.[12]

A measure to which the administration attached equal importance was adopted January 28, creating a separate legislative reference department to aid in efficient bill-drafting. Cox had already picked out the man to head the new agency, S. Gale Lowrie, who had served four years in the Wisconsin Legislative Reference Bureau under Charles McCarthy, its founder, and had directed the Cincinnati Municipal Reference Bureau, established by the Hunt administration in 1912. Cox placed great faith in this reform, arguing somewhat naïvely that if a bill was properly drafted the legislature would readily adopt it without change. That had not been the experience of the Wisconsin legislature, nor was it to be the case in the Ohio body. The General Assembly promptly established its independence by amending the administration bills, frequently destroying the best efforts of the legislative reference department to eliminate error.[13]

The watchful eye of the administration did not cease with the preparation of a bill. One of the Governor's secretaries kept a file on all measures, indicating their progress toward adoption and other pertinent facts. Such information formed the basis for frequent discussions with the Democratic leaders and also with their Republican counterparts. On only one or two issues did Cox consult with officials of the Progressive party, for their interest lagged and their promised legislative program was a limited one pledging support for measures already endorsed by the Democrats.[14]

The Democratic legislators were organized into groups of twelve men, with a party whip in charge of each group to make certain the members were all present when important bills were voted on. In the closing weeks of the session the regular machinery was supplemented by a steering committee in each chamber, composed of men the Governor had approved, who were empowered to choose bills from the calendar and give them priority in debate.[15]

Before the session ended on April 30, 1913, "Cox and his cabinet of politicians" were accused by opponents of cracking the whip and making the legislature "dance an accompaniment" or, to change the metaphor, of molding that body "until it became as plastic as clay in the master potter's hands." The friendly *Cleveland Plain Dealer* defended the solons against this charge, contending that they were not subservient, since they and the Governor, having been elected on the same platform with the same commission from the people, shared a common viewpoint. Clearly a community of purpose existed between executive and legislature. What is more, there were remarkably few "clay" figures in the state house. Cox was not indulging in hyperbole when he praised the members as surpassing all previous general assemblies "in earnestness, ability, and integrity." [16]

Like any other chief executive, the Governor would have preferred to complete his whole program in the regular session and free himself of legislative responsibility for the rest of his term. Although he came close to fulfilling this desire, he decided it would be wiser to delay action on the few controversial items remaining until a special session that he proposed to call the next year, rather than risk a hard fight for their adoption at the end of the regular session when the legislators were tired and their tempers frayed. More important, he was convinced that by such a postponement he would gain the time needed to organize an educational campaign among the people that would create a popular demand for these measures which the General Assembly would find irresistible. Furthermore, some of the hazards of calling a special session had been eliminated by the new amendment authorizing the governor to limit the agenda. The special session was convened on January 19, 1914, and lasted just four weeks. Cox carefully restricted the agenda to ten items and refused to allow discussion of other matters, despite the grumblings of Republican and Progressive party legislators that this was another example of the Governor's use of dictatorial powers.[17] In order to appraise the work of this General Assembly as a whole, I shall, in the following discussion of the legislative enactments, treat the two sessions together, with only an indication of the session at which each enactment was considered.

In the best sense of the word Cox was a master politician. Sensitive to the public temper, he judged it with remarkable accuracy. He preferred to persuade and cajole rather than force and domineer. At the same time he did not pussyfoot; he pushed his reforms to the limit that the legislative majority would accept. His first message to the Assembly on January 14, 1913, was an example. Ignoring the admonitions of faint-hearted friends, he presented a document of twelve thousand words, outlining in some detail fifty-six proposals. This was the most ambitious program of social welfare and democratic reform ever presented to Ohio's lawmakers, and much more advanced than the New Freedom program of the Democratic President, Woodrow Wilson. Although a major part of his recommendations were directed toward redeeming the constitutional mandate, the Governor did not stop there. He pressed for reforms endorsed in the party platform which the constitutional convention or the people had turned down, such as the short ballot, good roads, and classification of taxes, and he urged an extensive overhaul of the penal institutions and the state administration, as well as the school system. "In other days," he declared, "changes in government such as are made necessary everywhere by our industrial and social conditions, would have been wrought by riot and revolution. Now they are accomplished through peaceful evolution. He must be, indeed, a man of unfortunate temperamental qualities who does not find in this a circumstance that thrills every patriotic fibre of his being."[18]

Clearly one of the "changes in government" to be accomplished by "peaceful evolution" was completion of the long-sought reforms for more direct democracy. The twenty-sixth amendment, approved in September, had made mandatory the adoption of a direct-primary law, and a sweeping one was approved. All state and local officers save in villages of a population under two thousand, representatives to the national Congress, and members of controlling committees of political parties were to be nominated at primary elections. In addition, the act not only provided for the selection of delegates and alternates to the national party conventions by this method, but also introduced an official system for committing them to the electors' preferred presidential choice. Although the amendment had prescribed the Oregon Plan for nominating United States senators, this clause was made obsolete when Ohio and the requisite number of other states ratified the Seventeenth Amendment to the federal Constitution, eliminating the role of the legislature and making senatorial elections direct. Since ratification was completed too late for action in 1913, the legislature, in the special session of 1914, passed the necessary act providing for the nomination of senators at primary elections.[19]

Another mandatory amendment requiring legislative implementation was the initiative and referendum. First, the General Assembly was directed to prescribe a system of direct legislation for municipalities, an assignment fulfilled in a manner to satisfy the radical adherents of this reform. Under the law passed in 1913 the number of signatures required on both initiative and referendum petitions was held at the low figure of 10 per cent of the municipal electors; ordinances were to be initiated directly, instead of indirectly through the council, and might be voted upon at special elections.[20] By providing for the direct initiative, the legislature made the process for cities even more liberal than the process established for the state.

It was necessary, in the second place, for the legislature to specify the means of publicizing initiative and referendum measures and to safeguard the use of the system. Herbert Bigelow was placed in charge of drafting the appropriate publicity legislation. His bill provided for a pamphlet to be printed and distributed to each voter at state expense, listing the full title and text of each proposed law or amendment, the short title as it would appear on the ballot, and explanations of each proposal, limited to three hundred words, to be prepared by five persons who were to be named by the sponsors of the initiated proposal and who would work with a three-man legislative committee.

Though the measure easily passed the House, it was first

defeated in the Senate because of the general feeling that any bill with Bigelow's name attached must be "full of sleepers." Governor Cox and the secretary of state promptly got busy in its behalf. As a result the bill was reconsidered and passed nineteen to ten. Although the measure later had to be amended, it was not because of "sleepers" but because of inadequacies. It did not provide clearly for publicity on referendum petitions nor for an officially approved synopsis such as had accompanied each of the amendments submitted by the constitutional convention. These defects were corrected in 1914.[21]

The initial legislation to protect the initiative and referendum process from abuse was brief. It declared it a corrupt practice to offer or accept money for signing a petition and required organizations circulating petitions to list their expenses and the names of their agents. Cox had personally opposed the employment of paid solicitors from the beginning, but he yielded to the insistence of his Cleveland and Cincinnati friends that it would be impossible to obtain the requisite signatures without hiring such persons.[22]

The Governor's fear that it would be difficult to insure honest results if the peddling of petitions for pay were allowed was not unfounded. Certainly the original act proved wholly inadequate to deal with the malpractices which arose. During the summer of 1913 three measures passed by the legislature were subjected to the threat of referendum votes: a compulsory workmen's compensation law and two acts reforming the taxing system. The chief organization behind the referendums was the Equity Association of Cleveland, allegedly backed by Dan Hanna, among others. Cox and his friends believed that these were ruthless men whose intent was not only to defeat these particular laws but also to discredit the whole system of direct legislation. In a letter to Carl Friebolin the Governor wrote, "We drove these scoundrels out of the State House when the legislature was in session, but they have come in the back door under disguise of an alleged referendum petition which develops to be fraudulent." [23]

Preliminary investigations by the attorney-general had uncovered such wholesale fraud in the collection of signatures that Cox ordered a full-dress hearing, as he explained, to expose the abuses, clear the principle of the referendum from any odium, and establish the precedent that only honest referendum elections should be conducted. The revelations were startling. Hired circulators confessed to forging hundreds of signatures and blotching petitions with ink and grime to give them the appearance of having been much handled. Attorney-General Hogan summed up the testimony with ironic exaggeration: "Dead men, livery stables, vacant lots, empty houses, children, public parks, churches, stores, convicts, brick yards, public playgrounds, factories, flop houses, houses of ill-repute, and non-residents all have attempted to exercise the right of suffrage in Ohio."

Representatives and lawyers of the Equity Association walked out of the hearings, claiming that Secretary of State Graves had no authority to conduct them. When he threw out all the petitions for the three referendums because they were "so filled with fraud, corruption and crime that they constitute one solid mass of wrongdoing" and accused the Equity Association of perjury, the latter sought a writ of mandamus from the state supreme court to compel him to conduct the referendums. In a six-to-one decision the court denied the writ, sustaining Graves's action in conducting the investigation and rejecting the tainted petitions.[24]

At the special session in 1914 the legislature completely rewrote the protective law to proscribe the malpractices so recently perpetrated. For instance, willful misrepresentation of the content of a petition and the altering or erasing of names were added to the list of corrupt practices, and each petition was to bear a warning that whoever signed more than once was subject to prosecution and to contain a statement of what the solicitor received for collecting the signatures. The new law was passed by the necessary two-thirds vote as an emergency measure to safeguard any referendums on bills adopted in the session. Friends of direct legislation were satisfied that they had now protected the process against the worst evils, even though they recognized that public vigilance and good faith were the main bulwarks against a repetition of the first referendum frauds.[25]

A third mandatory constitutional amendment, designed to increase democratic controls by introducing a limited form of the recall, received the required legislative implementation. The act provided for the initiation of complaint petitions against officials alleged to be guilty of moral turpitude and other misconduct, to be followed by a trial before the governor for state officials and before the court of common pleas for local officials, with provision for review by the higher courts in both cases.[26]

Some of the legislators, not content with this half-measure, proposed a constitutional amendment for the full-fledged recall of all elective officials, including the judges, for whatever cause. Introduced in the House by Oscar E. Diser from Mahoning County, who had been nominated by both the Republicans and Progressives, it received the support of Bigelow, who tried to line up Democrats for the bill. Lacking administration support, however, and attacked by the Republican floor leader, Charles A. Reid, it failed to receive the necessary three-fifths vote. Another Progressive, James Nye of Toledo, offered Roosevelt's alternate proposal for the recall of judicial decisions. This resolution also was rejected, by a vote of sixty-four to thirty-one, the minority including the three Progressives, nineteen Republicans, and nine Democrats.[27]

Although some legislators were willing to attempt to amend the work of the constitutional convention with respect to the recall, none made an effort to overrule the popular decision on woman suffrage. The ladies were obliged to carry on their fight without legislative aid, initiating an amendment on their own, only to be defeated once again in the election of 1914. The legislature, however, did agree to submit to the electorate a second time the defeated amendment permitting women to hold official positions in institutions caring for females and children. They were right in believing that the voters in 1912 had misunderstood its intent, for this was the lone constitutional change to carry in the 1913 election.[28]

Another proposed amendment which Cox and the legislative leaders believed worthy of reconsideration was one to permit classification of property for tax purposes, an amendment which the constitutional convention had rejected. In spite of the protests of well-wishers, who pointed to the solid opposition of farmers, the Governor boldly advocated this amendment, coupled with a constitutional limit of fifteen mills on the general property tax. This ceiling, he felt, would allay the agrarians' fears that land would continue to bear the principal tax burden. Even though the legislature rejected the proposed resolution, such an amendment was initiated in 1914, only to be rejected by the people.[29]

Cox's recommendation that a tax limitation be written into the constitution evoked strong opposition from urban reformers, particularly the Cleveland group. They had fought the original imposition of such a ceiling by legislative enactment, the Smith 1 Per Cent Law of 1911. Although admittedly this act had contributed to the successful reappraisal of real property at 100 per cent of true value, it had failed miserably to draw intangibles on to the tax duplicate as its advocates had claimed it would. Furthermore, it placed most of the cities and their school systems in a financial strait jacket by rigidly limiting the amount of tax they could levy to meet the growing costs of municipal and educational services.[30]

At a meeting of the Ohio Municipal League in January, 1913, Newton Baker pleaded for the repeal of the Smith Act. To the majority, led by Mayor Henry Hunt, this seemed too extreme, however, and the League voted to endorse the principle but with modifications. A bill embodying this compromise was introduced into the General Assembly by Senator William A. Greenlund. It proposed to: remove all the internal limitations from the Smith Act; alter the membership of the local budget committees by replacing the prosecuting attorneys with the city solicitors in counties where the urban population exceeded the rural; increase the maximum city levy to ten mills, exclusive of state and county taxes as well as sinking fund and bond interest; permit the council to raise the limit by resolution, subject to a referendum.

Mayors Baker, Hunt, and Whitlock spoke before the Senate tax committee in favor of the bill and against the existing law, which the Cleveland mayor stigmatized as "conceived in iniquity and born in sin." But in the end the municipal reformers had to be satisfied with the administration-approved Kilpatrick bill, which removed the restrictions on the size of later tax levies and incorporated their ideas on the membership of the local budget committees, but reimposed the ten-mill limit exclusive only of sinking fund and bond interest. An act passed earlier in the session had already re-established a fifteen-mill maximum on taxes for all purposes, which a majority of the voters might approve. This had been made necessary by a supreme court decision which declared that the language of the original was ambiguous on this point.[31]

396

The determined urban progressives had still other proposals to win financial relief. They advocated two constitutional amendments: one to permit county home rule in taxation, the other to make state and local bonds tax free once again. Baker drafted a home-rule tax resolution which also allowed classification. Maurice Bernstein of Cleveland introduced it in the Senate, where it was approved twenty to ten, but it was ignored by the House. The other amendment was adopted by the legislature. Despite a vigorous campaign for it in the metropolitan press, it was defeated by twenty-eight thousand votes in the 1913 election.[32]

Finances were not the only municipal problems confronting the legislature. The amendment granting home rule to cities required implementation, since the General Assembly was still authorized to provide for the incorporation and government of all cities which failed to adopt their own charters. Shortly after his election Cox had asked Newton Baker to write whatever law or laws were necessary. The Cleveland mayor replied that the Ohio Municipal League, of which he was president, had a subcommittee working on the problem and that he would give it his personal attention.

The measure prepared called for three optional municipal-charter plans: the federal, the commission, and the city-manager. Recommended by Cox in his legislative message and endorsed by the League at its January meeting, this proposal became the basis for a bill drafted for the General Assembly by Professor Augustus R. Hatton of Western Reserve University. The chief controversial point was a provision for nonpartisan elections. In the final debate this was eliminated, together with some other important features such as the municipal court. Because of such deletions the League believed these à la carte plans to be so defective that it warned cities against adopting them. By 1916 only Westerville had experimented with one of these model charters; other cities preferred tailor-made plans of their own fashioning.[33]

A third municipal problem with which the legislature had to grapple related to utilities. Section 4 of the home-rule amendment granted cities the right to own and operate all public services including street railways; section 12 allowed them to issue bonds to construct or acquire these services, even beyond the

397

limits of bonded indebtedness prescribed by law, provided the lien was on the utility and not on the municipality itself and was accompanied by a franchise permitting the bondholders to operate the property in the event of foreclosure.[34] Friends of municipal ownership who had criticized the language of this latter section when it was adopted by the constitutional convention sought to amend it by legislative action. They desired to make all utility bonds a general lien on the municipality and to permit the city to sell them in small denominations privately, if it failed to find purchasers for them at public offerings. Don P. Mills of Cleveland sponsored a bill embodying these changes. It was passed at the first session, but with amendments so faultily drawn that Cox vetoed it. However, he included a recommendation for the bill's reconsideration by the special session, while making it clear that it was not an administration measure.

In the House debate in 1914, John Kramer, a Mansfield Democrat and member of the constitutional convention, contended that the Mills proposal would be a violation of the intent of the delegates to make municipal-utility bonds a lien solely on the public service and not on the city's general credit. Baker came posthaste to Columbus to persuade Kramer to shift his point of view, but without success. The Kramer contention was added as an amendment to the Mills bill, together with two other restrictive changes. In this form it was passed and sent to the Senate, which approved all of it except the Kramer amendment. Because of this stalemate a conference committee, which included Kramer, Mills, and Friebolin, was appointed to reconcile the differences. Neither the committee nor the two houses could agree, however, on the main point at issue. On final passage the Senate struck out every provision except the right of cities to sell bonds at private sale in small denominations, and the House accepted this version—a mere crumb to municipal-ownership partisans.[35]

Even more controversial than the utility-bond issue was the street-railway problem in Cincinnati, into which the legislature was drawn when Bigelow introduced a bill to revoke the Rogers Law of 1896 and annul the fifty-year franchise of the private traction company. Tom Johnson had suggested that such legislation might withstand a court test because of the constitutional provision that any special privilege granted by the legislature might be withdrawn. Since Cincinnati granted the only franchise under the Rogers Act, this bore the appearance of a special grant.

Bigelow presented his bill without first obtaining the concurrence of Henry Hunt, then demanded that the mayor publicly endorse it. To do so would have antagonized the conservative Democratic and Republican businessmen who had supported the administration, as well as frighten some of the middle-of-the-road reformers who were not prepared for such a radical step. Hunt refused, therefore, and offered an alternate proposal, which was introduced in the House by a Cincinnati Democrat, Thornton P. Snyder. This incorporated and made applicable to any city in the state the terms of a tentative agreement Hunt had reached with the Cincinnati traction company, which provided for an indeterminate franchise in place of a term franchise and gave the city an option to buy at the end of each five-year period, the price to be fixed by mutual agreement, by condemnation proceedings, or by the Ohio Public Utilities Commission.

Despite doubts about the Bigelow bill's constitutionality, the House passed it, persuaded by the preacher that it would be an effective club in dictating terms to the traction company. A week later, however, the House reversed itself by also approving the Snyder proposal. The contradictory action by the lower chamber left the decision to the Senate, which thereupon rejected the Bigelow measure and accepted the Snyder bill, but in an amended form. To reconcile the House and Senate versions of the Snyder proposal, a conference committee was voted. Friebolin, a member of the committee, consulted with Mayor Hunt and City Solicitor Alfred Bettman of Cincinnati, and John Stockwell of Cleveland to insure amendments which would satisfy those two cities, the only ones immediately interested. During the conference committee's session the utility lobby swooped down on the legislature to draw the teeth from the bill. So stiff was their resistance to an indeterminate franchise that the committee amended the proposal to apply only to the Cincinnati traction company, instead of to every type of utility in all cities. Their report was adopted by the General Assembly, the reformers accepting it as the best they could get. Though

399

of doubtful constitutionality, it did provide a remedy for the most pressing grievance, the street-railway franchise situation in Cincinnati.[36]

The issue of municipal control over utilities also entered into the larger problem of state control versus urban home rule in rate-making. Under the law adopted in 1910 and amended in 1911, cities were empowered to fix the rates of utility services provided within their limits, a right the home-rule amendment had confirmed in the general language authorizing municipalities "to exercise all powers of local self-government . . . not in conflict with general laws."[37] This power was attacked by utility companies, who feared that municipally owned plants would be permitted to sell their services for less than cost, with the loss to be made up through the general property tax.

When the issue came before the legislature, Cox was besieged by the gas and electric interests in Clevland, Dayton, Columbus, and Warren to make the Ohio Public Utilities Commission supreme in rate-making and to prohibit municipally owned services from being sold below cost. Mayor Baker, however, had already conferred with the Governor, and the two had reached an agreement whereby the existing power of municipalities over local utilities was not to be disturbed, but publicly owned plants were to be required to keep their records according to the same uniform accounting system required of all other utilities. This compromise was later approved by the Assembly.[38]

In other areas of business enterprise, however, the state did not share its regulatory power with the cities. A blue-sky law was approved which required all dealers in stocks and bonds to be licensed and to provide the state superintendent of banking with a prospectus of the securities being offered prior to sale, if the data were not already publicly available. The statute took full advantage of the new amendment permitting the state to regulate securities, and it received the endorsement of the large brokerage houses. Another permissive amendment, which extended state inspection to private banks, received legislative implementation. A third act declared fraudulent advertising a misdemeanor, and a fourth required a newspaper which had falsely maligned a person or group to publish a rejoinder to those maligned. Finally, the Antitrust Code was stiffened to make company directors and officials who knowingly carried out any agreement in restraint of trade liable to fine and imprisonment, and to outlaw combinations to control the price or supply of foodstuffs.[39]

In addition to these regulatory measures, which Cox insisted helped rather than harmed legitimate enterprises, other legislation was passed directly aiding business. The General Assembly adopted the Torrens system of registering land titles, which had been made constitutional by amendment, two laws favorable to insurance companies, and a fourth giving state banks the necessary authority to become members of the newly established Federal Reserve System.[40]

The favors to business were few, however, by comparison to the benefits bestowed upon labor. Cox, who had been endorsed by the Ohio Federation of Labor and received the bulk of the labor vote, did not forget his debt to the workingman. The key parts of his program were a compulsory workmen's compensation act and an industrial commission. A staunch advocate of a compulsory workmen's liability law, he had campaigned for the amendment which made it possible, and in his first message earnestly recommended its enactment as a common measure of justice to the workers and as a means of promoting industrial peace. His first thought was to place Newton Baker in charge of drafting such a bill in Cleveland where he could easily consult with top union officials, since the headquarters of the Ohio Federation of Labor was there. When the Cleveland mayor confessed to being too busy and too ill-informed to perform the task properly, Cox shifted the preparatory work to Columbus.

At a dinner meeting late in January he assembled Hogan, Nichols, Green, Friebolin, Finley, Wallace Yaple and Thomas Duffy of the state liability board of awards, and James Faulkner, Columbus correspondent of the *Cincinnati Enquirer*, to decide on the form of the bill. Their decision was to make the plan compulsory, require 100 per cent contribution from the employer, and establish a state monopoly, thus driving out the private insurance companies altogether. Senator William Green was accorded the honor of drafting and introducing the administration bill. Joint committee hearings were conducted nightly for a week in the Senate chambers, with the Governor a frequent spectator. The principal opposition came from representatives of the liability-insurance companies and employers ignorant of the content of the bill. Nevertheless, by the final hearing a number of manufacturers were reconciled to the administration plan, though insisting on two alterations: the right to be self-insurers outside the state fund and a modification of their responsibility for willful neglect. When the bill came before the Senate for debate, Cox yielded on these two points, and Green offered the amendments. With these changes it passed both houses unanimously.[41]

The strong legislative verdict, however, did not mean the end of opposition to the measure. Although it survived fraudulent efforts of the Equity Association and shyster lawyers to defeat it by a referendum vote, it was threatened again by the Republican legislature in 1915 during Governor Frank Willis' administration. The most serious breach was a decision of Frank Taggart, Republican superintendent of insurance, allowing liability companies to cover self-insurers. The effect of the "Taggart ruling" was to draw from the state fund companies which were the cream of the risks. When the Democrats returned to power in 1917, they closed this breach by amending the original act to prohibit the practice. Since that time this humanitarian measure, which Cox justly regarded as one of the great contributions of his administration, has been free from political assaults.[42]

Another labor amendment which required implementation was that giving the legislature a sweeping grant of power to fix minimum wages and maximum hours, as well as to enact other measures for the welfare of the workers. In his message to the General Assembly, the Governor had recognized "the obviously unjust conditions affecting the wages of women and children," but he had counseled a delay in action because there was not sufficient information at hand. He regretted the postponement of such a "question of live concern"; yet in view of the public ignorance on the subject, he said, a preliminary investigation must precede the adoption of a legislative remedy. The task of investigation was assigned to the newly created industrial commission.[43]

Although the labor groups acquiesced in this temporary disposition of the minimum-wage issue, the settlement of the maximum-hour question almost produced a head-on collision between them and the Governor. There was no conflict over implementing the eight-hour-day amendment for workmen engaged on any public work nor over limiting the hours for minors.[44] The issue that aroused controversy was the reduction of maximum working hours for women from ten to eight and the extension of the restriction to hotels and mercantile establishments previously exempted. Harry Vollmer, a militant labor representative from Cleveland, introduced an eight-hour bill in the House; Cox told the labor committee he would veto it unless it was changed to nine hours. In place of a blanket law he advocated the principle of administrative discretion, allowing the industrial commission to fix hours for women industry by industry. Such flexibility, he told the Assembly, was largely responsible for the successful regulation of labor conditions in Wisconsin.

The House labor committee bowed to the administration and reported out a nine-hour bill which applied to women working in hotels and mercantile establishments as well as to those working in factories. From the floor there was an effort to test the threat of Cox's veto by restoring the limitation of eight hours—an attempt that was narrowly defeated, fifty-seven to fifty-nine. The Senate, at first, rejected even the moderate administration proposal. However, after reconsideration it voted to accept the nine-hour limit for women but to enlarge its application to mercantile establishments only and not to hotels. After an effort to rewrite the measure in conference committee had failed, Vollmer urged the House to accept the Senate version, which was approved on the final day of the session.[45]

Still another controversy arose over an anti-screen bill for coal mines, which the amended constitution now permitted. When such a proposal was on the verge of passing the House, Cox publicly supported a resolution, introduced by a rural Democrat, calling for a governor-appointed commission to make a complete survey of conditions in the Ohio mines. William Green condemned the resolution as a mere subterfuge designed to placate the coal barons; Cox defended it as a necessary step to educate the public, who might otherwise defeat the reform by a referendum vote. The majority of the General Assembly agreed with the Governor; a commission was appointed, which reported unanimously in favor of paying the coal miners on a run-of-the-mine basis instead of on a screened-coal scale; and a bill embodying this recommendation passed in the special session of 1914.[46]

Workingmen, already embittered by these two controversies,

were further miffed by the Senate's action in pigeonholing a bill to abolish the black list and other antiunion practices of employers. At the end of the regular session the officers of the Ohio Federation of Labor asserted in a signed statement, "the Democratic party had failed to carry out its platform pledges . . . , [and] Governor Cox had broken faith with labor."[47]

The harshness of such criticism was undeserved. Cox, to be sure, shared the reluctance of most progressives to support labor reforms which would grant special favors to able-bodied adults, particularly male trade unionists, as had been proposed in the bill to outlaw antiunion practices. On the other hand, he was willing to accept governmental intervention to protect the safety and fair pay of all workers[48] as well as to regulate the bargaining conditions between employers and women and children by stipulating the maximum hours and minimum wages of their employment.

Furthermore, the working class was the chief beneficiary of the humanitarian reforms Cox espoused. One that directly affected them was a mothers' pension bill which had been forcefully endorsed in the first message of the Governor. He cited the extensive interest in such a measure among juvenile-court judges and the state inspectors in the department of workshops and factories. The Cuyahoga delegation, long interested in this reform, led in sponsoring it, Mills presenting a bill in the House and Greenlund in the Senate. The most influential figure behind it, however, was Henry Nell, secretary of the National Probation League, who had helped draft the Ohio proposal as well as those in a number of other states. It provided pensions to indigent mothers in amounts varying with the number of children, and assigned to the juvenile courts the administration of the system. Ohio was the seventh state to adopt such a law.[49]

Since the purpose of this legislation was not only to protect the family unit but also to relieve minors of the necessity of working to support the home, it was incorporated as part of a new Children's Code which was intended to gather together and revamp all laws affecting minors. George S. Addams, judge of the Cleveland Juvenile Court, had been the first to suggest such a compilation. Governor Harmon had seconded it and appointed Judge Daniel Babst of Crestline and Arthur D. Baldwin of Cleveland to perform the task, which they completed in time for the 1913 session. Cox urged its adoption, a course the General Assembly followed with only two dissenting votes in the Senate and four in the House. The first of its kind in the nation, this "Magna Carta of the children of Ohio" was an elaborate document, comprehensive in its provisions.

One section was devoted to the prohibition of child labor and the regulation of the employment of teen-age boys and girls and greatly strengthened the Reynolds Law of 1908. The minimum working age was raised from fourteen to fifteen years for boys and sixteen for girls in general industrial and commercial pursuits and made higher for both sexes in dangerous or morally deleterious occupations. A graduated scale of maximum hours was set for males under eighteen and females under twenty-one. Complementary action was taken in requiring compulsory education for boys until they were fifteen and for girls until they were sixteen.[50]

Even more far reaching were the code's provisions for reforms in the care of juvenile wards and delinquents. Juvenile courts, which had only existed before in the cities, were extended to every county, and justices of the peace and police judges were specifically denied jurisdiction over children. Separate detention homes or jails were made mandatory for minors, indeterminate sentences were prescribed, and the probationary system was broadened and strengthened.[51]

The old supervisory board of state charities was made responsible for assigning dependent and delinquent children committed by the juvenile courts to a private home or a public institution and for transferring these children from one place to another as required for their welfare. In addition the board was empowered to certify the suitability of all homes, private and public, for the care of the children who became wards of the state.[52] Commitment of minors by local officials to the wrong institution was one of the serious abuses of the existing system, and it threatened to destroy the whole reformatory plan. Women of hardened depravity had been sent to the girls' home; feeble-minded youths to the boys' industrial school. The power of transfer was to help eliminate the worst of these mistakes.[53]

The most important innovation in handling juveniles was the creation of a bureau of juvenile research. It had been recommended by the Governor, who, in turn, had borrowed the idea from Henry H. Goddard, Cox's principal advisor in penal reform and later director of the bureau. Since the bureau constituted an addition to the existing penal institutions of the state, it was placed under the direction of the state board of administration which managed all the other state services of this kind rather than under the board of state charities. The purpose of the bureau was to examine and diagnose treatment for all delinquent children who were assigned to it by the state board of administration. Each child was to be given the Binet-Simon test, the latest word in scientific child study; those who were found to be feeble-minded were to be assigned to one institution, those who had normal intelligence, but had committed an immoral act, to the boys' (or girls') home or reformatory; those who were average, but had been warped by their environment to foster homes. This program placed Ohio in the forefront of the nation, in a position comparable to the world leaders, France and Germany.[54]

As important to Cox as improvement in the treatment of delinquent children was reform of the whole penal system, which was in a deplorable condition when he took office. Since 1906 various commissions had investigated the situation and made recommendations which had been ignored or halfheartedly fulfilled. Contracting prison labor to private employers had been abolished supposedly by the Wertz Act of 1906, but vestiges of it lingered on; officials winked at the law and permitted favored contracts to continue. Insufficient effort had been made to replace this form of labor with employment on state projects. As a result many prisoners rotted in idleness. Funds had been allocated to renovate the penitentiary, but more were needed to complete the job. The old cell blocks were described as "unsanitary, unhealthy, and unfit for a dog kennel." "The tales those walls could tell of brutality, neglect, and inefficiency if they had but tongues," wrote an observer, "would make Ohio blush with shame. Nearly every state in the land would blush for itself in the same way, if the facts were known."[55]

Harmon had allowed the situation to drift from bad to worse because of his blinding interest in economy, his innate conservatism, and his lack of imaginative understanding. In 1908 he had vetoed an act to purchase a new penitentiary site in the country because he was opposed to the great expense. The appropriation voted in 1909 to renovate the penitentiary and to set aside a plot of farm land for the prisoners to cultivate at the state institution for the feeble-minded passed without his signature. In his final message to the legislature on January 6, 1913, he used the occasion to counter the known views of his successor on penal reform and to urge again that the penitentiary be left on its existing site, for the purpose of imprisonment, he insisted, was punishment and not the rehabilitation of the prisoner.[56]

Cox, while expressing his reluctance, felt obliged by conscience to take direct exception to his predecessor's remarks in his own message a week later. He could not subscribe to the opinion that the primary purpose of imprisonment was punishment. To him, "the underlying view . . . [was] betterment of the race, the reform of as many prisoners as possible, aid to their families, earned by the men confined, and a contribution to the next generation of fewer human shipwrecks." These "humanitarian consideration[s] must outweigh every thought of continuing the present abominable system simply because a considerable amount of money has been spent at the old prison." He recommended a prison farm where trusted convicts would help raise the food supply for state institutions. In addition, he asked that the system of penal labor be extended not only to farming, but also to work on the highways, quarrying, and the manufacturing of clothing and other articles for use by the state. He advocated that prisoners be paid a decent sum for their tasks in the form of a credit upon which either their families could draw or which would be available to the prisoners at the end of their sentences. Further reforms which he urged were the adoption of an indeterminate-sentence law, the creation of a parole board to recommend the release of prisoners for good behavior and to supervise the parolees, and the elimination of the custom of allowing judges to assign a convicted man to a particular institution. By the end of the regular session all of the Governor's recommendations had been adopted.[57]

Closely related to these reforms were some of the changes in judicial procedure made mandatory by the recently adopted constitutional amendments. One of the new statutes incorporated the alteration that required the gathering of evidence for presentation to the grand jury. It provided for the taking of depositions in criminal cases and guaranteed the right of the accused to be present in person or be represented by counsel when the depositions were taken. Another enacted the change demanded in the petit-jury procedure, providing for the concurrence of only three-fourths of the jurors to render a verdict in a civil suit.[58] At the same time, none of the permissive features in the amendments were approved, such as altering the size of the grand jury or regulating the use of expert witnesses and testimony in criminal procedure.

In his autobiography Cox singled out the reformation of the penal system as one of the three major contributions of his administration. The second was the Workmen's Compensation Act, and the third was the enactment of the Rural School Code.[59] Although the manner in which he prepared the ground for this important educational legislation through the appointment of a school commission and the assembling of a school congress is reserved for later discussion,[60] it seems appropriate to sketch in the details of the code in this chapter.

The first of the recommendations of Cox's school commission —efficient supervision of every school—was provided for in a series of bills. The principal bill established the county school district as the basic unit of organization for rural areas. Each county was to be subdivided by the county board of education into rural and village school districts, which had the privilege of combining by popular vote. The number of schools in each district was to be determined by geography and population; schools with a daily attendance below twelve were to be suspended and the children transported to another school at the expense of the local community. Responsibility for overall supervision was placed in the county superintendent appointed by the board, and the superintendent was to hold monthly discussions with the district superintendents on the efficiency of operation of the schools under their jurisdiction. The latter, selected by village presidents and rural education boards, carried on the direct work of guidance and supervision of the schools in their district. The hiring of teachers, however, was the responsibility of the district boards themselves.[61]

In spite of this emphasis on the county, the state itself was by no means relieved of supervisory control. According to a law passed in 1914, half the salary of each county superintendent was to be paid by the state, and, under the same law, the new constitutional office of state superintendent of public instruction was created, so that a close watch could be kept on the whole school system and particularly on the high schools. Furthermore, another law provided for the grading of schools according to pupil enrollment and curriculum and prescribed detailed standards of course offerings for each grade, including courses in domestic science and agriculture. The amount of state financial support was related to the school's position in the grading scale.[62]

The second recommendation of the school commission—the certification of teachers—was met by a law elaborate in its detail, the main purport of which was to enforce gradually a prerequisite of college or normal-school training. In order to enable applicants to meet the stiffened requirements, another act provided increased facilities for teacher instruction—the third major point in the recommendations of the school commission. Normal departments were to be established in village and rural high schools of the first grade to a maximum of three in each county, the state agreeing to pay $1,000 per year toward their maintenance; six model one-room schoolhouses were to be operated by each of the four state normal schools; and attendance at county teachers' institutes was encouraged by allowing teachers to draw their regular salary during the week they were there.[63] Although these laws were not always applied in the spirit intended and a subsequent generation found them inadequate, they marked a significant advance in their day by correcting the most marked inadequacies of Ohio's public education system.

Intimately related to the proposal for consolidated rural schools was the good-roads program. In response to the plea of the Governor and the impetus given by the Rural Life and Good Roads Conference held in March, 1913, the legislature voted a half-mill levy for a network of intercounty roads and main market highways. Counties were authorized to collect a one-mill tax to defray their one-half share of the expense, and townships were permitted a three-mill levy for local roads. It was anticipated that the state tax would provide $3,500,000 and change Ohio from the most backward of states to one in the forefront of the good-roads movement, a prophecy unhappily never fulfilled.[64]

Both the Rural School Code and the scheduled highway improvements were parts of Cox's program to make country life happier and healthier and thus to aid the farmer. Like many others he was disturbed by the cityward trend, fearing that, if it were not stemmed, the food supply for urban dwellers would be inadequate and the already high prices for commodities would mount even higher. While these two reforms assisted others besides farmers, the remaining parts of the Governor's farm program were directed exclusively at agricultural betterment. He placed great confidence in the gains to be made by consolidating all agricultural agencies under one head in the new agricultural commission, the functions of which are discussed in the next chapter. Yet more important to the Governor was the final point in his agricultural program, i.e., the revival and expansion of scientific research in farming and forestry. The state agricultural experiment station, placed under the new commission, was directed to carry on this work and demonstrate its findings on county experiment farms. Also, farmers' institutes, when properly certified, were to receive public aid, and the results of their investigations were to be published at state expense. Agricultural instruction was made mandatory in rural and village school districts. The momentum that the Cox administration gave to agricultural research benefited the farmers of the state for a long time thereafter.[65]

Closely related to the program of rural betterment was the conservation legislation adopted. The agricultural commission was assigned certain duties in this respect: the promotion of soil conservation, reforestation, and the protection of wild life. The office of superintendent of public works, created by constitutional amendment in place of the old board, was made responsible for the construction and operation of dams, reservoirs, and four state parks, as well as the canal system.[66] While this part of the program reflected administrative reorganization rather than the addition of new functions, the Conservancy Act, passed in the special session of 1914 as a result of the 1913 floods, was an important innovation on both counts.

In March, 1913, the rivers of Ohio went on a rampage following an unprecedented fall of rain. Among the cities most disastrously hit was Dayton, inundated with paralyzing effect by the waters of the Miami River. Determined to prevent a recurrence, a local citizens' committee made an intensive study of the best means of flood control, out of which grew the Miami Valley plan, which provided the basis for the Conservancy Law.

This act permitted the establishment of a new political subdivision, known as a conservancy district, to prevent floods, reclaim land, regulate or alter the courses of streams, and provide for irrigation. For the fulfillment of any of these purposes highways and railroads might be moved and whole villages condemned. Such a unit was to be set up by the judges of the common pleas courts of the proposed district upon petition of a specified number of freeholders. After the district was established, it was to be administered by three commissioners appointed by the court, and financed by bonds, tax levies, and special assessments against the property owners benefited. The first to be established was the Miami Conservancy District, which constructed a series of dams and reservoirs that have proved effective against floods ever since.[67] Because of the great success of this pioneer venture, it became a model for subsequent flood-control projects in the state.

When Ohioans surveyed this impressive array of legislation, most agreed that the Governor and the General Assembly had scarcely missed a single opportunity to build upon the foundations of the constitutional amendments. The laws that the progressives had been advocating for a decade were at last on the statute books. Though labor complained that not enough had been done in its behalf, the more frequent criticism was that the Cox administration had gone too far. Farmers protested particularly against the new commissions because of their traditional fear of executive authority; businessmen denounced the regulatory measures and the labor legislation, which, they predicted, would drive industry from the state; and conservatives were appalled by the volume and scope of the laws enacted. "Think of it—300 bills," moaned the *Ohio State Journal*, "enacted by a Democratic legislature, whose primary object is, or should be, governmental simplicity. Oh, shades of Jefferson —what have become of democratic Democrats, that they should pester a Democratic governor with a profusion of legislation whose needs nobody ever heard of?"[68]

But the conservatives missed the point. Cox and the progressive Democrats of Ohio, though they accepted Jefferson's ends, rejected his means. They were concerned with the needs of an urban industrial, not a rural agrarian, democracy, and with a positive, not a negative, role for government. Their purpose was to make government more responsive to the popular will, to use the power of the state to redress the balance in favor of the weaker economic groups, and to instill a broader humanity into the law. In keeping with these objectives they wished to make the machinery of the state government more efficient and effective.

1. Mercer, ed., *Ohio Legislative History*, [II], 28; Cox, *Journey through My Years*, 135–36. Cox's inaugural address was brief because he broke with traditional practice by placing his recommendations to the legislature in a separate message.

2. Cox, *Journey through My Years*, 135; *Ohio State Journal* (Columbus), January 14, 1913. The *Cleveland Plain Dealer* stated that Cox on the eve of his inauguration was one of the most popular governors-elect in a generation (issue for January 14, 1913).

3. The quotations are from the Governor's Message, January 14, 1913, in Mercer, ed., *Ohio Legislative History* [II], 30–31.

4. *Ohio State Journal*, December 1, 14–15, 1912; Cox, *Journey through My Years*, 136–37; James M. Cox to Newton D. Baker, November 15, 1912, Executive Documents–Correspondence of James M. Cox (MSS in the Ohio Historical Society, Columbus [hereafter referred to as Cox, Exec. Docs.]). Cox's correspondence during November and December, 1912, has been filed in the boxes of Executive Documents–Correspondence of Judson Harmon because of the overlap in dates.

5. Cox expressed his purpose to Baker in James M. Cox to Newton D. Baker, November 15, 1912, Cox, Exec. Docs. Finley's impressions are quoted from William L. Finley to James M. Cox, December 9, 1912, *ibid.* Cox has reported the aid of Commons and McCarthy in Cox, *Journey through My Years*, 137. Baker had grave reservations about the selection of Finley for this assignment, which he passed on to the Governor in Newton D. Baker to James M. Cox, November 18, 1912, Cox, Exec. Docs. However, Finley was as good as his word in working with Cox on appointments. He proved to be a man of a different stamp from his one-time associates, Harvey Garber and Edward Hanley. Cox had no reservations about Finley and the two remained close friends. (The author's interview with James M. Cox, June 29, 1949)

6. The author's interview with Carl D. Friebolin, August 1, 1949.

7. In the Senate the seven minority members were all Republicans; in the House thirty-three were Republicans and three were Progressives (*Report of the Secretary of State of Ohio* [1912], 711–13). Cox's defense was given in the *Ohio State Journal*, November 13, 1912, James M. Cox to Oscar Newman, December 7, 1912, Cox, Exec. Docs., and in James M. Cox to Walter F. Brown, November 16, 1912, W. F. Brown Papers.

8. George F. Burba, Cox's executive secretary, offered the speakership to Bigelow (the author's interview with Herbert S. Bigelow, September 26, 1949). Bigelow publicly announced his candidacy for the speakership, declaring that he would be opposed by the interests and lobbyists (*Cleveland Leader*, November 8, 1912). An example of the protests against Bigelow that Cox received is in Frank P. Miller to James M. Cox, November 12, 1912, Cox, Exec. Docs. However, most of the protests were made orally. The offer of the floor leadership to Bigelow was announced in the *Ohio State Journal*, November 13, 1912. The Bigelow quotation is from a public statement in *ibid.*, November 15, 1912. In a letter to Cox the Cincinnati preacher sought to soften the sound of his remarks by promising the Governor-elect his "hearty co-operation" in writing the great progressive principles into law. He also explained that he was declining the post of floor leader for fear that it would cause even more antagonism and embarrassment than his election to the speakership. (Herbert S. Bigelow to James M. Cox, November 14, 1912, Cox, Exec. Docs.)

9. James M. Cox to Newton D. Baker, November 15, 1912; Baker to Cox, November 18, 1912, Cox, Exec. Docs. Bigelow had previously conferred with Baker, hoping to gain the latter's support in his bid for the speakership, but the Cleveland mayor refused on the grounds that it was the policy of the Cuyahoga group to leave all organizational decisions to Cox (*Ohio State Journal*, November 9, 1912).

10. The selection of officers in the two branches of the legislature was reported in the *Ohio State Journal*, December 17–18, 1912. The qualifications of Swain, Lowry, Warnes, and Green are discussed in Mercer, ed., *Ohio Legislative History* [I], 331, 538, 638, and in Cox, *Journey through My Years*, 164. The use of Friebolin was discussed in *ibid.*, 164, and James M. Cox to the author, September 16, 1949.

11. The committee assignments were discussed and reported in the *Cleveland Plain Dealer*, January 5, 15, 1913; *Ohio State Journal*, December 17, 1912; January 5, 15–16, 1913. Examples of the important committee chairmanships assigned to the Cuyahoga delegation were: in the Senate, William A. Greenlund, liquor licenses and prisons; Carl Friebolin, judiciary; and Maurice Bernstein, privileges and elections; in the House, Don P. Mills, public utilities. The three major chairmanships given to the Hamilton County delegation were: in the House, Bigelow, cities; Robert Black, privileges and elections; in the Senate, Thomas M. Gregory, municipal affairs. In addition, the taxation and labor posts were placed in the hands of other progressive Democrats. Later Greenlund had the distinction of being appointed lieutenant-governor to fill out the unexpired term of Nichols, whom Cox had elevated to the vacant post of chief justice of the Ohio Supreme Court (*Ohio State Journal*, Jaunary 19, 1914).

12. When Cox was elected, he announced that he would not decide on appointments until after his inauguration; then after that had taken place, he quietly dropped the remark that he would make no appointments until the legislative program was completed (*Ohio State Journal*, January 26, 1913). The Lobby Regulation Act passed the Senate unanimously and the House by a vote of 114 to 5 (*ibid.*, January 17, 22, 1913). The text is in 103 O.L. 3 (1913). The legislators themselves committed the breaches in the law's enforcement by waiving the certificate requirement in the case of lobbyists they favored (*Youngstown Vindicator*, May 2, 1913). Cox, however, believed the act was on the whole effective (Cox, *Journey through My Years*, 161).

13. The text of the law is in 103 O.L. 8 (1913). Lowrie's background is drawn from the *Ohio State Journal,* January 19, 1913, and from the author's interview with S. Gale Lowrie, September 28, 1949. During Harmon's first administration the post of legislative reference librarian had been created in the state library, but it did not constitute a separate department. The text of the law establishing the librarian is in 101 O.L. 221 (1910).

14. Cox's collaboration with Democratic and Republican leaders in the General Assembly is discussed in Cox, *Journey through My Years,* 163–64; his conferences with the Republican leadership were applauded in the *Ohio State Journal,* January 25, 1913. An indication of the flagging interest of the Progressives in the legislative sessions was Walter Brown's lack of response to an invitation from the Governor to collaborate in drafting legislation and the failure to name the legislative committee authorized in December until nearly two months had elapsed. The purpose of the committee, Walter Brown declared, was to promote the short ballot, state and presidential primaries, and civil service. (*Ibid.,* February 9, 1913; James M. Cox to Walter F. Brown, November 16, 1912, W. F. Brown Papers) In addition, the three Progressives in the House were ardent advocates of labor reform (biographical sketch of James Nye in Mercer, ed., *Ohio Legislative History* [I], 609–10).

15. Cox, *Journey through My Years,* 163; *Ohio State Journal,* April 15–16, 1913. Friebolin was the chairman of the Senate steering committee.

16. The adverse characterizations appeared in the *Evening Repository* (Canton, Ohio), March 10, 1913, and the *Cleveland Leader,* April 20, 1913. The *Cleveland Plain Dealer's* defense is in the issue for May 1, 1913. Cox's praise was in a speech at a Lincoln's Birthday banquet of the Jefferson Club, in the *Ohio State Journal,* February 13, 1913. The *Toledo News-Bee,* generally critical, praised the independence of the legislators. It could only ferret out six Democratic members of the House to accuse of siding with special privilege. (Issue for March 22, 1913) An indication of the high moral tone of the General Assembly was its attack on the custom of dual pay. For many years it had been the practice to hire legislators as special counsels for state agencies during the months the Assembly was not in session. Even though no statute or constitutional provision prohibited the custom, a probe committee recommended that it be stopped before it became "a prominent mischief," and a law was passed subsequently at the special session prohibiting the lawmakers from drawing dual compensation. (*Ohio State Journal,* February 7, 17, 1914) The text is in 104 O.L. 252 (1914).

17. Art. III, sec. 8, Constitution of 1851 as amended in 1912; *Ohio State Journal,* January 27–28, 1914.

18. Governor's Message, January 14, 1913, in Mercer, ed., *Ohio Legislative History* [II], 30–58. The final quotation is at *ibid.,* 31. The press commentary appeared in the *Dayton Daily News,* April 22, 1913, the *Ohio State Journal,* January 15, 1913, and the *Cleveland Plain Dealer,* January 15, 1913.

It should be mentioned that not all of the constitutional amendments required further action. The following were self-executing: No. 7, permitting investigations by either house; No. 8, changing the governor's veto power; No. 18, limiting the power of the General Assembly in sepcial session; No. 34, establishing the double liability of bank stockholders; No. 39, altering the process of amending the constitution; and No. 41, the schedule. In addition, Cox made no recommendation on two permissive amendments: No.

15, regulating the use of expert witnesses and expert testimony; and No. 35, permitting the state to do its own printing.

19. The Direct Primary Law passed the House with little opposition and the Senate with one dissenting vote (*Ohio State Journal,* March 5, 21, 1913). The text is in 103 O.L. 476 (1913). Ohio ratified the Seventeenth Amendment on February 25, 1913; the text of the act of ratification is in 103 O.L. 974 (1913); the text of the act for primary elections of senators is in 104 O.L. 8 (1914).

20. The text of the bill is in 103 O.L. 211 (1913).

21. The history of the bill's enactment was reported in the *Ohio State Journal,* April 20, 1913; the text is in 103 O.L. 831 (1913). Bigelow admitted there were some "practical defects" in the act in his comments on the constitutional convention in Mercer, ed., *Ohio Legislative History* [I], 411. Cox expressed his chagrin to Baker that Bigelow, who had been entrusted with drafting such legislation, had failed to do a competent job (James M. Cox to Newton D. Baker, September 2, 1913, Cox Exec. Docs.). The subsequent amendment to the law provided that any organization proposing a law or amendment might submit a synopsis to the attorney-general. If he found it a truthful statement of the contents, he could so certify. In addition, such proposals might be submitted to the legislative reference department for aid in proper drafting. The text is in 104 O.L. 119 (1914).

22. *Ohio State Journal,* March 11, 1913. The text is in 103 O.L. 653 (1913). Cox had opposed the employment of paid solicitors in the Governor's Message, January 14, 1913, in Mercer, ed., *Ohio Legislative History* [II], 36. He believed that if the practice of soliciting signatures for pay had been prohibited, the initiative and referendum process would never have been brought into disrepute in Ohio as it was (James M. Cox to Senator Robert L. Owen, November 14, 1913, Cox Exec. Docs.).

23. The Equity Association was a cover for a group of liability insurance companies who were fighting the compulsory workmen's compensation bill because it would cut them out of some business (Cox, *Journey through My Years,* 143). The allegation of Hanna's backing was made by Attorney-General Hogan (*Youngstown Vindicator,* September 12, 1913). Hanna denied the connection to Cox (Dan R. Hanna to James M. Cox [September 14, 1913?], Cox, Exec. Docs.). Cox's views were expressed in a speech reported in the *Ohio State Journal,* July 12, 1913, and in James M. Cox to Carl D. Friebolin, August 11, 1913, Cox, Exec. Docs.

24. Cox's explanation is contained in James M. Cox to Charles H. Graves, August 7, 1913, Cox, Exec. Docs. The hearings were reported in the *Ohio State Journal,* August 21–23, 31, 1913, Hogan's summary in *ibid.,* August 28, 1913, Graves's statement in *ibid.,* August 22, 1913. The supreme court's denial of the writ was reported in *ibid.,* October 30, 1913, and in the *Toledo Blade,* October 29, 1913. The referendum fight on the Warnes Tax Law is discussed at greater length below in Chap. XV, pp. 429–30; 438 n. 18.

25. *Ohio State Journal,* January 28, February 4, 1914. The text is in 104 O.L. 119 (1914). In his autobiography Cox reiterated his faith in the initiative and referendum process because it made the people sovereign in fact as well as in principle (Cox, *Journey through My Years,* 123).

26. *Ohio State Journal,* December 15, 1912; March 20, April 16, 1913. The text is in 103 O.L. 851 (1913).

27. Consideration and defeat of the constitutional amendment for the recall of elective officials was reported in the *Ohio State Journal,* February 5,

March 19, 1913, for the recall of judicial decisions in *ibid.*, March 4, 8, 1913.

28. The submission of the woman-suffrage amendment is described in Harriet Taylor Upton, "Ohio," in Ida H. Harper, ed., *The History of Woman Suffrage* (6 vols.; New York, 1922), VI, 511–13. It was defeated by a vote of 335,390 for to 518,295 against (*Report of the Secretary of State of Ohio* [1914], 278). The amendment to permit women to hold certain offices passed by vote of 435,222 for, 255,036 against (*ibid.* (1913), 300–302). The text of the latter amendment is in 103 O.L. 992 (1913).

29. In the debate in the constitutional convention it had been pointed out that nineteen states already permitted classification of property for tax purposes and that the trend was in that direction (speech of George W. Harris in *Proceedings and Debates*, II, 1563). One of those who tried to dissuade Cox was William A. Greenlund. In replying to Greenlund the Governor defended his course by indicating that many groups eagerly supported classification, including business groups and building associations, and by emphasizing that he had coupled this proposal with a constitutional tax limitation. (W. A. Greenlund to James M. Cox, June 9, 1913; Cox to Greenlund, June 9, 1913, Cox, Exec. Docs.) The rejection by the legislature was reported in the *Ohio State Journal*, April 15, 19, 1913. The classification amendment was defeated by a vote of two to one: 223,873 for, 551,761 against (*Report of the Secretary of State of Ohio* [1914], 278).

30. Its failure to persuade taxpayers to list their intangibles is discussed in Oliver C. Lockhart, "Recent Developments in Taxation in Ohio," *Quarterly Journal of Economics*, XXIX (May, 1915), 494–98. Lowrie compiled a list of some of the services which cities had been forced to curtail: Cleveland had abandoned a mandatory audit of public accounts; Cincinnati had reduced its educational and municipal programs; Columbus had jeopardized its health program; Akron threatened to close her public library for a month; Dayton's city manager was pinch-hitting as safety director to save the salary of a separate officer. Cities were in this predicament because the rural solons who dominated the legislature would not allow them to tax themselves to maintain the services they desired. (S. Gale Lowrie, "Municipal Revenues in Ohio," *National Municipal Review*, IV [April, 1915], 258–61)

31. The meeting of the League was reported in the *Ohio State Journal*, January 23–24, 1913, the Greenlund bill in *ibid.*, February 6, 1913. The support of the three mayors and the Baker quotation are reported in *ibid.*, March 11, 12, 1913, the Kilpatrick bill in *ibid.*, April 17, 1913. The text is in 103 O.L. 552 (1913). The text of the fifteen-mill levy is in 103 O.L. 57 (1913). The supreme court decision was in *Roosevelt* v. *Village of Leipsic*, 87 Ohio 513 (1913). The Kilpatrick Law was one of the three threatened with a referendum in the summer of 1913, but the municipal reformers took no part in circulating the petition. That job was performed in a fraudulent manner by the Equity Association. As with the attempted referendum on the Warnes Act, the Association's sole purpose was to build up animosity against the Cox administration and to discredit the direct-legislation process. The only sop given to the urban reformers was the creation of a committee of five to study the sources of state and municipal revenues in an effort to find ways of increasing the latter without raising the general property tax. The text of the resolution is in O.L. 192 (1914).

32. The defeat of the first amendment in the legislature was reported in the *Ohio State Journal*, April 9, 11, 1913. The text of the second amendment, which was submitted to the voters, is in 103 O.L. 984 (1913). Press

support for the latter amendment is in the *Cleveland Plain Dealer,* October 16, 1913, the *Cincinnati Post,* October 19, 1913, the *Cincinnati Enquirer,* October 25, 1913, and the *Toledo Blade,* October 31, 1913. The *Ohio State Journal* reported a heavy farmer vote against it (*ibid.,* November 5–6, 1913). The vote was 312,232 for, 340,570 against (*Report of the Secretary of State of Ohio* [1913], 300–302). In 1915 an identical amendment was defeated again by a somewhat increased margin: 337,124 for, 401,083 against (*ibid.* [1915], 245).

33. James M. Cox to Newton D. Baker, November 15, 1912; Baker to Cox, November 18, 1912, Cox, Exec. Docs. Hatton's bill and its amendment by the Assembly were reported in the *Ohio State Journal,* January 25, February 21, April 17, 29–30, 1913. The text is in 103 O.L. 767 (1913). The League's warning and the reluctance of cities to adopt one of the model charters are discussed in Mayo Fesler, "The Progress of Municipal Home Rule in Ohio," *National Municipal Review,* V (April, 1916), 250.

34. Art. XVIII, secs. 4, 12, Ohio Constitution of 1851 as amended in 1912.

35. The Mills bill was reported in the *Ohio State Journal,* April 17, 1913; Cox's veto and subsequent recommendation are in *ibid.,* January 7, 1914. See the Governor's Proclamation, January 6, 1914, in Mercer, ed., *Ohio Legislative History* [II], 70–71. The Kramer amendment and Baker's opposition are reported in the *Ohio State Journal,* February 4, 1914, the subsequent history of the bill in *ibid.,* February 4, 6–7, 17, 1914. The text is in 104 O.L. 243 (1914).

36. Johnson's suggestion was reported in the author's interview with Herbert S. Bigelow, September 26, 1949; Hunt's reaction in the author's interview with Edward F. Alexander, September 28, 1949. The legislative course of the Bigelow and Snyder bills was reported in the *Ohio State Journal,* January 24, 17, February 5, March 12, April 1, 11, 19, 25, 1913, the adoption of the compromise measure in *ibid.,* April 30, 1913. The text is in 103 O.L. 726 (1913). In the opinion of Edward Alexander, at one time a close associate of Bigelow, the revocation-bill battle was a tactical error. In the first place, the fifty-year franchise ordinance provided that rates should be reviewed at the initiation of the city at the end of the first twenty-five years, which was only three years away in 1916. The franchise specified a five-cent maximum but did not prohibit a lesser rate. In the second place, by trying to knock out the traction company and establish municipal ownership in a rush, Bigelow lost the support of many among the reform group who were not prepared for such a radical step. Furthermore, years of experience with the George Cox machine had made Cincinnatians chary of placing additional enterprises under municipal control. Finally, Bigelow united the opposition of the business community by threatening the sanctity of contracts. (The author's interview with Edward F. Alexander, September 28, 1949) The issue of the sanctity of contracts was also raised by A. B. DuPont, next to Johnson the leading street-railway expert among the Cleveland reformers. In an open letter to Newton Baker, DuPont attacked the Bigelow revocation bill as unconstitutional because it violated the principle of home rule, placed in jeopardy every street-railway charter in the state, including the Tayler franchise, and threatened any future improvements and construction by companies holding franchises (A. B. DuPont to Newton D. Baker, March, 1913, Whitlock Papers).

37. Art. XVIII, sec. 3, Ohio Constitution of 1851 as amended in 1912.

38. *Ohio State Journal,* March 2, 21, April 19, 1913. This was incorporated in the bill, thus strengthening the powers of the Ohio Public Utilities Commission. The text is in 103 O.L. 804 (1913). The measure is discussed below in Chap. XV, pp. 431–32.

39. The texts of these acts are in 103 O.L. 743, 379, 43, 854, and 254 (1913), respectively. The tightening of the Antitrust Code did not lead to any wave of suits, because antitrust action had passed into the hands of the federal government.

40. The texts of these laws are in 103 O.L. 914, 713, 714 (1913), respectively.

41. The preliminary arrangements for drafting the bill are covered in James M. Cox to Newton D. Baker, November 15, 1912, and Baker to Cox, November 18, 1912, Cox, Exec. Docs.; and in Mengert, "The Ohio Workmen's Compensation Law," 18–20. The Governor's endorsement in his first message, January 14, 1913, is in Mercer, ed., *Ohio Legislative History* [II], 50–51. The legislative course of the bill is reported in the *Ohio State Journal,* January 22, 28, 31, February 6, 19, 27, 1913. The opposition is described in Mengert, "The Ohio Workmen's Compensation Law," 20–21, and in Cox, *Journey through My Years,* 138. The text is in 103 O.L. 72 (1913). Enabling legislation was also adopted to fulfill another constitutional mandate by removing any limitation in damage suits for wrongful death (103 O.L. 116 [1913]).

42. The "Taggart ruling" and its rejection are recounted in Mengert, "The Ohio Workmen's Compensation Law," 28–35. Cox's pride in this measure is revealed in Cox, *Journey through My Years,* 138–43, and in Hester E. Hosford, "Ohio's Contribution to Reform: an Interview with Governor James M. Cox," *Independent,* LXXV (September 4, 1913), 547.

43. Governor's Message, January 14, 1913, in Mercer, ed., *Ohio Legislative History* [II], 56. The Assembly passed a law directing employers to furnish the industrial commission data on hours, wages, and types of employment of women (*Ohio State Journal,* March 13, April 12, 1913). The text is in 103 O.L. 654 (1913). The functions of the Industrial Commission are described below in Chap. XV, p. 426.

44. The texts of these laws are in 103 O.L. 854 and 864 (1913), respectively.

45. Cox's views were expressed in the Governor's Message, January 14, 1913, in Mercer, ed., *Ohio Legislative History* [II], 37, and in the *Ohio State Journal,* March 7, 1913. The legislative course of the Vollmer bill is reported in *ibid.,* March 13, April 11, 19, 29-30, 1913. The text is in 103 O.L. 555 (1913).

46. The bill had already passed the Senate. Frank W. Thomas of Wood County introduced the resolution for the probe commission, which the Governor endorsed in a public letter to Representative Edwin N. Boggs of Belmont County. Finley urged the Democratic members of the legislature to support the Thomas resolution. (*Ohio State Journal,* March 14, 25, April 9–10, 1913) Green's condemnation was reported in *ibid.,* April 10, 1913. Cox discusses his own position at some length in Cox, *Journey through My Years,* 219–20. It was characteristic of the Governor that he went directly to the miners themselves and explained his policy, which they accepted in good faith (*ibid.,* 220). A five-man commission was appointed, headed by Judge Philip Crow, one of the ablest jurists in the state. The commission

reported in December, 1913, and its recommendations were adopted in February, 1914. (*Ohio State Journal*, December 18, 1913; January 7, 29, February 5, 1914) The text of the act is in 104 O.L. 181 (1914).

47. The bill was defeated in the House by a vote of forty-three to fifty-four, party lines being completely shattered. A much watered-down version finally passed the House but died in the Senate. (*Ohio State Journal*, January 28, March 20–21, 1913) The quotation is from the *Toledo News-Bee*, April 30, 1913.

48. The Mechanics' and Builders' Lien Amendment was written into the statute book; the Industrial Code was strengthened in several ways; the hours of work on railroads were regulated to insure rest for the operatives; and semimonthly payments of wages to manual and clerical labor were made mandatory. The texts of these laws are in 103 O.L 369, 819, 557, and 154 (1913), respectively.

49. The Governor's Message, January 14, 1913, in Mercer, ed., *Ohio Legislative History* [II], 57; *Cleveland Plain Dealer*, January 20, 1913; *Toledo News-Bee*, April 15, 1913. The text is in 103 O.L. 864 (1913). The other states with such legislation were: Illinois, 1911; Colorado, 1912; Washington, Utah, Minnesota, and New Jersey, 1913. Similar bills were pending in fourteen other states. (*Toledo Blade*, April 15, 1913)

50. The history of this legislation is told in Hastings H. Hart, "The Ohio Children's Code," *Survey*, XXX (July 19, 1913), 517–18. Cox's recommendation is in Governor's Message, January 14, 1913, in Mercer, ed., *Ohio Legislative History* [II], 57. The code's adoption by the legislature is in the *Ohio State Journal*, March 27, April 12, 1913. The text of the code is in 103 O.L. 864. These minimum age limits were the highest in the country (Faulkner, *The Quest for Social Justice*, 187).

51. The text of this statute is in 103 O.L. 864 (1913). The creation of separate juvenile courts to handle delinquent children was one of the greatest changes in criminal procedure during this period (Faulkner, *The Quest for Social Justice*, 182–83).

52. The state board of charities had been established originally and had continued to function as a supervisory and advisory body only. When the operation of the state penal and charitable institutions had been centralized in 1911, a new agency, the state board of administration, had been created to take charge. However, the assignment of operating functions to the state board of charities had begun in 1910 when it was empowered to enforce the Pay Patient Law, which required the relatives or guardians of a patient to pay for the support of the patient to the extent of their financial means. But these new responsibilities over the children who were wards of the state was a considerable extension of its operating function, and the board created a children's welfare department to carry them out. The new statute also directed the board to study procedures used elsewhere in treating defective children and to make recommendations to improve the operation of the institutions that cared for them in Ohio. (Mercer, ed., *Ohio Legislative History* [II], 414–16)

53. Cox cited these problems in his message of January 14, 1913, in Mercer, ed., *Ohio Legislative History*, [II], 39.

54. The influence of Goddard on Cox was stressed in the author's interview with Carl D. Friebolin, August 1, 1949. Goddard had presented his ideas in Henry H. Goddard, "The Basis for State Policy, Social Investigation

and Prevention," *Survey*, XXVII (March 2, 1912), 1852–56. The text of the law is in 103 O.L. 175 (1913); it is appraised in the *Ohio State Journal*, July 6, 1913. The first director of the bureau was Dr. Thomas H. Haines, professor of psychology at Ohio State University, who had served as first assistant physician of the Boston Psychopathic Hospital. Haines was assisted by three other psychologists, a bacteriologist, and a diagnostician in determining the physical defects of the patients, and by three fieldworkers with a knowledge of psychology in investigating the family histories of the youthful delinquents. Goddard was the director in 1917. (*Ibid.*, September 11, 1913; Mercer, ed., *Ohio Legislative History* [II], 337)

55. Cox stressed the need for reform of the whole penal system in his message of January 14, 1913, in Mercer, ed., *Ohio Legislative History* [II], 39–40. The quotations are from Isabel C. Barrows, "The Columbus Penitentiary," *Survey*, XXVI (September 23, 1911), 887 and 891, respectively.

56. Barrows, "The Columbus Penitentiary," 888; *Ohio State Journal*, January 7, 1913.

57. The Cox quotations and recommendations are drawn from his message of January 14, 1913, in Mercer, ed., *Ohio Legislative History* [II], 39–42. The texts of the statutes embodying these reforms are in 103 O.L. 725, 155, 551, 273, 29, 474, 887 (1913), respectively.

58. The texts of these laws are in 103 O.L. 443, 11–13 (1913), respectively.

59. Cox, *Journey through My Years*, 144–48.

60. See Chap. XV, pp. 433–35.

61. The bill passed the House by a vote of eighty-eight to twenty-seven, the Senate by twenty-three to eight. The most controversial feature was whether or not to have a county superintendent. (*Ohio State Journal*, January 29, February 5, 1914). The text of the law is in 104 O.L. 133 (1914).

62. The texts of these two laws are in 104 O.L. 225 and 125 (1914), respectively.

63. The texts of these laws are in 104 O.L. 100 and 155 (1914), respectively.

64. Cox's interest is revealed in Cox, *Journey through My Years*, 147–48; the conference is described below in Chap. XV, p. 434. The state half-mill road levy was reported in the *Ohio State Journal*, March 19, 23, 1913, the wishful prophecy in *ibid.*, April 20, 1913. The texts of the laws are in 103 O.L. 155 (amended on 863) and 449 (1913), respectively.

65. Cox's concern for agriculture is disclosed in James M. Cox to Alson Secor, October 17, 1913, Cox, Exec. Docs., and in the Governor's Message, January 14, 1913, in Mercer, ed., *Ohio Legislative History* [II] 52–54. The texts of the laws are in 103 O.L. 304 (1913) and 104 O.L. 168 (1914). The functions of the agricultural commission are discussed below in Chap. XV, pp. 426–27.

66. The texts of these statutes are in 103 O.L. 304 and 119 (1913), respectively.

67. The flood was reported in the *Ohio State Journal*, March 26–27, 1913; the text of the Conservancy Law is in 104 O.L. 13 (1914). Cox stresses its significance and the establishment of the Miami Conservancy District in Cox, *Journey through My Years*, 174–76.

68. Labor's complaints were voiced in the *Toledo News-Bee*, April 9–10,

21, 1913. Examples of farmers' protests are in R. H. Triplett to James M. Cox, March 8, 1913, Cox, Exec. Docs. Examples of businessmen's alarm are in: Colin Gardner Paper Co. to James M. Cox, March 21, 1913; Cleveland Furnace Co. to Cox, March 21, 1913; and Patterson-Sargent Co. to Cox, March 24, 1913 (Cox, Exec. Docs.). The quotation is in the *Ohio State Journal*, May 2, 1913. The news columns of this paper were not as hostile as its editorial page.

CHAPTER FIFTEEN

GOVERNOR COX AS ADMINISTRATIVE REFORMER
1912 ▪ 1914

Cox, who had contributed so much as legislative leader, played an even more commanding role in the reform of the state administration. The way had been prepared for him by several of the constitutional amendments which the voters had approved. But he often went well beyond the constitutional mandate in pressing for changes he believed necessary. Moreover, he took pains to select competent men who shared his sense of commitment to administer the new agencies. By his own example he sought to inculcate in others his feeling of urgency, dedication, and service.

Three of the amendments requiring legislative implementation were those ordering changes in the court structure to increase the efficiency of the judicial system. The Governor assigned to Carl D. Friebolin, Judge Louis H. Winch, and a Cleveland attorney, Fred L. Taft, the task of drafting the necessary proposals. In fulfillment of the terms of the amendments, the number of judges on the state supreme court was increased from six to seven, making the new complement a chief justice and six associate justices. New courts of appeal were organized, and a common pleas court was established in each county, with the option to combine it with the probate court in counties with a population of sixty thousand or less. Finally, the office of justice of the peace, no longer a constitutional position, was continued by an act endowing it with all the powers and duties it had possessed on September 3, 1912, except in cities where it was superseded by a municipal court.[1]

Friebolin, collaborating this time with Newton Baker and the Civic League of Cleveland, also framed another mandatory piece of legislation, a state-wide civil service bill. This measure embodied the best features of laws in other states. Administration of the system was given to a commission of three, appointed by the governor with Senate consent for six-year terms. Exemptions to the classified service were held to a minimum. Competitive examinations to determine eligibility, promotion by testing as well as by tenure, and efficiency ratings were all prescribed. Civil servants were protected from political assessments or other forms of coercion and prohibited from engaging in political activity. With little opposition the bill passed the Senate, but the House refused to accept it without an amendment extending the exemptions to election board clerks and assistants, bailiffs, and all laborers.[2]

Cox appointed three able men as the first commissioners: Samuel A. Hoskins and Charles Brown, Democrats, and Charles Bryson, Progressive. Hoskins, a prominent party man, had been a member of the constitutional convention; Brown was president of Findlay College; and Bryson, secretary of Ohio University, had led the fight against Republican standpatters in Athens County. In September, at Cox's behest, they traveled to Madison to study the Wisconsin Civil Service Department, reported to be the most efficient in the Union. "Wisconsin once again," the *Toledo Blade* declared, "[was] to be the school of Ohio state officials."[3]

For the dominant role the Governor believed the state should play in controlling the economic life and social welfare of its citizens, civil service reform was only one of the necessary organizational changes. Another was to concentrate political responsibility in the chief executive in order to insure harmony and efficiency in administration. In his first message to the legislators, Cox reminded them of the short-ballot pledge in the Democratic platform, and pointed out that the constitutional amendments creating the appointive offices of superintendents of public instruction and public works in place of their elective counterparts were indicative of the trend. He recommended that legislation be passed to make the office of dairy and food commissioner appointive by the governor and that of clerk of the supreme court appointive by that body, and also that a constitutional amendment be initiated to limit the elective state officers to two, namely, the governor and lieutenant-governor.[4]

The bill to make the clerkship of the supreme court an appointive office met little opposition, but the act calling for the appointment of the dairy and food commissioner, while approved, indicated that there was trouble ahead for the short-ballot reform. The Republicans, in violation of their platform pledge, voted solidly against the measure, along with twenty Democrats in the House.[5] The resolutions, two in number, proposing the short-ballot amendment for state, county, and township officials, were introduced by Stephen M. Young in January. A joint committee of the two houses held hearings on the resolutions during February and listened to addresses in favor of them by James Garfield, John Fackler, and John H. Clarke, who had helped to draft them, as well as by two other partisans, Newton Baker and Alfred Bettman. On March 6, the Senate passed the resolutions, but the following day a hostile House voted to table them. Cox promptly called in the chairmen of the three parties—William L. Finley of the Democratic committee, Walter Brown of the Progressive, and Harry M. Daugherty of the Republican—read them their party planks favoring the short ballot, and told them to get busy with their party representatives in the House. This turned the trick. On April 16 the House reconsidered the resolutions and adopted both by the necessary three-fifths vote, although not without the further assistance of the Democratic whip, Milton Warnes, who chased party recalcitrants from the cloakrooms to cast favorable votes.[6]

Nevertheless, this success meant the battle had only been half won. Before the ink was dry on the resolutions, Attorney-General Timothy Hogan was publicly attacking them as "another novelty, another nostrum," which would promote bossism, not reform. He was soon joined in the opposition by State Auditor Victor Donahey and State Treasurer John Brennan. These opponents found receptive audiences in the rural districts, where the traditions of Jacksonian democracy were strong. By fall Harry M. Daugherty and the Republican state committeemen were railing against the proposals. Their platform plank supporting the short ballot had never contemplated anything as radical as these amendments, they declared; the effect would be to concentrate power further in the hands of the Governor's machine. They played on popular prejudice and ignorance by raising the specter of another boss by the name of Cox. Although the short-ballot amendments were not without friends and received an excellent press, they were buried under an avalanche of negative votes in the November election of 1913, carrying only in Cuyahoga, Hamilton, and Lucas counties. In the rural counties the vote against them was as heavy as twelve to one. Despite defeat, the short-ballot partisans were not disheartened, for they had gained a hearing, and this, for them, was only the start of a long campaign.[7]

A third series of reforms in state administration pressed by Cox involved the creation of a budget system and the consolidation of departments in order to eliminate waste and costly duplication of services. The idea of a budget bureau was suggested to him by Gale Lowrie in a "cabinet" meeting, and a bill embodying the plan was introduced and adopted by the General Assembly on April 11. It directed the governor to prepare estimates for each state department and institution, to be presented biennially, and authorized him to appoint a budget commissioner to examine any part of the state administrative machinery for the purpose of improving efficiency and curtailing expenses. This power to probe gave real significance to the new office. The legislature appropriated $15,000 for the office, and Cox appointed an experienced accountant, W. O. Heffernan, recommended by Newton Baker, to head it. The fruits were harvested immediately. In the fall of 1913 Heffernan prepared a new budget which reduced by nearly one million dollars— a cut of 10 per cent—the general appropriation bill approved in the regular session the previous spring. The revised budget was submitted at the special session in 1914 and was accepted by the legislature with scarcely a change in the figures. Even though Republicans condemned the budget plan for increasing the "dangerous and autocratic power" of the Governor, they did nothing to alter the system once it was installed. Ohio was among the first of the states to adopt an efficient budget system and anticipated the federal government by eight years.[8]

A substantial portion of the savings that the Cox administration was able to realize in the revised appropriation bill had been made possible by the consolidations which had preceded it. The work Harmon had begun in centralizing the state administration was greatly expanded by Cox. The latter, for example, proposed an industrial commission to bring under one roof all the state agencies regulating the relations between labor and employers, of which there were seven. In asking for this legislation the Governor based his appeal not only on economy but also on the need to promote harmony in the field of industrial relations through a unified administration of policy.

Cox told the legislature there was "nothing new or experimental in this suggested consolidation." Wisconsin had done the pioneering work in introducing and administering such a plan. When the General Assembly began its hearing on the administration-drafted bill, Professor John R. Commons and members of the Wisconsin Industrial Commission were present to address the labor committees. Their testimony was reassuring on the point of employer opposition. Manufacturers in their state who protested most loudly when the agency was created, they reported, were now its strongest supporters. The bill passed the Senate with only two dissenting votes and the House by a majority of one hundred to sixteen. Actually the only vocal opposition came from labor representatives in the lower chamber, who feared that the bill granted the commission too much power.

The new commission was empowered to supervise every state function that related to labor. It was given charge of the new compulsory workmen's compensation program; it administered all the laws relating to the safety and health of employees; it enforced the legislation regulating the hours of labor of women and children; it was responsible for conducting free employment agencies; and it was directed to promote voluntary arbitration and conciliation. The commission's rules and regulations had the force of law, subject to review only by the Ohio Supreme Court. Cox's first appointments to the three-man industrial commission were Professor Matthew B. Hammond of Ohio State University and Wallace Yaple and Thomas Duffy, both of whom had served on the old state liability board of awards.[9]

A second area in which Cox recommended consolidation was agriculture. Here the evidence of the need for economy was even stronger than among the labor offices. After an examination

426

of twenty-five agricultural activities, the Governor found duplication in fourteen departments and triplication in eleven. For example, demonstrations, lectures, and publications prepared on a particular subject by one office were repeated by another, which was unaware of the activity of the first. Again savings were not Cox's only motive. He also wished to tighten the lax enforcement of the pure-food laws and to promote scientific farming. An appropriate measure was drafted by Gale Lowrie to create an agricultural commission, which was to absorb the duties and powers of seven offices and agencies. Senator John Cunningham, a Knox County farmer, introduced the bill. Although the Ohio State Grange inveighed against it in the joint committee hearings, it passed both houses with little debate and by safe margins.

The act authorized the agricultural commission to serve as an adviser to county agricultural societies, to promote soil conservation and reforestation, to prevent the spread of diseases and pests among livestock and crops, and to protect farmers and the public generally against false weights and measures and the misbranding of food products and chemical fertilizers. Problems of rural and farm financing were to be studied, in addition, by experts who were to visit European countries for the purpose. Cox appointed to the three-man commission men equal in competence to those he had invited to serve on the industrial commission: Alfred P. Sandles, a former secretary of the state board of agriculture, Sylvanus E. Strode, the dairy and food commissioner, and Homer C. Price, dean of the College of Agriculture of Ohio State University.[10]

Consolidation of state departments was one means of streamlining administration. Another was to remove the performance of certain functions from elective local bodies and entrust them to appointive state officials. Even though this change would run counter to the trend to grant municipalities a greater measure of home rule, it was necessary for the state to increase its police power, Cox insisted, over "projects of general human welfare that can only be kept uniform in their beneficence by operation of the state unit."[11]

The issue of centralization versus home rule was raised early in the session over the question of liquor licensing, which the voters had approved at the September referendum. The drys, who had opposed licensing, wanted the local communities to be responsible because of their past success in influencing smaller units, while the wets favored control by a state board. Cox, a personal dry, but opposed to prohibition, strongly recommended the wets' solution, hedged with proper safeguards, and an administration measure providing state control was introduced by Senator Greenlund. The question absorbed much of the time not only of the legislature but also of the Governor, whose "public and private offices were open at all times to the preacher as well as the brewer; to the anti-saloon workers and also the lobby for the liberal interests." After working hard and consistently for the Greenlund proposal, Cox finally had his way. Wayne B. Wheeler, state superintendent of the Anti-Saloon League, who had used all his renowned skill as a lobbyist to defeat the bill, paid him a high compliment: "The governor has the rare faculty of lining up more representatives and senators for a bill in which he is interested than anyone with whom I ever came in contact."[12]

Though Cox had hoped the licensing law would dispose of the liquor question, the "irrepressible issue" continued to plague the state. At the elections for the next three years, initiated laws or amendments were unsuccessfully presented to the voters to impose prohibition or to prevent it.[13] Cox's solution was short-lived, however, for the Republican legislature in 1915 scrapped the state-board plan in favor of county control.[14]

As controversial as the Liquor License Act was a bill to centralize the entire tax-assessing machinery of the state by replacing the local elective boards with commissioners appointed by the governor. Cox, as well as a number of tax experts, was prompted to introduce this reform because of the success already achieved in areas where unification had been introduced. The state tax commission, which Harmon had staffed with able appointees, had shown remarkable results in raising the valuations of railroads and other utilities, and in assessing the real property of the state at a figure close to its true value in money.[15]

These successful efforts, however, left one problem untouched, namely, the undervaluation of stocks, bonds, mortgages, and money in banks. The question was how to lure or force such intangible property out of hiding and on to the tax duplicate. Several solutions were offered, and Cox was willing to try them all. Still, he placed his immediate reliance on a proposal to centralize further the tax administration machinery by making the state instead of the counties and cities responsible for local assessments. The drafting of an appropriate bill was delegated to Chairman Robert M. Ditty of the tax commission, assisted by Professor Oliver C. Lockhart of Ohio State University and a special counsel from the attorney-general's office. The first draft contained so many objectionable features that Cox refused to support it and soon replaced Ditty with Alfred B. Peckinpaugh as head of the commission. A revised measure with the offending parts removed was finally introduced, sponsored by Milton Warnes. The Republicans, declaring that it proposed a system more Russian than Democratic, did their best to defeat it. Nevertheless the administration was able to hold its own members in line, and the bill passed on a strict party vote.

Designed to complete "the missing link" in tax administration, the law directed the state tax commission to supervise the assessment of all personal, as well as real, property in the state. In each county two commissioners, appointed by the governor and responsible to the commission, together with a staff of deputies, experts, and clerks were placed in charge of the appraisal work. Complaints were to be heard by a three-man board, and provision was made for full publicity of changes in the tax list. In effect the act substituted an annual for a quadrennial reappraisement of real estate.[16]

The Warnes Law, by centralizing the entire tax machinery in Columbus and abolishing the old system of local control by county auditors and city boards of review, and by introducing, in the opinion of one authority, "the most radical administrative change in taxation any state had undertaken," inevitably aroused opposition. Allen Ripley Foote voiced the point of view of Republican opponents when he attacked the act as a device to increase the Governor's political machine. The ruling cliques in the county auditors' offices condemned it because it meant a loss of patronage to them. Farmers criticized it for fear that it would raise their taxes. In an effort to capitalize on this discontent and discredit the Cox administration, the Equity Association selected this as one of the three bills which it sought to defeat by a referendum vote, an attempt which was thwarted by their maliciousness and the aggressiveness of the Governor.[17]

During the course of the referendum fight over the measure, Cox was highly embarrassed by an overzealous party member, Collin C. Meekison of Napoleon, who had assembled a list of the probable county tax commissioners and had solicited them by letter to prevent the circulation of petitions. Incensed by the blunder of this busybody, the Governor fired off a special-delivery letter ordering Meekison to recall every communication he had written and to stop at once this line of campaign. If there was to be a referendum, Cox continued, it must be entirely on the merits of the measure without a suggestion that anyone was being influenced in its support by possible preferment. Appointments would be made purely on a basis of "efficiency and integrity," he concluded.[18]

The Governor himself made positive efforts to insure the success of the new system. In making appointments he followed the standards expressed to Meekison with assiduousness. He directed the tax commission to advise all men selected for tax positions in the counties to cease any political activity, placed the clerical force under civil service, and conducted a seminar and a training school in the tax commission's office. When the returns showed an increase in the tax rolls in every county, he successfully sought a corresponding decrease in the schedule of tax rates. To set an example, he convened the legislature for a one-day special session on July 20, 1914, to vote a reduction in the state levy from .961 to .45 mill, estimated to save the taxpayers four million dollars.[19]

The Governor's radical experiment was destined to be a brief one. Despite the proven fact that the new system decreased the cost of assessing property and despite the Governor's efforts to show that it was the culmination of a reform in the tax system first advocated in the administrations of Foraker and McKinley, the Republicans were able to make political capital of the discontent it aroused. Once in office again in 1915, they restored the old system of local control by county auditors and elective boards of assessors. Nor did Cox, when re-elected a second time, try to re-enact the Warnes Law.[20]

Actually, in fulfilling its principal purpose of placing on the tax duplicate the vast intangible wealth of the state, even its friends confessed it had only been a modest success. Though it did increase the percentage of personal property values in the total returns from 34.2 per cent in 1913 to 39.3 per cent in 1914, there was still widespread evasion in reporting intangibles. Two thirds of this wealth, it was estimated, remained in hiding.[21]

A change second in importance only to the revamping of the tax machinery was that to increase the effectiveness of the public service commission in regulating public utilities. In his first message Cox had recommended several improvements. He proposed to make mandatory what had been permissive before and thus require each utility to report the valuation not only of its physical property but also of its intangible property. He recommended that certain loopholes be closed in the system of court review of the commission's orders. Furthermore, he wanted the commission to be able to draw upon the services of engineers and experts on the Ohio State University staff, as the Wisconsin commission did so effectively with its state university. It would be of reciprocal advantage, Cox thought, since students and professors would gain practical training and the state would get the work done at minimum cost.

The administration's bill embodying these improvements was drafted by two members of the old commission and two law professors from Ohio State University. It was introduced by Don P. Mills, and was approved by the General Assembly without serious alteration. It embodied all of the Governor's recommendations: compulsory valuation, a uniform accounting system for all utilities, provision for an enlarged staff and employment of members of the faculty of the state university, and appeal from the commission's orders directly to the state supreme court, thus eliminating delays in litigation. This law made the Ohio Public Utilities Commission (the new name given to the commission) one of the strongest among the states.[22]

In arguing for the extension of regulatory commissions, Cox had stressed their advantages to the public—advantages that would not be fully realized, however, unless experienced personnel exercised the control accurately and fairly. His appointments to the public utilities commission met his first criterion. Oliver H. Hughes, who had served with distinction on the old board, was retained. The two new commissioners were Charles C. Marshall, special counsel to the former commission and one of the authors of the new law, and Edward Doty, who had shown his remarkable political talents in the constitutional convention and was an expert on the physical valuation of steam railroads. A decision of the United States Supreme Court in the *Minnesota Rate Case* confirmed the fact that the act itself had met the Governor's other two specifications of reasonableness and fairness. After the announcement of the court's opinion, Doty wrote Cox that the Ohio valuation law was the only one "upon the statute books of any state or of the nation that provides for an appraisal of railroads and public-service corporations upon the reasonable basis" prescribed by the high tribunal.[23]

A reform of the state administration in which Cox took a personal hand was the management of the state penitentiary. His interest had been quickened by the "great work" being done at the Mansfield Reformatory by Dr. James A. Leonard and at the Cleveland Workhouse farm in Warrensville by Dr. Harris R. Cooley. "These institutions," Cox declared, "should be an inspiration to every citizen. The Warrensville farm is the greatest thing Cleveland has. It is an example that is leading to a nationwide reform and national benefit."

The Governor kept alive his enthusiasm for this cause by frequent contact with the prisoners. Unannounced and unexpected, he appeared at many a Sunday service in the penitentiary chapel. On his first visit in January he gave a brief extemporaneous talk, sketching his plans for the prison farm and for his wage proposal. When he told the inmates "the state doesn't want to mint any dollars from your tears," there were cheers, stamping of feet, smiling and weeping, among both the convicts and the officials. In later talks he promised personally to investigate cases of family hardship and destitution and to review promptly any parole request from those who believed they had been wrongly committed. He never pardoned a man without first giving him friendly counsel in an interview, a practice commended by Clarence Darrow, who followed Cox's practices with close interest. When a new warden was to be appointed the Governor persuaded the state board of administration to choose Preston E. Thomas, who had served nine years under Dr. Leonard and believed in the moral uplift and reformation of prisoners by training and constructive work.[24]

Cox was also given the opportunity to further a penal reform that he had long desired. The legislature authorized him to appoint a commission to select a farm site of a thousand to twenty-five hundred acres for a new penitentiary and to prepare plans for the grounds and buildings. The existing penitentiary in downtown Columbus had become hemmed in by the expansion of the city; there was no chance for the prisoners to receive the beneficial therapy of work in the fresh air and sunlight. Cox persuaded Drs. Leonard and Cooley, two of the most dedicated penal reformers in the state, to serve on the commission. Maude Ballington Booth, founder of the Volunteer Prisoners' League, after investigating the state's prison system in August, 1913, declared that the "new spirit" and "the humanitarian and make-men policy of the legislation enacted . . . already placed Ohio as the first state in the union in prison reform." Cox's contributions to this field rank with those of John Peter Altgeld in Illinois.[25]

The Governor's faith—which he shared with Johnson Democrats and Roosevelt Progressives alike—in the competence of the trained administrator to apply general rules to fit particular facts has been noted in the discussion of taxation and rate regulation. But this is only one of the ways in which the expert commission may serve. Another, that has been mentioned only briefly, is for it to publicize evils and thus prepare the electorate—particularly the middle-class voters — for their correction by *state* action. Cox, as already observed, insisted upon special commission reports to pave the way for two labor reforms: minimum-wage legislation and the anti-screen law for coal miners. Notice has also been taken of the commissions of experts appointed to study rural and farm credits, to investigate deficiencies in the judicial system, and to advise on a new penitentiary. But the most dramatic instance of the Governor's use of this device has still to be described, namely, the revamping of the Rural School Code. In handling this reform he gave both state and nation a brilliant lesson in the art of propaganda.

He persuaded the legislature to create a commission of three to be appointed by himself to make a survey of the schools, and he named as commissioners Edith Campbell, a dynamic Cincinnati schoolteacher and social worker, William L. Allendorf, a Sandusky banker, and Oliver J. Thatcher, a Republican member of the legislature and a former professor at the University of Chicago. These were selections designed to allay the fears of conservatives. In addition, the services of Horace L. Brittain, an expert from the bureau of municipal research in New York, were obtained to direct the survey. Enlisting the support of college professors and graduate students at Ohio State University, the commission investigated 1,370 schools, 600 of them one-room buildings, during the summer of 1913.[26]

While this body was collecting its facts, Cox began to focus public attention on the issue, first on the rural problem in general, then on the schools. By proclamation he issued a call for a conference (the first of its kind) to meet in Columbus in March to discuss rural life and the need for good roads. He appointed a committee of six, including, along with representatives from each of the two chambers, Dan Hanna, a leading champion of highway improvements, and Edith Campbell, whose energy, drive, and imagination were to make her the dominant person on this committee as well as on the school commission. During the two-day session, attended by fifteen hundred persons, the importance of good roads to rural communities was discussed along with other problems of interest to farmers, such as agriculture, rural schools, and home life. In the opening address Cox urged a system of market highways to aid the farmer, maintaining that they would reverse the city-ward trend and stimulate the back-to-the-farm movement. Miss Campbell made clear to everyone the interrelation between the good-roads movement and the program to improve the rural school system.[27]

In the fall, when the school commission had completed its study, the Governor proclaimed November 14 as School Survey Day. The slogan, "A light burning for school progress in Ohio," was carried to each district. In four thousand schools Cox's proclamation was read, followed by a short history of education in Ohio and a brief statement of the new school-survey plan. Children recited and read essays on the purposes of free education; their elders made speeches touching on the same subject. The effect was to awaken the interest of the people at the "grass roots" in the school issue and to make articulate a demand for change.[28]

Each group elected delegates to the school congress which the Governor had called for December 5 in Columbus, and which was to be the capstone of his propaganda campaign. On the eve of the meeting the commission released its proposals.

434

The reaction to the recommendations was hostile at the opening session. Those who feared that the suggested changes would tread on their toes voiced criticism at once. Some of it, however, was mere quibbling, for several opponents, after condemning the commission's proposals, proceeded to urge substantially the same changes. Slowly the note of hostility evaporated as friends of the recommendations began to speak. The Governor gave the main address, pacific in nature, and allayed the rumor that any new legislation would interfere with county home rule in school administration—the foremost cause of apprehension.

At the final session the following day, the school congress agreed to confine its attention to three main points in the school commission's report: efficient supervision of every school, sweeping reforms in the certification of teachers, and technical teacher training. The tide in favor of these proposals rose, swept on by Cox's fiery, persuasive speech. Put to a vote, they received an overwhelming endorsement. Delegates leaped to their feet, sang "America," and indulged in a round of hand-shaking congratulations. Such a demonstration was convincing proof to the doubting Thomases in the legislature of the popular enthusiasm for this reform, and the program was approved in the special session with little opposition, as previously noted.[29]

Cox brought Ohio into the national limelight. The governor-elect of Massachusetts announced his intention to learn all he could about the Ohio reforms at first hand. It was flattering indeed that such an old state should take the Ohio program as a model. In Chicago the *Record-Herald* pointed to the Ohio achievements and declared that Illinois must do as well. Many Ohioans took pride in the fact that their state, which once followed the banner of Wisconsin, seemed now to be carrying one herself. One admirer of the Governor continued the parallel by calling him the "La Follette of Ohio." [30] Although Cox and the legislature had won great reforms for the state, there was one part of the progressives' program they could not achieve—the fulfillment of municipal home rule, a contest that had to be fought city by city.

1. *Cleveland Plain Dealer,* January 19, 1913. The texts of the laws are in 103 O.L. 405, 673, 960, and 214 (1913), respectively. Municipal courts, which had existed only in Cleveland prior to this time, were established in

Cincinnati, Columbus, Dayton, Hamilton, and Youngstown by separate acts (103 O.L. 279, 292, 385, 345, 354 (1913), respectively). The legislature also permitted Cincinnati to introduce a new division of domestic relations in the court of common pleas. The judge who presided over this division was to hear all juvenile, divorce, and alimony cases. (104 O.L. 176 [1914])

2. The drafting of the law was reported in the *Ohio State Journal* (Columbus), November 21, 1912, the *Cleveland Plain Dealer*, January 15, 1913, and in Civic League of Cleveland to James M. Cox, December 5, 1912, Cox, Exec. Docs. The legislative course of the bill was recorded in the *Ohio State Journal*, March 14, April 29, 1913; the text of the law is in 103 O.L. 698 (1913). Some of the opposition to the bill was suppressed. William Green, for example, was hostile to a civil service system but voted for the bill on final passage for reasons of political expediency. (The author's interview with S. Gale Lowrie, September 28, 1949)

3. The backgrounds of the appointees were reported in the *Ohio State Journal*, August 19, 24, 1913, the trip to Wisconsin in *ibid.*, September 28, 1913, the quotation in the *Toledo Blade*, Setpember 26, 1913. See also Chap. XVII, footnote 26, below for later Republican efforts to weaken the law.

4. Governor's Message, January 14, 1913, in Mercer, ed., *Ohio Legislative History* [II], 33.

5. The vote on the second measure was reported in the *Ohio State Journal*, January 30, February 7, 1913; the texts of the laws are in 103 O.L. 10 and 24 (1913), respectively.

6. The hearings were reported in the *Ohio State Journal*, February 21, 1913, and *Cleveland Plain Dealer*, January 16, 1913. Cox's conference with the party leaders is described in a statement by W. L. Finley in *Ohio State Journal*, November 12, 1913, the legislative course of the amendments in *ibid.*, March 7–8, April 17, 1913. John H. Clarke's leadership in the short-ballot movement is described in Warner, *The Life of Justice Clarke*, 54.

7. Hogan's adverse remarks were reported in the *Ohio State Journal*, April 22, 1913, the opposition of other Democratic officers in *ibid.*, May 18, 1913, the Republican opposition in *ibid.*, October 23, 1913. The amendments were supported, however, by Republican United States Senator Theodore Burton, as well as by Washington Gladden, Arthur L. Garford, Henry L. Hunt, and Newton D. Baker. It was estimated that seventy-four newspapers, including most of the metropolitan dailies, supported the reform. (*Ibid.*, September 22, 1913; *Cleveland Leader*, November 1, 1913) The vote was as follows: short ballot for state officers, 239,126 for, 461,555 against; short ballot for county and township officers, 217,875 for, 449,493 against (*Report of the Secretary of State of Ohio* [1913], 300–302). In the following counties the amendments were defeated by majorities ranging between twelve to one and ten to one: Adams, Harrison, Monroe, Noble, Vinton, and Wyandot. The optimistic reaction of the short-ballot partisans was recorded in the *Ohio State Journal*, November 6, 10, 1913.

8. The adoption of the law was reported in the *Ohio State Journal*, February 20, April 12, 1913; the text is in 103 O.L. 658 (1913). The appropriation act is in 103 O.L. 600 (1913). The appointment of Heffernan is reported in the *Ohio State Journal*, May 14, 1913, the reduction in the general appropriation bill in *ibid.*, February 17, 1914. The text is in 104 O.L. 64 (1914). The subsequent history of the law and its significance are discussed in W. O. Heffernan, "State Budget Making in Ohio," *Annals of the American Academy of Political and Social Science*, LXII (November, 1915), 98–99, and in Cox, *Journey through My Years*, 163.

9. Cox's recommendation, including the quotation, is drawn from the Governor's Message, January 14, 1913, in Mercer, ed., *Ohio Legislative History* [II], 51–52; the legislative course of the bill was reported in the *Ohio State Journal*, February 19, 28, March 13, 1913. The text is in 103 O.L. 95 (1913). The commission appointments are in Mercer, ed., *Ohio Legislative History* [II], 346. The adoption of the laws that the new industrial commission had to administer and some of the problems relating thereto are discussed above in Chap. XIV, pp. 402–3.

10. Cox's recommendation is stated in the Governor's Message, January 14, 1913, in Mercer, ed., *Ohio Legislative History* [II], 52–54, the legislative history of the bill in the *Ohio State Journal*, February 15, March 19, April 16, 1913. The text is in 103 O.L. 304 (1913); the text of the act creating the special commission to study rural and farm financing is in 103 O.L. 150 (1913). The appointment of commissioners was reported in the *Ohio State Journal*, June 21, 1913. Other aspects of the administration's agricultural program are discussed above in Chap. XIV, p. 410. In 1915 the commission was abolished by a Republican-dominated legislature as an economy move to save salaries. However, some of the services of the commission were transferred to other boards. (*Ohio State Journal*, May 16, 1915)

11. Governor's Inaugural Address, January 13, 1914, in Mercer, ed., *Ohio Legislative History* [II], 28–29.

12. The controversy was reported in the *Ohio State Journal*, January 22, 29, March 7, April 18–20, 1913; Cox asserted his own position in Cox, *Journey through My Years*, 157–58. The two quotations are both from an interview with Wayne B. Wheeler in the *Ohio State Journal*, April 20, 1913. The text is in 103 O.L. 216 (1913). The law provided for a three-man commission, which was to appoint two licensing commissioners in each county. No commissioner was permitted to retain or hold any interest in the liquor business. Licensees were required to be of good moral character, operating only one place of business. The saloons were limited to one for every five hundred persons and could be reduced in number by a local referendum.

13. In the 1913 election the voters had to consider two initiated measures on the liquor question. One was a bill, proposed by the drys, to prohibit the shipment of liquor into "dry" territory. It received 360,534 affirmative votes to 455,099 negative ones. This was the first initiated bill presented to the electorate. The other was a constitutional amendment, initiated by the wets, to reduce the size of the legislature by consolidating rural counties into single-representative districts, the purpose of which was to reduce the preponderant strength in the General Assembly of the drys from the country areas. This was defeated by an even larger margin: 240,237 for, 418,114 against. (*Report of the Secretary of State of Ohio* [1913], 300–302)

In the 1914 election the issue reappeared, with the wets having the best of it. A prohibition amendment, the first to be submitted, was defeated by a vote of 504,177 to 588,329, and an amendment to permit home rule in deciding the issue of intoxicating liquors, desired by the wets, was approved, 559,872 to 547,254. The effect of this was to make all counties which had voted themselves "dry" under the Rose Local Option Law "wet" again except for districts which acted by separate election to close the saloons. (*Report of the Secretary of State of Ohio* [1914], 278; *Ohio State Journal*, November 5, 1914) The two forces resumed their fight in 1915. The drys resubmitted their prohibition amendment, which was defeated again, but by a narrower margin: 484,969 for, 540,377 against. In order to forestall the annual submission of the prohibition issue, the wets proposed a so-called stability amendment, which would prohibit for six years the resubmission of an amendment which had been defeated. Those who believed in the fundamental principles of direct legislation rallied with the anti-saloon forces to beat this insidious challenge. The vote was 417,384 for, 482,275 against. (*Report of the Secretary of State of Ohio* [1915], 245; the author's interview with Herbert Bigelow, September 26, 1949)

14. *Ohio State Journal*, May 9, 16, 1915.

15. See above Chap. IX, pp. 227–31.

16. The drafting of the bill was reported in the *Ohio State Journal*, December 15, 1912, and February 9, 1913. The wrangle between Cox and Ditty and the appointment of Peckinpaugh is in *ibid.*, April 29, 1913, the legislative course of the bill in *ibid.*, March 11, April 16, 1913. The text is in 103 O.L. 786 (1913).

17. The quoted characterization of the act is from Lutz, *The State Tax Commission*, 503; Allen Ripley Foote's remark was reported in the *Ohio State Journal*, June 1, 1913. An example of the opposition of the employees in the county auditors' offices is in Beriah E. Williamson to James M. Cox, November 11, 1913, Cox, Exec. Docs. The letters of complaint were so numerous from farmers that Cox prepared a form letter in reply. He told them that the purpose of the Warnes Law was to place thousands of dollars of personal property, which had escaped, on the tax duplicate; that the effect of this would be to lower farmers' taxes; and that they must wait until the results were known before passing judgment (James M. Cox to H. H. Prior, April 7, 1914, Cox, Exec. Docs.). The activities of the Equity Association are discussed above in Chap. XIV, pp. 393–94.

18. James M. Cox to C. C. Meekison, June 21, 1913, Cox, Exec. Docs. Meekison went so far as to attempt to steal referendum petitions from the safe of the Equity Association in Cleveland, was indicted for that, and found guilty (*Ohio State Journal*, August 7, 9–10, September 19, October 8, 1913).

19. Cox was commended by the Civic League of Cleveland for his firm endorsement of the merit system in the selection of tax assessors (Civic League to James M. Cox, December 5, 1913, Cox, Exec. Docs). The Governor's advice to the commission is in James M. Cox to Tax Commission of Ohio, October 31, 1913, *ibid.* The report on the changes in the schedule of rates in the counties is in secretary of the tax commission to Cox, September 21, 1914, *ibid.* At the special session the highway levy was cut from .5 to .3 mill, the education-fund levy from .451 to .15 mill, and a special levy to provide an insurance fund for state employees equal to 1 per cent of the payroll was dropped. Press comment is in the *Ohio State Journal*, December 5, February 2, July 21–22, 1914.

20. Cox discussed the merits of the system in his Special Message to the General Assembly, July 20, 1914, in the *Ohio State Journal*, July 21, 1914. See also Cox, *Journey through My Years*, 159–60. The act restoring the old system is in 105–106 O.L. 246 (1915). See also below Chap. XVII, p. 476.

21. The figures of increase are from the *Fifth Annual Report of the Tax Commission of Ohio* (1914), 5. The failure of the law to bring intangibles out of hiding is discussed in "Taxation in Ohio," *Report of the Civic League of Cleveland* (1915), 8–9.

22. Cox's recommendations are in Governor's Message, January 14, 1913, in Mercer, ed., *Ohio Legislative History* [II], 35–36. The drafting was done by Oliver H. Hughes and Charles C. Marshall, members of the old com-

mission, and William H. Page and John J. Adams, the two law professors (*Cleveland Plain Dealer,* January 18, 1913). The passage of the bill was reported in the *Ohio State Journal,* April 19, 1913. The text is in 103 O.L. 804 (1913).

23. The backgrounds of the appointees were reported in the *Ohio State Journal,* August 19, 26, October 14, 1913. The *Minnesota Rate Cases* are reported in 230 U.S. 352 (1913); the Doty quotation is in Edward W. Doty to James M. Cox, June 12, 1913, Cox, Exec, Docs. The problem of the commission's control over municipally owned utilities is discussed above in Chap. XIV, pp. 397–98.

24. Cox's commendation of the work of Leonard and Cooley was given in an interview in the *Cincinnati Post,* November 3, 1913; his visits to the penitentiary were reported in the *Ohio State Journal,* January 20, May 5, 1913. Darrow's interest in Cox's practices is stated in Cox, *Journey through My Years,* 151, 155. The appointment of Thomas is in the *Ohio State Journal,* April 27, 1913.

25. Authorization for the appointment of the commission was reported in the *Ohio State Journal,* April 10, 17, 1913; the text is in 103 O.L. 247 (1913). The other two members of the commission were Dr. Arthur F. Shepherd, a member of the state board of administration, and Senator William Greenlund. Their report recommending a new prison farm was submitted to the legislature. (*Cincinnati Post,* November 3, 1913) The Booth quotation is from an interview in the *Ohio State Journal,* August 25, 1913. Cox's leadership in enacting changes in the penal code are discussed above in Chap. XIV, pp. 406–7.

26. The action of the legislature and the Cox appointments were reported in the *Ohio State Journal,* March 8, 1913; the text of the law is in 103 O.L. 69 (1913). The investigations are described in: Cox, *Journey through My Years;* 144; "An Experiment in Co-operation," *Outlook,* CV (November 22, 1913), 603*; Oliver J. Thatcher, "Educational Reforms that Set a Whole State in Turmoil," *Survey,* XXXI (January 24, 1914), 494.

27. *Ohio State Journal,* February 10, March 13–14. The commentary on Edith Campbell came from the author's interview with S. Gale Lowrie, September 28, 1949. The highway legislation approved by the Assembly in response to this conference is described above in Chap. XIV, p. 409.

28. Thatcher, "Educational Reforms that Set a Whole State in Turmoil," 494; Cox, *Journey through My Years,* 144–46.

29. Cox gives a glowing account of the school congress in *Journey through My Years,* 146–47. Many members of the legislature attended both sessions of the congress (*Ohio State Journal,* December 6–7, 1913; Thatcher, "Educational Reforms that Set a Whole State in Turmoil," 494–95) The details of the school legislation are covered above in Chap. XIV, pp. 408–9.

30. The remark of the governor-elect of Massachusetts was reported in the *Ohio State Journal,* December 4, 1913. The statement from the *Chicago Record Herald* is in the issue for December 6, 1913. The characterization of the Governor is in Joseph C. Breitenstein to James M. Cox, May 5, 1913, Cox, Exec. Docs.

CHAPTER SIXTEEN

MUNICIPAL HOME RULE
1912 ■ 1916

ON OCTOBER 5, 1912, slightly more than a month after the adoption of the home-rule amendment, Mayor Newton Baker officially requested the Cleveland City Council to submit to the voters the question of framing a charter along with a provision for the election of a commission of fifteen to prepare the document. He reminded the council that this opportunity had come after years of struggle and that it was fitting for Cleveland to lead in this work, as that city had set the pace in the movement to emancipate the cities of Ohio. Acting upon his advice, the council passed the appropriate legislation and fixed the election date as February 4, 1913.[1]

Baker appointed a committee of nine to nominate a nonpartisan list of candidates to serve on the commission and persuaded the Democrats to endorse the panel selected. The *Cleveland Plain Dealer* in a series of editorials supported the charter and the slate. The nominees were able men. Among them were: Baker, Edward W. Doty, Carl Nau, Stephen S. Stilwell, and John E. Tuckerman, all devoted Johnson followers; Augustus R. Hatton, who had written the draft of the home-rule amendment; and Daniel E. Morgan, later city manager of Cleveland. The electorate voted four to one to adopt a new charter, simultaneously electing the nonpartisan ticket of fifteen unopposed candidates. Only one thing marred a complete triumph: the apathy of the citizens, two thirds of whom remained at home.[2]

The charter commission began its work at once. Since sentiment in favor of a strong mayor-council form of government
was overwhelming, the commission resolved unanimously to proceed on this basis, thereby precluding further discussion of the
alternative commission or council-manager plans. As chairman,
Baker kept the body on an even keel, acting more as an arbiter
than as an advocate of his own ideas. Citizens of every opinion
were invited to present their beliefs and recommendations, and
all of the meetings were open, a fact which inspired confidence
in the commission's work.[3]

When the charter was completed late in May, a month's
campaign was begun to secure its adoption. Mayo Fesler, the
militant secretary of the commission, who was, as well, secretary of the Municipal Association of Cleveland, prepared twenty
articles to explain the charter's contents, which the *Cleveland
Plain Dealer* published. The *Cleveland Leader* ran a less enthusiastic series from the pen of Harry L. Davis, a potential
Republican candidate for mayor. The chamber of commerce,
churchmen, and party leaders gave their endorsements. So slight
was the opposition that the *Cleveland Plain Dealer* pleaded for
constructive criticism which would enliven the campaign and
arouse voter interest. It dismissed as absurd, however, the canard
condemning the instrument for being "Baker-bossed." On the
first of July, in another light vote, Cleveland's new fundamental
law was approved two to one, the first home-rule charter in the
state. It was the spirit of Tom Johnson transmitted through
his disciples, especially Newton Baker, that had produced the
victory.[4]

Under the new charter, Cleveland restored the form of government the city had had from 1891 until 1902 when the
Municipal Code went into effect. The legislative power was
vested in a council chosen by wards, and all executive authority
was concentrated in the mayor, the only elective officer, who
appointed the heads of the seven departments of city government provided for in the charter. Sitting as a board of control,
the mayor and the seven departmental directors performed such
administrative functions as fixing the salaries of subordinates,
approving all contracts in excess of $1,000, and defining the
rate schedules of public utilities. A unique provision, borrowed
from German cities, permitted department heads to appoint ad-

visory boards and to consult with them. The chief executive was directly responsible for preparing an annual budget and for operating the civil service code, which was a model for the period. The civil service code in the charter placed division chiefs in each department under the merit system and required efficiency records to be maintained on each employee. Cleveland progressives were satisfied with the charter's sections on the initiative, referenum, and recall. Under them ordinances could be initiated upon the petition of only five thousand voters, referendums by 10 per cent of the voters at the last municipal election, recall of the mayor by fifteen thousand, and councilmen by six hundred. Municipal-ownership advocates won their demand that all franchises include the right of the city to purchase the property at a price excluding the value of the city's grants. Workingmen's support of the charter was assured by provisions establishing the eight-hour day and permitting the city to perform labor directly instead of by contract.

The charter's most controversial feature was the sections on the election system, which called for nominations by petition, a nonpartisan ballot, and election by preferential vote. Under the latter procedure, first introduced in Grand Junction, Colorado, in 1901, voters expressed their first, second, and other choices, the candidate receiving the highest combined total being the victor. The purpose of the system was to weaken the control of party organizations in municipal elections by the petition method of nomination and the nonpartisan ballot and, at the same time, to arrive at an approximate concensus of the majority will by counting the combined vote for a particular candidate. The serious flaw in the arrangement was the failure to weigh the first choice vote more heavily than the second or third choice vote. A candidate who had more first choice votes than his opponent could still lose to the latter on the combined total of votes each received.[5]

It was fitting that Baker should be re-elected in Cleveland's first mayoralty contest under the new charter. His principal opponent, Harry L. Davis, was a politician of small caliber. Backed by the *Cleveland Leader*, Davis hammered at the extravagance of the administration as reflected in the high city debt. Baker stood on his record of achievement, which included the enlarged municipal light plant nearing completion, the successful operation of the Tayler franchise and the three-cent street-railway fare, the construction of a new city hall, the settlment of the union-depot squabble, and the adoption of the charter which he had been so influential in framing. It was symbolic of the spirit of the charter that the campaign was entirely a home-rule affair; no outside speakers were imported, as had frequently been the practice before. In the balloting Baker led on both first choice and combined votes over Davis, his closest rival, but, because it was a three-cornered contest, Baker failed to receive a majority of the votes cast. The victor's margin of 4,553 votes was slim by comparison with the 17,000 votes by which he had led his Republican rival in 1911.[6] If this decline in popularity was disquieting to the reformers, they were nevertheless heartened by the assurance that the city's government under the new charter would be launched by its ardent friends, not its lukewarm supporters.

In Columbus, agitation for a new city government began in February, 1913, when the council voted unanimously to submit the charter question to the electorate on May 6. Although one group wanted the direct submission of a commission plan, they were overruled by another led by several Ohio State University professors who favored the selection of a body to frame the kind of instrument that would command majority support. The latter group had been formed on the last day of February, when five hundred representatives of some one hundred organizations assembled in Rankin Hall, with Washington Gladden in the chair, to establish the Municipal Charter League. William O. Thompson, president of Ohio State University, was elected president of the League, and Gladden was made a member of the executive committee. The purpose of the organization was to select a slate of fifteen candidates for the charter-drafting commission and to arouse interest in a new charter. A declaration of principles was adopted to which the League's nominees were to be committed: they included greater centralization of authority, the short ballot, and nonpartisan elections. The organization's failure to endorse the commission form kept alive the initial split, a cleavage which continued to impede the efforts to write a new charter.[7]

Although 162 men were placed in nomination for the charter commission, the League finally reduced the number to the required maximum of 15. Among them were advocates of every form of municipal government; eight were considered progressives, seven conservatives. Socialists and other dissident groups were expected to present their own tickets, but only two other candidates besides the League's finally appeared on the ballot. In an election that was even more dispirited than that in Cleveland, with only a fourth of the electorate participating, the decision to write a new charter carried three to one, and fourteen of the League candidates were elected.[8]

The Columbus Charter Commission organized with Martin A. Gemunder as chairman and C. W. Wallace as secretary. Not until fall did it begin intensive work, and then there were weeks of delay because of its inability to decide on the form of government. The division between advocates of a strong mayor-council form and those insisting on the city-manager plan was almost even. At first, the federal form was voted down, eight to seven. By an identical vote a resolution was adopted to proceed with a modified commission-manager scheme, which provided for a mayor in charge of the police and fire departments and a city manager to head all other departments. Criticized for even considering such a "mongrel," "incongruous" plan, the commission switched back to the federal form with a council of seven elected at large. After further struggle over the remaining details its work was finally completed in March, 1914.[9]

Since some of the Municipal Charter League members were embittered by the failure to adopt the commission-manager plan, it was not called together to campaign for the proposed change. Still, the charter was not without its friends. The chamber of commerce and other business and service organizations endorsed it. Because of the varied opposition, it was not surprising that the balloting on May 5, 1914, was close—the charter carried by only 1,042 votes.[10]

Though embracing the federal plan, the Columbus charter differed from Cleveland's instrument in important particulars. One theoretical advantage was the small council of seven elected at large. This was offset, however, by the greater dispersion of authority in the executive branch, where not only the major but also the city attorney and auditor were elected, and the treasurer was chosen by the council. The chief executive possessed little more power than he had under the existing Municipal Code; he continued to appoint the directors of public safety and of public service, and was authorized to appoint the head of a new department of welfare. The efficiency of city administration was increased by centralizing purchasing in a board and strengthening the merit system. There were provisions, too, for the initiative, referendum, and recall; the employment of direct labor; a nonpartisan ballot; and preferential voting; and the terms of municipal officials were extended from two to four years.[11]

At the first test of the new election provisions on November 2, 1915, nine nominees for mayor appeared on the ballot. It was necessary to count all three choices to select the winner, who was the popular Democrat, George Karb, who had already served two terms as the city's chief executive. The Republicans elected both the solicitor and the auditor and won five seats on the council; the Democrats and Socialists split the other two seats between them.[12] Such a party division among the municipal officers did not augur well for the initial operation of the new charter nor for the achievement of responsible government, which had been one of the principal goals. Still, the reformers were not disheartened, for power was concentrated in fewer hands than before, and increased efficiency was assured by other changes in the municipal machinery.

The third city to follow in the footsteps of Cleveland in adopting a federal form of government was Toledo. In view of the prominent role played by Whitlock in agitating for municipal home rule, it was surprising that Toledo trailed some of her sisters in drafting a charter. When the city council, on February 3, 1913, approved an ordinance to submit the question to the electorate, it appeared that action would be prompt.[13] But because of internal friction among the Independents, it was delayed until the regular municipal election in November.

Whitlock, their acknowledged leader, who had announced his intention to retire from politics at the end of his term, refused to take any initiative for fear of being committed so deeply that he could not withdraw. He confided to Clarence Darrow that he was weary of the mayor's job, which had become the "veriest slavery" to him, and that he longed to realize his dream of a literary career. And to Negley Cochran he added these further reasons for wishing to retire: his conviction that

445

the Independent movement should be tested to see whether it could continue without the leadership of Jones or himself; his feeling that he had done all he could for the city; and his need to earn more money. Therefore, he chose in 1913 to remain entirely aloof from the political maelstrom. To such men as Cochran and Peter Witt, with their instinctively combative natures, Whitlock's decision was incomprehensible. They pleaded with him to reconsider, and, if he would not run for mayor, at least pilot the Independent ship away from the rock of personal ambition on which it threatened to founder.[14] But no entreaties would move him.

The figure whose actions endangered the movement was Cornell Schreiber, the city solicitor. Ever since Whitlock's announcement of his forthcoming retirement, Schreiber had been grooming himself for mayor and organizing the municipal employees in behalf of his candidacy. In this he was defying one of the cardinal tenets of the Toledo nonpartisan movement, namely, that the office should seek the man and not the man the office. How skilful he had been in his preparations was soon revealed at the Independent Voters convention on August 26, 1913, when he was nominated for mayor on the first ballot by an overwhelming vote.[15]

Such open defiance of principle by a man who was far below the caliber of Jones or Whitlock was not to be countenanced by a number of the original sponsors of the Independent movement. Within a week Johnston Thurston, Charles S. Northup, Negley Cochran, and others announced their intention to name by petition a complete roster of officers, to be known as the Toledo Ticket. They planned to collect sufficient signatures to nominate Whitlock, then, should he continue to refuse to run, to substitute another candidate more satisfactory than Schreiber. When they failed to shake the mayor's resolution, they chose Judge Charles E. Chittenden to head the slate.[16]

The Republicans had already nominated Carl H. Keller for mayor. The Democrats backed Schreiber, placing his name in their party column, and the Progressives likewise endorsed him. The three-cornered race was a bitter one. Cochran's *Toledo News-Bee* anathematized Schreiber as the Benedict Arnold of the Independent movement. It scored Keller as a reactionary, identifying him with the street-railway interests. In retaliation the

Toledo Blade accused the *Toledo News-Bee* of having "hampered and hedged" Whitlock throughout his administration, concluding that the only interest of Cochran, Northup, and "their personal satellites" in Chittenden was "to hang onto the dominance in municipal affairs, which they have used and abused so long." This attack produced an exchange of letters between Cochran and Whitlock, in one of which the latter lamented: "Now that another municipal campaign is in progress, I suppose that this and other fictions will be repeated, although I had hoped that after four terms in the office I might be allowed to depart in peace with the feeling on the part of those who know me, that while I have been mayor, I have been—mayor."

An even more disturbing emotional issue, which was whispered about until Cochran boldly gave it expression, was of a religious character. Under the aegis of a group of militant Protestant churchmen calling themselves the Guardians of Liberty, anti-Catholic fanaticism was abroad again, rallying about the standard of Keller, endeavoring to fan prejudices and thus elect him on the religious question alone. The *Toledo News-Bee* deplored the revival of a sectarian war, even though the attacks were directed principally at Schreiber rather than Chittenden, and the paper reminded its readers that there were questions of greater import than the alleged Catholic menace, such as settlement of the traction issue.[17]

So intense was the mayoralty campaign that it completely overshadowed the campaign for the election of a charter commission. Furthermore, the election of the slate of candidates was complicated by the split among the Independents. The August convention of the Independent Voters party, which had now become a discredited body in the eyes of the old leaders, had selected a five-man nominating committee consisting of Independents and Republicans. That committee had named a nonpartisan panel of fifteen for the charter commission, composed of business, professional, and labor men, Walter Brown, and Whitlock, who had agreed to perform this last service for his city. Another ticket was placed in the field by the Republicans. The *Toledo Blade* supported the nonpartisan slate, while the *Toledo News-Bee* remained silent. The candidates conducted a listless campaign, confining their remarks to an expression of their charter views. Both Whitlock and Brown endorsed a strong mayor-council plan, nonpartisan elections, and popular referendums on franchises. The mayor reiterated his faith in the municipal ownership of public utilities.[18]

In the election of November 4 the Republicans made a clean sweep, electing every city officer and the entire council. Keller won by better than two thousand over the combined votes of Chittenden, second, and Schreiber, a poor third. Although this defeat marked the collapse of the Independent Voters party as a political force, the influence of their principles survived to guide the charter commission, which the electorate had approved in the same election.[19]

The quality of the charter was all the more remarkable since the citizens had chosen ten commission members from the Republican slate and only five from the nonpartisan. Whitlock was one of the survivors, but not Walter Brown. The Mayor's direct influence on the commission was practically nil, however, for he only attended a few meetings before departing for his new post as minister to Belgium, to which President Woodrow Wilson had appointed him. John M. Killits, a conservative judge, served as chairman, and another influential member was J. Kent Hamilton, a Republican. Almost nine months were spent in framing the charter, during which the commission drew its ideas from foreign as well as native sources. Both the city-manager and commission plans, though considered, were rejected in favor of the federal form.[20]

The charter commission's work received the enthusiastic endorsement of the *Toledo News-Bee* and *Toledo Blade*. Cochran told his readers that the new charter was desirable on two counts: it increased direct rule by the people and incorporated Sam Jones's nonpartisan principle. Nathaniel Wright, the *Toledo Blade* editor and a leading spirit in the Ohio Progressive party, urged its support "in the hopes of a greater Toledo with a freer Municipal Government and better official rule." Backed, in addition, by the former Independent Voters organization, it carried 21,028 to 16,466 at the regular November election in 1914. The interest in the gubernatorial race explains the large vote.[21]

The Toledo charter resembled Cleveland's more closely than it did Columbus'. The only elective officials were the mayor, vice-mayor, and councilmen. The legislative body was composed of fourteen chosen by wards. All executive power resided in the mayor, who appointed the six department heads specified, as well as the members of the civil service commission. The initiative, referendum, and recall were incorporated, although their use was circumscribed by the high percentage of signatures required. Referendums were made compulsory on public improvements costing $500,000 or more and on utility franchises. Municipal ownership of public services was specifically provided for, and the eight-hour day for all municipal employees was established. The most sacred provisions were those dealing with elections, embracing nomination by petition, the nonpartisan ballot, and preferential voting. The new instrument, which Jones had envisioned and the Independents fostered, established the best form of government Toledo had ever known.[22]

It was fitting that the first mayor to be chosen under the new charter in the election of 1915 was an unaffiliated candidate, Charles S. Milroy, a former law partner of Whitlock. During the campaign, he received the blessing of the *Toledo News-Bee* and *Toledo Blade,* the public approval of a handful of the old Independent crowd, and the support of Walter Brown. His opponents were Keller, whose administration had been lamentably weak, and George Murphey, a Democrat. Though Milroy ran behind Murphey in first-choice votes, he garnered enough in the second-choice column to defeat his nearest rival by 597.[23] Ironically, also in the 1915 election in Cleveland, Harry L. Davis defeated Peter Witt in an identical way. Conservatives and radicals alike now began to have mixed emotions about preferential voting, and the device was soon abondoned, first in Toledo, then in Cleveland.[24]

In contrast to these three cities, which adopted a plan familiar in outline and proven by experience, Dayton determined to experiment with a new form, the city manager plan. In part, the older mayor-council scheme had lost favor because of the citizens' distrust of its local partisans, Boss Edward Hanley and his Democratic henchmen, but, more important, it was rejected because of the complete breakdown of the municipal government when the great flood swirled over Dayton in March, 1913. In this grave crisis city officials wrung their hands in despair, incapable of devising means to meet the situation. The heads and managers of Dayton's factories had to take control, and organize rescue parties and provide food and clothing relief. This catastrophe opened the eyes of the citizens to the weakness and inefficiency of the existing government. If the industrialists were the saviors of the city, it was argued, why not adopt a form fashioned after the organization of a business concern? In essence that is what the city-manager plan is.[25]

This form of city government, first introduced in Staunton, Virginia, and adopted by a number of small cities, had been advocated a month before the flood by Lent D. Upson, director of the Dayton Bureau of Municipal Research. The founder of this agency was John N. Patterson, president of the National Cash Register Company and an enthusiastic convert to the new plan. Devoting to municipal affairs the same vigor and administrative skill with which he had made his company dominant in its field, he helped to organize the Citizens Committee of Dayton, composed of two hundred outstanding men, and then to nominate a charter commission (on which he himself agreed to serve) pledged to the city-manager form.[26]

Since both the Socialists and the Hanley Democrats had their own set of candidates, the interest in the contest was the liveliest in any of the cities. Throughout the campaign James Cox's *Dayton Daily News* urged support of *a* charter commission, but remained neutral in the fight between the Citizens Committee and the Hanley forces, opening its pages to both sides. Its editorials deplored the rancor which was generated. By building an organization from the precinct level up, to match that of the political machine, the Citizens Committee defeated the professionals at their own game. On election day, May 20, 1913, they hustled their friends to the polls in each ward, and won an overwhelming victory for their panel. The charter question itself carried five to one. A measure of the civic interest was the number who voted which amounted to 60 per cent of the electorate.[27]

Since the members of the charter commission agreed unanimously on the form, the commission could proceed to fill in the details at once. Four open meetings were held to permit individuals and groups to air their views. The Socialists asked in exchange for their support proportional representation; municipal ownership of utilities, including bakeshops, milk depots, and slaughterhouses; the eight-hour day for all city employees; and abolition of contract labor on public work. Since these demands were met only in part, and the city manager plan seemed capitalistic in form and origin, they were hostile. There was opposition also from Democratic politicians who raised the cry of "government by non-residents," and from other persons who clung to the old forms, fearing the destruction of the time-hallowed system of checks and balances. On the other hand, the full weight of the business community and the white-collar class was behind the charter; the *Dayton Daily News* dropped its neutrality and supported the change without reservation; and non-Socialist workers favored the proposal. On August 12, 1913, the city-manager plan was voted into force, 13,377 to 6,094, a decision in which 62 per cent of the electorate participated.[28]

The charter provided for a five-man commission elected at large for four-year terms. The member who received the highest vote became mayor. This body, whose functions were entirely legislative, was directed to select a city manager to take charge of administration, appoint the five department heads, and exercise all executive power. The people were safeguarded by the initiative, referendum, and recall, and municipal employees by the civil service system. Certain of the Socialists' demands were met in a permissive way: utility franchises were to include a provision for municipal ownership at the city's option, and the council was authorized to vote for the eight-hour day and the abolition of contract labor. However, their recommendation of proportional representation was ignored. The election provisions called for nomination by petition, a run-off primary, and a nonpartisan ballot.[29]

To insure continuity to the work begun and prevent the city government from reverting to the hands of the politicians, the founders of the Citizens Committee formed the Greater Dayton Association, with a membership of ten thousand and an annual budget of $50,000 assured for three years. In the fall the association placed a strong slate of four businessmen and one union laborer in the field. The Democrats were beaten so badly in the primaries that they made no contest at the general election. The Socialists provided the only opposition, but it was ineffective, and the Citizens' ticket won by majorities of five to seven

451

thousand. The *Dayton Daily News,* which had lapsed into silence during the campaign, congratulated the voters for electing men of such high character and promised the new commissioners its support.[30]

The new government proved a great boon to Dayton. Municipal services were vastly improved and broadened in scope. Streets were paved and cleaned, the water and sewer systems were enlarged, and garbage and ash collections were instituted. Vice was controlled by closing the red-light district and gambling places. The most remarkable advances were made in social betterment under a progressive, humanitarian preacher, Dr. D. F. Garland, who became the director of public welfare. He cleaned up the markets and bakeries, maintained milk stations and baby clinics, built playgrounds, ball parks, and a music hall in which he sponsored dances and concerts. He also introduced prison reforms, placing the prisoners on a farm, extending the parole system, and abolishing contract labor. Dayton took its place beside Cleveland and Toledo in the vanguard of civic and humanitarian reform.[31]

On two other counts Dayton's adoption of a city manager charter was important. First, the fact that it occurred in the same year as the tragic flood, when national interest was focused on the city, helped to dramatize this plan in the same way that the Galveston hurricane and tidal wave had publicized the commission form in 1901. Second, Dayton was influential in setting the pattern for the type of manager to be appointed. The post was first offered to George W. Goethals, who had won international fame as the builder of the Panama Canal. When he declined, the commission selected Henry M. Waite, another engineer, a graduate of the Massachusetts Institute of Technology and head of the Cincinnati Department of Pubic Works. Since he proved an excellent choice, other cities followed Dayton's lead in drawing managers from the same profession.[32]

Dayton was not the only Ohio municipality to experiment with this form of government. In Springfield, labor unions cooperated with merchant and trade associations in approving the creation of a charter commission in June and adopting the city-manager plan by a two-to-one vote on August 26, 1913. Ashtabula and Sandusky had followed suit by 1916. Since that time thirty-seven other Ohio cities have installed their own versions, the most notable being Cincinnati, Toledo, Hamilton, Ironton, and Xenia. Cleveland and Akron each tried the plan for a time, but then repealed it.[33]

Although the Galveston commission form was popular else-where at the time, Middletown and Salem were the only Ohio municipalities to try it; the voters in three others rejected it.[34] In general the urban electorate was extraordinarily cautious in writing home-rule charters. Of the eighty-two Ohio cities in 1916, only twenty-six had submitted the question, and of these only ten had won a new charter.[35] The outstanding failure was in Cincinnati.

There the battle became intertwined with the municipal-ownership issue, and the charter itself never received fair con-sideration on its own merits. The central problem was whether Cincinnati should purchase the street-railway lines immediately or at some later time. Bigelow, who had unsuccessfully tried to force a decision through the legislature with his revocation bill, founded the People's Municipal Ownership League in the spring of 1913 to carry on the fight at home. His intention was to initiate an ordinance for the appropriation of the traction system and other utilities and to submit it to the people. When the League's lawyers discovered that it was virtually impossible to frame such a proposal under the rigid, cumbersome state laws, they recommended to Bigelow early in May that the simpler procedure would be to adopt a home-rule charter with provision for municipal ownership by popular referendum. Their sug-gestion was approved. After a brief canvass, the League col-lected ten thousand signatures, more than enough to make mandatory the submission of the charter question to the elec-torate. Having no alternative, the reluctant council fixed the date for July 30, on which day a special referendum election was also to be held on the modification in the size and repre-sentation of the existing city council. Had it not been for the League's work in circulating petitions, there would have been no election on the charter question in the Queen City.[36]

Although not a candidate himself, Bigelow helped to organize the Civic and Labor Charter Committee to present a slate of candidates. Another ticket was sponsored by the Citizens Charter Committee and endorsed by the chamber of commerce, various businessmen's clubs, and the Federation of Catholic Societies.

453

Candidates on both panels were pledged to support the short ballot, civil service, the initiative, referendum, and recall, and nonpartisan elections. The nominees of the Citizens Charter Committee were committed to the principle of municipal ownership but not to the immediate appropriation demanded by the Civic and Labor group.[37]

Bigelow was the bogeyman of the campaign. The No Charter Committee, organized to attack him and destroy his influence, even urged the Citizens Committee to switch their ground and oppose the election of a commission, a proposition to which the latter group would not agree. The radical preacher struck back by branding his opposition as high-toned "thieves and grafters," and by castigating the labor group on the slate of the Citizens Charter Committee for infidelity in associating with representatives of the business world.

Despite the publicity created by the rancor of the campaign, only 40 per cent of the electorate cast their ballots at the election, and the decision to draft a charter carried by a bare 90 votes, 19,666 to 19,576. The nominees of the Citizens Charter Committee defeated their Civic and Labor opponents by a majority of about 5,000 votes. Bigelow decried the result as a defeat for the people; the victors declared it a rebuke to the demagogues.[38]

The work of the charter commission proceeded slowly, not reaching completion until late in the spring of 1914. The document framed was a good one in terms of clarity and arrangement, but tended to be conservative in content. It provided for a reduced council elected at large; a centralized executive; the merit system; popular control through the initiative, referendum, and recall; a nonpartisan ballot; and ample power to regulate utilities. Its municipal-ownership provisions, however, were considered a farce. Instead of introducing a direct plan, it stated that the appropriation of property should be done in the manner provided by state law, and further handicapped the purchase of public-service corporations by requiring that an ordinance for that purpose be approved by a two-thirds majority at a general election.[39]

The charter's chance for approval, tenuous at best, had not been improved by the change in the administration which had occurred at the November, 1913, election. The voters had turned

Henry Hunt out of office and restored the Republican gang to power. Though the young mayor had given the city its best administration in three decades—appointing able men to manage the municipal departments, raising government efficiency to a high level, stamping out the most offensive aspects of gambling and prostitution, and introducing a humanitarian spirit in the conduct of the city's welfare agencies—he had made enemies by his efforts to settle the traction issue. The radicals blamed him for being too generous toward the street-railway interests; the conservatives, many of whom were stockholders, accused him of offering too little. Furthermore, he was the butt of the discontent aroused by a strike of the traction-company employees. He caught the wrath of labor for threatening to call in the National Guard to quell the violence and disorder, and angered conservatives because City Solicitor Alfred Bettman had threatened during the strike to demand a receiver for the company for failing to render adequate public service. In this normally Republican city it required the vote of all friends of good government to elect a Democrat as mayor. Despite a very favorable press and endorsement by leaders of the Progressive party, Hunt lost by three thousand votes to the Republican candidate, the amiable, complacent Frederick Spiegel, "a social and political friend of George B. Cox." The Mayor attributed his defeat to the negative attitude of the Bigelow partisans, the failure of the public to understand his position on the traction issue, and the defection of Democrats opposed to civil service. Daniel Kiefer, speaking for the radicals, gave a different explanation: he suggested that the vote was a rebuke to Hunt for trying to satisfy the people with palliatives instead of fundamental reform.[40]

This breach, which had preceded and then been widened by the mayoralty election, had not been healed by the time of the charter campaign. Bigelow, by design, was absent from the city during most of the period and even on voting day. This, however, was not the only obstacle to the proposed charter. The Republican machine, always hostile, made its opposition more effective as soon as it had been returned to power. Doctrinaire Socialists attacked the nonpartisan-election provisions, and the charter lacked newspaper support. Though it received the endorsement of many business, service and church organizations, as well as the Democratic Central Committee, it went down to defeat on July 14, 1914, by a vote of 21,253 for, 17,823 against.[41]

When Cincinnati's interest in a home-rule charter revived in 1916, the Republican machine was still in power, having won 'by a landslide in 1915, and it was able to elect its own commission.[42] The instrument offered at this time was substantially the existing form of government, as prescribed in the old Municipal Code, with a few amendments. The council was preserved at the same size and basis of representation, and partisan elections were retained. The only change in the executive branch was to make the treasurer and city solicitor appointive by the mayor instead of elective, and the term of all municipal officers was lengthened from two to four years. Apparently this conservative document was what the voters wanted, for they adopted it by a large majority at the general election of November 6, 1917.[43] The reform wave which culminated in the adoption of the city-manager plan was not to occur until the early 1920's.[44]

Although the Ohio municipal reformers had expected a greater demand for new city charters than had been manifested, the failure to exercise this permissive right did not diminish the large measure of freedom that all cities had gained from state legislative control under the home-rule amendments, the exact extent of which has been the subject of a long series of court decisions. Newton Baker, writing twenty years later, declared that he and Brand Whitlock had hoped to write a *perfect* document which no judge would be called upon to interpret. Had this been their expectation in 1912, they would have had to consider their work a failure, for the amendment and the subsequent legislation under it have been the source of constant litigation.[45] But, at the time, they recognized the impossibility of writing an amendment which would spell perfection. They failed to win as much freedom for cities as they wanted, and the municipalities were by no means completely divorced from legislative control. On the other hand, the Ohio home-rule provisions were among the best as to form, and granted broader powers than those of any state except California. Furthermore, the judges have on the whole sustained the intent of the framers.[46]

An important exception to this general rule was the decision of the Ohio Supreme Court in one of the first test cases, decided in May, 1913. The case came before the court as a friendly suit to determine whether the municipal home-rule amendment was self-executing and, if it were, whether Toledo could build a municipal movie theater. John A. Schauck, then chief justice, spoke for the court, giving a negative answer to both questions. He contended that Toledo, which had not by then adopted its own charter, was still under the state Municipal Code, and the code did not allow municipal ownership of theaters. But even if the city possessed its own charter, he maintained, such a use of public funds would still be forbidden. The "exercise of functions which are appropriately exercised by caterers and impressarios," he insisted, were not included in the grant of "all powers of local self-government." The suggestion that motion pictures might be educational, he concluded, was gratuitous because that was not their natural object.[47]

The one judge to disagree, Robert M. Wanamaker, the Akron Progressive and the greatest champion of municipal sovereignty on the Ohio bench, wrote a sharp dissent. He argued that the amendment was self-executing and that a city had the right to establish a motion-picture theater or any other municipal service it desired. The majority opinion, he declared, made the home-rule provisions speak and mean what had never been intended and was therefore "simply judge-made constitution." "Did the people," he queried, "who had asked [for] bread get a brick and that of the 'gold' variety, too, all under the label on the ballot: Municipal Home Rule?"[48]

As has been so strikingly true in the history of the federal Supreme Court, where the dissent of yesterday has become the majority opinion of tomorrow, Judge Wanamaker's views came to prevail. Ten years later, after the Schauck doctrine had been overruled by implication in a number of cases, the Akron judge had the opportunity of writing an opinion for the court which destroyed any lingering hold it might have had. He gave as the settled conviction of the bench the opinion that the grant of powers of local self-government was automatic and belonged to the cities whether they had adopted a charter or not.[49]

Despite the original narrowness of the court's interpretation of this issue, the majority of the high tribunal were generous from the outset in allowing cities full freedom in framing their own governments. Three months after the decision in the

Toledo case, another questioned the legality of the election clauses of the Cleveland charter, which differed markedly from the state code in that they provided for nomination by petition, a nonpartisan ballot, and preferential voting. The court's opinion declared, "The provisions of a charter which is passed within the limits of a constitutional grant of authority to the city are as much the law as a statute passed by the general assembly; [and] municipal elections are and should be regarded as affairs relating to the municipality itself, . . . and are things that may be provided by the local government." In a concurring opinion Judge Wanamaker added a few remarks reminiscent of a stump speech: "It is high time to construe our constitution in the interest of a people's government instead of a party government . . . to shield the people's power and the people's property rather than to exploit them for the benefit of the political boss and the party machine. The people of a city cannot get real efficiency in the public business until they get real emancipation from the party boss." [50]

The fact that this decision was rendered by an evenly divided court sustaining the ruling of a lower tribunal robbed municipal reformers of some of the comfort this favorable verdict aroused. Nevertheless their concern proved to be unwarranted. In a Dayton civil service case the next year the majority upheld the municipal charter provisions which differed from the state statutes, and in 1915 the judges, without written opinions unanimously confirmed two other variations from the General Code in the Cleveland charter.[51] The one important exception to this rule has been the state supreme court's refusal to permit cities to alter judicial offices and functions, insisting that state sovereignty is supreme in this area.[52]

In interpreting the grant of municipal police powers the jurists have been more restrictive, in keeping with section three of the amendment itself, which states: "Municipalties shall have authority to exercise all powers of local self-government and to adopt and enforce within their limits such local police, sanitary and other similar regulations, *as are not in conflict with general laws.*" [53] The doctrine, as spelled out in the case books, has been that cities must accept the minimum state regulations, but may increase restraints and act in areas where the legislature has failed to enter. Moreover, no municipal regulatory ordinance involving the police power that conflicts with either a statute of a general nature or with the state or national constitution has been sustained by the courts.[54]

In drafting the provisions covering the municipal ownership, operation, and construction of utilities, the framers purposely made them as strong and unequivocal as they knew how. These sections the Ohio Supreme Court has interpreted as a grant of plenary power, derived directly from the constitution and not limited by the state code except as to statutory restrictions on taxes and debts and the review of rates to determine fairness.[55] It is true that the judiciary opposed the extension of services embraced by the term public utility, as in the Toledo movie-theater case; nevertheless, it has been generous in sustaining the right of every municipality, with or without a charter, to levy taxes and issue bonds against the general credit of the city to purchase a public-service corporation, provided the statutory limits are not exceeded.[56]

In the management of their fiscal affairs urban communities achieved the least freedom. Not only had the section of Article XIII of the Constitution of 1851 been retained which empowered the General Assembly to restrict cities in taxation, assessment, and contracting debt, but also its substance had been repeated in section thirteen of the new home-rule amendment, with the additional safeguard that laws might be passed requiring examination and reports of municipal finances.[57] Although home-rule partisans knew in 1912 that without yielding on this point they would not have carried their cherished reform, it continued to distress them. Baker expressed to Whitlock his feeling of disillusionment that "with all our solemn pains we did little more than put a new label on the back of our Statute book, for in all financial matters we are still ruled by the rustic garland that makes the member from Pike County our sovereign." The legislature has continued to insist upon exercising its prerogative, and the supreme court has upheld its right, clearly denying that the adoption of a charter altered state fiscal control in any aspect. The only leniency shown has been in permitting municipalities to levy taxes in areas not occupied by the state, such as those on occupations or payrolls.[58]

The home-rule amendment proved no panacea, but it did give urban communities the opportunity to attack old ills with new

459

forms of their own choice—the initiative, referendum, and recall, nonpartisan elections and preferential voting, the merit system, and permissive municipal ownership. It destroyed the pernicious abuse of special enactments inspired by partisanship or corrupt bargains. Civic pride was encouraged and the public conscience aroused wherever charters were adopted. Over the years they have been approved in cities embracing a majority of the urban population.[59] Finally, home rule provided the impetus that enabled the reform movement, heretofore confined to Cleveland, Toledo, Columbus, and Cincinnati, to spread and take root in such communities as Dayton, Springfield, and Middletown, which had not known before its stimulating effect.

1. Newton D. Baker to the City Council of Cleveland, October 5, 1912, in *Proceedings of the City Council, City of Cleveland*, XLV (1912), 716, 817, 844.

2. *The Municipal Bulletin* (The Civic League of Cleveland), (December, 1913), 10; *Cleveland Plain Dealer*, January 19, 22–29, 1913. The official count was 19,125 for, 5,218 against. Baker received 18,955 votes, the highest of all the candidates. (*Ibid.*, February 8, 1913)

3. *Cleveland Plain Dealer*, February 19, 21, 1913; "Twenty-five Years of Home Rule," 76.

4. *Cleveland Plain Dealer*, May 24, June 1–30, 1913; *Cleveland Leader*, June 1–30, 1913. Davis' concluding article was a veiled rejection of the charter, though he made no outright condemnation. The endorsements of the chamber of commerce and others appeared in the *Cleveland Plain Dealer*, June 30, 1913, the *Plain Dealer's* own plea in the issues for June 20, 26, 1913. The vote was 24,037 to 12,077 (*ibid.*, July 2, 1913). Baker commented upon the victory to his friend Whitlock: N. D. Baker to Brand Whitlock, July 2, 1913, Whitlock Papers.

5. *The Charter of the City of Cleveland, 1913.* An able commentary on the charter is in *The Municipal Bulletin* (The Civic League of Cleveland) (December, 1913), 3–9. The merits and defects of preferential voting are discussed in Charles M. Kneier, *City Government in the United States* (New York, 1934), 210–12.

6. *Cleveland Leader*, October 25–November 3, 1913; *Cleveland Plain Dealer*, October 19–November 3, 1913. The *Cleveland Press* also backed Baker. See the issues for October 17, 25–November 3, 1913. The vote for mayor was:

Candidates	First Choice	Second Choice	Third Choice
Baker	41,296	3,554	1,554
Davis	36,119	3,928	1,804
Robb	5,768	9,247	2,593

(*Cleveland Plain Dealer*, November 6, 1913).

7. The council vote was reported in the *Ohio State Journal* (Columbus),

February 18, 1913, the formation and work of the Municipal Charter League in *ibid.*, February 8, March 1, 14–15, 1913.

8. *Ibid.*, March 21, April 2, 4, 6, 9, 11, 1913. It was reported that four of those nominated by the League favored the commission plan. The vote as reported the morning after the election was 7,299 to 2,845. Undoubtedly these totals were increased by late returns. The press, however, commented on the empty polling booths and light interest, especially in the working-men's wards (*ibid.*, May 7, 1913).

9. The organization and work of the charter commission was reported in *ibid.*, May 14, September 10, October 17, November 19–20, 26, December 5, 1913; March 4, 1914. Washington Gladden endorsed some form of the council-manager plan before the commission (*ibid.*, October 8, 1913).

10. The campaign for, and endorsement of, the charter were reported in *ibid.*, March 30, April 5, 26, 1914. The vote was 8,500 to 7,458 (*ibid.*, May 6, 1914).

11. *Charter of the City of Columbus*, 1914, published in *ibid.*, May 6, 1914.

12. *Ibid.*, November 3–4, 1915.

13. *Toledo News-Bee*, February 4, 1913.

14. Whitlock's remarks are in Brand Whitlock to Clarence Darrow, May 7, 1911, Whitlock Papers, and Brand Whitlock to Negley Cochran, May 6, 1913, in Nevins, ed., *The Letters and Journal of Brand Whitlock*, I, 166–67. Cochran's pleas were in double-column editorials in the *Toledo News-Bee*, April 18, September 3, 1913, and in Negley D. Cochran to Brand Whitlock, September 3, 1913, Whitlock Papers. Witt's plea is in Peter Witt to Brand Whitlock, October 9, 1913, Whitlock Papers. The *Toledo Blade* also urged Whitlock to reconsider and run again (the issues for September 2–5, 16, 1913).

15. *Toledo News-Bee*, August 25–27, September 2, 1913; Johnson, *Toledo's Non-Partisan Movement*, 30–31. A recent authority defends the nomination of Schreiber because he had been city solicitor for four years and had been as militant as Whitlock in opposing the demands of the Toledo Railway and Light Company. Cochran's hostility to Schreiber is attributed to personal pique. (Randolph C. Downes, "The Toledo Political-Religious Municipal Campaign of 1913 and the Death of the Independent Party," Northwest Ohio Quarterly, XXX [Summer, 1958], 140–44)

16. *Toledo News-Bee*, September 3, October 3–4, 1913; *Toledo Blade*, September 3–5, 16, October 4, 1913.

17. The Republican nomination of Keller and Democratic endorsement of Schreiber were reported in the *Toledo Blade*, September 3, October 28, 30, 1913. Examples of the *Toledo News-Bee's* charges are in the issues for September 3–4, 29–30, October 3–4, 1913. Throughout October and espec-ially in the final week the *News-Bee* strained to create a stampede among the voters for Chittenden. Neither Jones nor Whitlock had ever received such strong and insistent support from Cochran, who seemed intent on electing the judge single-handedly. The *Blade's* attack is exemplified in the issue for October 6, 1913. The Whitlock quotation is in Brand Whitlock to Negley D. Cochran, October 7, 1913, in *Toledo News-Bee*, October 7, 1913. The revival of the anti-Catholic issue was reported in *ibid.*, October 14–15, 1913, and in Johnson, *Toledo's Non-Partisan Movement*, 30–31. Randolph Downes, however, has written the fullest account. He points out that neither Schreiber

nor Chittenden were Catholics, but it was feared that Schreiber, if elected
would reappoint the Catholic Joseph J. Mooney as director of public safety.
There was only one Catholic running for public office, J. F. McKenna, who
was seeking re-election to the school board, and he was defeated, as might be
expected. In addition to the wave of anti-Catholicism there was a revival of
the moral issue, which also played an important part in the election of Keller,
who promised to clean up the red-light district and to shut down the
gambling dens. (Downes, "The Toledo Political-Religious Campaign of 1913,"
148–61)

18. *Toledo Blade,* September 17, 29, October 8, 1913. Whitlock's and
Brown's views were reported in *ibid.,* October 29, 31, 1913.

19. The mayoralty vote was: Keller 16,897, Chittenden 9,507 Schreiber
4,073 (*ibid.,* November 5, 1913; *Toledo News-Bee,* November 5, 1913).
The vote on the charter question was 13,375 for, 4,822 against; it received
a majority in every ward in the city (*Toledo Blade,* November 6, 1913).

20. The organization and work of the charter commission are described
in the *Toledo Blade,* November 5–6, 1913, and in Killitts, ed., *Toledo and
Lucas County,* I, 297–303.

21. The *Toledo News-Bee's* endorsement was reported in the issues for
October 28–29, November 2, 1914; the *Toledo Blade's* in the issue for November
2, 1914. The election results and commentary thereon are in *ibid.,*
November 4–5, and in Killitts, ed., *Toledo and Lucas County,* I, 298–99.

22. The Toledo Charter of 1914 is analyzed in Killitts, ed., *Toledo and
Lucas County,* I, 299–303, and in H. T. Shenefield and J. Otis Garber,
Toledo Our Community (Chicago [1932]), 90–93. The influence of Jones
and the Independent Voters is stressed in Killitts, ed., *Toledo and Lucas
County,* I, 583–84.

23. The endorsement of the *Toledo News-Bee* is in the issues for October
25, 28–29, November 4, 1915, the *Toledo Blade's* in the issue for October
25, 1915. The election results were reported and commented upon in *ibid.,*
the *Toledo News-Bee,* November 3, 1915, and the *Ohio State Journal,*
November 4, 1915.

24. In the Cleveland mayoralty election the votes were: first choice,
Davis, 36,844, Witt 39,861; second choice, Davis 8,549, Witt 3,569. Witt
had asked for only first-choice votes, stating that those who desired someone
else were not his friends and that he would not play second fiddle (*Cleveland
Leader,* October 31, November 4, 1915). Toledo voted preferential balloting
out in 1916, Cleveland in 1923.

25. Burton J. Hendrick, "Taking the American City out of Politics,"
Harper's Monthly Magazine, CXXXVII (June, 1918), 108.

26. *Dayton Daily News,* February 19, April 21, 1913; *Toledo News-Bee,*
May 12, 1913; Stone, Price, and Stone, *City Manager Government,* 182.
A brief history of the city-manager plan is given in Kneier, *City Government,* 362–64.

27. The several slates of candidates were reported in the *Dayton Daily
News,* April 21, 1913; samples of editorial opinion in the *Daily News* are
in the issues for May 2–3, 8, 10, 17, 1913. The tactics of the Citizens'
Committee were described by Upson in a speech in Columbus reported in
the *Ohio State Journal,* October 5, 1913. The vote for drawing up a
charter was 11,542 for, 2,020 against. John N. Patterson led the Citizens'
ticket. (*Dayton Daily News,* May 21, 1913)

28. The Socialists' demands were reported in the *Dayton Daily News*, June 5, 10, 1913, the opposition of Democrats and others in *ibid.*, August 2, 5–12, 1913, and in Hendricks, "Taking the American City out of Politics," 109, the *Daily News*'s endorsement is in the issues for August 2, 5, 1913; the vote is in *ibid.*, August 13, 1913.

29. A résumé of the charter provisions was published in the *Dayton Daily News*, June 24, 1913.

30. The formation of the Greater Dayton Association was described by Upson in his Columbus speech, reported in the *Ohio State Journal*, October 5, 1913. The campaign and election were reported in the *Dayton Daily News*, October, *passim*, November 5, 1913, and in Stone, Price, and Stone, *City Manager Government*, 182–83.

31. Hendrick, "Taking the American City out of Politics," 111–13; Stone, Price, and Stone, *City Manager Government*, 183.

32. Stone, Price, and Stone, *City Manager Government*, 10–12, 55–56.

33. The adoption of the charter in Springfield was reported in the *Ohio State Journal*, August 27, 1913, that in Ashtabula and Sandusky in Fesler, "The Progress of Municipal Home Rule in Ohio," 248. Later adoptions are reported in Clarence E. Ridley and Orin F. Notling, eds., *The Municipal Year Book, 1949* (Chicago, 1949), 47–87. The other cities that adopted the city-manager plan were Cleveland Heights, East Cleveland, Painesville, Piqua, Sandusky, Bedford, Gallipolis, and Oakwood. The trial of the plan in Cleveland lasted only eight years, between 1923 and 1931; Akron's experience was even briefer. Political conditions, not a defect in the charter, were responsible for the abandonment of the plan in Cleveland. Newton Baker attacked the plan in the *Cleveland Plain Dealer*, October 20, 1929; February 5, 1930.

The most recent survey made by the Ohio Municipal League reveals that there are thirty-three Ohio cities with a council and manager, eight with a commission and manager, and that ten villages have also adopted the manager plan ("Council Manager Plan Developments," *National Civic Review*, L [November, 1961], 548–49).

34. The three were Akron, Canton, and Youngstown. See: *Ohio State Journal*, July 17, 1913; *Youngstown Vindicator*, February 1, 5, October 21, 27, 1913; Fesler, "The Progress of Municipal Home Rule in Ohio," 248–49. By 1917, five hundred American cities had adopted the commission plan (Kneier, *City Government*, 349).

35. The following cities rejected proposals to elect charter commissions: Zanesville, Norwood, Gallipolis, Amherst, Ironton, Jackson, Mansfield, Marietta, and Washington Court House. Lorain elected a commission which disbanded without submitting a charter. Six more rejected the charter submitted by the commission: Cincinnati, Ashland, and Elyria, in addition to Akron, Canton, and Youngstown. (Fesler, "The Progress of Municipal Home Rule in Ohio," 248–49)

36. *Cincinnati Commercial Tribune*, June 19, 1914.

37. *Cincinnati Enquirer*, July 21, 23, 1913; Pendleton, "Cincinnati's Traction Problems," 628.

38. The campaign was reported in the *Cincinnati Enquirer*, July 21–22, 1913. The results and commentary on the election are in *ibid.*, July 31, 1913, and in S. Gale Lowrie, "Cincinnati's Charter Campaign," *National Municipal Review*, III (October, 1914), 731.

39. Analyses favorable to the charter are in Lowrie, "Cincinnati's Charter Campaign," 731, and in Mayo Fesler to W. A. Knight, undated, in the *Cincinnati Enquirer*, July 11, 1914. For an unfavorable comment, see the *Cincinnati Commercial Tribune*, June 19, 1914.

40. Favorable views of the Hunt administration are presented in: *Cincinnati Post*, October 13, 1913; Taft, *City Management*, 15; A. Julius Freiberg, "Mayor Hunt's Administration in Cincinnati," *National Municipal Review*, III (July, 1914), 519–21. The traction controversy is reviewed in: *ibid.*, 520–21; Pendleton, "Cincinnati's Traction Problems," 624–26; the author's interview with Arthur C. Fricke, September 28, 1949. Hunt received the backing of the *Cincinnati Post* (issues for October 13, 22, 29, 1913) and the *Cincinnati Enquirer* (issues for October 23, 29, 1913). The vote was Spiegel 45,363, Hunt 42,251 (*ibid.*, November 6, 1913). The commentary on Spiegel is taken from the *Cincinnati Post*, October 13, 1913. The election commentary is drawn from the *Cincinnati Enquirer*, November 5, 1913, and from Freiberg, "Mayor Hunt's Administration in Cincinnati," 522–23.

41. The campaign is described in Lowrie, "Cincinnati's Charter Campaign," 730–32. The *Cincinnati Enquirer* attacked the charter as cumbersome and expensive (issues for July 1–12, 1914). Some of the Bigelow radicals declared they had voted against the charter and were glad it had been defeated. Many Democrats opposed it, despite the endorsement of their party officials, because of the provision for a council elected at large instead of by wards. (*Ibid.*, July 15, 1914) The vote was reported in *ibid.*, July 15, 1914. The provision for the recall of officials was presented separately and was also defeated.

42. In the 1915 election George Puchta, Republican, defeated Charles Sawyer, Democrat for mayor, 56,239 to 34,469; the majority of 22,000 was unprecedented (*Ohio State Journal*, November 4, 1915).

43. The Cincinnati Charter of 1916 and its acceptance are reported in "Cincinnati Adopts a Home Rule Charter," *National Municipal Review*, VII (January, 1918), 90.

44. Taft, *City Management*, 31 ff.

45. Baker's comment is in Baker, "Introduction," in Nevins, ed., *The Letters and Journal of Brand Whitlock*, I, xv. The amount of litigation under the Ohio home-rule amendment is not exceptional. All such constitutional grants to municipalities are expressed in broad language and necessitate, under our system of judicial review, the same interpretation by the state courts to determine the allocation of functions between cities and the state as the federal tribunals are called upon to make in deciding the distribution of power between the state and national governments under our federal constitution. This point is briefly discussed in Kneier, *City Government*, 64–70.

46. Their failure to win all the freedom for cities they wanted is noted in "Twenty-five Years of Home Rule," 76; the favorable comment on the amendment is made in Hatton, "Constitutional Municipal Home Rule," 82, and in Fesler, The Progress of Municipal Home Rule in Ohio," 250. Benjamin DeWitt cited the Ohio Supreme Court as being the most generous in its interpretation of the constitutional grant of home rule (DeWitt, *The Progressive Movement*, 297–98).

47. *State ex rel. City of Toledo v. Lynch*, 88 Ohio 71 (1913), 95, 97.

48. *Ibid.*, 141, 134; also quoted in the *Toledo News-Bee*, May 7, 1913,

and *Ohio State Journal,* May 10, 1913. The italics are Judge Wanamaker's.

49. The judges in the appellate court in 1921 no longer felt bound by Chief Justice Shauck's decision because the state's highest court had overruled it by implication in intervening cases (*City of Youngstown* v. *Arnold,* 112 Ohio App. 12 [1921]). Judge Wanamaker's opinion is in *Village of Perrysburg* v. *Ridgway,* 108 Ohio 245 (1923).

50. *Fitzgerald* v. *City of Cleveland,* 88 Ohio 338 (1913), 352–53, 347. Judge Wanamaker's remarks are in *ibid.,* 374–75. The city's case was argued by Assistant City Solicitor John N. Stockwell, who had first suggested the charter method of electing city officers (interview with Newton D. Baker in the *Ohio State Journal,* August 31, 1913).

51. The Dayton civil service case is *State* ex rel. *Lentz* v. *Edwards,* 90 Ohio 305 (1914). The first Cleveland case, involving changes in the organization of the sinking-fund commission, is in *State* ex rel. *Hile* v. *Baker,* 92 Ohio 506 (1915); the second, concerning the charter provisions dispensing with property owners' consents along street-railway lines, is in *Billings* v. *Cleveland Railway Co.,* 92 Ohio 478 (1915).

52. *State* ex rel.*Cherrington* v. *Hutsinpiller,* 112 Ohio 468 (1925).

53. Art. XVIII, sec. 3, Ohio Constitution of 1851 as amended in 1912. Author's italics.

54. An excellent study of all aspects of this problem that has provided many suggestive observations is Jack Fein Isakoff, "State Limitations upon the Municipal Ordinance Making Power in Ohio" (Master's thesis, Ohio State University, 1932), 195. In recent years the General Assembly has established pensions and maximum working hours for police and firemen, regulations which the cities have contested as violations of home rule. Each time the Ohio Supreme Court has upheld the legislation on the grounds that fire and police protection are of state wide interest and under control of the sovereign state. (*State* ex rel. *Strain* v. *Houston,* 138 Ohio 203 [1941]; *City of Cincinnati* v. *Gamble,* 138 Ohio 220 [1941]). Governor Cox agreed that municipal police powers must yield to state police powers in all projects that concern the general population of the state. His interpretation is noted above in Chap. XV, p. 427.

55. The Ohio Supreme Court has held that the constitutional provisions for municipal ownership and operation of utilities are self-executing, and are not subject to restrictions by the General Assembly nor to limitations by implication (*Pfau* v. *City of Cincinnati,* 142 Ohio 101 [1943]). The right of the Public Utilities Commission to review rates is discussed in *East Ohio Gas Co.* v. *Public Utilities Commission of Ohio,* 137 Ohio 225 (1940). The problem is discussed also in Isakoff, "State Limitations upon the Municipal Ordinance Making Power in Ohio," 163–65. The unsuccessful efforts to change the language of the amendment and to make utility bonds issued by a city in excess of the statutory limits a lien on the municipality instead of only on the utility itself are discussed above in Chap. XIV, pp. 397–98. The municipal reformers, however, did succeed in retaining home rule in the fixing of utility rates, although they had to agree that municipally owned utilities would follow the uniform accounting practices required of all privately owned utilities. See above, Chap. XIV, p. 400.

56. *State* ex rel. *City of Toledo* v. *Weiler,* 101 Ohio 123 (1920).

57. Art. XIII, sec. 6; Art. XVIII, sec. 13, Ohio Constitution of 1851 as amended in 1912.

58. Baker's comment is from N. D. Baker to Brand Whitlock, July 12, 1914, Whitlock Papers. The strict interpretation of this clause is in *State ex rel. City of Dayton* v. *Bisch*, 104 Ohio 206 (1922). The cases sustaining city levies on occupations and payrolls are *State* ex rel. *Zielonka* v. *Carrel*, 99 Ohio 220 (1919), and *Marion Foundry Co.* v. *Landes*, 112 Ohio 116 (1925). The legislature's exercise of its prerogative over municipal fiscal affairs and the opposition of urban reformers thereto in the 1913 session are discussed above in Chap. XIV, pp. 396–97; 416 n 30 and 31.

59. By 1961, 89 of the 192 cities of Ohio with a population of 5,000 or more had adopted home rule charters. Although they numbered less than half the total, they embraced considerably more than half the urban population of the state. Included among them were 7 of the 8 having a population of over 100,000 (the exception was Canton which defeated a charter proposal as recently as November, 1962) and all 4 of those in the 50,000 to 100,000 bracket. Emmett L. Bennett, "Ohio Local Self-Government with Exceptions," *National Municipal Review*, XXI (June, 1932), 362–63; "Council Manager Plan Developments," *National Civic Review*, L (November, 1961), 548–49; Mayor of Canton to the author, September 23, 1963. Few cities, however, took advantage of the model municipal charters approved by the legislature in 1913. They were considered so defective by urban reformers that they warned cities against them. These points are discussed above in Chap. XIV, p. 397.

CHAPTER SEVENTEEN

THE END OF AN ERA

As THE STATE ELECTION of 1914 approached, it became apparent that the Ohio electorate had lost its enthusiasm for reform and for those carrying that banner. One portent was the outcome of the municipal contests in 1913, with the defeats of Henry Hunt in Cincinnati, Charles Chittenden in Toledo, and George Marshall in Columbus, and the greatly reduced majority by which Newton Baker had been re-elected in Cleveland. The day after the municipal elections the *Cleveland Leader* interpreted the results in a statement which seemed to be only wishful thinking at the time but which later proved to be perspicacious: "Governor Cox would be far less shrewd and skilled in politics than he is if he could fail to perceive in the results of Tuesday's ballotings a plain warning that he has to face storms ahead. It is apparent to the merest novice in Ohio politics that a great recession of the Democratic tide has taken place in this state."[1]

Nor was this the only evidence of discontent. Farmers loudly opposed the centralization of the tax machinery and agricultural agencies. The Anti-Saloon League resented state control of liquor licensing, and saloonkeepers took offense at the Cox administration's enforcing the midnight-closing law and reducing the number of saloons in conformity with the constitutional amendment. Many businessmen objected to the compulsory workmen's compensation insurance, while labor was diffident, feeling that it had been bilked out of some of its just demands. Clearly these attacks worried the Democratic state leaders.[2]

467

The Progressive party added a note of uncertainty. Would it reunite with the Republican party or continue its independent organization? Its members were split on the matter. Dan R. Hanna, though a contributor to the party after the 1912 election, began urging a merger in the spring of 1913. His paper, the *Cleveland Leader,* in an effort to foment sentiment for such a move, applauded the Republican legislative caucus for initiating plans for amalgamation at the end of the 1913 session. Its star reporter claimed further that there was eagerness for fusion among the rank and file whom he had interviewed. Such a proposal was common sense, one of its editorials insisted, and the only way to end Democratic minority rule.[3]

Still a strong segment of the party opposed a union. Randolph W. Walton wrote that the *Cleveland Leader's* trial balloon had proved a blessing in disguise. "It had aroused the fighting spirit of the Progressives all over Ohio," he continued. "They are practically solid against amalgamation, in favor of going forward with the work of building up the . . . party." More important, these views were shared by the principal leaders, Walter Brown, Arthur Garford, and James Garfield. Brown reiterated his belief that soon the progressives of both parties would join together under a new label in opposition to their standpat brethren. In the municipal elections of 1913, the Progressives had found encouragement in the success of their candidates in the mayoralty contests in Akron and Canton.[4]

As a demonstration to the public that the majority of the party was against a merger, a rally of five hundred people was held in Columbus on January 3, 1914. Only a few malcontent committeemen failed to appear. Albert J. Beveridge, delivering the key address, extolled the virtues of Progressivism with ringing oratory. The party's future course was outlined in a series of resolutions presented by James Garfield as suggested platform planks. They included demands for prohibition and woman-suffrage amendments and a frontal attack on the Cox administration for interfering with home rule by centralizing authority in state commissions.

This gathering was followed by a Lincoln's Birthday dinner in Lima, at which all doubt about the party's continuation was cast aside when Garfield and Garford announced their candidacies under the Progressive label for governor and United

States senator respectively. The pattern of the second meeting was much the same as the first. Everett Colby of New Jersey, instead of Beveridge, brought the blessings of the national organization, similar resolutions were introduced again, and Governor Cox was denounced in bolder terms as a dictator responsible for the greatest machine in the state's history and blamed for forcing through the legislature poorly drafted laws.[5]

Despite this clear proof of majority sentiment, Dan Hanna, as late as the spring of 1914, still hoped for a reconciliation between the Progressives and the Republicans. Garfield, however, told a Columbus audience on May 20 that the Cleveland industrialist was barking up the wrong tree; the differences between the two parties were as irreconcilable as those between Republicans and Democrats. Three days later Garfield and Garford were at Oyster Bay to receive Roosevelt's final approval of an independent course.[6]

The opening gun of the Republican campaign had been fired by the legislative caucus at the beginning of the special session of 1914, when the members drafted a resolution asking Cox to enlarge the scope of the agenda to include repeal of the Warnes Tax Law and modification of the Liquor License Act to permit county home rule. This obvious political maneuver was roundly denounced by the Governor; nevertheless they had struck where the administration was most vulnerable. At a large rally in Columbus near the end of February this line of attack was continued, especially by two politically ambitious congressmen, Frank B. Willis and Simeon D. Fess. Other speakers leveled their barbs at Wilson, with a few blows directed at Roosevelt. Although a scattering of former Progressives attended, the Old Guard leaders were present in such numbers that a wit later referred to the get-together as "the embalmed beef banquet."[7]

By spring the Republican pre-primary campaign was in full swing. The two leading contenders for governor were the former state senator, David Tod of Youngstown, and Representative Frank B. Willis. Before entering Congress, Willis had been a teacher of political economy, history, and law at his alma mater, Ohio Northern University, and had served two terms in the Ohio House of Representatives from 1899 to 1903, where he had been a subservient member of the state organization. His political assets were a jovial personality, a rich, booming voice, and an evangelistic brand of oratory. However, because he was a dry, he was opposed in the primary by the urban party leaders, and he had to depend upon his own personal popularity, his record of undeviating party loyalty, and a small amateur organization headed by two newspaper men.[8]

The gubernatorial contest was overshadowed, however, by the race for the Republican senatorial nomination. First of all, the new method of selection by direct primary generated fresh interest, but the principal attractions were the candidates themselves. The incumbent, Theodore Burton, had bowed out. Unable to obtain the backing of the Scripps-McRae papers, which had supported him in 1908, and criticized by some of the Republican press, at odds with his party in the Senate and fearful of being drawn into a family row, he preferred to bide his time.[9]

The man chiefly responsible for this decision was Joseph B. Foraker, who emerged from retirement to fight again for the toga he had worn twice before. The reappearance of this lost leader, with the cloud of the Hearst disclosures still hovering about his person, threw alarm into the hearts of the party high command. In their desperate search for an opponent they selected one of Foraker's old lieutenants, Warren G. Harding. Reluctant at first to oppose his former boss, the Marion editor finally consented, at the pleading of Dan Hanna and the state organization. The most vicious attacks on Foraker came from Hanna, whose ire was aroused by a long standing antipathy to the former senator from Cincinnati inherited from his father and by the embarrassment to his fusion plans created by the candidacy of such a figure. The antimerger Progressives, on the other hand, rejoiced. Judge Wanamaker observed that Foraker was the logical man to represent the Republicans, for he was "the most brilliant exponent of stand-pattism and the party is essentially stand-pat."[10]

The Democratic pre-primary campaign had been slow in gaining momentum because Governor Cox had made it known early that he would seek renomination, and it was expected that he would be unopposed. This hope was shattered, however, when Congressman John J. Whitacre of Canton announced in a circular letter to Ohio Democrats in March that he was a nominee. He had the backing of a group of malcontents, calling themselves the True Democracy, led by Harvey Garber. Cox spent the spring and summer speaking before various groups, much of the time fending off attacks on the Warnes Law and the Liquor License Act.[11]

It appeared at first that there would be a close contest for the Democratic nomination for United States senator. John H. Clarke, "a pioneer progressive" who had run for the office in 1903, was determined to make a second try. He was the candidate of the Cleveland and Toledo progressives and the Scripps-McRae papers. Carl Friebolin was his manager. Opposing Clarke was Timothy S. Hogan, a popular Irish Catholic, who had twice been elected attorney-general, and who had gained renown prosecuting the referendum frauds. In the eyes of party progressives, however, he had fallen from grace for strenuously opposing the short-ballot amendments. But the contest between the two was short-lived, for in July Clarke withdrew to accept an appointment as a federal district court judge. The strategy of offering the judgeship to the Cleveland attorney was questioned at the time by a young congressman from Cleveland, Robert J. Bulkley, who insisted that his fellow townsman had an excellent chance to win the senatorial race. Nevertheless, President Wilson persisted in offering the appointment and Clarke accepted, content to escape from the turmoil of the primary campaign to the uncontested seat on the bench.[12]

On August 11 Ohio held its first state-wide direct-primary election. A light vote was expected because many of the foreign-born were too concerned about the welfare of relatives in Europe, now threatened by war, to discharge their civic duty, and the prognostication was realized. In the Democratic primaries Cox defeated Whitacre two to one, 137,553 to 65,841, and Hogan won by a plurality of 37,661 over his closest rival, though he failed to poll a majority. The combined vote for the Republican nominees for governor was 230,000, some 27,000 more than the Democratic total, Willis topping Tod by better than a 20,000 margin. Harding beat Foraker by 12,000, to the great joy of Hanna's paper, the *Cleveland Leader,* which prophesied: "He will help to draw back to the Republican ranks the few Progressives who have not yet decided to return, and he will aid in keeping the Republican party of this state always safely and soundly progressive and always the surest and most competent instrument the people of Ohio can find to execute their will."

471

The Progressive vote was extremely light, a harbinger of the disastrous results which were to face them in November. In the primaries Garfield polled only 7,081 for governor, and Garford only 6,571 for United States senator.[13]

Two weeks after the primaries the three parties met simultaneously in separate conventions in Columbus to write platforms and elect party officers. Cox was the dominant figure at the Democratic conclave, and in his address he set the stage for the proceedings. He characterized his first administration as "a term of promises fulfilled," to be followed, if he were re-elected, by "an era of legislative rest." It was important, however, that the laws "be tested by their friends, not their enemies." The resolutions committee, on which sat Baker, Bulkley, and William Greenlund, listened to arguments for a woman-suffrage plank and to labor's pleas for an eight-hour day for women, full crews and car limits on railway trains, and increased rates for workmen's compensation. All were rejected, and no fight was made for them on the floor. It was rumored that Baker would seek approval of an amendment to permit county home rule in taxation, but he was never heard from.

The platform, one of the shortest and most innocuous in a dozen years, endorsed Wilson, Pomerene, and Cox, and defended the laws adopted during the Governor's administration as the "Democratic interpretation of the people's will," singling out for special commendation the two most heavily attacked, the Warnes and Liquor License statutes. The declaration dodged woman suffrage and prohibition. The only new legislation requested was a federal workmen's compensation law. It reiterated Cox's pledge of the briefest possible session to consider only items of community interest. The convention completed its work by re-electing Edward L. Hanley, chairman of the state central committee, and William L. Finley, head of the executive committee.[14]

The Progressives adopted without dissent a set of resolutions drafted by Garfield, Nat Wright, and Walter Brown, who had been re-elected campaign manager. They began with a general indictment of both old parties for "their corrupt bosses and inept leadership," and continued with specific charges against Cox for abusing his executive power to build "a sinister political machine," for militating against the principle of home rule, and for "seeking to destroy the temperance laws of the state at the behest of the liquor interests with which he is politically allied." The heart of the platform was a series of planks drawn to attract three militant groups as allies. State-wide prohibition was endorsed to satisfy the drys, equality of voting rights for women to please the suffragists, and four demands proposed by the Ohio Federation of Labor to catch the workingman's vote.[15]

Before the convention adjourned it was clear that the Ohio Progressives were going to make the chief issue in the campaign moral, not economic, reform. Garford, whom the press characterized as being as "dry as a bleached bone," declared, "I am going out in this campaign and bust the liquor interests in the eye every chance I get." In making this their central theme they had their reward when a few days later the Prohibition party's central committee passed a resolution endorsing the Progressive platform and nominees and opposing a separate ticket. This was a logical decision, for the Bull Moose program embraced the one the Prohibitionists had been advocating since 1900.[16]

No such easy solution to the liquor question was found at the Republican convention hall, where it proved a major source of discord. Frank Willis, known to be closely associated with the Anti-Saloon League, favored a clear statement that the party would take no backward step. Although Harding supported his position, the big city leaders from Cincinnati, Cleveland, and Toledo, who had opposed Willis' nomination, threatened to walk out of the convention if the party took a direct slap at the wets. In the face of this opposition a weasel plank was adopted. Because of this intraparty division political wits dubbed Willis the "highball" candidate, part booze and part water. The failure to commit the Republicans to a strong stand placed the Anti-Saloon League in a dilemma. Would the rank and file be satisfied with the GOP resolution or would they support the politically weak Progressives, thus dividing the opposition and allowing the Democratic wets to win?

The rest of the Republican platform condemned Wilson for the Underwood Tariff and Cox for usurping legislative functions and exercising autocratic power; it denounced the Warnes Law and the administration tax policy in general; it advocated home rule in liquor control, reduction of expenditures in general but liberal appropriations for agriculture and for roads; it endorsed two of labor's demands, the eight-hour day for women and increased workmen's compensation benefits. Like its Democratic counterpart it was silent on woman suffrage.[17]

When the campaign began in September, the Republican orators at their opening in Akron marked out the party strategy. Harding, facing toward Washington, D. C., raised aloft the tariff issue and proposed the slogan, "Prosper America First." Willis, looking in the direction of Columbus, declared the issue was Governor Cox's misrule. Thus the two major themes were established, purposely designed to sidestep the embarrassing questions of temperance and suffrage. On the eve of election day Dan Hanna's *Cleveland Leader* rang the changes in its editorial column on the slogans of father Mark: "Vote for Willis and good times. Vote for Harding and prosperity. Vote for the whole Republican state ticket as a means of giving business a better chance and labor more work at better wages."[18]

The Progressives hammered on the prohibition and woman-suffrage issues. Roosevelt, who made a brief stumping tour, took up the dry cause, censoring "the natural affinities of whiskey and crooked politicians." He sought to soothe conservative fears of his radicalism by specifically opposing government ownership and urging regulation of trusts and tariffs instead. Lack of funds prevented the party from matching its efforts of 1912; there was no "Bull Moose Special" to carry the candidates on a whirlwind tour of the state.[19]

On the Democratic side the campaign suffered from a lack of positive issues. Following the Republican tactics of silence on the two most controversial subjects, their orators concentrated on a defense of the administration's record and the virtues of their tax program. Cox tried to turn the tables on the Republican charges of bossism by reviewing Willis' political history to show his past collaboration with such leaders of the Republican state machine as Cameron, McKinnon, and Guilbert, and to underscore his record of hostility to labor and of friendliness to corporate interests.[20]

The Democrats were beset with other difficulties. Because of the candidacy of the Irish Catholic, Timothy Hogan, they suffered from the wave of religious prejudice which had scarcely abated from the year before. Chalked on fences, billboards, and freight cars was the slogan, "Read the *Menace* and get the dope,

Go to the polls and beat the Pope." So great was the fanaticism that Cox was urged by many to make as few public appearances with Hogan as possible, advice he unhesitatingly rejected.[21] Furthermore, followers of Garber's True Democracy were busy undermining Cox among the old Bryanite wing of the party. Their effectiveness, however, was somewhat mitigated by a two-day tour of Bryan himself through the rural counties in support of Cox and Wilson. The most favorable advantage Cox possessed was his extensive endorsement by the metropolitan press, including the Wolfe papers in Columbus, the Scripps-McRae League, his own two papers in Dayton and Springfield, the *Cleveland Plain Dealer,* and the *Cincinnati Enquirer.*[22]

But such backing was not enough to overcome the opposition in the grass roots. The arc of the political pendulum which had moved leftward in the direction of the Democratic reformers since 1905, reaching its apex in 1912–13, had now abruptly swung the other way. The Republicans rolled up majorities in sixty-eight counties, the Democrats winning in only twenty, thus reversing the returns of the two preceding state contests. Those counties which had strayed before into either the Democratic or Progressive camp returned to the Republican fold. Willis won with a plurality over Cox of 29,270. Garfield failed to carry a single county, his vote dropping to 60,094, less than a third of Garford's total in 1912. Of the twelve major urban counties Willis won seven, Cox five, though the latter received a plurality of 22,448 on the combined vote. It was the rural areas that turned against the Democrats. Cox lost eleven counties which had heretofore been consistently loyal to the party, plus four doubtful ones. In the senatorial contest Harding was an even more decisive victor over Hogan. The Republicans made their victory complete by electing all the other state officers, a majority of both houses of the legislature, and thirteen of the twenty-two congressmen.[23]

The Democrats were shocked and mystified by the returns. Why, they asked, should the Cox administration have been defeated after carrying out a legislative program demanded, in effect commanded, by the people? The Governor felt the election had come too soon, before people had had an opportunity to realize the benefits from the new enactments. Other party analysts argued that he was the victim of his own reform laws, many of which trod on the toes of some voter group. Not only had the Warnes and Liquor License laws made enemies, but the liability-insurance agents were angered by the compulsory workmen's compensation act, which cut them out of a large portion of their business, and there was hostility among the village cliques against the new school code. In addition, there was a business slump, which generally militates against the party in power. Cox was probably correct, also, in his belief that many of his supporters did not bother to go to the polls, taking for granted his program and good administration. Willis, on the other hand, had been helped by the return of many Progressives to the Republican fold. Finally, it was probably true, as Theodore Roosevelt stated, that "the people are sick and tired of reformers and reform . . . ."[24]

Governor Frank Willis interpreted his victory as a mandate from the people to economize and decentralize, and such advice he dispensed to the legislature in his first message. As spelled out in legislation, his program embraced repeal of the Warnes Act and the restoration of control of tax assessments to local communities, the substitution of an unpaid state agriculture board for the commission and a dispersion of the latter's functions, and decentralization of the liquor-licensing system, though this law was repealed at a referendum in November, 1915. Business was not only given a breather through the forestalling of any further regulation, but was also the beneficiary of friendly enactments. Labor received no favors. The only one of their recommendations given serious attention, a bill to establish one day's rest in seven in industry, was killed in the final rush of business. Still more serious was the number of measures introduced threatening the gains already made, which drew a bitter condemnation from union leaders. The one major enactment of the session was a highway code, which had been drafted by a Cox-selected commission.[25]

Furthermore, Willis tried to disperse the excellent administrative staff his predecessor had assembled, asking for the resignation of all of the former governor's appointees in many of the chief agencies. His effort to force the retirement of Wallace Yaple and Thomas Duffy from the industrial commission was particularly unpopular with labor and even with some businessmen.[26] By the time of the 1916 campaign, the record of the

Republican administration had provided the Democrats with plenty of political ammunition.

The enigma of the approaching contest was the Progressive party. Some of the soothsayers had predicted, after its poor national showing in 1914, that all it could do was to prepare for a "decent burial." Opinion among the Ohio members remained divided as before. Symptomatic was the announcement by the Summit County Bull Moose of a "death banquet," countered, to be sure, by the declation of the Progressives in Franklin County that they would hold a "going forward" dinner.[27]

The man who had the power to make or break the party was the national leader, Theodore Roosevelt. Right after the 1914 election he had expressed doubts to Walter Brown whether the Progressives could "accomplish anything further," but he refused to commit himself either way. In 1915 he became absorbed in leading the drive for national preparedness and saw less and less of his party associates. He was changing his mind about the Republican conservatives, and they were softening toward him. By the summer of that year he had virtually decided against a separate ticket unless there was a political upheaval. Nevertheless a militant section of his party clung to the hope that when the time came he would again be their standard-bearer.[28]

Since 1916 was a presidential election year, national issues tended to overshadow those of the state, especially since the people were faced with problems growing out of the European war. Despite this, the presidential primary elections in Ohio were a tame affair in contrast to the contests of 1912. Wilson was the only candidate on the Democratic ballot, Burton, as Ohio's favorite son, the only candidate on the Republican. The selection of the four delegates-at-large introduced a modicum of excitment, but in each case the choices of the state administration won. The Democratic "Big Four" were Cox, Harmon, Campbell, and Pomerene; their Republican counterparts were Harding, Willis, William C. Proctor of Cincinnati, and John J. Sullivan. The Progressives, having failed to poll sufficient votes at the preceding election to participate in the primaries, held a state convention in Columbus to select all their delegates. The four posts of honor went to Garfield, Garford, Brown, and Myers Y. Cooper of Cincinnati. The representatives were uninstructed, and no platform or declaration of principles was approved. None of the leaders wished to place any obstruction in the path of unification with the Republicans.[29]

By prearrangement the GOP and the Progressives held their national conventions in Chicago simultaneously in June, 1916. For reasons that are neither logical nor clear, Roosevelt still had hopes that he would be chosen the common standard-bearer. There was never a chance, however, as far as the Republicans were concerned. The Progressive body was divided on the issue of amalgamation or independence. Practical politicians, such as Walter Brown and William Flinn, favored merger, whoever the Republican nominee might be; James Garfield and others whose loyalties were inextricably bound to the personality of the national leader wanted to bargain in the hopes of a double Roosevelt nomination; a small third group advocated the prompt nomination of a candidate to hold the party together. Although the antimerger faction won the first victory by electing Raymond Robins permanent chairman in place of Walter Brown, the organization choice, it proved a hollow victory because Roosevelt sent a letter urging co-operation with the Republicans, thus effectively checking antimerger sentiment.[30]

Garfield led the harmony move by sponsoring a resolution that was adopted to appoint a joint committee of ten, five from each party convention, to select a suitable candidate. The Progressives presented Roosevelt. The Republicans considered various men, among them Burton, but Charles Evans Hughes, whom the Bull Moose leader had declared acceptable, was the final choice. Roosevelt now balked, suggesting as alternatives General Leonard Wood or Henry Cabot Lodge. It was a striking indication of his thinking that he proposed no member of his own party. When the committee's effort to break the stalemate failed, the Republicans proceeded to nominate Hughes and the Progressives to name Roosevelt.[31]

But the latter disbanded without knowing whether they had made a real nomination or not. The Colonel wired the convention that he would decline to run until he knew Hughes's attitude toward the vital questions of the day. If the members preferred, he suggested, they could place his conditional refusal in the hands of the party's national committee. His friends pushed through a resolution putting into effect his recommendation, and the delegates departed for home, many feeling they had been betrayed. Immediately thereafter, George Perkins and Roosevelt began exerting pressure on the committee to accept Hughes. When its members met on June 26, the Colonel had already declared for the Republican nominee, an action the Progressive national officers endorsed by a vote of thirty-two to six, nine abstaining. Several of the dissenters, including Raymond Robins, announced they would probably support Wilson.[32]

The Democrats, who held their national convention the week of June 11, renominated President Wilson and Vice-President Thomas Marshall. They adopted with little dissension a platform drafted according to the President's wishes, which had been borne to the convention by Newton Baker, secretary of war since March, 1916, and Wilson's personal representative at the party conclave. Although most of the document was devoted to preparedness and neutrality, it also contained domestic planks framed to attract former Progressives, including an advanced social welfare program and woman suffrage. The resolution for woman suffrage did arouse a spark of controversy because it advocated an extension of equal suffrage state by state instead of nation-wide by constitutional amendment, as the suffragists wanted. The Ohio delegates enjoyed a greater prominence than they ever had before at a national Democratic gathering. In addition to Baker's key role, Pomerene served on the committee on resolutions. Harmon made one of the seconding speeches for Wilson's renomination, and William Finley was recommended to assist in the planning of the presidential campaign.[33]

On June 1, two weeks before the national party conclave, the Ohio Democrats had held a state convention in Columbus, but instead of adopting a declaration of principles, as originally planned, the meeting had turned into a "love feast" of oratory in praise of the national and state leaders. The work of drafting resolutions was deferred until a later date.[34]

The Ohio Republicans gathering on June 21, therefore, were the first to come forward with a state platform. Its promises were few. They included enactment of a law guaranteeing one day's rest in seven for industrial workers, abolishment of useless jobs and offices, provision of more good roads, protection of the workmen's compensation act, and legislation granting cities the right to vote on a modification of the financial limitations of the Smith-Kilpatrick statutes. Senator Harding received the heartiest ovation. Governor Willis, a candidate for renomination, was cheered without much enthusiasm, for many Republicans by this time had reservations about his administration. The event which produced the major excitement was Roosevelt's announcement of his support of Hughes, which Willis interrupted his speech to read. It created a tremendous uproar of cheers and singing.[35]

As a result of this declaration and the action of the national body, the Ohio Progressive organization precipitously began to disband. Arthur Garford and his financial angel, Henry H. Timken, accepted membership on the Republican State Central Committee in August. Walter Brown was anxious to return but not as a private. He waited for the psychological moment in order to re-enter as a party leader. This came in October, when the stress of the campaign forced the Republican organization to accept his terms. There were a few holdouts, like Randolph Walton, who proclaimed that he was still a Progressive and that Wilson was the only presidential candidate he could support.[36]

In the Republican primary election Willis was an easy victor for governor, and Myron T. Herrick defeated Harry M. Daugherty in the senatorial race. Such choices revealed how well the prestige of the party standpatters had survived the flux of time. In the Democratic primary contest Cox won handily over Alfred P. Sandles for the governorship, and Senator Atlee Pomerene was renominated three to one over John J. Lentz.[37]

On September 7 the Democrats held their second state convention to write a platform. Couched in as general terms as the 1914 document, it endorsed Wilson and Cox and their administrations, pledged support of Pomerene, condemned Willis' term in office, and promised financial relief for cities, though in even less explicit language than the Republicans had used.[38]

In the 1916 campaign Cox had two advantages which he had not possessed two years before. First, instead of having to defend his own administration, he could now attack Republican rule, vulnerable on many counts. He could point, as proof of the value of his reform program, to the few alterations that the opposition had made in it. Second, the True Democracy faction had dwindled. John J. Whitacre, for example, spoke from the same platform as Cox at the opening meeting. The Democratic nominee still had good press support, though less than in 1914.[39]

As far as the newspapers were concerned, the state contest was completely overshadowed by the national campaign. When the returns were counted, it was revealed that Wilson had performed the near miracle of carrying Ohio, the first Democratic presidential candidate since 1856 to win a majority of the votes cast in the state. In the previous three-cornered election of 1912, he had a large plurality over his nearest rival, Taft, but he was a minority choice. Wilson pulled votes for the rest of the ticket, running ahead of all the other Democrats, in contrast to 1912, when Cox led. The former Governor was returned this time by a record-thin margin of 6,616 votes. Despite this close shave, the party could rejoice in turning the tables on its Republican rivals. Pomerene kept his seat in the United States Senate, the only Democratic senator elected between New York and the Mississippi River north of the Mason-Dixon line. Moreover, the Democrats won thirteen of the twenty-two congressional seats and a majority in the state legislature.[40]

Of the twelve principal urban counties the Democrats captured the same five as in 1914, plus Summit; Wilson alone had a plurality in Mahoning; the Republicans won the other five. In Hamilton County the latter actually increased their lead because the Cincinnati German wards wanted to rebuke Wilson for his alleged pro-Allied sympathies and voted solidly against his party. Nevertheless, the Democrats had a combined vote in these twelve counties that was 27,015 greater than that of their rivals. What brought victory for their ticket, however, were the gains made in the rural areas. Particularly was this true in Cox's case. All of the reliably Democratic country counties were back in the fold and every doubtful one except Highland. The governor-elect's total was thirty-six counties, in contrast to the twenty in his column in 1914. From straw-vote polls conducted during the campaign it was estimated that the Democrats had gained more ballots from the collapse of the Progressive party than they had lost in its formation.[41]

In appraising the returns, the editor of the *Toledo Blade* believed the evidence was conclusive that the Republican leadership in Ohio had learned nothing from the trend of events. Party members with progressive tendencies had been sent to the woods. Every move of the organization had been toward "a return to the 'good old days' when the bosses bossed and the people could go hang." Cox's victory was heralded by the friendly *Cleveland Plain Dealer* as a personal vindication, proof that the voters preferred his record of progress, economy, and efficiency to his rival's reactionary and petty performance. But manifestly it was not a triumph of the reform spirit. The Cox of 1916 was not the Cox of 1912. Rebuffed by defeat in 1914, he had a diminishing faith in progressivism. In his campaign speeches he had stated that he had no new legislative program, had promised not to disturb business, and had declared for a short session. As good as his word, he sent the legislature home after a two-month session in 1917. The important thing, as he had stressed before, was not additional laws but a sympathetic and impartial administration of the reforms already adopted.[42]

Three months after Cox took office a second time, the United States entered the war in Europe. The conflict provided the final blow to the reform movement which had already lost its punch. In abandoning the fight, the Governor was not exceptional. Many of the old progressives had vanished altogether from the Ohio political scene. Jones and Johnson had died several years before; Whitlock had departed for Brussels to take the post of American minister to Belgium; Baker, who had intended to retire from politics to private law practice, had been persuaded to serve as secretary of war in Wilson's cabinet; Frederic Howe had gone to New York, where he became the commissioner of immigration at that port; and Henry Hunt had joined the army and later became an attorney in New York. Although Peter Witt and Herbert Bigelow wished to carry forward the cause of reform, they were hampered — Bigelow severely so—by their outspoken pacifism and alleged sympathy for Germany during the war.[43]

When peace returned there was no co-ordinated effort to revive the progressive movement in Ohio. Some of the former leaders refused to consider entering politics again because they wished to pursue careers in business or the law and earn a competence for their families, which the low municipal and state salaries inadequately provided. Coupled with this desire

was the feeling that their personal sacrifice was no longer justified because the people were tired of political and economic
reform and were only interested in prohibition, the Ku Klux
Klan, or schemes for "getting rich quick." Both Baker and
Whitlock shared Cox's belief that the main outline of their
program was complete; therefore, municipal and state politics
had lost their principal attraction for them. Moreover, Baker
became increasingly absorbed in international affairs, particularly
in a movement to persuade Americans to join the League of
Nations. Perhaps a more fundamental reason for their declining interest in reform at home was the fact that they lacked
the intensive ideological commitment to the cause that sustained
the first crusaders.[44] Jones and Gladden had been guided by
their own personal visions, Johnson by that of his mentor, Henry
George. But many others, such as Baker and Whitlock, had
lost their faith in George's primary remedy and had turned their
back on him altogether. It is of interest to note that the few
men whose efforts at political and economic reform continued
into the 1920's—men like Bigelow, Witt, and Robert Crosser—
were steadfast adherents of the Georgian gospel.[45]

Now that the narrative of Ohio's progressive movement has
been told, there remains for final consideration the significance
of its contribution and its place in history. First, and perhaps
foremost, the Ohio reformers clearly elevated the tone and
stature of government, both city and state. Not only did they
weed out the grafters who cheated the public in petty ways,
but they also exposed and drove from power the amoral politicians who used political office to promote their own selfish interests and those of their private clients. These reformers gave
vitality to the ideal that public office is a public trust and to
the corollary principle that the people's business is to be conducted as efficiently and honestly as possible. For the right-wing
leaders, such as Judson Harmon, this end was sufficient in itself.
Although the left-wing considered it only a minimum requirement, they, too, were dedicated to this principle. Thus, on the
basis of efficiency and honesty in government, Raymond Moley
considers Tom Johnson one of the best administrators any
reform movement has produced.[46] There can be little question,
under a similar appraisal, that James Cox was one of the outstanding governors of Ohio.

A second contribution of the reformers was the marked improvement in the machinery of government. At all levels, except the county, responsibility and authority became more concentrated in the hands of the chief executives, directly accountable to the people. The multiplicity of autonomous offices and agencies was reduced by bringing them under the top executive officers in the cities and in the state, loosely managed ex officio state boards composed of politicians were replaced by commissions of paid experts, and municipal boards were replaced by single department directors. The merit system in the civil service was expanded and made more efficient, first on the initiative of urban reformers, then by constitutional amendment for state, county, and city. The strong mayor-council plan adopted in Cleveland, Toledo, and Columbus, and Dayton's city-manager form proved successful innovations. Even though the spirit of these reforms has often been abused, the public business since they were instituted has been carried on at a much higher plane than at the turn of the century. The simplification of the mechanism of government has made many times more difficult boss and ring control, which thrives on the multiplication of offices and the attendant obscuring of lines of authority.

The many changes introduced in the election system are more difficult to evaluate. Certainly the naive faith of their advocates that they would purify politics and drive the representatives of privilege from power has not been realized. While the direct-primary system of nomination has had the vitrue of eliminating the most grievous abuses of the convention method, i.e., clique-domination and bribery, it has failed to bring forth consistently candidates strong in their devotion to the general public interest. Nor has the direct nomination and election of United States senators worked a radical change in the quality of the incumbents of that high office. It has prevented the crass practices of a Payne or a Brice in buying their way into the upper chamber, but, at the same time, it has tended to favor the mediocre man with a silvery voice and political sex appeal over the man of ability though with fewer gifts of speech, appearance, and manner. The people have shown that they can be fooled sometimes no matter what method of nomination and election is used.

The nonpartisan ballot, Samuel Jones's master principle, which became a fetish in the years from 1911 to 1915, has likewise failed to demonstrate all the benefits prophesied for it. It can almost be said that the nonpartisan ideal of voting for men and principles regardless of party labels had its most leavening influence before a ballot of that kind was legally permissible. In campaigning for this and other changes, adherents did their most effective work in breaking down voting patterns fired to a steel-like rigidity in the crucible of the Civil War, which had proved so useful to the bosses and special interests. By the time this reform swept the cities of Ohio and was extended to the state judiciary, independence in voting was already largely a fact. In helping to separate local from national issues, in emphasizing the individual rather than the party, this change has continued to serve a useful purpose, but it did not eliminate partisanship in judicial or urban elections save in Toledo, where the tradition of Jones and the Independents was the strongest.[47] Since national parties have their roots in local communities and party responsibility is necessary to the smooth functioning of our representative democracy, perhaps it is well that nonpartisanship has never gone beyond its present development.

Two other election reforms proved either to be faulty or of little consequence. The system of preferential voting, so popular when Ohio cities were writing their first home-rule charters, was tried and abandoned.[48] The other, the presidential-preference primary, is still in use, but the frequent practice of committing delegates to a "favorite son," regardless of his national prominence, then releasing them after the second or third ballot in the national convention, has defeated the hope that this device would register the popular will on the party's choice of a President.

What has been said in general about election reforms is equally applicable to the initiative, referendum, and recall. These forms of direct democracy have not produced the revolution in our representative system of government that the radical claimants hoped or the conservatives feared. The recall, only adopted in Ohio cities, has seldom, if ever, been used. The short two-year term of municipal officers made it practically superfluous from the beginning. The initiative and referendum have failed as important mediums for educating the public on the great questions of the day. Furthermore, these are weapons which can and have been used against the broad public interest to promote the selfish ends of well-organized minorities. On the

485

other hand, the initiative process has been used to great advantage in making municipal charter changes by mobilizing inarticulate opinion and overcoming the resistance of intrenched minority groups.[49] The referendum has been employed to defeat objectionable laws and has no doubt acted as a brake on unscrupulous attempts at legislation by special interests.

There can be little question that the tendency among reformers of this period was to lay too great a stress on change in the machinery of government. With some, indeed, this became an end in itself. But with others it was only a prelude to efforts to achieve economic and social reforms. Clearly, Samuel Jones, Tom Johnson, and their disciples never lost sight of these final objectives. Recognizing that the most serious ills of the day grew out of urban-industrial dislocations, they successfully shifted the focus of public interest from the needs of the old agrarian to the new urban society. Their cure for the maladjustments which Henry George had so vividly pictured was to restore economic equality, which the concentration of economic and political power in the hands of a few threatened to obliterate. All of them except Jones believed in the efficacy of competition; monopoly in every form was the monster to be destroyed.

In striking at the tax advantages of the privileged few, Johnson and his coterie made possible remarkable changes in the state tax structure. When he and his single-tax friends began their campaign, the system was chaotic and unjust. Although others wrote the new laws, it was the efforts and propaganda of the reformers that paved the way for the elimination of the most glaring favoritism and inequalities, for the rationalization of the tax structure, and for improvements in the machinery of taxation.

Also it was the educational work of the reformers that aroused the people to the menace of public utilities as the agents of much municipal and state corruption, and to the significance of the franchises in either abetting or preventing corruption. In this area of government, as in taxation, the achievements of the reformers were substantial. They brought the public-service corporations under effective control, checked their political influence, reduced their rates or charges, and, by introducing government ownership, developed a yardstick for rate-making. To be sure, their crusade to shift all urban utilities from private to public control lost its impetus with the First World War and the rise of communist Russia. Still, there has been no backward movement, and cities have continued to purchase street-railway systems, especially those that that are no longer profitable to private investors.[50]

Regulation of other businesses was also greatly increased in this period. Depositors were better protected by a more rigorous and extensive system of bank inspection and by the amendment providing for the double liability of stockholders in such institutions. Blue-sky legislation helped to safeguard the unwary investor. Laws to prohibit false labeling, fraudulent claims, and the sale of deleterious foods or medicines checked other antisocial abuses.

Laboring men and their families, whose interests as late as 1900 had been largely ignored, received many benefits. To be sure, the middle-class reformers looked upon trade unionism as another form of special privilege and opposed legislation which labor leaders regarded as necessary to the survival of unions. Moreover, they refused to support laws that might interfere with competitive bargaining between capital and able-bodied male workers over wages and hours. Nevertheless, the progressives did more for the labor force than any group had done before. Workingmen's homes and surroundings were improved through regulation of the construction and operation of tenements, and by the development of parks, playgrounds, sports fields, bathhouses, and dance halls. Equal attention was devoted to correcting evils in working conditions. Safety and health standards in mines, factories, and stores were stiffened and better enforced through an enlarged state inspection organization. Workmen's compensation was made compulsory; child labor was abolished; maximum hours for women in industrial pursuits were established; and the eight-hour day was enforced on public work as an example to industry.

Some of the most outstanding achievements of this era occurred in other humanitarian endeavors of the reformers. Such men as Jones and Whitlock in Toledo, Johnson and Cooley in Cleveland, and Cox and Leonard in the state infused a new spirit into the administration of the communities' wards and delinquents. Instead of dismissing them as pariahs, they respected these unfortunates as human beings for whose help and cure society has a responsibility. They used common sense in controlling the social evils of the saloon, prostitution, and gambling, and in the treatment of minor offenders. Much of the brutality and the corruption which were the curses of municipal police forces were swept away. The reformers were enlightened, too, in eradicating the most offensive aspects of prison conditions, in employing penal labor on state projects instead of private contracts, in introducing the indeterminate-sentence and parole systems, and in attempting to segregate different classes of offenders through analysis of their records and through psychological tests. Although in the light of present-day psychiatric knowledge it would appear that these reformers placed too much emphasis on environmental and economic factors as the source of delinquency and crime, their ideas were not without justification, for the squalid tenements and the bare subsistence level of wages of thousands in the labor force did, indeed, sap the moral sense of many individuals and break down their inner controls.

The Ohio experience in this era was not unique, as the many references throughout the text to parallel reforms in other cities and states have indicated. Substantial reform movements appeared in Philadelphia, Kansas City, Minneapolis, Los Angeles, and San Francisco. Reform spread to the states of the Middle West, the West, and the South; and four of them, Wisconsin, Oregon, California, and New Jersey, experienced comparable waves of reform.[51] Progressivism became a national movement during the administration of Theodore Roosevelt and continued into the presidency of Woodrow Wilson. The nationalization of the progressive program of reform was made inevitable by the nation-wide structure of the American economy.

This trend that was so well marked in the progressive period became even stronger during and after the First World War. The result has been the increasing necessity of federal economic controls of business, labor, and agriculture, and the corresponding restriction of the area of effective action by the states. Furthermore, programs touching the welfare of all Americans—for example, social security, health, education, conservation, and regional planning—also require the co-ordinated action of the federal government. Hence, it is not surprising that the major reform movements since 1917 have been conducted at the national level. Some of the old Ohio progressives have participated in them.

Peter Witt was state chairman in the campaign for Robert M. La Follette and his Progressive party ticket in 1924, while Frederic Howe stumped for the Wisconsin senator in the East.[52] When Franklin D. Roosevelt initiated the New Deal in 1933, Ohio progressives again joined that nation-wide movement of reform. Howe was appointed consumers' counsel in the agricultural adjustment administration; Henry Hunt served under Harold Ickes in the department of the interior; Bigelow and Crosser supported the New Deal program in the House of Representatives and Robert J. Bulkley in the Senate. Several others, like Peter Witt and former Justice John H. Clarke, although not active participants, were staunch partisans of the New Deal.[53] James M. Cox, who had known the President well since 1920, when the Ohioan was the presidential nominee and Roosevelt was the vice-presidential candidate on the Democratic ticket, served as one of the American representatives to the World Monetary and Economic Conference in London in 1933. However, Cox's initial enthusiasm for Roosevelt and his program waned, and he became critical of the President's administrative methods and labor policy.[54] Even more critical of the New Deal were Baker and Whitlock. Baker denounced it for its frightful extravagance and dictatorial coercion; Whitlock, who had remained an expatriate in Europe since the war, condemned it for its inflationary policies which hurt all people like himself living on fixed incomes.[55]

The Second World War and the problems of postwar America have made big government in Washington even more necessary. The federal government continues to pre-empt many areas of regulation and public welfare that had been available to the states in the progressive era. It seems unlikely, therefore, that either Ohio or any other state will experience again such a movement of reform.

Yet something remains. The legacy of Jones and Johnson is seen in the remarkable record of efficient and humane government which their respective cities of Toledo and Cleveland have enjoyed in the intervening years. The spirit of the Cincinnati progressives had a late flowering, in the charter movement initiated in 1925 in that city, but has continued ever since.[56] However, perhaps the most significant contributions of Ohio's progressives have been the identification of privilege as the foremost enemy of democracy, the restoration of faith in an informed public as democracy's best hope, and the recognition that successful leadership in reform demands both a keen intellect and a warm heart.

1. *Cleveland Leader,* November 6, 1913.

2. James Cox has emphasized these voices of discontent in his autobiography, *Journey through My Years,* 178–83.

3. Dan Hanna was listed as a contributor to the Progressive party in E. H. Hooker to A. L. Garford, January 4, 1913, Garford Papers. The merger sentiment appeared in the *Cleveland Leader,* May 1–3, 1913.

4. The Walton quotation is from Charles L. Thurber to A. L. Garford, May 29, 1913, Garford Papers. Thurber was secretary of the Ohio Progressive Executive Committee. Brown's statement appeared in the *Ohio State Journal* (Columbus), May 11, 1913. The Progressives' encouragement from the mayoralty victories was reported in *ibid.,* November 5, 1913.

5. The Columbus rally was reported in the *Ohio State Journal,* January 3–4, 1914, the Lincoln's Birthday dinner in Lima in *ibid.,* the *Cincinnati Enquirer,* and the *Toledo Blade,* February 13, 1914.

6. It was reported that Hanna had held two meetings in an effort to reconcile the two parties. Hanna himself had returned to the Republican fold. (*Ohio State Journal,* May 17, 1914). George Perkins had tried to prevent Hanna from abandoning the Progressives, but the latter was adamant (Dan R. Hanna to George W. Perkins, March 8, [1914], W. F. Brown Papers). Garfield's speech was reported in the *Ohio State Journal,* May 21, 1914, his and Garford's meeting with Roosevelt in *ibid.,* May 24, 1914.

7. The resolutions of the Republican legislative caucus and Cox's reaction were reported in the *Ohio State Journal,* January 23–24, 1914, the Columbus rally in *ibid.,* February 27, 1914. The wit was Randolph W. Walton, an ardent Progressive, whose witticism appeared in *ibid.,* August 26, 1914.

8. The Republican pre-primary campaign was reported in *ibid.,* March 5, April 5, 1914. The biographical data on Willis are drawn from: Gerald E. Ridinger, "The Political Career of Frank B. Willis" (Ph.D. dissertation, Ohio State University, 1957), 2–45, 58; Mercer, ed., *Ohio Legislative History* [II], 91–93; Cox, *Journey through My Years,* 179–80; and Cox's disclosures in the 1914 gubernatorial campaign, *Ohio State Journal,* October 8, 25, 1914. The testimony on Willis' legislative activities, 1899 to 1903, was provided Cox under affidavit by C. H. Gerrish, a Columbus Republican.

9. *Ohio State Journal,* April 7, 1914. Burton had requested the support of the Scripps-McRae papers at a conference with Negley Cochran. With blunt frankness the Toledo editor told the Senator that his record had been wishy-washy in the Senate and that none of the league papers would lift a finger for him. (The author's interview with Hal DeRan, January 28, 1950. DeRan was present at the conference.) Burton's reasons for retirement are explored in detail in Crissey, *Burton,* 224–38.

10. Foraker opened his campaign headquarters in Cincinnati on April 4 (*Ohio State Journal,* April 5, 1914). Harding's reluctance to run and his

consent were reported in *ibid.*, April 10, May 24, 28, 1914. Hanna's attacks on Foraker appeared in *ibid.*, May 24, 1914; Wanamaker was quoted in *ibid.*, May 24, 1914.

11. The Democratic pre-primary campaign was reported in *ibid.*, March 5, 1914, and in Cox, *Journey through My Years*, 182–83. Examples of Cox's speeches are in the *Ohio State Journal*, March 12, April 10, 1914.

12. *Ohio State Journal*, June 11, 1913; January 4, July 3, 1914; *Youngstown Vindicator*, March 30, 1914; the author's interviews with Carl D. Friebolin, August 1, 1949, and Robert J. Bulkley, July 31, 1949; Warner, *The Life of Justice Clarke*, 55–57, 59–60. Two other candidates were also in the senatorial race, John J. Lentz of Columbus and John Zimmerman of Springfield, but they were no match for Hogan.

13. The primary election returns for all parties were reported in the *Ohio State Journal*, August 12–13, 16, 21, 1914. The vote in the Democratic senatorial contest was: Hogan 90,669, Lentz 53,008, and Zimmerman, 39,925. In the Progressive party primary both Garfield and Garford were unopposed. The quotation appeared in the *Cleveland Leader*, August 13, 1914.

14. The proceedings of the Democratic convention and the platform were reported in the *Ohio State Journal*, August 23, 25–26, 1914, and the *Dayton Daily News*, August 25–26, 1914.

15. The proceedings of the Progressive convention and the platform were reported in the *Ohio State Journal*, August 21, 26–27, 1914, and the *Cleveland Leader*, August 26, 1914. The four labor demands were an eight-hour day and minimum-wage legislation for women, one day's rest in seven for all workers, extension of the safety laws, and improvement of the workmen's compensation act.

16. Garford was so characterized in the *Ohio State Journal*, August 27, 1914; the endorsement of the Progressive platform and nominees by the Prohibition party's central committee was reported in *ibid.*, August 28, 1914.

17. The proceedings of the Republican convention and the platform were reported in *ibid.*, August 26–27, 1914; the characterization of Willis was quoted in the *Toledo Blade*, August 25, 1914.

18. *Ohio State Journal*, September 27, 1914; *Cleveland Leader*, November 2, 1914.

19. Speeches exemplifying the emphasis on these two issues are in the *Cleveland Plain Dealer*, October 29–30, 1914. Roosevelt spoke in Cleveland, Toledo, and Columbus (*Cleveland Leader*, September 29, 1914; *Toledo Blade*, September 30, 1914; *Ohio State Journal*, September 29, 1914). Garford expended only about $15,000 in his campaign for the United States Senate, half of which sum came from Henry H. Timken. Walter Brown contributed $2,000, Garford and his wife, $2,500, and there was a bank loan of $3,000. (Statement of campaign receipts and expenditures in the Garford Papers)

20. *Ohio State Journal*, September 26, October 8, 25, November 2, 1914.

21. Cox discusses the anti-Catholic feeling at some length in his autobiography, *Journey through My Years*, 178–79.

22. Bryan's tour was reported in the *Ohio State Journal*, October 9, 15, 1914. Cox lists the support of these newspapers in his autobiography, as well as that of the *Portsmouth Times, Canton News, Cambridge Jeffersonian,* and *Sidney News* (Cox, *Journey through My Years*, 185). Support for Cox

in the *Cincinnati Enquirer* was not in the form of editorials, which were noncommittal, but in the news articles signed by James W. Faulkner, the paper's Columbus correspondent and an admirer of the Governor.

23. *Report of the Secretary of State of Ohio* (1914), 262–64, 273–74, 285–94, 609, 611; *Ohio State Journal*, November 4–5, 7, 1914. The vote for governor was: Willis 523,074, Cox 493,804, Garfield, 60,094, Scott Wilkins (Socialist) 51,441. The vote for United States senator was: Harding 526,115, Hogan 423,748, Garford 67,509, E. L. Hitchens (Socialist) 52,803.

24. The explanations for Cox's defeat are drawn from Cox, *Journey through My Years*, 179–83, 185, and from the *Youngstown Vindicator*, November 5, 1914. The Roosevelt quotation is from Theodore Roosevelt to James R. Garfield, November 9, 1914, T. Roosevelt Papers.

25. Willis' interpretation of his victory and his message to the assembly were reported in the *Youngstown Vindicator*, November 5, 1914, the *Ohio State Journal*, January 12, 1914, and in Ridinger, "The Political Career of Frank B. Willis," 79–82. The review of the legislative session in Willis' first year is drawn from the *Ohio State Journal*, April 25, May 16, 30, 1915, the *Cleveland Plain Dealer*, May 21–22, 1915, and the *Toledo News-Bee*, June 2, 1915. The provisions of the Warnes Law are discussed in Chap. XV, p. 429 above. The act to decentralize control of liquor licensing was one of two defeated at the November election. The other was a congressional gerrymandering bill. Both had been passed after pressure from Willis. Their defeat was considered a personal rebuke to the Governor and his administration. (*Dayton Daily News, Ohio State Journal*, November 3–4, 1915) The system of liquor licensing is described in Chap. XV, pp. 427–28 and footnote 12; the agricultural commission is discussed in Chap. XV, pp. pp. 426–27 and footnote 10.

26. *Ohio State Journal*, April 10, 1915. The qualifications of Yaple and Duffy are discussed above in Chap. XV, p. 426. An attempt was also made to rewrite the Civil Service Law to increase the exemptions from the service, an effort that was thwarted by the Ohio Civil Service Association, which publicized this threatened breach of the Republican platform pledge (*Ohio State Journal*, May 8–9, 1915). See also Chap. XV, p. 423. Willis' patronage problems and disillusionment over them are discussed in Ridinger, "The Political Career of Frank B. Willis," 89–92, 113.

27. *Ohio State Journal*, November 8, 1915.

28. Roosevelt expressed his doubts in Theodore Roosevelt to Walter Brown, November 9, 1915, T. Roosevelt Papers. This discussion of Roosevelt's attitude and the hopes of his followers is based on Mowry, *Theodore Roosevelt and the Progressive Movement*, 320–29, and Garraty, *Right-Hand Man*, 317–20, 327–30.

29. The presidential primary elections were reported in the *Ohio State Journal*, April 16, 22, 23, 1916, the selection of delegates-at-large in *ibid.*, April 26–27, 1916, the Progressive convention in *ibid.*, May 7, 1916.

30. Roosevelt's hopes are analyzed by Mowry. He suggests that the Colonel's expectations may have been based on his great desire for the office, the wishful thinking of his friends, or Lodge's action in deliberately misleading him for his (Lodge's) own profit. (Mowry, *Theodore Roosevelt and the Progressive Movement*, 345) The proceedings of the Progressive convention are covered in: *ibid.*, 348–49; Garraty, *Right-Hand Man*, 334-52; Harold L. Ickes, "Who Killed the Progressive Party?", *American Historical Review*, XLVI (1940-41), 318, 322–24; *Toledo Blade*, June 8–10, 1916; *Ohio State Journal*, June 6–10, 1916.

31. The maneuvers of the two conventions in selecting a presidential nominee are critically described in: Ickes, "Who Killed the Progressive Party?", 325, 328; Mowry, *Theodore Roosevelt and the Progressive Movement*, 328–29, 350–54; Garraty, *Right-Hand Man*, 345–51. At the Republican convention Senator Warren G. Harding gave the keynote speech, and Theodore Burton was offered the nomination for the vice-president, which his manager rejected (*Ohio State Journal*, June 8, 1916; Crissey, *Burton*, 242–47).

32. Mowry, *Theodore Roosevelt and the Progressive Movement*, 354–60; *Toledo Blade*, June 22, 26–27, 1916.

33. *Cleveland Plain Dealer*, June 16–17, 1916; *Ohio State Journal*, June 13, 16, 1912. A detailed account of the convention is in Ray Stannard Baker, *Woodrow Wilson: Life and Letters* (8 vols.; New York, 1927–38), VI, 254–61; a brief critical analysis is in Link, *Woodrow Wilson and the Progressive Era*, 233–34.

34. *Cleveland Plain Dealer, Youngstown Vindicator, Toledo News-Bee,* June 2, 1916.

35. *Toledo Blade*, June 22, 1916.

36. The action of Garford and Timken was reported in the *Ohio State Journal*, August 20, 1916, Brown's in *ibid.*, October 29, 1916, Walton's statement in *ibid.*, September 10, 1916.

37. *Ibid.*, August 9, 1916.

38. *Ibid., Dayton Daily News*, Setpember 8, 1916; *Toledo News-Bee*, September 7, 1916.

39. The Democratic campaign was reported in the *Cleveland Plain Dealer* and *Dayton Daily News*, October 1–November 2, 1916, and the *Ohio State Journal*, September 29, 1916. The Scripps-McRae papers refused to endorse Cox again, although they were strong for Wilson (*Toledo News-Bee*, October 26–November 6, 1916).

40. *Report of the Secretary of State of Ohio* (1917), 239, 244, 255–56, 265. The votes were: for President, Wilson 604,161, Hughes 514,753; for governor, Cox 568,218, Willis 561,602, Tom Clifford (Socialist) 36,908, J. H. Dickason (Prohibition) 7,347; for United States senator, Pomerene 571,488, Herrick 535,391. The significance of Pomerene's victory was noted in the *Ohio State Journal*, November 12, 1916.

41. The rebuke of Wilson by the German voters in Cincinnati was reported in the *Cincinnati Enquirer*, November 8, 1916; the straw poll was recorded in the *Ohio State Journal*, November 19, 1916.

42. The *Toledo Blade* quotation is from the issue for November 8, 1916, the *Cleveland Plain Dealer* appraisal from the issue for November 9, 1916. The Democrats were also helped by the disorganization of the Republicans in Ohio (Ridinger, "The Political Career of Frank B. Willis," 115–17). The aim and character of the legislative session of 1917 are described in Cox, *Journey through My Years*, 194–95. Although a substantial number of bills were passed, they contained, for the most part, refinements on the program previously enacted.

43. Howe's appointment as commissioner of immigration and his subsequent career are related in Howe, *The Confessions of a Reformer*, 255 ff. The information on Hunt is from the author's interview with Herbert Bigelow, September 26, 1949. Witt made the offending remarks in the campaign for mayor of Cleveland in 1915 (*Cleveland Plain Dealer*, October 26, 1915; the author's interview on July 31, 1949, with Robert J. Bulkley, who was Witt's campaign manager).

Bigelow was captured by a white-robed mob in Newport, Kentucky (opposite Cincinnati) and beaten in October 1917. It was alleged that he had been disloyal in offering a prayer for "the repose of the Kaiser's soul." In the opinion of his friends, however, there was little doubt that the mob had been instigated by business and political groups on both sides of the Ohio river because of Bigelow's part in defeating a street-railway franchise grant. They were determined to teach the preacher-in-politics "a lesson." The terror was effective. For ten to twelve years thereafter Bigelow was reviled and men were afraid to have his name associated with their cause. Time, however, made people forget, and by the end of the 1920's Bigelow's good name was reestablished in the community. (The author's interview with Edward F. Alexander, September 28, 1949; *Cincinnati Post,* May 13, 1929; Edward F. Alexander, "An Epic in City Government" [MS in the Historical and Philosophical Society of Ohio, Cincinnati, 1949], 5).

44. These are some of the reasons assigned by Newton Baker in his reply to a questionnaire, published under the title of "Where are the Pre-War Radicals?" *Survey,* LV (February 1, 1926), 556–57. Baker's views were corroborated by Alfred A. Benesch, one of the young men in the Cleveland circle of reformers, who went out of office with Baker and formed a law partnership with John Stockwell (the author's interview with Alfred A. Benesch, March 8, 1946). Whitlock's reasons for retiring are stated in his correspondence with his friends quoted above in Chap. XVI.

45. The author's interview with Peter Witt, March 8, 1946; with Herbert Bigelow, September 26, 1949; Robert Crosser to the author, October 28, 1947; Wittke, "Peter Witt", 374–77; Cramer, *Baker,* 41; Brand Whitlock to Newton D. Baker, June 23, 1920, in Nevins, ed., *The Letters and Journal of Brand Whitlock,* I, 304.

46. Raymond Moley, *27 Masters of Politics in a Personal Perspective* (New York, 1949), 10. Moley was in Cleveland during Johnson's 1907 mayoralty campaign and knew the Mayor's administration at first hand.

47. The persistence of the nonpartisan movement in Toledo has been traced from 1913 to 1934, when the electorate adopted the city-manager plan and proportional representation. In this period only three mayors sponsored by national parties were elected. (O. Garfield Jones, "Some Non-Partisan Patterns" [MS in the possession of O. Garfield Jones, Toledo, Ohio])

48. See Chap. XVI, p. 449.

49. This has been particularly true in Cincinnati and Toledo (Alexander, "An Epic in City Government," O. Garfield Jones, "Charter History of Toledo" [MS in the possession of O. Garfield Jones, Toledo, Ohio]).

50. Cleveland, for example, purchased its street-railway system in 1944.

51. George E. Mowry, *The Era of Theodore Roosevelt, 1900–1912* (New York, 1958), 65, 71–80.

52. Wittke, "Peter Witt," 374. Witt returned to the Democratic fold to support Alfred E. Smith for President in 1928, as well as to run for governor in the Democratic primary—a race that he lost to Martin L. Davey. Witt's last effort to win public office was the Cleveland mayoralty election of 1931, in which he was defeated by Ray T. Miller. (*ibid.,* 374) Howe's support for La Follette is reported in Hoyt Landon Warner, "Frederic Clemson Howe," *Dictionary of American Biography,* XXII, 327.

53. Warner, "Frederic Clemson Howe," 327; author's interviews with Herbert Bigelow, September 26, 1949; with Robert J. Bulkley, July 31, 1949;

Wittke, "Peter Witt," 375; Warner, *The Life of Justice Clarke,* 189–97. Clarke was persuaded to support the constitutionality of Roosevelt's so-called court-packing proposal of 1937 in a nationwide radio address (*ibid.,* 194–97.)

54. Cox, *Journey through My Years,* 346, 420–22.

55. Cramer, *Baker,* 259–71; Warner, *The Life of Justice Clarke,* 191–94; Samuel M. Jones, III, "Brand Whitlock: Years of Expatriation, 1922–1934," *Northwest Ohio Quarterly,* XXXII (Autumn, 1960), 183–84.

56. Taft, *City Management,* 31 ff.

BIBLIOGRAPHY

THE PRINCIPAL SOURCES for this history in the approximate order of their importance are newspapers, articles in popular magazines and scholarly journals, manuscript collections, interviews, published autobiographies and biographies, and official records. The Ohio press of the period reported local and state politics more thoroughly than the same papers do today. Debates in the legislature received ample space, and, since no official transcript is kept, this remains the only record. Special correspondents frequently sounded out political conditions or public opinion throughout the state. William S. Couch's articles for the *Cleveland Plain Dealer* in the summer of 1905 on bossism in Ohio municipalities were the equal in accurate reporting of Lincoln Steffens' muckraking series on St. Louis, Pittsburgh, Minneapolis, Cincinnati, and other cities. Such newspapers as the *Cleveland Plain Dealer, Youngstown Vindicator,* and members of the Scripps-McRae League were influential voices in behalf of reform. They did more than record opinion; they sought to mold it in favor of reform. Especially powerful was the Scripps-McRae chain, with papers in Cleveland, Cincinnati, Toledo, Columbus, and Akron, relentlessly exposing graft or the suspicion of boodle, continuously attacking the utility interests, and pushing radical reform not only by means of news articles and editorials but by direct lobbying for key measures. Hence, a study of the press is significant both for the record of the times and for its own role in Ohio's reform movement.

Magazine articles supplemented the newspaper material at many points. The contributions of individual ones are mentioned in the itemized bibliography below. National interest in Ohio as measured by the attention received in the popular periodicals rose with the

497

elections of Samuel M. Jones and Tom L. Johnson, slacked off in the years between 1905 and 1909, and reached a new peak from 1910 to 1914. In the first part of the period the *Arena* followed the Ohio scene closely, publishing three of Jones's own essays, and two articles about him, as well as sketches of Tom Johnson.* Although the *Arena* was apparently the most interested, it was not the only muckraking magazine to find good copy in Ohio. *McClure's Magazine* followed up Steffens' exposure of George B. Cox with George Kibbe Turner's sequel on Cincinnati's political conditions seven years later, assigned Burton J. Hendrick to interview Judson Harmon. and commissioned Judge A. Z. Blair to write up the voting frauds in Adams County, which he was prosecuting. In 1911 *Hampton's Magazine* published four chapters of Johnson's autobiography, *My Story,* and an article on Boss Cox by Frank Parker Stockbridge. Essays by Frederic C. Howe and Stockbridge in *Everybody's* described reform in action in Cleveland and the state. The *American* ran a series of thumbnail sketches, leading off with Albert J. Nock's portrait of Brand Whitlock and George Creel's of Perry Knapp, followed by four from the pen of Whitlock briefly delineating Newton Baker, Herbert Bigelow, Daniel Kiefer, and Henry T. Hunt.

The *Outlook* was a favorite medium in which Howe, Jones, and Gladden aired their views. It was one of the most steadfast followers of the Ohio scene in every aspect. Another outlet was the *Independent,* which printed essays by Jones, Bigelow, James M. Cox, and two members of the constitutional convention. From 1910 to 1912 the *Review of Reviews* recognized Ohio, publishing articles on Harmon, on vote-selling in Adams County, and on the constitutional convention. At the height of the progressive period, the *Survey,* a periodical devoted to humanitarian causes, reported on the labor, educational, and penal reforms taking place in the state.

Nor was Ohio neglected in the scholarly journals. Edward W. Bemis wrote on the Cleveland street-railway situation for the *Quarterly Journal of Economics;* O. C. Lockhart wrote on taxation for the same journal. Robert Crosser explained Ohio's initiative and referendum amendment, W. O. Heffernan the new budget commission, and Max May taxes and politics in Cincinnati, in the *Annals of the American Academy of Political and Social Science.* The *American Political Science Review* ran articles on the legislative sessions, the constitutional convention, and the model-charter law. In the *National Municipal Review,* founded in 1912, the home-rule amendment, charter campaigns, and city administrations were

---

* Titles and exact references are omitted because they may readily be found under the author's name in the itemized bibliography which follows.

described in detail. Seldom before or since has Ohio received so much attention in national periodicals as it did from 1899 to 1903, and from 1910 to 1914. Though not so influential in shaping public opinion as the newspapers, the popular magazines were not without effect in advancing reform.

For so recent a historical period the collections of private papers and letters of the Ohio progressives are not so numerous or voluminous as the investigator could wish. Frederic C. Howe, Harris R. Cooley, Henry Hunt, and Judson Harmon left nothing. Very few letters of Herbert S. Bigelow remain. Washington Gladden's correspondence is in the main devoted to non-political subjects. There is one volume of letters of Tom L. Johnson in the Cleveland City Hall, which covers the last two and a half years of his life, during only one of which he was mayor of Cleveland. More helpful are two small boxes of material Peter Witt saved after cleaning out his office, yet much of it relates to his special street-railway interests. The John H. Clarke Papers contain only a handful of letters for the years prior to 1916. The collection of Robert Crosser papers includes files on the initiative and referendum and municipal home rule which he collected for the use of the committees considering those subjects in the Ohio Constitutional Convention of 1912, but there is little on Ohio politics. Atlee Pomerene's papers are heavily weighted on the national side, slighting state affairs.

Fortunately, there are some important exceptions to the generalization made above. The official letter file of Ohio's governors is rewarding, more so for James M. Cox's administration than for Judson Harmon's. Cox placed among these papers his extensive correspondence during the months of November and December, 1912, when he was governor-elect. They constitute an invaluable record of his preliminary preparations for the legislative session of 1913. Recently there have been two most significant discoveries: a substantial collection of Samuel Milton Jones's letters and papers, which had been "lost" in his factory, consisting of his correspondence during the years he was mayor, 1897–1904, and other materials; and a voluminous file of Newton D. Baker's personal letters, which had lain forgotten in the basement of Cleveland City Hall, stretching over the period from July, 1896, to January, 1899, and then from September, 1903, to May, 1916. The Baker papers in the Library of Congress, however, contain only a handful of items dating prior to 1916. On the other hand, the Library of Congress' collection of Brand Whitlock papers is voluminous and valuable. Although the record is concentrated on Toledo affairs, there are many references to Ohio politics and numerous letters to Whitlock from the Cleveland and Cincinnati reformers, as well as from Lincoln Steffens,

Albert Jay Nock, and Clarence Darrow. The most important of Whitlock's own letters have been published in Allan Nevins, ed., *The Letters and Journal of Brand Whitlock.*

Other collections on Ohio history in the progressive era are the papers of some of the leading Republicans and Theodore Roosevelt Progressives: Theodore E. Burton's papers, particularly for the Cleveland mayoralty election of 1907; the papers of Charles Dewey Hilles, who was Taft's campaign manager in 1912 and who began receiving reports from Ohio and other states on the political situation as early as 1910; the letters of Arthur L. Garford, the Progressive party candidate for governor in 1912; and the papers of Walter F. Brown, which are unfortunately very meager because his executors destroyed much of his correspondence at his request.

An attempt has been made to fill in the many gaps in the written record by interviews and correspondence with direct participants or contemporary observers. In interpreting many facets of the Cleveland scene, Peter Witt, Robert J. Bulkley, Alfred A. Benesch, Charles A. Otis, and two newspaper reporters, Leo Weidentahl and Henry P. Boynton, were helpful. Jesse Dowd Stafford, an intimate friend of Whitlock and his wife, aided in re-creating the personality of the Toledo mayor. Many twists in the complicated skein of Cincinnati politics were unraveled by Herbert S. Bigelow, Graham P. Hunt, and Edward F. Alexander. Boynton, Bigelow, and Alexander assisted in identifying Ohio single taxers and their contributions. Certain obscurities about the organization of the constitutional convention were clarified by Bigelow, Boynton, and John D. Fackler. James M. Cox, Carl Friebolin, and S. Gale Lowrie aided in illuminating the legislative sessions of 1913 and 1914. In addition Friebolin and Hal C. DeRan provided suggestive leads on personalities and events.

The lack of manuscript material remaining is partially compensated by the wealth of published autobiographies and biographies of the major participants. There is Tom Johnson's sincere apologia, *My Story;* Whitlock's charming, graceful reminiscences of his career to 1914, *Forty Years of It;* Howe's candid *Confessions of a Reformer;* Gladden's thoughtful, mellow *Recollections;* Cox's rambling *Journey through My Years;* and Jones's sketch of his early life in the *New Right,* as well as the homely expression of his philosophy in *Letters of Love and Labor.* Carl Lorenz, critically though not maliciously, examines the Cleveland mayor's character and program in *Tom L. Johnson.* A more sympathetic study is Eugene C. Murdock's "Buckeye Liberal, a Biography of Tom L. Johnson," his Ph.D. dissertation, parts of which have been published under the title "Cleveland's Johnson," in the *Ohio Historical Quarterly.* The biographies of Newton D. Baker by Frederick Palmer and C. H. Cramer offer only brief treatments of his Cleveland period. The Cramer study, nevertheless, is very helpful in giving a well-rounded and balanced picture of the somewhat controversial Baker. *E. W. Scripps* by Negley Cochran all but ignores Ohio politics. Samuel Milton Jones III, has written a full-dress biography of his grandfather's successor, which has been published in a series of articles under the title "Brand Whitlock," in the *Northwest Ohio Quarterly*. It is a thoughtful and often penetrating portrait. A perceptive general study of reform in Cleveland and Toledo is Robert H. Bremner's "The Civic Revival in Ohio," the title of a number of articles based on his Ph.D. dissertation and published in the *American Journal of Economics and Sociology*.

There are excellent portrayals of two of the leading figures on the conservative side. Herbert Croly's sympathetic interpretation is still the standard biography of Marcus A. Hanna; Thomas Beer's treatment is impressionistic and romanticized. Everett Walters has written an able, impartial life of Joseph Benson Foraker. However, Foraker's autobiography is of little help, and the same is true of T. Bentley Mott's *Myron T. Herrick,* which skims over the Ohio phase of his career, and Forrest Crissey's *Theodore E. Burton,* which is "colorful," superficial, and poorly organized.

The printed official records, though not abundant, are important. *Reports* of the special tax commissions of 1893 and 1908, as well as those of the permanent board established in 1910, illuminate that subject. The *Proceedings* of the special house committee on the municipal code in 1902 reveal the many conflicting views on city government presented at the hearings. The voluminous *Proceedings and Debates* of the constitutional convention of 1912 is not only a detailed record of the action taken by that body, but the speeches mirror opinion on most of the leading issues of the day. All election statistics, except municipal ones, which are not reported, are drawn from the *Annual Reports* of the secretary of state, the content of statutes from *Ohio Laws,* and the state supreme court opinions from *Ohio State Reports.*

PRIMARY SOURCES

Manuscript Collections

Newton D. Baker Papers. Cleveland City Hall.
Newton D. Baker Papers. Library of Congress.

Herbert S. Bigelow Papers. Historical and Philosophical Society of Ohio, Cincinnati, Ohio.

Walter F. Brown Papers. Ohio Historical Society, Columbus, Ohio.

Theodore E. Burton Papers. Western Reserve Historical Society, Cleveland, Ohio.

John H. Clarke Papers. Western Reserve University, Cleveland, Ohio.

Robert Crosser Papers. Ohio Historical Society, Columbus, Ohio.

Executive Records—Correspondence of Ohio Governors: Judson Harmon, January 1, 1909—December 31, 1912; James M. Cox, January 1, 1913—December 31, 1914. Ohio Historical Society, Columbus, Ohio.

Arthur L. Garford Papers. Ohio Historical Society, Columbus, Ohio.

Washington Gladden Papers. Ohio Historical Society, Columbus, Ohio.

Charles Dewey Hilles Papers. Yale University, New Haven, Connecticut.

Tom L. Johnson Papers. Cleveland City Hall.

Samuel Milton Jones Papers. Toledo Public Library.

Atlee Pomerene Papers. Kent State University, Kent, Ohio.

Theodore Roosevelt Papers. Library of Congress.

Brand Whitlock Papers. Library of Congress.

Peter Witt Papers. In the possession of Mrs. Helen Witt Cummins, Cleveland, Ohio.

Other Unpublished Material

ALEXANDER, EDWARD F. "An Epic in City Government." Historical and Philosophical Society of Ohio, Cincinnati, 1949.

BREMNER, ROBERT H. "The Civic Revival in Ohio: The Fight against Privilege in Cleveland and Toledo 1899–1912." Unpublished Ph.D. dissertation, Ohio State University, 1943.

CAMPBELL, THOMAS E. "Background for Progressivism: Machine Politics in the Administration of Robert E. McKisson, Mayor of Cleveland 1895–1899." Unpublished Master's thesis, Western Reserve University, 1960.

FORD, HARVEY S. "The Life and Times of Golden Rule Jones." Unpublished Ph.D. dissertation, University of Michigan, 1953.

FREY, ROYAL D. "The Ohio Constitutional Convention of 1912." Unpublished Master's thesis, Ohio State University, 1950.

HARRIS, GEORGE B. "The Ohio Republican State Convention of 1912 and Its Effect on United States History." In the possession of George B. Harris, Cleveland, Ohio.

HERRING, JEAN ADELE. "Harris Reid Cooley." Unpublished Master's thesis, Ohio State University, 1949.

ISAKOFF, JACK F. "State Limitations upon the Municipal Ordinance Making Power in Ohio." Unpublished Master's thesis, Oho State Unversity, 1932.

JAGSCH, ALMA. "Washington Gladden, Prophet of Social Justice." Unpublished Master's thesis, Ohio State University, 1935.

JOHNS, LATTIMER. "Taxation of Railroads in the State of Ohio." Unpublished Master's thesis, Ohio State University, 1912.

JONES, O. GARFIELD. "Charter History of Toledo." In the possession of O. Garfield Jones, Toledo, Ohio.

———. "Some Non-Partisan Patterns." In the possession of O. Garfield Jones.

KOCH, HERBERT F. "An Ohio Warwick: Something of the Life and Times of George Barnsdale Cox." Historical and Philosophical Society of Ohio, Cincinnati, 1946.

MURDOCK, EUGENE C. "Buckeye Liberal: A Biography of Tom L. Johnson." Unpublished Ph.D. dissertation, Columbia University, 1951.

RAWLINSON, GORDON R. "Tom Johnson and His Congressional Years." Unpublished Master's thesis, Ohio State University, 1958.

RIDINGER, GERALD E. "The Political Career of Frank B. Willis." Unpublished Ph.D. dissertation, Ohio State University, 1957.

Author's Interviews

Edward F. Alexander, Cincinnati, Ohio, September 28, 1949.

Alfred A. Benesch, Cleveland, Ohio, March 8, 1946.

Herbert S. Bigelow, Cincinnati, Ohio, September 26, 1949.

Henry Percy Boynton, Cleveland, Ohio, October 3, 1949.

Robert J. Bulkley, Cleveland, Ohio, July 31, 1949.

James M. Cox, Dayton, Ohio, June 29, 1949.

Hal DeRan, Columbus, Ohio, September 20, 1949, and Fremont, Ohio, January 28, 1950.

John D. Fackler, Cleveland, Ohio, October 7, 1949.

Arthur C. Fricke, Cincinnati, Ohio, September 28, 1949.

Carl D. Friebolin, Cleveland, Ohio, August 1, 1949.

Robert N. Gorman, Cincinnati, Ohio, October 18, 1959.

Joseph C. Hostettler, Cleveland, Ohio, March 23, 1946.

Graham P. Hunt, Cincinnati, Ohio, September 28, 1949.

S. Gale Lowrie, Cincinnati, Ohio, September 28, 1949.

William F. Maag, Jr., Youngstown, Ohio, September 11, 12, 1951.

Carl Matson, Cleveland, Ohio, June 15, 1946.

Charles A. Otis, Cleveland, Ohio, October 4, 1949.

Jesse Dowd Stafford, Toledo, Ohio, August 15, 1946.

Leo Weidenthal, Cleveland, Ohio, April 13, 1946.

Peter Witt, Cleveland, Ohio, March 8, 1946.

Official Records

Amendments to the Constitution of Ohio Proposed by the Constitutional Convention. Columbus, 1912.

Annual Messages of Mayor Samuel M. Jones to the Common Council of the City of Toledo, 1897–1903.

Annual Reports of the Departments of Government of the City of Cleveland, 1900–1915.

Annual Reports of the Secretary of State of Ohio, 1897–1917.

Annual Reports of the Tax Commission of Ohio, 1910–16.

Bates' Annotated Revised Statutes of Ohio. 3 vols., 3d ed. (revised to 1902). Columbus, 1902.

"Commercial Valuation of Railway Operating Property in the United States, 1904," United States Bureau of the Census *Bulletin,* No. 21.

Ellis, Wade H., ed. *The Municipal Code of Ohio.* Cincinnati, 1903.

First Quadrennial Assessment of Real Property for the City of Cleveland. Cleveland, 1910.

The General Code of the State of Ohio. 4 vols. Cincinnati, 1910.

Journal of the Constitutional Convention of the State of Ohio. Columbus, 1912.

Ohio Constitution of 1851 (as amended to 1917).

Ohio Laws, 94–107 (1900–1917).

Proceedings of the City Council, City of Cleveland, 1901–13.

Proceedings of the Special Committee on the Municipal Code. (75th General Assembly of Ohio, Extraordinary Session). 1902.

Proceedings and Debates of the Constitutional Convention of Ohio, 1912. 2 vols. Columbus, 1912.

Report of the Honorary Commission Appointed by the Governor to Investigate the Tax System of Ohio and Recommend Improvements Therein. 1908.

Report of the Railroad Commission of Ohio, 1911.

Report of the Tax Commission of Ohio, 1893.

Revised Ordinances, Special, City of Cleveland. 1907.

Court Cases

Adams Express Co. v. *Ohio State Auditor*, 166 U.S. 185 (1897).

Billings v. *Cleveland Railway Co.*, 92 Ohio 478 (1915).

Bryant v. *Akron Metropolitan Park District*, 281 U.S. 74 (1930).

City of Cincinnati v. *Gamble*, 138 Ohio 220 (1941).

City of Cincinnati v. *Trustees of the Cincinnati Hospital*, 66 Ohio 440 (1902).

City of Youngstown v. *Arnold*, 112 Ohio App. 12 (1921).

Clements Construction Co. v. *City of Cleveland*, 67 Ohio 197 (1903).

East Ohio Gas Co. v. *Public Utility Commission of Ohio*, 137 Ohio 225 (1940).

Exchange Bank of Columbus v. *Hines*, 3 Ohio 1 (1853).

Express Co. v. *The State*, 55 Ohio 69 (1896).

Fitzgerald v. *City of Cleveland*, 88 Ohio 338 (1913).

Floyd v. *Manufactures Light and Heat Co.*, 111 Ohio 57 (1924).

Galveston, Harrisburg and San Antonio Railway Co. v. *Texas*, 210 U.S. 217 (1908).

Jones v. *State of Ohio* ex rel. *Walbridge*, 66 Ohio 75 (1902).

Karlinger v. *Board of Control* (Cleveland), 60 Ohio 489 (1898).

Marion Foundry Co. v. *Landes*, 112 Ohio 166 (1925).

The Minnesota Rate Cases, 230 U.S. 352 (1913).

Ohio Tax Cases, 232 U.S. 577 (1914).

Pfau v. City of Cincinnati, 142 Ohio 101 (1943).

Platt v. Craig, 66 Ohio 75 (1902).

Roose v. Village of Leipsic, 87 Ohio 513 (1913).

Southern Gum Co. v. Laylin, 66 O.S. 578 (1902).

State ex rel. Attorney-General v. Beacom, 66 Ohio 491 (1902).

State ex rel. Cherrington v. Hutsinpiller, 112 Ohio 468 (1925).

State v. Cincinnati, 52 Ohio 419 (1895).

State v. Jones, 51 Ohio 492 (1894).

State ex rel. City of Dayton v. Bish, 104 Ohio 207 (1922).

State ex rel. City of Toledo v. Lynch, 88 Ohio 71 (1913).

State ex rel. City of Toledo v. Weiler, 101 Ohio 123 (1920).

State ex rel. Hile v. Baker, 92 Ohio 506 (1915).

State ex rel. Johnson v. Annual State Board of Equalization for Railroads, 65 Ohio 544 (1902).

State ex rel. Kemp v. Clarke, 68 Ohio 463 (1903).

State ex rel. Knisely v. Jones, 66 Ohio 453 (1902).

State ex rel. Lentz v. Edwards, 90 Ohio 305 (1914).

State ex rel. Sheets v. Cowles, 64 Ohio 162 (1901).

State ex rel. Strain v. Houston, 138 Ohio 203 (1941).

State ex rel. Zielenka v. Carrel, 99 Ohio 220 (1919).

State v. George B. Cox, Record in Case No. 16466, Court of Common Pleas of Hamilton County, Ohio (March 31, 1911).

Village of Perrysburg v. Ridgway, 108 Ohio 245 (1923).

Western Union Telegraph Co. v. Mayer, 28 Ohio 521 (1876).

Newspapers

Cincinnati Enquirer, 1899–1917.

Cincinnati Post, 1905–13.

Cleveland Leader, 1899–1917.

Cleveland Plain Dealer, 1899–1917.

Cleveland Press, 1899–1915.

Columbus Evening Dispatch, 1911–16.

Dayton Daily News, 1900–1917.

Ohio State Journal (Columbus), 1899–1917.

Toledo Blade, 1897–1917.

Toledo Bee, 1897–1903.

Toledo News-Bee, 1903–17.

Youngstown Vindicator, 1900–1917.

Pamphlets

BATES, THEODORE M.; AKINS, A. E.; and DODGE, MARTIN. *Your Servant or Your Master.* [Cleveland, 1909].

BEMIS, EDWARD W. *Report of Prof. Edward W. Bemis on the True Value of Ohio Railroads for the Purpose of Taxation.* [Cleveland (?), 1903(?)].

BIGELOW, HERBERT S. *Initiative and Referendum, Speech of Herbert S. Bigelow in Ohio Constitutional Convention, March 27, 1912.* Columbus, 1912.

BURNHAM, DANIEL H.; CARRERE, JOHN M.; and BRUNNER, ARNOLD W. *Report on the Group Plan of the Public Buildings of the City of Cleveland.* (2d ed.) [Cleveland], 1907.

CHASE, HARVEY S. *The Work of the Bureau for Uniform Municipal Reporting, Auditing and Accounting in the State of Ohio.* n.p., 1903.

Civic League of Cleveland. *Municipal Bulletin* (December, 1913).

DERTHICK, F. A. *Revision of the Tax System of Ohio.* n.p., 1906.

DITTY, ROBERT N. *Judson Harmon of Ohio, a Man of Deeds, Not Words.* Columbus, [1912(?)].

KOHLER, FRED. *Common Sense, a Golden Rule.* Buffalo, 1909.

McDOUGALL, THOMAS. *Address on the Taxation of the Property of Street Railways, Gas, Electric Light and Other Quasi Public Corporations before the Senate and House Committee on Taxation at Columbus, February 25, 1896.* Cincinnati, 1896.

The New Ohio. n.p. [1914].

PATTISON, JOHN M. *Inaugural Address of Hon. John M. Pattison, Governor of Ohio Delivered at Columbus, Ohio, January 8, 1906.* n.p. [1906].

RYAN, DANIEL J. *Taxation Suggestions for Relief, State and Municipal.* n.p., 1892.

SALEN, CHARLES P. *The City's Opportunity.* Cleveland, [1896(?)].

Shall Franchises Worth $600,000,000 Remain Untaxed in Ohio? n.p. [1906].

A Story of Progress in Ohio during Governor Judson Harmon's Administration. Columbus [1911].

Taxation in Ohio Discussed by the Commercial Club of Cincinnati, December 23, 1895. [Cincinnati, 1896(?)].

This Is Herman C. Baehr. [Cleveland, 1909].

What Herman C. Baehr Will Do. [Cleveland, 1909].

ZANGARLE, JOHN A. *Untaxed Wealth of Cleveland and Why.* [Cleveland(?), 1917(?)].

Articles in Periodicals and Essays in Collected Works

ANTRIM, ERNEST I. "Ohio Constitutional Convention," *Independent,* LXXII (June 27, 1912), 1423–26.

ARBUTHNOT, C. C. "Mayor Baker's Administration in Cleveland," *National Municipal Review,* V (April, 1916), 226–41.

BAKER, NEWTON D. "The Challenge of the City," *Social Year Book* (The Cleveland Federation for Charity and Philanthropy). Cleveland, 1913.

———. "Tom Loftin Johnson," *The Dictionary of American Biography,* ed. DUMAS MALONE, Vol. X, 122–24.

———. "A Labor Policy for Cleveland," *Cleveland Chamber of Commerce Reports and Addresses* (1923).

BARROWS, ISABEL C. "The Columbus Penitentiary," *Survey,* XXVI (September 23, 1911), 886–91.

BEMIS, EDWARD W. "The Cleveland Street Railway Settlement," *Quarterly Journal of Economics,* XXIV (May, 1910), 550–60.

———. "The Street Railway Settlement in Cleveland," *Quarterly Journal of Economics,* XXII (August, 1908), 543–75.

———. "The Significance of Mayor Johnson's Election," *Arena,* XXIX (June, 1903), 582–85.

———. "Tom L. Johnson's Achievements as Mayor of Cleveland," *Review of Reviews,* XLIII (May, 1911), 558–60.

BIGELOW, HERBERT S. "From Pulpit to Stump," *Independent,* LXI (November 1, 1906), 1036–37.

BLAIR, ALBION Z. "Seventeen Hundred Rural Vote Sellers: How We Disfranchised Voters in Adams County," *McClure's Magazine,* XXXVIII (November, 1911), 28–40.

BOGART, ERNEST L. "Recent Tax Reforms in Ohio," *American Economic Review*, I (September, 1911), 505–18.

"Bribery as a Local Custom," *Outlook*, XCVII (January 14, 1911), 42–44.

BURBA, GEORGE F. "Ohio Law for Workmen's Compensation," *Review of Reviews*, XLVIII (July, 1913), 90–93.

CARLTON, FRANK T. "The Golden Rule Factory: The Late Mayor Jones' Contribution toward the Solution of Industrial Problems," *Arena*, XXXII (October, 1904), 408–10.

CASSON, HERBERT N. "Draining a Political Swamp," *Arena*, XXI (1899), 768–72.

The Chronicler. "Among Those Present," *Ohio Magazine*, I (1906), 76–83; II (1907), 320–28.

"Cincinnati's Charter Commission," *National Municipal Review*, VI (November, 1917), 720–22.

"Cincinnati Adopts a Home Rule Charter," *National Municipal Review*, VII (January, 1918), 90.

Civic League of Cleveland. *Municipal Bulletin* (December, 1913).

CLOPPER, E. N. "Ohio's Child Labor Relief Law," *Survey*, XXIII (March 26, 1910), 981–82.

COKER, F. W. "Administration of Local Taxation in Ohio," *Annals of American Academy of Political and Social Science*, XLVII (May, 1913), 182–98.

COOLEY, HARRIS R. "Tom L. Johnson's Full Day's Work," *The Public*, XIV (July 21, 1911), 685–87.

COX, JAMES M. "Governor Judson Harmon," *Independent*, LXXI (November 2, 1911), 954–59.

CREEL, GEORGE, and GORDON, SLOANE. "What Are You Going to Do about It—the Shame of Ohio," *Cosmopolitan*, LI (October, 1911), 599–610.

CREEL, GEORGE. "Perry D. Knapp," *American Magazine*, LXXII (July, 1911), 306–8.

CROSBY, ERNEST. "Golden Rule Jones, the Late Mayor of Toledo," *Craftsman*, VII (1904–5), 530–47, 679–88.

CROSSER, ROBERT. "The Initiative and Referendum Amendments in the Proposed Ohio Constitution," *Annals of the American Academy of Political and Social Science*, XLIII (September, 1912), 191–202.

CUSHMAN, RORERT E. "Voting Organic Laws: Action of the Ohio Electorate in the Revision of the State Constitution in 1912," *Political Science Quarterly*, XXVIII (June, 1913), 207–29.

DAVENPORT, H. J. "The Taxation of Unearned Increment," *Proceedings of the National Tax Conference* (1907), 294–303.

DICK, CHARLES. "Charles H. Grosvenor," *Ohio Magazine*, II (March, 1907), 185–89.

———. "Marcus A. Hanna," *Ohio State Archaeological and Historical Quarterly*, XIII (1904), 355–74.

DITTY, ROBERT M. "Uniform Rule and Tax Limit Legislation in Ohio," *Proceedings of the Sixth Annual Conference National Tax Association* (Madison), 1913, 215–33.

ELLIS, WADE H. "The History of the Standard Oil Company in Ohio," *Ohio Magazine*, IV (January, 1908), 2–10.

———. "Taxation in Ohio," *Ohio Magazine*, I (September, 1906), 274–87.

ELSON, HENRY W. "The Fourth Constitutional Convention of Ohio," *Review of Reviews*, XLV (March, 1912), 337–40.

———. "Making a New Constitution for Ohio," *Review of Reviews*, XLVI (July, 1912), 83-86.

"An Experiment in Co-operation," *Outlook*, CV (November 22, 1913), 603–4.

"Extension of Street Railway Franchises, Report of Special Committee, February 21, 1901," *Cleveland Chamber of Commerce Reports and Addresses* (1901-3).

FAIRLIE, JOHN A. "Financial Provisions of the New Municipal Program," in *A New Municipal Program*, ed. C. R. WOODRUFF. New York, 1919. pp. 199–217.

FESLER, MAYO. "Municipal Home Rule," "The Ohio Municipal Conference," and "Home Rule for Ohio Cities," *National Municipal Review*, I (April–October, 1912), 284–85, 302, 475–76, 714–16.

———. "Municipal Home Rule in Ohio: Supreme Court Upholds Cleveland's Charter," *National Municipal Review*, II (October, 1913), 678–79.

———. "The Progress of Municipal Home Rule in Ohio," *National Municipal Review*, V (April, 1916), 242–51.

FILLEBROWN, C. B. "The Single Tax," *Proceedings of the National Tax Conference* (1907), 286–93.

FLOWER, BENJAMIN O. "A New Champion of the People's Cause," *Arena*, XXVIII (November, 1902), 534–42.

———. "Two Notable Reform Victories in Ohio," *Arena*, XXIX (June, 1903), 651–55.

FOOTE, ALLEN RIPLEY. "Relation of Franchise Taxation to Service Rates," *Proceedings of the National Tax Conference* (1907), 655–61.

FREIBERG, A. JULIUS. "Cincinnati Situation," *Proceedings of the National Conference on Good City Government* (1906), 124–34.

———. "Mayor Hunt's Administration in Cincinnati," *National Municipal Review*, III (July, 1914), 517–24.

FURZBAY, HARVEY G. "The Anti-Saloon League," *North American Review*, CLXXVII (September, 1903), 434–39.

GALBREATH, CHARLES B. "Vote on the Ohio Constitution," *Independent*, LXXIII (December 19, 1912), 1407–10.

GARFIELD, JAMES R. "A Review of President Roosevelt's Administration," *Outlook*, XCI (February 20, 1909), 389–93.

GILBERTSON, H. S. "Progressive Charters for Ohio Cities," *American City*, IX (August, 1913), 121–23.

"Dr. Gladden's Election," *Outlook*, LXIV (April 14, 1900), 855–56.

GLADDEN, WASHINGTON. "The Case against the Labor Union," *Outlook*, XCVII (February 25, 1911), 465–71.

———. "The Church and the Labor Question," *Outlook*, XCVIII (May 6, 1911), 35–40.

———. "Crosslights and Counter Claims," *Outlook*, XCVII (April 15, 1911), 827–32.

———. "Industry and Democracy," *Outlook*, XCVII (March 18, 1911), 589–95.

———. "The Reason for the Unions," *Outlook*, XCVII (March 4, 1911), 497–502.

———. "The Cosmopolis City Club," *Century*, N.S. XXIII (January, 1893), 395–406.

———. "The Influence of Public Service Corporations on City Government," *Proceedings of the National Conference for Good City Government* (1900), 164–75.

———. "Mayor Jones of Toledo," *Outlook*, LXII (May 6, 1899), 17–21.

———. "Public Service Companies and City Governments," *Outlook*, LXVI (October 27, 1900), 502–8.

GODDARD, HENRY H. "The Basis for State Policy, Social Investigation and Prevention," *Survey*, XXVII (March 2, 1912), 1852–56.

GORDON, SLOANE. "Judson Harmon of Ohio," *Review of Reviews*, XLII (September, 1910), 298–309.

HALE, WILLIAM BAYARD. "Judson Harmon and the Presidency," *World's Work*, XXII (June, 1911) 14,446–59.

HARD, WILLIAM. "Brand Whitlock, Mayor of Toledo," *World To-Day*, XI (1906), 700-701.

HARDING, WARREN G. "Joseph Benson Foraker," *Ohio Magazine*, III (October, 1907), 197-202.

"Judson Harmon—His Record and His Views," *Outlook*, C (January 27, 1912), 175–83.

"Harmonics of Harmon," *Current Literature*, I (January, 1911), 32–35.

HART, HASTINGS H. "The Ohio Children's Code," *Survey*, XXX (July 19, 1913), 517–18.

HATTON, AUGUSTUS RAYMOND. "Constitutional Municipal Home Rule," in *A New Municipal Program*, ed. C. R. WOODRUFF. New York, 1919. pp. 73–94.

HAUSER, ELIZABETH J. "The Woman Suffrage Movement in Ohio," *Ohio Magazine*, IV (February, 1908), 83–92.

HAWORTH, PAUL LELAND. "Mayor Johnson of Cleveland," *Outlook*, XCIII (October 23, 1909), 469–74.

HAYDEN, WARREN S. "The Street Railway Situation in Cleveland," *Proceedings of the Cincinnati Conference for Good City Government and the Fifteenth Annual Meeting of the National Municipal League* (1909), 403–16.

HEFFERAN, W. O. "State Budget Making in Ohio," *Annals of American Academy of Political and Social Science*, LXII (November, 1915), 91–100.

HENDRICK, BURTON J. "Judson Harmon: Progressive Candidate," *McClure's Magazine*, XXXVIII, (April, 1912) 619–24.

——. "Mayor Tom's Successor," *World's Work*, XXVII (April, 1914), 670–78.

——. "Taking the American City out of Politics," *Harper's Monthly Magazine*, CXXXVII (June, 1918), 106–13.

HOPKINS, WILLIAM ROWLAND. "The Street Railway Problem in

Cleveland," *American Economic Association, Economic Studies,* I (1896), 283–376.

HOPWOOD, E. C. "Newton D. Baker's Administration as Mayor of Cleveland and Its Accomplishments," *National Municipal Review,* II (July, 1913), 461–66.

HOSFORD, HESTER E. "Ohio's Contribution to Reform: An Interview with Governor James M. Cox," *Independent,* LXXV (September 4, 1913), 547–50.

HOWE, FREDERIC C. "Best Governed Community in the World," *World's Work,* III (February, 1902), 1723–28.

——. "Cleveland, a City Finding Itself," *World's Work,* VI (October, 1903), 3988–99.

——. "City in the Life Saving Business," *Outlook,* LXXXVIII (January 18, 1908), 123–27.

——. "The City of Cleveland in Relation to the Street Railway Question," *Bulletin of the Municipal Association of Cleveland* (1897).

——. "Education of Cleveland through Its Chamber of Commerce," *Outlook,* LXXXIII (July 28, 1906), 739–49.

——. "Golden Rule Chief of Police," *Everybody's,* XXII (June, 1910), 814–23.

——. "New Constitution of Ohio," *Survey,* XXVIII (September 21, 1912), 757–59.

——. "Taxation of Quasi-Public Corporations in the State of Ohio and the Franchise Tax," *Annals of the American Academy of Political and Social Science,* XIV (September, 1899), 157–80.

HUEBNER, GROVER G. "Five Years of State Railroad Regulation," *Annals of the American Academy of Political and Social Science,* XXXII (1908), 138–56.

HUNT, HENRY T. "Obligations of Democracy," *Yale Review,* N.S. VI (April, 1917), 586–99.

——. "Obstacles to Municipal Progress," *American Political Science Review,* XI (February, 1917), 76–87.

ICKES, HAROLD L. "Who Killed the Progressive Party?", *American Historical Review,* XLVI (1940-41), 306–37.

JOHNSON, TOM L. "Address at the National Anti-Trust Conference, Chicago, February 13, 1900," *The Public,* XIV (April 21, 1911), 373–79.

——. "Nine Year's War with Privilege," *Hampton's Magazine,* XXVII (July, 1911), 3–18.

———. "Inequalities of Taxation," *Hampton's Magazine*, XXVII (August, 1911), 192–205.

———. "My Fight against a Three Cent Fare," *Hampton's Magazine*, XXVII (September, 1911), 373–78.

———. "Three Cent Fare Fight in Cleveland," *Hampton's Magazine*, XXVII (October, 1911), 491–504.

"Johnson and the Cleveland Clergy," *Arena*, XXXV (April, 1906), 430–32.

JONES, SAMUEL M. "American Workingmen and Religion," *Outlook*, LXV (July 14, 1900), 640–42.

———. "Government by the Golden Rule," *Munsey's Magazine*, XXVIII (1902–3), 506–9.

———. "Municipal Expansion," *Arena*, XXI (1899), 766–67.

———. "The Non-Partican in Politics," *Independent*, LV (August 20, 1903), 1963–66.

———. "Patience and Education the Demands of the Hour," *Arena*, XXV (May, 1901), 544-46.

———. "Plea for Simpler Living," *Arena*, XXIX (April, 1903), 345–48.

———. "The Way to Purify Politics," *Independent*, LIV (February 27, 1902), 512–13.

"Samuel Milton Jones: The Golden Rule Mayor by 'One Who Knew Him,'" *Arena*, XXXV (February, 1906), 126–32.

KENNY, JOHN T. "Ohio—the Legislature That Elected Mr. Hanna," *Arena*, XXI (1899), 311–26.

KLINE, VIRGIL P. "The Other Side of the Standard Oil Controversy," *Ohio Magazine*, IV (March, 1908), 193–201.

LAPP, JOHN A. "Public Utilities," *American Political Science Review*, VI (November, 1912), 576–78.

"Latest Ideas in Constitution Making," *Chautauquan*, LXVII (July, 1912), 101–2.

LOCKHART, OLIVER C. "Recent Developments in Taxation in Ohio," *Quarterly Journal of Economics*, XXIX (May, 1915), 480–521.

———. "Taxation in Ohio," *American Economic Review*, II (September, 1912), 729–30.

LOWRIE, S. GALE. "Cincinnati's Charter Campaign," *National Municipal Review*, III (October, 1914), 730–33.

———. "Municipal Revenues in Ohio," *National Municipal Review*, IV (April, 1915), 254–56.

——. "Ohio Model Charter Law," *American Political Science Review*, VII (August, 1913), 422–24.

McCLURE, W. FRANK. "Cleveland's New Methods of Care for Her Wards," *Chautauquan*, LXI (December, 1910), 90–106.

MACKOY, HARRY BRENT. "Judson Harmon," *Independent*, LXIX (September 29, 1910), 694–99.

MARTZOLFF, CLEMENT L. "Ohio: Changes in the Constitution," *American Political Science Review*, VI (November, 1912), 573–76.

——. "Recent Ohio Legislation Conforming to the Demands of the New Constitution," *American Political Science Review*, VII (November, 1913), 639–47.

MATTHEWS, WILLIAM O. "Taxation, the Unit Rule of Assessment: A Hope for the Future," *Proceedings of the National Tax Conference* (1907), 551–94.

MAXWELL, ROBERT S., ed. "A Document on the Progressive Campaign of 1912," *Mississippi Valley Historical Review*, XXXVI (June, 1949), 113–15.

MAY, MAX B. "Cincinnati. (a) Citizens Municipal Party. (b) Honest Election Committee," *Annals of the American Academy of Political and Social Science*, XXVII (1906), 405–7.

——. "New Municipal Code," *Annals of the American Academy of Political and Social Science*, XXI (1903), 125–28.

——. "Taxation in American Cities: Cincinnati," *Annals of the American Academy of Political and Social Science*, XXVIII (1906), 157–59.

"Mayor Johnson's Victory and National Politics," *Arena*, XXXVIII (December, 1907), 710–12.

MENGERT, HERBERT R. "The Ohio Workmen's Compensation Law," *Ohio Archaeological and Historical Quarterly*, XXX (1921); 1–48.

MERRELL, JOHN B. "Samuel M. Jones: The Mayor," *Commons*, IX (August, 1904), 351–55.

Municipal Association of Cleveland, *Municipal Bulletin*, XV (1911).

"The Municipal Problem," *Outlook*, XCVIII (September 4, 11, 18, 25, 1909), 13–14, 55–56, 90–92, 141–42.

NICHOLS, HUGH L. "Judson Harmon," *Ohio Archaeological and Historical Quarterly*, XLI (1932), 137–50.

NOCK, ALBERT JAY. "Mayor of Toledo, Ohio," *American Magazine*, LXIX (1909–10), 599.

NORTON, WILLIAM J. "Chief Kohler of Cleveland and His Golden Rule Policy," *Outlook*, XCIII (November 6, 1909), 537–42.

"Ohio's New Constitution," *Chautauquan,* LXIX (January, 1913), 128–29.

"Ohio's Rebuilt Constitution," *Literary Digest,* XLV (September 12, 1912), 405–6.

ORTH, SAMUEL P. "The Municipal Situation in Ohio," *Forum,* XXXIII (June, 1902), 430–37.

PENDLETON, ELLIOTT HUNT. "Cincinnati's Traction Problems," *National Municipal Review,* II (October, 1913), 617–28.

———. "Address," *Proceedings of the Cincinnati Conference for Good City Government and the Fifteenth Annual Meeting of the National Municipal League* (1909), 4–5.

——— and Others. "Militant Political Work for Better Governed Cities," *Proceedings of the Pittsburgh Conference for Good City Government and the Fourteenth Annual Meeting of the National Municipal League* (1908), 98–99.

PHILLIPS, DAVID GRAHAM. "Tom Johnson," *Appleton's Booklovers Magazine,* VII (April, 1906), 457–60.

"A Preacher's Winning Fight for Democracy," *Literary Digest,* XLV (November 16, 1912), 923.

"Progress of Municipal Home Rule in Ohio," *American City,* X (February, 1914), 150–53.

PURDY, LAWSON. "Improved Tax Laws for Ohio," *Proceedings of the Thirteenth Annual Meeting of the Ohio State Board of Commerce, Second Session* (1906), 37–52.

"Report of the Committee on Legislation," *Cleveland Chamber of Commerce Reports and Addresses* (1906).

"Report of the Special Committee on Proposed Municipal Electric Plant," *Cleveland Chamber of Commerce Reports and Addresses* (1903).

"Report of the Special Committee on Street Railway Conditions and Referendum," *Cleveland Chamber of Commerce Reports and Addresses* (1908).

"Report of the Street Railway Committee," *Cleveland Chamber of Commerce Reports and Addresses* (1911).

"Report of the Street Railway Franchise Committee," *Cleveland Chamber of Commerce Reports and Addresses* (1906).

"Report of the Committee on Taxation of the Cleveland Chamber of Commerce," *Cleveland Chamber of Commerce Reports and Addresses* (1908).

"Revising the Ohio Constitution," *Outlook*, C (March 9, 1912), 514–15.

RYAN, DANIEL J. "Influence of Socialism on the Ohio Constitution," *North American Review*, CXCVI (November, 1912), 665–72.

SALEN, CHARLES P. "The Democratic Opportunity," *Ohio Magazine*, IV (March, 1908), 220–31.

SAWYER, CHARLES. "The Ohio Constitution: A Reply and a Rejoinder," *North American Review*, CXCVII (February, 1913), 275–79.

SCHINDEL, JOHN R. "The Paine Law in Ohio," *Proceedings of the Cincinnati Conference for Good City Government and the Fifteenth Annual Meeting of the National Municipal League* (1909), 249-57.

SHAW, ALBERT. "A National Lesson from Adams County," *Review of Reviews*, XLIII (February, 1911), 171–80.

SHEPARD, WALTER J. "Legislative Session in Ohio," *American Political Science Review*, IV (May, 1910), 231–37.

SIKES, GEORGE C. "The City Government Questions in Ohio," *Outlook*, LXXI (August 23, 1902), 1008–10.

———. "Tom L. Johnson, Mayor of Cleveland," *World To-Day*, XI (1906), 698–99.

"Statement of the Purpose and Effect of the Amendments to the Constitution of Ohio to Be Voted on September 3rd, 1912," *Cleveland Chamber of Commerce Reports and Addresses* (1912).

STEFFENS, LINCOLN. "Ohio: A Tale of Two Cities," *McClure's Magazine*, XXV (July, 1905), 293–311.

STOCKBRIDGE, FRANK PARKER. "The Biggest Boss of Them All," *Hampton's Magazine*, XXVI (May, 1911), 616–29.

———. "Ohio Wide Awake," *Everybody's Magazine*, XXVII (November, 1912), 696–707.

"Taxation in Ohio," *Report of the Civic League of Cleveland* (1915).

"Taxation: Report of Special Committee," *Cleveland Chamber of Commerce Reports and Addresses* (1895).

TAYLOR, GRAHAM. "Washington Gladden," *Survey*, XL (July 13, 1918), 422.

"10 Hour Law before Ohio's Supreme Bench," *Survey*, XXVII (November 18, 1911), 1195–96.

THATCHER, OLIVER J. "Educational Reforms That Set a Whole State in Turmoil," *Survey*, XXXI (January 24, 1914), 494–95.

TURNER, GEORGE KIBBE. "The Thing above the Law, the Rise and Rule of George B. Cox and His Overthrow by Young Hunt and the Fighting Idealists of Cincinnati," *McClure's Magazine,* XXXVIII (March, 1912), 575–91.

"Twenty-five Years of Home Rule," *Greater Cleveland,* XIII (December 30, 1937), 73–76.

UPSON, LENT D. "Comment on the Dayton Charter," *National Municipal Review,* IV (April, 1915), 266–72.

———. "City Manager Plan of Government for Dayton," *National Municipal Review,* II (October, 1913), 639–44.

UPTON, HARRIET TAYLOR. "Ohio," in *The History of Woman Suffrage,* ed. IDA HUSTED HARPER, Vol. VI. 6 vols. New York, 1922. pp. 508–19.

"Brand Whitlock: Mayor, Novelist, Democrat," *Arena,* XXXVII (June, 1907), 193–208.

WHITLOCK, BRAND. "Adventure in Democracy," *Harper's Weekly,* LVIII (January 31, 1914), 19–21.

———. "Newton D. Baker," *American Magazine,* LXXII (September, 1911), 559–60.

———. "Backing Up an Independent Mayor," *Charities and the Commons,* XVII (1906–7), 240–42.

———. "Herbert S. Bigelow," *American Magazine,* LXXV (December, 1912), 30.

———. "The City and Civilization," *Scribner's Magazine,* LII (November, 1912), 623–33.

———. "The City and the Public Utility Corporation," *World To-Day,* XIX (September, 1910), 957–64.

———. "Daniel Kiefer," *American Magazine,* LXXIV (September, 1912), 549–53.

———. "The Elimination of Graft," *World To-Day,* XVIII (June, 1910), 594–98.

———. " 'Golden Rule' Jones," *World's Work,* VIII (September, 1904), 5308–11.

———. "Henry T. Hunt," *American Magazine,* LXXIV (July, 1912), 297.

———. "Tom Johnson of Cleveland," *Human Life,* V (August, 1907), 3–5.

WHITNEY, E. B. "Judson Harmon," *North American Review,* CLXXXVII (June, 1908), 831–37.

518

WILCOX, DELOS F. "How the Chicago and Cleveland Street Railway Settlements Are Working Out," *National Municipal Review,* I (April, 1912), 630–38.

WITT, PETER. "Those Tax Burdens, Who Pays Them?", *American City,* XLIX (December, 1934), 66.

———. "The Vision of Tom L. Johnson," *The Public,* XIV (July 21, 1911), 684–85.

WOODRUFF, CLINTON ROGERS. "The American Municipal Situation," *Proceedings of the Cincinnati Conference for Good City Government and the Fifteenth Annual Meeting of the National Municipal League* (1909), 87–141.

———. "Municipal Government in Ohio," *Yale Review,* XII (1903–4), 121–40.

Books

ALLEN, PHILIP LORING. *America's Awakening: The Triumph of Righteousness in High Places.* New York, 1906.

AVERY, ELROY McK. *A History of Cleveland and Its Environs.* 3 vols. Chicago, 1918.

BABSON, ROGER W. *Cox—the Man.* New York, 1920.

BAKER, NEWTON D. *Progress and the Constitution.* New York, 1925.

———. *Frontiers of Freedom.* New York, 1918.

BOGART, ERNEST L. *Financial History of Ohio.* ("University of Illinois Studies in the Social Sciences," Vol. I, Nos. 1 and 2.) 1912.

CLARK, CHAMP. *My Quarter Century of American Politics.* 2 vols. New York, 1920.

CLARK, FREDERICK C. *State Railroad Commissions and How They May Be Made Effective.* ("American Economic Association Publications," Vol. VI, No. 6.) 1891.

COCHRAN, NEGLEY D. *E. W. Scripps.* New York, 1933.

COX, JAMES M. *Journey through My Years.* New York, 1946.

CROLY, HERBERT. *Marcus Alonzo Hanna, His Life and Work.* New York, 1912.

———. *The Promise of American Life.* New York, 1909.

DARROW, CLARENCE. *The Story of My Life.* New York, 1932.

DEWITT, BENJAMIN PARKE. *The Progressive Movement.* New York, 1915.

DOYLE, JOHN H. *A Story of Early Toledo.* Bowling Green, Ohio [1919].

[EVANS, N. W.] *A History of Taxation in Ohio.* Cincinnati, 1906.

FORAKER, JOSEPH BENSON. *Notes of a Busy Life.* 2 vols. Cincinnati, 1916.

GALBREATH, CHARLES B. *History of Ohio.* 5 vols. Chicago, 1925.

GEORGE, HENRY. *Progress and Poverty.* New York, 1879.

———. *Social Problems.* New York, 1883.

GLADDEN, WASHINGTON. *The Labor Question.* Boston, 1911.

———. *Organized Labor and Capital.* Philadelphia, 1904.

———. *Recollections.* Boston, 1909.

———. *Social Facts and Forces.* New York, 1897.

HARMON, JUDSON. *Messages and Other Official Papers of Judson Harmon Governor of Ohio, 1909–1913.* Columbus, 1909–13.

HARPER, IDA HUSTED, ed. *The History of Woman Suffrage.* 6 vols. New York, 1922.

HOWE, FREDERIC C. *The City the Hope of Democracy.* New York, 1905.

———. *The Confessions of a Reformer.* New York, 1925.

———. *The Modern City and Its Problems.* New York, 1915.

———. *Wisconsin: An Experiment in Democracy.* New York, 1912.

JOHNSON, TOM L. *My Story.* Edited, with an Introduction, by ELIZABETH J. HAUSER. New York, 1911.

JONES, SAMUEL M. *Letters of Love and Labor.* 2 vols. Toledo, 1900–1901. Republished in a single volume with an Introduction by BRAND WHITLOCK under the title *Letters of Labor and Love,* Indianapolis, 1905.

———. *The New Right.* Edited by HERBERT N. CASSON, with an Introduction and chapter on "Co-operation and Profit Sharing" by N. O. NELSON, New York, 1899.

KENNEDY, CHARLES E. *Fifty Years of Cleveland, 1875–1925.* Cleveland, 1925.

KILLITS, JOHN M., ed. *Toledo and Lucas County, Ohio, 1623–1923.* 3 vols. Chicago, 1923.

LA FOLLETTE, ROBERT M. *Autobiography.* Madison, 1913.

LIPPMANN, WALTER. *Drift and Mastery.* New York, 1914.

LLOYD, HENRY DEMAREST. *Wealth against Commonwealth.* New York, 1894.

LORENZ, CARL. *Tom L. Johnson.* New York, 1911.

McCARTHY, CHARLES. *The Wisconsin Idea.* New York, 1912.

McRAE, MILTON A. *Forty Years in Newspaperdom.* New York, 1924.

MARSHALL, EDWIN J. *The Law Governing Private Corporations in Ohio.* Cincinnati, 1903.

MERCER, JAMES K., ed. and comp. *Ohio Legislative History.* 6 vols. Columbus [1914]–1926.

MOLEY, RAYMOND. *27 Masters of Politics in a Personal Perspective.* New York, 1949.

MORRIS, CHARLES E. *Progressive Democracy of James M. Cox.* Indianapolis, 1920.

MOTT, T. BENTLEY. *Myron T. Herrick, Friend of France.* New York, 1929.

MYERS, ALLEN C. *Bosses and Boodle in Ohio Politics.* Cincinnati, 1895.

NEWCOMB, H. T. *Municipal Socialism, the Conservative Victory in Cleveland.* Washington, D.C., 1905.

ORTH, SAMUEL P. *The Centralization of Administration in Ohio.* New York, 1903.

——. *A History of Cleveland, Ohio.* 3 vols. Cleveland, 1910.

PALMER, FREDERICK. *Newton D. Baker.* 2 vols. New York, 1931.

POST, LOUIS F. *The Prophet of San Francisco.* New York, 1930.

POWELL, THOMAS E., ed. *The Democratic Party of the State of Ohio.* 2 vols. n.p., 1913.

RANDALL, EMILIUS O., and RYAN, DANIEL J. *History of Ohio, the Rise and Progress of an American State.* 5 vols. New York, 1912.

SCRIBNER, HARVEY, ed. *Memoirs of Lucas County and the City of Toledo.* 2 vols. Madison, 1910.

SHAW, ARCHER H. *"The Plain Dealer," One Hundred Years in Cleveland.* New York, 1942.

SHENEFIELD, H. T., and GARBER, J. OTIS. *Toledo Our Community.* Chicago [1932].

STEFFENS, LINCOLN. *Autobiography.* New York, 1931.

——. *The Letters of Lincoln Steffens.* Edited by ELLA WINTER and GRANVILLE HICKS. 2 vols. New York, 1938.

——. *The Shame of the Cities.* New York, 1905.

——. *The Struggle for Self-Government.* New York, 1906.

TAFT, CHARLES P. *City Management, the Cincinnati Experiment.* New York, 1933.

WHITE, WILLIAM ALLEN. *Masks in a Pageant.* New York, 1939.

WHITLOCK, BRAND. *Forty Years of It.* New York, 1914.

———. *The Letters and Journal of Brand Whitlock.* Edited, with a Biographical Introduction, by ALLAN NEVINS, and an Introduction by NEWTON D. BAKER. 2 vols. New York, 1936.

———. *On the Enforcement of Law in Cities.* Indianapolis, 1910.

WILLIAMSON, CHARLES C. *The Finances of Cleveland* ("Columbia University Studies in History, Economics and Public Law," Vol. XXV, No. 3.) 1907.

WINTER, NEVIN O. *A History of Northwest Ohio.* 3 vols. New York, 1917.

W[ITT], P[ETER]. *Cleveland before St. Peter.* Cleveland, 1899.

WOODRUFF, CLINTON ROGERS, ed. *City Government by Commission.* New York, 1911.

———, ed. *A New Municipal Program.* New York, 1919.

WRIGHT, HENRY C. *Bossism in Cincinnati.* Cincinnati, 1905.

SECONDARY SOURCES

Articles in Periodicals and Essays in Collected Works

AUMANN, FRANCIS R. "The Course of Judicial Review in the State of Ohio," *American Political Science Review,* XXV (May, 1931), 367–77.

———. "Ohio Government in the Twentieth Century: From Nash to White (1900–1931)," in HARLOW LINDLEY, comp., *Ohio in the Twentieth Century, 1900–1938.* (*The History of the State of Ohio,* ed. CARL WITTKE, Vol. VI.) 6 vols. Columbus, 1942–43. pp. 3–54.

BENNET, EMMETT L. "Ohio—Local Self-Government with Exceptions," *National Municipal Review,* XXI (June, 1932), 357–63.

BREMNER, ROBERT H. "The Civic Revival in Ohio," and other articles in the same series under various subtitles, in *American Journal of Economics and Sociology,* VIII (1948–49), 61–68, 151–61, 299–310, 413–22; IX (1949–50), 239–53, 369–76; X (1950–

51), 87–91, 185–206, 301–12, 417–28; XI (1951–52), 99–110; XII (1952–53), 189–200, 305–10; XIV (1954–55), 71–74; XV (1955–56), 195–202.

———. "Tom L. Johnson," *Ohio State Archaeological and Historical Quarterly*, LIX (January, 1950), 1–13.

CARLTON, FRANK T. "Labor in the Twentieth Century," in HARLOW LINDLEY, comp., *Ohio in the Twentieth Century, 1900–1938*. (*The History of the State of Ohio*, ed. CARL WITTKE, Vol. VI.) pp. 94–119.

CHANDLER, ALFRED D., JR. "The Origins of Progressive Leadership," in *The Letters of Theodore Roosevelt*, ed. ELTING E. MORRISON and JOHN M. BLUM, Vol. VIII, Appendix III, 1462–65.

COLE, ARTHUR C., "Judson Harmon," *The Dictionary of American Biography*, ed. DUMAS MALONE, Vol. VIII, 276–78.

CONNELLY, GORDON M., and FIELD, HARRY H. "The Non-Voter— Who He Is, What He Thinks," *Public Opinion Quarterly*, VIII (September, 1944), 175–87.

"Council Manager Plan Developments," *National Civic Review*, L (November, 1961), 548–49.

DESTLER, CHESTER McA. "The Toledo Natural Gas Pipe-Line Controversy," *Northwest Ohio Quarterly*, XV (April, 1943), 76–110.

DOWNES, RANDOLPH C. "The Toledo Political-Religious Municipal Campaign of 1913 and the Death of the Independent Party," *Northwest Ohio Quarterly*, XXX (Summer, 1958), 137–63.

FALCONER, JOHN I. "Agricultural Changes," in HARLOW LINDLEY, comp., *Ohio in the Twentieth Century, 1900–1938*. (*The History of the State of Ohio*, ed. CARL WITTKE, Vol. VI.) pp. 120–34.

FLYNN, JOHN T. "Mark Hanna—Big Business in Policies," *Scribner's Magazine*, XCIV (August, 1933), 85–90, 118–28.

FORDYCE, WELLINGTON G. "Nationality Groups in Cleveland Politics," *Ohio State Archaeological and Historical Quarterly*, XLVI (1937), 109–27.

GIST, GENEVIEVE B. "Progressive Reform in a Rural Community: The Adams County Vote-Fraud Case," *Mississippi Valley Historical Review*, XLVIII (June, 1961), 60–78.

JONES, SAMUEL MILTON III. "Brand Whitlock," and other articles in the same series under various subtitles, in *Northwest Ohio Quarterly*, XXXI (1958–59), 7–37, 94–112, 126–37, 156–69; XXXII (1959–60), 7–14, 61–78, 117–31, 173–86; XXXIII (1961), 91–104.

Jones, Wilbur D. "Marcus A. Hanna and Theodore E. Burton," *Ohio Archaeological and Historical Quarterly*, LX (January, 1951), 10–19.

Link, Arthur S. "What Happened to the Progressive Movement in the 1920's?", *American Historical Review*, LXIV (July, 1959), 833–51.

Mann, Arthur. "British Social Thought and American Reformers of the Progressive Era," *Mississippi Valley Historical Review*, XLII (March, 1956), 672–92.

Murdock, Eugene C. "Cleveland's Johnson," and other articles in the same series under various subtitles, in *Ohio Archaeological and Historical Quarterly*, LXII (October, 1953), 323–33; *Ohio Historical Quarterly*, LXIII (October, 1954), 319–35; LXV (January, 1956), 28–43; LXVI (October, 1957), 375–90; LXVII (January, 1958), 35–49.

Noble, R. E., Jr. "Henry George and the Progressive Movement," *American Journal of Economics and Sociology*, VIII (April, 1949), 259–69.

Pershing, Benjamin H. "Membership in the General Assembly of Ohio," *Ohio Archaeological and Historical Quarterly*, XL (1931), 222–83.

Rodabaugh, James H. "A Decade of Reform," *Saturday Review of Literature*, XXVIII (January 6, 1945), 24–25.

———. "Arthur L. Garford," *Museum Echoes* (Ohio Historical Society), XXVIII (July, 1953), 51–54.

———. "Samuel M. Jones—Evangel of Equality," *Northwest Ohio Quarterly*, XV (January, 1943), 17–46.

Starring, Charles R. "Hazen S. Pingree: Another Forgotten Eagle," *Michigan History*, XXXII (June, 1948), 129–49.

Warner, Hoyt Landon. "Frederic Clemson Howe," *The Dictionary of American Biography*, ed. Dumas Malone, Vol. XXII, 326–28.

Weed, John M. "The Travelled Ways," and "Business—As Usual," in Harlow Lindley, comp., *Ohio in the Twentieth Century, 1900–1938.* (*The History of the State of Ohio*, ed. Carl Wittke, Vol. VI.) pp. 135–58, 159–97.

Weisenburger, Francis P. "General Isaac R. Sherwood," *Northwest Ohio Quarterly*, XIV (April, 1942), 42–53.

"Where Are the Pre-War Radicals?", *Survey*, LV (February 1, 1926), 556–66.

WIEBE, ROBERT H. "Business Disunity and the Progressive Movement, 1901–1914," *Mississippi Valley Historical Review,* XLIV (March, 1958), 664–85.

WISH, HARVEY. "Altgeld and the Progressive Tradition," *American Historical Review,* XLVI (July, 1941), 813–31.

WITTKE, CARL. "Mr. Justice Clarke—A Supreme Court Judge in Retirement," *Mississippi Valley Historical Review,* XXXVI (June, 1949), 27–50.

———. "Peter Witt, Tribune of the People," *Ohio Archaeological and Historical Quarterly,* LVIII (October, 1949), 361–77.

Books

AARON, DANIEL. *Men of Good Hope.* New York, 1951.

ALBURN, WILFRED HENRY, and ALBURN, MIRIAM RUSSELL. *This Cleveland of Ours.* 4 vols. Cleveland, 1933.

BAKER, RAY STANNARD. *Woodrow Wilson, Life and Letters.* 8 vols. New York, 1927–38.

BEER, THOMAS. *Hanna.* New York, 1929.

BLUM, JOHN M. *The Republican Roosevelt.* Cambridge, Mass., 1954.

———. *Woodrow Wilson and the Politics of Morality.* Boston, 1956.

BRYCE, JAMES. *The American Commonwealth.* 2 vols. new edition. New York, 1912.

CATLIN, GEORGE B. *The Story of Detroit.* Detroit, 1923.

CHAMBERLAIN, JOHN. *Farewell to Reform.* New York, 1933.

COPE, ALEXIS. *History of the Ohio State University, 1870–1910.* (*History of the Ohio State University,* ed. THOMAS C. MENDENHALL, Vol. I.) Columbus, 1920.

CRAMER, C. H. *Newton D. Baker: A Biography.* Cleveland, 1961.

CRAVEN, AVERY. *Democracy in American Life: A Historical View.* Chicago, 1941.

CRISSEY, FORREST. *Theodore E. Burton, American Statesman.* Cleveland and New York, 1956.

DOCKERAY, JAMES CARLTON. *Public Utility Taxation in Ohio.* ("The Ohio State University Studies, Contributions in Economics," No. 2.) 1938.

FAULKNER, HAROLD UNDERWOOD. *The Quest for Social Justice.*

(A History of American Life, ed. ARTHUR M. SCHLESINGER and DIXON RYAN FOX, Vol. XI.) New York, 1931.

FILLER, LOUIS. Crusaders for American Liberalism. New York, 1939.

FITZPATRICK, EDWARD A. McCarthy of Wisconsin. New York, 1944.

FORCEY, CHARLES. The Crossroads of Liberalism. New York, 1961.

GARRATY, JOHN A. Right-Hand Man: The Life of George W. Perkins. New York, 1957.

GEIGER, GEORGE H. The Philosophy of Henry George. New York, 1933.

GLAD, PAUL W. The Trumpet Soundeth: William Jennings Bryan and His Democracy 1896–1912. Lincoln, Neb., 1960.

GOLDMAN, ERIC F. Rendezvous with Destiny: A History of Modern American Reform. New York, 1952.

HOFSTADTER, RICHARD. The Age of Reform: From Bryan to F.D.R. New York, 1955.

———. The American Political Tradition and the Men Who Made It. New York, 1948.

JOHNSON, WALTER. William Allen White's America. New York, 1947.

JOHNSON, WENDELL F. Toledo's Non-Partisan Movement. Toledo, 1922.

JORDAN, PHILIP D. Ohio Comes of Age, 1873–1900. (The History of the State of Ohio, ed. CARL WITTKE, Vol. V.) Columbus, 1943.

KNEIER, CHARLES M. City Government in the United States. New York, 1934.

LINDLEY, HARLOW, comp. Ohio in the Twentieth Century, 1900–1938. (The History of the State of Ohio, ed. CARL WITTKE, Vol. VI.) Columbus, 1944.

LINK, ARTHUR S. Wilson: The Road to the White House. Princeton, 1947.

———. Wilson, the New Freedom. Princeton, 1956.

———. Woodrow Wilson and the Progressive Era, 1910–1917. New York, 1954.

LUTZ, HARLEY LEIST. The State Tax Commission. ("Harvard Economic Studies," Vol. XVII.) 1918.

McGeary, M. Nelson. *Gifford Pinchot: Forester-Politician.* Princeton, 1960.

Mann, Arthur. *Yankee Reformers in the Urban Age.* Cambridge, Mass., 1954.

Miller, William D. *Memphis during the Progressive Era, 1900–1917.* Memphis, Tenn., 1957.

Morison, Elting E., and Blum, John M., eds. *The Letters of Theodore Roosevelt.* 8 vols. Cambridge, Mass., 1951–54.

Mowry, George E. *Theodore Roosevelt and the Progressive Movement.* Madison, Wis., 1946.

———. *The California Progressives.* Berkeley and Los Angeles, 1951.

———. *The Era of Theodore Roosevelt, 1900–1912.* New York, 1958.

Noble, David W. *The Paradox of Progressive Thought.* Minneapolis, Minn., 1958.

Noble, Ransom E., Jr. *New Jersey Progressivism before Wilson.* Princeton, 1946.

Nock, Albert J. *Henry George.* New York, 1939.

Patton, Clifford W. *The Battle for Municipal Reform: Mobilization and Attack, 1875–1900.* Washington, D.C., 1940.

Pinchot, Amos. *History of the Progressive Party, 1912–1916.* Edited, with a Biographical Introduction, by Helene Maxwell Hooker. New York, 1958.

Pringle, Henry F. *The Life and Times of William Howard Taft.* 2 vols. New York, 1939.

Regier, C. C. *The Era of the Muckrakers.* Chapel Hill, N.C., 1932.

Ridley, Clarence E., and Nolting, Orin F., eds. *The Municipal Year Book 1949.* Chicago, 1949.

Roseboom, Eugene H., and Weisenburger, Francis P. *A History of Ohio.* Rev. edition. Columbus, 1958.

Schlesinger, Arthur M. *The Rise of the City.* (*A History of American Life,* eds. Arthur M. Schlesinger and Dixon Ryan Fox, Vol. X.) New York, 1933.

Stone, Harold A.; Price, Don K.; and Stone, Kathryn H. *City Manager Government in the United States, a Review after Twenty-five Years.* Chicago, 1940.

WALTERS, EVERETT. *Joseph Benson Foraker, an Uncompromising Republican.* Columbus, 1948.

WARNER, HOYT LANDON. *The Life of Mr. Justice Clarke.* Cleveland, 1959.

WERNER, M. R. *Bryan.* New York, 1929.

YOUNG, ARTHUR NICHOLS. *The Single Tax Movement in the United States.* Princeton, 1916.

ZINK, HAROLD. *City Bosses in the United States, a Study of Twenty Municipal Bosses.* Durham, N.C., 1930.

INDEX

Adams, John., 438–39 n. 22

Adams, Theodore, 139 n. 24

Adams County, Ohio, 267–68, 288–90 n. 48, 290 n. 49; see Corrupt Practice Act

Adams Express Co. v. Ohio State Auditor, 102 n. 12

Addams, George S., 404

Addams, Jane, 29

Administrative reform: constitutional amendments: affecting legislative probes of state offices, 327–28, affecting the powers of the governor, 327, concerning printing by the state, 328, making certain state offices elective, 327, 352 n. 72, providing for the removal of state and local officers, 324; introduction of a budget system, 425; of state government, 391, 483; *see also* Short ballot; Women, eligibility for certain offices; Recall

Agricultural reform, 433–34, 473; expansion of scientific research and instruction, 410; state agricultural commission, 427, 437 n. 10, 467, 476; *see also* Ohio Agricultural Commission

Akers, William, 55

Akron, Ohio, 416 n. 30, 453, 463 n. 33 and n. 35, 468

Akron Press, 169 n. 22

Alexander, Edward F., 417 n. 36

Allen, Charles L., 373

Allen, John E., 168 n. 18

Allendorf, William L., 433

Alsdorf, Walter A., 228, 232

Altgeld, John Peter, 155–56, 175, 433

American Book Company, 145

American Protective Association, 10–11, 25, 43, 132

Amherst, Ohio, 463 n. 35

Anderson, Carl C., 263

Anderson, David F., 311 n. 26, 312, 314–15, 344 n. 6, 344–45 n. 9, 348 n. 39

Andrews, LaForrest R., 275, 292 n. 67

Ankeny, Horace, 168 n. 15

Anti-catholicism: in Ohio, 10–11, 474–75; in Toledo, 153, 447, 461–62 n. 17; in Youngstown, 132; *see also* Toledo, Ohio; Youngstown, Ohio

Anti-imperialism, 121, 124, 129, 132

Anti-Saloon League; *see* Ohio Anti-Saloon League

Antitrust: code strengthened, 400, 418 n. 39; denunciation of trusts, 23–24, 71, 121, 129, 132; government ownership of trusts, 24, 31, 44; Ohio campaign, 6–7; Ohio legislation, 7, 24; regulation of trusts and proposals of Roosevelt Progressives, 359, 474

Antrim, Ernest I., 345–46 n. 17, 348 n. 44

Archbold, John D., 220

537

7n.m